Windows® XP All-i[...] Desk Reference For Dummies, 2nd Edition

Behind the Security Center

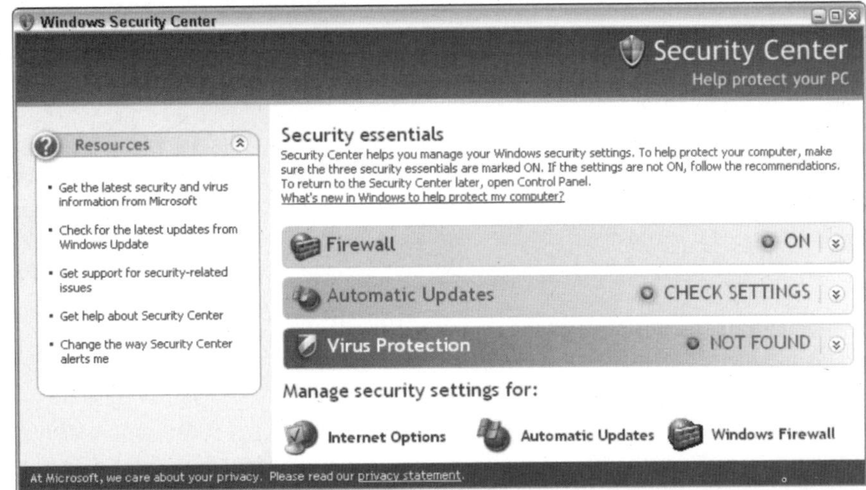

1. Windows Firewall is responsible for more weird Windows XP behavior than all other festering problems combined. If you can't connect into or out of your computer, disable the firewall momentarily (see Book II, Chapter 4). Your system will be vulnerable for a few minutes — but you may save yourself hours (or days!) of headaches from trying to run down the problem.
2. Microsoft really wants you to download and install Windows patches automatically. Given its track record, do you trust the company? Get all the facts — not just the Party Line — in Book II, Chapter 5.
3. The Windows Security Center is notorious for not recognizing perfectly legitimate antivirus programs. If Windows doesn't identify your AV program, don't fret. Follow the nostrums in Book II, Chapter 6 to turn the red light off — and remember that Microsoft is working on its own antivirus products to peddle.

Make Windows Run Faster

If Windows XP runs too slowly, buy more memory (that is, RAM).

If you're up to 512MB of memory and Windows XP *still* runs too slowly, buy a new PC, bucko. Don't bother trying to upgrade: It's expensive, time consuming, and you won't be happy with the results. Give the old PC to the kids or a worthwhile charity or use it as a boat anchor. The PC won't mind.

Item 7463-9.

For more information about Wiley Publishing, call 1-800-762-2974.

For Dummies: Bestselling Book Series for Beginners

Windows® XP All-in-One Desk Reference For Dummies,® 2nd Edition

Don't PANIC!

The five most common causes of computer-induced insanity — and their cures:

5. If there's no mouse cursor on the screen or the cursor won't move no matter how much you move the mouse, shut the computer down, make sure the mouse is plugged in, and restart the computer. If that doesn't work, flip the mouse over and use your fingernail to scrape off built-up gunk, pull the ball out if there is one, and clean the inside with a cotton swab and a touch of isopropyl alcohol. If the cursor still won't move, throw the stupid thing away. Mice are cheap. Sheesh.
4. If you suddenly can't get at your e-mail or get on the Web even though you could get to it yesterday and you haven't changed anything at all, chill. Chances are good that your Internet Service Provider (the place your computer dials into) is having problems. Come back in a few hours. DON'T CHANGE YOUR SETTINGS.
3. If you can't find a file that was sitting around yesterday, chances are good it's either in the Recycle Bin or you dragged it somewhere weird. Double-click the Recycle Bin icon. If your file is there, double-click it and then click Restore. If your file isn't there, choose Start⇨Search, click the kind of file you're looking for, and ask Rover (yes, that's his name) to go look for it.
2. If you spend the money to buy an expensive piece of hardware — a new video card, a second hard drive, a fancy force-feedback mouse, or a different cable modem — spend a little bit more money and have the retailer install it. Life's too short.
1. If the stupid computer won't work right, turn it off. Go read a book or watch a movie. Get some sleep. Come back when you're not so tied up in knots. Few pursuits in the history of humanity are as frustrating as trying to get a recalcitrant computer to behave itself.

Three Fatal Flaws

Every single Windows XP user — from the first-time novice to the most grizzled veteran — needs to understand three vital points about Windows XP:

- Windows XP hides a key piece of information from you that can help you identify and avoid viruses. The next time you use Windows XP, take a few seconds and make it show you "filename extensions" — the little piece at the end of each file's name, usually three characters long (for example, `.doc` or `.exe` or `.bat`), that dictates how Windows treats the file. See Book I, Chapter 3 for complete details on showing file extension names.
- Windows XP will beg, bully, and cajole you into divulging all sorts of information about yourself, and *you don't have to give in*. From the Registration Wizard to Windows Messenger, to .NET Passport and MSN and a dozen places in between — *all* of that information is optional. Don't hand out any more than you feel comfortable giving. There's nothing illegal, immoral, or habit-forming about telling Windows Messenger, for example, that your name is William Gates III. Read Book IX, Chapter 4 for more on this.
- Windows XP does not have built-in antivirus protection. You need to buy, install, frequently update, and religiously use an antivirus package. Choosing one specific manufacturer's package over another's isn't nearly as important as getting AV software installed, updated, and working. All of the major antivirus packages work well.

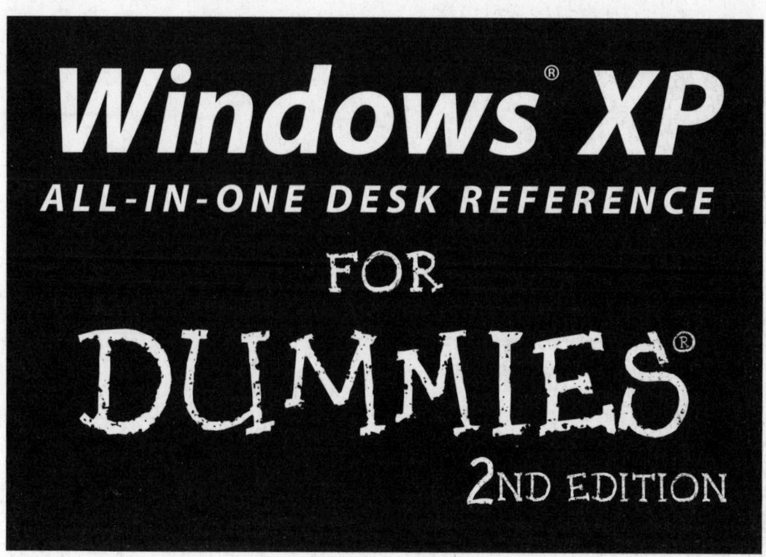

by Woody Leonhard

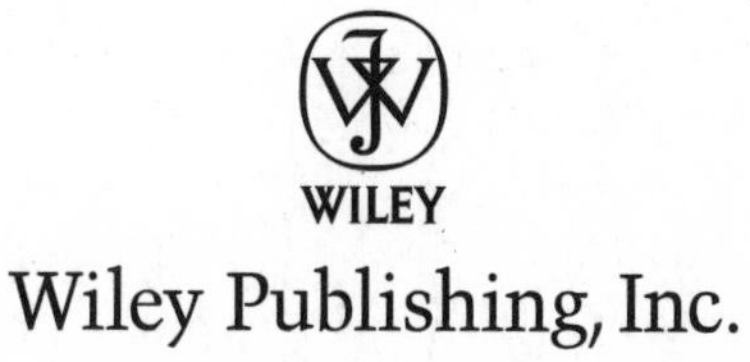

Wiley Publishing, Inc.

Windows® XP All-in-One Desk Reference For Dummies®, 2nd Edition

Published by
Wiley Publishing, Inc.
111 River Street
Hoboken, NJ 07030-5774

Published by Wiley Publishing, Inc., Indianapolis, Indiana

Published simultaneously in Canada

For general information on our other products and services or to obtain technical support, please contact our Customer Care Department within the U.S. at 800-762-2974, outside the U.S. at 317-572-3993, or fax 317-572-4002.

Wiley also publishes its books in a variety of electronic formats. Some content that appears in print may not be available in electronic books.

Library of Congress Control Number: 2004112223

ISBN: 0-7645-7463-9

Manufactured in the United States of America

10 9 8 7 6 5 4 3 2 1

2B/QU/RQ/QV/IN

About the Author

Curmudgeon, critic, and self-described "Windows Victim," **Woody Leonhard** runs `www.AskWoody.com`, the Web's single best source of up-to-the-nanosecond news about Windows and Office — warts and all. Check it out for answers to your most pressing questions, no-bull analysis of Microsoft's latest gaffes, and all sorts of information that you can't find anywhere else.

With a couple dozen computer books under his belt, Woody knows where the bodies are buried. He was one of the first Microsoft Consulting Partners and a charter member of the Microsoft Solutions Provider organization. He's a one-man major Microsoft beta testing site and delights in being a constant thorn in Microsoft's side. Along with several co-authors and editors, he's won an unprecedented six Computer Press Association Awards and two American Business Press Awards.

Woody currently lives with his son and two dogs in Phuket, Thailand, where he's working on an action-adventure novel set in Saudi Arabia. Most mornings you can see him jogging on Patong Beach with the dogs, and then guzzling a latte at Starbucks. Feel free to drop by and say, "Sawadee krap!" Microsoft hit squads, please take a number and form a queue at the rear of the building.

About the Contributors

Justin Leonhard drew recognition as the first teenager to publicly crash Office XP. He put together the main peer-to-peer network used in this book, tested it with the toughest applications Windows XP handles — games — and generated several interesting bug reports in the process. He was admitted to Mensa International at the age of 14, works sporadically on his PADI Rescue Diver certification, and spends his spare time playing video games. Justin has developed a singular knack for, uh, challenging his teachers.

Pakdee Noosri ("Lek") claims the #1 spot as Woody's Research Assistant. He's also the lead Webmeister for `www.AskWoody.com`. Lek holds a degree in Computer Science from Prince of Songkla University, Phuket Campus. He's an accomplished swimmer, Thai comic book guru, photographer — and one of the nicest people in the business.

Guy Wells knows wireless like the back of his hand. He also built the advanced Windows Media Center PC used in this book, from scratch, all by himself. A tinkerer of the first degree, Guy sometimes remembers to put the screws back in the case. He often hangs out on eBay and other places of ill repute. A frequent international traveler, he's in the process of earning his Dive Master certification.

Katherine Murray has been using technology to write about technology since the early 80s. With more than 40 books to her credit (spanning genres from technical to trade to parenting to business books), Katherine enjoys working on projects that teach new skills, uncover hidden talents, or develop mastery and efficiency in a chosen area. Katherine gets the biggest kick out of writing about technologies that help people communicate better — in person, in print, by e-mail, or on the Web. For the last 14 years, Katherine has owned and operated reVisions Plus, Inc., a publishing services company that uses many different programs — one of which, of course, is Microsoft Windows.

Jonathan Sachs discovered computers as a freshman at Oberlin College. He worked as a student staff member of the college computer center for three years and graduated with an A.B. in Physics. He moved on to DePaul Law School, graduated, passed the Illinois bar, and relocated to the San Francisco area, where he's currently employed as a programmer. He lives with two cats in a house in the East Bay hills. Jonathan has published three books and several magazine articles on computer topics — and one science fiction story. In his spare time, he grows vegetables, reads, and, in a small way, sells used books through eBay.

Dedication

To Rubye Hannah Leonhard (nee Holmes), who had the knowledge to teach me what I needed to know, and the wisdom to let me learn for myself.

We love you, Mom.

— Woody, Add, and Justin

Author's Acknowledgments

Thanks so much to Melody Lane, Linda Morris, Jean Rogers, and Jim Kelly, who guided the second edition of this book on its often-harrowing journey. Claudette Moore and Debbie McKenna once again proved themselves to be agents of the first degree. And a special thanks to Christian Simpson of euromantix music, London (`www.euromantix.com`), for helping me sort through the arcana of Windows Media Center Edition. Most of all, thanks to the folks at Microsoft who realized that the original Windows XP was badly in need of a makeover, and for the hard work and dedication it took to get Windows XP Service Pack 2 out the door. I know you guys 'n' gals didn't really want to work on a Service Pack, but the world needed it.

Publisher's Acknowledgments

We're proud of this book; please send us your comments through our online registration form located at `www.dummies.com/register/`.

Some of the people who helped bring this book to market include the following:

Acquisitions, Editorial, and Media Development

Project Editor: Linda Morris

Acquisitions Editor: Melody Layne

Copy Editor: Jean Rogers

Technical Editor: Jim Kelly

Editorial Manager: Leah Cameron

Permissions Editor: Laura Moss

Media Development Manager: Laura VanWinkle

Media Development Supervisor: Richard Graves

Editorial Assistant: Amanda Foxworth

Cartoons: Rich Tennant (`www.the5thwave.com`)

Production

Project Coordinator: Kristie Rees

Layout and Graphics: Andrea Dahl, Lauren Goddard, Denny Hager, Joyce Haughey, Stephanie D. Jumper, Melanee Prendergast, Jacque Roth, Heather Ryan, Julie Trippetti

Proofreaders: Melissa D. Buddendeck, John Greenough, Carl Pierce, Dwight Ramsey

Indexer: Rebecca R. Plunkett

Publishing and Editorial for Technology Dummies

Richard Swadley, Vice President and Executive Group Publisher

Andy Cummings, Vice President and Publisher

Mary Bednarek, Executive Acquisitions Director

Mary C. Corder, Editorial Director

Publishing for Consumer Dummies

Diane Graves Steele, Vice President and Publisher

Joyce Pepple, Acquisitions Director

Composition Services

Gerry Fahey, Vice President of Production Services

Debbie Stailey, Director of Composition Services

Contents at a Glance

Table of Contents

Book IV: Adventures with Internet Explorer 379

Introduction

Welcome to the second edition of *Windows XP All-in-One Desk Reference For Dummies* — the no-bull, one-stop Windows reference for the rest of us. Microsoft has made many changes to Windows XP since it first rolled off the assembly line in October 2001. Most important: Massive security changes — and even a few improvements — to make it harder for the bad guys to take over your computer, turn it into a zombie, clobber your files, and/or make it spew infected messages to every e-mail address stored in every nook and cranny of your PC.

While the online world has grown fangs since the halcyon days of October 2001, the world of entertainment has blossomed. Windows XP — particularly the Windows Media Player, support for digital cameras and camcorders, and the special-purpose/extra-cost Windows XP Media Center Edition — expanded to fill the void, dragging millions of new PC users, kickin' and screamin' and rockin' and rollin', into the 21st century.

With all the bad press that Microsoft has drawn (and, in many cases, earned), it's easy to lose sight of one key fact: Windows XP is the first PC operating system that *works*. At least, most of the time, on most PCs, running most kinds of applications. It's the closest thing we humans have ever had to a universal experience: Taxi drivers in Hong Kong swear at Windows XP with as much fervor as sheepherders in Estonia; hagglers sipping coffee in a souq in Kuwait talk about the latest Windows XP worms with the same awe and worry as hagglers downing lattes in Manhattan.

We're all in this big, leaky boat together. Sobering thought, that.

About This Book

Windows XP All-in-One Desk Reference For Dummies, 2nd Edition, takes you through the Land of the Dummies — with introductory material and stuff your grandmother could (and should!) understand — and then continues the journey into more advanced areas, where you can really put Windows to work every day. I don't dwell on technical mumbo-jumbo, and I keep the baffling jargon to a minimum. At the same time, though, I tackle the tough problems you're likely to encounter, show you the major road signs, and give you a lot of help where you'll need it the most.

Whether you want to set up a quick, easy, reliable network in your home office or you want to cheat at Solitaire, this is your book. Er, I should say *nine* books. I've broken the topics out into nine different minibooks so you'll find it easy to hop around to a topic — and a level of coverage — that feels comfortable.

I didn't design this book to be read from front to back. It's a reference. Each chapter and each section is meant to focus on solving a particular problem or describing a specific technique. Sections toward the beginning of a chapter are more tutorial. Sections near the end of a chapter take the bull by the horns and squeeze.

Windows XP All-in-One Desk Reference For Dummies, 2nd Edition, should be your reference of first resort, even before you consult Windows XP's Help and Support Center. There's a big reason why: Windows Help was written by hundreds of people over the course of many, many years. Some of the material was written ages ago, and it's confusing as all get-out, but it's still in Windows Help for folks who are tackling tough "legacy" problems. Some of the terminology in the Help files is inconsistent and downright misleading, largely because the technology has changed so much since some of the articles were written. The proverbial bottom line: I don't duplicate the material in the Windows XP Help and Support Center, but I will point to it if I figure it'll help you.

Conventions

I try to keep the typographical conventions to a minimum:

- ✦ The first time a buzzword appears in text, I italicize it and define it immediately. That makes it easier for you to glance back and re-read the definition.
- ✦ When I want you to type something, I put the letters or words in bold. For example: "Type **William Gates** in the Name text box." If you need to press more than one key on the keyboard at a time, I add a plus sign between the keys' names. For example, "Press Ctrl+Alt+Delete to initiate a Vulcan Mind Meld."
- ✦ I set off Web addresses and e-mail addresses in monospace. For example, my e-mail address is `woody@AskWoody.com` (true fact), and my Web site is at `www.AskWoody.com` (another true fact).

There's one other convention, though, that I use all the time. I always, absolutely, adamantly include the filename extension — the period and (usually) three letters at the end of a filename, such as `.doc` or `.vbs` or `.exe` — when talking about a file. Yeah, I know Windows XP hides filename extensions by default, but you can and should go in and change that. Yeah, I know that Bill G. hisself made the decision to hide them, and he won't back off. (At least, that's the rumor.)

I also know that hundreds — probably thousands — of *Microsoft employees* passed along the ILOVEYOU virus, primarily because they couldn't see the filename extension that would've warned them that the file was a virus. Uh, bad decision, Bill.

(If you haven't yet told Windows XP to show you filename extensions, take a minute now and hop to Book I, Chapter 3, and get Windows XP to dance to your tune.)

What You Don't Have to Read

Throughout this book, I've gone to great lengths to separate out the "optional" reading from the "required" reading. If you want to learn about a topic or solve a specific problem, follow along in the main part of the text. You can skip the icons and sidebars as you go, unless one happens to catch your eye.

On the other hand, if you know a topic pretty well but want to make sure you've caught all the high points, read the paragraphs marked with icons and make sure that information registers. If it doesn't, glance at the surrounding text.

Sidebars stand as "graduate courses" for those who are curious about a specific topic — or stand knee-deep in muck, searching for a way out.

Foolish Assumptions

I don't make many assumptions about you, dear reader, except for the fact that you're obviously intelligent, well-informed, discerning, and of impeccable taste. That's why you chose this book, eh?

Okay, okay. Least I can do is butter you up a bit. Here's the straight scoop. If you've never used Windows before, bribe your neighbor (or, better, your neighbor's kids) to teach you how to do three things:

- ✦ Play Solitaire
- ✦ Get on the World Wide Web
- ✦ Shut down Windows and turn off the computer

That covers it. If you can play Solitaire, you know how to turn on your computer, use the Start button, click, drag, and double-click. After you're on the Web, well, heaven help us all. And if you know that you need to click Start in order to Stop, you're well on your way to achieving Dummy Enlightenment.

And *that* begins with Book I, Chapter 1.

Organization

Windows XP All-in-One Desk Reference For Dummies, 2nd Edition, contains nine minibooks, each of which gives a thorough airing of a specific topic. If you're looking for information on a specific Windows XP topic, check the headings in the Table of Contents or refer to the Index.

By design, this book enables you to get as much (or as little) information as you need at any particular moment. Want to know how to jimmy your Minesweeper score to amaze your boss and confound your co-workers? Look at Book I, Chapter 6. Worried about cookies? Try Book IV, Chapter 3. Also by design, *Windows XP All-in-One Desk Reference For Dummies,* 2nd Edition, is a reference that you reach for again and again whenever some new question about Windows XP comes up.

Here are the nine minibooks, and what they contain:

Book I: A Windows XP Overview: What Windows can and can't do. What's inside a PC, and how does Windows control it? Do you really need Windows XP? How do you upgrade? What is activation, and why you should be concerned? Adding users — with a particular nod to security. Manipulating files. Using the Windows taskbar and shortcuts. Getting help. Performing searches. Cheating at the Windows games. Burning CDs. The care and feeding of hard drives. Using the built-in applications for word processing and image manipulation. How is Windows XP Professional different from Windows XP Home?

Book II: Customizing Your Windows eXPerience: Personalizing the desktop with themes, colors, backgrounds, and the like. Avoiding Active Desktop. Mouse Pointers. Screen Savers. ClearType. Changing the Start menu. Using the Quick Launch toolbar. Dealing with the Security Center: Windows Firewall, Windows Update, and adding antivirus software.

Book III: Windows XP and the Internet: Expanding your reach through the Internet with dial-up, DSL, or cable modems. Outlook Express: Your tool for managing e-mail and newsgroups. Chatting and more with Windows Messenger.

Book IV: Adventures with Internet Explorer: Working with Internet Explorer. Working with Web pages intelligently. E-mailing, saving, and printing Web pages. Using the History folder. Maintaining favorites. Searching. Personalizing Internet Explorer. Speeding it up. The truth about cookies.

Book V: Connecting with Microsoft Network: MSN Explorer for busy people. Using Passport to get an ID and set your password. Setting up your own home page. E-mail and newsgroups.

Book VI: Adding and Using Other Hardware: Cameras, scanners, printers, audio, memory, memory sticks, monitors, and more. Choosing the right products and getting them to work.

Book VII: Joining the Multimedia Mix: Windows Media Player, Windows Movie Maker, digital cameras, camcorders, and other video devices. Ripping from audio CDs. Burning your own CDs. Digital licensing. Printing and sharing pictures.

Book VIII: Windows Media Center: What is it, really? How to pick a good Windows Media Center PC. Installation and set up. Running MCE for you and me.

Book IX: Setting Up a Network with Windows XP: Concepts behind peer-to-peer and client/server networking. How to build your own network quickly, easily, and reliably. Wi-Fi and other ethereal wireless topics. Protecting your network and your privacy.

Icons

Some of the points in *Windows XP All-in-One Desk Reference For Dummies*, 2nd Edition, merit your special attention. I set those points off with icons.

When I'm jumping up and down on one foot with an idea so absolutely cool I can't stand it anymore, that's when I stick a Tip icon in the margin. You can browse through any chapter and hit the very highest points by jumping from Tip to Tip.

Pssssst. Want to know the *real* story? Not the stuff Microsoft's Marketing Droids want you to hear, but the kind of information that'll give you some insight into this lumbering beast in Redmond? You'll see it all next to this icon, and on my eponymous Web site.

You don't need to memorize the stuff marked with this icon, but you should try to remember that there's something special lurking about.

Achtung! Cuidado! Thar be tygers here! Any place you see a Warning icon, you can be sure that I've been burnt — badly — in the past. Mind your fingers. These are really, really mean suckers.

Okay, so I'm a geek. I admit it. Sure, I love to poke fun at geeks. But I'm a modern, new-age sensitive guy, in touch with my inner geekiness. Sometimes I just can't help but let it out, ya know? That's where the Technical Stuff icon comes in. If you get all tied up in knots about techie stuff, pass these by. (For the record, I managed to write this whole book without telling you that an IP Address consists of a unique 32-bit combination of network ID and host ID, expressed as a set of four decimal numbers with each octet separated by periods. See? I *can* restrain myself sometimes.)

Where to Go from Here

That's about it. Time for you to crack the book open and have at it.

Don't forget to bookmark my Web site, `www.AskWoody.com`. It'll keep you up to date on all the Windows XP news you need to know — including notes about this book, the latest Windows bugs and gaffes, patches that are worse than the problems they're supposed to fix, and much more — and you can submit your most pressing questions, for free consultation from The Woodmeister hisself.

See ya! `woody@AskWoody.com`

Book I

A Windows XP Overview

The 5th Wave
By Rich Tennant
©RICHTENNANT
Good thing I had my laptop with me. Try turning it over now!

Contents at a Glance

Chapter 1: Introducing Windows XP

In This Chapter

- Where Windows XP fits into The Grand Scheme of Things
- What Windows can (and can't) do for you
- Dissecting your computer
- Installing and activating Windows XP
- Getting help

So you're sitting in front of your computer, and this thing called Windows XP is staring at you. The screen you see — the one with the peoples' names on it — is called a Welcome screen, but it doesn't say "Welcome" or "Howdy" or even "Sit down and get to work, bucko." It says only that you have to click your user name in order to start, but you don't have any idea what a user name is, why you have to have one, what Windows has to do with anything, and why in the %$#@! you can't bypass all this garbage, log on, and get your e-mail.

Good for you. That's the right attitude.

Someday, I swear, you'll be able to pull a PC out of the box, plug it into the wall, turn it on, and get your e-mail — bang, bang, bang, just like that, in ten seconds flat. If you want the computer to do something, you'll say, "Computer, get me my e-mail," just like Scotty in the *Star Trek* movies.

No matter what anyone may tell you, computers are still in their infancy. Maybe my son will see the day when they're truly easy to use, when the marketing hype about "intuitive" and "seamless" and "user friendly" actually comes true. I doubt that I will.

In the meantime, those of us who are stuck in the early 21st century have to make do with PCs that grow obsolete before you can unpack them, software that's so ornery you find yourself arguing with it, and Internet connections that surely involve turtles carrying bits on their backs.

Windows XP is one of the most sophisticated computer programs ever made. It cost more money to develop and took more people to build than any previous computer program, ever. So why is it so blasted hard to use? Why doesn't it do what you want it to do the first time? For that matter, why do you need it at all?

That's what this chapter is all about.

What Windows Does (And Doesn't Do)

Someday, you'll get really, really mad at Windows. I guarantee it. When you feel like putting your fist through the computer screen, tossing your Windows XP CD in a bonfire, or hiring an expensive Windows expert to drive out the devils within (insist on a Microsoft Certified System Exorcist, of course), read through this section. It may help you understand why and how Windows has limitations. It also may help you communicate with the geeky rescue team that tries to bail you out, whether you rely on the store that sold you the PC, the smelly guy in the apartment downstairs, or your eight-year-old daughter's nerdy classmate.

Hardware and software

At the most fundamental level, all computer stuff comes in one of two flavors: either it's hardware, or it's software. *Hardware* is anything you can touch — a computer screen, a mouse, a CD. *Software* is everything else: e-mail messages, that letter to your Aunt Martha, pictures of your last vacation, programs like Microsoft Office. If you have a roll of film developed and put on a CD, the shiny, round CD is hardware — you can touch it — but the pictures themselves are software. Get the difference?

Windows XP is software. You can't touch it. Your PC, on the other hand, is hardware. Kick the computer screen and your toe hurts. Drop the big box on the floor and it smashes into a gazillion pieces. That's hardware.

Chances are very good that one of the major PC manufacturers — Dell, HP/Compaq, IBM, Gateway/eMachines, Toshiba, Sony, and the like — made your hardware. Microsoft, and Microsoft alone, makes Windows XP. The PC manufacturers don't make Windows. Microsoft doesn't make PCs, although it does make other kinds of hardware — video game boxes, keyboards, mice, and a few other odds and ends.

When you first set up your PC, Windows had you click "I accept" to a licensing agreement that's long enough to wrap around the Empire State Building. If you're curious about what you accepted, a printed copy of the End User License Agreement is in the box that your PC came in or in the CD packaging (if you bought Windows XP separately from your computer). If you can't find your copy, choose Start⇨Help and Support. Type **eula** in the Search text box and press Enter.

When you bought your computer, you paid for a license to use one copy of Windows on the PC that you bought. The PC manufacturer paid Microsoft a royalty so that it could sell you Windows along with your PC. You may think that you got Windows from, say, Dell — indeed, you may have to contact Dell for technical support on Windows questions — but, in fact, Windows came from Microsoft.

Now you know who to blame, for sure.

Why do PCs have to run Windows?

The short answer: You *don't* have to run Windows on your PC.

The PC you have is a dumb box. (You needed me to tell you that, eh?) In order to get the dumb box to do anything worthwhile, you need a computer program that takes control of the PC and makes it do things such as show Web pages on the screen, respond to mouse clicks, or print résumés. An *operating system* controls the dumb box and makes it do worthwhile things, in ways that mere humans can understand.

Without an operating system, the computer can sit in a corner and count to itself, or put profound messages on the screen, such as `Non-system disk or disk error. Insert system disk and press any key when ready`. If you want your computer to do more than that, though, you need an operating system.

Windows is not the only operating system in town. The single largest competitor to Windows is an operating system called Linux. Some people (I'm told) actually prefer Linux to Windows, and the debates between pro-Windows and pro-Linux camps can become rather heated. Suffice it to say that, oh, 99 percent of all individual PC users stick with Windows. You probably will, too.

A terminology survival kit

Some terms pop up so frequently that you'll find it worthwhile to memorize them, or at least understand where they come from. That way, you won't be caught flatfooted when your first-grader comes home and asks if he can download a program from the Internet.

If you really want to drive your techie friends nuts, the next time you have a problem with your computer, tell them that the hassles occur when you're "running Microsoft." They won't have any idea if you mean Windows, Office, Word, Outlook, or any of a gazillion other programs.

A *program* is *software* (see preceding section) that works on a computer. Windows, the *operating system* (see preceding section), is a program. So are computer games, Microsoft Office, Microsoft Word (which is the word processor part of Office), Internet Explorer (the Web browser in Windows), the Windows Media Player, those nasty viruses you've heard about, that screen saver with the oh-too-perfect fish bubbling and bumbling about, and so on.

A special kind of program called a *driver* makes specific pieces of hardware work with the operating system. For example, your computer's printer has a driver; your monitor has a driver; your mouse has a driver; Tiger Woods has a driver. Several, actually, and he makes a living with them. Would that we were all so talented.

Sticking a program on your computer, and setting it up so that it works, is called *installing*.

When you crank up a program — that is, get it going on your computer — you can say you *started* it, *launched* it, *ran* it, or *executed* it. They all mean the same thing.

If the program quits the way it's supposed to, you can say it *stopped, finished, ended, exited,* or *terminated*. Again, all of these terms mean the same thing. If the program stops with some sort of weird error message, you can say it *crashed, died, cratered, croaked, went belly up, GPFed* (techspeak for "generated a General Protection Fault" — don't ask), or employ any of a dozen colorful but unprintable epithets. If the program just sits there and you can't get it to do anything, you can say the program *froze, hung, stopped responding,* or *went into a loop*.

A *bug* is something that doesn't work right. (A bug is not a virus! Viruses work right far too often.) Admiral Grace Hopper often repeated the story of a moth being found in a relay of an ancient Mark II computer. The moth was taped into the technician's log book on September 9, 1947, with the annotation "1545 Relay #70 Panel F (moth) in relay. First actual case of bug being found."

The people who invented all of this terminology think of the Internet as being some great blob in the sky — it's "up," as in "up in the sky." So if you send something from your computer to the Internet, you're *uploading*. If you take something off the Internet and put it on your computer, you're *downloading*.

And then you have *wizards*. Windows comes with lots of 'em. They guide you through complex procedures, moving one step at a time. Typically, wizards have three buttons on the bottom of each screen: Back, Next (or Finish), and Cancel (see Figure 1-1). Wizards remember what you've chosen as you go from step to step, making it easy to experiment a bit, change your mind, back up, and try a different setting, without getting all the check boxes confused.

That should cover about 90 percent of the buzzwords you hear in common parlance.

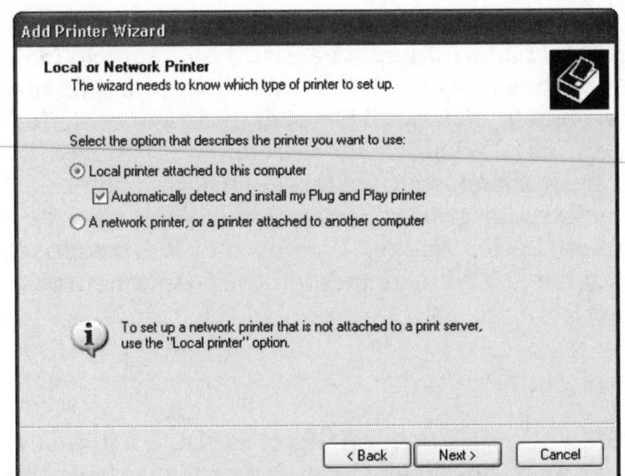

Figure 1-1: The Add Printer Wizard helps you connect printers to your computer.

Where Windows Has Been

Unlike Windows Me (which is a barely warmed-over remake of Windows 98) and Windows 2000 (which should've been called Windows NT 5.0), Windows XP is quite different from any operating system that has come before. To understand why Windows XP works so differently, you need to understand the genetic cesspool from which it emerged.

Let's start at the beginning: Microsoft licensed the first PC operating system, called DOS, to IBM in late 1981. MS-DOS sold like hotcakes for a number of reasons, not the least of which is that it was the only game in town. None of this sissy graphical stuff; DOS demanded that you type, and type, and type again, in order to get anything done.

The rise of Windows

The 'Softies only started developing Windows in earnest when the company discovered that it needed a different operating system to run Excel, its spreadsheet program. Windows 1.0 shipped in November 1985. It was slow, bloated, and unstable — some things never change, eh? — but if you wanted to run Excel, you had to have Windows.

Excel 2.0 and Windows 2.0 shipped in late 1987. This breathtaking, revolutionary new version of Windows let you overlap windows — place one window on top of another — and it took advantage of the PC/XT's advanced computer chip, the 80286. Version 2.1 (also called Windows 286) shipped in June 1988, and some people discovered that it spent more time working than crashing. My experience was, uh, somewhat different. Windows 286 came on a single diskette.

Windows 3.0 arrived in May 1990, and the computer industry changed forever. Microsoft finally had a hit on its hands to rival the old MS-DOS. When Windows 3.1 came along in April 1992, it rapidly became the most widely used operating system in history. In October 1992, Windows for Workgroups 3.1 (which I loved to call "Windows for Warehouses") started rolling out, with support for networking, shared files and printers, internal e-mail, and other features you take for granted today. Some of the features worked. Sporadically. A much better version, Windows for Workgroups 3.11, became available in November 1993. It caught on in the corporate world. Sporadically.

eNTer NT

At its heart, Windows 3.*x* was built on top of MS-DOS, and that caused all sorts of headaches: DOS simply wasn't stable or versatile enough to make Windows a rock-solid operating system. Bill Gates figured, all the way back in 1988, that DOS would never be able to support an advanced version of Windows, so he hired a guy named Dave Cutler to build a new version of Windows from scratch. At the time, Dave led the team that built the VMS operating system for Digital Equipment Corp's DEC computers.

When Dave's all-new version of Windows shipped five years later in August 1993, Windows NT 3.1 ("New Technology"; yes, the first version number was 3.1) greeted the market with a thud. It was awfully persnickety about the kinds of hardware it would support, and it didn't play games worth squat.

NT and the "old" Windows

For the next eight years, two entirely different lineages of Windows co-existed.

The old DOS/Windows 3.1 branch became Windows 95 (shipped in August 1995, "probably the last version of Windows based on DOS"), Windows 98 (June 1998, "absolutely the last version of Windows based on DOS, for sure"), and then Windows Me (Millennium Edition, September 2000, "no, honest, this is really, really the last version of Windows based on DOS").

On the New Technology side of the fence, Windows NT 3.1 begat Windows NT 3.5 (September 1994), which begat Windows NT 4.0 (August 1996). Many companies still use Windows NT 4 for their servers — the machines that anchor corporate networks. In February 2000, Microsoft released Windows 2000, which confused the living daylights out of everybody: In spite of its name, Windows 2000 is the next version of Windows NT and has nothing at all in common with Windows 98 or Me.

Microsoft made oodles of money milking the DOS-based Windows cash cow and waited patiently while sales on the NT side gradually picked up. Windows NT 5.0, er, 2000 still didn't play games worth squat, and some hardware gave it heartburn, but Windows 2000 rapidly became the operating system of choice for most businesses and at least a few home users. Still is, for many of them.

Merging the branches

Windows XP — in my opinion, the first must-have version of Windows since Windows 95 — officially shipped in October 2001. Twenty years after Microsoft tiptoed into the big time with MS-DOS, the Windows XP juggernaut blew away everything in sight.

Some people think that Windows XP (the XP stands for eXPerience, according to the marketing folks) represents a melding or blending of the two Windows lineages: a little Me here, a little 2000 there, with a side of 98.

Ain't so. Windows XP is 100 percent, bona fide NT. Period. Not one single part of Windows Me — or any of the other DOS-based Windows versions, for that matter, not to mention DOS itself — is in Windows XP. Not one.

That's good news and bad news. First, the good news: If you can get Windows XP to work at all on your old computer, or if you buy a new PC that's designed to use Windows XP, your new system will almost certainly be considerably more stable than it would be with Windows Me or any of its progenitors. The bad news: If you know how to get around a problem in Windows Me (or 98 or 95), you may not be able to use the same tricks in Windows XP. The surface may look the same. The plumbing is radically different.

Windows XP evolves

The original Windows XP, for all its faults, came shining through as a workhorse of the first degree. If you could get it installed, it almost always worked right. Microsoft waited nearly a year — until September 2002 — to release its first Service Pack, a massive collection of 300 bug fixes and security patches to the original version of Windows XP.

Actually, Microsoft released two "Service Pack 1" versions, and therein lies a legal story of clashing titans, Microsoft and Sun. The original version of Windows XP didn't include Sun's programming language, Java (otherwise known as JVM, or the Java Virtual Machine), which is used on many Web sites. Sun was miffed: In order to run Java programs on Web pages, original Windows XP users had to download and install a copy of Java, separately, and Sun felt (rightly) that Microsoft was using its monopoly on the desktop to hinder the spread of Java. After a series of legal wranglings that made the Keystone Cops look staid, Microsoft decided to put Java in Service Pack 1, and the version of SP1 that went out in September 2002 included Java. Sun was miffed again — something about oral orifices on gift horses, I think. Back to court. In February 2003, Microsoft released Service Pack 1a, which only differed from Service Pack 1 in that it *didn't* include Java. If you wanted Java, you had to download it from `www.java.com`. 'Course that happened eons (well, okay, 14 months) before Microsoft agreed to pay Sun $2 billion to settle all its open disputes and improve "interoperability" between Sun and Microsoft products — including Java and Windows. Go figger.

Microsoft continued to improve on Windows XP, with new versions of Windows Media Player, Windows Movie Maker, Windows for telephones, Windows for toasters, Windows for telephones attached to toasters with integrated roasters and coasters and more. But, hands down, the most impressive new product to come out of Redmond in the post-Windows XP era has to be Windows XP Media Center Edition, a program that runs on top of Windows XP and gives you tremendous control over your television, cable, satellite, stereo system — everything for the couch potato except the couch.

Simultaneously, black-hat cretins all over the world discovered that PCs attached directly to the Internet running Windows XP had "Kick Me" signs posted all over them. Microsoft responded with security patches and patches to patches and patches to patches to patches. Bill stopped all the work at Microsoft to run a month-long "security lockdown." The net result: more patches and patches to patches and . . . well, you get the idea.

Thus, nearly two years after Service Pack 1, Windows XP users got treated to Service Pack 2, a huge roll-up of new features and patches, and patches disguised as features. Some things never change.

The Future of Windows

When Windows XP got beaten to a pulp by a few dozen relentless virus and worm writers, and courts around the world found Microsoft guilty of all manner of egregious behavior, the company's tune changed quickly. We stopped hearing so much about Microsoft's breast-beating plans to dominate every nook and cranny of computerdom. In some cases — Microsoft's decision to stop keeping financial information in .NET Passports, for example — Microsoft stopped sounding so much like a convicted monopolist bull in a china shop and more like a socially responsible, trustworthy team player.

I remain skeptical.

The next version of Windows, code-named Longhorn, remains a great unknown. This much is certain: It will be very different from the Windows XP you know today. Between a new user interface, bolted-to-the-walls security, greatly improved storage and retrieval capabilities, searching and indexing from the get-go, DVD support par excellence, and a new communications subsystem, Longhorn improvements look great. On paper.

At the same time, Microsoft is moving out of the business of selling software into the business of renting it — and charging for the "glue" that binds companies, individuals, buyers, and sellers together. Whether either of those shifts makes the lives of Windows users easier remains to be seen. But the profitability of it all beckons, loud and clear.

Now's a great time to dig into Windows XP and get to know it. Future versions of Windows may well seem anticlimactic, compared to this one.

Anatomy of a Computer

Here's how it usually goes. You figure you need to buy a new PC. So you spend a couple of weeks brushing up on the details — bits and bytes and kilobytes and megabytes and gigabytes — and comparison shopping. You end up at your local Computers Were Us shop, and this guy behind the counter convinces you that the absolutely best bargain you'll ever see is sitting right here, right now, and you'd better take it quick before somebody else nabs it.

Your eyes glaze over as you look at yet another spec sheet and try to figure out one last time if a RAM is a ROM and how a CD-R differs from a CD-RW and whether you need a DVD-R or DVD+R. In the end, you figure the guy behind the counter must know what he's doing, so you plunk down your plastic and pray you got a good deal.

The next Sunday morning you look in the paper and discover you could've bought twice as much machine for half as much money. The only thing you know for sure is that your PC is hopelessly out of date, and the next time you'll be smarter about the whole process.

If that describes your experiences, relax. It happens to everybody. Take solace in the fact that you bought twice as much machine for the same amount of money as the poor schmuck who went through the same process last month.

In this section, I try to give you just enough information about the inner workings of your PC so that you can figure out what you have to do with Windows. The details will change from week to week. But these are the basics.

Inside the big box

The big box that your computer lives in is sometimes called *a CPU,* meaning Central Processing Unit (see Figure 1-2). Right off the bat, you're bound to get confused, unless somebody clues you in on one important detail: The main computer chip inside that big box is *also* called a CPU. I prefer to call the big box "the PC" because of the naming ambiguity, but you have probably thought of a few better names.

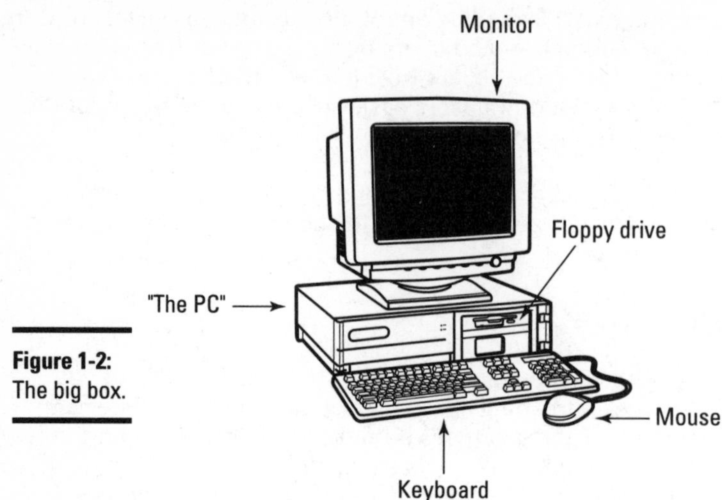

Figure 1-2: The big box.

The big box contains many parts and pieces (and no small amount of dust and dirt), but the crucial, central element inside every PC is the *motherboard* (see Figure 1-3). Attached to the motherboard you'll find

- **The *processor* or CPU:** This gizmo does all the computing. It's probably from Intel or AMD or one of their competitors. People who sell computers rate the processors by speed, measured in MHz (megahertz) or GHz (gigahertz, 1 GHz = 1,024 MHz). Windows XP runs like a slug on anything slower than 300 MHz or so.

  If you're buying a new computer, the speed really doesn't mean much, unless you're designing airplane wings, reshooting *Jurassic Park,* or you play a lot of games on your PC. Ignore the salesperson. If you want to improve Windows XP performance, your money should go to more memory (see next) or a fast Internet connection.

- **Memory chips and places to put them:** Memory is measured in MB (megabytes). Windows XP runs on a machine with 64MB — I've done it — but you usually want 256MB or more. Most computers allow you to add more memory to them, and boosting your computer's memory to 512MB from 256MB makes it much snappier, especially if you run memory hogs such as Office, PageMaker, or Photoshop. If you leave Outlook 2003 open and work with it all day, and run almost any other major program at the same time, 512MB will make a big difference.
- **Lots of other stuff:** You'll never have to play with this other stuff, unless you're very unlucky.

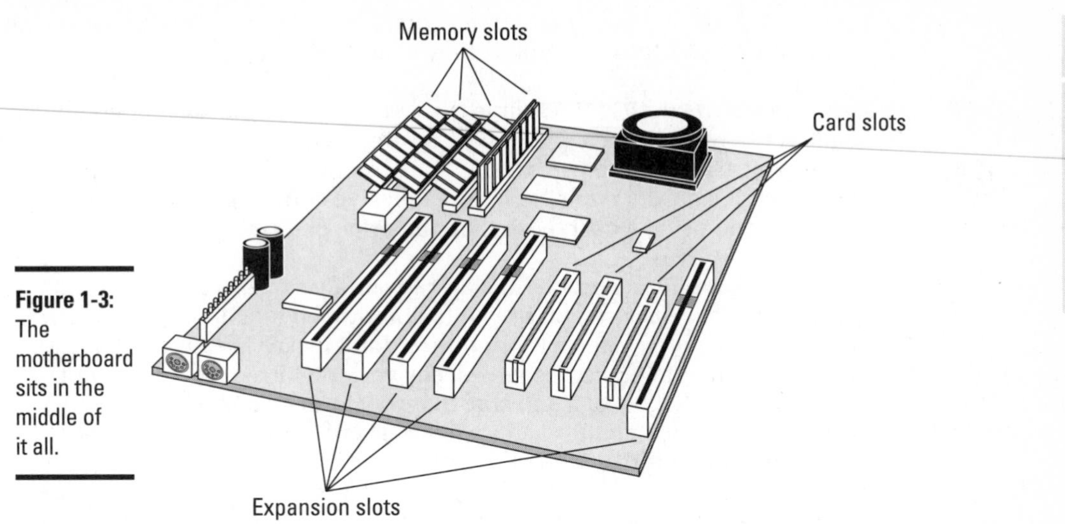

Figure 1-3: The motherboard sits in the middle of it all.

Never let a salesperson talk you into eviscerating your PC and upgrading the CPU: A 2.0 GHz PC doesn't run a whole lot faster than a 1.6 GHz PC. Memory upgrades don't mean much beyond 512MB: You'll see a noticeable improvement in performance up to the 512MB mark, especially if you run multiple memory-hungry applications at the same time (I won't mention Office 2003 by name), but very little improvement beyond that. Instead of nickel-and-diming yourself to death on little upgrades, wait until you can afford a new PC, and give away your old one.

If you decide to get more memory, have the company that sells you the memory install it. The process is simple, quick, and easy — if you know what you're doing. Having the dealer install the memory also puts the monkey on their back if a memory chip doesn't work or a bracket gets snapped.

What you see, what you get

The *computer monitor* or *screen* — you may think of it as a hoity-toity TV — uses technology that's quite different from what you have in your television set. A TV scans lines across the screen from left to right, with hundreds of them stacked on top of each other. Colors on each individual line vary all over the place. The near-infinitely variable color on a TV combined with a comparatively small number of lines makes for pleasant, but fuzzy, pictures.

By contrast (pun absolutely intended, of course), a computer monitor works with dots of light, called *pixels*. Each pixel can have a different color, but the maximum number of different colors that can appear on the screen at one time is limited. As a result, computer monitors are much sharper than TV tubes, but if the number of on-screen colors is restricted, pictures shown on the monitor won't look as good as they would on a TV set.

Although it's theoretically possible to use a TV set as a makeshift computer monitor, the result leaves much to be desired. So-called *scan converters* allow you to plug a TV set into the back of your computer, but text ends up so murky that it's hardly readable. Very expensive converters sharpen text — but in the end usually cost more than the price of a new monitor.

LCD monitors or *flat screens* hold many advantages over traditional monitors: The lines are always straight; the units don't weigh much, they're small and they don't use much electricity; and they don't flicker like fireflies in heat. On the other hand, the flatties are expensive; individual pixels on an LCD screen can and do go black and stay that way forever; and a high-quality well-adjusted traditional monitor can always deliver a better, richer picture — if you're snooty about that kind of thing.

Most people set up Windows XP to run at 1024 x 768 pixels — that is, their monitors show 1024 pixels across the screen, with 768 running up and down — on 17 inch or smaller conventional monitors or 15-inch LCD monitors. Some folks have screens (and eyes!) that are good enough to run 1280 x 1024. Others limp along at 800 x 600. The more pixels you can cram on a screen — that is, the higher the *screen resolution* — the more information you can pack on the screen. That's important if you commonly have more than one word-processing document open at a time, for example. At 800 x 600, two open Word documents placed side by side look big but fuzzy, like viewing them through a dirty magnifying glass. At 1280 x 1024, those same two documents look sharp, but the text may be so small that you have to squint to make it out.

A special-purpose computer stuck on a board called a *graphics adapter* creates everything that's shown on your computer's screen. The graphics adapter has to juggle all the pixels and all the colors — so if you're a gaming fan, the speed of the adapter's chip can make the difference between a zapped alien and a lost energy shield. People who sell graphics adapters for home and office rate them in accordance with both their resolution and their *color depth,* and the two are interrelated: A graphics adapter that can handle 1024 x 768 pixels on the screen with 64,000 colors showing simultaneously may be able to show 1280 x 1024 pixels, but only 256 simultaneous colors.

If you don't like the graphics adapter that shipped with your computer, you can always buy a new one. But beware of one big potential problem. The drivers that ship with new graphics adapters — the programs that allow Windows XP to control the graphics adapter — are notorious for being buggy and unstable. Think twice before buying a new graphics adapter, and always update the driver to the latest version by following the instructions on the manufacturer's Web site: Don't bother installing the software that came on the CD in the box.

Computer monitors are sold by size, measured diagonally, like TV sets. Just like TV sets, the only way to pick a good computer screen over a run-of-the-mill one is to compare them side by side or to follow the recommendation of someone who has.

Managing disks

Your PC's memory chips hold information only temporarily: Turn off the electricity, and the contents of main memory goes bye-bye. If you want to reuse your work, keeping it around after the plug has been pulled, you have to save it, typically on a disk. The following are the most common types of disks:

- **Floppies:** The 1.44MB floppy disk drives that were ubiquitous on PCs for many years are becoming an endangered species — most new PCs (especially laptops) no longer come with floppy disk drives. Still, it's going to make more than a few silver bullets and strands of garlic to get rid of them completely.

  You probably know how to put a floppy disk into a drive (right-side up with the slidey-metal-thing pointing into the PC). You may not know how to get a recalcitrant floppy out of the drive. Sometimes the slide starts bowing, and the floppy hangs when you press the eject button. If that happens to you, get a long pair of thin tweezers — stamp collector's tongs work great — turn off your PC, unplug it, grab the diskette between the prongs of the tweezers and gently pry the diskette out. You have to get the tweezers all the way down beyond the tip of the slide, so longer is definitely better.

- **Hard drives:** Get the biggest, cheapest one(s) you can; electronic pictures swallow up an enormous amount of space. While it's generally true that more expensive hard drives seem to be more reliable than cheaper ones, objective numbers are hard to come by, and individual results will vary all over the place. Speed doesn't matter much, and the technology (ATA, EIDE, SCSI) matters even less.

  If you buy a new hard drive, have the dealer install it. You have to worry about lots of permutations and combinations, and it simply isn't worth the effort. Life's too short.

- **CD and DVD drives:** Of course, these drives work with CDs and DVDs, which can be filled with data or contain music or movies. Although Windows XP will play an audio CD automatically, you may have to jump through some extra hoops to get it to play DVDs. See the section on "Multimedia galore," later in this chapter, for details.

- **CD-R drives:** These drives let you create (*burn*) your own CDs. After you burn a CD in a CD-R drive, you generally can't reburn it. If you *can* get Windows XP to reburn a CD, you might not be able to play the reburned disc in a CD player — or even in another PC. *Caveat burnor.*

✦ **CD-RW drives:** These drives not only allow you to burn CDs; they're also reusable. The CD-RW drive, in conjunction with CD-RWs, lets you burn and reburn to your heart's content.

Most older audio CD players — like the one you probably have in your car or your home stereo — will play only CDs that are burned with a CD-R drive. You can't reburn audio CDs.

✦ **CD-R/CD-RW drives:** Many drives nowadays can create both CD-Rs and CD-RWs, just to confuse everybody. You need CD-Rs if you're going to burn audio CDs. You probably want CD-RWs for everything else, even though the blank discs themselves cost more than blank CD-Rs.

✦ **DVD-RW/DVD+RW drives:** If you think the CD terminology is confusing, wait till you look at DVDs. The DVD world is divided into two camps: DVD-R ("DVD slash R"), which uses one method for encoding and reading data; and DVD+R ("DVD plus R"), which uses a completely different (and incompatible) method.

If you're going to buy a DVD recorder, get one that'll burn both DVD-RW and DVD+RWs. That gives you the option of creating "-R" discs if you need to play them in a "-R only" player. In general, when burning DVDs for use on other PCs, buy the cheapest discs you can find that don't turn themselves into pixie dust. When burning DVDs for use in a commercial DVD player, use brand name discs and DVD+R.

✦ **USB Flash Drive:** Treat them like lollipops. Half the size of a pack of gum, and able to hold an entire PowerPoint presentation or two or six, flash memory should be your first choice for external storage space or for copying files between computers. Pop one of these guys in a USB slot (see the next section) and suddenly Windows XP knows it has another drive — except this one's fast, portable, and incredibly easy to use. Make sure you get USB 2.0 support, and only pay for password protection if you need it. The rest of the "features" are just, uh, Windows dressing.

This list is by no means definitive: There are Jaz disks, Zip drives, and recordable media that sing till the cows come home.

Making PC connections

Your PC connects to the outside world using a bewildering variety of cables and connectors. The most common are as follows:

✦ **USB (Universal Serial Bus) cables:** These cables have a flat connector that plugs into your PC. The other end is usually shaped like a D, but different pieces of hardware have different *terminators*. ("I'll be back . . .") USB is the connector of choice for just about any kind of hardware — printers, scanners, MP3 players, Palm/pocket computers, portable hard drives, even mice. If you run out of USB connections on the back of your PC, get a USB hub with a separate power supply and plug away.

✦ **RJ-45 connectors:** These are the most common kind of network connectors. They look like overweight telephone plugs (see Figure 1-4). One end plugs into your PC, typically into a *NIC* (Network Interface Card, pronounced "nick"), a network connector on the motherboard, or a network connector on a card that slides into a port (a so-called "PC Card" or "PCMCIA Card"). The other end plugs into your network's hub (see Figure 1-5), switch, or possibly into a cable modem, DSL box, router, or other Internet connection-sharing device.

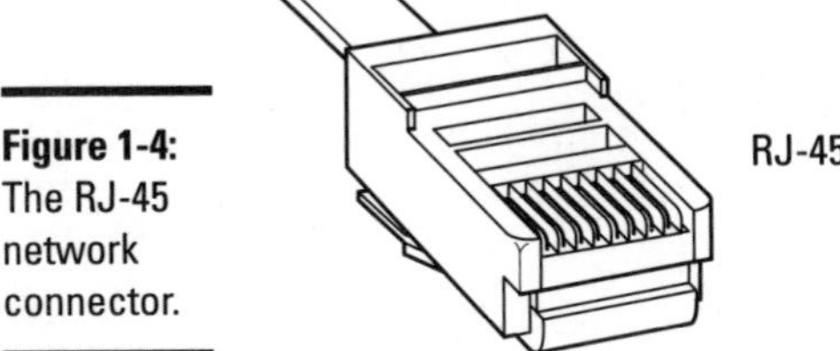

Figure 1-4: The RJ-45 network connector.

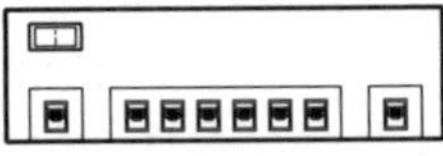

Figure 1-5: A network hub.

✦ **PS/2 or mini-DIN connectors:** These are round connectors with six pins and a plastic hump that prevents you from getting the connector twisted around in the wrong direction (see Figure 1-6). Ancient technology that works great. Commonly found on keyboards and mice.

If you have a mouse and a keyboard, both with PS/2 connectors, but your PC sports only one PS/2 slot, not to worry! Most cable manufacturers have Y connectors that allow you to attach two PS/2 devices to a single port. Surprisingly, both the mouse and the keyboard can co-exist with nary a hiccup. Try `www.cablestogo.com`.

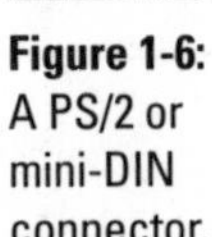

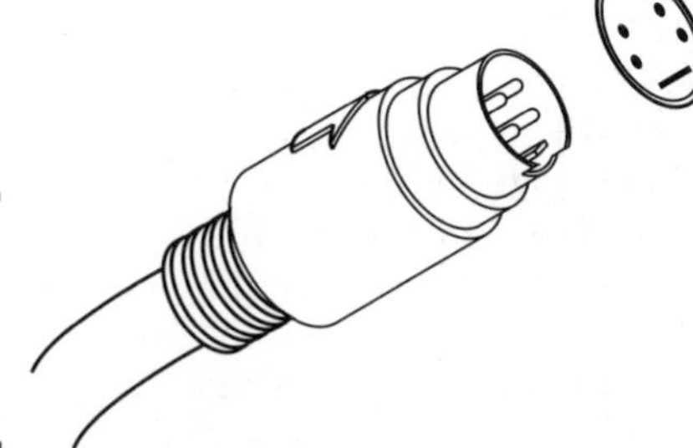

Figure 1-6: A PS/2 or mini-DIN connector.

- **Parallel and serial ports:** These are the long (parallel, 25-pin, with 13 pins on top and 12 on the bottom) and short (serial, 9-pin, five on top and four on the bottom) connections on the back of your computer. The serial port is notoriously slow, and both kinds sometimes fall apart — which is particularly disconcerting when you unscrew a connector and a nut falls off inside your computer. If you have a choice, choose USB.

Futzing with sound

If you plug your computer's speakers directly into the back of the PC, the whole process won't strain any little gray cells (see Figure 1-7).

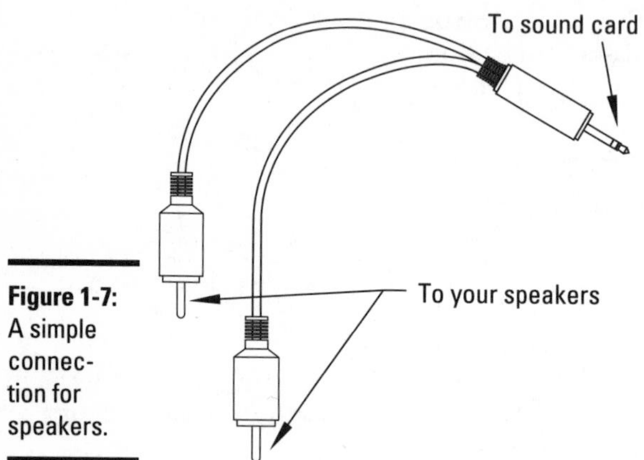

Figure 1-7: A simple connection for speakers.

Most Windows XP users care about sound, and many find that tiny, tinny speakers meticulously paired with an underaspirated amp sound about as bad as Leonard Nimoy singing *The Star Spangled Banner.* (No offense, Leonard, okay?)

Chances are pretty good that you are running Windows XP on a PC with at least a little oomph in the audio department. If so, you have to be concerned about four different sound jacks because each one does something different. Your machine may not have all four. (Are you feeling inadequate yet?) Here's how they are usually marked, although sometimes you have to root around in the documentation to find details:

- **Line in:** A stereo input jack. Feeds a stereo signal into the PC. Not used very often, but it can be handy if you need to record a radio program or digitize something on audio tape.

- **Mike in:** Almost exclusively used for voice-recognition systems, where you speak into the microphone and the computer attempts to convert your speech into text. There are lots of gotchas, particularly when selecting microphones. See `www.woodyswatch.com/office/archtemplate.asp?v6-n30` for details.
- **Line out:** A stereo output jack that bypasses the computer's internal amplifier. This is the source for the highest-quality sound your computer can produce.
- **Headphone or speaker out:** Goes through the internal amplifier. Use this jack for headphones or speakers, but avoid it in all other situations.

PC manufacturers love to extol the virtues of their advanced sound systems, but the simple fact is that you can hook up a rather plain-vanilla PC to a home stereo and get great sound. Just connect the "line out" jack on the back of your PC to the "Aux in" jack on your home stereo. *Voilà!*

Do You Need Windows XP?

If you haven't yet decided whether Windows XP or Windows XP Media Center Edition is worth the plunge, this section should help you make up your mind.

You can safely skip this section, unless you have to justify the upgrade to the boss — or your spouse. Trust me. You want Windows XP — and you may want the Media Center, too. Read on to find out why.

It just works

In the vast majority of cases, Windows XP works far more reliably than any other version of Windows. One of the main reasons why: Windows XP successfully protects itself from programs that try to overwrite its crucial files. The end — or at least the severe curtailing — of "DLL hell," where incompatible versions of programs overwrite each other, goes a long way toward increasing Windows XP's reliability.

Although rooting around inside Windows XP is certainly an order of magnitude more complex than in Windows 98 or Me, you're much less likely to dig into the bowels of Windows XP, unless you're running some really weird, relatively old hardware or trying to coax a hopelessly ancient game into action.

Multimedia galore

If you want to use your computer for music, pictures, video, and the like, Windows XP has plenty of good news for you: Microsoft finally gets it. Well, more than it used to, anyway.

Workgroups and domains

When you attach computers to each other (that is, you network them), you can choose from two inherently different ways to go. In a *client/server network,* which Microsoft calls a *domain,* one computer (the server) controls access to all the others (the clients). On the other hand, in a *peer-to-peer network,* which Microsoft calls a *workgroup,* all of the computers are equal, with no single computer standing out above all the rest.

Client/server networks abound in large companies, where central control is crucial. Network Administrators set up security rules, grant access where needed, allow new users to get onto client PCs, and generally ride herd on the entire network. Usually the server(s) hold important corporate files and backup copies of key files on the client computers. Usually the major networked printers hang off of the server(s). Usually all Internet access goes through the server(s). Usually.

Peer-to-peer networking, on the other hand, doesn't get hung up in the kind of security and central administration that client/server networks take for granted. For example, a typical user on a peer-to-peer network can share a disk drive so that anybody on the network can see it. On a client/server network, you'd have to call in the Network Administrator.

At the risk of over-simplifying, peer-to-peer networking works best in homes and small offices where security isn't a major concern. Client/server networking works best in larger companies with significant security needs — and a budget to match. Network Administrators don't come cheap.

One of the most controversial parts of Windows XP is its limited support (some would say "lack of support") for the MP3 audio format. A lot of misinformation is floating around about Windows XP and MP3, so let me set the record straight:

- ✦ If you have MP3 files, Windows XP will play them, no hassle, no sweat. You can e-mail MP3 files, burn CDs and DVDs full of them, copy and trade them to your heart's content, and Windows XP helps you every inch of the way.
- ✦ On the other hand, if you are trying to convert audio CD tracks to MP3 format (a process called *ripping*), Windows XP won't help much — for many reasons, but two stand out:
    - Microsoft would have to pay a royalty for the technology that allows audio CD tracks to be converted to MP3. Microsoft doesn't want to pay a royalty for every copy of Windows XP that's sold, so it doesn't ship fully functional MP3 ripping technology in the box with Windows XP. You have to pay extra for it, find the ripper somewhere else and install it on your machine, or get the ripper some other way — perhaps along with your MP3 player.

  - Microsoft has no incentive for building MP3 ripping technology into Windows XP. Some wags (this one included) feel that Microsoft could've done something more to support MP3 ripping if it wanted to badly enough. But it doesn't want to. Microsoft wants the world to change to its own WMA audio file format for a bunch of reasons, not the least of which is the fact that WMA discourages piracy.

✦ No matter where you stand on the ethical questions surrounding piracy, Microsoft can clearly make a lot of money helping companies sell (non-pirated) music files. It doesn't make squat from pirated copies.

Windows XP does not include DVD support, straight out of the box. Again, licensing considerations take the brunt of the blame. Unless DVD playback software came with your DVD player or PC, you have to find, pay for, and install DVD playback software before Windows XP will play DVDs.

Windows XP also includes digital camera support that's automatic, full-featured, and probably better than the software that shipped with your camera. Add the slide show feature built into Windows Explorer, and digital imaging takes a giant leap forward.

Easy multiuser support

Windows XP/Home makes setting up multiple users on the same machine very easy:

✦ Each user can have his or her own password or decide not to use a password at all.

✦ With Windows XP/Home, you don't have to memorize user names or passwords: one click and you're in.

✦ You can switch among users quickly and easily. So if your daughter wants to check her Hotmail quickly while you go get a sandwich, all it takes is a click.

✦ Your programs keep running when you switch users, unless you specifically close them down.

Windows XP/Pro, straight out of the box, retains the old you-gotta-know-yer-user-id-and-password-to-get-in bias, and it won't allow you to switch quickly between users, but in a corporate environment with centralized access controls, that makes sense. (You can change Windows XP/Pro to make it act like Windows XP/Ho me, though — and you can add some password restrictions to Windows XP/Home accounts.)

Making networks easy

Windows XP finally delivers on Microsoft's promise to make simple networking simple. That's no small accomplishment, as anyone who's struggled with assembling and maintaining a network can readily attest. In most cases, putting together a small network of Windows XP, 2000, Me, and 98 PCs is as easy as connecting the wires and running a wizard. Really.

The good news extends well beyond the mechanics of pulling together a network. Windows XP makes sharing an Internet connection among many machines easy, whether they're running Windows XP, 2000, Me, or even lowly Windows 98. Sharing a printer with any other computer on a network takes a few clicks. Sharing a disk drive takes even less effort.

Do you need Windows XP/Pro?

Windows XP/Pro costs a whole heckuvalot more than Windows XP/Home, but for many folks, both at home and at the office, Windows XP/Home beats the pants off Windows XP/Pro. The arguments, both, uh, Pro and Con, may get esoteric and techie very quickly. What's a Dummy to do?

Fortunately, the situation isn't nearly as difficult as you may think. In most situations, if you get to pick the version of Windows XP that's right for you, you want Windows XP/Home. If somebody else makes the decision — presumably a corporate IT department or some such — they probably choose Windows XP/Pro, simply because it fits into the existing PC network better.

You should buy Windows XP/Pro if

- ✦ You want to set up a secure, client/server network (see sidebar "Workgroups and domains"). If you think Windows XP/Pro itself is expensive, wait until you see the bill for this one.
- ✦ Your company wants you to use Windows XP/Pro. They probably have good reasons to spend the extra bucks, mostly centered around security, central administration, and automated backup.
- ✦ While you're on the road, you need to dial into your computer at work and use it directly from your laptop. That demands a feature called Remote Desktop, which runs only with Windows XP/Pro.
- ✦ The machine you're currently using runs Windows 2000 Pro (or Windows NT 4), and you want to upgrade it directly to Windows XP, carrying across all of your settings.

You can upgrade directly from Windows 98 or Windows Me to either Windows XP/Home or Windows XP/Pro, and bring all of your settings with you. See the next section, "Upgrading to Windows XP — A Brain Transplant."

Windows XP/Pro comes in handy in a corporate environment in a few minor ways. For example, it handles Roaming Profiles, which let you log onto any computer on the network and retrieve your settings, and it has built-in security hooks that let you get at folders even when the server is not working (so-called Offline Folders) — but none of the other Windows XP/Pro features are show stoppers.

What about Windows XP Media Center?

If you're an inveterate toy freak, you don't need me to answer that question.

But if you're kind of sitting on a fence, and you don't want to throw away a few thousand bucks on some piece of technology that's sure to be obsolete in a couple of years, consider this:

✦ Windows XP Media Center Edition (affectionately known as MCE) is a program that runs on top of Windows XP. That means MCE inherits all of the truly rich capabilities of Windows XP itself, including the Windows Media Player, which is a crucial component of MCE.

In the same breath, it also means that MCE inherits all of the problems in Windows XP itself, and adds another layer of bugs and potential security problems. A quick glance through Microsoft's Knowledge Base will rapidly confirm that even MCE gets the buggy blues.

✦ Some people love the MCE approach — a keyboard and TV-style remote, typically sitting on a couch or coffee table, that let you get at the more common multimedia capabilities functions quickly and easily. It's a great way to drive a big screen TV. Some people would rather just sit at their PC to watch a movie, or prop a portable up on the coffee table and get rid of the software middleman.

✦ On the other hand, Microsoft's marketing clout means that all sorts of new features — particularly the kind that require cooperation with satellite and cable TV companies — are sure to appear on MCE systems at the earliest possible instant. With MCE, you're driving the best, and the rest of the industry knows it.

No matter how you look at it, Windows XP Media Center Edition is still in its infancy. Unlike many other Microsoft products, though, this youngster appears to be here to stay.

Upgrading to Windows XP — A Brain Transplant

If your current machine runs Windows 98 or Me, you can upgrade to Windows XP by simply starting Windows, inserting the Windows XP CD into the CD drive, and following the instructions.

If you decide that Windows XP isn't your cup of tea, you can remove it and restore your old Windows 98 or Me system, intact. Here's how:

1. **Choose Start➪Control Panel.**
2. **Click Add and Remove Programs.**
3. **Click Windows XP, and then click Add/Remove.**
4. **Pick the option to Uninstall Windows XP, and click Continue.**

If your current machine runs Windows NT 4 or Windows 2000, you can upgrade to Windows XP/Pro directly with the CD. However, you will not be able to automatically uninstall Windows XP and revert to NT 4 or 2000.

If your current machine runs Windows 95 or NT 3.*x*, you won't be able to upgrade. Your only option is to erase Windows from your hard drive (never a simple proposition) and perform a clean install from scratch (see the section, "Considering a clean install," for sobering enlightenment). Chances are good that your Windows 95 or NT 3.*x* system isn't powerful enough to run Windows XP very well anyway. It's far better to wait until you can afford a new PC that comes with Windows XP preinstalled.

Windows Upgrade Advisor/Hardware Compatibility List

Before you upgrade an existing PC to Windows XP, you should check the machine to make sure there are no known problems. Microsoft distributes a program called the Windows XP Upgrade Advisor that reaches into the innermost parts of your PC and reports on potential problems with the upgrade. You can download the Windows XP/Home Upgrade Advisor from `www.microsoft.com/windowsxp/home/howtobuy/upgrading/advisor.asp`. The Windows XP/Pro advisor is at `www.microsoft.com/windowsxp/pro/howtobuy/upgrading/advisor.asp`. You may also find a copy of both advisors on a free CD at your friendly local computer shop.

Microsoft used to publish a master list of all hardware that's passed muster for Windows XP — a so-called Windows Hardware Compatibility List — but that useful tool has been supplanted by a piece of marketing fluff called the Windows Catalog (`www.microsoft.com/windowsxp/pro/upgrading/compat.mspx`). The Windows Catalog consists of paid advertising, which is worse than useless. (The same could be said, in spades, about Windows Marketplace.) Read the fine print at the bottom of the page: "The Windows Catalog is provided for informational purposes only and Microsoft makes no representations and warranties, either expressed, implied, or statutory, regarding the products, manufacturers, compatibility of the products available within, or the Windows Catalog." What a crock.

There's a tremendous, unbiased list of Windows XP compatibility problem reports covering every imaginable piece of hardware and software available at `www.ntcompatible.com/compatibility.html`. In spite of its name, the NT Compatible Web site deals with Windows NT, 2000, and XP.

Considering a clean install

Windows XP is an enormously complex program. In the best of all possible worlds, if you upgrade from your current version of Windows — be it 98, Me, NT 4, or 2000 — to Windows XP, the upgrade routines successfully grab all of your old settings, get rid of the extraneous garbage that's floating around on your old machine, and install a stable, pristine copy of Windows XP, ready for you to take around the block.

Unfortunately, the world is not always a pretty place, and your hard drive probably looks like a bit-strewn sewer. Historically, Windows has been considerably less stable for upgraders than for those who perform a *clean install* — wiping out the contents of the hard drive and starting all over again. All the flotsam and jetsam left from an old version of Windows invariably mucks up the works with the new version.

A clean install is not for the faint of heart. No matter how hard you try, you will lose data, somewhere, somehow — it always happens, even to those of us masochists who have been running clean installs for a decade. If you value everything on your computer, go for the simple upgrade. If you want your PC to run smoothly, think about a clean install.

The following is my general procedure for a clean install, on computers that can start from the CD drive, in very broad terms:

1. **Download and install Revelation from SnadBoy software at `www.snadboy.com` (see Figure 1-8).**

   Use Revelation for a few days (or weeks!) to retrieve any passwords that you may have stashed away.

2. **Make sure that you have current CDs for all the software that you normally use.**

   If the programs require passwords/installation keys, you need the passwords, too.

3. **Back up everything. Twice.**

   If you have a Windows XP computer handy, and you can attach it to the PC that you're upgrading through a network or a direct-connect cable, you may want to try a Vulcan Mind Meld, er, the Windows XP Migration Wizard. Use it to transfer all your files and settings over to the other PC, temporarily. Follow the instructions in the next section, "Using the

Migration Wizard," to pick up the settings before you perform the upgrade and stick them on the temporary machine. Then follow the instructions again to move them from the temporary PC back to your (freshly upgraded) original PC.

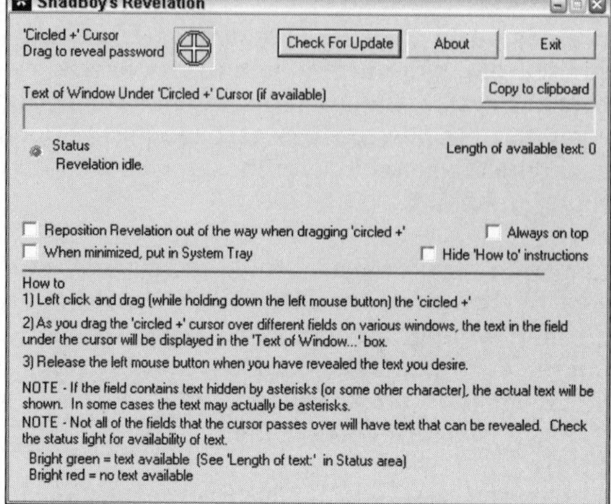

Figure 1-8: SnadBoy's Revelation lets you see passwords that appear as ****** on the screen.

4. **Insert the Windows XP installation disc in the CD drive, and then choose Start➪Shut Down to go through a full shut down.**

   Windows XP may offer to install itself while you're trying to shut down. If it does, click Cancel. Power off the PC and wait at least a full minute.

5. **Turn the power on.**

   If the PC is capable of starting ("booting") from the CD, you see a line on the screen that says something like `Press any key to boot from CD.` Press the Enter key.

6. **Go through the steps indicated by the installer to delete the primary partition.**

   That wipes out all the data on the hard drive.

7. **Pick your jaw up from the floor, kick yourself twice for being so obstinate, pat yourself on the back for starting out fresh, and follow through with the rest of the installation.**

   Windows XP does a good job of taking you through the steps. Just follow along. The only really tricky part of the installation: Windows XP has to restart your PC early in the installation process. When that happens, you'll probably get that `Press any key to boot from the CD` message again. This time — the second time you see the message — ignore it. Let Windows XP start itself from the hard drive.

Clean installs rate right up there with root canals and prostate exams. Nobody in their right mind will try one, unless they really want to make sure that Windows will run smoothly. That said, I try to perform a clean install on all of my systems at least once a year. It can make a big difference.

Using the Migration Wizard

Windows XP's Files and Settings Transfer Wizard (better known as the Migration Wizard) makes transferring certain kinds of settings and data files between two computers comparatively easy. It sounds great and works well, as long as you don't expect too much. You need to be aware of several limitations:

✦ The PC you're transferring files and settings "to" must be running Windows XP. If at all possible, it should be connected to the PC that you're transferring settings "from." The "from" PC can be running Windows 95, 98, Me, NT 4, 2000, or XP.

The Files and Settings Transfer Wizard can send a humongous amount of data from one PC to another. You can schlep diskettes from one machine to another, if you have a few spare hours (or days). Far better, though, is if you can get both PCs talking to each other on a network. Failing that, you can buy a special cable called a "Serial PC to PC Transfer Cable" that plugs into the serial slots on both PCs (the slots you may be using for printers). The wizard will work with any of 'em.

✦ The wizard can't install your old programs on your new PC. You have to do that yourself, manually, one at a time, generally from the original CDs that the programs came on.

If you use the Files and Settings Transfer Wizard but you don't install all of your old programs on your new PC, weird things may happen on the new PC. You may double-click on a file in Windows Explorer, for example, and have Windows XP say that it can't find the program associated with the file. Outlook may have trouble displaying a file attached to a message. Nothing earth-shattering will happen, mind you, but it can be annoying.

✦ The wizard picks up only data files and some Windows Registry entries. That means you can't expect it to pull across all of your passwords, and some copy-protection schemes (on games, for example) may go haywire.

On the plus side, though, the Files and Settings Transfer Wizard doesn't pick up much of the garbage that seems to accumulate in every Windows PC, which means you can use it without gumming up your new computer. Too much.

Here are the kinds of things you can expect to go across in a transfer:

✦ Data files from your Windows desktop, the My Documents folder (including My Pictures and My Music, if you have those in the My Documents folder), and the Shared Desktop and Documents folders.

- Other files scattered around your hard drive(s), as long as Windows recognizes them as common data files.

The Files and Settings Transfer Wizard really chooses which files to transfer based on the filename extension. It looks for filename extensions that are commonly associated with data files, such as `.doc` or `.jpg`. See the section on showing filename extensions in Book I, Chapter 3 for a lengthy tirade on this topic.

- Settings for Windows (desktop, screen savers, taskbar options, and the like), Windows Explorer, Internet Explorer (including your list of Favorites), and Outlook Express.
- All of your Microsoft Office settings.

To use the File and Settings Transfer Wizard, follow these steps:

1. **Make sure Windows XP is up and running on the "to" PC.**

   Get your hardware installed, set up your users, and run Windows XP long enough to be familiar with it.

2. **Log on the "to" PC as the user who's supposed to receive all the files and settings from the "from" PC.**

   If both the "to" and "from" PCs are connected to your network, choose Start⇨My Network Places or Start⇨My Computer to make sure that the network connection is up and kicking. If they aren't connected to the same network, get a Serial PC to PC Transfer Cable and attach it to the serial ports on both PCs.

3. **Choose Start⇨Files and Settings Transfer Wizard, if it's on the Start menu.**

   If it isn't, choose Start⇨All Programs⇨Accessories⇨System Tools⇨Files and Settings Transfer Wizard.

4. **Follow the steps in the wizard (see Figure 1-9).**

   The exact steps vary depending on the method you're using to transfer the data. If you have many large documents or picture files, plan on spending a few hours. If you're transferring by diskette, don't be surprised if it takes a day.

If you perform a scorched-earth clean install of Windows XP (see the preceding section), you can use the Files and Settings Transfer Wizard twice to drag most of your data (but none of your programs!) through the upgrade, even though you delete everything on your hard drive in the process of upgrading. All it takes is an intermediary machine running Windows XP that holds your settings while the old PC is wiped clean. For the first run of the Files and Settings Transfer Wizard, use the intermediary machine as the "to" machine. Then upgrade the old PC. Finally, run the Files and Settings Transfer Wizard again, this time using the intermediary machine as the "from" machine. Works like a champ.

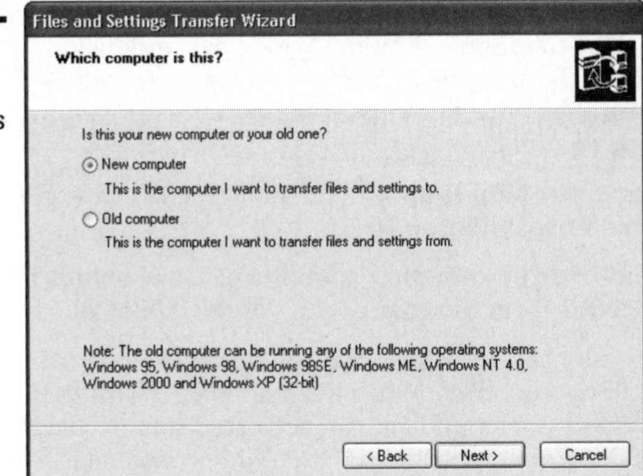

Figure 1-9: The Files and Settings Transfer Wizard can send most (but not all) of your important information from an old PC to a new one.

Product Activation

When you buy a copy of Windows XP in a shrink-wrapped box, you're allowed to install it on one — and only one — PC.

When you buy a new PC with Windows XP preinstalled, Windows stays with the PC. You can't transfer Windows XP from the original, bundled machine to a different machine. Microsoft uses a technique called "BIOS locking" to make sure that the copy of Windows XP that ships with a PC stays tied to that specific PC, forever and ever. See Fred Langa's expose at `www.langa.com/newsletters/2001/2001-09-10.htm` for a detailed explanation of what's involved.

There are some ifs, ands, and buts floating around (for example, what if you upgrade to Windows XP and the next day your PC suddenly dies?), but in general, you can't copy Windows XP and pass around pirate CDs to your buddies or install a single copy on all the machines in your home. If you have three PCs, and you want to run Windows XP on all of them, you have to buy three copies of Windows XP, either in shrink-wrapped boxes or preinstalled on new machines.

Corporate licenses are a little different. I talk about them at the end of this section.

Windows XP enforces this one-Windows-one-PC licensing requirement with a technique called *Windows Product Activation,* or WPA. Here's how WPA works:

1. **The Windows XP installer makes you type the unique 25-character code that's printed on the case of your Windows XP CD.**

Later, the Product Activation program looks at various serial numbers inside your PC — the processor, network card, and disk drives, among others — mixes them together, and produces a second 25-character code that identifies your PC. Those 50 characters, taken together, are called the *Installation ID*.

2. **When you *activate* Windows XP (see Figure 1-10), you give Microsoft that 50-character Installation ID.**

   Microsoft checks to see whether anybody else has submitted the 25-character code from the case of the Windows XP CD.

   - If nobody else has activated that 25-character code from the CD case, or if the 25-character code has been activated with that specific Installation ID (which means you activated this particular copy of Windows XP from the same PC twice), Microsoft sends back a 42-character *Confirmation ID*. Both the Installation ID and the Confirmation ID are stored on your PC.
   - If that 25-character code has already been used on a different PC, though, you get a polite message on your machine saying, `According to our records, the number of times that you can activate Windows with this product key has been exceeded. Please enter a different product key, and then click Retry.` You're given further instructions for contacting Microsoft, if you feel the need.

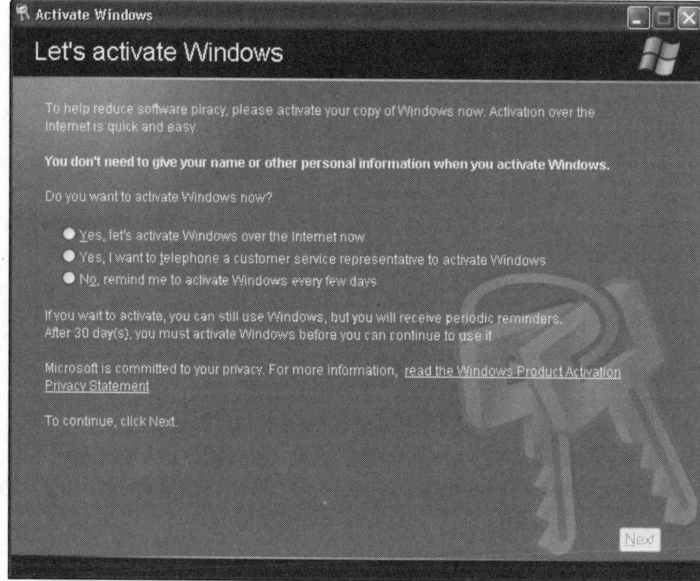

Figure 1-10: The Windows Product Activation Wizard.

3. **Every time Windows XP starts, it recalculates the 25-character code that's based on the various serial numbers inside your PC.**

   If the code matches the one that's stored on your PC, and the Confirmation ID is good, Windows takes off.

4. **On the other hand, if the recalculated 25-character code doesn't match your original code, pandemonium breaks loose.**

   Your hard drives start spinning at twice their normal speed, your keyboard gets short-circuited with your PC's power supply, and the local constabulary receives an urgent fax from Redmond with a preapproved no-knock search warrant. Okay, okay. I'm exaggerating a little bit. Here's what really happens:

   - If Windows decides that you've only made a few changes to your PC — replaced a hard drive, say, or even changed the motherboard — it lets you start Windows anyway.
   - On the other hand, if Windows determines that you've made too many changes, it refuses to start and insists that you contact Microsoft for a new Confirmation ID. That starts the activation cycle all over again. Microsoft has full details at `www.microsoft.com/piracy/basics/activation` and `www.microsoft.com/technet/prodtechnol/winxppro/evaluate/xpactiv.mxpx`.

If you bought your PC with Windows XP preinstalled, it was activated before you ever got it.

If you bought and installed Windows XP yourself, though, the activation time clock takes over. From the day you install Windows XP, you have 30 days to activate it. Windows tries to get you to activate it while you're installing. Failing that, it continues to remind you, relentlessly, as the 30 days tick away. Reinstalling Windows XP won't bypass the activation requirement.

Activating via the Internet makes the whole process of generating, sending, and receiving ID codes invisible: All you know is that the process worked, and you can continue to use the software you bought. If you activate by telephone, though, you have to be sitting at your computer with your Windows XP installation CD handy. You get to read a bunch of numbers to the rep on the other end of the phone line, and she reads a bunch of numbers back to you so that you can type them into the WPA Wizard.

Surprisingly, Windows XP still works a little bit, even after the activation period has expired, and even though it won't start. For example, a modem attached to a PC that hasn't been activated can still dial out, if it's set up for Internet Connection Sharing.

As the Activation Wizard screens emphasize (see Figure 1-11), activation is not the same as registration. When you activate Windows XP, your computer sends Microsoft a 50-character Installation ID — *and nothing else*. When you register Windows XP, you send Microsoft your name, address, telephone number, and any other information that the screens can extract from you.

Activation is a given: You have to activate Windows XP or it dies. Registration, on the other hand, is entirely optional — and basically useless for Dummies everywhere. (What? You think Microsoft wants your mailing address to send you a product recall? A birthday card? Sheeesh.) You have no reason in the world to register Windows XP. Don't do it.

Big companies with big bucks don't have to put up with Windows Product Activation. (One guess why.) Any company that buys Windows XP via a site license — that is, buys many copies at a time — gets a special version that doesn't require activation.

If you hear rumors on the Internet about a key that magically bypasses Windows Product Activation, chances are very good that it's a corporate key that somebody is passing around the Net. Microsoft can, and has, blocked access to Service Packs and updates for people who used the most widely available and well-known pirated keys. (Don't confuse these hamfisted, widely disseminated pirate keys with the results of "keygen" programs, which produce unique, untraceable, fully functional keys. Big difference.) Cracking Windows XP is illegal, immoral, and fattening. Don't do it.

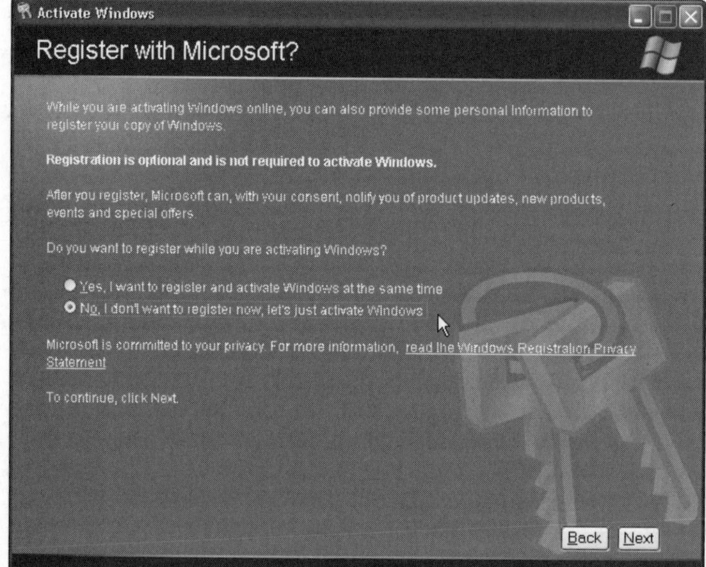

Figure 1-11: You can (and should) activate without registering.

What if the Wheels Fall Off?

So what should you do if Windows XP dies?

- ✦ If you got Windows XP bundled with a new PC, scream bloody murder at the vendor who sold you the %$#@! thing. Don't put up with any talk about "it's a software problem; Microsoft is at fault." If you bought Windows XP with a new PC, the company that sold you the machine has full responsibility for making it work right.
- ✦ If you upgraded from Windows 98 or Windows 98 SE to Windows XP, you can always uninstall Windows XP and go back to your old operating system, as unpalatable as that may seem. Follow the instructions in the section, "Upgrading to Windows XP — A Brain Transplant."
- ✦ If you upgraded from Windows NT 4 or 2000 and you didn't go through a clean install, try that. You don't have much to lose, eh? Follow the instructions in the section, "Considering a clean install."
- ✦ If you've done a clean install and Windows XP still falls over and plays dead, man, you have my sympathies. Check with your hardware manufacturer and make sure you have the latest BIOS version installed. (Make sure you get an instruction book; changing the BIOS is remarkably easy, if you follow the instructions.) Hit the newsgroups online, check out the NT Compatible Web site, `www.ntcompatible.com/compatibility.html`, or drop by my WOPR Lounge, `www.wopr.com/lounge`, to see if anybody there can lend a hand. If all else fails, admit defeat, and reinstall your old operating system. Again, life's too short.

Chapter 2: A Windows XP Orientation

In This Chapter

- **Logging on**
- **Adding users**
- **Moving around the desktop**
- **Working with windows (that's "windows" with a wittle w)**

This chapter explains how to add new users, and how to find your way around the Windows windows. If you're an old hand at Windows, you know most of this stuff — such as mousing and interacting with dialog boxes — but I bet some of it will come as a surprise. If you're new to Windows, this is the place where you start paying your dues. In particular, you find out things such as how to add and delete users, and why you may want to avoid Microsoft Passport. Not to worry. When you get past the terminology, the concepts won't hurt a bit.

Most of all, you need to understand that you don't have to accept all of the defaults. What's best for Microsoft isn't necessarily best for you, and a few quick clicks can help make your PC more usable, more secure, and more . . . *yours*.

Controlling Who Gets On

Windows XP assumes that, sooner or later, more than one person will want to work on your PC. All sorts of problems crop up when several people share a PC. I get my screen set up just right, with all my icons right where I can find them, and then my son comes along and plasters the desktop with a shot of Alpha Centauri. He puts together a killer teen Media Player playlist, and "accidentally" deletes my Grateful Dead playlist in the process.

It's worse than sharing a TV remote.

Windows helps keep peace in the family — and in the office — by requiring people to *log on*. The process of logging on (also called *signing on*) lets Windows keep track of each person's settings: You tell Windows who you are, and Windows lets you play in your own sandbox.

Having personal settings that activate when you log on to Windows XP isn't heavy-duty security, at least in the Home version of Windows XP. (Windows XP/Pro beefs up security substantially, particularly if you're connected to a big corporate network, but makes you jump through many more hoops.) In Windows XP/Home, your settings can get clobbered, and your files deleted, if someone else tries hard enough. But as long as everybody sharing the PC cooperates, the Windows XP logon method works pretty darn well.

The Welcome screen

When it's ready to get started, Windows XP greets you with a *Welcome screen* — variously called a "Logon screen" or a "Signon screen" as well — like the one shown in Figure 2-1. The screen lists all the users who have been signed up to use the computer. It may also show a catch-all user called "Guest." (I guess that sounds better than "Other" or "Hey, you!")

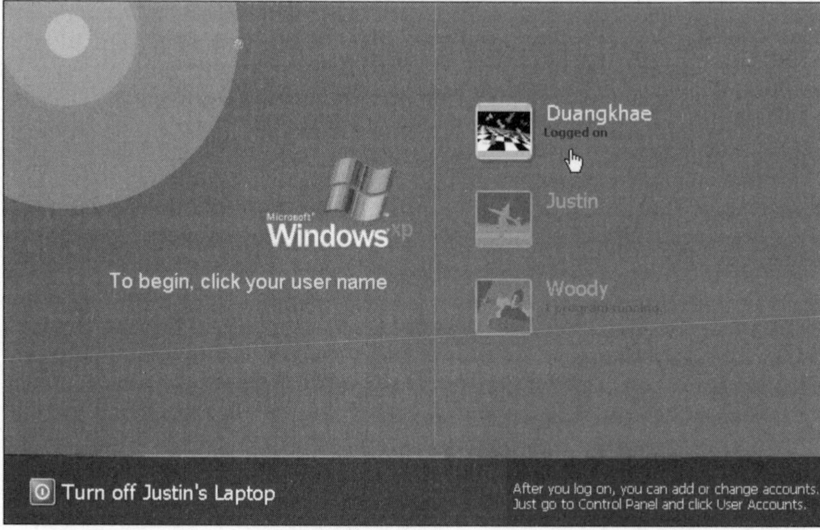

Figure 2-1: The Welcome screen helps Windows keep users from bumping into each other.

You can set up a Guest account to grant very limited capabilities to anyone who hasn't been formally set up on that specific PC. (I explain how to set up the Guest account and new users in the next section, "Adding users.") Unless you assign a password to a specific account, nothing prevents a guest — friend, foe, or mother-in-law — from clicking on one of the other icons and logging on under an assumed identity: In general, Windows XP/Home relies on the gentlemanly conduct of all participants to keep its settings straight.

And if you can't rely on gentlemanly conduct, you need to set up a password. I talk about how you do that in the section, "Changing user settings."

Adding users

After you log on by clicking your name on the Welcome screen, you can add more users quite easily. Here's how:

1. **Choose Start⇨Control Panel⇨User Accounts.**

   You see the User Accounts window, as shown in Figure 2-2.

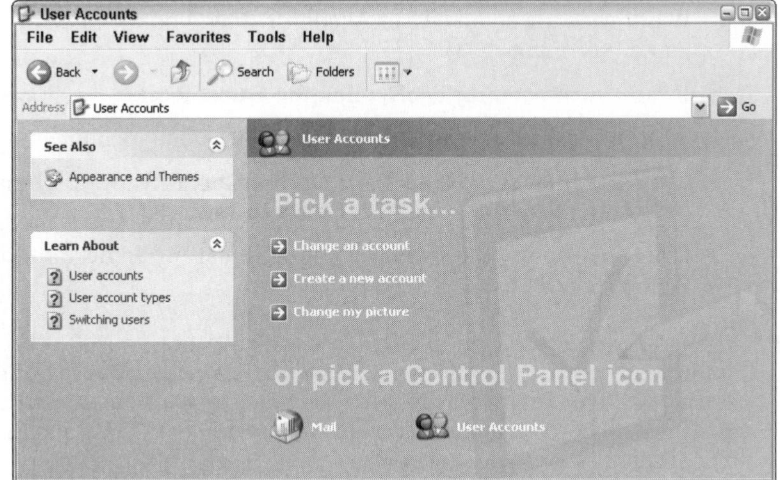

Figure 2-2: Perform all kinds of account maintenance in the User Accounts screen.

2. **Click the task marked Create a New Account.**
3. **Enter an account name and click Next.**

   You can give a new account just about any name you like: first name, last name, nickname, titles, abbreviations. No sweat. Even weird punctuation marks make it past the Windows censors: The name "All your base@!^" works fine.

4. **Tell Windows if you want the account to be a Computer Administrator account or a Limited account. Click Create Account.**

   The choice of Administrator versus Limited account status isn't nearly as straightforward as Microsoft's description would lead you to believe. I have the whole skinny in the section, "Using account types," later in this chapter, but I swear by this easy litmus test: If the person who will be using this account is gullible or new to the seamier side of Windows, give 'em a Limited account.

   You're done. Rocket science. The name now appears on the Welcome screen.

The Guest account is a special Limited account that comes in handy if many different people need to use a computer, but you don't want any of them to be able to get at important information — or run potentially destructive programs. To make the Guest account available on your computer

1. **Choose Start⇨Control Panel⇨User Accounts.**

   You get the User Accounts dialog box in Figure 2-2.

2. **In the lower-right corner, click the icon that says User Accounts.**

   Windows shows you a User Accounts dialog box with all of the users listed (see Figure 2-3).

3. **If the Guest account is off, click the Guest icon.**

   Windows asks if you want to turn on the Guest account.

4. **Click the button marked Turn On the Guest Account. Then click the X button to close the User Accounts window.**

   From that point, Windows will show "Guest" as an account on the Welcome screen.

If you only have a few people who sporadically use your PC, take the time to set up Limited accounts for each of them. That way, your PC will save their settings and make them available the next time each person logs on. But if you have more than a handful of guests, enable the Guest account, and have all of them use the Guest account.

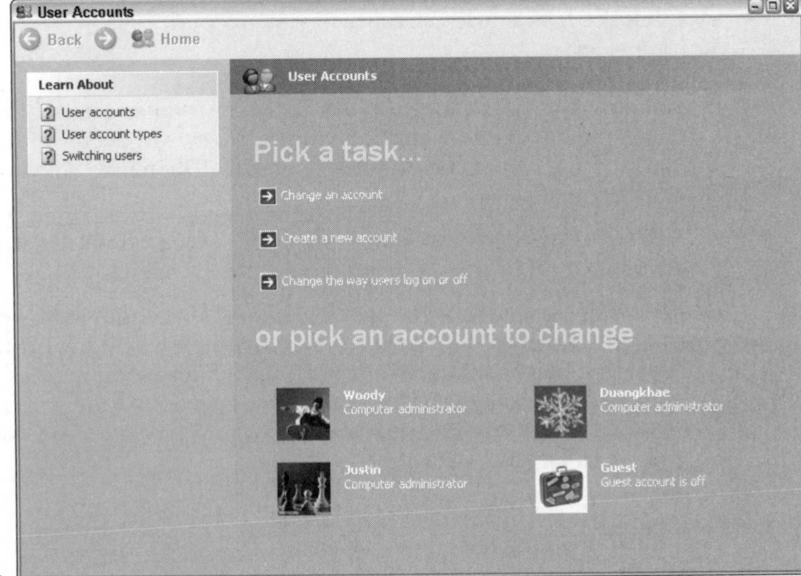

Figure 2-3: Turn on the Guest Account from this User Accounts screen.

Don't enable the Guest account unless you need it. One more account is just one more potential hole for a slobbering cretin virus writer to exploit.

Changing user settings

If you pick an account from the User Account screen, which you bring up by choosing Start➪Control Panel➪User Accounts, Windows immediately presents you with five options. (See Figure 2-4.) Click on any of these options to begin the chosen task. Here's what the options entail:

- **Change the name:** Modifies the name displayed on the Welcome screen and at the very top of the Start menu, while leaving all other settings intact. Use this option if you want to change the name on the account only — for example, if "Bill" wants to be called "William."

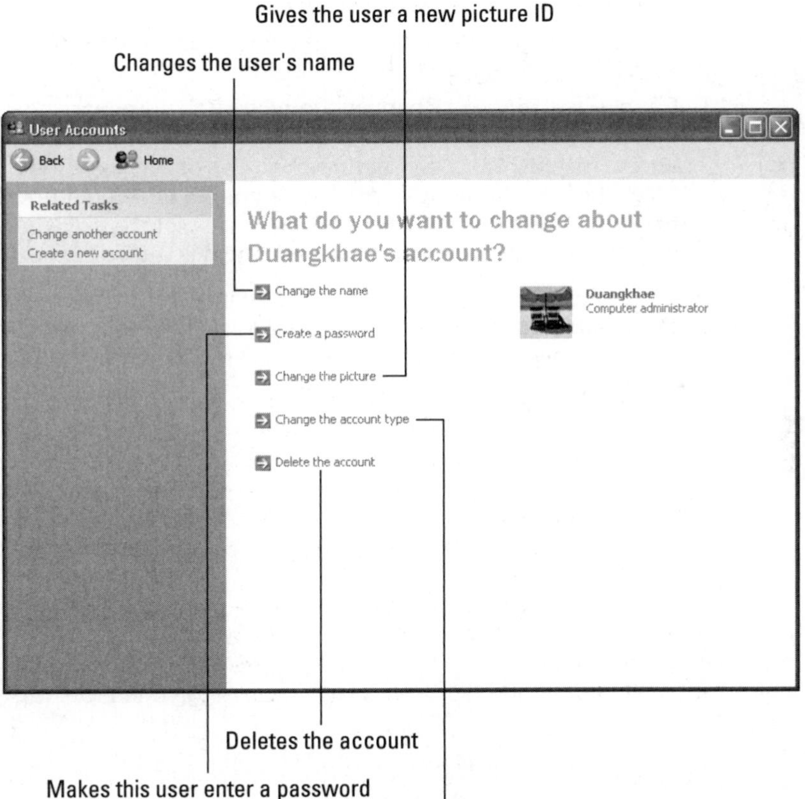

Figure 2-4: Maintain another individual's account.

- **Create a password:** Requires users to enter a password whenever they start Windows. They can't get past the Welcome screen (using their own account) without it. This is a weird setting because you can change it for other people: You can force "Bill" to use a password when none was required before. Worse, you specify the initial password when you set up an account this way, so Bill would have to pry the password out of you before he can log on.

Passwords are cAse SenSitive — you must enter the password, capitals and all, precisely the way it was originally typed. If you can't get the computer to recognize your password, make sure the Caps Lock key is off. That's the number one source of logon frustration.

If you decide to put a password on your account, take a couple of minutes to run the Forgotten Password Wizard (choose Start➪Help and Support and type **forgotten password wizard**). This nifty little program creates a diskette that you can use to unlock your password and get into your account, even if your precocious seven-year-old daughter changed it to MXYPLFTFFT. You have to run the wizard just once; the diskette it creates will always unlock your account.

- **Change the picture:** Changes the picture that appears next to the user's name on the Welcome screen, the Start menu, and in the User Accounts areas. You can choose a picture from any of the common file types: GIF, BMP, JPG, or PNG. Windows offers a couple dozen pictures to choose from, but you can reach out and grab any picture, anywhere. If you pick a big picture, Windows automatically scales it down to size.
- **Change the account type:** Lets you change accounts from Computer Administrator to Limited and back again. The implications are somewhat complex; I talk about them in the next section.
- **Delete the account:** Allows you to deep-six the account, if you're that bold (or mad, in all senses of the term). Windows offers to keep copies of the deleted account's My Documents folder and desktop, but warns you quite sternly and correctly that if you snuff the account, you take along all the e-mail messages, Internet Favorites, and other settings that belong to the user. Definitely not a good way to make friends.

Okay, I fibbed — you can't make all of those changes to other peoples' accounts if you're a lowly Limited user. In fact, you must be a designated Computer Administrator before Windows grants you such power. But therein lies a different, muddled story, which I relate to you in the next section.

Using account types

All Windows XP/Home users can be divided into two groups: the haves and the have-nots. The haves are called *Computer Administrators*. The have-nots are called *Limited*. That's it. "Limited." Kinda makes your toes curl just to think about it.

A Limited user, running his Limited account, can only do, uh, limited things:

- ✦ Run programs that are installed on the computer (but he can't install new programs)
- ✦ Use hardware that's installed on the computer (but he can't install new hardware)
- ✦ Create and use documents/pictures/sounds in his My Documents/ My Pictures/My Music folders, as well as in the PC's shared folders
- ✦ Change his password or switch back and forth between requiring a password for his account and not requiring one
- ✦ Change the picture that appears next to his name on the Welcome screen and the Start menu

On the other hand, Computer Administrators can change anything, anywhere, at any time, with the sole exception of getting into folders marked Private. Computer Administrators can even change other users' passwords — a good thing to remember if you ever forget your password.

In order to mark a folder as Private — and thus keep other users from getting into it — you must be using the Windows NT file system, known as *NTFS*. If Windows XP was installed on your computer when you bought it, chances are good that it's using NTFS. If you upgraded from Windows 98 or Me to Windows XP/Home, though, there's a very big chance you aren't using NTFS. To find out if you're using NTFS, and to mark a folder as Private if it's possible, follow the steps detailed in Book I, Chapter 3, in the section about making a folder private.

When you install Windows XP/Home, every account that's set up is considered a Computer Administrator account. It may appear at first blush as if every account should have Computer Administrator privileges. Ain't so. If you start Windows XP with a Computer Administrator account, and you accidentally run a virus or a worm or some other piece of bad computer code, you can kiss your keister goodbye. On the other hand, if you start Windows XP with a Limited account and then launch a worm, the amount of damage the worm can do is, uh, limited by the restrictions on your account. In most cases, that means the malware can delete files in My Documents, and probably in Shared Documents, but that's just about the extent of the damage — in particular, the virus can't install itself into the computer, so it won't run over and over again, and it may not be able to replicate. Poor virus.

Most experts recommend that you use a Limited account for daily activities, and only switch to an Administrator account when you need to install software or hardware, or get at files outside the usual shared areas. Most experts ignore their own advice: It's the old do-as-I-say-not-as-I-do syndrome. It's also a bit of a head-in-the-sand approach, because viruses and other malware *can* clobber stuff, even if you're running as a Limited user.

The best compromise I've found: Use Limited accounts for people who are most likely to shoot themselves in the foot.

Avoiding Microsoft Passport

On the surface, *Microsoft Passport* dazzles as a wonderful idea: It's a central location where you can put all the consumer-related information you'll need to interact with vendors over the Web, not to mention chat with other people using Windows Messenger, download stock prices, customize weather forecasts, send and receive e-mail using Microsoft's own Hotmail e-mail service, open a bank account, trade stock, and on and on.

If you choose Start➪Control Panel➪User Accounts and then select your own account in the User Account screen, you have the option of signing up for Microsoft Passport — or linking your local PC to your existing Passport — as shown in Figure 2-5.

How much do you trust Microsoft to protect your privacy? That seems to be the root question when any discussion of Microsoft Passport hits the ether. Most people don't trust Microsoft much farther than they can throw a cow. (With a tractor and two barns attached.)

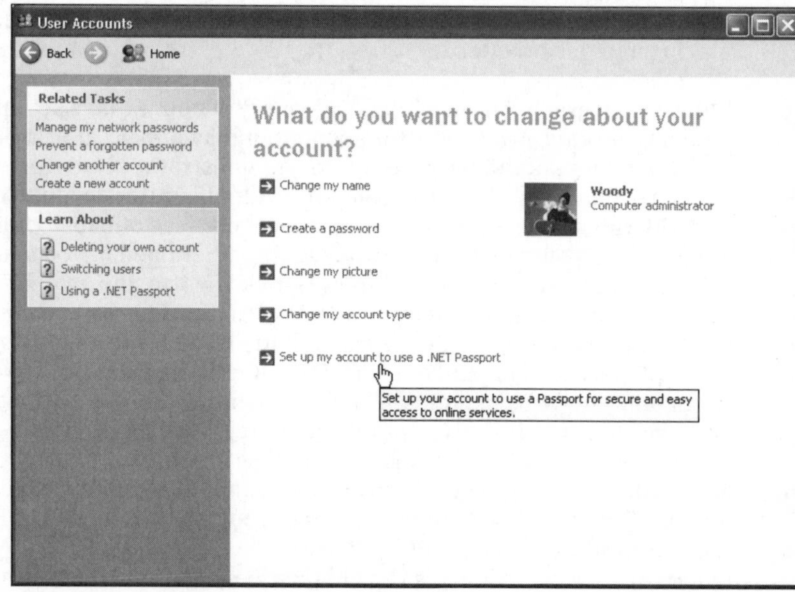

Figure 2-5: When you bring up your account, you have the choice of hitching up to Microsoft Passport.

On the face of it, the Passport seems innocuous: Type in your name, pick an ID and a password, and these wonderful features become available. Beneath the surface, though, you have to realize that Microsoft holds the keys to all of the Passport data. If you trust Microsoft (in this case, I do), the only real problem with Passport is a growing sense of Big Brother's imminent arrival. If you don't trust Microsoft, don't give your personal information — even something as simple as a list of your favorite stocks.

On the other hand, if you don't sign up for Passport, you can't use Windows Messenger for instant chatting, can't use Hotmail for e-mail on the Web, can't ask someone to take over the controls at your computer and help you with Remote Assistance, can't put Microsoft's dubious stock ticker on your Windows desktop, and on and on.

What's a person to do?

Many folks strike a balance between privacy and convenience by getting a Passport, but being very vigilant about the kinds of information they hand over to Microsoft's ever-expanding database. You may find that a workable solution, too. Just be aware that Passport data collection can be a two-way street: If you use a Passport to get onto a site, there's a chance that the site will send gathered information back to Microsoft. I don't mean to make you paranoid, but almost anything that you enter on any Web page hooked up to Passport could end up sitting in a Microsoft database.

I cover Microsoft Passport extensively in Woody's Windows Watch (my free e-mail newsletter, `www.woodyswatch.com`), and each time I learn something new about Passport, the new info seems to fall into the Big Brother category. If you decide to use Passport, understand that Microsoft will hold any information you enter. And make sure you stay on top of the latest developments with Passport. It's another one of those areas that requires constant vigilance.

Don't be too surprised if you see reference to ".NET Passport" and maybe "Windows Passport" in various trade publications. Passport has gone through more skin changes than a rattler. Version 1.1 shipped in the original Windows XP, but Version 2.0 came online shortly afterward, and then there was Version 3.0 and . . . well, you get the idea. The Passport Privacy Policy has been updated almost every month for years. No matter what you call it — Microsoft Passport, Windows Passport, .NET Passport — and no matter what version you're using, the basic idea behind Passport hasn't changed.

At any rate, if you want to sign up for Microsoft Passport and have your account on your PC linked to that big MS Passport logbook in the sky, follow these steps:

1. **Choose Start⇨Control Panel⇨User Accounts.**
2. **Choose your own account.**

3. **Click Set Up My Account to Use a .NET Passport.**

   You are transported to Microsoft's Web site, where you can consummate the relationship.

Deleting yourself

AHA! I bet you saw it.

Did you compare Figure 2-4 to Figure 2-5? Bonus Dummies Merit Points if you noticed the subtle difference. (One hundred Dummies Merit Points are redeemable for one Severe Bragging Right at any local Dummies store. Tell 'em Woody sent ya.)

You can't delete your own account.

Windows has to protect itself. Every PC must have at least one user signed up as Computer Administrator. If Windows XP lost all of its Administrators, no one would be around to add new users or change existing ones, much less to install programs or hardware, right?

Although you and I could probably think of a few dozen ways to ensure that a PC always has at least one Computer Administrator, Microsoft has chosen a rather straightforward approach. First, you can't turn yourself into a Limited user if you're the only Computer Administrator left. Second, you can't delete your own account.

Betwixt the two of those requirements, Windows XP is assured of always having a minimum of one Administrator available at its beck and call.

The Basics

As soon as you log onto the computer, you're greeted with an enormous expanse of near-nothingness, cleverly painted with a pretty picture of a wheat field. Or is it Bill Gates' front yard? Hard to tell.

The desktop

Your Windows destiny, such as it is, unfolds on the computer's screen. The screen that Windows shows you every time you start is called the *desktop,* although it doesn't bear much resemblance to a real desktop. Try putting a pencil on it.

The first time you start Windows, your desktop looks something like the one shown in Figure 2-6.

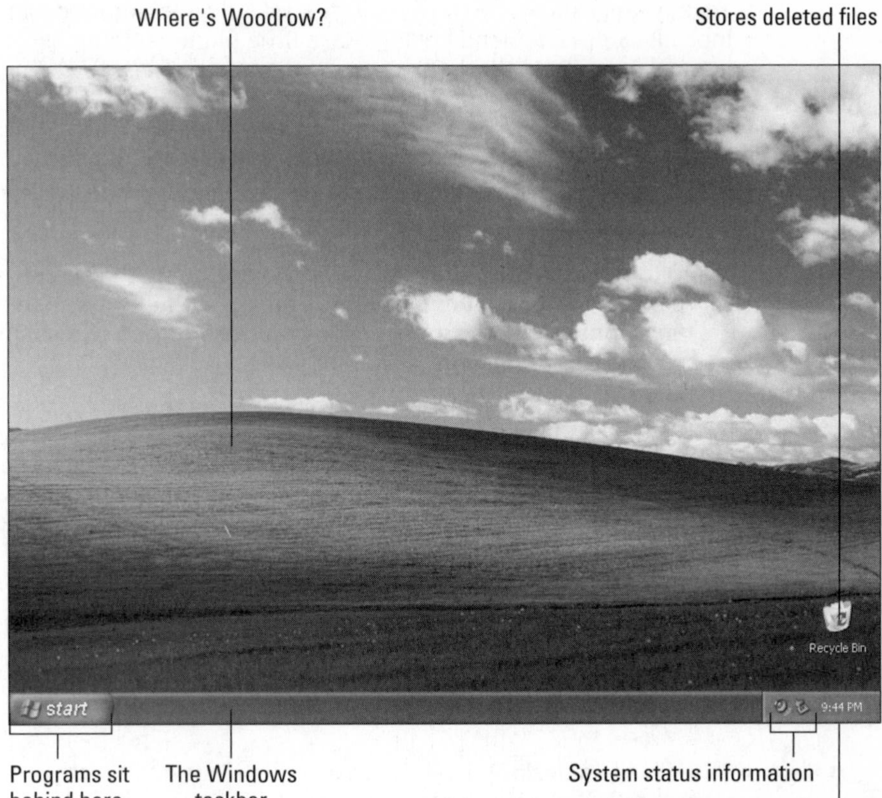

Figure 2-6: The bone-stock Windows XP/Home desktop.

Although the number and appearance of objects scattered on your computer monitor varies depending on who sold you the computer and what was included when you bought it, chances are pretty good that you have only a few pictures — they're called *icons* — sitting on the desktop. In Figure 2-6, one icon appears, the Recycle Bin icon, where Windows sticks everything you've thrown away.

Your desktop probably looks different from the one in Figure 2-6. For one thing, you're bound to have a handful of icons sitting around. If you bought a new computer with Windows XP preinstalled, chances are good that the manufacturer sold some desktop real estate to a software company or an Internet Service Provider. (Oh yeah, the AOLs and Nortons of the world compensate the Dells and HPs for services rendered.) If you see an icon you don't like, right-click it and choose Delete. Good riddance to bad rubbish.

Yeah, yeah, I know. The terminology stinks: The Windows desktop doesn't look like a desktop. And calling those little pictures "icons" seems a bit, uh, iconoclastic, given that real icons are exquisite *objets d'art,* rendered in paint on wood. The price of progress, I guess.

When you get past the verdant fields rolling across your screen, the rest of the desktop isn't very inspiring, although plenty of surprises await as you begin clicking:

- **Windows taskbar:** Runs all along the bottom of the screen, keeps you posted on what your computer is doing — which computer programs are running, where you're visiting on the Internet, and almost anything else that requires your attention.
- **Notification area:** Also known to techies as the *system tray.* This area sits on top of the taskbar on the right side and tells you the time, but it also lets you know what Windows is doing behind the scenes. For example, if you're using a modem to connect to the Internet, little modem lights down here reassure you that the connection hasn't frozen. Other tiny icons in the notification area may control your speaker volume or tell you if you're logged on to Windows Messenger.
- **Start button:** Located in the lower left of the desktop. This button gives you access to everything your computer can do. Click it and you see the Start menu — *menu* being geekspeak for a list of things that you can click. Look for all the details in Book I, Chapter 3.

The Windows desktop looks simple enough, but don't fool yourself: Underneath that calm exterior sits the most sophisticated computer program ever created. Hundreds of millions of dollars went into creating the illusion of simplicity — something to remember the next time you feel like kicking your computer and screaming at the Windows gods.

Mousing

Your computer's mouse serves as the primary way of interacting with Windows, but you already knew that. You can click on the left mouse button or the right mouse button, or you can roll the wheel in the middle (if you have one), and the mouse will do different things, depending on where you click or roll. But you already knew that, too.

If you're left handed, you can interchange the action of the left and right mouse buttons — that is, you can tell Windows XP that it should treat the left mouse button as if it were the right button, and the right button as if it were the left. The swap comes in handy for some left-handers, but most southpaws I know (including my son) prefer to keep the buttons as is, because it's easier to use other computers if your fingers are trained for the "normal" setting. To switch left and right mouse buttons, follow these steps:

1. **Choose Start⇨Control Panel⇨Printers and Other Hardware⇨Mouse.**
2. **Click the Buttons tab.**
3. **Select the Switch Primary and Secondary Buttons check box.**
4. **Click OK.**

Making the mouse behave

Here are a few important rodent things you may not know:

✦ To move an item on the Windows desktop — a process called *dragging* — click the left button, move the mouse, and then release the button. On laptops with a touch pad, you can tie your fingers up in knots trying to replicate the click-move-release shuck 'n' jive. Chances are good that the touch pad recognizes a swift tap as the beginning of a drag. Check the documentation and practice a bit.

Windows has a feature called ClickLock that can come in handy if you have trouble holding down the left mouse button and moving the mouse at the same time — a common problem for laptop users who have fewer than three hands. When Windows uses ClickLock, you hold down the mouse button for a while (you can tell Windows exactly how long) and Windows "locks" the mouse button. To turn on ClickLock

1. **Choose Start⇨Control Panel⇨Printers and Other Hardware⇨Mouse.**
2. **On the Buttons tab, select the Turn on ClickLock check box.**
3. **Immediately click the Settings button and adjust the length of time you need to hold down the mouse button for ClickLock to kick in.**

Note that you can test the ClickLock time length setting by clicking next to Settings for ClickLock and dragging the box around.

✦ You can roll over items on the desktop too quickly! When you're spelunking around Windows XP trying to get a feel for what's happening, go slowly. The word for it is *hovering* — that's when you let the mouse pointer sit in one place for a few seconds. You'll be surprised at how often Windows flashes information on the screen in response to hovering.

✦ Although almost everyone catches on to single-clicking, given a few tries, many people have trouble with double-clicking, and here's the reason why: Windows ain't that smart. If you click twice, Windows has to figure out if you wanted to make two single-clicks or one double-click — and that's surprisingly difficult. Windows watches as you click. You have to click twice, quickly and without moving the mouse in between clicks, for Windows to identify the two clicks as a double-click. If you have trouble getting Windows to recognize your double-clicks, you're probably moving the mouse just a bit too far between the clicks for a double-click to "take."

If you have consistent problems with Windows recognizing your double-clicks, try adjusting the double-click speed:

1. **Choose Start⇨Control Panel⇨Printers and Other Hardware⇨Mouse.**
2. **Click the Buttons tab.**
3. **Double-click the folder on the right side, as a test to see how much leeway Windows gives you.**
4. **Adjust the Double-click speed slider as needed to suit your leisurely lifestyle.**

✦ The best way to get the feel for a new mouse? Play one of the games that ships with Windows. I recommend Minesweeper and Solitaire. Try clicking in unlikely places, double-clicking, or right-clicking in new and different ways. Bet you'll discover several wrinkles, even if you're an old hand at the games.

Inside the computer, programmers measure the movement of mice in units called *mickeys.* Nope, I'm not making this up. Move your mouse a short distance and it has traveled a few mickeys. Move it to Anaheim, and it's put on a lot of mickeys.

Pointers on pointers

When you move the mouse around on your desk, the *pointer* (also called the *cursor*) on the screen moves around in concert. Table 2-1 shows the pointers you encounter most often when using Windows. Click one of the mouse buttons while the pointer is sitting on something and it may (or may not) react.

Table 2-1 Standard Windows Mouse Pointers

When a Pointer Looks Like This	*It Means*	*And Windows Is Trying to Tell You This*
[arrow pointer]	*Normal*	The mouse is ready for action. Move it around the screen, and point and click to get work done.
[hand pointer]	*Hot*	Windows has found a "hotspot" — a *hyperlink* in geekspeak — and if you click while this pointer is showing, you are transported to the linked location.
[vertical resize pointer]	*Ready to resize*	Hold down the left mouse button and move the mouse forward and backward on your desk ("up" and "down" as you're looking at the Windows desktop) to make a window taller or shorter.

When a Pointer Looks Like This	It Means	And Windows Is Trying to Tell You This
	Ready to resize	Same as the preceding pointer, except it makes the selected window fatter or skinnier as you move the mouse left and right.
	Expand or shrink to fit	Click and drag on a window's corner, and the picture expands or shrinks to fit.
	Kinda busy	You can keep doing whatever you're doing, but Windows may be a bit slow because it's working on something else. If Windows gets to be too slow, grab a latte.
	Out to lunch	Windows is really, really busy and doesn't want to be disturbed. You may be able to move the pointer around a bit, but you won't get much done.
	Pick a pic	Windows expects you to draw or choose a part of a picture (for example, if you're selecting Uncle Ernie's head for cropping). When the pointer is like this, click in the upper-left corner of the picture, hold down the mouse button, and release it when you get to the lower-right corner.
	Move	Instead of resizing the selected area (see the preceding), you move the entire selected area, all at once.
	Help	Click on something to get help. If you don't want help, press Esc on the keyboard and the pointer returns to normal.
	Text allowed	Click when the mouse pointer looks like an I-beam and you can type text where you clicked.
	No way	Windows shows you this pointer if you're trying to do something that can't be done — trying to move a printer into a word-processing document, for example.

One other thing to note is what's called *skid pads.* If you see a faint stair-step triangle in the lower-right corner of a window, you can probably use the four resizing arrows to make the window larger or smaller.

If Windows shows you one of its "busy" pointers, you go out to have a latte, and lunch, and run through a quick 18 holes, and come back only to discover that the busy pointer is still there, chances are pretty good that Windows is *hung.* (That's a technical term, okay? Don't laugh. You can also say that Windows *went belly up* or that it *crashed* or *froze* or *died* or *bit the big one.*)

If Windows hangs, hold down the Ctrl key and, without letting go of it, press the Alt key and, without letting go of the preceding two, press the Del key. (That's called a *three-finger salute* or a *Vulcan Mind Meld.*) The Windows Task Manager appears, and you can (usually) use it to close down whatever is ailing Windows.

If you encounter one of the resizing pointers while working with a picture, remember that different programs use the resizing pointers differently: Some may cut off ("crop") parts of a picture as you resize it, while others may stretch or shrink the picture as you drag. Usually, you can use some combination of the Shift and Ctrl keys to convince the program to behave itself: Hold down the Ctrl key while resizing, for example, and the program may start stretching the picture instead of cropping it. Experiment. If all else fails, you can always start over again.

The point where typed text gets inserted onto the screen is called the *insertion point* (more rocket science). Various word processors show the insertion point differently, but Word uses a solid vertical line. Don't be too surprised if some old cuss — yours truly included — calls the insertion point a "cursor." That's a throwback to the Cro-Magnon days when word processors worked more like typewriters, and the blinking cursor kept track of where text would go.

Using the right button

Windows XP allows you to right-click just about anywhere and choose from a context-sensitive list of actions to be performed on the item you've clicked. For example, you can right-click on a disk drive and choose to search the disk drive; you can right-click on a printer and make the printer stop printing. The choices that appear when you right-click on an item are called a *shortcut menu* (sometimes also called a *right-click menu* or a *context menu*). In Figure 2-7, you can see an example of the context menu that appears when you right-click on a blank portion of the Windows desktop.

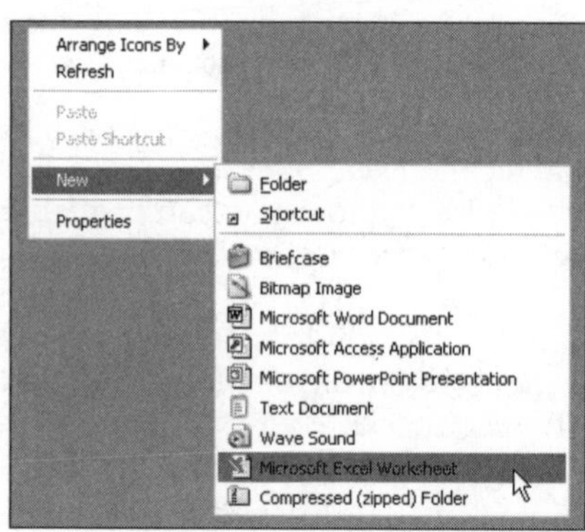

Figure 2-7: The right-click shortcut menu for the Windows desktop, with Microsoft Office installed.

Mice need to be cleaned! If you start having problems with a sluggish mouse — one that jumps, stalls, or doesn't move around the screen the way it should — you should immediately turn the beast upside down and clean it. If you see a rubber ball, pop the lid off, take out the ball, blow on it, and clean off the roller contacts inside (you may need a cotton swab and some isopropyl alcohol). Regardless of whether the mouse has a ball, the feet need to be cleaned from time to time — use your fingernails and scrape gently.

Windows

Most of the time that you spend working with Windows is spent working with, uh, windows. The kind with the little "w" — the rectangles that appear all over your screen. Each part of a window has a name and a specific function.

Many people spend most of their time on the computer working in Word 2003, which is the word processor in Office 2003 and the word processor used by Outlook 2003 for composing e-mail messages. You may have a copy of it on your machine. Look at Figure 2-8 for an overview of the components of the Word 2003 window, and what they represent.

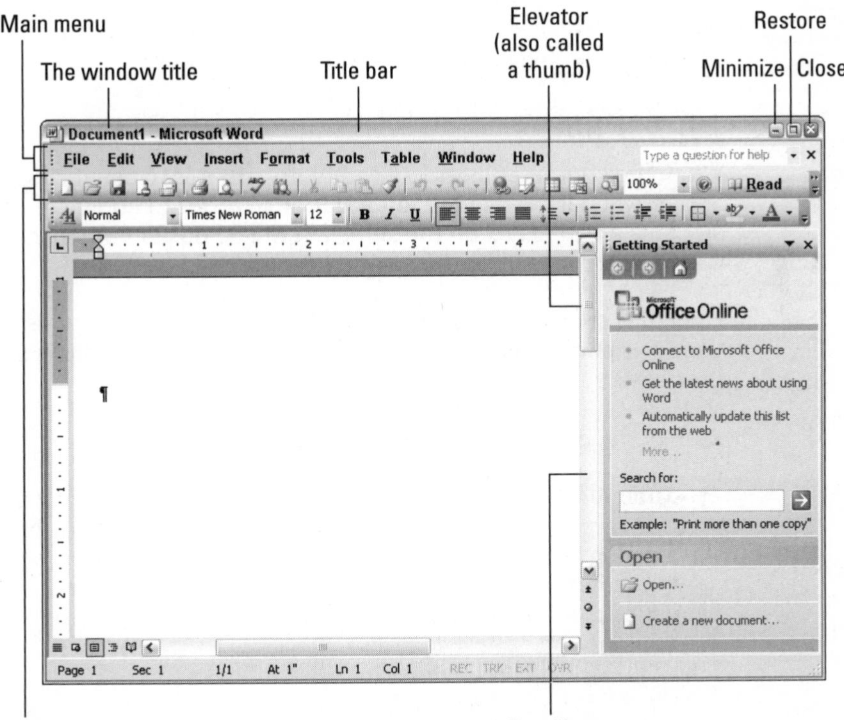

Figure 2-8: Word 2003's window.

A few details worth noting

- The window title appears both in the title bar — that is, the bar across the top of the window — and (usually) in the Windows taskbar, way down at the bottom of the screen. That makes it easy for you to identify which window is which and to switch among them by clicking on the taskbar. (I say "usually" because sometimes the boxes in the taskbar get stacked up; see the section on the Windows taskbar in Book I, Chapter 3.)
- Clicking the Minimize button makes the window disappear but leaves the title down in the Windows taskbar, so you can bring the window back with just a click.
- Clicking the Restore button "restores" the size of the window. That is, if the window doesn't take up the whole screen and you click the restore button, it expands to take up the full screen. On the other hand, if the window is taking up the whole screen and you click on the restore button, it reduces in size to occupy a portion of the screen. I have no idea why that's called restoring.
- Clicking the X button removes the screen entirely — even from the Windows taskbar — most commonly by shutting down the program that's using the window.

Many windows can be resized by clicking and dragging an edge or a corner. See the preceding section on "Mousing" for details.

Dialog boxes

When the computer interacts with you — that is, when it has a question to ask, or when it needs more information in order to complete a task — it usually puts a *dialog box* on the screen. A dialog box is nothing more or less than a window that requires your attention.

Figure 2-9 shows a dialog box that illustrates how the various standard Windows components can be used to extract information from unsuspecting Dummies.

Each of the parts of a window has a name:

- **Title:** A dialog box's *title* appears at the top of the dialog box, but the title rarely appears in the Windows taskbar. This is one of the ways that a dialog box is different from a garden-variety window (see the preceding section): You can usually hop directly to a regular ol' window by clicking in the taskbar. To find a lost dialog box, you frequently have to hunt around.

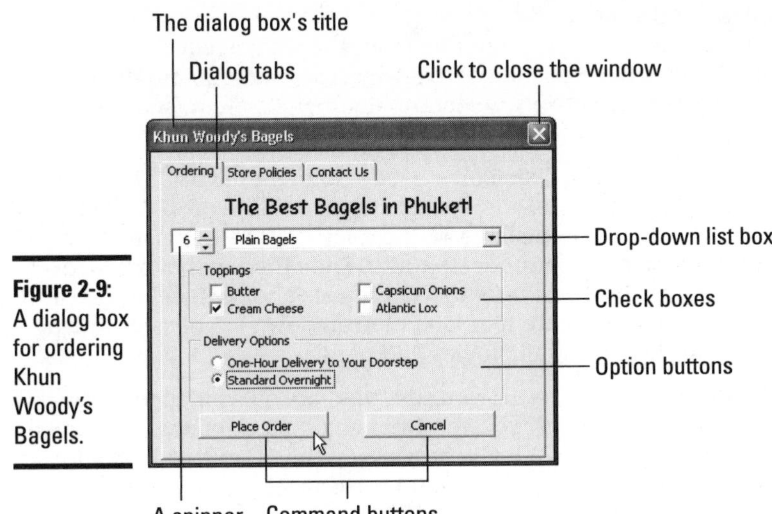

Figure 2-9: A dialog box for ordering Khun Woody's Bagels.

Those "things" that appear on dialog boxes are called *controls*. (Sounds a whole lot better than "things," true?) Windows comes with many controls, and most of the controls you see from day to day are drawn from the standard control toolbox. Standard controls are a real boon to us Dummies because they work the same way, all the time, no matter where you are in Windows.

- **The X (Close) button:** The X button almost always appears on a dialog box, but the other two buttons that you often see on a regular window — Restore and Minimize — rarely show up on dialog boxes. Clicking the X button almost always makes the dialog box go away.
- **Tabs:** Those funny-looking index tabs (usually just called *tabs*) are supposed to remind you of filing tabs. Click on a tab, and you bring up a whole bunch of settings, which are usually related — at least, some programmer somewhere thought they were related.

You can usually hop from one part of a dialog box to the next by pressing the Tab key. Press Shift+Tab to move backward. If you see an underlined letter in a dialog box — called an *accelerator key* — hold down the Alt key and press the letter, and you go directly to that location. In some dialog boxes, pressing Enter is the same as clicking OK (unless you've used the Tab key to move around). In other dialog boxes, though, pressing Enter doesn't do anything.

- **Spinners:** These are almost always placed right next to numbers, with the number hooked up so that it increases when you click the up arrow and decreases when you click the down arrow. Sometimes you can bypass the spinner entirely, select the number, delete it, and type whatever you want.
- **Drop-down lists:** These lists come in two different flavors. With one kind, you're limited to the choices that appear in the drop-down list: If the item you want is in the list, you just pick it; if the item isn't there, you're up the ol' creek without a paddle. The other kind of drop-down list lets you type in whatever you want if your choice doesn't appear in the list. Programmers hate that kind of drop-down list because it lets you do things like order anchovies and pepper sauce on your bagels.
- **Check boxes:** *Check boxes* let you say "yes" or "no," independently, to a whole bunch of choices; if you see a bunch of check boxes, you can pick one or none or all of 'em. *Option buttons,* on the other hand, only let you choose one out of a group — no more, no less.

Back in the good old days (he says, stroking his long, white beard), option buttons were called *radio buttons.* They act like the buttons on a radio: Push one, and a station plays; push a different button, and a different station kicks in. You can't have two different buttons pushed in at the same time. Old-fashioned radios had mechanical buttons that would pop in and out, reminiscent of the way Windows radio buttons work. But you aren't old enough to remember those old radios, are you? Me neither.

- **Command buttons:** These buttons tell the dialog box to get on with it. Click a command button, and the dialog box does something.

Usually it's pretty obvious when you can change things in a dialog box: Text that can't be changed generally appears against a gray background, for example, whereas text that can be changed frequently appears on a white background. Unfortunately, programmers aren't the most consistent folks in the world, and sometimes what you see on the screen is a bit, uh, nonstandard. Utterly random, in some cases.

Files and folders

"What's a file?" Man, I wish I had a nickel for every time I've been asked that question.

A file is a, uh, thing. Yeah, that's it. A thing. A thing that has stuff inside of it. Why don't you ask me an easier question, like "What is a paragraph?" or "What is the meaning of life, the universe, and everything?"

A file is a fundamental chunk of stuff. Like most fundamental chunks of stuff (say, protons, or Congressional districts, or ear wax), any attempt at a definitive definition gets in the way of understanding the thing itself. Suffice it to say that a Word document is a file. An Excel workbook is a file. That photograph your cousin e-mailed you the other day is a file. Every track on Nine Inch Nails' latest CD is a file, but so is every track on every audio CD ever made. Trent Reznor isn't *that* special.

File and folder names can be very long, but they can't contain the following characters:

```
/ \ : * ? " < > |
```

Files can be huge. They can be tiny. They can even be empty, but don't short-circuit any gray cells on that observation.

Three things I know for sure about files:

- ✦ Every file has a name.
- ✦ Files — at least, files that aren't empty — contain bits, the 1s and 0s that computers use to represent reality (a tenuous concept under the best of circumstances).
- ✦ Windows lets you work with files — move them, copy them, create them, delete them, and group them together.

Folders hold files and other folders. Folders can be empty. A single folder can hold millions — yes, quite literally *millions* — of files and other folders.

Three things I know for sure about folders:

- ✦ Every folder has a name.
- ✦ Windows creates and keeps track of a whole bunch of folders, like
    - **The My Documents folder** for each user on the PC. That's where Windows and Microsoft Office usually put new documents that you create.
    - **The My Pictures and My Music folders** inside each user's My Documents folders. Windows — including the Media Player — tend to store your pictures and music files in these folders.
    - **The Shared Documents folder**, which includes Shared Pictures and Shared Music folders, to make it easy to share documents, pictures, and music with other people who use your PC or other people on a network, if you have one. For more info on sharing documents, see Book I, Chapter 3.
- ✦ Windows lets you move, copy, create, delete, and put folders inside of other folders.

If you set them up right, folders can help you keep track of things. If you toss your files around higgledy-piggledy, no system of folders in the world will help.

To look at the files and folders on your machine that you're most likely to bump into, choose Start⇨My Documents. You see something like the list shown in Figure 2-10.

The picture of My Documents that you see in Figure 2-10 comes from a part of Windows called *Windows Explorer,* which can help keep your files and folders organized. Many of the things that you can do in Windows Explorer, you can also do elsewhere. For example, you can rename files in the Open dialog box in Word by choosing File⇨Open — but it's hard to beat the way Windows Explorer enables you to perform powerful actions quickly and easily. I talk about Windows Explorer in Book I, Chapter 3.

If you're looking at My Documents on your computer, and you can't see the period and three-letter ends of the filenames (such as `.doc` and `.xls`) that are visible in Figure 2-10, don't panic! You need to tell Windows to show them — electronically knock Windows upside the head, if you will. I explain how in Book I, Chapter 3 in the section about showing filename extensions.

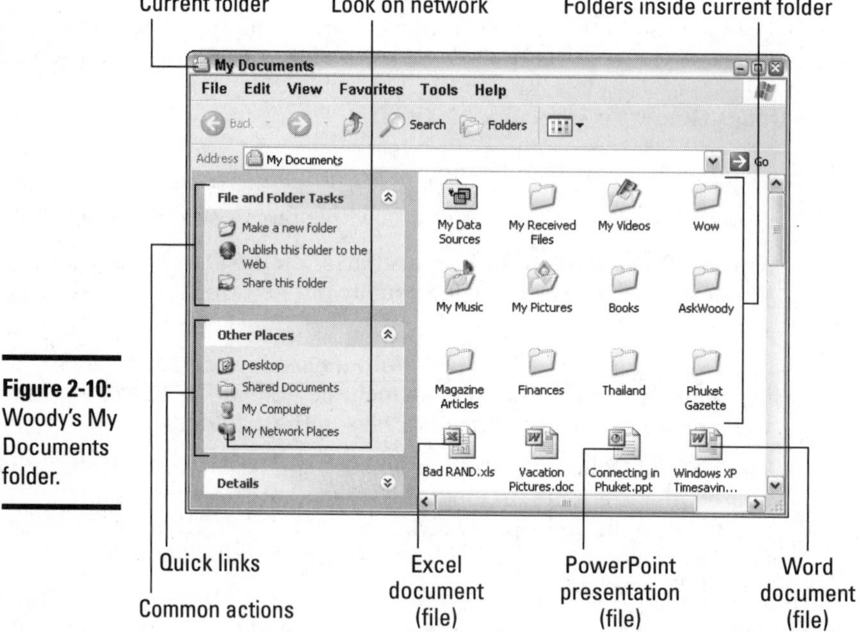

Figure 2-10: Woody's My Documents folder.

Chapter 3: Running Windows from Start to Finish

In This Chapter

- Showing filename extensions
- Taking control of your files
- Getting to know a button named Start
- Logging off

In this chapter, I explain how to get Windows kick-started, and what you should (and shouldn't!) do to tell the beast where you want it to go. Admit it. The first time you were told that you had to click the Start button in order to tell your computer to stop, you felt like you'd fallen down the rabbit hole, didn't you?

Windows XP ships with built-in networking, and if you have a network, you should be concerned about who can get at the files on your computer. This chapter tells all, cutting through the techie bafflegab in a way that you can understand.

This chapter includes the most important tip I have to offer new Windows users, a tip that will pay for this book, all by itself, if it keeps you from getting infected by just one virus. Details are in the later section, "Showing filename extensions." Read it. Believe it. Tell your friends about it. Tattoo it on the inside of your eyelids.

Starting with the Start Button

Microsoft's subverting the Rolling Stones classic *Start Me Up* for advertising may be ancient history by now, but the royal road to Windows XP still starts at the Start button. Click it, and you get the Start menu, which looks something like the one shown in Figure 3-1.

The Start menu looks like it's etched in granite, but it isn't. You can change almost anything on it:

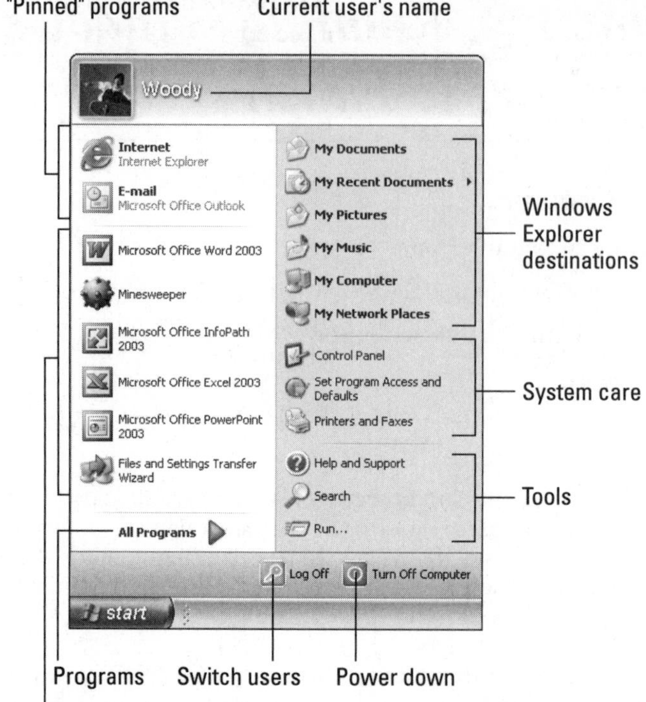

Figure 3-1: Woody's Start menu.

- To change the name or picture of the current user, see Book I, Chapter 2.
- To remove a program from the "pinned" programs list or the recently used programs list, right-click on it and click Remove from This List.
- To add a program to the "pinned" programs list, use Windows Explorer to find the program (see the section, "Using Windows Explorer," later in this chapter), right-click on the program, and click Pin to Start Menu.

If you bought a new computer with Windows XP preinstalled, the people who make the computer may have sold one of the spots on the Start menu. Think of it as an electronic billboard on your desktop. Nope, I'm not exaggerating. I keep expecting to bump into a Windows XP machine with fly-out Start menu entries that read, oh, "Surveys have shown⇨Near and far⇨That people who drive like crazy⇨Are⇨Burma Shave." You can always delete those pesky Start menu billboards by right-clicking on them and choosing Remove from This List.

Don't expect a whole lot of consistency in the way adjacent Start menu items behave.

You may expect that the recently used program part of the Start menu would list the programs you've used most recently. And it does. Sorta. Partly. Now and then. Microsoft stacks the deck, so MSN Explorer (which connects to Microsoft's for-pay MSN service) may stay on the list a whole lot longer than other programs.

Some programs are more equal than others, eh?

Internet

Windows XP ships with Internet Explorer 6 (IE6), Microsoft's flagship Web browser. To bring up IE6, choose Start⇨Internet/Internet Explorer, and you'll be surfing on the Web, as shown in Figure 3-2.

Internet Explorer is so important that I devote Book IV to it.

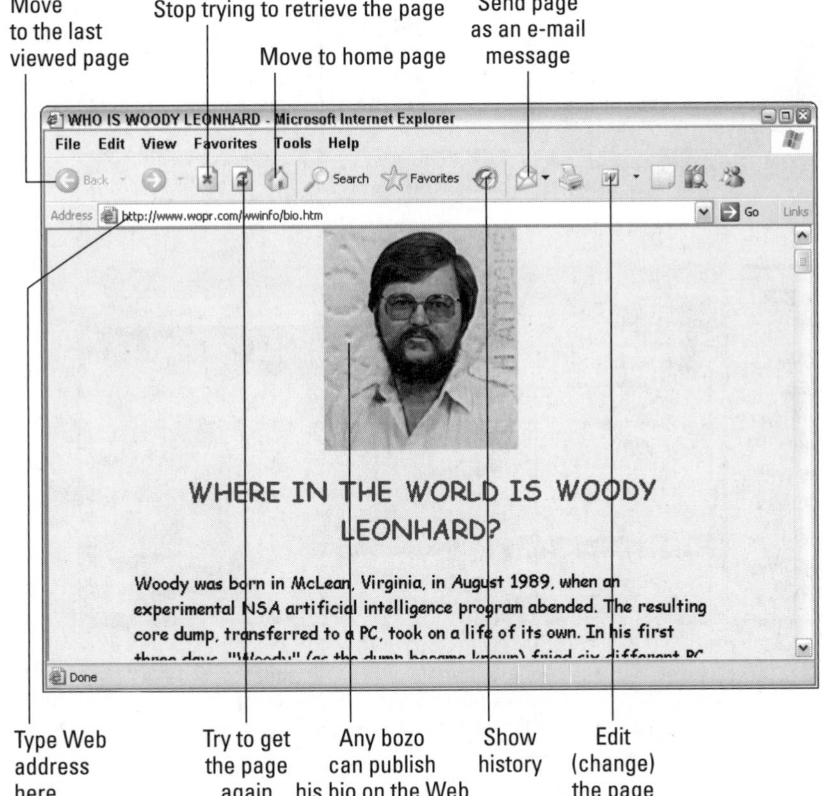

Figure 3-2: Internet Explorer 6 in action.

E-mail

Windows XP ships with a versatile e-mail program called Outlook Express. Outlook Express also handles *newsgroups,* the places on the Internet where people can freely exchange ideas, gossip, tips, and fertilizer. Choose Start➪E-mail/Outlook Express and it appears, as shown in Figure 3-3.

If you bought a PC with Microsoft Office installed, you are undoubtedly using Outlook — which, in spite of the sound-alike name and superficial similarities in appearance, is very different from Outlook Express. Trying to understand Outlook by reading about Outlook Express is like trying to understand cars by reading about incarnation. This Dummies book covers Outlook Express. It doesn't cover Outlook. No way, no how. (If you want more information about Outlook, check out *Outlook 2003 For Dummies* by Bill Dyszel, published by Wiley Publishing, Inc.)

Outlook Express lets you compose and read e-mail messages. It also has an address book and a program for reading Internet newsgroups. I talk about Outlook Express at length in Book III, Chapter 3.

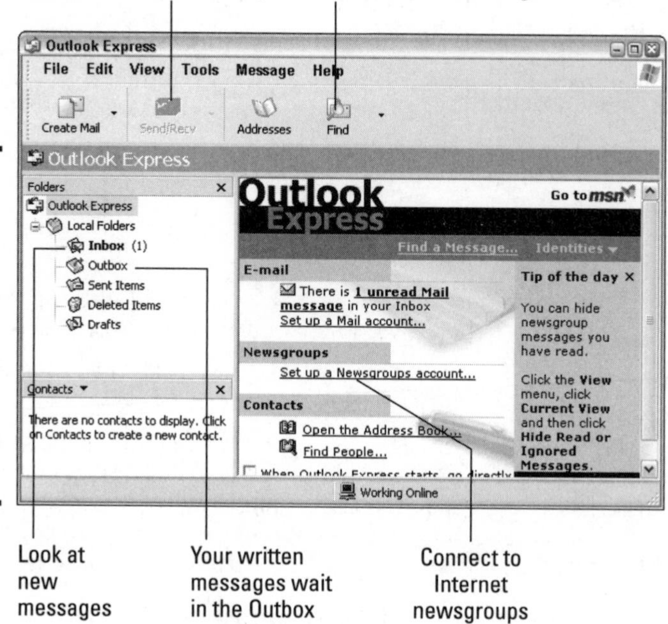

Figure 3-3: Outlook Express, the free, fast e-mail program, comes with an address book and newsgroup reader.

Media Player

Windows XP includes Microsoft's Media Player, a multifaceted tool for playing, organizing, ripping, and burning audio and video files.

If you're new to the topic, don't be flummoxed. The terminology is a bit obtuse, but if you've lived with computers for more than a few days, you're already accustomed to clear-as-mud jargon. Here are the biggies:

- **MP3:** A way of storing digital music that's become very popular because it allows you to squeeze big audio files into tiny MP3 files, without much degradation in sound quality. MP3 stands for MPEG3, but nobody cares about that anyway. My son insists that MP3 means "Mario Party 3." It does.
- **WMA:** Microsoft's challenger to MP3 (short for Windows Media Audio). A typical WMA file is about half the size of a corresponding MP3, so you fit about twice as many songs into the same amount of room. In addition, music publishers can use WMA to limit the number of times a file is copied or the period of time a WMA track can be played. Copyright protection is the number-one reason why music publishers love WMA, and the number-one reason why many normal folks aren't really happy about it.
- **Ripping:** The process of converting audio CD tracks into MP3 or WMA format computer files. You stick an audio CD into your PC, and Windows Media Player (or another ripper) pulls the audio tracks off the CD and converts them into MP3 or WMA files.
- **Burning:** What you do when you create — or write to — a CD. It's also what you do if you are trying to make a living from music that's being ripped off by copyright abusers.

Choose Start⇨Windows Media Player (or Start⇨All Programs⇨Windows Media Player), and you see the odd-shaped amoeba shown in Figure 3-4.

My Documents, My Pictures, My Music

Figure 2-10 in Book I, Chapter 2 shows you the contents of my My Documents folder. (I guess that makes it a list of my My Documents documents, right?) Windows Explorer lets you look at your folders in various ways, called *views,* and you can switch from view to view depending on what you're trying to do, your mood, or the phase of the moon.

The view shown in Figure 2-10 in Book I, Chapter 2 is called Tiles view; it is, at once, the most visually impressive and the most cumbersome view Windows offers. If you get tired of seeing those big icons and you choose

View➪Details, you get the succinct list shown in Figure 3-5 (alternatively, you can click the Views button and choose a view from the list that appears).

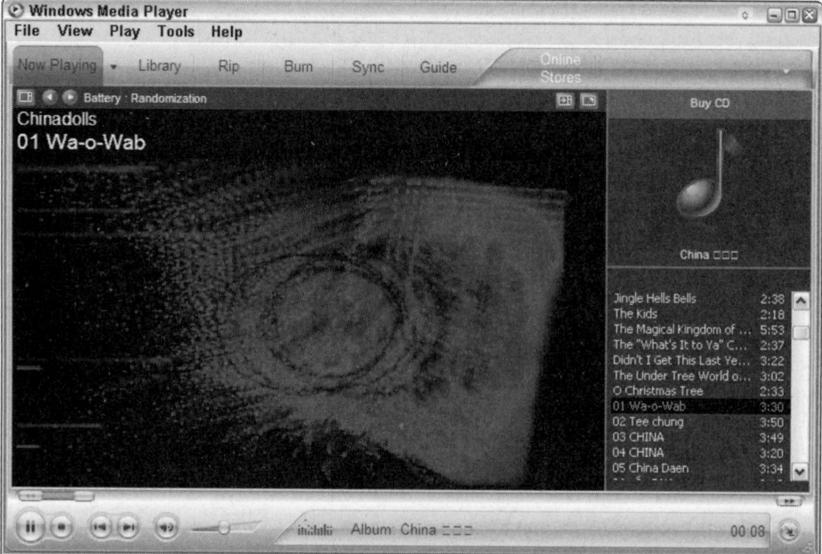

Figure 3-4: Windows Media Player, version 10.

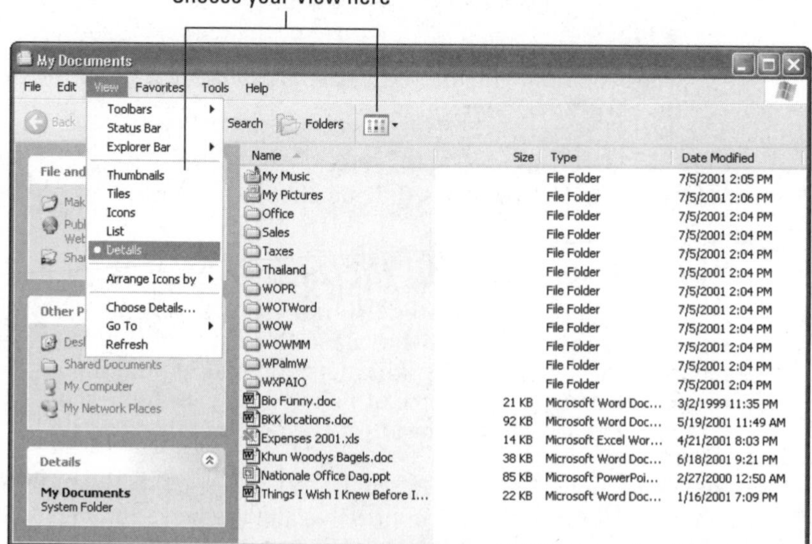

Figure 3-5: My Documents showing the Details view.

The following are the views you can use:

- **Thumbnails:** Shows small versions (called *thumbnails*) of graphics files, along with a few surprises: tiny pictures of the first slide in PowerPoint presentations, small pictures of enclosed graphic files on file folders, even album cover art on identified My Music albums.
- **Tiles:** Gives large icons but makes no attempt to show you a small version of picture files. Documents are identified by what application "owns" them and how big they are.
- **Icons:** Trims down the large size of the Tiles but sacrifices document details.
- **List:** Simply lists filenames. This view is a good choice for looking at folders with lots and lots of files.
- **Details:** Shows filenames, sizes, and types. In most folders, the Details list also includes the date when the file was created, but for music and pictures, artist names and titles appear.

  In Details view, you can sort the list of files by clicking on one of the column headings — name, size, and so on. You can right-click on one of the column headings and click More to change what the view shows (get rid of Type, for example, and replace it with Author).
- **Filmstrip:** Shows thumbnails of pictures across the bottom of the screen, with a Play button below the selected picture, as shown in Figure 3-6. (This view is available only in picture folders.)

Within the My Documents folder sit two more folders that you can get to directly from the Start menu. If you choose Start⇨My Pictures, the Windows Explorer appears with the My Pictures folder open. Choose View⇨Filmstrip and your pictures look like the ones shown in Figure 3-6.

Double-click on a picture and it appears in the Windows Picture and Fax Viewer. At that point, you can easily zoom in and out on the picture, print it, copy it to a floppy, or even change the picture.

If you choose Start⇨My Music, and then choose View⇨Thumbnails, you see the My Music folder (shown in Figure 3-7), which appears with its own special set of actions in the pane on the left.

If you use the Windows Media Player to rip audio CDs, it places all the songs from a single CD into a folder, tucks each of those folders into a big folder for each artist, and puts the artists' folders into My Music. The covers appear, up to four on a folder, when you use Thumbnail view.

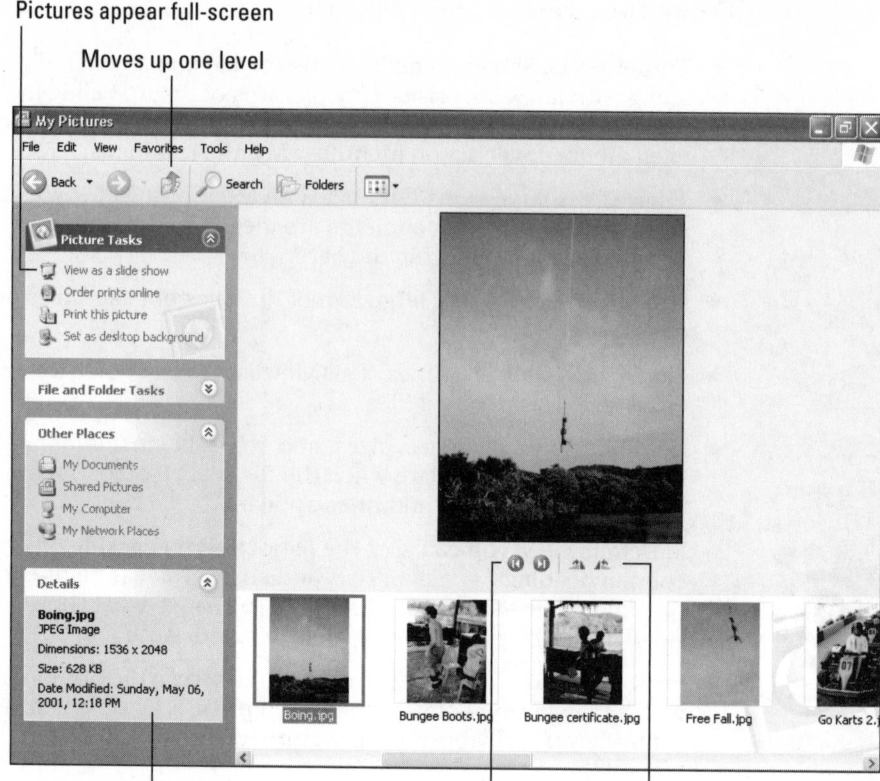

Figure 3-6: The My Pictures folder in Filmstrip view.

My Recent Documents

Windows keeps track of documents as you open them, maintaining a list of documents that you have opened most recently. Taking a leaf from the "HUH?" School of Computer Design, Microsoft's Usability Lab decided that Windows XP/Pro users should see the list on the Start menu, whereas Windows XP/Home users should not. If you like, you can tell Windows that you want to be able to get at that list. Here's how:

1. **Right-click Start and click Properties.**
2. **Click the Customize button.**
3. **Click the Advanced tab.**
4. **Select the List My Most Recently Opened Documents check box, and then click OK twice.**

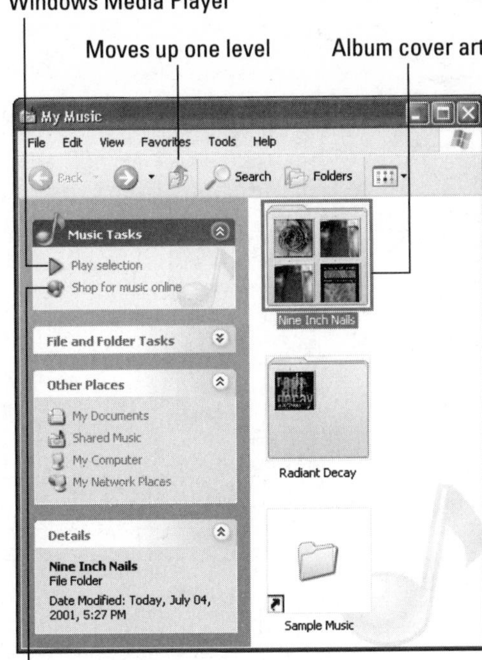

Figure 3-7: The My Music folder in Thumbnail view.

When the Most Recently Opened Documents list is enabled, an entry called My Recent Documents appears on your Start menu. If you choose Start➪ My Recent Documents, Windows presents you with a list of the 15 documents that you opened most recently (see Figure 3-8). If you want to open a listed document again, pick it from the list, and Windows does the rest.

Take this list with a grain of salt. Windows doesn't always get all of the files listed correctly.

If you want to wipe out the list of files that you've opened recently — hey, ain't nobody's business but your own — try this:

1. **Right-click Start and choose Properties.**
2. **Click the Customize button.**
3. **Click the Advanced tab.**
4. **Click Clear List, and then click OK twice.**

   All of the entries in your My Recent Documents menu disappear.

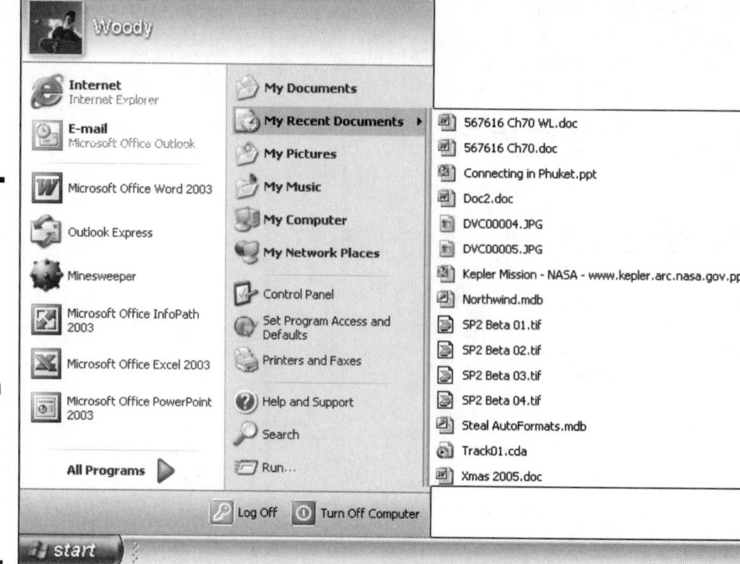

Figure 3-8: The documents that you opened most recently can appear on your Start menu, if you know how to set it up.

My Computer

Choose Start⇨My Computer, and Windows shows you the highest level of folders on your machine, in addition to a list of all the drives (see Figure 3-9). You can use this bird's-eye view to "drill down" to various nooks and crannies in your folders and in the folders of all the other people who use your PC.

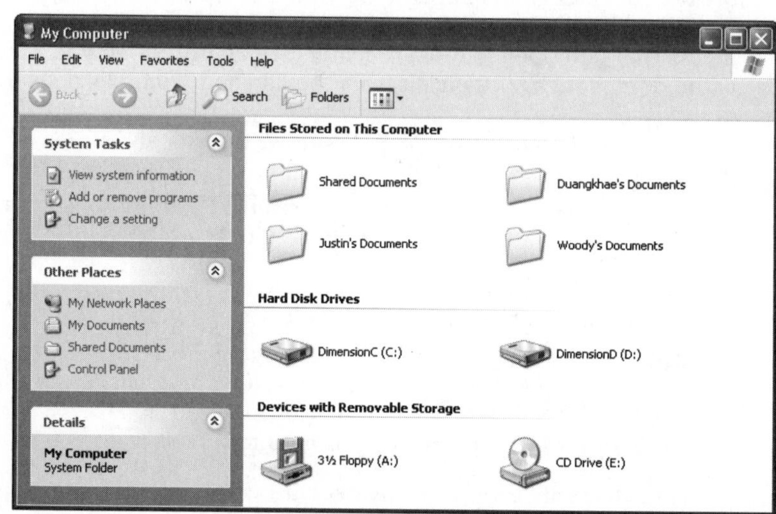

Figure 3-9: My Computer.

For a traditional (that is, pre-Windows XP) view of the contents of your computer that enables you to easily navigate down to the lowest level, click the Folders icon. You see all of your folders and how they're interrelated in the pane on the left (see Figure 3-10).

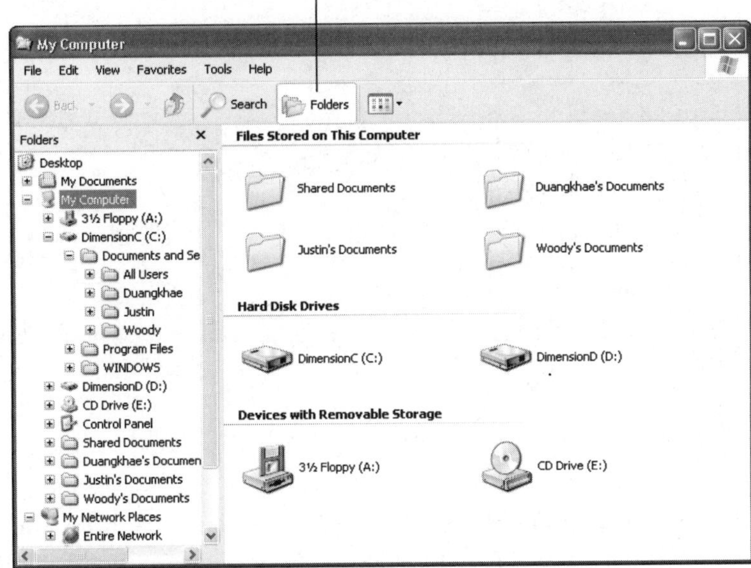

Figure 3-10: My Computer, showing folders in the left pane.

Control Panel

The inner workings of Windows XP reveal themselves inside the mysterious (and somewhat haughtily named) Control Panel. Choose Start⇨Control Panel to plug away at the innards (see Figure 3-11).

I cover various Control Panel components (they're called *applets*) at various points in *Windows XP All-in-One Desk Reference For Dummies,* but the lion's share of the discussion appears in Book I, Chapter 7.

The main components of the Control Panel are as follows:

✦ **Appearance and Themes:** Change what your desktop looks like — wallpaper, colors, mouse pointers, screen saver, icon size and spacing, and so on. Set screen resolution (for example, 1024 x 768 or 800 x 600) so that you can pack more information onto your screen — assuming your eyes (and screen) can handle it. Make the Windows taskbar hide when you're not using it, and change the items on your Start menu. Change what Windows Explorer shows when you're looking at folders.

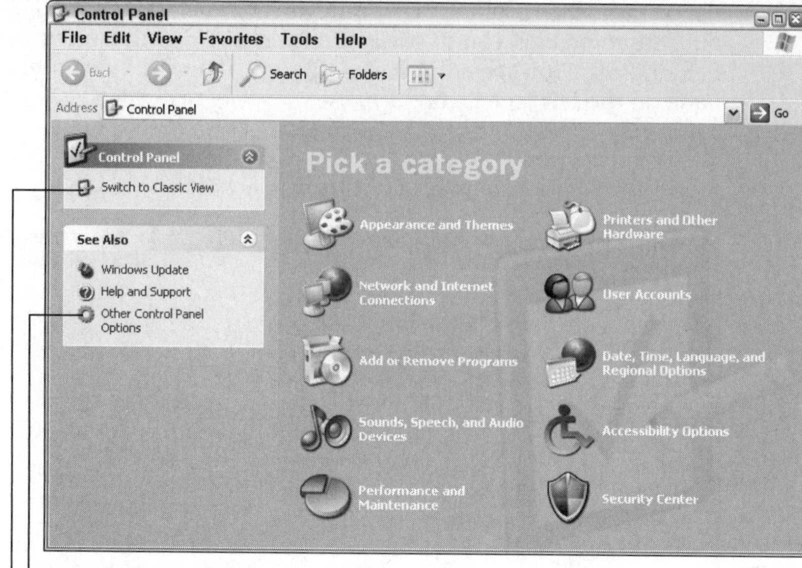

Figure 3-11: The Control Panel.

- **Printers and Other Hardware:** Add or remove printers and connect to other printers on your network. Troubleshoot printers. Set up and modify Windows faxing. Install, remove, and set the options for scanners and digital cameras. Control the options on mice, game controllers, joysticks, and keyboards. Set up dialing rules and other modem arcana.

If you use a modem for your Internet connection, Windows faxing may not do what you expect. You may have to disconnect from the Internet before you send or receive a fax, for example. Many people use J2 fax (`www.j2.com`) because it treats faxes like e-mail. Outbound faxes are converted to e-mail on your PC using J2's programs, and then they are sent to J2, which routes the fax to a local fax machine at your destination, thus bypassing long-distance telephone charges. Inbound faxes get delivered to your e-mail inbox.

- **Network and Internet Connections:** Set up a network. Configure Internet Explorer and its startup page, history files, cookies, AutoComplete, and so on. Set up Internet connections, particularly if you're sharing an Internet connection across a network, or if you have a cable modem or DSL.
- **User Accounts:** Add or remove users from the Windows welcome screen. Enable the "Guest" account (see Book I, Chapter 2). Change

account characteristics, such as the picture, password requirement, direct connection with .NET Passport, and so on.

- **Add or Remove Programs:** Add and remove specific features in some programs (most notably Windows XP).
- **Date, Time, Language, and Regional Options:** Set the time and date — although double-clicking the clock on the Windows taskbar is much simpler — or tell Windows to synchronize the clock automatically. Here you can also add support for complex languages (such as Thai) and right-to-left languages, and change how dates, times, currency, and numbers appear.
- **Sounds, Speech and Audio Devices:** Control volume, muting, and so on, but those functions are usually better performed inside the Windows Media Player. You can also choose a Sound scheme, which is something like a desktop theme, except that it involves the pings and pongs you associate with Windows events (for example, the music that plays when Windows starts, or the cling! you hear when you try to click on something you shouldn't). Speech choices cover only text-to-speech output — the "Danger, Will Robinson!" voice you hear when the computer tries to read something out loud.
- **Accessibility Options:** Change settings to help you see the screen, use the keyboard or mouse, or have Windows flash part of your screen when the speaker would play a sound.
- **Performance and Maintenance:** Use an enormous array of tools for troubleshooting and adjusting your PC, and making it work when it doesn't want to. Unfortunately, it also includes all the tools you need to shoot yourself in the foot, consistently and reliably, day in and day out. Use this part of Control Panel with discretion and respect.

Help and Support

Windows XP includes an online help system that's quite good in places, marginal in some areas, and very, uh, in tune with the Microsoft Party Line everywhere. To bring up the system, choose Start⇨Help and Support. The Help system (shown in Figure 3-12) connects to the Internet, if possible, and updates its "hot topics" list.

I cover the Help system inside and out in Book I, Chapter 4.

Search

Windows XP jumbles an odd assortment of "searchables" in the Search feature. Choose Start⇨Search and you see what I mean (see Figure 3-13). I talk about Search extensively in Book I, Chapter 5.

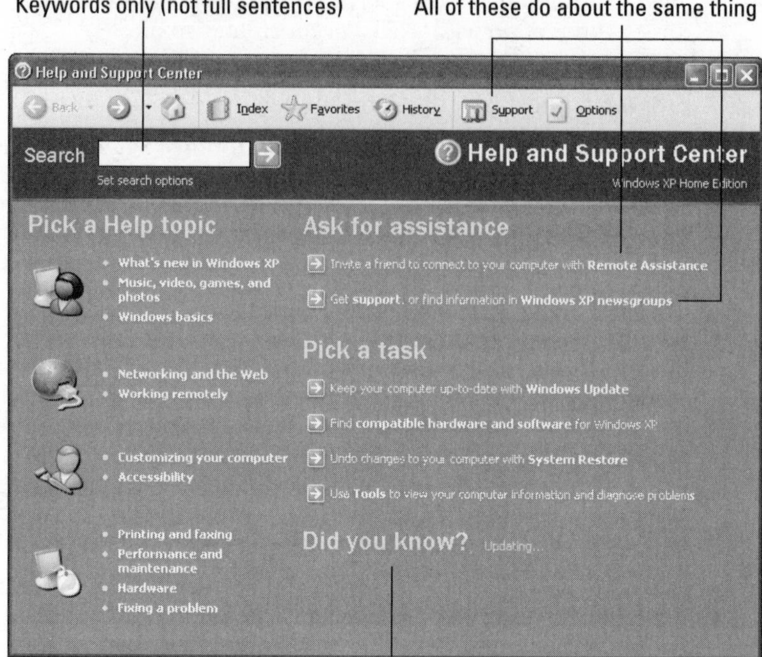

Figure 3-12: Help and Support feels your pain.

Run

Harkening back to a kinder, gentler age, where you had to type (and type and type and type) to get anything done at a computer, the Run box lets you type program names and have Windows run the programs. It also recognizes Web addresses.

What's that I hear? Scoffing? Perhaps a little snort and a rejoinder about buggy whips and five-cent cigars? Oh ye of little faith!

Here. Try this. Choose Start⇨Run, type **calc** (see Figure 3-14), and press Enter. I defy you to find a quicker, easier way to run the Windows calculator.

Okay, okay. That calc thing isn't much more than a parlor trick that you can try at home. In fact, the Run box is pretty thoroughly outdated and something you don't want to use on a regular basis. You may find unusual situations where you need it, but with any luck you'll never encounter one of them.

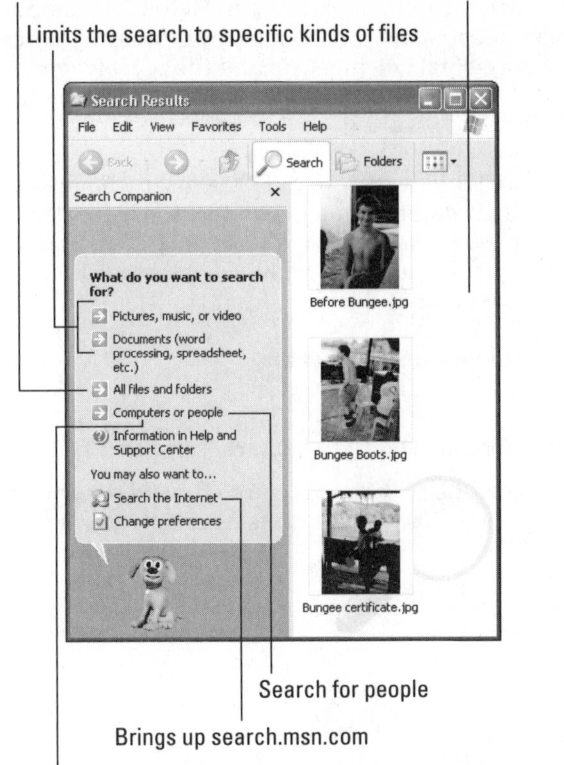

Figure 3-13: Searching with Windows XP.

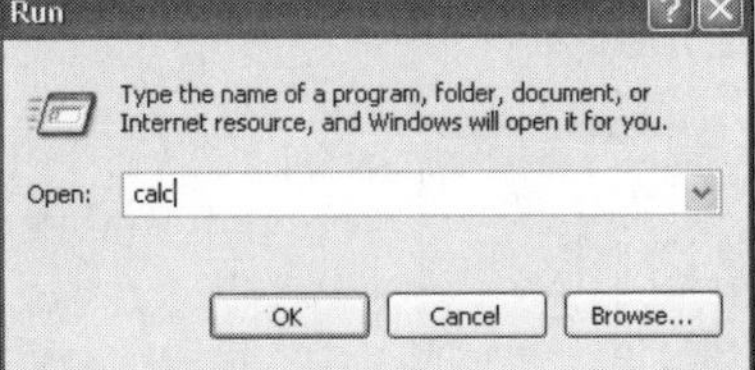

Figure 3-14: The Run box.

All Programs

Almost all of the programs on your computer are accessible through the All Programs menu. To see it, choose Start➪All Programs. Figure 3-15 shows you what the Games folder in All Programs looks like.

Those right-pointing arrowheads that you can see to the right of Accessories, Games, Microsoft Office Tools, and Startup in Figure 3-15 simply indicate that you have more choices to make. You can let your mouse pointer hover over an arrowhead-endowed Start menu entry and the *pop-out menu* appears. Or if you're the impatient type, you can click on the menu entry to make the pop-out appear faster.

Are you an inveterate Windows 98/Me/NT/2000 user who misses her old Start menu — the single-column menu, with its little icons, that automatically tucked away menus items you didn't use very often? You can bring the old buzzard back to life, if you insist, and have it replace this new-fangled version of the Start menu. Here's how:

1. **Right-click Start and click Properties.**
2. **Click the Start Menu tab.**
3. **Choose the button marked Classic Start Menu and click OK.**

   Personally, I prefer the new Start menu to the old one, but it's nice to know that you can go back to the classic version, if you like.

Figure 3-15: The Games folder in the Start menu's All Programs menu.

Organizing the contents of the All Programs menu is very easy:

- To copy or move an item on the All Programs menu to a different location on the All Programs menu, right-click it, drag it to the new location (you can navigate anywhere on the menu, even into the pop-out menus), release the right mouse button, and choose Copy or Move.
- To sort all of the items on the All Programs menu alphabetically (with folders sorting higher than programs), right-click on any folder or program and choose Sort by Name.

Getting Around

Your PC is a big place, and you can get lost easily. Microsoft has spent hundreds of millions of dollars to make sure that Windows points you in the right direction and keeps you on track through all sorts of activities.

Amazingly, some of it actually works.

Using Windows Explorer

If you're going to get any work done, you have to interact with Windows. If Windows is going to get any work done, it has to interact with you. Fair 'nuff.

Computer geeks refer to the way Windows interacts with people as the *human interface.* As far as I'm concerned, that jargon's more than a little presumptuous. We poor, downtrodden Windows victims should refer to people-machine interactions as the *stupid computer interface.* About time to put the horse before the cart, sez I.

Now that you have the terminology turned right-side-out, you can easily understand where Windows Explorer fits into the Grand Scheme of WinThings. Windows Explorer lies at the center of the stupid computer interface. When you want to work with Windows — ask it where it stuck your wedding pictures, show it how to mangle your files, tell it (literally) where to go — you usually use Windows Explorer.

If you choose Start➪My Documents or Start➪My Computer or Start➪My Pictures or My Music or My Network Places, Windows Explorer jumps to your command like an automated bird dog, pointing at whatever location you selected. When you run a search with Start➪Search, Windows Explorer takes the reins.

This book is littered with pictures of Windows Explorer. If you look through this chapter, you see Windows Explorer in many of its guises: working on the My Documents folder (refer to Figures 3-5, 3-17, 3-18), My Pictures (refer to

Figure 3-6), My Music (refer to Figure 3-7), My Computer (refer to Figures 3-9 and 3-10), and viewing the results of a search (refer to Figure 3-13).

Windows Explorer takes a snapshot of your hard drive and presents that snapshot to you. If the contents of the hard drive change, the snapshot is *not* automatically updated, which can be a real problem. Say you're using Windows Explorer to leaf through the files in My Documents. You suddenly realize that you need to write a letter to your Aunt Emma, so you start Word and write the letter, saving it in My Documents. If you switch back to Windows Explorer, you may not be able to see the letter to Aunt Emma: The snapshot may not be updated. Disconcerting. To force Windows Explorer to update its snapshot, you can close it down and start it again, or you can press F5.

The following are some Windows Explorer high points:

- **The name of the current folder appears in the title bar.** If you click once on a file or folder, details for the selected file or folder appear in the Details box in the lower-left corner. If you double-click on a folder, it becomes the current folder. If you double-click on a document, it opens. (For example, if you double-click on a Word document, Windows fires up Word and has it start with that document open and ready for work.)

- **Almost any actions that you want to perform on files or folders show up in the File and Folder Tasks list in the upper-left corner of Windows Explorer.** Provided you know the secret, that is! You have to click once on a folder before the list of folder actions becomes visible; and you have to click once on a file before you can see the list of file actions. So if you're trying to copy a file, and you don't see Copy File in the list of File and Folder Tasks, click the file you want to copy first. When you do, Copy This File shows up in the list of Tasks.
- **You can open as many copies of Windows Explorer as you like.** That can be very helpful if you're scatterbrained like me . . . er, if you like to multitask, and you want to look in several places at once. Simply choose Start⇨My Documents (or My Computer, whatever), and a totally independent copy of Windows Explorer appears, ready for your finagling.

Creating files and folders

Usually, you create new files and folders when you're using a program; you make new Word documents when you're using Word, say, or come up with a new folder to hold all of your offshore banking spreadsheets when you're using Excel. Programs usually have the tools for making new files and folders tucked away in the File⇨Save and File⇨Save As dialog boxes. Click around a bit and you'll find them.

But you can also create a new file or folder directly in My Documents quite easily, without going to the hassle of cranking up a 900-pound gorilla of a program:

1. **Move to the location where you want to put the new file or folder.**

   For example, if you want to stick a new folder called Revisionist Techno Grunge in your My Music folder, choose Start➪My Documents and double-click on the My Music folder. (If you want to show off, you could just choose Start➪My Music, which does the same thing.)

2. **Right-click a blank spot in your chosen location.**

   By "blank" I mean "don't right-click on an existing file or folder," okay? If you want the new folder or file to appear on the desktop, right-click any empty spot on the desktop.

3. **Choose New (see Figure 3-16) and pick the kind of file you want to create.**

   If you want a new folder, click Folder.

4. **Windows creates the new file or folder and leaves it with the name highlighted, so that you can rename it by simply typing.**

Arrange Icons By
Refresh
Paste
Paste Shortcut
New
Properties

Folder
Shortcut
Briefcase
Bitmap Image
Microsoft Word Document
Microsoft Access Application
Microsoft PowerPoint Presentation
Text Document
Wave Sound
Microsoft Excel Worksheet
WinZip File

Figure 3-16: Right-click an empty location and pick New to create a new file or folder.

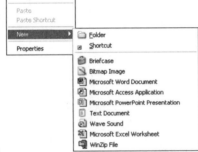

Modifying files and folders

Modifying files and folders is easy — rename them, delete them, move or copy them — if you remember the trick: Click once and wait.

The whole world's in a rush. When I'm learning something new, I tend to try a lot of different things all at once, and that plays havoc on computers. They're only human, ya know? When it comes to working with files and folders, it's important that you wait for the computer to catch up with you. In particular, when you're trying to rename, move, copy, or delete a file, *click once and wait* while the computer figures out what you can do and shows you the legal choices in the File and Folder Tasks area.

If you double-click on a file, Windows interprets your action as an attempt to open the file and start working on it. Double-click on a Word document, for example, and Word springs to life with the document loaded, ready to rumble.

If you simply click a file, though — just click once, and wait a second until the computer catches up — Windows offers a whole range of options for your consideration. In Figure 3-17, I clicked once on a Word document, and Windows gave me all sorts of choices in the File and Folder Tasks area, over on the left.

If you want to copy or move more than one file (or folder) at a time, select all of the files (or folders) before choosing the action in the File and Folders Tasks area. To select more than one file, hold down the Ctrl key while clicking, or click and drag around the outside of the files and folders to "lasso" them. You can also use the Shift key if you want to choose a bunch of contiguous files and folders — ones that are next to each other. Click the first file or folder, hold down the Shift key, and click the last file or folder.

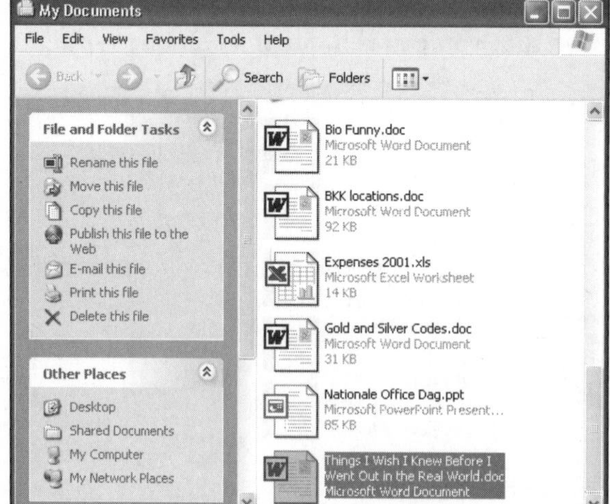

Figure 3-17: Click once and wait to perform minor surgery on a file.

The options for folders (see Figure 3-18) are a little bit different from those for files. In particular, Windows allows you to share a folder but not a file — Windows isn't set up to share individual files. Windows allows you to print a file but not all the files in a folder; to print all the files in a folder, you have to go into the folder and print each file individually. But even though the details are ever-so-slightly different, the principle remains the same: If you want to muck around with folders or files, *click once and wait.*

Click once and wait is, far and away, the easiest way to rename, move, copy, delete, e-mail, or print a file. It's also the least error-prone because you can see what you're doing, step by step.

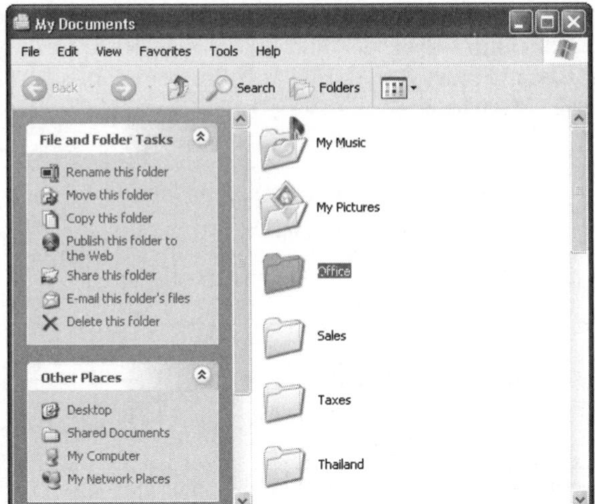

Figure 3-18: Folder tasks vary just slightly from file tasks.

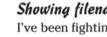

Showing filename extensions

I've been fighting Microsoft on this topic for many years. Forgive me if I get a little, uh, steamed — yeah, that's the polite way to put it — in the retelling.

Every file has a name. Almost every file has a name that looks more or less like this: `Some Name or Another.ext`.

The part to the left of the period — `Some Name or Another`, in this example — generally tells you something about the file. The part to the right of the period — `ext`, in this case — is called a *filename extension,* the subject of my diatribe.

Filename extensions have been around since the first PC emerged from the primordial ooze. They were a part of the PC's legacy before anybody ever talked about "legacy." Somebody, somewhere decided that Windows wasn't going to show filename extensions any more. (My guess is that Bill Gates himself made the decision, about five years ago, but it's only a guess.) Filename extensions were considered dangerous: too complicated for the typical user; a bit of technical arcana that novices shouldn't have to sweat.

Garbage. Pure, unadulterated garbage.

The fact is that nearly all files have names like `Letter to Mom.doc` or `Financial Projections.xls` or `ILOVEYOU.vbs`. But Windows, in its infinite wisdom, shows you only the first part of the filename. It cuts off the filename extension. So you see Letter to Mom, without the `.doc` (which brands the file as a Word document), Financial Projections without the `.xls` (a dead giveaway for an Excel spreadsheet), and ILOVEYOU without the `.vbs` (which is the filename extension for Visual Basic programs). Table 3-1 lists many common filename extensions.

Table 3-1 Common Filename Extensions

Extension	*Type of File*
bas, bat, exe, com, dll, vb, vbs, vbe, js, jse*	Different kinds of programs
txt, asc	Text
cpl, ini, inf, msi, pif, reg, scr	System files
chm, hlp, hta, htm, html	HTML files, typically for Web sites, Help, or formatted e-mail
avi, bmp, gif, jpg, wmf, mpg	Various kinds of graphic files
mp3, wav, wma, mid	Sound files
doc, dot	Microsoft Word
xls, xla, xlt	Microsoft Excel
ppt, pot	Microsoft PowerPoint
pst	Microsoft Outlook

** Italicized names indicate file types that have been used to propagate viruses and other malware. This is far from an exhaustive list, and the guys in black hats are finding new approaches every day.*

Every time you see a file mentioned in Windows, you see a little icon next to the filename. For example, Word documents have an icon that looks like a sheet of paper with a flying W on top. Excel worksheets sport grids with a big X. PowerPoint presentation icons look like Pac Man in drag, but you get the point. (Take a close look at Figure 3-17, and you'll see what I mean.) The icon is directly tied to the filename extension. All `.doc` files have the flying W icon. All `.xls` files get grids with Xs. All `.ppt` files get Pac Man. Uh, Pac Men. Whatever. Graphics files — `.gif` and `.jpg` and `.bmp` among others — sometimes use a small rendition of the picture inside for the icon.

I really hate it when Windows hides filename extensions, for four big reasons:

✦ If you can see the filename extension, you can usually figure out what kind of file you have at hand (refer to Table 3-1). That can be really important when, for example, you get an e-mail message with a file called ILOVEYOU attached to it. Millions of people — even experienced Microsoft geeks, who should know better — received bogus messages, opened the ILOVEYOU file, and got infected with the ILOVEYOU virus. Many of those people would've been tipped off if they had told Windows that they wanted to see the full filename, `ILOVEYOU.vbs`. Bagle and Netsky brought the world's e-mail to a grinding halt by spewing plausible-sounding files with hidden filename extensions.

- It's almost impossible to get Windows to change filename extensions if you can't see them. For example, while writing this book, I wanted to create a new text file called `White.htm`. I couldn't do it. Finally, I had to haul in Windows Notepad and use an undocumented trick in the Save dialog box to get the extension changed. (I typed **"White.htm"** with quotes. Really intuitive, huh?)
- Microsoft Outlook forbids you from sending or receiving specific kinds of files, based solely on the filename extension. If you can't see the filename extension, you don't stand a snowball's chance of figuring out why Outlook is being so draconian.
- You bump into filename extensions anyway. No matter how hard Microsoft wants to hide filename extensions, they show up everywhere — from the `Readme.txt` files mentioned repeatedly in Microsoft's official documentation, to discussions of `.jpg` file sizes on Web pages, and a gazillion places in between.

To make Windows show you filename extensions, curl your right hand into a ball, extend your index finger, and stick your thumb straight up in the air. Point your index finger at your computer's screen, make your eyes bulge waaaaay out like Jim Carrey, and shout as hysterically as you can, "Show me filename extensions, sucka, or I'm gonna getcha!"

Oops. Wait a second. I got carried away a bit. Sorry. To make Windows show you filename extensions, follow these steps:

1. **Bring up Windows Explorer (by, say, choosing Start⇨My Documents).**
2. **Choose Tools⇨Folder Options and click the View tab.**

   You see the Folder Views Advanced Settings dialog box, as shown in Figure 3-19.
3. **Deselect the Hide Extensions for Known File Types check box.**
4. **Click the Apply to All Folders button at the top of the dialog box, click Yes, and then click OK.**

While you're here, you may want to change two other settings if you can avoid the temptation to delete or rename files that you don't understand. Select the Show Hidden Files and Folders option button if you want Windows to show you all of the files that are on your computer. Also consider deselecting the Hide Protected Operating System Files (Recommended) check box. Sometimes you really need to see all of your files, even if Windows wants to hide them from you.

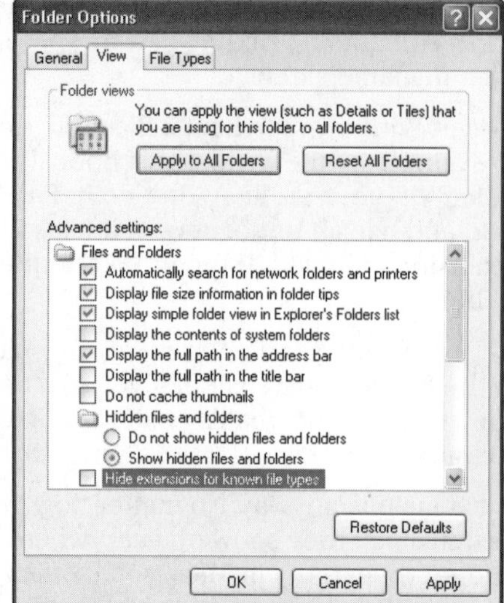

Figure 3-19: Show me the filename extensions!

Sharing folders

Sharing is good, right? Your mom taught you to share, didn't she? Everything you need to know about sharing you learned in kindergarten — like how you can share your favorite crayon with your best friend and get back a gnarled blob of stunted wax, covered in mysterious goo.

Windows XP/Home supports four kinds of sharing. Unfortunately, "sharing" means different things in different contexts, and the devil (as you surely know by now) can be in Windows' details. Here's a quick guide to the four kinds of sharing that you find lurking in various parts of Windows, how to make them work, and what they really entail.

Sharing on one computer

The simplest form of sharing is with other people who use your computer: They log on with a user name that's different from yours, and you want them to be able to get a specific file or folder. In fact, in Windows XP/Home, just about anybody can get to any of your files, at any time. Sharing with other people on your computer is more about making it easy for them to find the files they need, as opposed to preventing them from seeing files that they shouldn't see. Thus, I think of this simple approach to sharing as "sticking your file or folder in a place where other people may think about looking for it." It's all about location, location, location.

Windows has a folder called Shared Documents that looks and acts a lot like My Documents. Inside Shared Documents, for example, you find folders called Shared Music and Shared Pictures.

The Shared Documents folder has three cool but minor characteristics that make it a special place:

- Windows Explorer makes it easy to get to the Shared Documents folder with a link to Shared Documents in the Other Places box on the left side of the screen. You can see it in Figures 3-5, 3-9, and 3-17. A Shared Music link shows up on the left when you're in My Music (refer to Figure 3-7), and Shared Pictures appears in My Pictures, too (refer to Figure 3-6). You get the idea.
- The Shared Documents folder is shared across your network (if you have one). I talk about sharing among computers on a network in the next section.
- Limited users, such as the Guest account, can get into the Shared Documents folder but not into other My Documents folders (see the section about using account types in Book 1, Chapter 2 for details).

Aside from those three minor points, the only real advantage to putting a file or folder in Shared Documents is the location: People may think to look there when they go rooting around looking for stuff.

To put a file or folder in the Shared Documents folder — and thus make it "shared" in this sense of the term — you have to physically move it. The following is the easiest way to do that:

1. **Bring up Windows Explorer (choose, say, Start⇨My Documents), and click on the files and/or folders that you want to put in the Shared Documents folder.**
2. **In the File and Folder Tasks box on the left, click Move This File or Move This Folder.**
3. **In the Move Items dialog box (see Figure 3-20), pick a location in or under the Shared Documents folder where you want the chosen files and/or folders to go.**

   To see the folders inside another folder, click the plus sign (+). Click the folder where you want to move the document or folder.
4. **Click the Move button.**

The Windows XP documentation suggests that you click and drag the file(s) and/or folder(s) that you want to share to the Shared Documents folder in the Other Places box on the left of the Windows Explorer screen. I strongly recommend that you *not* follow those instructions. Dropping the files in the wrong "Other" place is too easy. More than that, using drag and drop gives you no opportunity to see any folders that may be sitting underneath the Shared Documents folder. That's a sure way to stack tons of unrelated files in one messy folder. It's also an invitation to disaster — or at least massive confusion — if Windows encounters duplicated folder names.

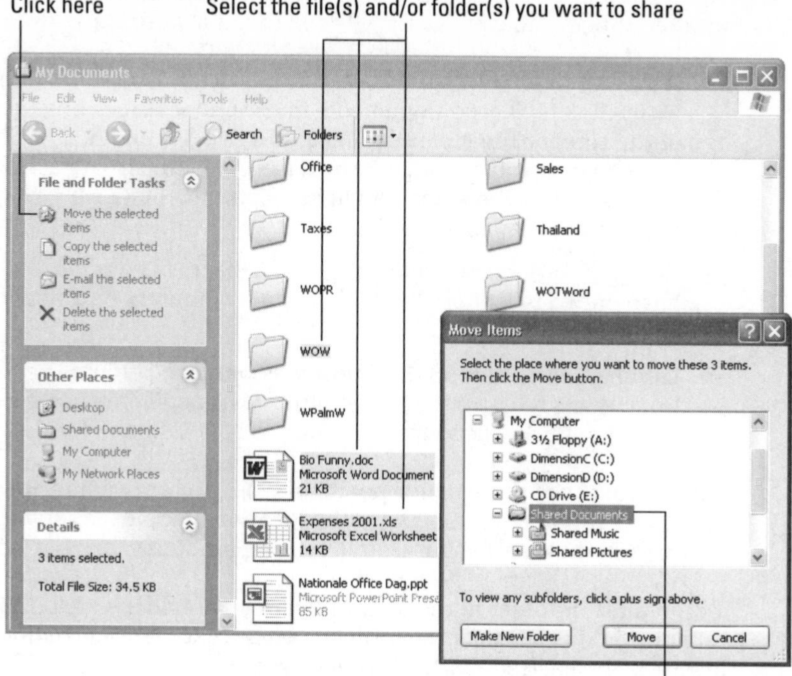

Figure 3-20: Moving files and folder to the Shared Documents folder.

After you move the file or folder, you may have a hard time finding it! For example, if you use Word to create a document and you then move the document to the Shared Documents folder, Word isn't notified that the file has been moved. In Word, if you choose File and then click the name of the document, Word won't be able to find it. Ditto if you use Word's Task Pane to try to open the document. The only way you can open the document from within Word is to choose File⇨Open and browse to the file's new location in the Open dialog box.

Sneak-in-any-time-you-like sharing

The Windows Shared Documents approach to sharing files on a single computer works, but it really doesn't do much, particularly in Windows XP/Home where any user (except a Limited user; see Book I, Chapter 2) can get into any folder (except those marked Private; see the section, "Making a folder private," later in this chapter) with a couple of clicks.

I get a big kick out of Microsoft's description of the Shared Documents folder, in the Windows Help file. It goes like this: "Billy can put his homework in Shared Documents so that Dad can check his work. And Mom can put digital pictures from the family vacation in Shared Pictures so that the whole family can see them." Gawrsh. I can smell the bread baking in the oven. Or is that the family cat frying in the microwave? *BILLLLYYYYYY!*

Time for a dose of reality here, folks. If Billy is using Word to type up his homework, he'll probably save the work in his My Documents folder. (In fact, if Billy's as smart as I think he is, he'll use a separate folder inside of My Documents for each class's assignments.) Dad won't have any problem finding the homework file. All he has to do is choose Start⇨My Computer, double-click Billy's Documents, and double-click the homework file.

Mom can put the family photo album in Shared Pictures if she wants, but Billy and Dad can find the pictures almost as easily in Mom's My Pictures folder. Again, they only have to choose Start⇨My Computer, double-click Mom's Documents, and double-click Mom's Pictures, and they're in like Flynn.

Unless you take very specific steps to make a folder private (described in the upcoming section, "Making a folder private"), any file you put on a computer running Windows XP/Home is immediately and easily available to anyone who can stumble up to the mouse. Other people who use your computer may take a gander inside the Shared Documents folder to find what they're looking for, but Shared Documents is only a convenient dumping ground. There's no security, no privacy, no way, no how.

Sharing on your network

This is real sharing.

Windows XP lets you identify specific folders (or entire disk drives) that are to be shared with other people on your network. You can also tell Windows whether those other people should be able to only read the files in the folders, or whether they are also allowed to change the files.

Windows XP does not allow you to share individual files across a network. You can either share a folder (which may include other folders and certainly includes files), or you can share an entire drive. But single files won't work.

With Windows XP/Home, the sharing choices are quite straightforward: A folder (or drive) is either shared or it isn't. A shared folder (or drive) can be read-only or read-write. That's it. Anybody on the network can get at a shared folder or drive. There's no additional authorization, no secret password, no clandestine handshake, no list of who can get in and who can't.

In Windows XP/Pro, security options are legion — and chances are very good that you have little choice about security settings. That's why there are Network Administrators, eh?

Windows sets up the Shared Documents folder, detailed in the preceding two sections, for network sharing. So any files or folders that you move into the Shared Documents folder are "automagically" shared across the network — you needn't lift a finger.

Before you try to share a folder or drive on your network, you have to set up the network. D'OH! For instructions, see Book IX, Chapter 2.

If you don't mind lifting a finger once or twice, you can easily share a folder on your network:

1. **Bring up Windows Explorer (for example, choose Start⇨My Documents).**
2. **Right-click on the folder that you want to share, and choose Sharing and Security.**
3. **In the folder's Properties dialog box (see Figure 3-21), select the Share This Folder on the Network check box.**

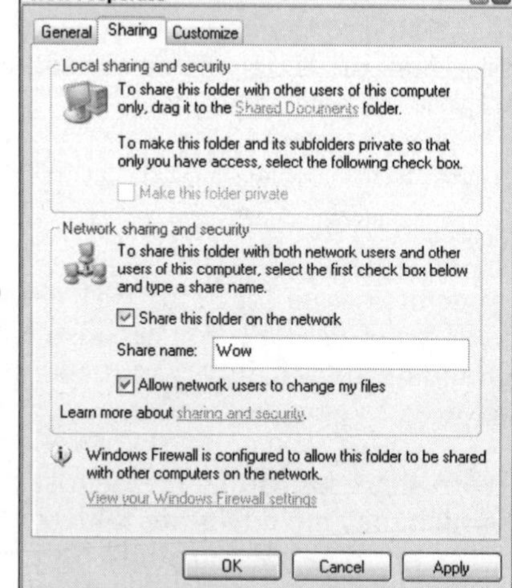

Figure 3-21: Share a folder called Wow by using the Properties dialog box.

4. **Type a name that other people on the network will find enlightening.**

   Officially, that name is known as a *share name,* but any ol' moniker will work.

5. **If you want to give read-write access to every Tom, Dick, and Harry who can get on the network, select the Allow Network Users to Change My Files check box.**

Click OK, and the shared folder becomes accessible from all the computers on your network. For example, if I choose Start➪My Network Places on a computer connected to the computer that holds the folder shown in Figure 3-21, Windows Explorer lets me get into the newly shared folder, as shown in Figure 3-22.

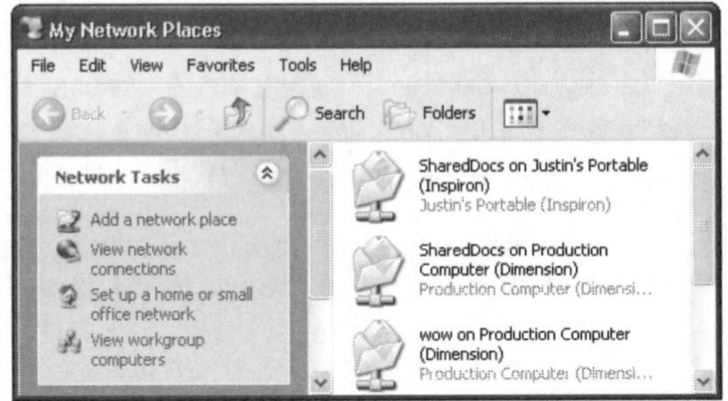

Figure 3-22: The new shared folder Wow, accessible from the network.

When you share a folder on your network, all of the files and folders inside the shared folder are shared, too.

The process for sharing an entire drive is only slightly more difficult, but considerably more intimidating, than sharing a folder:

1. **Choose Start➪My Computer to bring up My Computer in Windows Explorer.**
2. **Right-click the drive that you want to share.**

   Note that you can share CD drives, floppy disk drives, and just about any kind of drive.
3. **Choose Sharing and Security.**

   Windows responds with a rather odd statement: `To protect your computer from unauthorized access, sharing the root of a drive is not recommended. If you understand the risk but still want to share the root of the drive, click here.` (Bafflegab alert: The *root* of a drive is the whole drive, including all the folders on the drive.)

   Setting up an entire drive for sharing (by right-clicking the drive choosing Sharing and Security) elicits a message from Windows about "the risk" of sharing an entire drive. Somewhat predictably, I've never found an explanation of "the risk" or its presumably dire consequences in any Windows documentation. Suffice it to say that granting access to an entire drive lets anybody on your network get at everything on the drive. If you're sharing your C: drive, granting access to the drive probably includes the Windows folder (which contains Windows itself), the Program Files folders (which contain most of the programs on your computer), settings for everybody on the computer — the whole enchilada.

4. **Click If You Understand the Risk but Still Want to Share the Root of the Drive, Click Here.**
5. **Select the Share This Folder on the Network check box. Type a name for the drive that's intelligible to other people.**

   If you want to give everyone on the network write access, select the Allow Network Users to Change My Files check box. Click OK and the drive becomes accessible from anywhere on the network.

When sharing CD drives, Jaz drives, and even floppy disk drives, including a description of the drive in the share name is often a good idea. That way, you know what the drive can handle before you try to use it, so you won't find yourself frustrated by repeated attempts to, oh, transfer a 2.3MB photo to a 1.44MB floppy disk drive.

"Sharing" files on the Internet

When you put a file on the Internet, Microsoft calls it "sharing" sometimes (see, for example, the Windows Help file on sharing) and "publishing" other times (see the Windows Explorer File and Folder tasks box). I call it "storing." There's a difference, but I'll spare you the semantic argument.

Once upon a time, you could grab free storage space on the Internet and park your files indefinitely: The companies that provided the free space also ran advertisements to defray the costs. Alas, like so many other good ideas that failed to meet the reality test, free Internet storage space seems to have gone the way of the Tyrannosaurus Rex. Now, while you may be able to find a "free" trial offer, in the end, you have to pay.

The files you store on the Internet can be for your use only. Or you can give your friends and neighbors your site ID and password, and they can get at your files, too. That's where "sharing" comes into the picture: Store a file on the Internet, give your buddy a password, and he can retrieve the file and stick it on his computer.

Sharing a file on the Internet — I call it "storing" a file on the Internet — has nothing to do with making your own Web site or cranking out a home page. The sharing that's accessible from Windows Explorer (Windows also calls it "publishing") is nothing more or less than the ability to store a file on the Internet, much the same way as you would store the file on your own hard drive — except that a several billion people can get at it, if they know the password. To see if there are any low-cost alternatives accessible from Windows XP, click Start⇨My Network Places and in the task pane on the left, click Add a Network Place. You will probably be directed to MSN and offered a free trial, but there may be other options.

Making a folder private

Under the right circumstances, Windows XP/Home allows you to designate certain folders as *Private*. Private folders aren't accessible to anyone other than their owner.

In order to mark a folder as private, you must meet the following criteria:

- **You must be using *NTFS* (the Windows NT File System) on the drive that contains the folder.** NTFS contains numerous security enhancements that weren't around in earlier Windows file systems. If you bought your PC with Windows XP preinstalled, it's likely (but not certain!) that you're using NTFS on all of your drives. If you upgraded from Windows NT or Windows 2000 to Windows XP, it's likely (but again, not certain) that all of your drives use NTFS. If you upgraded from Windows 98 or Me, you probably *aren't* using NTFS.

  TIP: To see whether a drive uses NTFS, choose Start⇨My Computer. Right-click on the drive and pick Properties. The File System entry near the top of the Properties dialog box should say NTFS. If it says FAT-32, you won't be able to mark a folder as private.

- **The folder has to be one of your folders.** You can mark My Documents as private, or you can mark any folder inside of My Documents (such as My Pictures or My Music) as private. You can also mark any folder inside your branch of the Documents and Settings folder. When you mark a folder as private, every folder inside of that folder automatically becomes private.
- **You should assign a password to your account.** Windows allows you to mark a folder as private even if you don't have a password-protected account, but it warns you that you're trying to do something very silly. If your account is not password protected, anybody can pretend to be you when they log on and simply open the private folder.
- **As soon as you have a password, you should run the Forgotten Password Wizard and create a diskette that allows you to log on to the PC if you forget your password!** Make sure the diskette is stored in a secure place. For more information on passwords and the Forgotten Password Wizard, see the section about changing user settings in Book I, Chapter 2.

Windows taskbar

If you have more than one program running, the fastest way to switch from one program to another is via the Windows taskbar, as shown in Figure 3-23.

With a few small exceptions, each running program carves out a chunk of space on the Windows taskbar. If more than one copy of a program is running (not an unusual state of affairs for Windows Explorer, among others) or if a program has more than one file open (common in Word, for example) and Windows runs low on real estate in the taskbar area, the chunks are grouped together, with the number of open documents in front of the program name.

If you click on the button marked 4 Microsoft Word (as shown in Figure 3-23), for example, you see a list of the four documents that Word currently has open. Click on one of those documents, and Word comes up with that document loaded for bear.

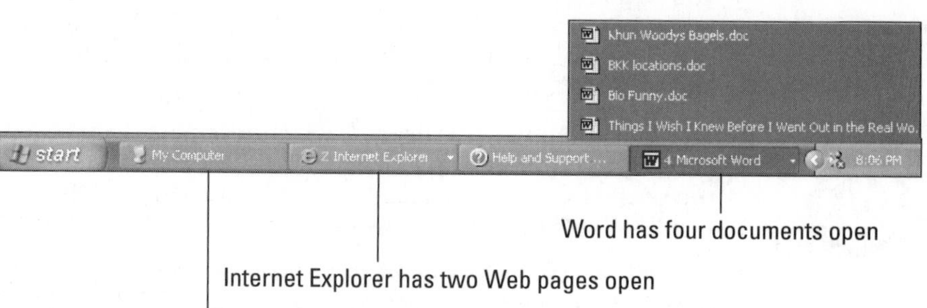

Figure 3-23: The Windows taskbar makes switching among programs easy.

The Windows taskbar has many tricks up its sleeve, but it has one capability that you're likely to need. *Auto-Hide* lets the taskbar shrink down to a thin line until you bump your mouse pointer way down at the bottom of the screen. As soon as your mouse pointer hits bottom, the taskbar pops up. Here's how you teach the taskbar to Auto-Hide:

1. **Right-click an empty part of the taskbar.**

   Usually the area immediately to the right of the Start button is a good place.

2. **Click Properties.**

   The Taskbar tab should be visible.

3. **Select the Auto-Hide the Taskbar check box, and then click OK.**

If you don't want to hunt around for the mouse — or if your mouse has suddenly gone out to lunch — Windows XP has a feature called Coolswitch that lets you switch among running programs, while (insert your best W.C. Fields impression here) your fingers never leave your hands . . . er, your fingers never leave the keyboard. Wink, wink. Just hold down the Alt key and press Tab. When you get to the program you want, release the Alt key. Bam!

Shortcuts

Sometimes life's easier with shortcuts. (As long as the shortcuts work, anyway.) So, too, in the Windows XP realm, where shortcuts point to things that can be started. You may set up a shortcut to Word and put it on your desktop. Double-click on the shortcut, and Word starts, the same way as if you chose Start⇨All Programs⇨Microsoft Word.

You can set up shortcuts that point to the following:

- Programs, of any kind
- Web addresses such as `www.woodyswatch.com/signup`
- Documents, spreadsheets, databases, PowerPoint presentations, and anything else that can be started in Windows Explorer by double-clicking on it
- Specific chunks of text inside documents, spreadsheets, databases, presentations, and so on (they're called *scraps*)
- Folders (including the weird folders that are inside digital cameras), even the Fonts folder and others that you may not think of
- Drives (hard disk drives, floppies, CDs, Jaz drives, the works)
- Other computers on your network, and drives and folders on those computers
- Printers (including printers attached to other computers on your network), scanners, cameras, and other pieces of hardware
- Dial-up network connections

Shortcuts can do many amazing things. For example, you can set up a shortcut to a specific network printer on your desktop. Then, if you want to print a file on that printer, just drag the file onto the shortcut. Windows XP takes care of all the details.

There are many different ways to create shortcuts.

Say you use the Windows calculator all the time, and you want to put a shortcut to the Windows calculator on your desktop. Here's an easy way to do it:

1. **Right-click any blank spot on the desktop.**
2. **Choose New⇨Shortcut.**

   The Create Shortcut Wizard appears (see Figure 3-24).
3. **Click Browse.**
4. **In the Browse for Folder dialog box, click My Computer, click the C: drive, click Windows, and then click system32.**

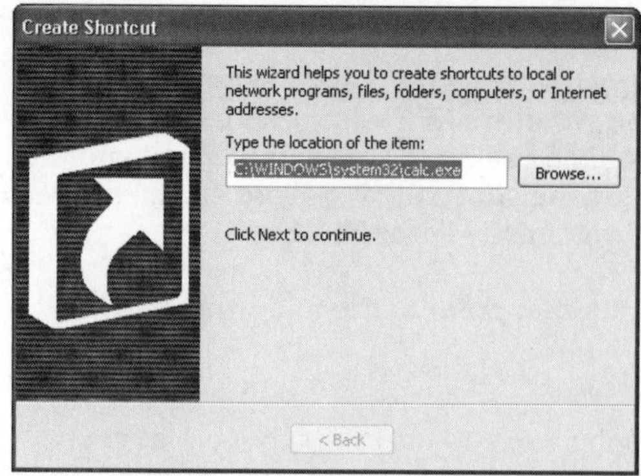

Figure 3-24: Use the Create Shortcut Wizard to put a shortcut on your desktop.

Scroll way down to `calc.exe` (if you haven't told Windows that you want to see filename extensions, you see only "calc" — follow the instructions in the earlier section, "Showing filename extensions," to get full filenames showing).

5. **Click** `calc.exe` **and click OK.**
6. **Click Next, type a good, descriptive name like** Calculator**, and click Finish.**

Any time you double-click the Windows Calculator shortcut on your desktop, the Calculator comes to life.

You can use a similar procedure for setting up shortcuts to any file, folder, program, or document on your computer or any networked computer.

Often, the hardest part about setting up a shortcut is finding the program that you want the shortcut to refer to. In the preceding example, you saw how the Windows Calculator is located in the system32 folder, which in turn sits inside the Windows folder (techie shorthand is `C:\Windows\system32`). Many other Windows programs are in the system32 folder. If you're looking for the Microsoft Office XP programs, they're probably in `C:\Program Files\Microsoft Office\Office10`, while Office 2000 programs are most likely in `C:\Program Files\Microsoft Office\Office`. The Fonts folder sits in `C:\Windows`. In general, if you're looking for programs, your best bet is to look in the Program Files folder first and then in Windows.

You have many other ways to skin the shortcat . . . uh, skin the shortcut cat. When you're working in Windows Explorer, you can right-click many types of files and folders, drag them to new locations — other folders, the desktop, even the Start menu or the Quick Launch Toolbar — release the mouse button, and click Create Shortcuts Here.

Quick Launch Toolbar

While the taskbar can get cramped at times, many Dummies are willing to give up a little bit of taskbar room for a fancy one-click program launcher called the Quick Launch Toolbar. The Quick Launch Toolbar sits next to the Start button (see the following figure), and you can fill it with a handful of little icons that will start your favorite programs.

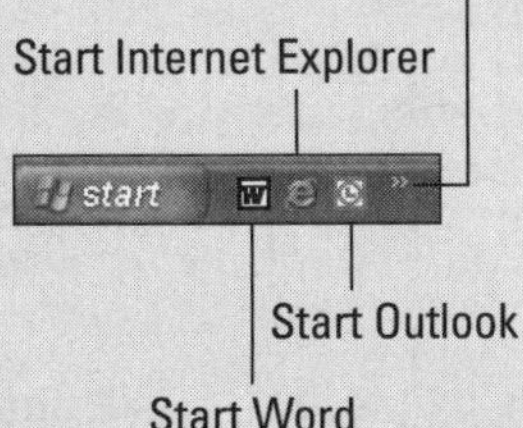

The Quick Launch Toolbar may already be visible on your machine, depending on how it was set up. If it isn't visible, you have to turn it on manually. To turn on the Quick Launch Toolbar, follow these steps:

1. **Right-click a blank part of the taskbar.**

   The area immediately to the right of the Start button is a good place.

2. **Click Properties.**

   You should see the Taskbar tab.

3. **Select the Show Quick Launch check box, and then click OK.**

The Quick Launch Toolbar first appears with three icons: Internet Explorer, Show the Desktop, and Windows Media Player. If you've installed Microsoft Office, Outlook probably shows up as an icon in the Quick Launch Toolbar, too.

You can add or delete icons on the Quick Launch Toolbar — and resize the toolbar, too, if you know the trick. Here's how to do both at the same time, after you use the preceding steps to show the Quick Launch Toolbar:

1. **Right-click a blank part of the taskbar, and deselect the Lock the Taskbar check box.**

   That allows you to resize the Quick Launch Toolbar.

2. **Bring up Windows Explorer (choose Start⇨My Computer, for example) and find a program, document, or other file that you want to put on the Quick Launch Toolbar.**

   Hint: if you have Office 2003 installed, Word is probably `C:\Program Files\Microsoft Office\Office11\winword.exe`.

3. **Click the file that you want to put on the Quick Launch Toolbar and drag the icon to your preferred location on the Quick Launch Toolbar.**

4. **Right-click the new icon, and click Rename.**

   Whatever name you type appears above the icon when you hover your mouse over the icon.

5. **Repeat Steps 3 and 4 as many times as you like, to bring in as many Quick Launch Toolbar items as you like.**

6. **When you're done, click and drag the "perforated" line at the right edge of the Quick Launch Toolbar, resizing it to take as much (or as little) room as you like. Then right-click a blank part of the taskbar and select the Lock the Taskbar check box.**

Judicious use of the Quick Launch Toolbar can save you gobs of time.

Believe it or not, Windows thrives on shortcuts. They're everywhere, lurking just beneath the surface. For example, every single entry on the Start menu is a (cleverly disguised) shortcut. The icons in the Quick Launch Toolbar are all shortcuts. Most of Windows Explorer is based on shortcuts — although they're hidden away where you can't reach them. So don't be afraid to experiment with shortcuts. In the worst-case scenario, you can always delete them. Doing so gets rid of the shortcut, but doesn't touch the original file at all.

Here's yet another way to create a shortcut. Say you want to put a shortcut to a network printer on your desktop. Try this:

1. **Choose Start⇨Control Panel and click Printers and Other Hardware.**
2. **Click View Installed Printers or Fax Printers.**
3. **Right-click the printer that you want to be shortcutted. (Uh, the printer you want the shortcut to go to? The shortcuttee? Somebody run and get me the Funk and Wagnalls.)**
4. **Click Create Shortcut.**

   Windows displays the dialog box shown in Figure 3-25. You'll find that "Create Shortcut" is a common option when right-clicking almost anything in Windows XP.
5. **Click Yes, and the shortcut that you wanted appears on your desktop.**

Figure 3-25: The quick way to put a shortcut to a network printer on your desktop.

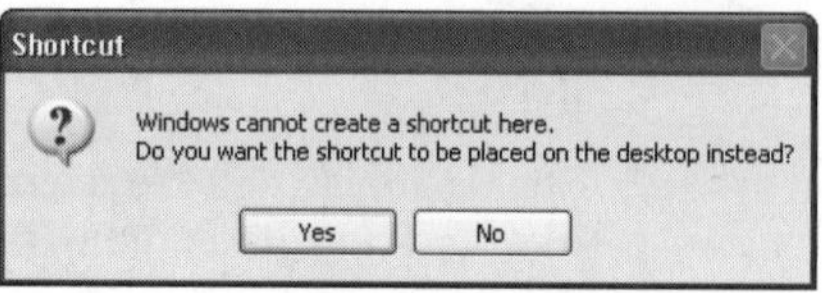

Recycling

When you delete a file, it doesn't go to that Big Bit Bucket in the Sky. An intermediate step exists between deletion and the Big Bit Bucket. It's called *purgatory* — oops. Wait a sec. Wrong book. (*Existentialism For Dummies*, anybody?) Let me try that again. Ahem.

The step between deletion and the Big Bit Bucket is called the Recycle Bin.

When you delete a file or folder on your hard drive — whether by selecting the file or folder in Windows Explorer and pushing the Delete key, or by right-clicking and choosing Delete — Windows doesn't actually delete anything. It marks the file or folder as being deleted but, other than that, doesn't touch it at all.

Files and folders on floppy drives, and on network drives, really *are* deleted when you delete them. The Recycle Bin doesn't work on floppies or on drives attached to other computers on your network.

That's a good news/bad news state of affairs.

The good news: If you ever accidentally delete a file or a folder, you can easily recover the "deleted" file from the Recycle Bin.

The bad news: All of those deleted files take up space on your hard drive. The space won't be reclaimed until you go through the steps necessary to empty the Recycle Bin — and thus truly delete the files.

To rummage around in the Recycle Bin, and possibly bring a file back to life, double-click the Recycle Bin icon on the Windows desktop. Windows Explorer takes you to the Recycle Bin, as shown in Figure 3-26.

To restore a file or folder (sometimes Windows calls it "undeleting"), click on the file or folder, and then click Restore This Item in the Recycle Bin Tasks box in the upper-left corner. You can select a bunch of files or folders by holding down the Ctrl key as you click.

Figure 3-26: The Recycle Bin, where all good files go when they kick the bucket.

To reclaim the space being used by the files and folders in the Recycle Bin, click Empty the Recycle Bin in the Recycle Bin Tasks box. Windows asks if you really, really want to get rid of those files permanently. If you say yes, they're gone. Kaput. Curtains. You can never get them back again.

After you empty the Recycle Bin, the deleted files and folders are permanently gone. If you've been keeping backups, though, you might be able to resurrect an old file or folder. See the section on backup in Book I, Chapter 7.

Logoff

Last things last, I always say.

Windows XP/Home allows you to have more than one person logged on to a PC simultaneously. That's very convenient if, say, you're working on the family PC checking Billy's homework when you hear the cat screaming bloody murder in the kitchen, and your wife wants to put digital pictures from the family vacation in the Shared Pictures folder while you run off to check the microwave.

The ability to have more than one user logged onto a PC simultaneously is called *Fast User Switching,* and it has advantages and disadvantages:

- **On the plus side:** Fast User Switching lets you keep all of your programs going while somebody else pops onto the machine for a quick jaunt on the keyboard. When they're done, they can log off, and you can pick up precisely where you left off before you got bumped.
- **On the minus side:** All of the idle programs left sitting around by the inactive ("bumped") user can bog things down for the active user. You can avoid the overhead by logging off before the new user logs on.

If you want to disable Fast User Switching, choose Start⇨Control Panel and click User Accounts. In the lower-right corner, click the icon marked User Accounts. At the bottom of the Pick a Task list, click Change the Way Users Log On or Off. Then deselect the Use Fast User Switching check box.

You probably won't be surprised to find that you have to click Start in order to log off or switch users. Simply choose Start⇨Log Off, and then click Switch User or Log Off.

To further confuse matters, many computers — especially portables — can go into *Hibernate* or *Standby* mode (variously called Suspend, or Suspend to File, or any of a handful of out-to-lunch synonyms). The primary differences between the two modes are as follows:

- In *Standby* mode, the PC shuts off the monitor and hard drives but keeps everything in memory so it can "wake up" quickly.

✦ In *Hibernate* mode, the PC shuts off the monitor and hard drives and shuffles a copy of everything in memory to the hard drive before going night-night. It takes longer to wake up from Hibernate mode because the contents of memory have to be pulled in from the hard drive.

If your portable runs out of power while in Standby mode, you're up the creek without a paddle. If it's in Hibernate mode (and Hibernate mode is working properly — not always a given!), running out of juice poses no problem at all: Plug the PC back into the wall and it comes out of Hibernate mode, brings its memory back from the hard drive, and picks up where you left off.

Not all computers support Standby mode or Hibernate mode. Some older computers don't handle either mode. Other computers can do both. If you have a choice, the guidelines are quite simple:

✦ If there's any chance that your PC will run out of power while in Standby mode, don't use it. Hibernate instead.

✦ If you have to bring your machine back up quickly (say, for a presentation, or to take sporadic notes), use Standby mode.

To go into Standby or Hibernate mode, choose Start⇨Turn Off Computer. You see a dialog box with the recommended mode as your first option (see Figures 3-27 and 3-28).

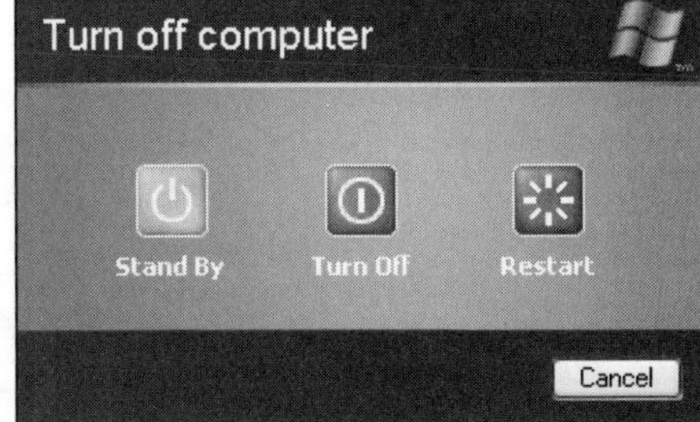

Figure 3-27: Go into Standby mode.

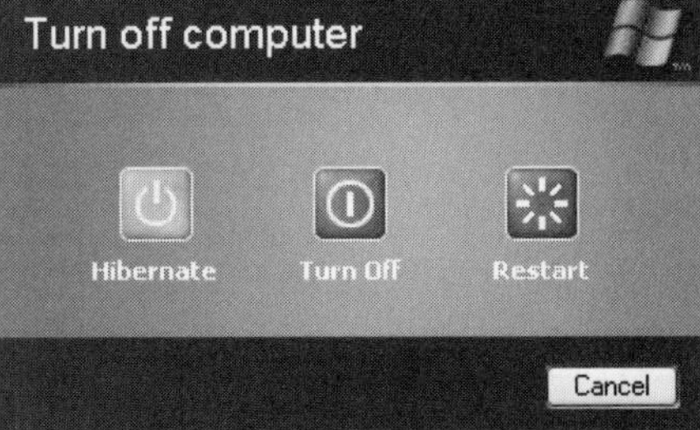

Figure 3-28: Or use Hibernate mode.

If your PC supports both Standby and Hibernate mode, hold down the Shift key while the Turn Off Computer dialog box is on the screen. Windows obliges by changing back and forth between Standby and Hibernate.

You should always turn your computer off the "official" way, by choosing Start➪Turn Off Computer➪Turn Off. If you just flip the power switch off, Windows can accidentally zap files and leave them unusable. Windows needs time to make sure that everything is in order before turning the lights off. Make sure it gets the time it needs by using the official method for shutting down.

Chapter 4: Getting Help with Windows XP

In This Chapter

- Windows XP Help: A resource of first resort
- Remote Assistance
- Searching for help in all the right places
- More help when you're ready to give up

Think of this chapter as help on Help. When you need help, start here.

Windows XP ships with acres and acres — and layers and layers — of Help. Some of it works well. Some of it *would* work well, if you could figure out how to get to the right help at the right time.

This chapter tells you when and where to look for help. It also tells you when to give up and what to do after you've given up. Yes, destroying your PC is an option. But you may have alternatives. No guarantees, of course.

This chapter also includes detailed, simple step-by-step instructions for inviting a friend to take over your computer, via the Internet, to see what is going on and lend you a hand *while you watch*. I believe this Remote Assistance capability is the most powerful and useful feature ever built into any version of Windows.

This chapter shows you what you can do when you're ready to tear your hair out.

Meet the Help and Support Center

When you choose Start➪Help and Support Center, Windows XP presents you with a wide array of choices. Many of the top-level choices that you see in Figure 4-1 "drill down" to the same bits of information; by giving you many different ways to get to that information, Microsoft hopes to make finding what you need easier for you, even if you don't know the answer to your question in advance — a common problem in all versions of Windows Help.

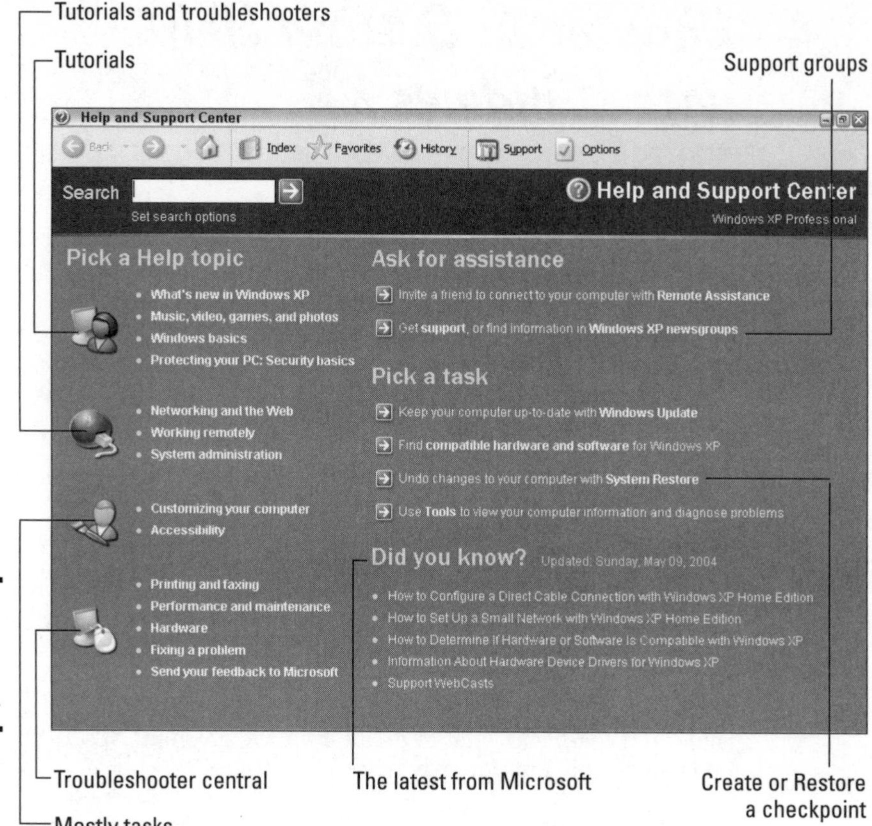

Figure 4-1: Help and Support's cheery face.

The Help and Support Center gives you only the Microsoft Party Line. If a big problem crops up with Windows XP, you find only a milquetoast report here. If you want searing insight or unbiased evaluations, look elsewhere. Like, oh, in this book, for example.

Windows Help morsels fall into several categories:

✦ **Overviews, articles, and tutorials:** Explanatory pieces aimed at giving you an idea of what is going on, as opposed to solving a specific problem.

✦ **Tasks:** Step-by-step procedures for solving a single problem or changing a single setting.

✦ **Walkthroughs:** Marketing demos . . . uh, multimedia demonstrations of capabilities that tend to be, uh, light on details and heavy on splash.

✦ **Troubleshooters:** Take you through a series of (frequently complex) steps to help you identify and resolve problems.

The Help and Support Center exists primarily to reduce Microsoft's support costs, which is both good and bad. Microsoft has tried hard to enable you to solve your own problems. That's good. At the same time, Microsoft has made it pretty difficult to figure out how to pick up the phone and chat with somebody in Product Support Services. That's bad. I spill the beans — and give you some much better alternatives — at the end of the section, "How to Really Get Help," later in this chapter.

The Help and Support Center window puts a happy face on an otherwise sobering (and bewildering!) topic. After you click past the sugarcoating, you find a few gotchas that you should know about:

- Few Dummies will want to jigger with the Search Options, except to increase the number of hits that are reported (see the later section, "Running an Effective Search"). The Help and Support Center already looks in all the places it can; your only options are to cut off certain types of searches entirely — and any limitations you apply carry forward to the next search.
- Live, one-on-one support from Microsoft is notoriously uneven. One day you get a support rep who can solve your problem in the blink of an eye. The next day you spend hours on hold, only to be told that you need to reformat your hard drive and reinstall Windows. If you get bumped up to "Level 2" live support, you're more likely to find someone who knows what he or she is doing, but you have to persist to "Level 3" before you get to talk to a real, live, breathing guru. Few customers have the patience or the savvy to convince Microsoft product support droids to escalate their problem to Level 3.
- When Troubleshooters work, they work well, but they cover only the most basic problems and the most direct solutions.
- Although Remote Assistance is a great idea, in practice the idea has plenty of problems: Both you and your assistant have to be connected to the Internet (or to the same local network); you should probably establish a telephone connection prior to setting up the session; and if firewalls exist between you, Remote Assistance might not work at all. See the section, "Connecting to Remote Assistance," later in this chapter, for lots of details.
- Windows newsgroups on the Internet are unmoderated, which means anybody can post anything. Many well-meaning support group participants dole out utterly execrable advice.
- Sometimes Windows Updates are worse than the problem they're supposed to fix. I usually wait for an update to be in general circulation for at least a week before I apply it to my machine. That way, Microsoft has a chance to withdraw or reissue problematic updates (of which there are many). And I wait at least a month to apply hardware driver updates, unless they solve a specific problem that's been killing me.

✦ The Hardware and Software Compatibility lists leave much to be desired. If a piece of hardware or software that you want to buy appears on the list, it's probably at least a little bit compatible. If it isn't on the list, you can't really draw much of a conclusion.

It never hurts to run a System Restore checkpoint when Windows is firing on all cylinders. The worst possible time to create a checkpoint? When your system has gone to the dogs. Right now, while you're thinking about it and Windows makes you smile from ear to ear, follow the instructions in Book I, Chapter 7 to run a checkpoint. That way, when the inevitable falling out occurs, you'll have something to fall back on.

How to Really Get Help

You use the Help and Support Center when you need help and support, right? Well, yes. Sorta.

In my experience, the Help and Support Center works best when

✦ You want to learn about what functions big pieces of Windows perform, and you aren't overly concerned about solving a specific problem (for example, "What is Windows Media Player"?).

✦ You have a problem that's easy to define ("My printer won't print").

✦ You have a pretty good idea of what you want to do, but you need a little prodding on the mechanics to get the job done ("How do I change my desktop's picture?").

The Help and Support Center won't do much for you if you have only a vague idea of what's ailing your machine, if you want to understand enough details to think your way through a problem, if you're trying to decide on what hardware or software to buy for your computer, or if you want to know where the XP bodies are buried.

For all of that, and much more, you need an independent source of information. Like this book, for example.

My Web site, `www.AskWoody.com`, can come in handy, especially if you're trying to decide whether you should install Microsoft's latest security patch of a patch of a patch. AskWoody.com answers questions, too! Drop by from time to time to see what's happening.

If you can't find the help you need in the Help and Support Center or at AskWoody.com, expand your search for enlightenment in this order:

- Far and away the best way to get help involves simple bribery. Buttonhole a buddy who knows about this stuff, and get her to lend you a virtual hand. Promise her a beer, a pizza, a night on the town — whatever it takes. If your friend knows her stuff, it'll be cheaper and faster than the alternatives. If you can cajole your machine into connecting to the Internet — and get your friend to also connect to the Internet — Windows XP makes it easy for a friend to take over your computer while you watch with a feature called Remote Assistance, which I discuss in the next section, "Connecting to Remote Assistance."
- If your buddy is off getting a tan at Patong beach, you may be able to find help elsewhere on the Internet. See the section, "Getting Help on the Web," later in this chapter.
- If all else fails, you can try to contact Microsoft by e-mail. You may qualify for free e-mail support using something called Microsoft Online Assisted Support. The best way to find out if you qualify, and connect with a support droid if you do, is to jump through the prescribed hoops:
  1. **Choose Start⇨Help and Support.**
  2. **Under the Ask for Assistance list, click Get support, or find information in Windows XP newsgroups.**
  3. **In the Support box, click Get Help from Microsoft.**
  4. **You connect to Microsoft's support site on the Internet, and at that point, you have a chance to review what support is available to you and how much it will cost.**
- As a last resort, you can try to contact Microsoft by telephone. Heaven help ya.

Microsoft offers support by phone — you know, an old-fashioned voice call — but some pundits (including yours truly) have observed that you'll probably have more luck with a psychic hotline. Be that as it may, the telephone number for tech support in the USA is (425) 635-3311; in Canada, it's (905) 568-4494.

Connecting to Remote Assistance

Raise your hand if you've heard the following conversation:

> Overworked Geek, answering the phone: "Hi, honey. How's it going?"
>
> Geek's Clueless Husband: "Sorry to call you at work, but I'm having trouble with my computer."
>
> OG: "What kind of trouble?"
>
> GCH: "I clicked on the picture and it went into Microsoft, you know, and I tried to look at this report my boss sent me, but the computer said it couldn't."

OG: "Huh?"

GCH: I'm sure you've seen this a hundred times. I clicked on the picture but the computer said it couldn't. How do I look at the report?"

OG: "Spfffft!"

GCH: "What's wrong? Why don't you say anything? You have time to help the other people in your office. Why can't you make time for me?"

OG wonders, for the tenth time that day, how she ever got into this bloody business.

At one time or another you may have been on the sending or the receiving end of a similar conversation — probably both, come to think of it. In the final analysis, one thing's clear: When you're trying to solve a computer problem — whether you're the solver or the solvee — being able to look at the screen is worth ten thousand words. Or more.

Windows XP includes a feature called Remote Assistance that lets you call on a friend to take over your PC. The interaction goes something like this:

1. **You create a special message inviting your friend to take over your computer and fix the problem.**
2. **You send the message to your friend, either by standard e-mail, via MSN Messenger or Windows Messenger, or by giving your friend a file.**
3. **Your friend receives the message and responds by clicking on a specific link.**
4. **Your PC displays a message saying that your friend wants to take over.**
5. **If you give the go-ahead, your friend takes complete control of your machine. You watch as your friend types and clicks, just as you would if you knew what the heck you were doing. Your friend solves the problem as you watch.**
6. **Either of you can break the connection at any time.**

The thought of handing your machine over to somebody on an Internet connection probably gives you the willies. I'm not real keen on it either, but Microsoft has built some industrial-strength controls into Remote Assistance. If you like, you can limit your friend to simply observing, instead of taking over the controls of your computer. You can also require your friend to type in a password before the session gets started. And you can put a time limit on the invitation: If your friend doesn't respond within an hour, say, the invitation gets cancelled.

Plenty of pitfalls lurk around the edges of Remote Assistance, but it mostly rates as an amazingly useful, powerful capability. The following are among the potential problems:

- Both of you have to be connected to the Internet, or to the same local network. If you can't get connected to the Internet — especially if that's the problem you're trying to solve — you're outta luck.
- If you have a dial-up Internet connection, you have to *stay connected* from the time you create the invitation through the time you send the invitation, while your friend responds, and all the way until the time that the Remote Assistance session ends. You can't hop on the Internet, send an invitation, break your Internet connection, and then dial back an hour later to get the Remote Assistance session going.
- Both of you have to be running Windows XP or some other operating system that supports Remote Assistance.
- One of the following must be true so that you can send the invitation, and your friend can use the invitation to get connected to your PC:
  - Both of you have to be logged on to MSN Messenger or Windows Messenger.
  - You must be able to send, and your friend must be able to receive, e-mail with an attachment that includes a hot link.
  - You must be able to send a file to your friend — possibly over a network or by simply handing your friend a floppy.
- If a firewall is between either of you and the Internet, it may interfere with Remote Assistance. Windows Firewall (the firewall that's included in recent versions of Windows XP) doesn't intentionally block Remote Assistance, but other firewalls may. If you can't get through, either contact your system administrator, or dig into the firewall's documentation, and unblock "Port 3389" — that's the communication channel Remote Assistance uses.

You — the person with the PC that's going to be taken over — must initiate the Remote Assistance session. Your friend can't tap you on the shoulder, electronically and say something like (with apologies to Dire Straits): "You an' me, babe, how 'bout it?"

When you're ready to set up the connection for Remote Assistance, here's what you need to do:

1. **Make sure your friend is ready.**

   Call him or shoot him an e-mail and make sure he's going to have his PC on, connected to the Internet, and running Windows XP. Also, make sure that he will have MSN Messenger or Windows Messenger cranked up, will be checking e-mail frequently, or will be waiting for you to hand him a file or make one available on your network.

   Make sure you can contact your friend using your selected method: If he's going to use MSN Messenger or Windows Messenger, make sure you're able to send messages back and forth; if you're using e-mail, make sure he's in your Address Book and send him a test message to make sure you have his e-mail address down pat; if you're going to send a diskette by carrier pigeon, make sure the pigeon knows the route and has had plenty of sleep.

2. **When you contact your friend, make up a password and give it to him.**

   It doesn't have to be fancy — a single letter or number will do — and it shouldn't be a password you use for anything else. It's a one-timer that will be valid only for this single Remote Assistance session.

3. **Get on the machine that will be zombified (the one that your Remote Assistance friend will take over), and make sure it's connected to the Internet.**

4. **Choose Start⇨Help and Support to bring up the Help and Support Center (refer to Figure 4-1).**

5. **Under the Ask for Assistance list, click Invite My Worthless Brother-In-Law to Rummage Through All Of My Secret . . . wait a sec . . . click Invite a Friend to Connect to Your Computer Using Remote Assistance.**

6. **In the Remote Assistance pane, click Invite Someone to Help You.**

7. **You have three choices for notifying your assistant, as shown in Figure 4-2.**

   A. If your assistant has MSN Messenger or Windows Messenger running, and you have decided to contact each other that way, sign in to Messenger. You have to pick your friend's e-mail address and then click Invite This Person.

   B. If your assistant is waiting for an e-mail message from you, type his address in the space provided and click Invite This Person.

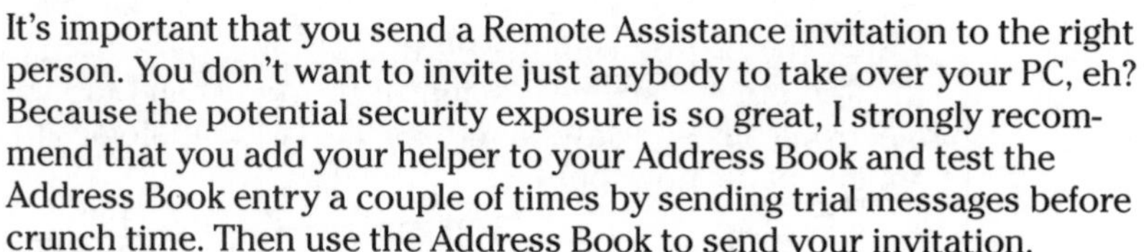

It's important that you send a Remote Assistance invitation to the right person. You don't want to invite just anybody to take over your PC, eh? Because the potential security exposure is so great, I strongly recommend that you add your helper to your Address Book and test the Address Book entry a couple of times by sending trial messages before crunch time. Then use the Address Book to send your invitation.

   C. If your assistant expects to get a file from you (and this option really isn't any more advanced than the other two, in spite of what the option says), click Save Invitation As a File (Advanced).

8. **The Remote Assistance program asks you to type your name, to set a time limit for the invitation to expire (recommended: one hour), and to type a password (no limitation on length or form). If you're communicating via e-mail, you're also allowed to type a message to your friend. Just follow the easy steps.**

   When the Remote Assistance program finishes, one of three things happens, depending on how you're communicating with your friend:

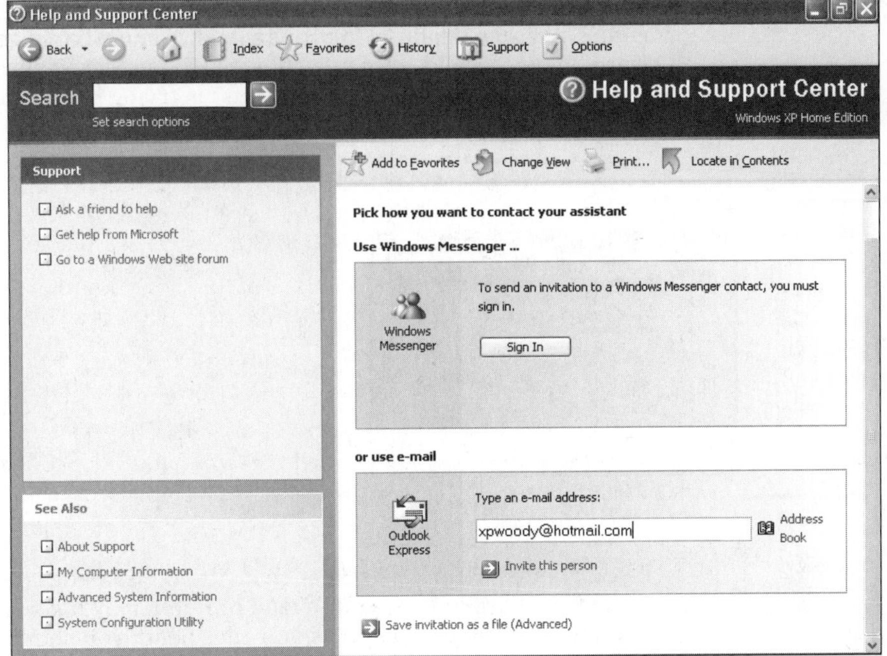

Figure 4-2: The three methods for sending a Remote Assistance invitation.

A. If you're using MSN Messenger or Windows Messenger, your friend (who's identified in the Windows interactions as, ahem, the *Expert*) receives a computer-generated instant message inviting him to help you, much like the message shown in Figure 4-3.

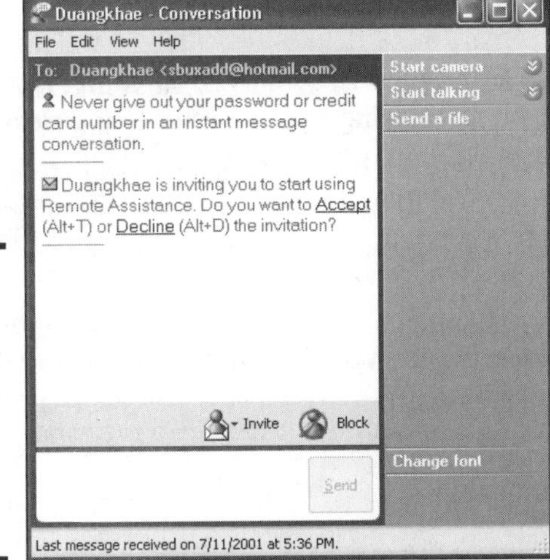

Figure 4-3: Windows Messenger-based invitation to offer Remote Assistance.

B. If you're using e-mail, the Remote Assistance program generates an e-mail message destined for your friend. You probably get an e-mail warning message like the one shown in Figure 4-4, saying that some renegade program (like, uh, Windows) is trying to send an e-mail message on your behalf. Just click the Send button.

Figure 4-4: E-mail security halts your attempt to send a message to your helpful friend.

If you create a Remote Assistance invitation that goes out via e-mail, using this B procedure, your e-mail program may *not* send the invitation automatically. As soon as you click Send, you should immediately start your e-mail program (choose Start⇨E-mail) and make sure that the invitation isn't languishing in your Outbox.

C. If you're working with a file, you need to tell Windows where to put the file called `RAInvitation.msrcincident`. The file easily fits on a diskette, or you may want to save it on a network drive. That's the file you should deliver to your friend.

9. **Your friend, the Expert, has to initiate the Remote Assistance session. The method for starting the session varies depending on how he got your invitation:**

   A. If you're using MSN Messenger or Windows Messenger, your friend can start helping you by clicking Accept (refer to Figure 4-3).

   B. If you're using e-mail, your friend receives a message that looks like the one in Figure 4-5. To initiate the Remote Assistance session, he must open the attached document and respond Yes to the Remote Assistance request shown in Figure 4-6.

   C. If your friend opens the file `RAInvitation.msrcincident`, he sees the message shown in Figure 4-6. Clicking Yes initiates the Remote Assistance session.

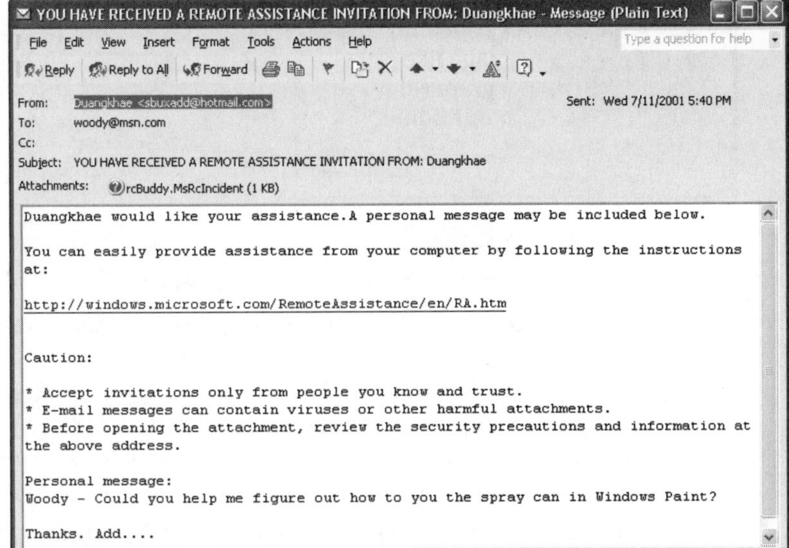

Figure 4-5: The e-mail message sent to your friend, the helper.

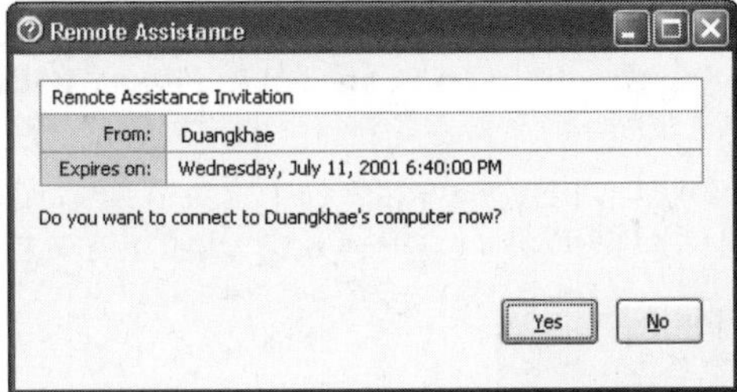

Figure 4-6: To start the Remote Assistance session, your friend clicks Yes.

If your friend attempts to open the file RAInvitation.msrcincident and gets an error message saying that he must choose a program to open the file, he's not using Windows XP. As of this writing, only Windows XP can initiate a Remote Assistance session. At some point in the future, Microsoft possibly will make Remote Assistance available with other operating systems. For the latest information, choose Start⇨Help and Support, and type **Remote Assistance** in the Search text box.

10. **After your friend, the Expert, initiates a Remote Assistance session, you need to allow him onto your machine.**

    After he does his part (by clicking Accept in an Instant Message or clicking Yes in the Remote Assistance request), you see the message shown in Figure 4-7.

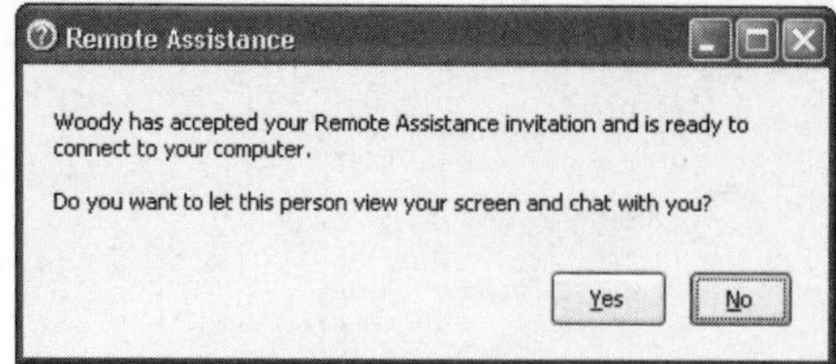

Figure 4-7: Accept or reject the Remove Assistance session.

11. **Click Yes and two things happen simultaneously.**

    First, your computer sprouts a Remote Assistance dialog box, like the one shown in Figure 4-8.

    Second, your friend's computer — which is to say, the "Expert's" computer — receives a Remote Assistance dialog box that looks a little bit like yours, but it also has a viewing box that displays everything on your screen. (See Figure 4-9.)

12. **If your friend wants to take control of your PC, he needs to click the Take Control icon in the upper-left corner of the Remote Assistance window.**

    If he does that, your machine warns you that the "Expert" is trying to take control, displaying the dialog box shown in Figure 4-10.

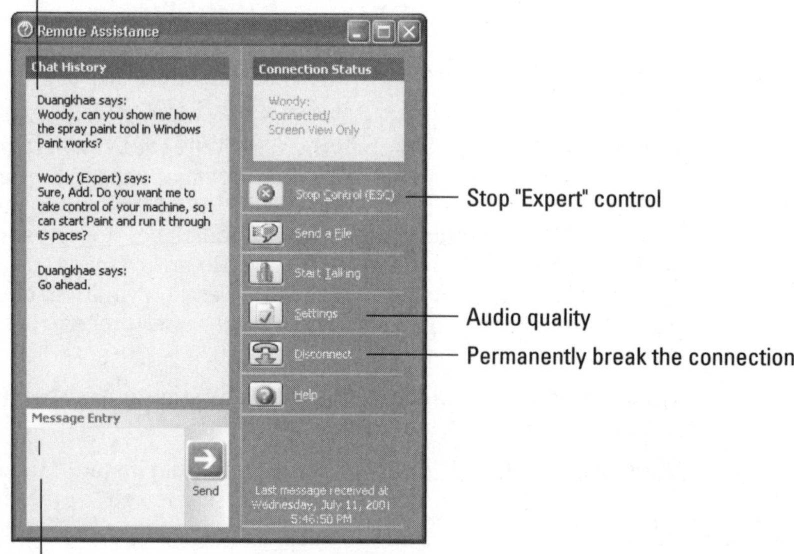

Figure 4-8: The Remote Assistance control dialog box that appears on your machine.

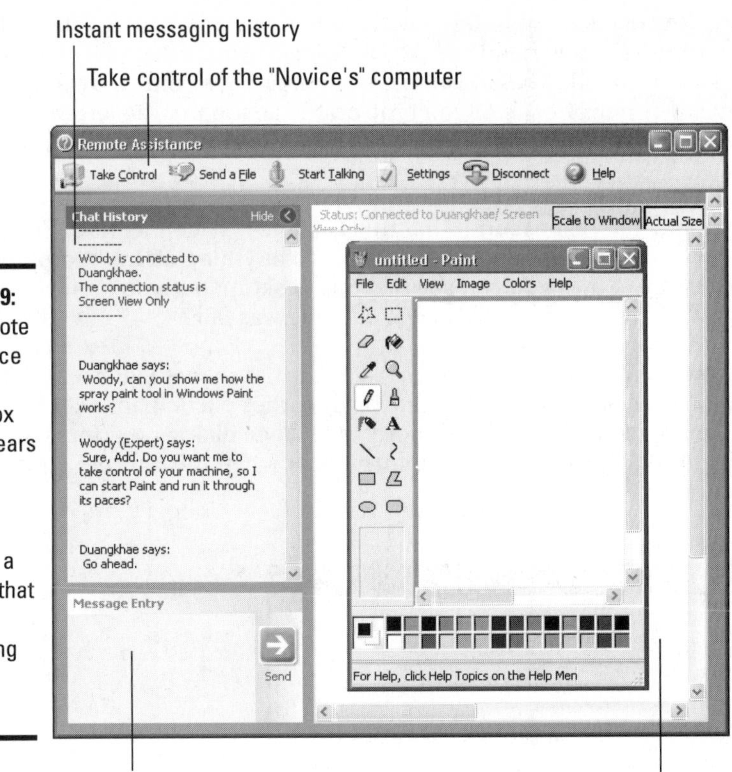

Figure 4-9: The Remote Assistance control dialog box that appears on your friend's machine includes a window that shows everything on your desktop.

13. When you (the "Novice") have given your blessing, your friend (the "Expert") sees the message shown in Figure 4-11 on his screen.

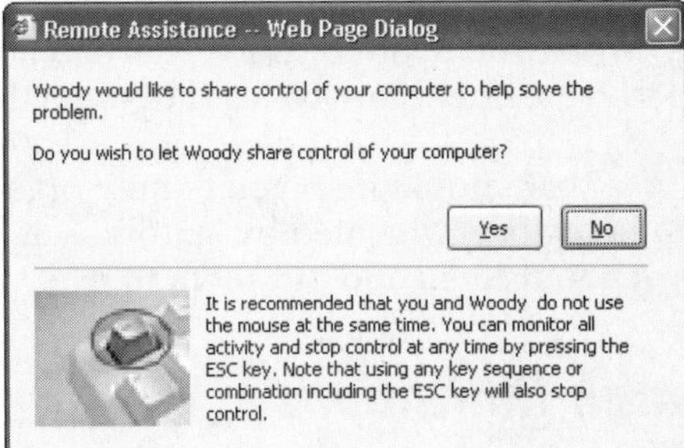

Figure 4-10: You must give your permission before your friend can take control of your computer.

After a Remote Assistance session is under way and you've released control to your friend, your friend can do anything to your computer that you can do. Anything at all. Both of you have simultaneous control over the mouse pointer. If either or both of you type on the keyboard, the letters appear on-screen. You can stop your friend's control of your computer by pressing the Esc key.

Your friend can rest assured that this is a one-way connection. He can take control of your computer, but you can't do anything on his computer. He can see everything that you can see on your desktop, but you aren't allowed to look at his desktop at all. Whoever said life was fair?

All good things come to an end, or at least that's what I've been told. Remote Assistance sessions end when one or the other participant clicks the Disconnect icon, closes the Remote Assistance dialog box (for example, by clicking the X in the upper-right corner), or when the Internet connection goes away.

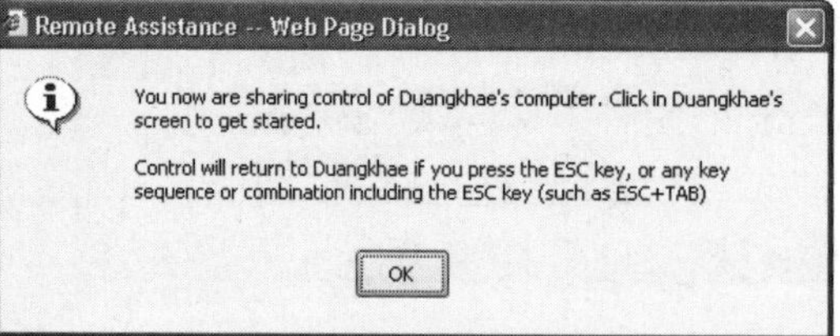

Figure 4-11: You friend is in the driver's seat.

Running an Effective Search

Windows Help has been set up for you to jump in, find an answer to your problem, resolve the problem, and get back to work.

Unfortunately, life is rarely so simple. So, too, with Help. Chances are good that you won't dive into Help until you're feeling very lost. And once you're there, well, it's like the old saying, "When you're up to your <insert favorite expletive here> in alligators, it's hard to remember that you need to drain the swamp."

Windows Help has a few tools that should help you to stay organized — to keep your <expletive> from being overwhelmed by 'gators — if you make a conscientious effort to learn about them and put them to use.

Understanding search limitations

If you're looking for sophisticated search capabilities, Windows Help isn't going to impress you. It has no natural language feature, so you can't ask a question such as "How do I install a digital camera?" and expect a decent response. All searches are for keywords. The words you type are the words that Windows Help uses.

Still, Windows Help has some flexibility and built-in know-how, as displayed in Table 4-1.

Table 4-1 Windows Help Search Combinations

If You Search for This	*Help Returns This*
mouse keyboard	All entries referring to either *mouse* or *keyboard*
mouse and keyboard	All entries that refer to both *mouse* and *keyboard*
mouse not keyboard	Entries that refer to only *mouse*, and do not refer to *keyboard*

When Windows Help searches the Knowledge Base, it doesn't seem to recognize the "not" command mentioned in Table 4-1. For example, searching the Knowledge Base for "start menu" and "start not menu" returns the same results. Looks like a bug to me.

Setting search options

The Windows XP Help and Support Center gives you surprisingly few options for controlling the destiny of your searches.

Although your choices are few, two Search changes make sense for most Dummies:

1. **Choose Start⇨Help and Support.**
2. **Click the Options icon in the upper-right corner of the screen.**
3. **In the Options box, click Set Search Options.**

   You see the Set Search Options pane, as shown in Figure 4-12.
4. **If you want Windows Help to show you more than 15 results from each of its searches — a choice that slows down searches but increases your chances of finding an answer you need — consider setting the Return Up To XX Results Per Provider to 50.**
5. **If you dislike the way Windows Help highlights all the "matched" words when it shows you the results of a search, deselect the Turn On Search Highlighting check box.**

   I *hate* search highlighting: Looking at a Help page with the same word highlighted over and over again gives me a headache. This one change makes all the difference between a useful Help search capability and a garish overblown sideshow, far as I'm concerned.

6. **Click the X (Close) button in the upper-right corner to leave the Help and Support Center.**

   Your new settings are saved.

Collapsing the view

After you find the help you're looking for, you frequently want to keep the Help text in front of you, but you couldn't care less about the search pane, the index, or any of those fancy icons.

If you click the Change View icon, Windows Help retracts all of the unnecessary pieces, leaving the screen refreshingly uncluttered. Compare Figure 4-13 to Figure 4-12.

When you want the Search text box back, just click the Change View icon again, and Windows Help returns to its usual out-of-the-shell configuration.

Keeping your Favorites

Compared to Internet Explorer, Windows Help maintains a very unsophisticated list of Favorites. You have a couple ways to use Favorites:

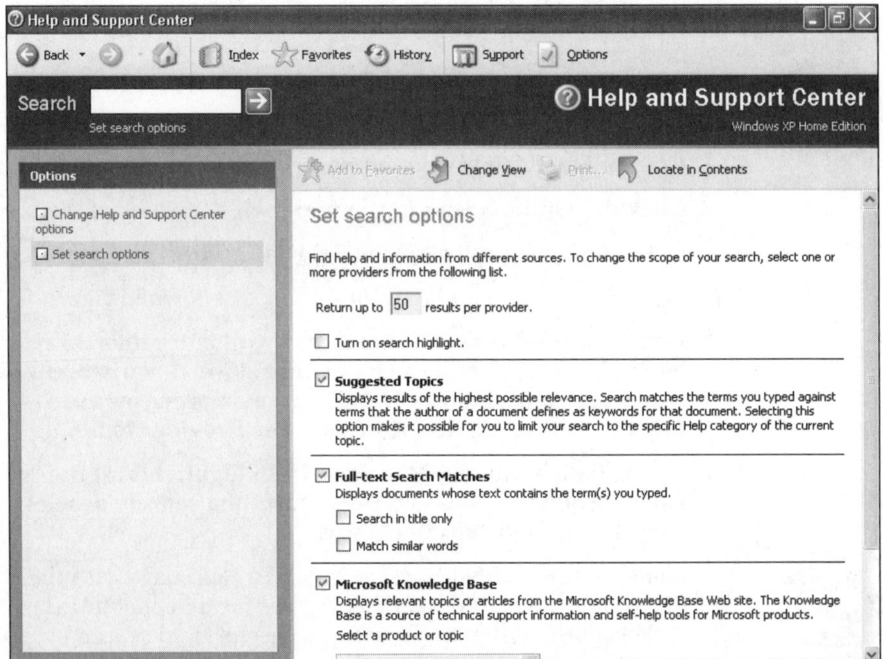

Figure 4-12: Slim pickins for search options.

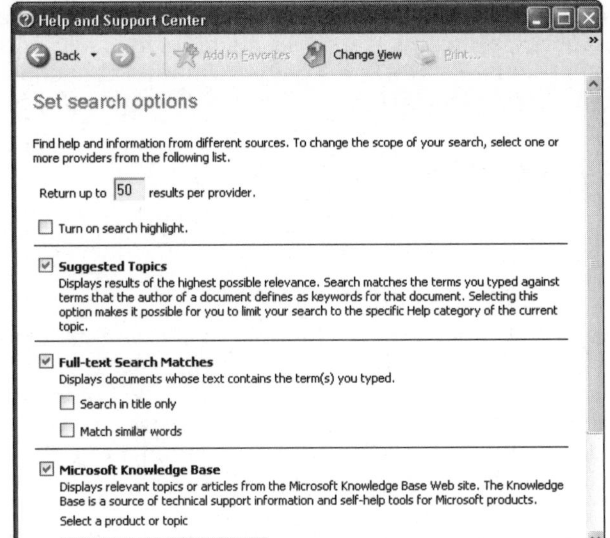

Figure 4-13: Click the Change View icon, and Windows Help pulls in all the unnecessary appendages.

- ✦ When you bump into a Help topic that you want to be able to find again, click the Add to Favorites icon (to the left of the Change View icon in Figure 4-14).
- ✦ To bring up your list of Favorites, click the Favorites icon at the top of the Help window.

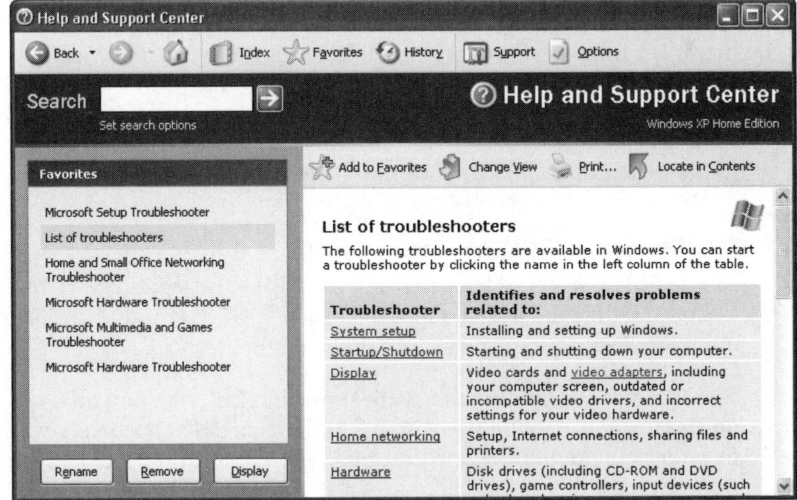

Figure 4-14: Windows Help's unsophisticated list of Favorites.

When you're running through a Troubleshooter that shuts down Windows, the Troubleshooter text warns you that a restart is imminent. Adding the Troubleshooter to your Favorites list before Windows shuts down is always a good idea, in case Windows Help has trouble finding its way back.

Hopping to the Table of Contents

Introducing one of Windows XP Help's great unsung features: the ability to jump from a Help topic straight to the topic's location in the Table of Contents.

What? You say you haven't seen the Help Table of Contents? Oh ye of little faith! There's a good reason why you haven't seen it. Microsoft goes to great lengths to hide it in Windows XP. Earlier versions of Windows made it very easy to leaf through the Table of Contents — there was a little Contents tab, prominently displayed in the Help panel, which brought up the TOC. Not so in Windows XP.

If you want to look at the Windows XP Table of Contents, you must first search for a topic using the techniques outlined in this section or find a topic in the Index (see the next section, "Working through the index") *before* you can jump to the Table of Contents. That's a lot like requiring you to pull a book off a library shelf before you're allowed to look at the card catalog, but sometimes Windows works in mysterious ways.

When you've found a topic that interests you, simply click the Locate in Contents button to jump to the TOC. If Help is kind enough to let you into the TOC at that point (and it may block your attempt, saying the topic is only available from Search or the Index), you can leaf through related topics.

If you try to use Windows XP's Help to get help on, uh, Windows XP Help, you're in for a merry ride. For example, if you search for the topic "Getting Help," you'll find an eloquent discourse on the virtues of Windows Help's Contents tab. Of course, Windows XP Help doesn't *have* a Contents tab. A foolish consistency is the hobgoblin of little minds, eh?

Working through the index

Just as this book has an index, so, too, does the Windows Help and Support Center. To find the index, click the Index icon. The index appears, as shown in Figure 4-15.

The Windows Help index is quite thorough but, like any index, relies heavily on the terminology being used in the Help articles themselves. That leads to frequent chicken-and-egg situations: You can find the answer to your question quite readily if you, uh, know the answer to the question. Or if you know the terminology involved (which is nearly the same thing, eh?).

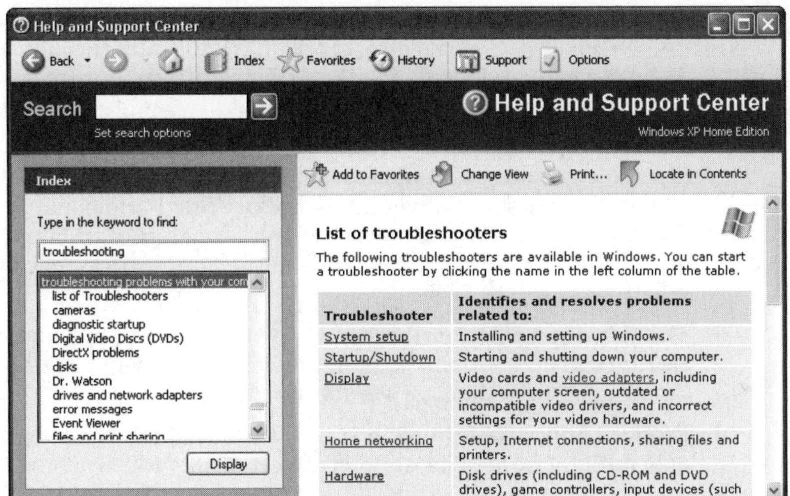

Figure 4-15: The Help index.

Generally, typing keywords in the Search text box is the best way to approach a problem, but the index comes in handy from time to time. Don't hesitate to use it.

Getting Help on the Web

Of course, the single greatest source of information about Windows XP is the single greatest source of information about *everything* — the Web. The Windows Help and Support Center weaves in and out of the Web in a multitude of ways.

Whenever you use the Windows Help and Support Center to search for an answer to a question, it's vitally important that you get hooked up to the Web. Microsoft posts answers to its most-often-asked questions. Thousands of 'Softies are actively involved in keeping the answers as accurate as time and corporate discretion permit.

The following are the best sources I've found for Windows Help and information:

- **The Microsoft Knowledge Base:** This is the mother lode, the source of information that all of Microsoft's tech support people use. Find it at `http://search.support.microsoft.com/kb/c.asp`.
- **AskWoody.com:** The Knowledge Base shows you Microsoft's Official Party Line. `www.AskWoody.com` gives you the rest of the story.

- **Google:** Type in the key words of your question, and you can usually find an answer — although you may have to wade through a lot of chaff. As with any search engine, it works better if you already know the answer to your question. Check it out at `www.google.com`.
- **Windows newsgroups:** These are a great source of information, but you have to remember that not everybody posting to the newsgroups knows whereof they speak. To get there, choose Start⇨Help and Support and in the Ask for Assistance corner, click on Get Support or Find Information in Windows XP Newsgroups. Then in the Support box, click Go to a Windows Web Site Forum.
- **The Windows Update site:** You can get to this site by choosing Start⇨Help and Support and, in the Pick a Task list, clicking Keep Your Computer Up-To-Date with Windows Update.
- **Product Support Options:** If you're curious about the tech support available directly from Microsoft, what you qualify for, and how much it will cost, hit `http://support.microsoft.com` and search for Product Support Options.
- **User Web sites:** Several free user-helping-user Web sites focus on Windows problems (and even a few solutions!). My site, the WOPR Lounge (`www.wopr.com/lounge`), draws thousands of people every day.

Chapter 5: Searching Your Machine and Beyond

In This Chapter

- Secrets for powerful searches on your computer
- Automatic Indexing Service — less wait, more weight
- Search Companion strategy: Throw Rover a bone
- Best ways to search the Web

Computers store lots and lots of stuff. As long as you're churning out the stuff, life goes along pretty easily. Sooner or later, though, the time comes when you have to find some stuff — the right stuff — and that's when the stuff hits the fan.

Windows XP includes a powerful search feature with a cute name — Search Companion — and a cloying mascot, a mutt called Rover.

This chapter explains how to make Rover sit up, heel, fetch, and . . . play dead.

If you want to understand how Windows performs searches, you have to be able to see filename extensions — the short (usually three-letter) part of each file's name following the period that identifies the file's type, such as `.doc` and `.jpg`. Windows XP does not show you filename extensions unless you specifically tell it to. In order to make heads or tails out of anything in this chapter, make Windows show you filename extensions by following the steps outlined in Book I, Chapter 3.

Exploring the Search Companion

If you choose Start⇨Search, you bring the Search Companion to life, with Rover (see Figure 5-1) sitting ever-so-patiently at the bottom of the pane, tail wagging, waiting to help you fetch whatever you like.

Rover exists solely to reduce your anxieties: a nice, cuddly pooch to reassure you that Windows XP is so friendly and helpful. Rover just wants to roll over and get scratched like a, well, like a companion. C'mere Rover. Good boy.

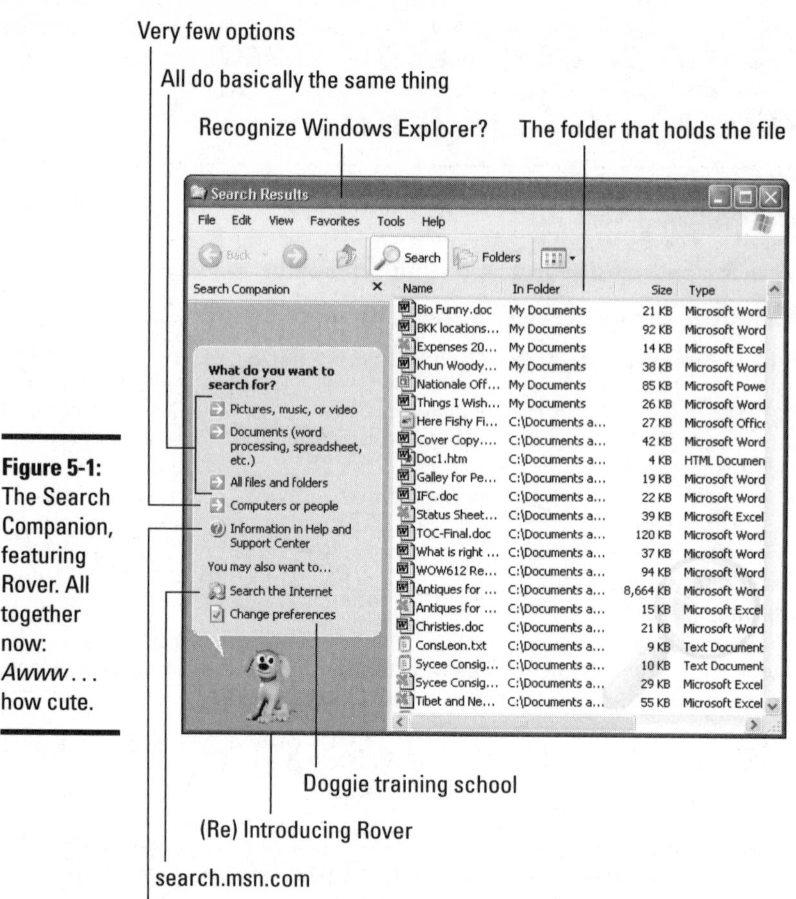

Figure 5-1: The Search Companion, featuring Rover. All together now: *Awww*... how cute.

Of course, Microsoft knows very well that if you're searching for something, you're probably in a panic — a file isn't where you put it, you need it now, and you're about ready to scream bloody murder at the stupid computer or commit some heinous act.

If you can't find a file or a folder, you crank up Search Companion. You probably figured that out. Search Companion also claims that it looks for computers, people, and places on the Internet. It does. Sorta.

You may not know that Search Companion can be jimmied to bypass Microsoft's proprietary Internet search site, `http://search.msn.com` — a trick that makes Internet searching a lot faster and more powerful. Details are in the section, "Searching the Internet," later in this chapter.

If the Search Companion screen shown in Figure 5-1 looks familiar, it should. In fact, Search Companion is a pane inside Windows Explorer. You can see the striking similarities as shown in Figure 5-2.

What you can find

When you bring up the Search Companion by choosing Start⇨Search (refer to Figure 5-1) or clicking the Search icon in any Windows Explorer window (refer to Figure 5-2), Rover offers to search for the following:

- **Pictures, music, or video:** Choosing this option leads Rover (see Figure 5-3) to ask whether you want to limit your search to Pictures and Photos, Music, and/or Video. You can select as many check boxes as you like; if you don't select any, Windows assumes that you want to search for all the categories. Windows then runs a full search (as described in a section later in this chapter, "Looking for Files and Folders") but narrows down the search to files with specific filename extensions, as shown in Table 5-1.

  Note that the contents of the file don't matter: Windows XP doesn't look inside the file to see if it contains, oh, a JPEG image, for example. The Search Companion cares about only the filename extension.

- **Documents (word processing, spreadsheet, and so on):** Like the Pictures, Music, or Video option, choosing Documents leads to a full search, limited to the specific filename extensions shown in Table 5-1.
- **All files and folders:** This leads to the full search described in the later section, "Looking for Files and Folders."

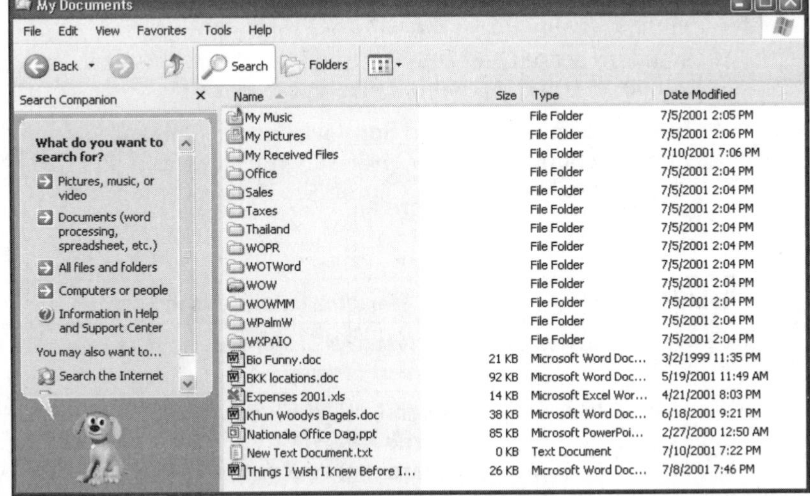

Figure 5-2: Click the Search icon in Windows Explorer and the Search Companion appears.

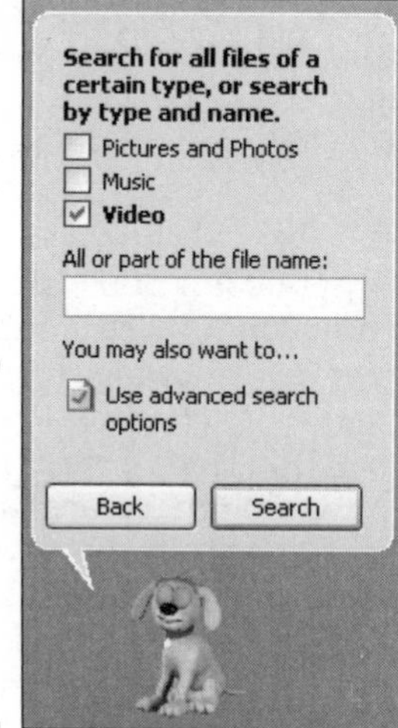

Figure 5-3: Narrowing down the search based on filename extensions.

✦ **Computers or people:** The computer side of this search (assuming you leave the computer name box empty) is identical to choosing Start⇨My Network Places and clicking View Workgroup Computers.

The people side of the search leads to your Outlook Express (not Outlook) Address Book. From there, you can also use OE's crude interface to look in the Bigfoot, VeriSign, or WhoWhere directories.

Don't bother using Start⇨Search to find people on the Internet. As of this writing, none of the three options work very well: The VeriSign directory is very tiny, the Bigfoot directory doesn't seem to be hooked up to Windows, and the WhoWhere link seems to be broken, too. If you're serious about finding somebody on the Web, use Internet Explorer to go to one of the standard search engines: `www.anywho.com` works well, as do `people.yahoo.com` and `www.whowhere.lycos.com`.

✦ **Information in Help and Support Center:** This option opens up the Help and Support Center, precisely the same as if you had chosen Start⇨Help and Support Center. See the preceding chapter for full details.

Table 5-1 Filename Extensions in Search

Choose This Type of File	*And Windows Limits the Search to Files with These Common Filename Extensions**
Pictures and Photos	ANI, ART, BIT, BMP, CDR, CGM, CMP, DIB, EPS, GIF, JPG, TIF, PCX, PNG, PS, WMF
Music	AIF, AIFF, ASF, CDA, FAR, MID, MP3, RAM, RMI, WAV, WMA

Choose This Type of File	And Windows Limits the Search to Files with These Common Filename Extensions*
Video	ASF, ASX, AVI, MMM, MPG, WMV
Documents	ASC, ASP, AW, CHI, CHT, DBF, DOC, DOT, HTM, HTML, MDB, MSG, OBD, PDD, POT, PPS, PPT, PUB, RTF, SAM, TIF, TXT, WRI, XLA, XLL, XLS, XLT

** This list is far from exhaustive; yes, TIF appears in two lists*

The Search Companion also allows you to search the Internet. I go into details about this option in the section, "Searching the Internet," later in this chapter.

What you can't find

Surprisingly, Windows XP Search Companion doesn't search Outlook or Outlook Express e-mail messages unless you turn on the Indexing Service (discussed in the section, "Indexing service," later in this chapter). If you want to look for text in a message, or even a message Subject line, Windows XP can't do it.

Office XP and Office 2003 — specifically Word 2002 and 2003 — can reach inside Outlook e-mail messages and search for text, Subject lines, senders, receivers, and the like. Word also supports AND/OR search arguments, narrowing searches to specific Outlook folders, and much more. If you have Office XP or Office 2003, you should use this vastly more powerful search tool:

1. **Start Word 2002 (the version of Word in Office XP) or Word 2003.**
2. **In Word 2002, if the task pane isn't visible on the right side of the screen, bring it up by choosing View⇨Task Pane. Click the down-arrow to the right of the task pane title and select Search.**

   If you're using Word 2003, choose File⇨File Search.
3. **If Basic Search appears in the title, click Advanced Search at the bottom of the task pane.**

   The Advanced Search task pane appears. (See Figure 5-4.)
4. **To restrict the search to specific Outlook folders, pick a folder from the Search In drop-down list.**
5. **Select Outlook Items/E-mail Messages from the Results Should Be drop-down list.**
6. **Put together your search criteria in the upper part of the task pane, and click the Search button.**

Office XP and 2003 can use Windows XP's Indexing Service to great effect. See the "Indexing service" section, later in this chapter, for details.

Phrasing a search query

You have two different, almost mutually exclusive, ways to ask a computer to look things up:

- **Keyword searches:** These searches take the words you specify and look for those words. In some cases, keyword searches can be augmented by the *qualifiers* LIKE, AND, or NOT. So you may have the Search Companion look for files with the names **blue or dolphin**, and you get back a list of files with either **blue** or **dolphin**, or both, in their names.

Figure 5-4: If you need to search for Outlook e-mail messages, your only choice is the Word 2002 (Office XP) or Word 2003 Advanced Search task pane.

- **Natural language searches:** These searches, on the other hand, expect you to ask a question in the form of a question (with apologies to Alex Trebek). Thus, you might ask your computer, **What color are dolphins?** and get back a list of Web sites that discuss dolphins' colors.

Windows XP's Search Companion combines both search methods, but in a very specific way. If you're looking for Web sites, you're expected to ask a question — that is, Windows uses a natural language search approach when going out to the Internet. For everything else, you should type only keywords.

It's an odd dichotomy that you may find irritating, or confusing, or both.

Looking for Files and Folders

Maybe you need to find all of the handouts you typed for your Porcine Prevaricators seminar. Maybe you remember that you have a recipe with tarragon in it, but you can't remember where in the world you put it. Maybe you accidentally moved or deleted all of the pictures of your trip to Cancun, or Windows Media Player suddenly can't find your MP3s of the 1974 Grateful Dead tour.

Good. You're in the right place.

People generally go looking for files or folders on their computers for one of two reasons. Perhaps they vaguely remember that they used to have something — maybe a Christmas letter, a product description, or a great joke — and now they can't remember where they put it. Or they have been playing around with Windows Explorer, and whatever they thought was sitting in a specific place isn't there anymore.

In either case, the solution is to make Windows XP do the work and go searching for your lost files or folders.

If you choose Start⇨Search, the Search Companion dog Rover (refer to Figure 5-1) gives you a chance to narrow down your search, in advance, by choosing Pictures, Music, or Video, or Documents. If you know in advance what kind of file you're looking for, those choices can hone in on specific file types (refer to Table 5-1). If you don't know exactly what you're looking for, though, it's just as easy to go straight to the full-fledged search — the choice marked All Files and Folders.

Rover the Searching Agent

First things first: You can get rid of the dog. Banish him to the doghouse. Trade him in for a newer model — or at least a different one. You can simply tell him to get lost. He won't mind. Here's how:

1. **Bring up the little mutt by choosing Start⇨Search (see Figure 5-1).**
2. **Click Change Preferences at the bottom of the screen.**

   You see the question "How Do You Want To Use Search Companion?" in the screen that appears.
3. **To completely rid yourself of the critters, click Without an Animated Screen Character.**
4. **If you think you have a tiny chance of finding a character more to your liking, click With a Different Character, and peruse the ensuing rogues' gallery.**

Do you really, really need to get a life? Here's how to tell. Click on Rover (or whichever cloying character you have chosen as your Search Companion), and then click Do a Trick. Go ahead. I dare ya.

Those little Search Companion characters — they're called *Agents* — are stored in ACS files. If you search for `*.acs` files (see "Using wildcards" later in this chapter), you can find a handful of them scattered in various places on your hard drive. If you come across other ACS files — Office XP and 2003 have a bunch of them, for example, probably tucked away in hidden folders — and put the files in the `\Windows\srchasst\chars` folder, they are available for you to choose as an alternative to Rover.

Making the most of simple searches

Can you remember what's in the file you're looking for? Can you remember at least part of the file's name? Nine times out of ten, that's all you need.

Forgive me if you've read this already, but you absolutely must make Windows XP show you filename extensions — the characters following the period toward the end of the filename, such as `.exe` or `.bat`. Read up on filename extensions, and why they're so important to see, in Book I, Chapter 3. Then follow the steps listed there to tell Windows XP to show you filename extensions.

The best approach to performing a simple search depends on whether you know for an absolute, dead-certain fact what kind of file you're dealing with. The following sections describe how it works in the best of all possible worlds.

Searching for pictures, music, or video

Here's what to do if you know for an absolute, dead-certain fact that the file you want is a picture, photo, music file, and/or video:

1. **Choose Start⇨Search.**

   You see Rover (refer to Figure 5-1) or something like him (or, if you're lucky, nothing at all!).

2. **Click Pictures, Music, or Video.**

   You see the Search pane (refer to Figure 5-3).

3. **Pick the kind of file you're looking for.**

   If you know anything at all about the file, type it in the text box marked All or Part of the File Name. Windows is a whole lot smarter than this dialog box would have you believe. For example, if you search for Music files and you type **Ludwig** in the box, Windows will find Beethoven's 9th Symphony, even though Ludwig doesn't appear in the filename. Try it. You'll see.

All of the advanced search options described in the section, "Digging deeper with advanced searches," are available by choosing Use Advanced Search Options.

4. **If you don't find the file you want, crank up the Windows Media Player and see whether you can find it from there. I talk about Windows Media Player in Book VII, Chapter 1.**

Searching for a document

Here's what to do if you are absolutely, completely certain that the file you want is a document — which is to say a text file (with the `.txt` filename extension), Word document (`.doc`), Excel workbook (`.xls`), PowerPoint presentation (`.ppt` or `.pps`), or one of the other documents listed in Table 5-1:

1. **Choose Start⇨Search.**
2. **Click Documents (Word Processing, Spreadsheet, and so on).**

   You see the pane shown in Figure 5-5.

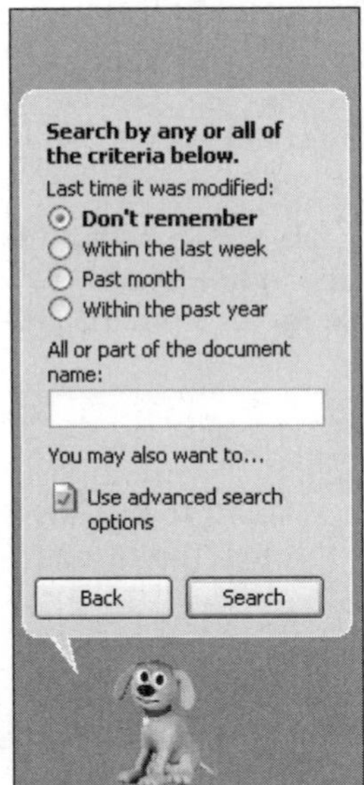

Figure 5-5: Tell Rover to search for documents.

3. **Tell Rover how to narrow down the search.**

   If you can remember the last time that the document was modified — not created or opened, but changed — select the appropriate option button. There's no wiggle room. If you select the Within the Last Week option button, and you last modified the file eight days ago, it won't show up in the search.

If you can remember any part of the filename, type it in the text box. The Search Companion matches any file with a name that includes the characters you've typed. (See Table 5-2.)

Table 5-2 Simple Filename Matches

Type This	*And You Will Match*	*But You Will Not Match*
a	`a.xls`	`b.xls`
bug	`bed bug.txt`	`abu ghanim.txt`
add	`madden.ppt`	`dad.ppt`
wood	`woody.doc`	`woo.doc`

Search Companion recognizes the key words OR and AND. If you type **new or recent** in the All or Part of the Document Name box, Rover brings back files such as `new pictures.jpg` and `recent songs.mp3`. If you type two words in the All or Part of the Document Name box, Rover assumes you mean AND.

The search for filenames is quite literal, and filename extensions are included if you have Windows show filename extensions. So if you show filename extensions and you enter **txt**, you see all of your `.txt` text files.

All of the advanced search options described in the section, "Digging deeper with advanced searches," are available by choosing Use Advanced Search Options.

4. **If you don't find the file you want, try the option called Change File Name or Keywords (see Figure 5-6). This option enables you to easily switch over to searching for text inside the documents (see Figure 5-7).**

Searching for All Files and Folders

If you aren't absolutely, totally, utterly certain that you want to find a picture, photo, music file, video, or document, it's best to tell Rover to fetch everything matching your criteria, and sift through the results yourself. Here's how:

1. **Choose File⇨Search.**
2. **Click All Files and Folders, and go for a full-fledged search.**

   When you do, you get the search pane shown in Figure 5-8.
3. **Help Rover find your file.**

   The filename part of the search is identical to the details I discussed in Table 5-2. If you have filename extensions showing, and you type **doc** in this text box, for example, you get a list of all the `.doc` files on your computer.

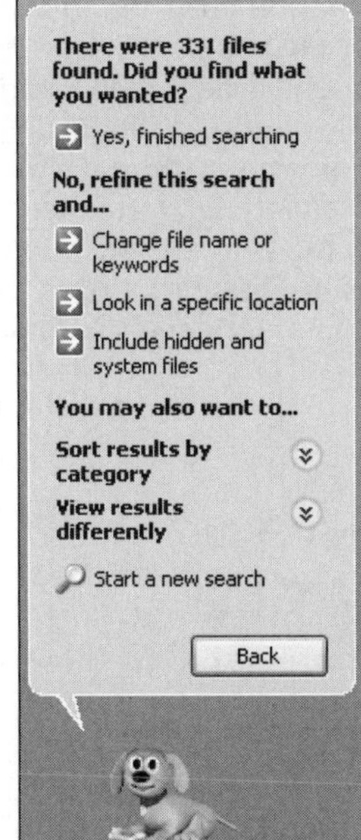

Figure 5-6: Frequently people forget filenames but can think of keywords inside the document.

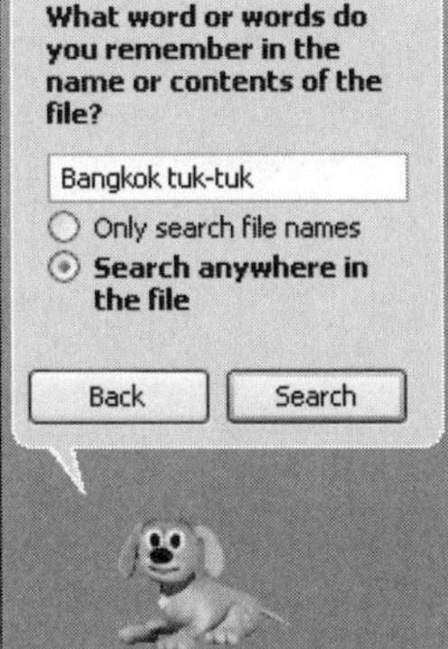

Figure 5-7: Type a keyword that's unique to the file, if you can think of one.

The A Word or Phrase in the File text box jumps through some interesting hoops. If you type a single word, Search Companion looks for that word, of course. If you type a phrase like **back in a minute**, Search Companion looks for that precise phrase, with spaces and punctuation exactly the way you specify.

Search Companion also looks for information attached to a file — information you may not see if you open the file. It's called *metadata,* and I gave you an example of a metadata search earlier when I said that Search would find Beethoven's 9th if you look for **Ludwig**. Media files usually have metadata attached to them with information about the content. Microsoft Office documents always have metadata attached to them. You can see Office metadata by bringing up the Office application (such as Word, Excel, or PowerPoint) and choosing File⇨Properties. The file's metadata appears on the tabs marked Summary and Custom.

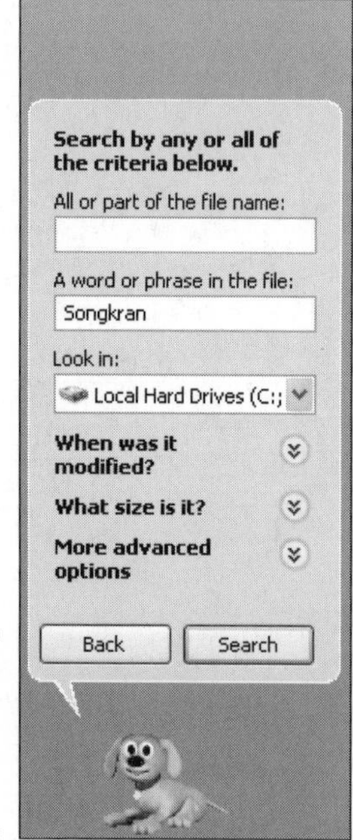

Figure 5-8: The full-fledged search.

The Look In drop-down list enables you to pick the starting point of the search. If you want to search your entire network (a process that could take many hours!), click the down-arrow and choose Browse⇨My Network Places⇨Entire Network.

Windows XP warns you not to share an entire hard drive (see Book I, Chapter 3) for several reasons, and this is a big one: Searching every shared hard drive on your network is as simple as firing up Search Companion and choosing Look In/Entire Network. And you can search for anything.

4. **Click the Search button and the Search Companion returns the names of files that match all of your criteria. (In geek terms, they're "ANDed" together.)**

   If you tell Rover that you want to see files with **woody** in all or part of the filename, with the phrase **blew it again** in the file, Search Companion returns only files with names that match AND contain the indicated phrase. So a file named `woodrow.doc` containing the phrase "blew it again" wouldn't make the cut. Nor would a file called `woody.txt` with the text "blewit agin."

That's the lowdown on simple searches. Much more power awaits, in the next parts of this chapter.

Using wildcards

Windows XP's Search Companion lets you use *wildcards,* which are symbols that substitute for letters. The easiest way to describe a wildcard is with an example. ? is the single-letter wildcard. If you tell Rover to look for files named **d?g.txt**, the mutt dutifully retrieves `dog.txt` and `dug.txt` (if you have files with those names), but it doesn't retrieve `drag.txt` or `ding.txt`. The ? matches one — and only one — character in the filename.

Search Companion recognizes two wildcards. ? matches a single character, and * matches multiple (zero or more) characters. (See Table 5-3.)

Table 5-3 Wildcards for Filenames

This	*Matches This*	*But Not This*
`d?g.txt`	`dog.txt, dug.txt`	`drag.txt, ding.txt`
`ne*w.mp3`	`new.mp3, neosow.mp3`	`ne.mp3, new.doc`

Wildcards work with only file and folder names. The A Word or Phrase in the File text box (refer to Figure 5-8) does *not* recognize wildcards.

Digging deeper with advanced searches

The full-fledged search dialog box (refer to Figure 5-8) has three buttons: When Was It Modified?, What Size Is It?, and More Advanced Options.

If you click the (inappropriately named) When Was It Modified? button, you have a chance to specify when the file you're looking for was last changed (in computerese, *modified* means changed). As you can see in Figure 5-9, though, you aren't limited to the modified date. In fact, Search Companion searches for files based on the date that they were created or last opened (*accessed* in computer lingo) as well.

If you click the What Size Is It? button, Search Companion lets you pick the file size. In my experience, people are amazed at how big files get, so if you use this option, allow yourself lots of breathing room on the high side.

Finally, the More Advanced Options selection (see Figure 5-10) holds six possibilities:

✦ Type of File lists all of the filename extensions that your computer recognizes, except that you don't get to see the filename extensions; you have to make do with the hokey names. If you have Microsoft Office installed, the list of types starting with "Microsoft" goes on forever (my list in Office XP includes one called Microsoft FrontPage Dont Publish — an all-time classic). If you know the filename extension that you're looking for, this is the worst place to tell Search Companion what kind of file you want, because the hokey names can be so ambiguous. Instead, if you know the filename extension that you want, use a wildcard search using the filename extension in the All or Part of the File Name text box (for example, enter ***.mpeg** to find all the `.mpeg` files, or ***.ani** to find all the `.ani` files).

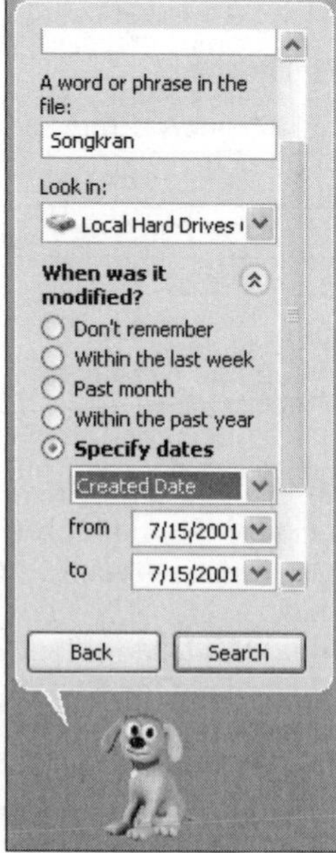

Figure 5-9: Narrow your search based on the date that the file was last changed, created, or opened.

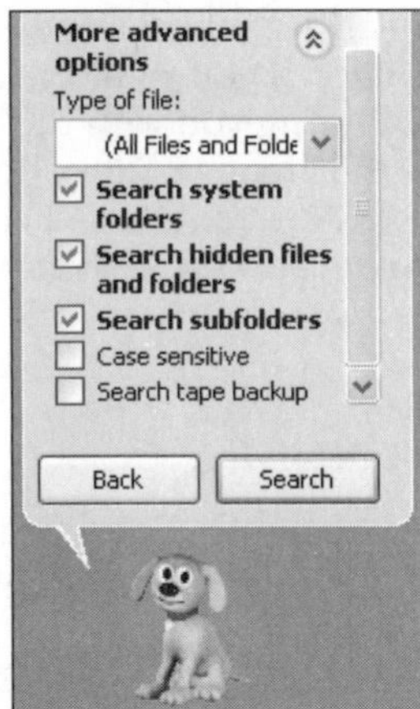

Figure 5-10: A hodge-podge of additional Search criterion.

- Select the Search System Folders check box, and Search Companion looks in the Windows, Documents and Settings, and Program Files folders.
- Select the Search Hidden Files and Folders check box, and Search Companion looks in any files or folders that are marked Hidden.

Hidden files and folders aren't really hidden. They're just marked a certain way so that Windows Explorer won't show them — unless you tell Windows Explorer to show hidden files and folders. To hide a file or folder, choose Start⇨My Documents to start Windows Explorer. Right-click on the file or folder, and click Properties. At the bottom of the Properties dialog box, in the Attributes area, select the Hidden check box. Now your file or folder is hidden from view. To make Windows Explorer show hidden files and folders, follow the steps described in Book I, Chapter 3.

- Selecting the Search Subfolders check box tells Search Companion that you want to look in the folder specified in the Look In drop-down list, as well as in all folders inside of that folder. You almost always want to have this check box selected.
- In spite of what you read in other books, the Case Sensitive check box has nothing to do with filenames. If you select this check box, Search Companion matches the case of the text you type in the A Word or Phrase in the File text box. So if you type **Blue Mango** in the box and check this box, Search Companion looks for the text "Blue Mango" inside files, but passes on both "blue Mango" and "BLUE mango."

  Filenames are never case sensitive. Ever. My Documents and my documents always refer to the same folder.
- Select the Search Tape Backup check box only if you are using Windows XP's Backup feature.

If you've managed to read to this point, you're probably serious about searching. Good on ya, as they say Down Under. If you want the Search Companion to cut to the chase and stop bothering you with the "helping" screens that divert you to searching for specific kinds of files, do this:

1. **Choose Start⇨Search and bring up Rover and the Search Companion (refer to Figure 5-1).**
2. **Click Change Preferences.**
3. **Click Change Files and Folders Search Behavior.**
4. **Click Advanced — Includes Options to Manually Enter Search Criteria. Recommended for Advanced Users Only (see Figure 5-11).**

After you change to Advanced, the Search Companion always starts up, ready to perform a full-fledged search (refer to Figure 5-8).

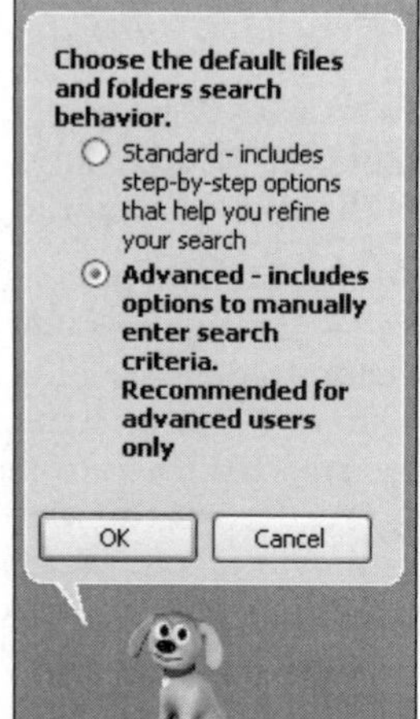

Figure 5-11: If you've read this far, you're an advanced user.

Saving a search

Do you find yourself repeating the same searches over and over again? Maybe you need to look in BearShare's Download folder to see if those MP3s have finally arrived. Or you want to look at a list of invoices for your number-one customer. Only a real dummy would do the same thing over and over again when the computer can do the work. A *For Dummies* dummy, on the other hand, knows that he can save and reuse searches 'til the cows come home.

If he reads this book, anyway.

Here's how you save and reuse a search:

1. **Choose Start⇨Search to bring up the Search Companion.**
2. **Set up your search.**

   In Figure 5-12, for example, I've instructed Rover to fetch all the MP3 files in the My Music folder that are less than a week old.
3. **Click the Search button and run the search.**

   This is the trick. It doesn't matter whether or not you really want to run the search. You have to if you're going to save the search to use in the future.
4. **Choose File⇨Save Search.**

   Windows XP offers to save a file called `Files named @.mp3.fnd` or something equally obtuse. (See Figure 5-13.)
5. **Navigate to a convenient location (if you put the search on your desktop, it'll always be handy); give the search a more descriptive name, if you like; and click Save.**
6. **Any time you want to run the saved search, double-click the FND file and click the Search button. Voilà!**

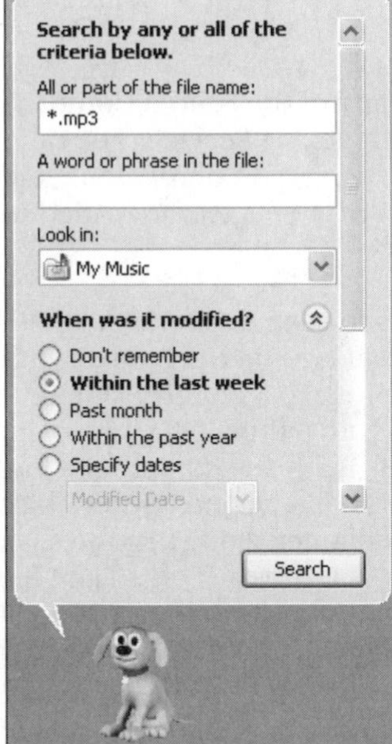

Figure 5-12: To save and reuse a search, set up a search the way you want it, and then run the search.

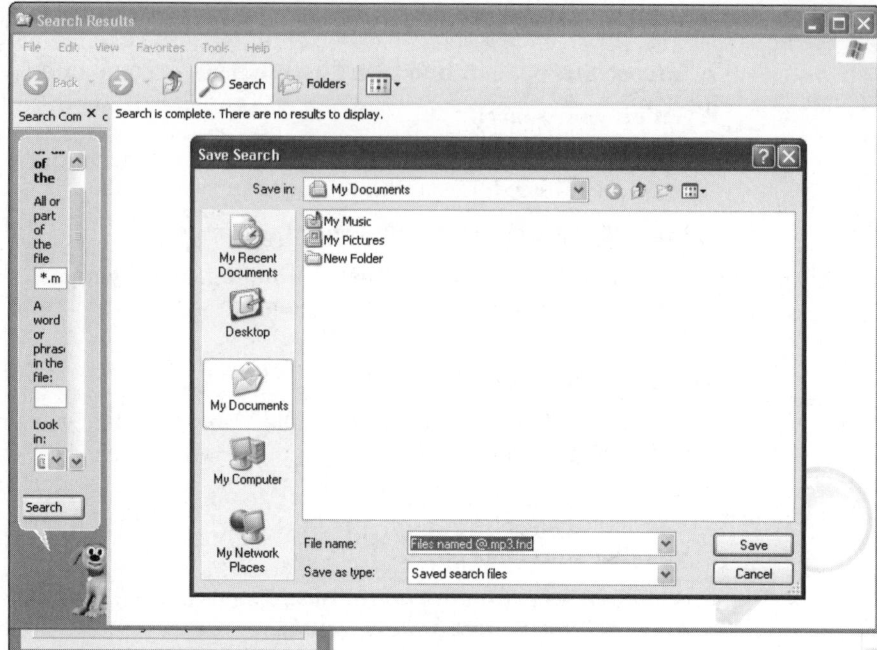

Figure 5-13: The saved search has a strange filename, ending in .fnd.

Indexing service

If you choose Change Preferences in any of the Search Companion dialog boxes, you see an option called With Indexing Service (For Faster Local Searches). Click that line and you see a Search Companion dialog box — select Yes, Enable Indexing Service to turn on a feature called Indexing Service.

Indexing is a fancy way for computers to scan documents, build and store indexes, and then retrieve documents based on the indexes in response to your searches. Sounds difficult? In principle, it's pretty simple: The computer waits until you aren't doing anything; then it starts looking, methodically, at every file on your hard drive(s). Say the computer's looking at a file called `Woody da Dummy.doc`. Inside the file, the computer discovers the words "jumping jack flash." It builds an index entry that says, among other things, "the word *jumping* is in `Woody da Dummy.doc`." Then it builds another index entry that says, "the word *jack* is in `Woody da Dummy.doc`." And so on. When you ask for all the files that contain the word *jack,* the Indexing Service realizes immediately that `Woody da Dummy.doc` should be included on the list.

In practice, indexing is one whole heckuvalot more difficult than you may imagine. The biggest problem Microsoft had, for years, was the intrusiveness of the bloody indexer: You'd be typing along, pause a few seconds to think, and WHAM! All of a sudden this crazy program had taken over your machine. Resume typing, and you had to wait an eternity to regain control of your PC. I'm very happy to say that, in Windows XP (and only Windows XP, in my eXPerience), indexing finally works.

If it's turned on, Windows XP Indexing Service hooks into Microsoft Office XP and Office 2003. So if you perform a search in Office, what you see is what Windows XP delivers.

I have had no end of problems getting Windows XP to use the index created by the Indexing Service: There's an entire section of my book *Windows XP Timesaving Techniques For Dummies* (Technique 19) published by Wiley Publishing, Inc. that shows you how to determine if the Indexing Service saves time — indeed, if Windows XP itself will even *use* the index. As far as I'm concerned, the only reason you would want to turn on the Indexing Service is to speed up searches inside Office XP and/or Office 2003, or if you're willing to jump through the extra hoops involved in working with the Computer Management Console (see later in this section). If you don't search in Office very much, and you don't want to force yourself to use the Computer Management Console, turning on the Indexing Service is a waste of your time.

You can really get your hands dirty with complex searches, providing that the Indexing Service is running. For example, in Figure 5-14, I use the NEAR operator to ask the Indexing Service to return a list of all files where the word *read* appears within 50 words of the word *write*.

To find out more about the Indexing Service's query language and to run a query, follow these steps:

1. **To start the Windows Computer Management Console, choose Start⇨Control Panel, click Performance and Maintenance, click Administrative Tools, and then double-click Computer Management.**
2. **In the Computer Management Console, in the left pane, double-click on Services and Applications. Then click to expand Indexing Service; then System; then Query the Catalog.**
3. **Now you can run your search, or you can get help by choosing Action⇨Help and then clicking Indexing Service in the Help system.**

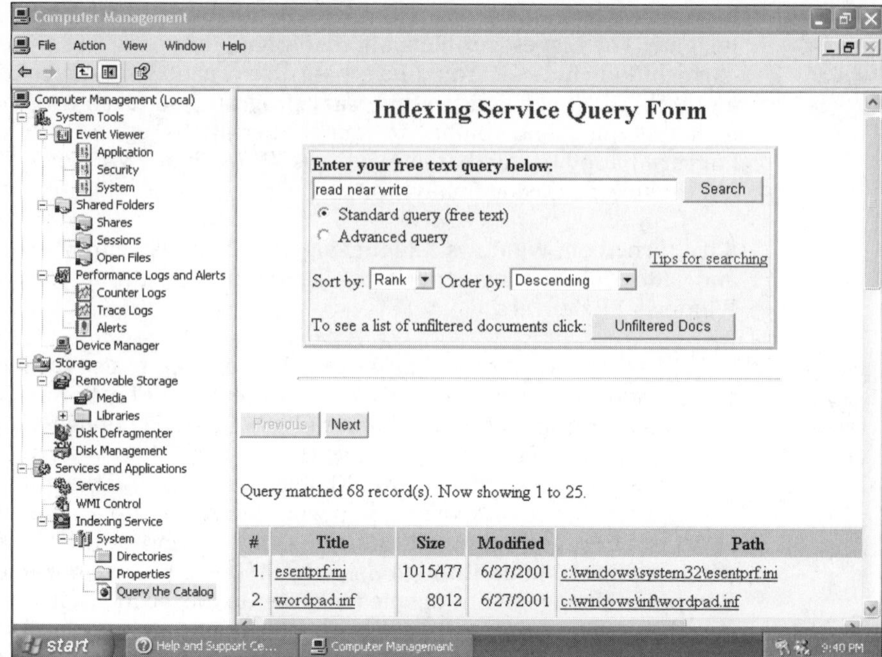

Figure 5-14: You can make very complex searches with the Indexing Service's query language.

Searching the Internet

If you tell Rover to search the Internet, he tells you to type your question in a complete sentence. Click the Search button, and the Search Companion steers you directly to — you guessed it — Microsoft, Rover's master. In Figure 5-15, you can see that the typed question **What is the sound of one hand clapping?** was transformed by the Search Companion into **sound one hand clapping**, and then it was sent directly to `search.msn.com`.

Nothing is particularly bad about `search.msn.com`, but I find it annoying. For example, when I ran the search in Figure 5-15, MSN Search hit me with a pop-up ad (you can see the message that a pop-up ad was blocked in the screen shot if you squint real hard). The fact that Microsoft hit me with a pop-up ad makes my blood boil — but the fact that Internet Explorer's pop-up blocker caught it gives me some hope. Talk about Microsoft's left hand not knowing what the right hand is clicking. . . .

As far as I can tell, all the people who live in Redmond, Washington (the home of Microsoft) have cable modems or DSL in their offices and homes, and they aren't particularly concerned about how much, uh, offal gets shoved down their data pipes. If you happen to live just about anywhere else in the world, though, you may think differently.

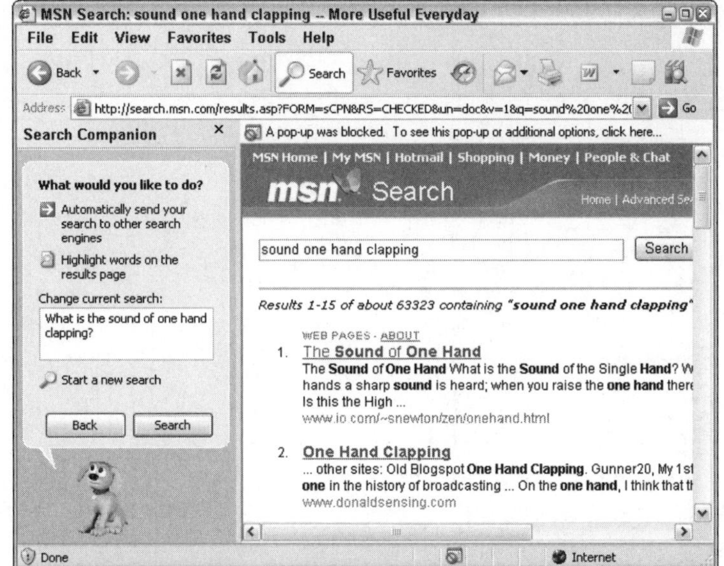

Figure 5-15: Rover goes directly to `search.msn.com` — and gets hit with a pop-up ad.

The good news is that you can easily banish `search.msn.com` to the same doghouse that Rover vacated and have your Internet searches use a Web site that doesn't bury half its screens in ads. Here's how:

1. **Choose Start⇨Search to bring up the Search Companion (refer to Figure 5-1).**
2. **Click Change Preferences.**
3. **Click Change Internet Search Behavior.**
4. **Pick the Web-based search engine that you like best, and click OK.**

   In Figure 5-16, I chose Google.

After you change your default search engine, every time you ask Search Companion to search the Internet, it uses the engine you've chosen. See Figure 5-17 and note how little useless information appears on the screen with a Google search. No pop-up, either. Wonder why I switched?

Web-based search engines change every day. I have no guarantee that my search engine of choice now will be the same six months from now. If you use the Search Companion to perform searches on the Web, be sure to check every few months to see whether a competing Web-based search engine works better than the one you're using.

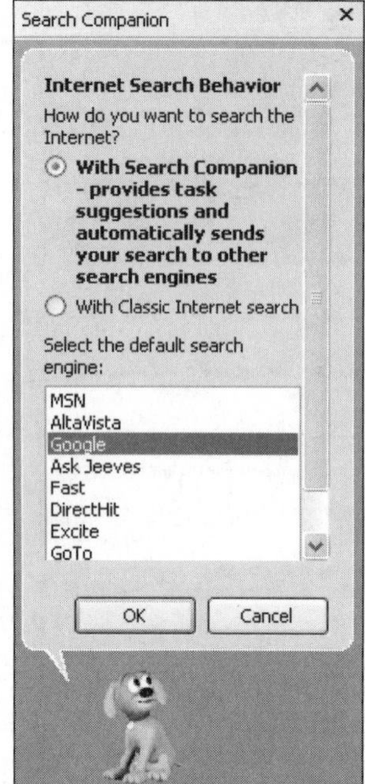

Figure 5-16: Change your default Internet search engine in the Internet Search behavior screen.

Figure 5-17: A Google search is fast, efficient — and usually comes up with good matches, the first time.

If you're serious about searching on the Web, Rover and the Search Companion will irritate you sooner or later. To go directly to the Web and take it on, *mano a mano*; see Book IV, Chapter 3.

Chapter 6: Getting the Basic Stuff Done

In This Chapter

- Cheating at the Windows games (I know that's what you're looking for)
- Burning your CDs without singeing your fingers
- Taking control of your PC, using Task Manager, when a program goes haywire
- . . . And lots of boring stuff you need to know anyway

You bought your PC to get things done, right? I guess it depends on what you mean by "things." Certainly you need to know how to write a letter, even if you don't have Microsoft Office installed on your PC. Draw pictures. You should figure out how to use the Windows Calculator program, even if the thought of employing a $2,000 tool to solve a $2 problem leaves you feeling a little green.

Hey, I have to talk about that stuff somewhere.

On a somewhat less mundane level, this chapter also contains Windows game "cheats." Amaze your friends! Strike terror into the hearts of your enemies. They'll cheer or they'll weep when you show them Minesweeper scores that look like the national debt of a small country.

This chapter also digs into the truly cool Windows XP support for burning CDs.

Beating Windows Games

You really bought this book because you heard it had all the game cheats, didn't you? C'mon, admit it.

What? Your boss doesn't like you playing games on the company PC? Remind her that Windows games are, singularly, the best way to brush up on your mousing skills, take your mind off work for a brief spell, and take a break from all the typing. How do you spell Repetitive Motion Syndrome?

Windows XP ships with 11 games, many of which are quite good.

Solitaire

Venerable classic *Solitaire,* the oldest Windows game of all (see Figure 6-1) — dating back to the prehistory of Windows 3.0, with a copyright that reaches back to 1981, for heaven's sake — still captures the hearts and spare cranial cycles of millions. To get it going, choose Start⇨All Programs⇨Games⇨ Solitaire. But you've probably done that a hundred times already, haven't you?

If you don't know the rules for Solitaire in general, ask the guy sitting next to you on your next flight. The Windows version of Solitaire

- ✦ Won't let you pull a card from inside a stack.
- ✦ Lets you undo only your last move. If you flip over a card that's face-down in one of the stacks, you can't undo the flip.
- ✦ Restricts you to putting Kings in open stacks.

Scoring a Solitaire game makes cricket look like child's play. To get the full details on Standard and Vegas scoring, choose Help⇨Contents, and then navigate to Solitaire⇨Choose a Scoring System.

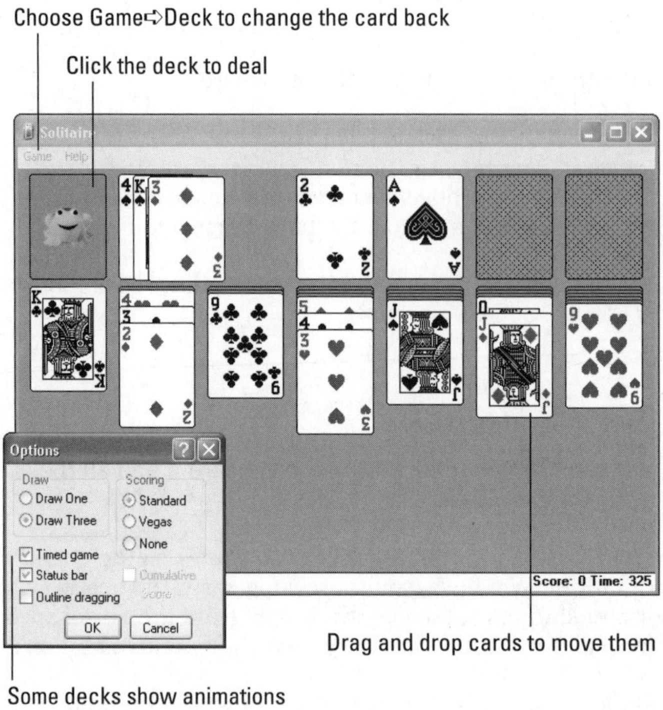
Choose Game⇨Deck to change the card back
Click the deck to deal
Options
Draw
Draw One
Draw Three
Scoring
Standard
Vegas
None
Timed game
Status bar
Outline dragging
Cumulative
Score
OK
Cancel
Score: 0 Time: 325
Drag and drop cards to move them
Some decks show animations

Figure 6-1: Windows Solitaire, the mother of all Windows games.

One little cheat works if you have Solitaire set up to turn over three cards at a time. To make it turn over just one card, press Ctrl+Alt+Shift and click the deck. This is a particularly valuable cheat if you're using Vegas scoring. (Vegas rules let you go through the deck three times if you have Solitaire set to turn over three cards at a time, but you can go through only once if Solitaire is set to turn over one card at a time.) If you use the Ctrl+Alt+Shift trick and turn over one card at a time, you can go through the entire deck three times — a real boon for Vegas scorekeeping.

FreeCell

FreeCell, Microsoft's first Solitaire variant, mimics the card game of the same name. To get it going, choose Start➪All Programs➪Games➪FreeCell (see Figure 6-2).

The first page of the FreeCell Help file tells you that "It is believed (although not proven) that every game is winnable."

Ah, what fools these mortal Help files be.

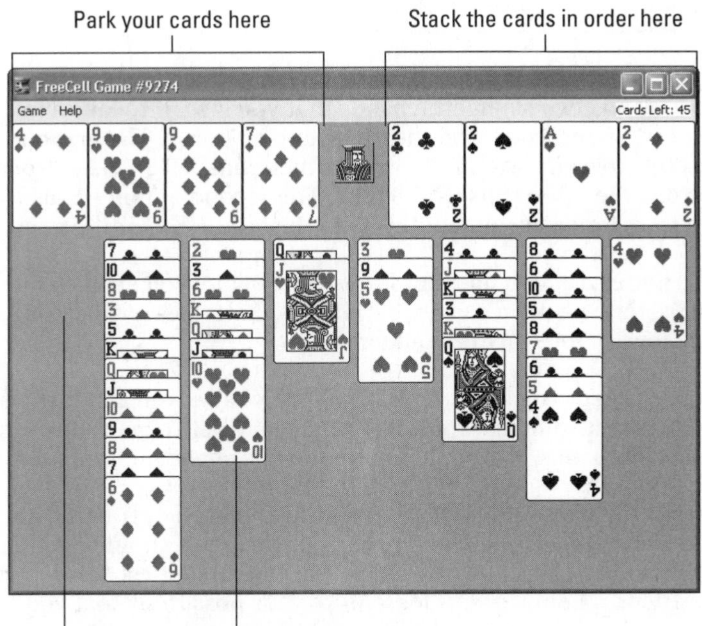

Figure 6-2: FreeCell should stimulate a few more gray cells.

FreeCell lets you replay the same hands, over and over, by assigning numbers to specific starting card combinations. To play hand number 50,000, for example, choose Games⇨Select Game, type **50000**, and click OK. That's a nifty trick if you want to play the same hand at home and then do it again at work, or if you want to challenge a friend on a different machine to a duel.

All of the games numbered from 1 to 32000 are winnable, except for game 11982. Yes, there are people who study these things. No, they don't have lives. See `www.freecell.org` for details.

While a game is in progress, press Ctrl+Shift+F10. You receive one of the funniest dialog boxes in Windows (see Figure 6-3). If you click Abort and then click any card, you win immediately. Sorta. The cards are stacked in the correct slots, but not in the right order. Your score is updated to reflect a win.

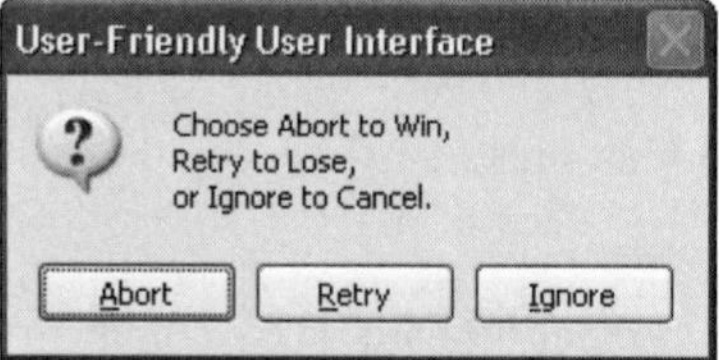

Figure 6-3: Click Abort to win at FreeCell every time.

FreeCell has two symmetric hands that you'll want to take a look at. Choose Games⇨Select Game, and then type either **-1** or **-2**. The first option, -1, generates two rows for each suit, one of which runs A-3-5-7-9-J-K, from top to bottom; the other runs Q-10-8-6-4-2. The second option, -2, also generates two rows for each suit, but this time they run A-K-Q-J-10-9-8 and 7-6-5-4-3-2.

Oh. I better mention one tiny, little detail, before you defenestrate this book — that is, throw it out a convenient window. Both the -1 and -2 games are impossible to win. You can't beat either of them.

FreeCell keeps track of how many hands you've won and lost, and how long your current winning (or losing) streak may be. To get to the scores, choose Game⇨Statistics. You see a list like the one shown in Figure 6-4.

Ah, but there's another trick — one I bet you've never heard about, no matter how much you love FreeCell. If you aren't afraid of getting your hands a little dirty, you can jigger your own statistics. Amaze your family and friends. Confuse your foes. Make your boss think that you have an IQ in the upper triple digits. Yes, you can do it.

FreeCell stores its scores in the Windows Registry. By switching a few numbers in the Registry, you can have FreeCell say that you've won thousands of hands, and lost few (or none!). How do you think I got the 511-hand winning streak shown in Figure 6-4?

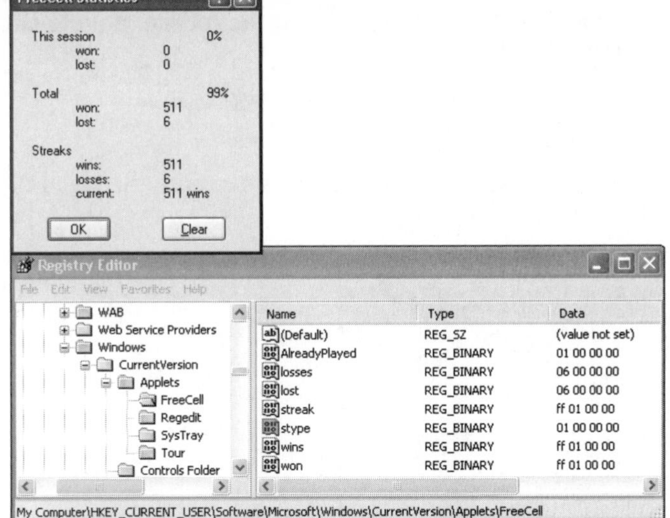

Figure 6-4: Perfect scores in FreeCell are only a hack away.

To set your own scores in FreeCell, you have to go into the Windows Registry. No doubt you've been warned from the day you were born that the Registry is a dangerous, scary place. Balderdash. In fact, 99 percent of the Registry hacks that are published in the magazines and books don't do much in Windows XP. They aren't worth the effort. That's why you won't see any hacks in this book. Except for the game hacks. They work great.

You can set each of the four scores in FreeCell — Total Won, Total Lost, Streak Wins, and Streak Losses — to any number between 0 and 4,294,967,295. You can also tell FreeCell whether your streak is a winning streak or a losing streak. Follow these easy steps:

1. **Choose Start⇨Run.**
2. **Type** regedit **in the Open text box and click OK.**

   You see the Windows Registry Editor, the High Priest of Windows XP. I can see the beads of sweat on your forehead already. No, this isn't a scary place. At least, not *that* scary. Just be careful while you're here. Follow my instructions. Don't go changing anything willy-nilly, okay?
3. **Choose Edit⇨Find.**

   The Find dialog box appears.
4. **In the Find What text box, type** FreeCell **(no space; capitalization doesn't matter) and press Enter.**

   The Registry Editor moves to a location that looks a lot like the place shown in Figure 6-4. This is where the FreeCell settings live.

5. **To see how the Registry entries work, change FreeCell's Total Won number to 511. On the right side of the screen, double-click on the line marked** `won`**.**

   The Edit Binary Value dialog box appears.

6. **Press Del on your keyboard four times.**

   That should wipe out any value that's currently sitting in the Value data box. (See Figure 6-5.)

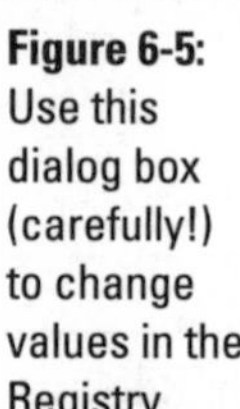

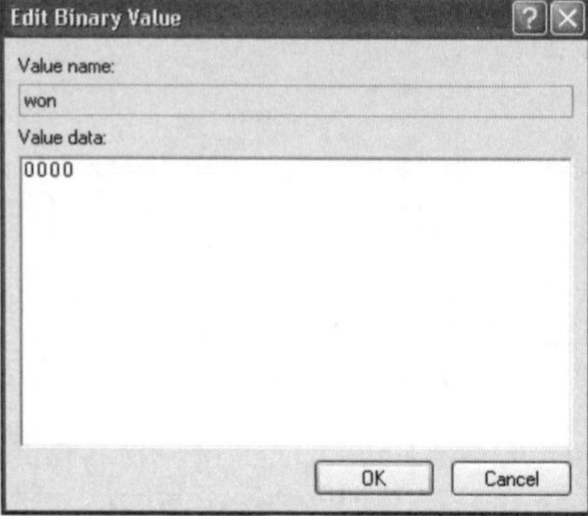

Figure 6-5: Use this dialog box (carefully!) to change values in the Registry.

7. **Type** ff010000 **and press Enter.**

   In case you were wondering, `ff010000` is the value 511, written in a weird way. Table 6-1 gives you a bunch of common values, and their equivalents in FreeCell notation. The Registry Editor shows that you have changed the value of `won` to 511, er, `ff010000`. Great!

The weird notation used by FreeCell is called *little-endian hexadecimal*. If you want to add more values to Table 6-1, you can. Convert the decimal number you want to 8-digit hexadecimal (using, say, the Windows Calculator program, discussed in the later section, "Calculating"). Take the last pair of hex digits and make them the first pair of the FreeCell value. Take the next-to-last pair and make them the second pair in the FreeCell value, and so on. Example: 511 in decimal is `00 00 01 ff` in hexadecimal, so the FreeCell value for 511 is `ff 01 00 00`. Try it. You'll see.

8. **Choose Start⇨All Programs⇨Games⇨FreeCell to crank up FreeCell, choose Game⇨Statistics to bring up the Statistics dialog box, and verify that FreeCell honestly believes that you have won 511 hands!**

9. **Go back to the Registry Editor and change the values for Total Lost (Registry key** `lost`**), Streak Wins (key** `wins`**), and Streak Losses (key** `losses`**). Use Table 6-1 to pick some common values.**

10. **Tell FreeCell that your current streak is a winning streak.**

To do so, double-click `stype` (Streak Type, eh?), press Del four times, type **01000000**, and press Enter. (If you want to make FreeCell think you're on a losing streak, type **00000000**.)

11. **Choose File➪Exit to get out of the Registry Editor.**

Table 6-1 Values for FreeCell Registry Hacking

Number	*What You Should Enter*	*Number*	*What You Should Enter*
0	00000000	255	ff000000
1	01000000	256	00010000
2	02000000	257	01010000
3	03000000	511	ff010000
10	0a000000	512	00020000
11	0b000000	1000	e8030000
15	0f000000	1001	e9030000
16	10000000	10,000	10270000
17	11000000	100,000	a0860100
100	64000000	1,000,000	40420f00
101	65000000	1,000,000,000	00ca9a3b
254	fe000000	4,294,967,295	ffffffff

Spider Solitaire

When you get the hang of it, Spider Solitaire is every bit as addictive as the two older Windows Solitaire siblings. Get Spider going by choosing Start➪All Programs➪Games➪Spider Solitaire.

The easiest way to learn Spider Solitaire is to start with a single suit — Spider gives you that option when you start. Basically, you have to move cards around in descending order (see Figure 6-6), and you can mix and match suits to your heart's content (pun intended). When you have a descending sequence (K to A) in a single suit, the entire sequence gets removed. When you get stuck, click the spider card deck and Spider Solitaire deals another row of cards.

Spider Solitaire stores its scores in the Windows Registry, just like FreeCell. You can use a technique very similar to the one I describe in the preceding section to hack the Registry and change your scores — it's almost identical to the method for Minesweeper as well. Look for the Registry values under `HKEY_CURRENT_USER\Software\Microsoft\Spider`. One bit of warning: Make sure that Spider Solitaire is *not* running when you change the Registry. Spider has a nasty habit of resetting Registry values when it finishes, regardless of whether you want it to or not.

Figure 6-6: Spider Solitaire allows you to mix suits in intermediate steps, but ultimately you have to match them to win.

Spider Solitaire has a boss button — push the Esc key when the boss comes by and Spider quickly minimizes itself.

Minesweeper

One of the most absorbing, simple games ever created — and a longtime personal favorite of Bill Gates — is Minesweeper, which has been around since the days of Windows 3.1.

The concept is pretty simple: Click on a square and a number appears, indicating the number of adjacent squares that contain mines (see Figure 6-7). Click on a square that contains a mine and you lose. Play against the clock.

If you've never tried Minesweeper, you're in for a treat — even inveterate computer game-haters take a liking to this one.

Minesweeper holds oodles of options:

- Click Game and choose from Beginner (a 9 x 9 box playing field with 10 mines), Intermediate (a 16 x 16 field with 40 mines), and Expert (16 x 30 with 99 mines). Minesweeper automatically keeps high-score figures for each.

- ✦ Alternatively, you can choose Game➪Custom and tell Minesweeper how many squares you want to see and how many mines should be scattered on the field.
- ✦ If you think a square contains a mine, and you want to, uh, remine yourself of that fact, right-click on the square. A flag appears, warning you that once upon a time, you thought a mine might be here. Right-click on the same square a second time, and you see a question mark — probably to remind you that you once thought there was a mine here, but now you're not so sure, and maybe you really ought to click on the sucker to see whether it blows up. Right-click on the square a third time, and it goes back to normal.

Whenever you want to see the best times and who holds the records, choose Game➪Best Times. The Fastest Mine Sweepers dialog box, shown in Figure 6-7, appears.

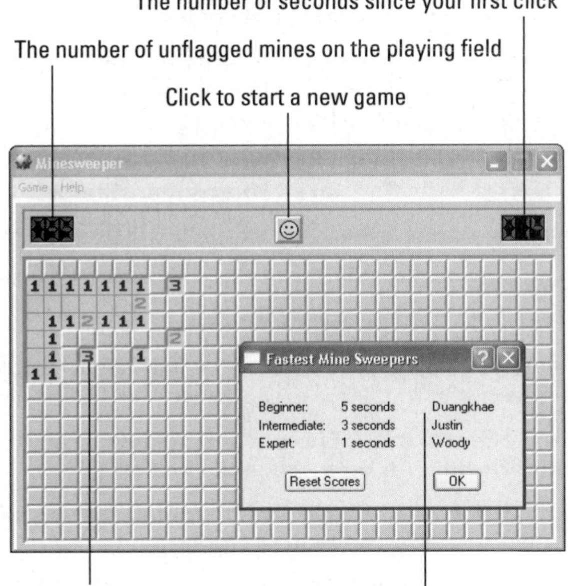

Figure 6-7: The Expert Minesweeper playing field.

There was a well-known cheat for Minesweeper that used to work in older versions of Windows, but doesn't appear to work in Windows XP. (At least, we here at Dummies Central can't get it to work.) Maybe you'll be luckier. In older versions, any time Minesweeper is running, you can type **xyzzy** and press Ctrl+Enter. From that moment on, every time you put the mouse over a "good" square — one that doesn't contain a mine — Minesweeper flashes a tiny, tiny, single white dot in the far upper-left corner of the Windows desktop. And every time you put the mouse over a "bad" square, Minesweeper puts a single black dot in the far upper-left corner. You may have to change your background or wallpaper to see it, but it's there. Click when you see the white dot, and you'll win every time.

Earlier versions of Minesweeper had a "stop-the-clock" cheat: Start the clock by clicking on a square; then hold down both mouse buttons and the Esc key at the same time. That stopped the clock. Unfortunately, that cheat doesn't work in Windows XP either. At least, I couldn't get it to work.

Oh yes, you can hack the Windows Registry to set the fastest Minesweepers names and times for the statistics dialog box shown in Figure 6-7. Here's how:

1. **Make sure Minesweeper is *not* running.**
2. **Choose Start⇨Run.**
3. **Type** regedit **in the Open text box and click OK.**

   That brings up the Windows Registry Editor and, as I warn in the section on FreeCell, you have to be careful while you're here. Follow my instructions. Don't go changing anything willy-nilly.
4. **On the left side of the screen, click the + boxes and navigate to HKEY_CURRENT_USER⇨Software⇨Microsoft⇨winmine.**
5. **On the right side of the screen, double-click the line marked** `Name1`.

   You see a dialog box called Edit String, like the one shown in Figure 6-8.
6. **Type a new name in the Value Data text box.**

   The new name shows up in the Fastest Mine Sweepers dialog box as the fastest minesweeper in the Beginner category.
7. **Double-click the line marked** `Time1`**, click Decimal, enter the Beginner category winner's time (in seconds), and click OK.**
8. **Repeat the process for** `Name2` **and** `Time2` **(for the Intermediate winner) and** `Name3` **and** `Time3` **(for the Expert winner).**
9. **Choose Start⇨All Programs⇨Games⇨Minesweeper to get Minesweeper going, and click Game⇨Best Times to bring up the Fastest Mine Sweepers dialog box and bask in the glory!**
10. **Get out of the Registry Editor by choosing File⇨Exit.**

    You don't want to leave the Registry Editor open any longer than necessary.

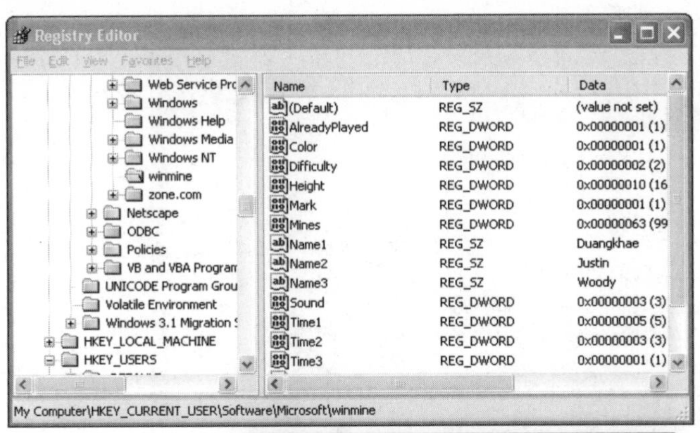

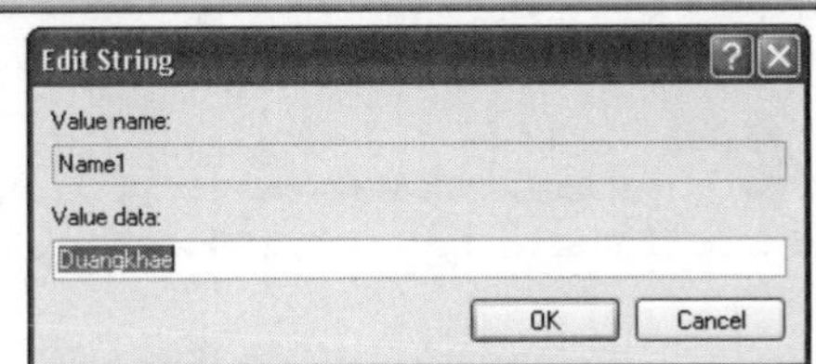

Figure 6-8: The name of the fastest Minesweeper in the Beginner category is stored as Name1.

Hearts

If you know how to play Hearts, the Windows one-player version will help you hone your skills. Windows XP plays a mean game of Hearts. Choose Start⇨All Programs⇨Games⇨Hearts to get it going.

The people who wrote the Hearts program insist that the computer doesn't "look" at your cards — or any other player's cards — when deciding what to play.

Believe it or not, you can cheat at Hearts and make Windows show you the contents of all your opponents' hands (see Figure 6-9). Follow these steps:

1. **You have to run Hearts on your computer at least once before you can make the changes necessary to cheat. If you've never run Hearts, choose Start⇨All Programs⇨Games⇨Hearts, enter your name, and click OK.**
2. **Choose Start⇨Run.**
3. **Type** regedit **in the Open text box and click OK.**

   That brings up the Windows Registry Editor and, as I warn in the section on FreeCell, you have to be careful while you're here. Follow my instructions. Don't go changing anything you aren't supposed to be changing.
4. **On the left side of the screen, click the + boxes and navigate to HKEY_CURRENT_USER⇨Software⇨Microsoft⇨Windows⇨CurrentVersion⇨Applets⇨Hearts.**

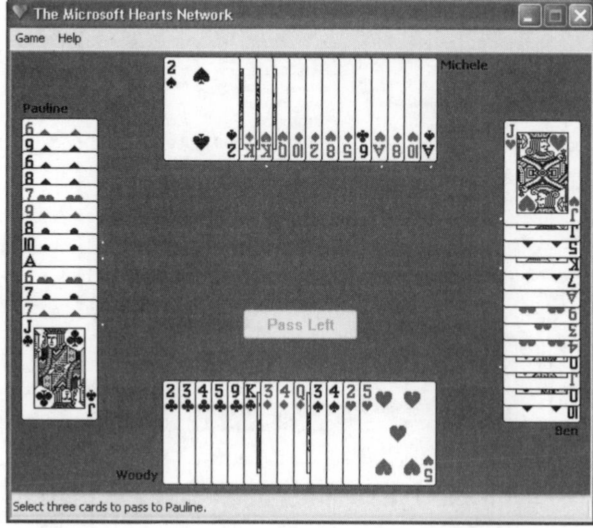

Figure 6-9: The Hearts cheat shows you all of the cards in your opponents' hands.

5. **Choose Edit➪New➪String Value.**

   The Windows Registry creates a new value called, imaginatively, `New Value #1`, and highlights the new value so that you can change its name.

6. **Type** ZB **and press Enter twice.**

7. **In the Value Data box, type** 42**, and press Enter.**

   Your Registry should have a new string value called ZB, with a value of 42, as shown in Figure 6-10. (Douglas Adams fans may pause to ponder whether Zaphod Beeblebrox and the ultimate answer to Life, the Universe, and Everything may have a bearing on this setting.)

8. **Move back to Hearts (or start it if it isn't running by choosing Start➪All Programs➪Games➪Hearts). Press Ctrl+Alt+Shift+F12 all at the same time.**

   Your opponents' cards are now visible. To hide them, press Ctrl+Alt+Shift+F12 again.

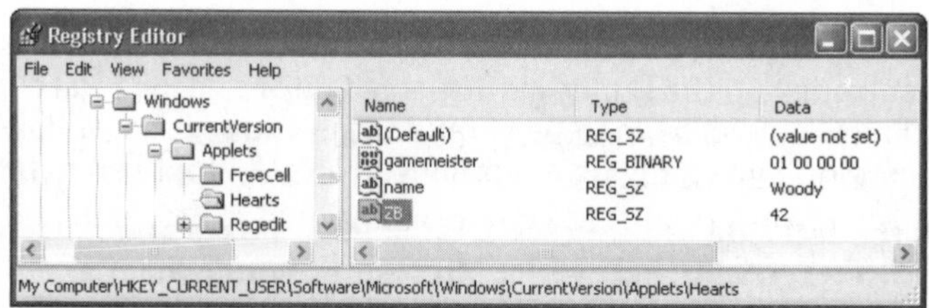

Figure 6-10: This is what you need to make Hearts show you everybody's cards.

9. **Choose File➪Exit to get out of the Registry Editor.**

   You don't want to leave the Registry Editor open any longer than necessary.

Hearts has a boss button — push the Esc key when the boss comes by and Hearts quickly minimizes itself.

Pinball

Although it will never come close to the real thing, Windows 3D Pinball - Space Cadet (that's the official name) does have some good graphics, decent sound, and "nudge" features that make it fun.

The game itself is far more complex than it appears at first blush. You're trying to advance from Space Cadet to Fleet Admiral by completing missions. Full details appear in the Pinball Help file, which you can see by choosing Help➪Help Topics.

When you start Pinball for the first time, you have to hold down the spacebar on the keyboard to launch the ball, which isn't the least bit obvious. After you're over that hump, though, the game is pretty easy: The left flipper is the Z key and the right flipper is the / key.

Several locations on the Internet claim to have *trainers* for Space Cadet. A trainer alters the program itself to give you extra capabilities. The Space Cadet trainers all claim to give you more than three balls — the major restriction in the game.

You can hack the Windows Registry to change Pinball scores and winners' names, but the technique is substantially more difficult than that for FreeCell, Spider Solitaire, or Minesweeper. Look in the Registry key HKEY_CURRENT_USER➪Software➪Microsoft➪Plus! ➪Pinball➪Space Cadet. The big trick: The key called Verification is supposed to contain the sum of all the high scores, plus the sum of the ASCII values of each character in all the names. (What's an ASCII value? If you have to ask, you don't want to know. Trust me.) Good luck.

Pinball also has a boss button — push the Esc key when the boss comes by and in a split second, Pinball minimizes itself and turns off the sound.

Internet games

The five Internet games offered for free in Windows XP — Backgammon, Checkers, Hearts, Reversi, and Spades — all connect to Zone.com (`http://zone.msn.com`), a gaming site on the Web. It probably won't surprise you one little bit to discover that Zone.com is actually part of MSN.com, which (surprise!) is a division of Microsoft.

Many corporate Internet firewalls block access to Zone.com. Can't imagine why, can you?

The Internet games have three big selling points: They're free; they hook you up with other players from all over the world, automatically, with no hassle; and they're decent (if uninspiring) versions of the games advertised.

The Internet games have one big disadvantage: They're really just ads. Microsoft wants you to play the games so that you'll be tempted to sign up for a Zone.com membership. When you have a (free) membership, Microsoft tries to get you to pay for the more sophisticated games. Nothing is inherently wrong with Zone.com, mind you, but you have many choices for online games. If you think you may be interested, start with the Multiplayer Online Games site, `www.mpogd.com`, or use any common Web search site to look for *online games.*

Burning CDs

Windows XP includes simple, one-click (or two- or three-click) support for creating CDs. You need a CD recorder (a CD-R or CD-RW drive) to make your own CDs, of course, but most PCs these days have them built in. For those stuck in a PC time warp, if you buy a cheap CD-RW drive that attaches to your PC via a USB cable, your most difficult job will be pulling it out of the Styrofoam padding. See Book VI, Chapter 1, for more about installing external devices.

Understanding CD-R and CD-RW

Before you burn a CD, you should understand the fundamental differences between CD-R and CD-RW, the two most popular technologies. Most CD writers these days can burn both CD-Rs and CD-RWs. You have to choose the kind that suits your situation:

- **CD-Recordable (CD-R):** These discs can be played in audio CD players, but they cannot be erased. You can record to a CD-R more than once (up to its capacity) if you use multisession. See `www.roxio.com/en/support/cdr/multisession.html` for more information.
- **CD-Record/Write (CD-RW):** These discs can be erased, and the erased area can be rewritten with new stuff. The downside is that these discs will not work in some audio CD players (particularly older ones). See `www.roxio.com/en/support/cdr/howrecworks.html` for more information.

Both CD-Rs and CD-RWs can hold data or music. Both CD-Rs and CD-RWs can be recorded multiple times, until they run out of space. Both CD-Rs and CD-RWs can hold 74 minutes of music or 650 MB of data. Some CD-Rs can go all the way up to 80 minutes of audio, or 700 MB of data. (Yeah, yeah. Some CD-Rs are supposed to go way beyond that, but I don't trust 'em, and you shouldn't, either.)

DVD is not the same as CD-R or CD-RW. You can't create DVDs using a CD-R or CD-RW drive; to burn a DVD, you must have a DVD burner.

Some drives are *combo drives,* meaning that they will read DVD/CD/CD-R/CD-RW and write CD-Rs and CD-RWs; however, you can't burn a DVD with these drives. DVD recorders are available but there are two competing of formats that aren't always compatible. Fortunately, the DVD burners available nowadays are almost always capable of burning in both formats; see `www.cdburner.ca/dvd-format-faq.htm` for more information.

Burning with Windows

The first time you try to burn a CD with a new CD writer, work with data files instead of picture files or music. Start out with the easiest possible scenario (simple data files) before you work your way up to the most complex (audio CDs). That increases your chances of finding and solving problems when they're easiest to tackle.

When you have a CD-R or CD-RW drive installed and working, transferring your files to CD couldn't be simpler. ***Note:*** If you want to copy music files, don't follow these instructions. Use the Windows Media Player (WMP). I tell you how to use Windows Media Player in Book VII, Chapter 1. WMP has all sorts of bells and whistles that are specific to music, and it does a fine job of burning music CDs with all the ancillary information about artists, titles, and so on.

Follow these steps to burn a CD with data files:

1. **Locate the files (picture, data, program, and so on) you want to burn to the CD by choosing Start⇨My Documents, Start⇨My Pictures, Start⇨My Computer, or Start⇨My Network Places.**

   Yes, you can pull files off your network.

2. **Select the files that you want to put on the CD.**

   All of the standard selection methods work:

   - Click once on a file to select it, or Ctrl+click to select multiple files.
   - Click on one file, hold down the Shift key, and click on a different file to select all the files in between.

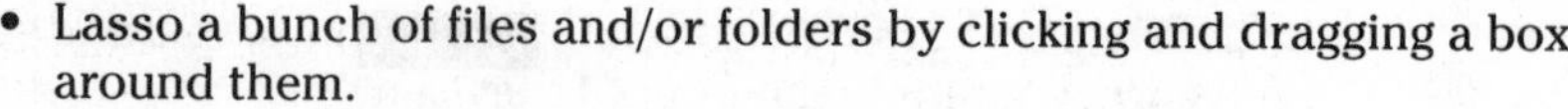

- Lasso a bunch of files and/or folders by clicking and dragging a box around them.

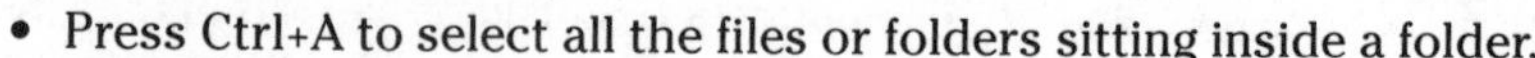

- Press Ctrl+A to select all the files or folders sitting inside a folder.

You may want to switch views so that you can see more files at once when selecting them. Choose View➪List to see the largest number of files at once.

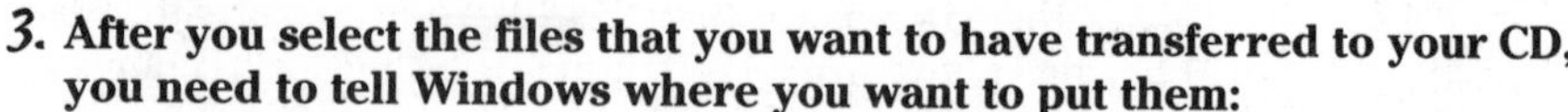

3. **After you select the files that you want to have transferred to your CD, you need to tell Windows where you want to put them:**

   - If the Copy to CD command is available in the task pane on the left — it is available if you are inside a folder that holds pictures (as shown in Figure 6-11) — click Copy to CD.
   - If the Copy to CD command is not available — which means that the current folder has documents and data files, for example — click Copy This File (or Copy This Folder, or Copy Selected Items, *mutatis mutandis*), and pick the CD-R drive as the destination.

   Each time you click Copy to CD, Windows copies the files you have selected into a temporary storage area, waiting for you to transfer the files, *en masse,* to the blank CD. As the files are being copied, Windows puts a CD-R icon in the notification area, near the time in the lower-right of the screen, with a balloon that says `You have files waiting to be written to the CD. To see the files now, click this balloon.`

4. **Continue selecting files in this manner until you have all the files you want.**

5. **When you're done gathering files, click the balloon in the lower-right corner of the screen to see Windows' collection of files that are waiting to be burned on the CD.**

   Alternatively, choose Start➪My Computer and navigate to the CD-R drive. You see the files you've chosen, grayed out to indicate that they're in a temporary waiting area (see Figure 6-12).

6. **Make sure that you want to burn all the chosen files. If you change your mind about any of them, just click on the file or folder and press Del.**

   You can move files around to different folders while in the temporary storage area, rename them — just about anything. When you have everything set up the way you want it, click Write These Files to CD in the CD Writing Tasks pane. Windows starts the CD Writing Wizard (see Figure 6-13).

7. **Follow the wizard, inserting a CD when prompted (see Figure 6-14).**

   When the CD Writing Wizard is done, your files have been transferred to the CD. Probably. At least, that's the theory.

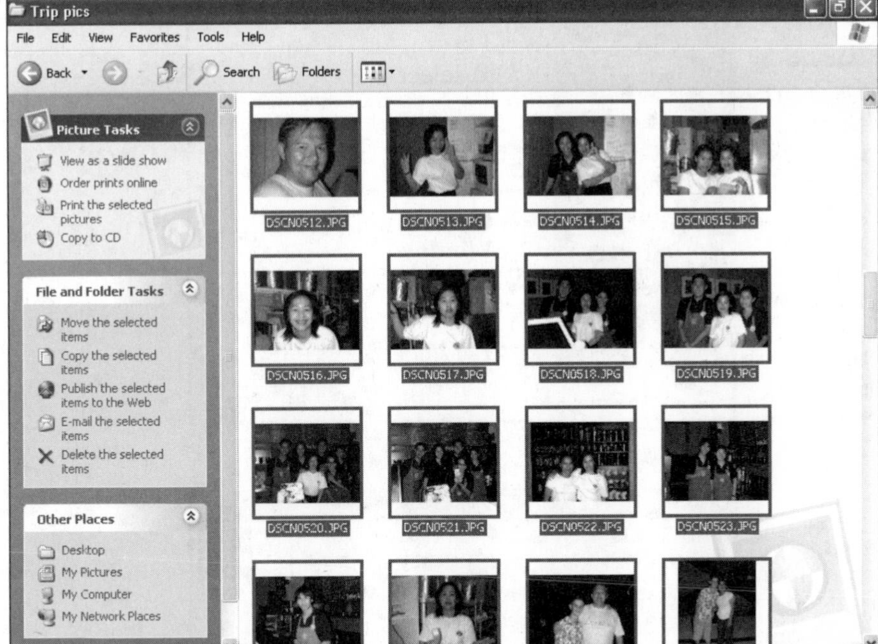

Figure 6-11: Select the files that you want to burn and click Copy to CD, if the command is available.

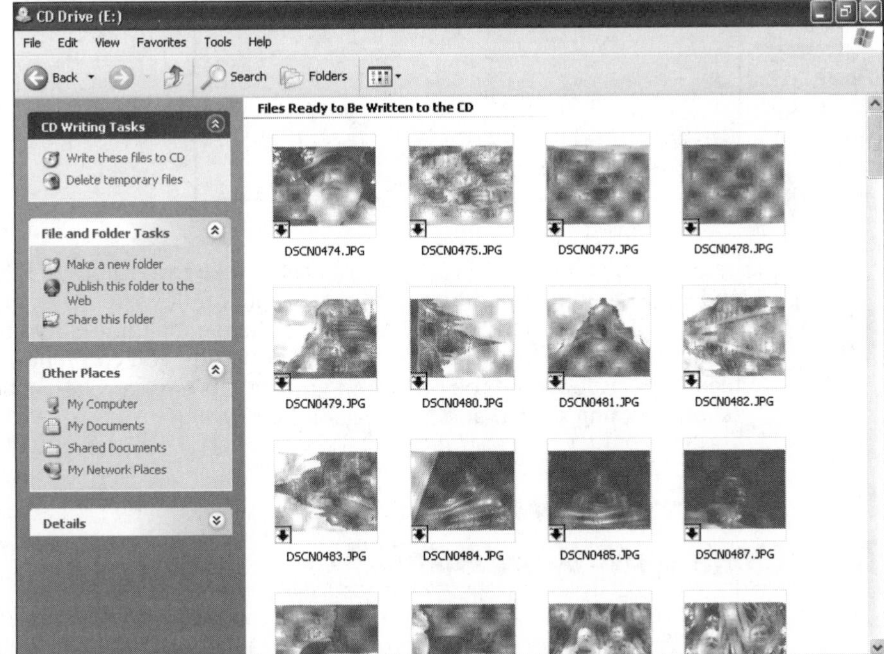

Figure 6-12: Files being held in a temporary area, prior to being copied to the CD.

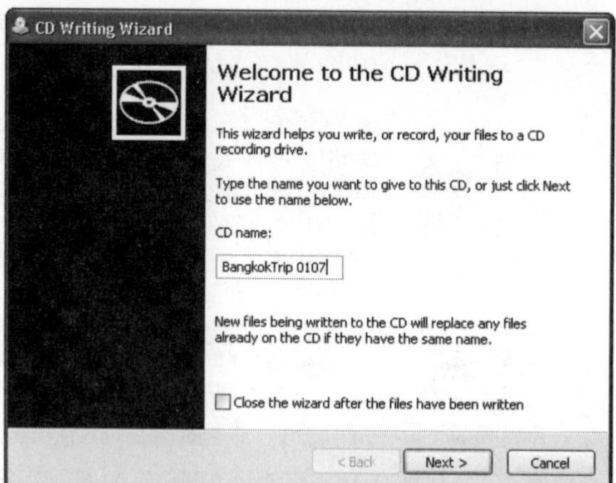

Figure 6-13: After you choose the files, the CD Writing Wizard steps you through the entire burning process.

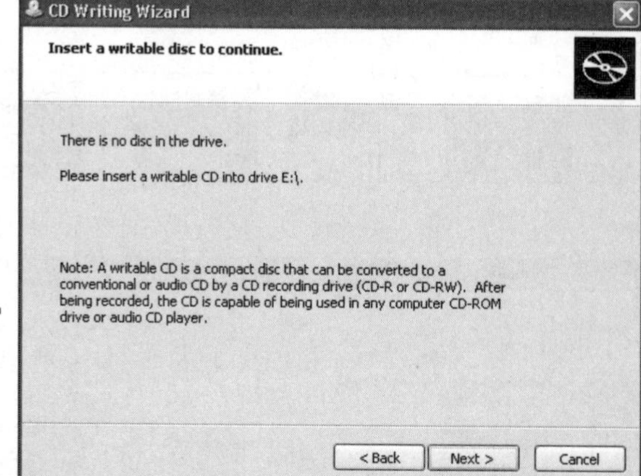

Figure 6-14: Insert a CD when prompted.

Immediately after the CD has been burned, take the CD out of the burner, and try to read it on a different machine. (If you have no other machine, take it out of the drive and try to read it on the same machine.) If you do this immediately, and the CD is screwed up, hopefully you can remember which files were supposed to be on it, and you should have a relatively easy time reconstructing the CD and burning a new one.

Using the Free Word Processors That Come with Windows XP

If you're serious about word processing, you undoubtedly have Microsoft Word (and probably even Microsoft Office) installed already. Word is a great program — and one that will serve you well, along with the other useful programs in the Office suite. Personally, I've been swearing at Office for almost a decade — my first four books were about it.

On the other hand, if you only mess around the periphery of word processing, with an occasional letter to Mom or a diatribe to the local newspaper, you'll be relieved to know that Windows XP includes two programs that you can use for simple word processing. While WordPad and Notepad are not word processing powerhouses like Word, they can help a little bit — as long as you don't have any great expectations, anyway.

Running Notepad

Reaching back into the primordial WinOoze, Notepad was conceived, designed, and developed by programmers, for programmers — and it shows. Although Notepad has been vastly improved over the years, many of the old limitations still pertain. Still, if you want a fast, no-nonsense text editor (certainly nobody would have the temerity to call Notepad a word processor), Notepad's a decent choice.

Notepad understands only plain, simple, unformatted text — basically the stuff you see on your keyboard. It wouldn't understand formatting like **bold** or an embedded picture if you shook it by the shoulders, and heaven help ya if you want it to come up with links to Web pages.

On the other hand, Notepad's shortcomings are, in many ways, its saving graces. You can trust Notepad to show you exactly what's in a file — characters are characters, old chap, and there's none of this frou-frou formatting stuff to munge things up. Notepad saves only plain, simple, unformatted text; if you need a plain, simple, unformatted text document, Notepad's your tool of choice. To top it off, Notepad's fast and reliable. Of all the Windows programs I've ever met, Notepad is the only one I can think of that's never crashed on me.

To start Notepad, choose Start⇨All Programs⇨Accessories⇨Notepad, or double-click on any text (`.txt`) file in the Windows Explorer. You see something like the file shown in Figure 6-15.

Notepad can handle files up to about 48MB in size. (That's not quite the size of the *Encyclopedia Britannica,* but it's close.) If you try to open a file that's larger, a dialog box suggests that you open the file with a different editor.

When you first start Notepad, it displays a file's contents in the 10-point Lucida Console font. That font was chosen by Notepad's designers because it's relatively easy to see on most computer monitors.

Just because the text you see in Notepad is in a specific font, don't assume for a moment that the data in the file itself is formatted. It isn't. The font you see on the screen is just the one Notepad uses to show the data. The stuff inside the file is plain-Jane, unformatted, everyday text.

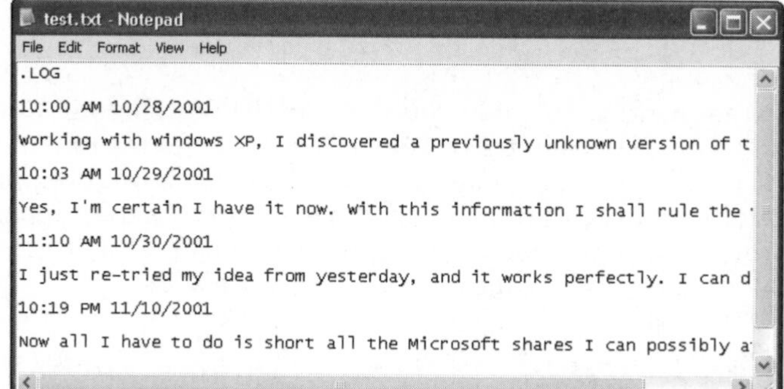

Figure 6-15: Notepad in its initial form.

If you want to change the font that's displayed on the screen, choose Format⇨Font and pick from the offered list. You don't need to select any text before you choose the font because the font you choose is applied to all the text on the screen — and it doesn't affect the contents of the file at all.

If you look at Figure 6-15, you'll notice that text extends way off the right side of the screen. That's intentional. Notepad, being ever-true to the file it's attached to, skips to a new line only when it encounters a line break — usually that means a carriage return (or "Enter key"), which typically occurs at the end of every paragraph.

Notepad allows you to wrap text on-screen, if you insist, so that you don't have to go scrolling all the way to the right to read every single paragraph. To have Notepad automatically break lines so that they show up on the screen, choose Format⇨Word Wrap.

Notepad has one little trick that you may find amusing — possibly worthwhile. If you type **.LOG** at the beginning of a file, Notepad sticks a time and date stamp at the end of the file each time it's opened.

Writing with WordPad

If you really want and need formatting — and you're too cheap to buy Microsoft Word — Windows XP's WordPad will do. If you've been locked out of Word by Microsoft's nefarious Office (De)Activation Wizard, you'll no doubt rely on WordPad to keep limping along until Microsoft can reactivate you.

If you find yourself reading these words because Office has slipped into "reduced functionality mode" (gawd, I love that phrase!), take heart, but be forewarned: If you aren't careful, you can really clobber your Word files by saving them with WordPad. If you have to edit a Word 97, 2000, 2002, or 2003 document with WordPad, always follow these steps:

1. **Make a copy of the Word document, and open the copy in WordPad.**

   Do *not* edit original Word documents with WordPad. You'll break them as soon as you save them. Do *not* open Word documents in WordPad, thinking that you'll do a Save As and save with a different name. You'll forget.

2. **When you get Word back, open the original document, choose Tools⇨Compare and Merge Documents. Pick the WordPad version of the document, and click Merge.**

   The resulting merged document probably looks like a mess, but it's a start.

3. **Use the Revisions Toolbar (which is showing) to march through your original document and apply the changes you made with WordPad.**

   This is the only reliable way I know to ensure that WordPad doesn't accidentally swallow any of your formatting.

WordPad works much the same as any other word processor, only less so. Its feature set reflects its price — you can't expect much from a free word processor. That said, WordPad isn't encumbered with many of the confusing doodads that make Word so difficult for the first-time e-typist, and it may be a decent way to start learning how simple word processors work.

To get WordPad going, choose Start⇨All Programs⇨Accessories⇨WordPad (see Figure 6-16).

Like a Word document or a text file, Rich Text Format (RTF) is another type of file. RTF documents can have some simple formatting, but nothing nearly as complex as Word 97, for example. Many word-processing programs from many different manufacturers can read and write RTF files, so RTF is a good choice if you need to create a file that can be moved to a lot of places.

If you're just starting out with word processing, keep these facts in mind:

✦ To format text, select the text you want to format; then click the formatting you want from the toolbar, or choose Format⇨Font.

✦ To format a paragraph, you can simply click once inside the paragraph and choose the formatting from the toolbar, or choose Format⇨Paragraph. Alternatively, you can select all the text in the paragraph, or in multiple paragraphs, before applying the formatting.

✦ General page layout (such as margins, whether the page is printed vertically or horizontally, and so on) is controlled by settings in the Page Setup dialog box. To get to the Page Setup dialog box, choose File⇨Page Setup.

✦ Tabs are complicated. Every paragraph starts out with tab stops set every half inch. You set additional tab stops by choosing Format⇨Tab, but the tab stops you set up work only in individual paragraphs: Select one paragraph and set a tab stop, and it works only in the selected paragraph; select three paragraphs and set the stop, and it works in all three.

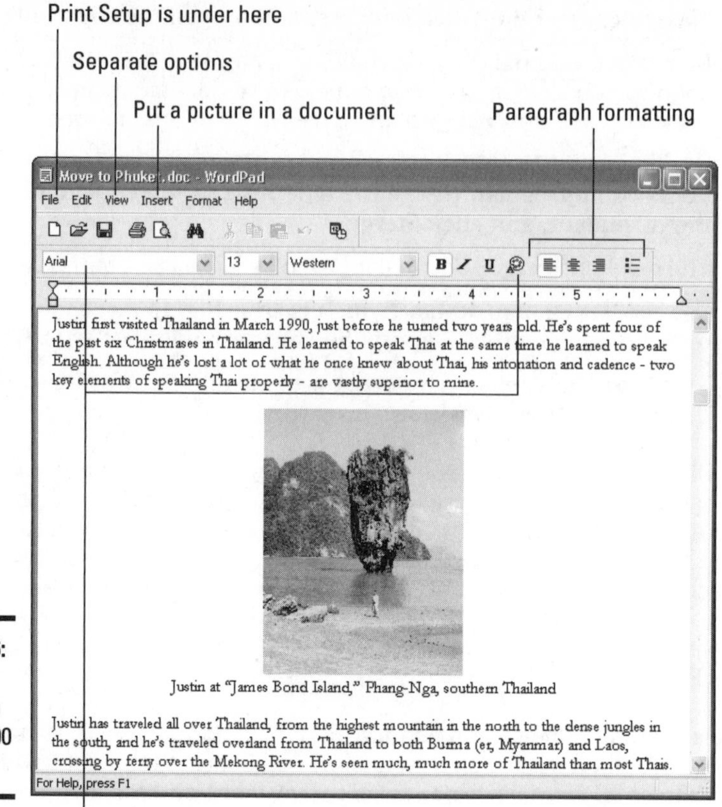

Figure 6-16: WordPad working on a Word 2000 document.

WordPad treats tabs like any other character: A tab can be copied, moved and/or deleted, sometimes with unexpected results. Keep your eyes peeled when using tabs and tab stops. If something goes wrong, hit Edit⇨Undo immediately and try again.

WordPad lacks many of the features that you may have come to expect from other word processors: You can't even insert a page break, much less a table. If you spend any time at all writing anything but the most straightforward documents, you'll outgrow WordPad quickly.

Taming Character Map

Windows XP includes a utility called Character Map that may prove a lifesaver if you need to find characters that go beyond the standard keyboard fare — "On Beyond Zebra," as Dr. Seuss once said. Using the Character Map, you can ferret odd characters out of any font, copy them, and then paste them into whatever word processor you may be using (including WordPad).

Windows ships with many fonts — collections of characters — and several of those fonts include many interesting characters that you may want to use. To bring up the Character Map, choose Start⇨All Programs⇨Accessories⇨ System Tools⇨Character Map. You see the screen shown in Figure 6-17.

You can use many characters as pictures — arrows, check marks, boxes, and so on — in the various Wingdings fonts (see Figure 6-18). Copy them into your documents, and increase the font size as you like.

Downloading document viewers

Although it won't compensate for a locked-out copy of Office, Microsoft has quite a number of free file viewers and format converters. You can't use a viewer to edit documents or even print them, but you will be able to see what the file contains.

The Word 97/2000 file viewer, in particular — a program called `wd97vwr32.exe` — allows you to view any Word 97 or Word 2000 document. It also makes an attempt at showing Word 2002 (the version of Word in Office XP) and Word 2003 documents, but Microsoft won't guarantee that you'll see everything. You don't have to buy anything; the viewer is free.

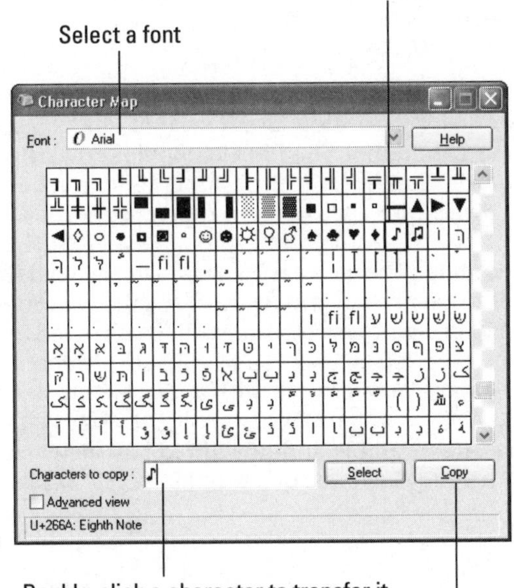

Figure 6-17: Windows Character Map lets you find odd characters in all of your fonts.

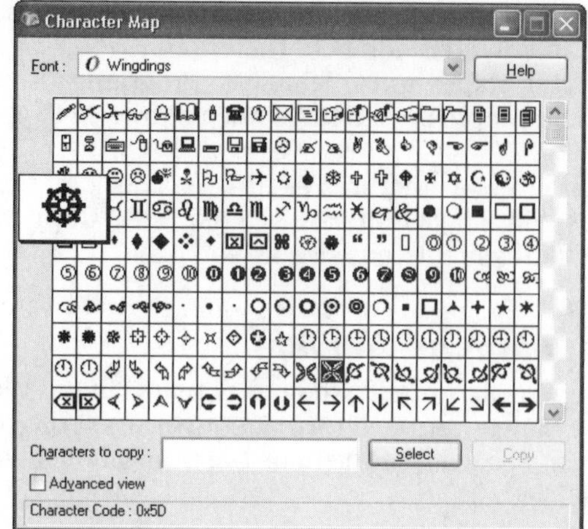

Figure 6-18: Wingdings contains many unusual and useful pictures, disguised as fonts.

As of this writing, Microsoft distributes free document viewers for the following files:

- **Word 97 and 2000 documents.** This viewer also works with most Word 2002 ("Word XP") and 2003 documents.
- **Excel 97 and 2000 spreadsheets.** The viewer works with most Excel 2002 and 2003 spreadsheets, but you should be very cautious about trusting it with critical data.
- **PowerPoint 97, 2000, and 2002 ("PowerPoint XP") presentations.** Think of this viewer as a slide show program that lets you see the presentation, regardless of whether you have a copy of PowerPoint installed. This is the only viewer that Microsoft has upgraded in recent years, and it may not show PowerPoint 2003 presentations properly.

Why hasn't Microsoft updated the viewers? A more cynical soul than I would note that Microsoft doesn't make any money with the file viewers — so why should they give a hairy rat's patootie? If you really, really need an accurate viewer for Office XP or Office 2003 files, get a free 30-day evaluation version of the software, and let it expire. You'll be left with a bloated but accurate viewer.

To see the viewers that are available and download any viewers you or your friends may want, go to `www.microsoft.com/office/000/viewers.asp`.

Calculating

Windows XP includes a very capable calculator. Actually, it contains two very capable calculators. Before you run out and spend twenty bucks on a scientific calculator, check out the two you already own!

To run the calculator, choose Start➪All Programs➪Accessories➪Calculator. You probably see the standard calculator.

To use the calculator, just type whatever you like on your keyboard, and press Enter when you want to carry out the calculation. For example, to calculate 123 times 456, type **123 * 456** and press Enter.

The following are several calculator tricks:

- You can use your mouse to "press" the keys on the calculator — an approach that's very slow and quite error prone.
- Nope, an X on the keyboard doesn't translate into the times sign. I don't know why, but computer people have had a hang-up about this for decades. If you want "times" you have to press the asterisk on the keyboard — the * or Shift+8 key.
- You can use the number pad, if your keyboard has one, but to make it work you have to get "Num Lock" going. Try typing a few numbers on your number pad. If the calculator sits there like a dodo and doesn't realize that you're trying to type into it, press the Num Lock key. The calculator should take the hint.

Of all the applications in Windows, you'd think that the %$#@! calculator would let you select the number in the read-out window so that you could copy it or paste over it, using any of the Windows-standard methods. Huh-uh. No way. Calculator limits you to copying the entire contents of the read-out (with Edit➪Copy or Ctrl+C) or overwriting all of the read-out (with Edit➪Paste or Ctrl+V). The calculator doesn't even have the usual File menu, so you can save anything, print anything (like an audit tape), or even perform a File➪Exit. Ahhhh! Don't get me started.

If you need to do some fancy-shmancy calculatin', choose View➪Scientific to bring up the scientific version of the Windows Calculator program, shown in Figure 6-19.

The scientific calculator slices and dices and cooks dinner, too. For details on all of the options, choose Help➪Help Topics.

If you're hacking your Windows games, especially FreeCell, the way I explained in the "FreeCell" section of this chapter, you should know how to use the scientific calculator to convert decimal numbers to hexadecimal, the same way as those guys in white lab coats. Here's how:

1. **Select the Dec option button so that the calculator knows you're typing a decimal number.**
2. **Type in the number.**
3. **Select the Hex option button.**

That's all there is to it. Tough, huh?

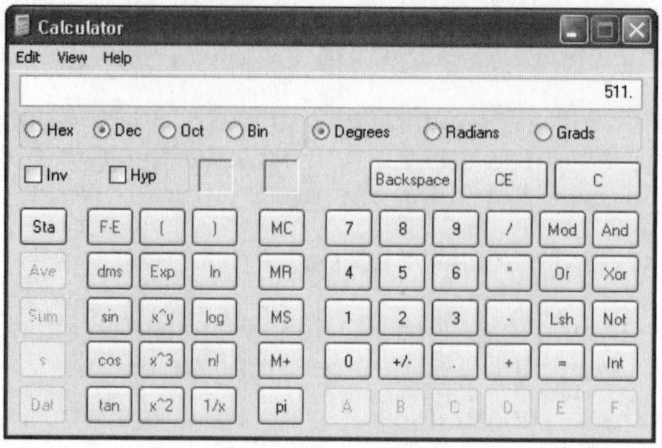

Figure 6-19: The full-functioned scientific calculator.

I suppose you could always toss your tie over your shoulder, moan and groan about how hard converting these stupid numbers is, and then gnash your teeth a bit as you click. It would certainly impress the boss. Or the neighbors. The gnashing teeth would go a long way to cover that hex-eating grin on your face.

And I bet you always thought computer science was a difficult subject.

Painting

Nobody would ever mistake Windows Paint for a real graphics program. It's a just-barely-good-enough application for manipulating existing pictures, and it helps you convert among the various picture file formats (JPEG, GIF, and so on), but it's certainly no competition for a real drawing tool like CorelDraw or a photo-editing tool like Microsoft Photo Editor or Adobe Photoshop.

That said, you can have a lot of fun with Windows Paint. To bring it to life, choose Start⇨All Programs⇨Accessories⇨Paint. You see a screen like the one shown in Figure 6-20.

Opening, saving, and closing pictures in Paint is a snap; it works just like any other Windows program. Scanning pictures into Paint goes like a breeze (choose File⇨From Scanner or Camera). Where you're bound to get in the most trouble is in free-form drawing, which can be mighty inscrutable until you understand the following:

- ✦ You select a line color (used by all of the painting tools as their primary color) by clicking the color on the palette (near the bottom of the window).
- ✦ You select a fill color (used to fill the inside of the solid shapes, such as the rectangle and oval) by right-clicking the color.
- ✦ Many of the painting tools let you choose the thickness of the lines they use — in the case of the spray can, you can choose the heaviness of the spray — in the box that appears after you select the tool.

General rules for editing are a lot like what you see in the rest of Windows — select, copy, paste, delete, and so on. The only odd editing procedure I've found is for the free-form selection tool. If you click on this tool and draw an area on the picture, Paint responds by selecting the smallest rectangle that encloses the entire line that you've drawn. It's . . . different.

You can specify the exact size of your picture by choosing Image⇨Attributes.

Free-form drawing

Click eyedropper; then click picture to select color

Select by drawing a line

Select by drawing a rectangle

Available colors

Current line color and fill color

Draw a straight line

Type text over the top of the picture

Figure 6-20: Don't let Windows Paint drive you off the deep end.

Getting Older Programs to Work

Program compatibility rates as one of the big nightmares in Windows XP. So many programs have been written for the PC, for so many years, that Windows XP has absolutely no way to handle all of them in all circumstances.

The designers of Windows XP knew that they could never be all things to all people, so they built a very tricky safety net into Windows XP. In essence, Windows XP can behave to a remarkable extent like any earlier version of Windows. So if you have a program that worked under Windows 95, say, and it doesn't work under Windows XP, you can tell Windows XP to pretend like it's Windows 95, and see if the offending program can be tricked.

The Program Compatibility Wizard doesn't work all the time, but it does trick squirrelly programs frequently enough to make the process worth a try. It makes Windows XP act like Windows 95, 98, Me, NT 4, or 2000. Follow these steps to use the Program Compatibility Wizard:

1. **Choose Start➪All Programs➪Accessories➪Program Compatibility Wizard.**

   You awaken the wizard, as shown in Figure 6-21.

2. **The wizard searches for programs on your hard drive (or on CD) and asks you to pick the program that's giving you problems.**

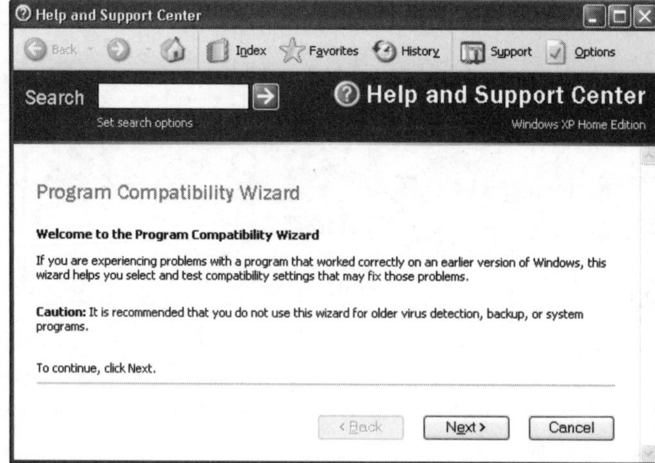

Figure 6-21: The Program Compatibility Wizard tricks old programs into cooperating with Windows XP.

3. **The wizard then wants to know which version of Windows the program is expecting.**

   This can be a bit of a turkey shoot. I have a trash can full of programs that never ran under *any* version of Windows, despite advertising to the contrary. But if you ever got the program to run under *any* earlier version of Windows, start with that version.

4. **The wizard wants to know if the program was designed to run with specific color settings (256 colors) or screen resolutions (640 x 480 or 800 x 600).**

   It also allows you to turn off Windows XP themes — the fancy graphics that Windows XP uses to make it look different from earlier versions of Windows. In my eXPerience, it doesn't hurt to turn themes off on any program that's hiccupping with Windows XP.

5. **Try to run the program.**

   If it works, the wizard enables you to easily have those settings kick in every time you run the program. If it doesn't work, the wizard offers to try other settings.

Ultimately, if the program doesn't work, you're up a creek, unless you can convince the program manufacturer that Windows XP compatibility is the most important "new" feature that they can add to their product. (Which it is.)

Using Sneaky Key Commands

Windows XP includes two well-buried key commands that everyone should know about. Neither of the key combinations works if your machine is hopelessly frozen, but in most normal circumstances, they should help a lot, especially if a program isn't behaving the way it should.

Conjuring up the Task Manager

Windows XP has a secret command post that you can get to if you know the right handshake. Uh, key combination. Whatever. The key combination works all the time — unless Windows is seriously out to lunch — as long as you're a designated Administrator. If you use Windows XP/Home, you probably are an Administrator. If you use Windows XP/Pro, you probably are not. (For a discussion of Administrators, see the section on using account types in Book I, Chapter 2.)

To bring up the Task Manager, hold down the Ctrl, Alt, and Del keys simultaneously. Task Manager should appear with a list of all the applications that are currently running (see Figure 6-22).

With Task Manager, you can do the following:

✦ Click an application, and then click the End Task button to initiate an orderly shutdown of the application. Windows tries to shut down the application without destroying any data. If it's successful, the application disappears from the list. If it isn't successful, it presents you with the option of summarily executing the application (called End Now to the less imaginative) or simply ignoring it and allowing it to go its merry way.

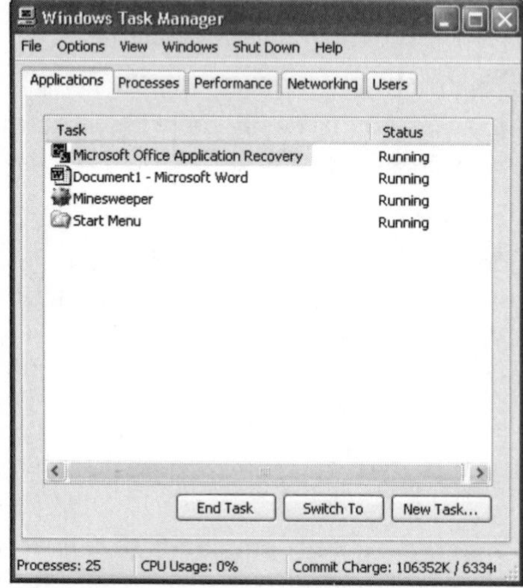

Figure 6-22: Task Manager gives you absolute control over the running applications.

✦ Click an application, and then click Switch To, and Windows brings up the switched-to application. This is very convenient if you find yourself stuck somewhere — in a game, say, that won't "let go" while it's taken control of your system — and you want to jump over to a different application.

✦ Click Shut Down on the menu bar. From that point, you can switch users, log off, hibernate, restart, or completely shut down the computer.

This is an orderly shutdown, so if you have an application that's hung so badly that it won't terminate itself, you have to tell Windows XP to End Now and risk losing all the unsaved data in the application.

Task Manager goes way beyond application control. For example, if you have a somewhat dominant techie gene (it runs in the family), you may be tickled to watch the progress of your computer on the Performance monitor, which is in the Task Manager on the Performance tab (see Figure 6-23).

Switching coolly

Windows includes a quick, easy way to switch among running applications without diving for the mouse to click on the Windows taskbar. It's known as the CoolSwitch (yes, that's the technical term for it), and it works on any computer, any time, unless Windows is totally out to lunch.

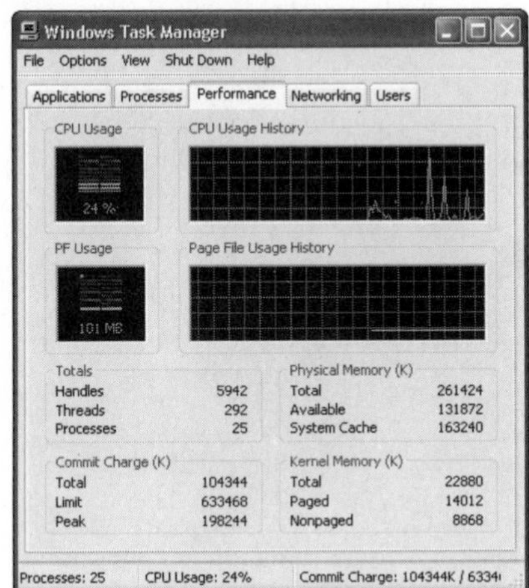

Figure 6-23: Performance monitor keeps track of every imaginable part of your computer — and some you probably couldn't imagine in your worst nightmares.

Which happens sometimes.

To use the CoolSwitch, hold down the Alt key and press Tab. You see something like the screen shown in Figure 6-24.

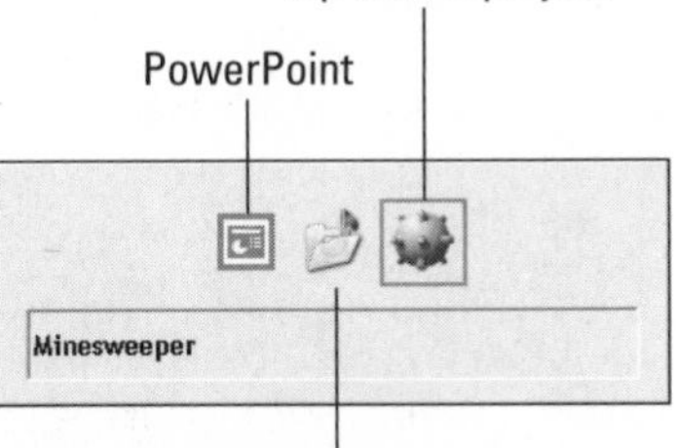

Figure 6-24: The Windows XP CoolSwitch.

As you press Tab over and over again, Windows cycles through the running programs. When you arrive at the program that you want to run, simply let go of the Alt key, and the selected program comes to life.

Cool, eh?

Chapter 7: Maintaining Your System

In This Chapter

- Keeping track of the programs installed on your PC
- Using Windows Messenger and MSN Messenger — or zapping them both
- Working with disks
- Scheduling boring things so that your computer does them automatically
- Storing more and spending less with Zips

Into every Windows XP's life a little rain must fall.

Or something like that.

Microsoft claims it has sold more than 200 million copies of Windows XP. With two major service packs under its belt, every nook and cranny of Windows XP has been exercised thoroughly — by 200 million *ex post facto* beta testers. That's the main reason why Windows XP has a well-deserved reputation for working pretty darn well, on almost all computers.

Still, Windows XP is a computer program, not a Cracker Jack toy, and it's going to have problems. The trick lies in making sure you don't have problems, too.

This chapter takes you through all of the important tools you have at hand to make Windows XP do what you need to do, to head off problems, and to solve problems as they (inevitably!) occur.

Windows Update — the big, complicated system that (usually) helps your system reach out to Microsoft's computers, and then retrieve and apply security patches — falls under the Security Center umbrella and, as such, is discussed in Book II, Chapter 5.

Installing and Removing Programs

Windows only lives to serve — or so I'm told — and, more than anything, Windows serves programs. Most of us spend our time working inside programs such as Outlook or Word or PageMaker. Windows acts as traffic cop and nanny, but doesn't do the heavy lifting. Programs rule. Users rely on Windows to keep the programs in line.

Windows XP includes a one-stop shopping point for adding and removing programs. To get to it, choose Start⇨Control Panel⇨Add or Remove Programs. You see the Add or Remove Programs dialog box, as shown in Figure 7-1.

When Windows talks about changing programs, it isn't talking about making minor twiddles — this isn't the place to go if you want Microsoft Word to stop showing you rulers, for example. Add or Remove Programs is designed to activate or deactivate big chunks of a program — graft on a new arm or lop off an unused head (of which there are many, particularly in Office). If you look at Figure 7-2, you can see the kind of grand scale I'm talking about: In Add or Remove Programs, you may tell Excel that you want to use its Analysis ToolPak add-in for financial analysis. Similarly, you may use Add or Remove Programs to completely obliterate Office's Speech Recognition capabilities. That's the kind of large-scale capability I'm talking about.

Windows XP itself doesn't do much in Add or Remove Programs. The main function of Windows is as a gathering point: Well-behaved programs, when they're installed, are supposed to stick their uninstallers in Add or Remove Programs. That way, you have one centralized place to look when you want to get rid of a program. Microsoft doesn't write the uninstallers that Add or Remove Programs runs; if you have a gripe about a program's uninstaller, you need to talk to the company that made the program.

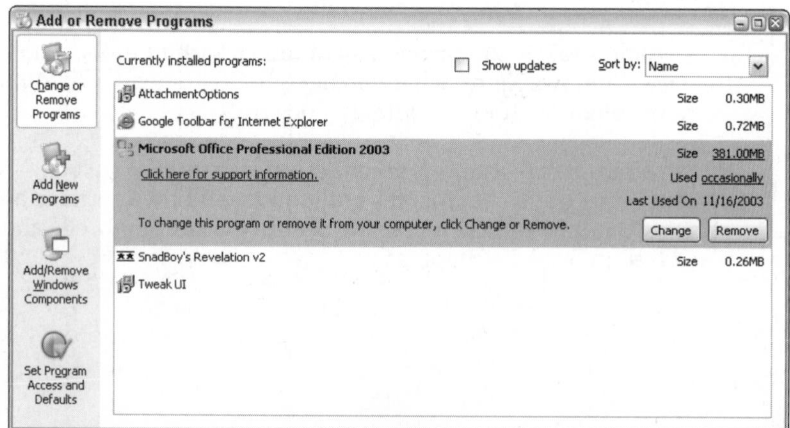

Figure 7-1: Add or remove programs.

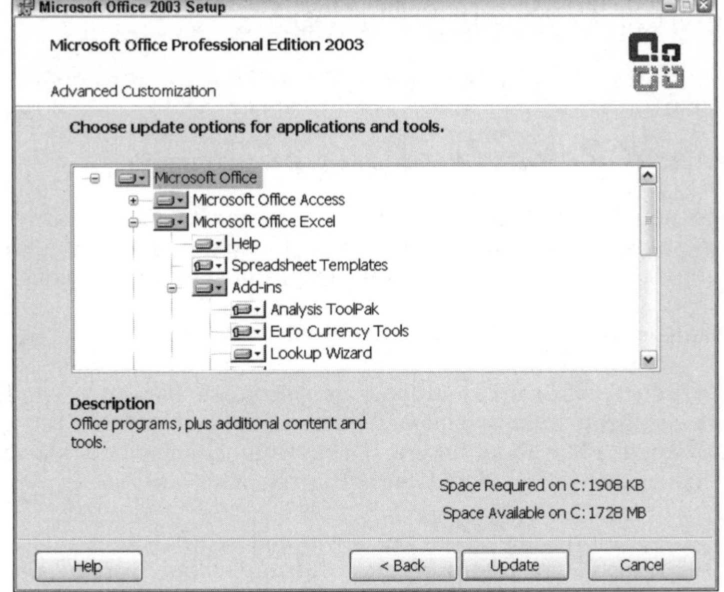

Figure 7-2: The Office 2003 Setup dialog box, as seen from Windows Add or Remove Programs.

Several school-of-hard-knocks comments pertain:

✦ In practice, you should never use Add or Remove Programs to add programs. If you want to install a program, do what savvy Dummies always do: Put the CD in the CD drive and follow the instructions. It's a whole lot easier that way.

✦ You rarely use Add or Remove Programs to remove parts of a program. Either you try to add features in a program that you forgot to include when you originally installed the program — most commonly with Office — or you want to delete a program entirely, to wipe its sorry tail off your hard drive.

Why sweat the small stuff? When you install a program, install all of it. Even Office 2003, in all its bloated glory, only takes up 600MB if you install every single far-out filter and truculent template — 800MB if you get suckered into installing the Outlook 2003 Business Contact Manager. With hard drives so cheap they're likely candidates for landfill, it never pays to cut back on installed features to save a few megabytes.

✦ Many uninstallers, for reasons known only to their company's programmers — I won't mention Adobe by name — require you to insert the program's CD into your CD drive before you uninstall the program. That's like requiring you to show your dog's vaccination records before you kick it out of the house.

When you start a program's uninstaller, you're at the mercy of the uninstaller and the programmers who wrote it. Windows doesn't even enter into the picture.

Installing and Removing Parts of Windows

Most people never use big parts of Windows XP. Some parts are made with very specific functions in mind and, with two exceptions, the average Person on the Street rarely encounters the requisite specific situations.

Thank heaven.

The two exceptions? Fax support and automatic backup in Windows. Neither gets installed unless you make the trek to retrieve it. Fax is relatively simple and benign; I talk about it here. Backup is much meaner; I talk about it in the "Backup/Restore" section, later in this chapter.

Windows' support for faxing has never been great. Although it's theoretically possible for you to get the Windows fax application working, one great Achilles' heel hampers you: If you have just one modem and it's connected to the Internet, you can't use it to send or receive faxes! Funny how Microsoft glosses over that detail, eh?

The smartest Dummies I know don't try to use Windows for faxing. Instead, they have a standalone fax machine (connected to its own telephone line, of course), or they use a fax service such as j2 Messenger (`www.j2.com`). j2's software lets you send faxes as easily as you print: Choose File⇨Print⇨Send with j2 Messenger, and the program turns your fax into an e-mail message. When you send the message to j2 headquarters — along with all your other e-mail — it's routed to a location close to the recipient, converted into a fax and then actually faxed for you, generally at a fraction of the cost for a long-distance phone call. j2 also offers inbound fax delivery: Your correspondent sends a fax to a specific phone number, the fax is converted to e-mail, and the e-mail is sent to you — all within a matter of seconds.

If the preceding caveat hasn't warned you off, here's how you install the Windows fax software. The same general procedure works for installing other obscure parts of Windows:

1. **Choose Start⇨Control Panel⇨Add or Remove Programs to bring up Add or Remove Programs.**
2. **Click Add/Remove Windows Components to bring up the Windows Components Wizard (see Figure 7-3).**

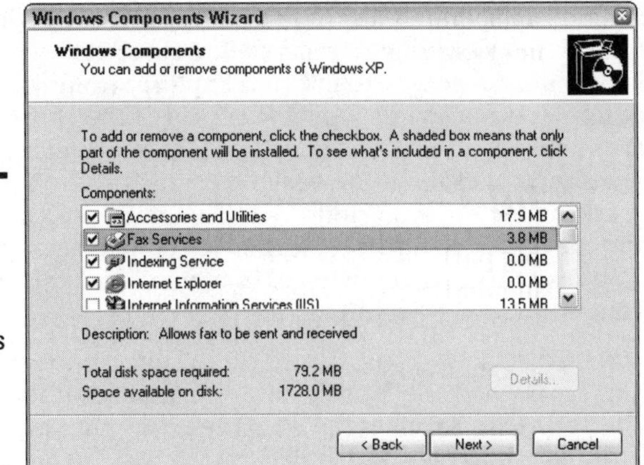

Figure 7-3: Install unusual Windows components in Add or Remove Programs.

3. **Find the component that you want to add.**

   In this case, because you're trying to add fax support, select the Fax Services check box. In general, you may have to click on a likely sounding component, and then click the Details button to see which subcomponents are available.

4. **Insert the CD that Windows came on so that Windows can pull the component off the CD and install it on your PC.**

   You may be required to restart Windows. In any case, by the time the wizard is done, your new component should be available and ready to use.

If you performed a typical installation of Windows XP/Home, the following list covers the components that you installed and have available:

- All the Accessories and Utilities are installed.
- Fax Services aren't installed. Follow the preceding instructions to install Windows faxing, but make sure you understand the limitations.
- Indexing Service is installed.
- The only Management and Monitoring Tools available are for an obscure Internet network management standard called SNMP, or Simple Network Management Protocol. You can look up SNMP in the Windows Help and Support Center, but if you need to look it up, you probably don't need it.
- Internet Explorer and MSN Explorer are installed. You can get rid of them here, if you really want to.

If you read the fine print, you'll discover that Add/Remove Windows Components isn't really offering to remove Internet Explorer. This option, ahem, "Adds or removes access to Internet Explorer from the Start menu and the desktop." In other words, you can get rid of the shortcut to IE from the Start menu (Windows XP, as it ships in plain-vanilla systems, doesn't have a shortcut to IE on the desktop) using this option. Not exactly what you expected, eh? Windows relies on IE for all sorts of services, including the ability to interpret formatted e-mail messages, and many more. You can no more uninstall IE than you can uninstall your cerebral cortex — no matter what the courts say.

- Under Networking Services, you can add three subcomponents — RIP Listener, which works with NetWare's Router Information Protocol Version 1; Simple TCP/IP Services, an obscure group that includes Quote of the Day; and Universal Plug and Play support, which comes into question only if you have UPnP devices installed (confusingly, UPnP isn't related to Plug 'n Play, the industry-wide standard for identifying hardware).
- Other Network File and Print Services includes support for only UNIX (and Linux) computers to print on printers connected to your PC.
- The software to automatically Update Root Certificates (digital security certificates for Microsoft products) is installed and running.
- Windows Messenger — Microsoft's instant messaging/chat program — is installed by default, and runs incessantly. See the section on chatting with Windows Messenger in Book III, Chapter 4 for more information.

Maintaining Disks

E pur, si muove.
Even so, it does move.

Galileo, to his inquisitors, April 30, 1633

Disks (floppies, hard drives, and other types of storage media) seem to cause more computer problems than all other infuriating PC parts combined. Why? They move. And unlike other parts of computers that are designed to move — printer rollers and keyboard springs and mouse balls, for example — they move quickly and with ultra-fine precision, day in and day out.

I go into details about the various kinds of disks and their plusses and minuses in the section on managing disks in Book I, Chapter 1. If you're unfamiliar with the inner workings of the beasts, that's a good place to start.

Like any other moving mechanical contraption, an ounce of disk prevention is worth ten tons of cure. Unlike other moving mechanical contraptions, a good shot of WD-40 usually won't cure the problem.

Formatting: NTFS versus FAT32

If you'll forgive a slightly stretched analogy, the surface of a floppy diskette or the surface of the platters inside a hard drive is a lot like a blank audio cassette tape. You know, the kind you can buy for 29 cents at a discount store. The surface of a floppy diskette is coated with some sort of magnetic gunk that somehow magically stores electrical impulses, holds onto them, and then spits them back when you want them.

Audio cassette tapes are amazingly forgiving — ever turn one into an accordion with a lousy capstan? — but diskettes and hard drives generally aren't so forgiving. Disks try to pack a lot of data into a small space, and because of that, they need to be calibrated. That's where *formatting* comes in.

When you format a disk, you calibrate it: Mark it with guideposts that tell the PC where to store data and how to retrieve it. Every floppy diskette and every hard drive has to be formatted before it can be used. Chances are good that the manufacturer formatted your disk before you got it. That's comforting, because every time a disk gets reformatted, everything on the disk gets tossed out, completely and irretrievably. *Everything.*

If you feel like you have to completely wipe out everything on a disk (even a USB flash drive or Compact Flash card) and start over, you can reformat it in one of two ways:

- Choose Start⇨My Computer to bring up Windows Explorer, right-click on the drive you want to reformat, click Format, and click Start. As long as you're a designated Administrator (see the section on using account types in Book I, Chapter 2), you receive the dialog box and warning shown in Figure 7-4.
- Reformat your hard drive as part of a complete (re)installation of Windows XP. See the section on considering a clean install in Book I, Chapter 1 for details.

Reformatting a hard drive really does obliterate everything. You not only lose your documents, pictures, programs, and e-mail messages; if they're on the zapped hard drive, you also lose all of your settings, your passwords, and anything you've done to customize Windows. It's a drastic step.

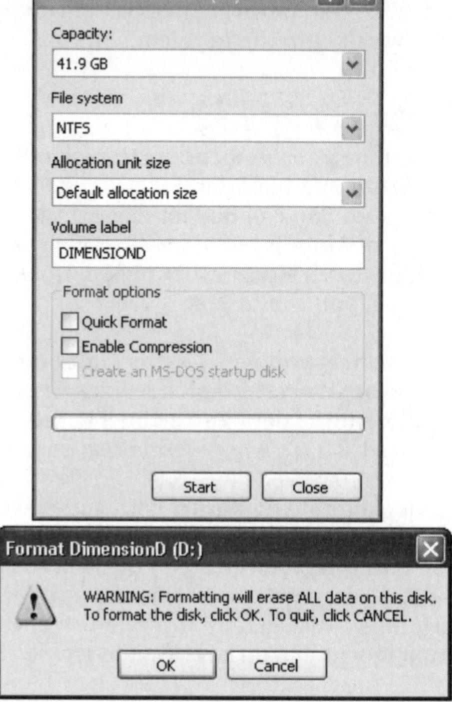

Figure 7-4: The scorched-earth approach to completely obliterating all the data on a drive and starting over again.

The primary choice you have to make when formatting or reformatting a hard drive — or even buying a preformatted hard drive — is which of the two competing file systems you should employ:

✦ **FAT32:** Stands for 32-bit File Allocation Table, as if that means anything to an honest chap. FAT32 is the old DOS/Windows 98/Me method for storing data on a hard drive. You may want to use FAT32 if you have disk utility programs that you absolutely have to run that absolutely require FAT32 (check the manufacturer's Web site). You may also want to stick with FAT32 if you intend to run two different versions of Windows on the same machine (a process called *multiple booting,* which, thankfully, is way beyond the scope of this book), or if you find yourself occasionally using an ancient emergency Windows 95/98/Me boot diskette to bring an old system back to life: They understand only FAT.

If you really want to use one PC to start up with many different operating systems — Windows 95, 98, Me, NT 3.51, NT 4, 2000, Linux, whatever — start with the instructions at `www.microsoft.com/windowsxp/pro/using/howto/gettingstarted/multiboot.asp`.

✦ **NTFS:** Stands for Windows NT File System. NTFS isn't quite as Neolithic as FAT32. NTFS includes built-in support for security and compression. It's the file system of choice in almost all circumstances.

As long as you're a designated Administrator (see Book I, Chapter 2 on using account types), formatting a drive for NTFS is as simple as choosing NTFS in the File System drop-down list in the Format dialog box. You can also convert an existing FAT32 drive or *partition* (part of a drive) to NTFS by using an arcane command called `convert`. For details, search the Windows Help and Support Center for *convert ntfs.* Windows has no analogous command to convert NTFS drives (or partitions) to FAT32.

If you install Windows XP on a PC that's running Windows 98 or Me, Windows offers you an opportunity to change any existing FAT32 drives (or partitions) to NTFS. Unless you have a very specific reason for sticking with FAT32, letting the system convert the drive is a good idea.

If you have a big hard drive, you may be forced to use NTFS. Windows XP won't format a hard drive larger than 32GB for FAT32. Windows has good reasons for this restriction, but the upshot is that really big drives need NTFS.

Performing periodic maintenance

Hard drives die at the worst possible moment. A hard drive that's starting to get flaky can display all sorts of strange symptoms: Everything from long, long pauses when you're trying to open a file to completely inexplicable crashes and other errors in Windows itself.

Windows XP comes with a grab bag of utilities designed to help you keep your hard drives in top shape. One of them runs automatically every time your system shuts down unexpectedly, like when the dog finally bites through the power cord: The next time you start your system, Windows scans your hard drives to see whether any pieces of files were left hanging around.

You can spend a lot of time futzing around with your hard drives and their care and feeding if you want, but as far as I'm concerned, just three utilities suffice: Check Disk, Cleanup, and Disk Defragmenter. You have to be a designated Administrator (see the section on using account types in Book I, Chapter 2) to get them to work.

Running an error check

If a drive starts acting weird — for example, you get errors when trying to open a file, or Windows crashes in unpredictable ways — run the Windows error-checking routines.

If you're an old hand at Windows — or an even older hand at DOS — you probably recognize the following steps as the venerable `CHKDSK` routine, in somewhat fancier clothing.

Follow these steps to run Check Disk:

1. **Choose Start⇨My Computer.**
2. **Right-click the drive that's malfunctioning and click Properties.**
3. **On the Tools tab, click Check Now.**

   The Check Disk dialog box appears (see Figure 7-5).
4. **In most circumstances, you want to select the Scan for and Attempt Recovery of Bad Sectors check box, and then click the Start button.**

   If you don't want to sit and wait and wait and wait for Windows to finish, you probably want to select the Automatically Fix File System Errors check box, too.

As long as you aren't using any files on the hard drive that Windows is scanning, Windows performs the scan on the spot and reports back on what it finds. If you are using files on the hard drive, however — and that always happens if you're scanning the drive that contains Windows itself — Windows asks whether you want to schedule a scan to run the next time you restart your machine. If you say yes, you have to turn the computer off and then turn it back on again before Windows runs the scan. (Note that merely logging off isn't sufficient.)

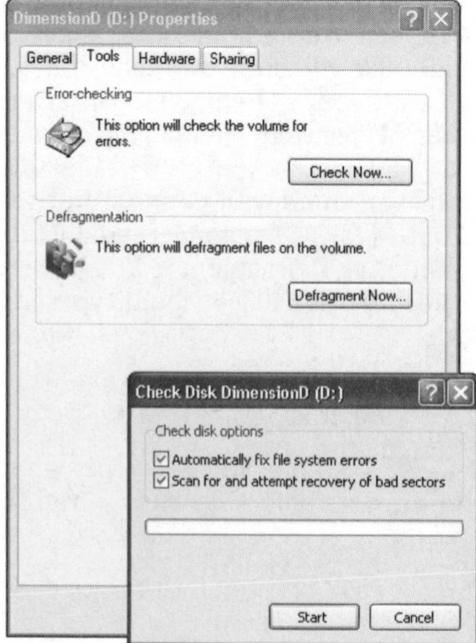

Figure 7-5: Use Check Disk to perform a complete surface scan.

Scheduling cleanups

In addition to running an error check from time to time, I use the Windows Task Scheduler to periodically go through and remove temporary files that I don't need, with a utility called Cleanup. I tell you how to do that in the section, "Scheduling Task Scheduler," later in this chapter.

Defragmenting a drive

Every week or so (or whenever I'm thinking about it), I run the Windows Disk Defragmenter on all my hard drives. This is quite different from the Check Disk routine (refer to Figure 7-5), which concentrates on the surface of the hard drive and whether it has been corrupted. Files become *fragmented* — scattered in pieces all over a hard drive — when Windows dynamically creates and deletes files. Having many fragmented files on a hard drive tends to slow down processing because Windows has to jump all over to reassemble a file when you ask for it. Windows Disk Defragmenter focuses on putting the pieces of files back together, in contiguous slots, so that Windows doesn't have to scamper all over the hard drive to read an entire file. To run the defragmenter, follow these steps:

1. **Turn off your antivirus program, and any other programs that might be running.**

   AV programs are notorious for gumming up defrags. Any program that goes out to your hard drive can interrupt the defrag.

2. **Choose Start⇨All Programs⇨Accessories⇨System Tools⇨Disk Defragmenter.**

   Alternatively, you can navigate to the drive in question, right-click it, click Properties, click Tools, and click Defragment Now (refer to Figure 7-5).

3. **Click the drive that you want to work on, and then click Analyze.**

   Windows XP checks to be sure that the files are put together properly, and then it advises you about whether a defragmentation run is worthwhile (see Figure 7-6).

4. **To run the defragmenter, click the Defragment button.**

5. **Break out that novel you've always wanted to read. This can take a long, long time.**

   While Windows is defragmenting, it keeps you posted on its progress at the bottom of the Disk Defragmenter window (see Figure 7-7), but don't be surprised if the "percent complete" figure freezes for a while and then jumps inexplicably.

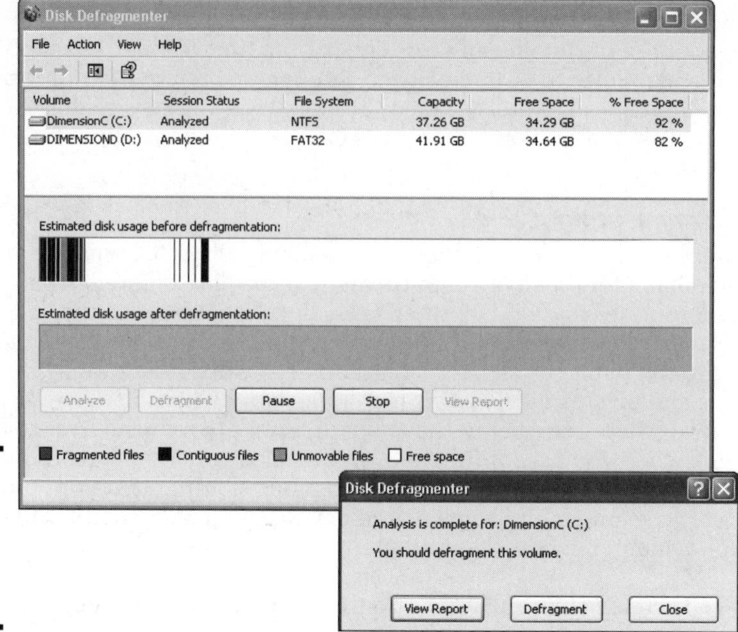

Figure 7-6: The defragmenter's Analyze phase.

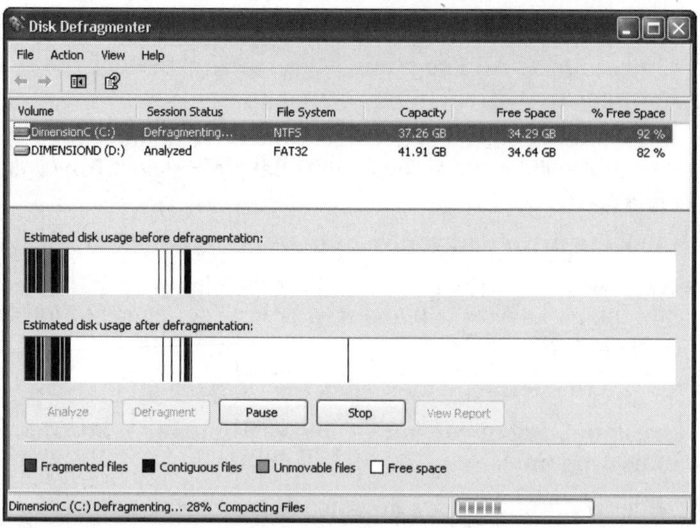

Figure 7-7: Follow the progress of the defragmenter at the bottom of the window.

Use those three tools regularly — Check Disk, Cleanup, and Disk Defragmenter — and your hard drives will thank you. Profusely.

Backup/Restore

Windows XP/Pro comes with a very thorough (and very complex) backup and restore capability called Automated System Recovery, or ASR. The Backup part of ASR works through a wizard. If your computer is hooked up to a Big Corporate Network, and all the pieces are in place and working properly, the Restore part can kick in, at your command, when you reboot the computer — even if your system was so thoroughly messed up you had to replace the hard drive.

If you think you're going to click a couple of times and get automatic backups from Windows XP, you're in for a very rude awakening. While working with ASR isn't as complex as, say, setting up and maintaining a Big Corporate Client/Server Network, mastering ASR will certainly take you more than a day, assuming you already have a Ph.D. in Computer Science. Check the Windows XP Help and Support Center for the topic *ASR* and you'll see why.

Earlier versions of Windows let you boot your PC with a special diskette called an Emergency Repair Disk (or Emergency Boot Disk in very early versions). Windows XP doesn't have an ERD. All of the functions of the old ERD have been subsumed by ASR. Yes, that means you can't boot to Windows XP directly from diskette anymore.

In general, if Windows won't boot at all, you need to haul out your installation CD and boot from the CD. If your computer won't boot from a CD, for whatever reason, Microsoft has a set of seven diskettes that will let you start your computer, and get you to the point where you can run Windows from the CD. See `www.bootdisk.com` for details.

If you're using Windows XP/Pro and you need automatic backups through your Big Corporate Network (you probably do!), and your network isn't already set up to handle backups, your only realistic choice is to bring in somebody who knows ASR and have them configure it for you. Usually, the designated stuckee is your favorite whipping boy, the Network Administrator. ASR kinda goes hand in hand with other Big Corporate Network chores.

What if you're using Windows XP/Home? Ah, have I got a gotcha for you.

Back in the weeks leading up to Windows XP's release, Microsoft announced that it would ship ASR and its backup subsystem with Windows XP/Pro, but would *not* include any sort of automatic backup with Windows XP/Home. That brought a hailstorm of criticism from two different perspectives: the "XP/Home users need backup just as much as XP/Pro users" contingency and the "Windows has always had a backup routine even if nobody ever used it" contingency. Both contingencies won.

Microsoft does, indeed, ship ASR Backup with Windows XP/Home — if you know where to find it. Except, uh, well, er, there's no ASR Restore to go along with it. That makes Windows XP/Home's backup just about as useful as a Ferrari Testarossa with no wheels. Or a transmission, engine, seats, or brakes.

If you really, really want to install ASR Backup (better known as NTBackup) in Windows XP/Home, even though there's no built-in restore, put the Windows XP/Home CD in a convenient drive and wait for the Welcome to Microsoft Windows XP screen. Choose Browse this CD➪Valueadd➪MSFT➪NTBACKUP. Make sure you read (and understand!) the warning in the file `readme.txt` before running the installer.

Scheduling Task Scheduler

Windows XP has a built-in scheduler that runs just about any program according to any schedule you specify — daily, weekly, monthly, middle of the night, on alternate blue moons.

The scheduler comes in handy in two very different situations:

- **When you always want to do something at the same time of day.** Perhaps you always want to dial up the Internet at 6:15 every morning, so that your machine is connected by the time you drag your sorry tail into your desk chair. Or maybe you want to run a PowerPoint presentation every morning at 7:30, so that your boss hears the tell-tale sounds as she walks by your cubicle. (And who said Dummies aren't Devious?)
- **When you want to make sure that the computer performs some mundane maintenance job when it won't interfere with your work time.** Thus, you may schedule disk cleanups every weekday at 2:00 in the afternoon because you know you'll always be propped up in the mop closet taking a snooze.

Any discussion of scheduled tasks immediately conjures up the old question, "Should I leave my computer running all night, or should I turn it off?" The fact is that nobody knows which is better. You can find plenty of arguments on both sides of the fence. Suffice it to say that your computer has to be on (or suspended) for a scheduled task to run, so you may have to leave your computer on at least one night a week (or a month) to get the maintenance work done.

You find absolutely no debate about one "should I leave it on" question, though. Everybody in the know agrees that running a full surface scan of your hard drive daily is a bad idea. (Specifically Check Disk, see the "Performing periodic maintenance" section, earlier in this chapter.) A full scan simply inflicts too much wear and tear on the hard drive's arms. It's kind of like forcing yourself to fly every morning just to keep your shoulders in shape.

One of the most important uses of the Task Scheduler is driving a Windows file cleanup program called, imaginatively, Cleanup. I talk about it earlier in this chapter in the section, "Maintaining Disks." Here's how to get Cleanup scheduled — and how to use the Task Scheduler in general:

1. **Make sure you have at least one user set up with Administrator privileges and a password.**

   The Task Scheduler requires that you supply it with a user name that has a password, and a password that's valid *at the time Task Scheduler runs*. If you change the password in Windows, you have to go back into the Task Scheduler and change the password there. Otherwise, the scheduled task won't run, and you may not find out about it until months later.

   To set up an account with a password, see Book I, Chapter 2. For a quick overview of the problem, see `http://support.microsoft.com/?kbid=311119`. For several solutions, see *Windows XP Timesaving Techniques For Dummies*, Technique 21, written by yours truly and published by Wiley Publishing, Inc.

2. **Choose Start⇨All Programs⇨Accessories⇨System Tools⇨Scheduled Tasks to get the Task Scheduler going.**

   Yes, your instincts are correct if you looked at the Scheduled Tasks windows and thought that something appeared familiar. All of Windows XP's Scheduled Tasks appear in a folder called Scheduled Tasks. The tasks themselves are just files, and the Add Scheduled Task icon is just a wizard. If you ever need to look at the Scheduled Tasks on a PC connected to your network, look for the Scheduled Tasks folder.

3. **Double-click the icon marked Add Scheduled Task.**

   The Scheduled Task Wizard appears with a frou-frou introductory screen.

4. **Click Next.**

   You see a list of some available programs, as shown in Figure 7-8.

   Does the list in Figure 7-8 look like an odd assortment of programs? It is. The Scheduled Task Wizard takes all the programs listed on the Start menu, alphabetizes them, and throws them all in this list. Literally. If you want to schedule a program that isn't on the Start menu, you have to click the Browse button.

5. **In this example, assume that you want to schedule regular Disk Cleanup runs, so click Disk Cleanup, and then click Next.**

   You can tell Windows how frequently you want to run Disk Cleanup by selecting one of the Daily, Weekly, Monthly, and so on option buttons in the window that appears.

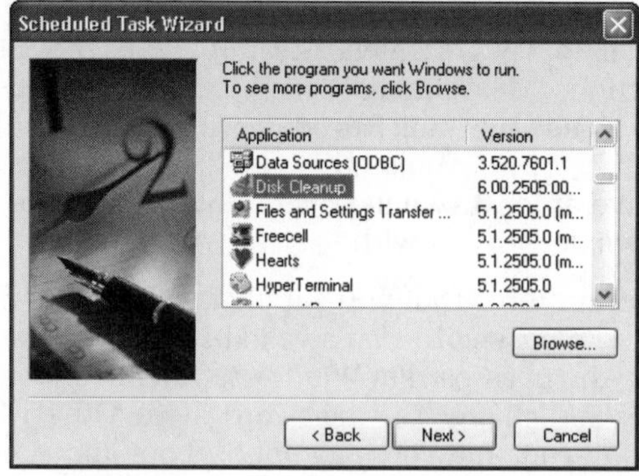

Figure 7-8: To schedule regular Disk Cleanup runs, choose Disk Cleanup.

6. **Click Next again, and you can set the exact schedule — which days, what times.**
7. **Click Next again, and the Scheduled Task Wizard asks you to provide security information (see Figure 7-9).**

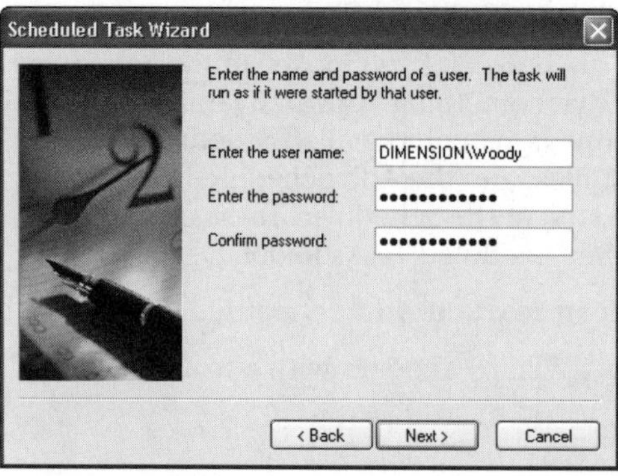

Figure 7-9: A scheduled program runs only if you have sufficient authority to run it manually.

This is an important screen because it reinforces the point that you aren't given any special security privileges just because you're scheduling a program. The program runs only if you have the authority to make it run. (See the section on using account types in Book I, Chapter 2.)

8. **In the very last step, you can set Advanced Properties for the scheduled task.**

The advanced properties include telling Windows XP what to do if the task takes a verrrry long time to complete; whether the task should go into hibernation if something else happens on the computer (presumably you're awake in the wee hours, banging out an assignment); and whether Windows should wake up the computer if it's hibernating or run the task if the PC is using batteries at the time.

The Windows Disk Cleanup program has a handful of settings that you may want to twiddle (see Figure 7-10). The System Schedule Wizard doesn't have any way to allow you to pick and choose your options for a scheduled program. The solution? Run Disk Cleanup once by hand (choose Start⇨All Programs⇨Accessories⇨System Tools⇨Disk Cleanup). Disk Cleanup remembers the settings that you applied when you ran it manually, and it uses those settings every time you run it with the Task Scheduler. Many other Windows programs work the same way.

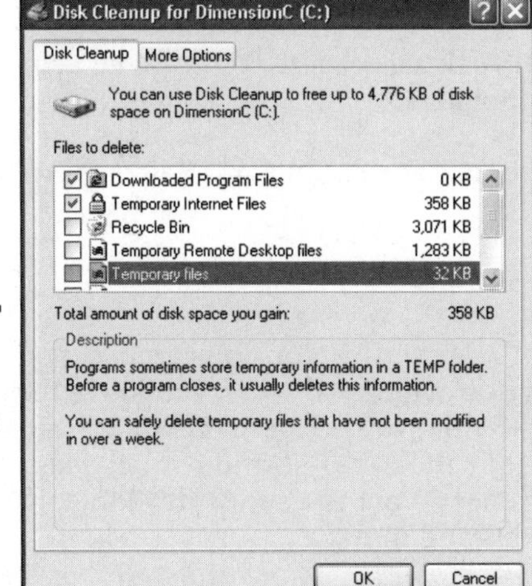

Figure 7-10: Disk Cleanup lets you choose what kinds of files will be deleted.

Zipping and Compression

Windows XP supports two very different kinds of file compression. The distinction is confusing but important, so bear with me.

File compression reduces the size of a file by cleverly taking out parts of the contents of the file that aren't needed, storing only the minimum amount of information necessary to reconstitute the file — *extract* it — into its full, original form. A certain amount of overhead is involved because the computer has to take the time to squeeze extraneous information out of a file before storing it, and then the computer takes more time to restore the file to its original state when someone needs the file. But compression can reduce file sizes enormously. A compressed file often takes up half its original space — even less, in many cases.

How does compression work? That depends on the compression method you use. In one kind of compression, known as Huffman encoding, letters that occur frequently in a file (say, the letter *e* in a word-processing document) are massaged so that they take up only a little bit of room in the file, while letters that occur less frequently (say, *x*) are allowed to occupy lots of space. Instead of allocating eight 1's and 0's for every letter in a document, say, some letters may take up only two 1's and 0's, while others could take up 15. The net result, overall, is a big reduction in file size. It's complicated, and the mathematics involved get quite interesting.

Windows XP's two file compression techniques are as follows:

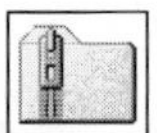

- Files can be compressed and placed in a "Compressed (zipped) Folder," with an icon to match.
- Files, folders, or even entire drives can be compressed using NTFS's built-in compression capabilities.

For a description of NTFS, see the "Formatting: NTFS versus FAT32" section, earlier in this chapter.

Here's where things get complicated.

NTFS compression is built into the file system: You can use it only on NTFS drives, and the compression doesn't persist when you move (or copy) the file off the drive. Think of NTFS compression as a capability inherent to the hard drive itself. That isn't really the case — Windows XP does all the sleight-of-hand behind the scenes — but the concept will help you remember NTFS compression's limitations and quirks.

Although Microsoft would have you believe that "Compressed (zipped) Folder" compression is based on folders, it isn't. A "Compressed (zipped) Folder" is really a file — *not* a folder — but it's a special kind of file called a Zip file. If you've ever encountered Zip files on the Internet (they have a filename extension of `.zip` and they're frequently manipulated with programs such as WinZip, `www.winzip.com`), you know exactly what I'm talking about. Zip files contain one or more compressed files, and they use the most common kind of compression found on the Internet. Think of "Compressed (zipped) Folders" as being Zip files, and if you have even a nodding acquaintance with ZIPs, you'll immediately understand the limitations and quirks of "Compressed (zipped) Folders." Microsoft calls them "Folders" because that's supposed to be easier for users to understand. You be the judge.

If you have Windows show you filename extensions — see my rant about that topic in the section on showing filename extensions in Book I, Chapter 3 — you see immediately that "Compressed (zipped) Folders" are, in fact, simple Zip files.

Table 7-1 shows a quick comparison of NTFS compression and Zip compression.

Table 7-1 NTFS Compression versus "Compressed (Zipped) Folders" Compression

NTFS	*Zip*
Think of NTFS compression as a feature of the hard drive itself.	Zip technology works on any file, regardless of where it is stored.
The minute you move an NTFS compressed file off an NTFS drive — by, say, sending a file as an e-mail attachment — the file is uncompressed, automatically, and you can't do anything about it: You'll send a big, uncompressed file.	You can move a "Compressed (zipped) Folder" (actually a Zip file, with a .ZIP file name extension) anywhere, and it stays compressed. If you send a Zip file as an e-mail attachment, it goes over the ether as a compressed file. The person receiving the file can view it directly in Windows XP, or he can use a product such as WinZip to see it.
A lot of overhead is associated with NTFS compression: Windows has to compress and decompress those files on the fly, and that sucks up processing power.	Very little overhead is associated with Zip files. Many programs (for example, antivirus programs) read Zip files directly.
NTFS compression is great if you're running out of room on an NTFS formatted drive.	"Compressed (zipped) Folders" (that is to say, Zip files) are in a near-universal form that can be used just about anywhere.
You have to have Administrator privileges in order to use NTFS compression.	You can create, copy, or move Zip files just like any other files, with the same security restrictions.
You can use NTFS compression on entire drives, folders, or single files. They cannot be password protected.	You can Zip files or folders, and they can be password protected.

If you try to compress the drive that contains your Windows folder, you won't be able to compress the files that are currently in use by Windows.

To use NTFS compression on an entire drive, follow these steps:

1. **Make sure that you are a full-fledged Administrator (see Book I, Chapter 2).**
2. **Choose Start⇨My Computer and right-click the drive that you want to compress. Click Properties and then click the General tab (see Figure 7-11).**

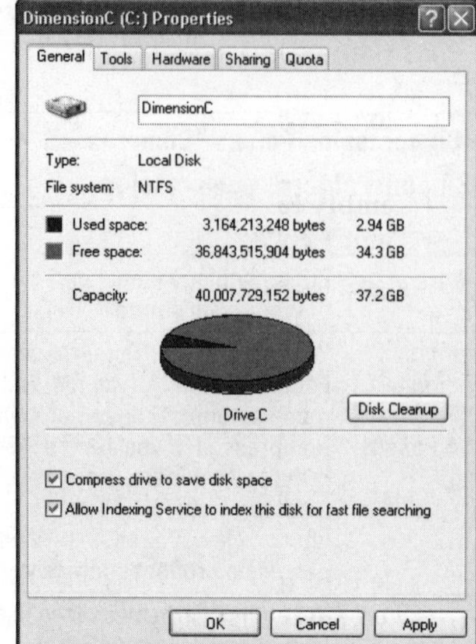

Figure 7-11: NTFS Compression is available only on drives formatted for NTFS.

3. **If the drive is formatted with NTFS (see the section, "Formatting: NTFS versus FAT32," earlier in this chapter), you see a check box saying Compress Drive to Save Disk Space. Select this check box.**
4. **Click OK.**

   Windows asks you to confirm that you want to compress the entire drive. Windows takes some time to compress the drive — in some cases, the estimated time is measured in days. Good luck.

To use NTFS compression on a folder or single file, follow these steps:

1. **Make sure that you are a full-fledged Administrator (see Book I, Chapter 2).**
2. **Navigate to the folder or file you want to compress (for example, choose Start⇨My Documents or Start⇨My Computer). Right-click on the file or folder you want to compress. Click Properties and click the Advanced button on the General tab.**

   The Advanced Properties dialog box appears.
3. **Select the Compress Contents to Save Disk Space check box, and then click OK.**

To uncompress a file or folder, go back into the Advanced Properties dialog box (right-click the file or folder, click Properties, and then click Advanced) and deselect the Compress Contents to Save Disk Space check box.

To use Zip compression, er, "Compressed (zipped) Folders," you must first create a Zip file, er, a "Compressed (zipped) Folder." Here's how:

1. **Choose Start⇨My Documents to navigate to the folder that you want to contain your new Zip file.**

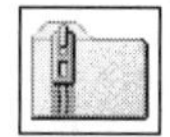

2. **Right-click in any convenient empty location within the window and choose New⇨Compressed (Zipped) Folder.**

   Windows responds by creating a new Zip file, with a `.zip` filename extension, and placing it in the current folder.

   The new file is just like any other file — you can rename it, copy it, move it, delete it, send it as an e-mail attachment, save it on the Internet, or do anything else to it that you can do to a file. (That's because it *is* a file.)

3. **To add a file to your "Compressed (zipped) Folder," simply drag it onto the zipped folder icon.**
4. **To copy a file from your Zip file (uh, folder), double-click the zipped folder icon, and treat the file the same way you would treat any "regular" file (see Figure 7-12).**

Figure 7-12: Zipped files can, with a few minor restrictions, be treated the same as any other files.

5. **To copy all of the files out of your Zip file (folder), click Extract All Files in the Folder Tasks pane.**

   You see the Windows XP Compressed (zipped) Folders Extraction Wizard (see Figure 7-13), which guides you through the steps.

The Compressed (zipped) Folders Extraction Wizard places all the copied files into a new folder with the same name as the Zip file — which confuses the living bewilickers out of everybody. Unless you give the extracted folder a different name from the original Compressed (zipped) Folder, you end up with two folders with precisely the same name sitting on your desktop. Do yourself a huge favor and feed the wizard a different folder name while you're extracting the files.

Nico Mak's WinZip compression utility runs rings around Windows XP's built-in "Compressed (zipped) Folder" features. Check out `www.winzip.com` for details.

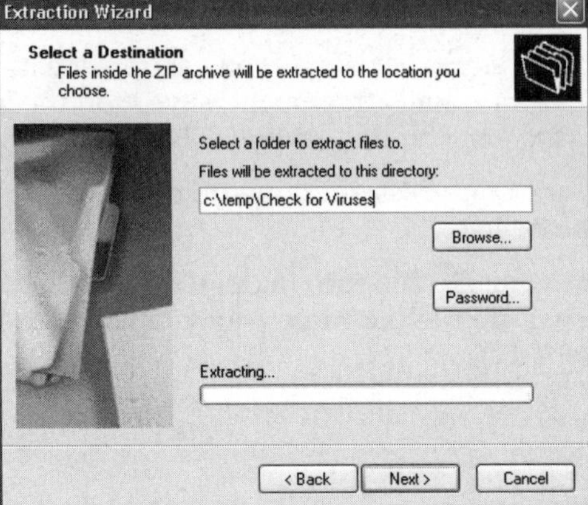

Figure 7-13: To copy all of the files out of the Zip file, "extract" them using this wizard.

Creating Checkpoints and System Restore

Ever get the feeling that things were going right?

Moments later, did you get the feeling that something must be wrong *because* things are going right?

Now you understand the gestalt behind System Restore. If you take a snapshot of your PC from time to time, when things are going right, it's relatively easy to go back to that "right" time when the wolves come howling at the, uh, Gates.

Windows XP automatically takes System Restore snapshots — called *checkpoints* — when it can tell that you're going to try to do something complicated, such as install a new network card. Unfortunately, Windows can't always tell when you're going to do something drastic — perhaps you have a new CD player and the instructions tell you to turn off your PC and install the player *before* you run the setup program. So it doesn't hurt one little bit to run checkpoints from time to time, all by yourself.

Here's how to generate a System Restore checkpoint:

1. **Wait until your PC is running smoothly.**

   No sense in having a checkpoint that propels you out of the frying pan into the fire, eh?

2. **Make sure you're set up as an Administrator (see Book I, Chapter 2).**

3. **Choose Start➪All Programs➪Accessories➪System Tools➪System Restore.**

   You get to choose between setting up a checkpoint and restoring to an earlier checkpoint.

4. **Select the Create a Restore Point option (see Figure 7-14) and click Next.**

5. **Type a descriptive checkpoint name (such as** Things Are Finally Working Okay**) and click Create.**

   Windows automatically brands the checkpoint with the current date and time.

6. **Windows creates a restore point with little fanfare and lets you go on your merry way.**

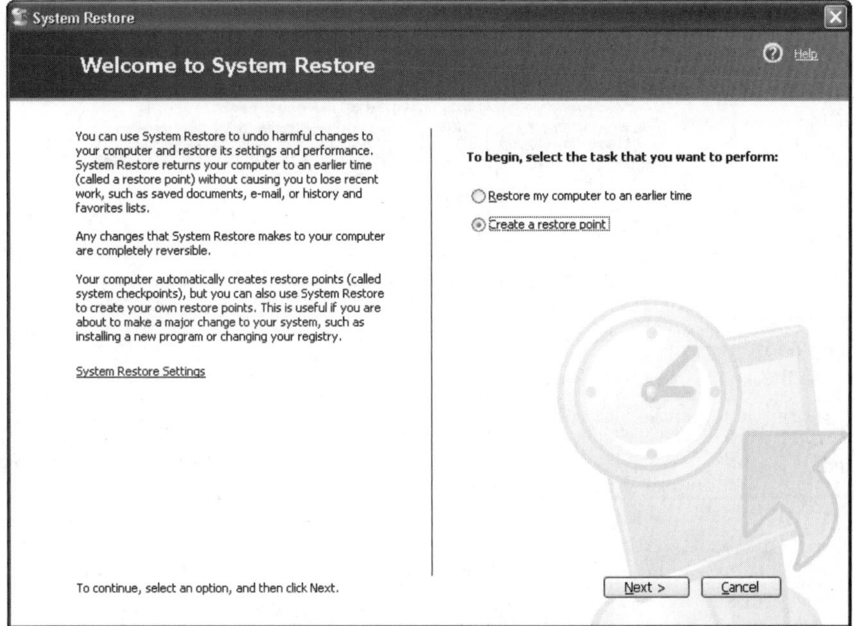

Figure 7-14: Windows XP creates checkpoints on demand.

If you ever need to restore your computer to a previous state, follow these steps:

1. **Save your work and then close all running programs.**

   System Restore doesn't muck with any data files, documents, pictures, or anything like that. It only works on system files. Your data is safe.

2. **Choose Start⇨All Programs⇨Accessories⇨System Tools⇨System Restore.**
3. **Select the Restore My Computer to an Earlier Time option and click Next.**
4. **Select the date and specific checkpoint that you want to restore to (see Figure 7-15).**
5. **Windows shuts down, restarts, and restores itself to the point you chose.**

System Restore is a nifty feature that works very well.

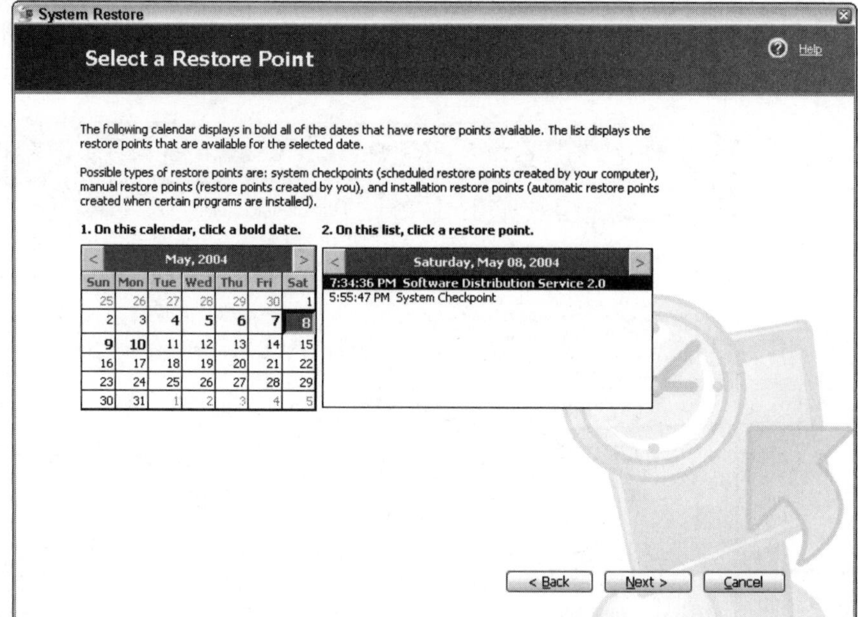

Figure 7-15: Choose the checkpoint that you need.

Chapter 8: Focusing on Windows XP/Professional

In This Chapter

- **Determining if you need Windows XP/Pro**
- **Finding out what to do if you have Windows XP/Pro and you want Windows XP/Home**
- **Finding out what to do if you have Windows XP/Home and you need Windows XP/Pro**
- **Taking advantage of Windows XP/Pro's features**

With certain specific exceptions (for example, the discussion of client/server networking in Book IX, Chapter 1), *Windows XP All-in-One Desk Reference For Dummies*, 2nd Edition, is aimed directly at the Windows XP/Home user.

Why? With few exceptions, Windows XP/Pro has nothing to offer the garden-variety Dummy. Hey, you can throw away that extra hundred bucks if you want to. But I'd much rather that you spent it on something worthwhile — like, oh, a copy of *Windows XP Timesaving Techniques For Dummies* (written by yours truly and published by Wiley Publishing, Inc.), for example. Not that I'm biased or anything.

This chapter looks at the exceptions — why you may want to pay extra for Windows XP/Pro, and what to do with Windows XP/Pro if you get it, either voluntarily or by corporate edict.

Differentiating Windows XP/Pro and Windows XP/Home

On the surface, Windows XP/Home and Windows XP/Pro look very different. Just from the get-go, the installers make different assumptions about the kind of network that you want to establish. Windows XP/Home sports a friendly point-and-click Welcome screen, while Windows XP/Pro requires you to log on — and that, in turn, means you have to know your logon I.D. and password before you can even begin. In Windows XP/Home, you can easily switch among multiple users on the same machine. In Windows XP/Pro, switching users is about as easy as switching offices at CIA headquarters.

Underneath the surface, though, the products are remarkably similar. Almost all of the features in Windows XP/Pro are also in Windows XP/Home, and they behave in precisely the same way. Even the CDs for Windows XP/Home and Windows XP/Pro are very nearly identical — only a handful of files differ. Windows XP/Pro users can even tell Windows to use the easy Welcome screen and fast user switching, if they're so inclined, providing the PC isn't connected to a Big Corporate Network.

That's not accidental. Microsoft designed it that way, at least for this version of Windows. Redmond's Product Managers used to promise us that some future version of Windows would provide "more value" for the Windows XP/Pro sucker, er, purchaser than the Windows XP/Home purchaser. But for now the pickins are slim indeed, and Microsoft seems to have its hands full just plugging the security holes.

Weighing the advantages of Windows XP/Home

Windows XP/Home's main advantage lies more in what it *doesn't* have than in what it does have, if ya know what I mean.

Windows XP/Home assumes that you don't want or need a lot of file protection. Windows XP/Home won't tie into a sophisticated corporate security system. It doesn't recognize the heavy-duty security built into Windows NT Server or Windows 2000 Server or Windows Server 2003.

Starting with Windows 2000 Advanced Server, Big Corporate Network security comes in the guise of the Active Directory, a comprehensive tool for managing computers on a client/server network, as well as managing users, system resources (such as printers and Internet connections), and the interactions among all of the pieces. Active Directory is a world unto its own, with so many technical nooks and crannies that it has spawned an entirely new breed of Network Administrators, charged specifically with the care and feeding of the AD beast.

On the flip side, most small business users don't want or need the overhead inherent in a heavy-duty security system — Network Administrators don't come cheap, and do-it-yourself network administration rates right up there with do-it-yourself proctology. Home users almost never want to subject themselves to the extra hassle.

Windows XP/Home's lessened security requirements buy you a lot of extra goodies. The following are features that you will find in Windows XP/Home, but won't find in Windows XP/Pro:

- ✦ Simple logon via the point-and-click Welcome screen.
- ✦ No need to memorize a user name or password, unless you really want to (see Book I, Chapter 2).

✦ Fast switching among users, so that you can let little Billy surf the Internet real quick while you run and check on the cat.

If you have a Windows XP/Pro system that is not connected to a client/server network (that's a Big Corporate Network, or a "domain" in Microsoft parlance), you can make Windows XP/Pro treat users just like Windows XP/Home. Choose Start➪Control Panel➪User Accounts➪Change the Way Users Log On or Off. Using the settings in the User Accounts dialog box, you can tell Windows to use the Windows XP/Home-style Welcome screen, and/or allow fast switching among users.

All of the added Windows XP/Pro security comes via client/server networking — which Microsoft calls a *domain*. For much more information about client/server and domains, see Book IX, Chapter 1.

Of course, the other big advantage to Windows XP/Home is the price. If you're buying Windows in a shrink-wrapped package off the shelf, Windows XP/Home costs about a hundred dollars less than Windows XP/Pro. If you're buying a new PC, Windows XP/Home may be free, while Windows XP/Pro — if it's available at all — costs a pretty penny or two or ten. Thousand.

Have you ever seen those signs from the PC manufacturers that say, "We recommend Windows XP/Pro"? I've seen them on Web sites, in computer shops, in newspaper ads, even on billboards. You know *why* the manufacturers recommend Windows XP/Pro? Because they make more money selling it!

Weighing the advantages of Windows XP/Pro

If you need Windows XP/Pro, you probably already know it — or somebody in your company has told you, in no uncertain terms, that you need it, bucko, so you better get with the system.

There's a reason why corporate IT folks can be so, uh, insistent (that's the polite term, anyway) about you installing Windows XP/Pro. They're concerned about security, and for good reason. If you run Windows XP/Home on your PC, and you manage to get hooked into the Big Corporate Network — you know, the one that runs on the Big Corporate Server — you and your PC represent a significant security risk.

Here's a common high-risk security scenario (computer security types love to use the term *scenario,* so I'm humoring them):

1. **You install Windows XP/Home on your portable computer; then you lug that computer into the office and plug it into the Big Corporate Network.**
2. **You get onto the Big Corporate Network using, say, the technique described in the section, "Converting Windows XP/Home to Windows XP/Pro," later in this chapter.**

3. **You use your itty-bitty portable's modem to dial out to the big, bad Internet, and you don't use the Windows Firewall. Ba-da-bing, ba-da-boom, you've opened a hole into your company's network.**

That kind of security breach is hardly unique to Windows XP/Home — it's been around for a long time — but the widespread availability of Windows XP/Home and its simple networking setup makes it a big, big target. Security folks, understandably, don't like having machines on "their" network that poke gaping holes in their carefully crafted protection plans.

Security concerns go beyond simple modem back doors. Windows XP/Pro sports all sorts of security features that Windows XP/Home can't match:

- **Full integration with Active Directory:** That means, with Windows XP/Pro, you can use Active Directory on the Big Corporate Network to control who uses your PC and what they can do on your PC (and on the network as a whole) — and official Network Administrators are in charge of the whole shootin' match.
- **Domains:** Even if your company doesn't use Active Directory, Windows XP/Pro takes full advantage of the features Microsoft builds into all of its client/server networks *(domains)*. Lots of capabilities are associated with domains, including the ability to predefine access privileges for groups of users and assign each individual user to a specific group.

With Windows XP/Pro, if you have the Network Administrator's blessing, you can control access to individual files. With Windows XP/Home, the lowest-level control is for entire folders.

- **Encryption:** Windows XP/Pro lets you encrypt individual files and folders using the NTFS file system's built-in encryption routines (for a description of NTFS, see Book I, Chapter 2). Windows XP/Home lets you mark folders as Private, thus making it difficult for other people to get at them, but encryption goes one step further by scrambling the contents. NTFS encryption is notoriously difficult to crack.

Windows XP/Pro's file encryption capability strikes a resounding chord with many portable PC users who are concerned about losing their portables and having all of their data accessible to the cretin who ran away with the machine. If you carry around sensitive data, and you don't want to encrypt individual files (using, say, the Microsoft Office encryption routines), Windows XP/Pro may be a good choice, based on this one feature alone.

Windows XP/Pro also includes a couple of features that are lacking in Windows XP/Home and that make it easier to use in a corporate (read: client/server) environment:

✦ **IntelliMirror:** This feature makes it easy (well, at least *possible*) for Network Administrators to *push* installations of operating systems — force networked computers to install specific pieces of software. IntelliMirror allows push installs of entire operating systems, components, some applications, and their upgrades, onto all PCs connected to the Big Corporate Network.

If everybody comes into the office one morning and discovers that, oh, Word doesn't work right, chances are pretty good that somebody in IT pushed upgrades onto all the machines. Microsoft Office patches, in particular, are notorious for not working right the first time.

✦ **Roaming User Profiles:** Windows configures itself to your preferences, no matter which PC you use on the network.

Finally, Windows XP/Pro has a grab bag of additional features that a few users may want:

✦ **Remote Desktop:** This feature allows you to take over your office computer while you're on the road. The computer at the office has to be running Windows XP/Pro — Windows XP/Home won't cut the mustard. The computer that's traveling can be running just about any version of Windows, from Windows 98 on.

If you're seriously considering Remote Desktop (see the Windows Help and Support Center topic *Remote Desktop*), make sure you take a look at Remote Assistance (see Book I, Chapter 4). Although the two are inherently different — for example, you have to explicitly initiate a Remote Assistance session from the "zombie" computer; and you have to have someone physically present on the zombie computer to click a couple of buttons — in many respects they accomplish the same thing. Remote Assistance is much, much easier to install and use. It's also arguably more secure. Remote Desktop requires Windows XP/Pro on the zombie computer — and any version of Windows can reside on the "controller" — and Remote Assistance requires Windows XP (Home or Pro) on both computers.

✦ **Personal Web Server:** This feature lets you build a Web site on your Windows XP/Pro machine. (It's actually Internet Information Services version 5.1.) Anyone who has access to the files on your machine will be able to view your personal Web pages using a browser, just as if they were on the Internet.

✦ **Dual-CPU Support:** If you own a computer with two CPU chips, you need to run Windows XP/Pro if you want to take advantage of both of them. Windows XP/Home uses only one chip, no matter how many chips you have installed.

✦ **Multilingual User Interface:** Only Windows XP/Pro can have its language changed on the fly, so you can see dialog boxes in different languages. Or so I'm told.

If you want to upgrade your current Windows 2000 PC to Windows XP — that is, install Windows XP on top of Windows 2000 and carry along all of your settings and applications — you have to pay for Windows XP/Pro. Windows XP/Home won't install over the top of Windows 2000, although it will install over Windows 98 or Me. I give full details in Book I, Chapter 1.

Making a buying decision

Want to know which version of Windows XP to buy? Here's *Woody's Tried-and-True Quick Windows XP/Pro/Home Decision Tree For Dummies:*

- ✦ If you're going to install Windows XP on a computer that will be attached to a Big Corporate Network, chances are awfully good that the Network Administrator will insist that you use Windows XP/Pro. Do it.
- ✦ If you decide that you really have to set up your own Big Corporate Network — with all the security capabilities that entails — don't buy Windows XP/Pro or Windows XP/Home just yet. Do yourself a favor and hire a Network Administrator with Active Directory experience and a long list of satisfied customers to scope out your situation *before* you open that particular vein and let it bleed. Uncle BillyJoeBob down at the local Computers Were Us shop doesn't make the grade.

You should consider becoming your own Network Administrator only if you seriously wish to pursue a new full-time career — and you have a very high tolerance for pain. It helps to have several screws loose, too.

- ✦ If you're going to install Windows XP on a portable computer and you're worried about somebody walking away with the computer and the data, get Windows XP/Pro and immediately encrypt your sensitive folders. (You need to be using the NT File System, NTFS, in order to encrypt a drive. See the discussion in Book I, Chapter 2.)

To encrypt the My Documents folder with Windows XP/Pro, choose Start➪My Documents. On the left in the task pane, click Share This Folder. On the General tab, click Advanced. Then select the Encrypt Contents to Secure Data check box.

- ✦ If you need to be able to connect to your office computer while you're on the road, and nobody's around to push a couple of keys while you're gone (to get Remote Assistance going), you probably want Remote Desktop. Go ahead and buy Windows XP/Pro.
- ✦ If the PC you're using right now has Windows 2000 or Windows NT 4 installed on it, and you want to upgrade to Windows XP over the top of the old Windows, you need Windows XP/Pro because Windows XP/Home won't do the upgrade. Be very wary of this approach, though, because in-place upgrades are notoriously fragile.
- ✦ Look hard at the list of Windows XP/Pro features in the section, "Weighing the advantages of Windows XP/Pro." If you find a feature that you absolutely can't live without, get Windows XP/Pro.

In the vast majority of cases, you either connect to a Big Corporate Network and will thus require Windows XP/Pro, or you'll be happy as a dog in a butcher shop with Windows XP/Home.

Changing Your Mind

What? You got the wrong version of Windows XP?

Don't worry. Happens all the time. Keep on reading to find out what to do.

Converting Windows XP/Home to Windows XP/Pro

By far the most common mismatch arises when someone (I'll raise my hand here) buys Windows XP/Home for a particular machine, but decides he should've bought Windows XP/Pro.

If you really need Windows XP/Pro and all that it contains, Microsoft will sell you an upgrade kit, complete with CD, that fills in the gaps. Check with your friendly local ye olde software shoppe.

In many cases, though, all you really need is a Windows XP/Home machine that can get at stuff stored on the Big Corporate Network. If that's the case, not to worry. Have I got a trick for you — all it takes is a logon I.D. and password for the Big Corporate Network.

Say you have a portable PC that's running Windows XP/Home, and you want it to do double duty. At home — or, say, in a small field office — you want it to run on the regular, old, everyday Windows XP/Home network. But when you plug it into the docking station at the main office, you want to use the portable to get into your Big Corporate Network.

No problem. Here's my favorite way to do it:

1. **Warn your Network Administrator that you're going to be sticking a Windows XP/Home machine on the Big Corporate Network.**
2. **Get the PC working on the home (or field office) peer-to-peer network (which Microsoft calls a *workgroup*).**

   That may involve installing Windows XP/Home or customizing it. Follow all the steps for installing a network in Book IX, Chapter 2.
3. **When the PC is working with the home or field office network, bring it into the main office and fire it up.**
4. **Attach the PC to the Big Corporate Network.**

   You probably plug in a cable or a card or both.

5. **Choose Start⇨My Network Places.**
6. **Click View Workgroup Computers.**
7. **In the Other Places pane, click Microsoft Windows Network.**
8. **Choose the Big Corporate Network.**

   In Figure 8-1, I chose the client/server network called Sabai. The alternative, Mshome, is the default Windows XP/Home peer-to-peer network.
9. **Windows requires you to enter a valid I.D. and password for the Big Corporate Network. Enter it, click OK, and you're in (see Figure 8-2).**

In some cases, this little trick may be all you need to run Windows XP/Home on your Big Corporate Network.

Converting Windows XP/Pro to Windows XP/Home

What if you bought Windows XP/Pro and all you want is Windows XP/Home?

Hey, that's easy, too. You can't get your money back, but you can readily convince a Windows XP/Pro machine to look and act pretty much like a Windows XP/Home machine.

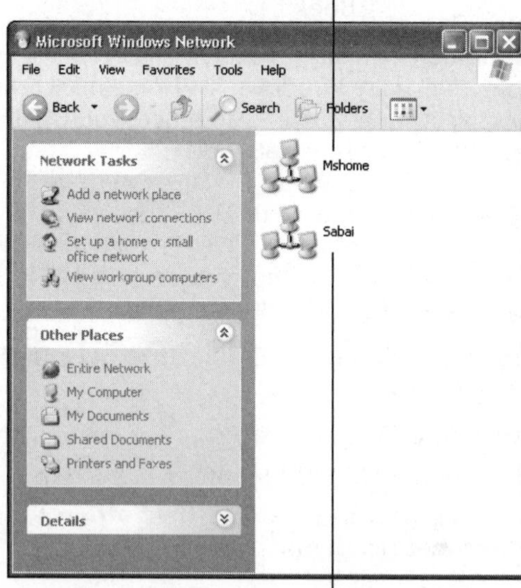

Figure 8-1: Getting to the Big Corporate Network from a Windows XP/Home PC.

Figure 8-2: The computers on the Sabai client/server network, as viewed from a Windows XP/Home PC.

You may want to change two cosmetic differences between Windows XP/Home and Windows XP/Pro:

- ✦ Windows XP/Home shows the Quick Launch Toolbar; Windows XP/Pro does not. (The Quick Launch Toolbar is a bunch of little icons immediately to the right of the Start button.) For instructions on how to show the Quick Launch Toolbar, see Book I, Chapter 3.
- ✦ Windows XP/Pro puts an item called My Recent Documents on the Start menu; Windows XP/Home does not. See Book II, Chapter 2, if you want to turn it off.

If you install Windows XP/Pro rather blindly — or if you bought a new PC with Windows XP/Pro preinstalled — it may think that it should belong to a network called Workgroup. Unless you've changed the settings, Windows XP/Home computers think that they belong to a network called Mshome.

Here's how to convince a default Windows XP/Pro machine to look for a Windows XP/Home network:

1. **Choose Start⇨Control Panel.**
2. **Click Performance and Maintenance; then click System.**
3. **On the Computer Name tab (see Figure 8-3), click Change.**
4. **In the Computer Name Changes dialog box that appears, select the Workgroup option button and type in the Windows XP/Home (peer-to-peer workgroup) network's name.**

Unless you've gone to Herculean lengths to change it, the name is Mshome (see Figure 8-4).

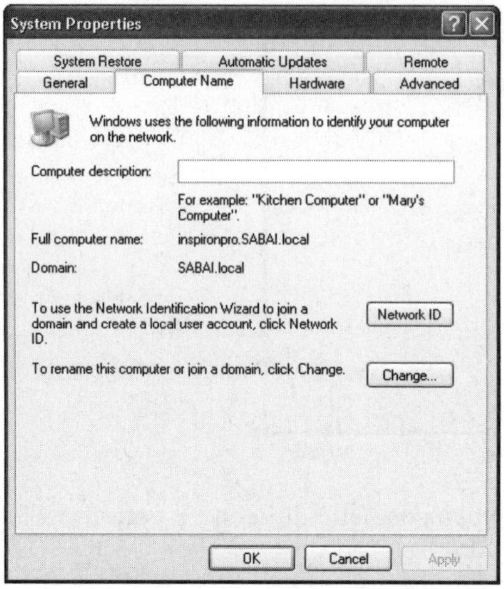

Figure 8-3: Tell Windows XP/Pro to attach the PC to a different network by going through the Computer Name tab.

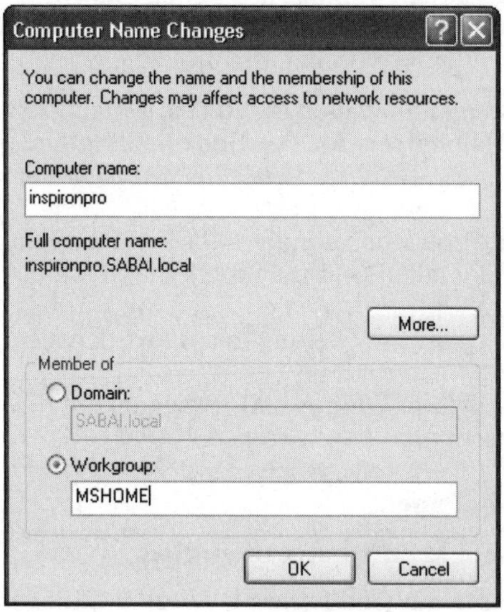

Figure 8-4: Switching your Windows XP/Pro machine from a Domain (client/server network) to a Workgroup (peer-to-peer network).

5. **Click OK twice.**

   The PC takes a few minutes to get its bearings, but if you have a peer-to-peer network running, you should be able to verify the change by choosing Start⇨My Network Places.

You can use this same technique to switch a Windows XP/Pro machine back to a Big Corporate Network. When you get to the Computer Name Changes dialog box shown in Figure 8-4, simply select the Domain option button.

WARNING!

Even though it may not appear to be that way, the Computer Name text box in the Computer Name Changes dialog box (refer to Figure 8-4) is case sensitive. If you're trying to get connected to a domain called Sabai and you type **SABAI**, Windows XP won't be able to find it — at least, it didn't on my network. That's true, even if the name appears as all-caps in the dialog box.

Installing Windows XP/Pro

Installation of Windows XP/Pro proceeds almost identically to installation of Windows XP/Home, with one key difference. (I discuss installing Windows XP/Home at length in Book I, Chapter 1.)

The key difference: During installation, you encounter a dialog box that asks, "Do You Want to Make This Computer a Member of a Domain?" Although it may not be immediately obvious, you have three choices:

- Select the No, This Computer Is Not on a Network or on a Network without a Domain check box. That sets the computer up for peer-to-peer (workgroup) networking. See Book IX, Chapter 2 for details.
- Select the No, This Computer Is Not on a Network or on a Network without a Domain check box and type a name in the Make This Computer a Member of the Following Workgroup text box. This choice sets up the computer for peer-to-peer networking on the network that you pick. If you want the Windows XP/Pro machine to get along with a typical Windows XP/Home network, type **MSHOME** in that text box.
- Select the Yes, Make This Computer Part of the Following Domain check box and type a domain name into the indicated text box.

If you choose to make your computer part of a domain, Windows XP/Pro asks you to supply an Administrator I.D. and password for the domain. If you can do that, Windows XP/Pro reaches out to the server adds you to the network — er, domain.

Figures 8-5 and 8-6 show a newly installed Windows XP/Pro machine called INSPIRONPRO that has added itself to the Active Directory on a server running Windows 2000 Advanced Server.

If you're installing Windows XP/Pro on a PC that's connected to a Big Corporate Network, try to con the Network Administrator into looking over your shoulder at the very end of the installation. She'll be able to provide the appropriate logon I.D. and password at the key moment, so that your machine gets added to the network with a minimum of fuss and bother. Saying "please" works wonders. Bribery works better.

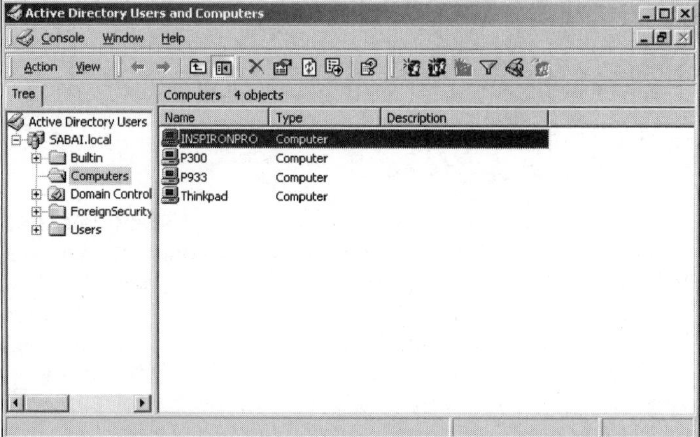

Figure 8-5: Supply an Administrator I.D. and password during Windows XP/Pro installation, your PC is added to the Active Domain.

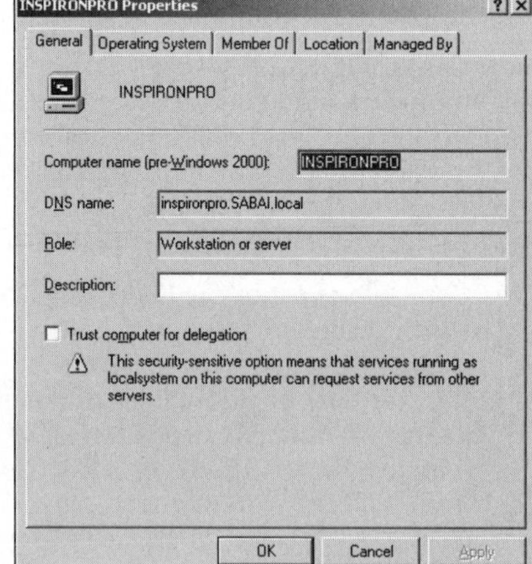

Figure 8-6: Full details from the newly installed machine are added to the server's Active Domain database.

Book II

Customizing Your Windows eXPerience

Contents at a Glance

Chapter 1: Personalizing Your Desktop

In This Chapter

- **Finding the *real* story on how Windows puts together your desktop**
- **Taking control of each desktop level**
- **Seeing why you're better off ignoring some of the fancy stuff**
- **Establishing a Super Boss Key — a key combination that immediately starts a screen saver**
- **Making your folders stand out**

It's your desktop. Do with it what you will.

I've never bumped into a complete description of how the Windows desktop gets tossed together, so you Dummies go to the head of the class. You may think it'd be easy for a computer to slap windows on the screen, but it isn't. In fact, Windows XP uses seven separate layers to produce that Windows eXPerience — and you can take control of every layer. I show you how in this chapter.

I also include a discussion of Desktop Themes, backgrounds in Windows Explorer, and custom pictures for folders. Pretty cool stuff, especially when you see CD album covers plastered on My Music folders.

Most importantly, I include instructions for creating a Super Boss Key in the section called "Selecting Screen Savers." When you press a key combination that you choose — say Alt+F10 — a Windows screen saver immediately springs into action. If you've ever been surprised when the boss walked in as you were dusting off your résumé, day trading, or playing a mean game of Minesweeper, you now know how to cover your tracks. You're welcome.

Recognizing Desktop Levels

The Windows XP desktop — that is, the stuff you see on your computer screen — consists of seven layers (see Figure 1-1).

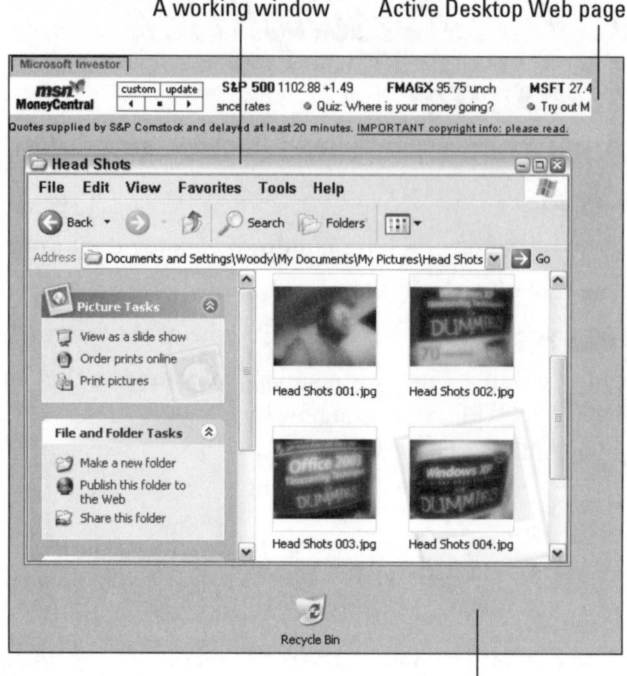

Figure 1-1: The Windows XP desktop.

For a quick change of pace, Desktop Themes change all seven layers, all at once. I talk about Desktop Themes in the section, "Using Desktop Themes," later in this chapter.

Here are the seven settings that control how Windows dishes up your desktop:

- ✦ At the very bottom, the Windows desktop has a *base color,* which is a solid color that you see only if you don't have a background picture or if your chosen background doesn't fill up the entire screen. Most people never see their Windows base color because the background usually covers it up. I tell you how to set the base color and all of the other Windows colors — for dialog boxes, the taskbar, the works — in the section, "Setting Colors in Windows XP."
- ✦ Above the base color lives the Windows *background.* (Microsoft used to call it *wallpaper,* and you'll see that name frequently.) You may be familiar with the rolling hills background — the one Microsoft calls Bliss — because it's the one that ships with Windows XP.

The people who sold you your computer may have ditched Microsoft's Bliss background and replaced it with some sort of dorky ad. I tell you how to get rid of the ad and replace it with a picture you want in the section, "Picking a Background."

- On top of the background, Windows lets you put pictures, Web pages, and just about anything you can imagine. Microsoft even has a little stock ticker and weather map that you can download and stick in this layer. This is the so-called *Active Desktop* layer and, by and large, it's a disaster. I tell you why in the section, "Avoiding the Active Desktop."
- Windows puts all of its desktop icons on top of the Active Desktop layer. Bone-stock Windows XP includes only one icon — the Recycle Bin. If you bought a PC with Windows XP preinstalled, chances are good that the manufacturer put lots of additional icons on the desktop, and you can easily get rid of them. I tell you how in the section, "Controlling Icons."
- Above the icons you (finally!) find the program windows — the ones that actually do work. You know, little things like Word, Excel, and the Media Player.
- Then you have the mouse, which lives in the layer above the program windows. The complete lowdown on standard mouse pointers — how they work and what they do — appears in the section on pointers in Book I, Chapter 2. If you want to change the picture used for the pointer, I talk about fancy mouse pointers in the section, "Changing Mouse Pointers," later in this chapter.
- At the very top of the desktop food chain sits the screen saver. The screen saver kicks in only if you tell Windows that you want it to appear when your computer sits idle for a spell. I talk about that beast in the section, "Selecting Screen Savers."

If you have more than one user on your PC, each user can customize every single part of the seven layers to suit his or her tastes, and Windows XP remembers every setting, bringing it back when the user logs on. Much better than getting a life, isn't it?

Setting Colors in Windows XP

Windows XP ships with three designer color schemes: Blue (the default scheme, which you probably use), Olive Green (which looks just as bad as you might imagine), and Silver (rather, uh, self-consciously techno-blah). To change color schemes, follow these steps:

1. **Right-click any empty part of the Windows desktop and choose Properties.**

   The Display Properties dialog box appears.

2. **Click the Appearance tab (see Figure 1-2).**
3. **From the Color Scheme drop-down list, choose Default (blue), Olive Green, or Silver, and then click OK.**

   Windows changes the base color — that is, the color of the Windows desktop when no background appears or the background doesn't fit (see the section, "Picking a Background") — as well as the title bar color of all windows and dialog boxes, the color of the Windows taskbar, menu highlight colors, and a dozen other colors scattered in various places throughout Windows.

You aren't confined to Microsoft's three-color world. In fact, you can pick and choose many different Windows colors, individually, although some of them appear on-screen only if you tell Windows to use the Windows Classic Style of windows and buttons — the old-fashioned pre-XP style, where windows had squared off edges and OK buttons weren't so boldly sculpted.

If you're terribly nostalgic for old-fashioned Windows windows, choose Windows Classic Style from the Windows and Buttons drop-down list shown in Figure 1-2.

If you ever need to shoot pictures of the computer's screen, you will probably want to get rid of the distracting background and turn the desktop itself white. (That's how all the screens shown in the figures in this book were shot.)

To set the desktop's base color to white — regardless of whether you use Windows XP Style or Windows Classic Style windows and buttons — follow these steps:

1. **Right-click any empty part of the Windows desktop and choose Properties.**

   The Display Properties dialog box appears.
2. **Click the Appearance tab (see Figure 1-2).**
3. **Click Advanced.**

   You see the Advanced Appearance dialog box, as shown in Figure 1-3.
4. **Make sure that Desktop appears in the Item drop-down list; then click the down-arrow under Color 1, and click the white color swatch in the upper-left corner.**
5. **Click OK twice.**

   Your desktop base color is now set to white, although you may have to change (or get rid of) your background in order to see it. I talk about strangling and axing the background in the next section. Stand back, Lizzie Borden.

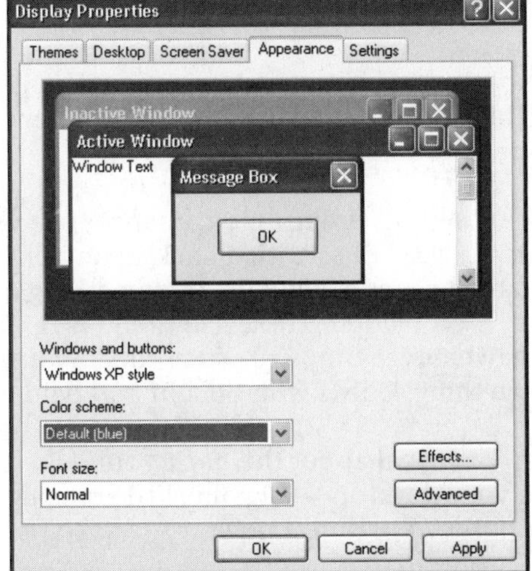

Figure 1-2: The three major Windows XP color schemes are accessible here.

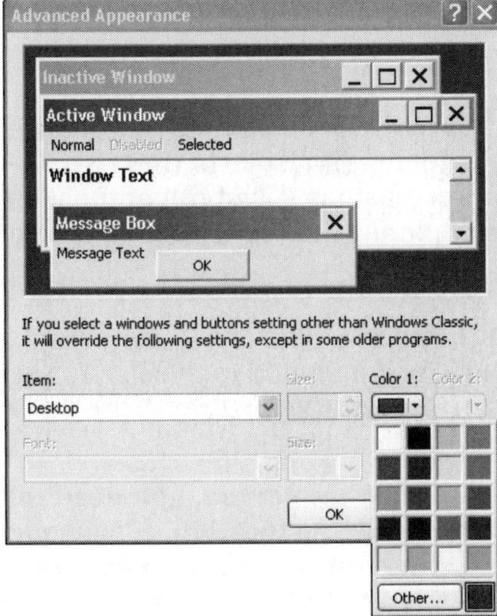

Figure 1-3: Individual color settings can be applied in the Advanced Appearance dialog box.

The Advanced Appearance dialog box (refer to Figure 1-3) seems to be saying that you have to use Windows Classic windows and buttons in order to see changes made in the Advanced Appearance dialog box. At least, I *think* that's what the dialog box says. (Sometimes this computer gobbledygook really confuses me.) Read it and see what you think. Anyway, if you're spooked and think that you have to switch back to the old Windows Classic windows and buttons in order to change your base color, not to worry: Just follow the steps and you'll be fine. Trust me.

Picking a Background

Windows XP, straight out of the box, ships with a picture of rolling verdant hills as the background. This background is peaceful and serene — Microsoft calls it "Bliss" — and it's boooooooring.

If you bought a PC with Windows XP preinstalled, chances are very good that the manufacturer has replaced Bliss with a background of its own choosing — maybe the manufacturer's own logo or something a bit more subtle, like "Buy Wheaties." Don't laugh. The background is up for sale. PC manufacturers can include whatever they like. You probably have an AOL icon on your desktop. Same thing. Guess who bought and paid for that?

There's nothing particularly magical about the background. In fact, Windows XP will put *any* picture on your desktop — big one, little one, ugly one, even a picture stolen straight off the Web. Here's how:

1. **Right-click on any empty part of the Windows desktop and choose Properties.**

   The Display Properties dialog box appears.

2. **Click the Desktop tab.**

   In the Background box, Windows XP lists pictures from the Windows folder and the My Pictures folder. (It also lists Web pages — files with HTM or HTML as filename extensions — in both of those folders.) Windows ships with lots of pictures in the Windows folder.

3. **Scroll through the Background box and pick the picture you want.**

   If you don't see the picture you're looking for — surprisingly, pictures in the Shared Pictures folder aren't included in this list, for example — click the Browse button and go find the picture. A preview of the picture appears in the little screen in the dialog box.

4. **If your picture is too big to fit on the screen, you need to tell Windows how to shoehorn it into the available location. If your picture is too small to cover up the entire screen, you need to tell Windows what to do with the extra room. You do both in the Position drop-down list, as described in Table 1-1.**

Table 1-1 How Windows Resizes Desktop Pictures

Position	*If the Picture Is Too Big*	*If the Picture Is Too Small*
Center	Windows carves a piece out of the middle of the picture and puts it on the screen.	Windows puts the picture in the center of the screen and fills the unoccupied part of the screen with the base color. *

Position	*If the Picture Is Too Big*	*If the Picture Is Too Small*
Tile	Windows takes a suitably sized piece out of the upper-left corner of the picture and uses it as the background.	Windows puts one copy of the picture in the upper-left corner of the screen, and then "*tiles*" (repeats) additional copies of the picture to fill up the remainder of the screen.
Stretch	Windows squishes the picture to fit the dimensions of the screen. If you're working with a photo, the effect is almost always horrible.	Windows stretches the picture so that it fits. Think Torquemada — it looks awful with a photo.

** See the discussion of base color in the section, "Setting Colors in Windows XP."*

Selecting None for a background means that you don't want Windows XP to use a background at all: It should let the base color show through, unsullied.

5. **If you tell Windows to put your too-small picture in the Center of the screen in the Position drop-down list, you can use the Color box as a quick way to set the base color.**
6. **Click the Apply button.**

   Windows changes the background according to your specifications but leaves the Display Properties dialog box open so that you can change your mind.
7. **Click OK.**

   The Display Properties dialog box disappears.

Many people are mystified by the Color box on the Display Properties dialog box because it doesn't seem to do anything. In fact, Color kicks in only when you choose Center for the Position and when the picture you've chosen as a background is too small to occupy the entire screen.

Changing the base color in the Advanced Appearance dialog box (see Figure 1-3) also changes the color on the Desktop tab and vice versa.

Windows XP lets you right-click a picture — a JPG or GIF file, regardless of whether you're using Windows Explorer or Internet Explorer — and choose Use as Desktop Background. When you do that, the picture appears as the background, with Position set to Stretch (if the picture is too big for the screen) or Tile (if the picture is not too big for the screen).

Avoiding the Active Desktop

You can read all the way through the Windows XP help files and never find a single mention of "Active Desktop," although it's featured prominently in Windows 98, Me, and 2000 product literature — touted as one of the big reasons to upgrade to those old dinosaurs, in fact.

There's a reason why. Active Desktop, introduced years ago in Internet Explorer 4, has a reputation for sucking up computer power and crashing Windows, inexplicably and unpredictably, with gleeful abandon. Believe me, you've never seen a program as gleeful as Active Desktop about crashing Windows 98.

Microsoft has completely abandoned the terminology, but the technology remains in Windows XP. And if you use it right, you'll discover that it isn't as bad as it used to be.

I believe Alexander Pope called that "damning with faint praise."

The concept is simple enough: Windows XP lets you put pictures and Web pages (even tiny Web pages, called *live content*) on top of your desktop background but underneath the Windows icons. In practice, you shouldn't have any problem at all putting static things — such as a picture, a calendar, or other stuff that doesn't change — on top of the background. But you're begging for trouble if you toss "live" things — such as stock market tickers — in there.

Static material sitting on top of the desktop's background doesn't make many demands on Windows. Live things can tie up your PC, your Internet connection, and your life. If you want live content — news feeds, weather updates, commodities prices, Webcam shots of corn growing in Kansas — open up Internet Explorer and work directly with the source.

To put items on top of your desktop's background but underneath the icons, follow these steps:

1. **Right-click any open space on the desktop and choose Properties.**
2. **In the Display Properties dialog box, click the Desktop tab, and then click the Customize Desktop button.**

   The Desktop Items dialog box appears.
3. **In the Desktop Items dialog box, click the Web tab (see Figure 1-4).**

   Although the check box is marked Web Pages, in fact you can put any picture or Web page (including any HTML file located on the Web or on your hard drive) in the Active Desktop layer. The way you do it is a little strange.

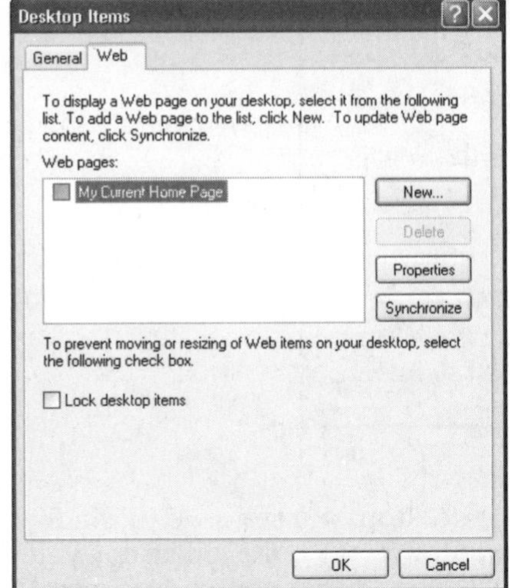

Figure 1-4: Choose Active Desktop items here by selecting the check box in front of the item.

4. **Add the picture or Web page to the Web Pages list. Then select the check box next to the picture or page, and Windows actually adds it to the Active Desktop.**

   For example, My Current Home Page appears as one of the options in the Web Pages list, but it isn't actually shown on top of your desktop background because the check box in Figure 1-4 isn't checked. Confusing? You bet it is.

5. **Add new pictures or Web pages to the Web Pages list by clicking the New button.**

   You see the New Desktop Item dialog box, as shown in Figure 1-5.

   You can follow the New Desktop Item dialog box's suggestion and click Visit Gallery, but be forewarned: The mini-Web pages Microsoft offers in the Microsoft Desktop Gallery are very limited — the stock ticker and weather map you can see in Figure 1-1, plus a sports news page and a satellite tracker — and they haven't been updated in years. That's because they're "live content" and live content drags down your PC's performance and makes it less stable. Don't go there.

6. **Click Browse and navigate to any pictures that you want to put on top of your desktop background. (Pictures are fine: They're *static* and won't hurt anything.)**

7. **When you're done gathering all the pictures you want, go back to the Desktop Items dialog box (refer to Figure 1-4), select the check boxes in front of any pictures that you definitely want to put on the desktop, and click OK twice.**

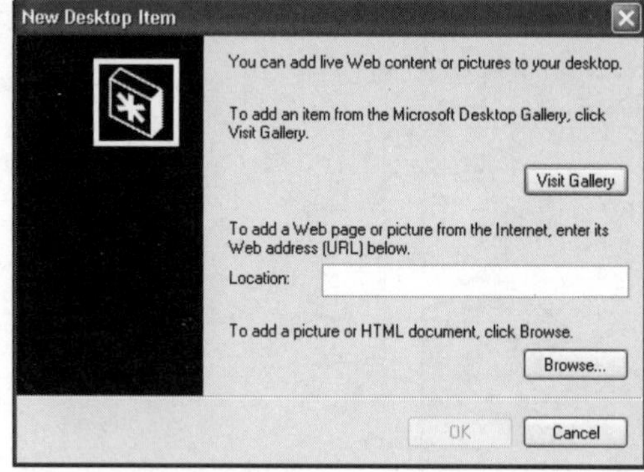

Figure 1-5: Preselect Active Desktop items — add them to the Web Pages list — using this dialog box.

When you get back to the desktop, you see a weird window with your picture inside of it — a window that's quite unlike any you've ever seen (see Figure 1-6). You may have to hover your mouse near the top of the picture to coax Windows into showing you the window's gray top part.

8. **If you get tired of the picture, click the X in the upper-right corner of the window, as shown in Figure 1-6, or navigate back to the Web Pages list (see Step 5 in this list) and deselect the check box in front of the picture's name.**

If you remove an Active Desktop picture by clicking the X in the upper-right corner of the weird window, the only way to bring the picture back is by bringing up the Web Pages list in the Desktop Items dialog box and select the check box in front of the picture's name.

If you select the Lock Desktop Items check box in the Desktop Items dialog box (refer to Figure 1-4), Windows won't show the gray top part of any of the weird windows in the Active Desktop, even if you hover your mouse near the top of the pictures 'til the cows come home. Without the gray top part showing, you can't move or resize any of the weird Active Desktop windows, so they stay put.

Controlling Icons

Windows XP sticks icons above the Active Desktop items (see the preceding section, "Avoiding the Active Desktop") but below are the real, working windows — the ones you use every day to get things done.

Windows XP, straight out of the box, ships with exactly one icon: the Recycle Bin. Microsoft found that most people appreciate a clean desktop, devoid of icons — but it also found that hiding the Recycle Bin confused the living daylights out of all its guinea pigs (uh, Usability Lab Test Subjects). So Microsoft compromised by making the desktop squeaky-clean, except for the Recycle Bin: Bliss and a Recycle Bin. Who could ask for more?

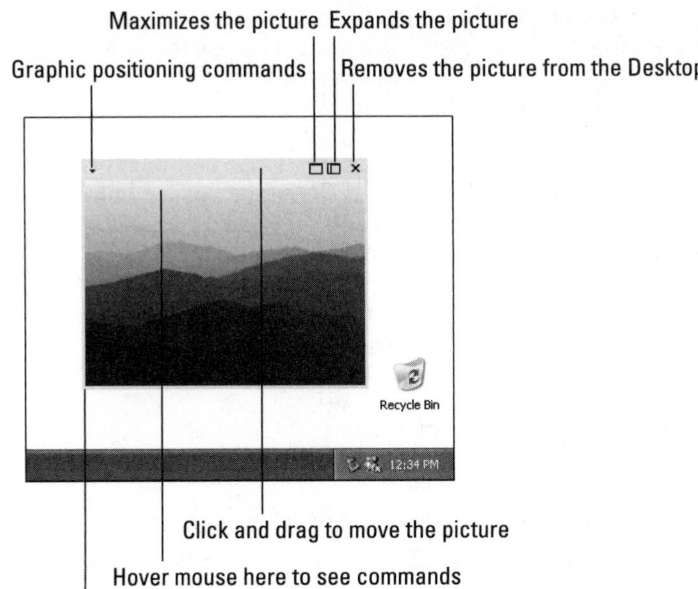

Figure 1-6: Your chosen pictures(s) appear in special Active Desktop window(s).

If you bought a PC with Windows XP preloaded, you probably have so many icons on the desktop that you can't see straight. That desktop real estate is expensive, and the manufacturers get a pretty penny for dangling the right icons in your face. Know what? You can delete all of them, without feeling the least bit guilty. The worst you'll do is delete some shortcut to a manufacturer's tech support software, and if you really need to get to the program, the tech support rep on the telephone can tell you how to find it from the Start menu.

Windows XP gives you several simple tools for arranging icons on your desktop. If you right-click on any empty part of the desktop and choose Arrange Icons By, you see that you can do the following:

- ✦ Sort icons by name, size, type (folders, documents, shortcuts, and so on), or the date that the icon was last modified.
- ✦ *Auto Arrange* icons — that is, have Windows keep them arranged in an orderly fashion, with the first icon in the upper-left corner, the second one directly below the first one, the third below it, and so on.
- ✦ If you don't want them arranged automatically, at least you can have Windows *Align to Grid,* so you can see all of the icons without one appearing directly on top of the other.

In general, you can remove an icon from the Windows desktop by right-clicking on it and choosing Delete, or by clicking it once and pressing the Delete key. Unfortunately, PC manufacturers are wise to this trick, and they often disable the Delete function on icons that they want to remain on your desktop.

Some icons are hard-wired: If you put a Word document on your desktop, for example, the document inherits the icon of its associated application, Word. Same goes for Excel worksheets and text documents and recorded audio files.

Icons for shortcuts, however, can be changed at will. (I talk about shortcuts in Book I, Chapter 2.) Follow these steps to change an icon — that is, the picture — on a shortcut:

1. **Right-click on the shortcut.**
2. **Click Properties.**
3. **In the Properties dialog box, click the Change Icon button.**
4. **Pick an icon from the offered list, or click Browse and go looking for icons. Windows abounds with icons. See Table 1-2 for some likely hunting grounds.**
5. **Click OK twice, and the icon is changed.**

Table 1-2 Places to Look for Icons

Contents	*File*
Everything	`C:\Windows\System32\shell32.dll`
Computers	`C:\Windows\explorer.exe`
Communication	`C:\Windows\System32\hticons.dll`
Household	`C:\Windows\System32\pifmgr.dll`
Folders	`C:\Windows\System32\syncui.dll`
Old programs	`C:\Windows\System32\moricons.dll`

Lots and lots (and lots and lots) of icons are available on the Internet. Use your favorite search engine, and search for "free Windows icons."

Windows XP gives special treatment to five icons: the Recycle Bin (which can't be removed from the desktop unless you go into the Windows Registry with a blunt axe), My Documents, My Computer, My Network Places, and Internet Explorer. To control the appearance of those icons

1. **Right-click any open space on the desktop and choose Properties.**

2. **In the Display Properties dialog box, click the Desktop tab, and then click the Customize Desktop button.**
3. **In the Desktop Items dialog box, click the General tab.**
4. **Select and/or deselect each of the four check boxes — My Documents, My Computer, My Network Places, and Internet Explorer — depending on whether you want the associated icon to appear on the desktop.**
5. **To change an icon (that is, the picture itself), click the icon to select it, and then click the Change Icon button.**

   Now you can look inside any files you want, looking for icons. Refer to Table 1-2 for some ideas.

   Notice that one of the icons in the Desktop Items dialog box is marked Recycle Bin (full). In fact, that isn't the icon for a full Recycle Bin. Ain't true. There *is* no icon for a full Recycle Bin. If the Recycle Bin gets full, Windows has apoplexy and shoots you a dialog box to ask whether it can empty the Bin. In fact, the icon shown appears when anything at all is in the Recycle Bin.
6. **When you're done, click OK twice.**

   Your new icons appear on the desktop.

The politically correct way to remove icons on the desktop is via the Desktop Cleanup Wizard.

The Desktop Cleanup Wizard cleans up only shortcuts. (I talk about shortcuts in Book I, Chapter 2.) It doesn't touch data files, folders, or anything else you might be parking on your desktop. Nor does it affect My Documents, My Computer, My Network Places, and Internet Explorer, which have to be handled individually, per the preceding instructions.

To run the Desktop Cleanup Wizard, follow these steps:

1. **Right-click any open space on the desktop and choose Properties.**
2. **In the Display Properties dialog box, click the Desktop tab, and then click the Customize Desktop button.**
3. **In the Desktop Items dialog box, click the General tab.**
4. **Make sure that the Run Desktop Cleanup Wizard Every 60 Days check box is selected.**

   You certainly want Windows XP to remind you every couple of months that you can tidy up.
5. **Click the Clean Desktop Now button.**

   The Desktop Cleanup Wizard starts. You see a welcome screen. Ho-hum.

6. **Click Next.**

   The wizard presents you with a list of shortcuts on your desktop, along with the dates that they were most recently used (see Figure 1-7).

   The Desktop Cleanup Wizard doesn't pick up all shortcuts on the desktop. But it does get the vast majority of them.

7. **Select the check boxes next to all the shortcuts that you want to have removed from your desktop, and then click Next.**

   If it doesn't exist, Windows creates a new folder on your desktop, called Unused Desktop Shortcuts, and moves all the selected shortcuts to that folder.

Figure 1-7: Take rarely used shortcuts off your desktop with the Desktop Cleanup Wizard.

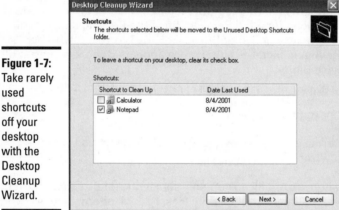

Changing Mouse Pointers

Believe it or not, Microsoft has spent many thousands of person-hours honing its mouse pointers. The pointers you see in a standard Windows XP installation have been selected to give you the best visual "clues" possible, without being overly distracting. I go into great detail on the standard mouse pointers and what they do in the section on pointers in Book I, Chapter 2.

What? You think they're boring? Yeah, me too.

You can control your mouse pointer destiny in three different ways:

- By choosing a new Desktop Theme, which replaces all of your pointers, along with the background, screen saver, and virtually everything else that can be customized. I talk about Desktop Themes in the later section, "Using Desktop Themes."

- By selecting and changing individual pointers — so you can turn, say, the Windows "I'm busy but not completely tied up" mouse pointer (which Windows calls Working In Background) into, oh, a dinosaur.
- By changing all of your pointers, wholesale, according to schemes that Microsoft has constructed.

To change individual pointers or to select from the prefab pointer schemes, follow these steps:

1. **Choose Start⇨Control Panel⇨Printers and Other Hardware⇨Mouse.**

   The Mouse Properties dialog box appears.
2. **Click the Pointers tab (see Figure 1-8).**
3. **To change all the pointers at the same time, pick a new pointer scheme from the Scheme drop-down list.**

   You can choose from purely functional sets of pointers (such as extra large pointers to use for presentations or pointers inverted to show solid black blobs) or fun sets (such as Conductor, Dinosaur, or Hands).
4. **If you want to bring back the original scheme, choose Windows Default (System Scheme), which is the one you started with.**

If the selected pointer is animated the animation appears here

A Scheme replaces all pointers

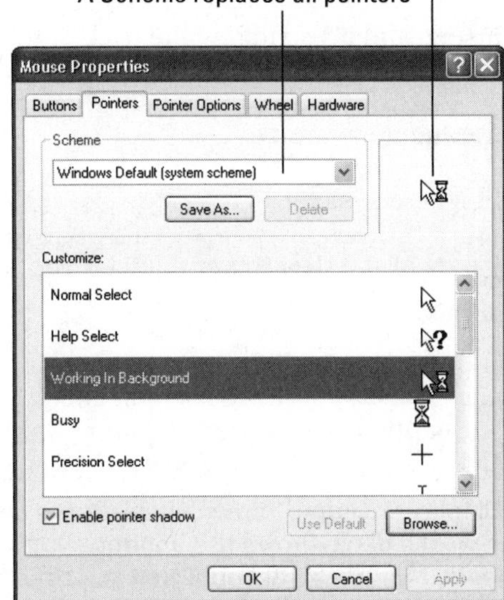

Figure 1-8: Mouse pointers can all be changed.

5. **To change an individual pointer, click the pointer in the Customize box, and click Browse.**

   Windows shows you all of the available pointers — which number in the hundreds. Choose the pointer you want, and click Open.

6. **If you want to change an individual pointer back to the original pointer for the particular scheme that you have chosen, click the pointer in the Customize box and click Use Default.**

7. **When you settle on a set of pointers that appeal to you, click Save As, and give your new, custom scheme a name so that you can retrieve it at any time.**

8. **Click OK.**

   Windows starts using the pointers you've chosen.

Selecting Screen Savers

Windows screen savers are absolutely, totally, utterly, 100 percent for fun. Ten years ago, screen savers served a real purpose — they kept monitors from "burning in" the phosphors in frequently used parts of the screen. Nowadays, monitors aren't nearly as prone to burn-in (or burnout — would that were the case with humans!), and saving screens rates right up there with manufacturing buggy whips on the obsolescence scale. Flat-panel LCD monitors (such as a laptop's screen) don't have phosphors, so there's nothing to burn.

Still, screen savers are amusing, and if you follow the trick in this section, they serve one truly important function: A screen saver makes an excellent front for a "Super Boss Key" — a key that you can push whenever Da Boss makes an unexpected, unwanted appearance.

Follow these steps to select a screen saver:

1. **Right-click any empty part of the desktop and click Properties.**

2. **Click the Screen Saver tab.**

   Most of the settings on this tab are self-explanatory, but one can be a bit confusing: the On Resume, Display Welcome Screen check box. That check box controls what happens when the computer "wakes up" after the screen saver has kicked in.

   - If the On Resume, Display Welcome Screen check box is selected, when the computer wakes up, it shows the Windows logon screen. If the user who was logged on has an account that requires a password, she will have to re-enter the password in order to get back into Windows. (I talk about passwords in the section on changing user settings in Book I, Chapter 2.)

- If the On Resume, Display Welcome Screen check box is deselected, when the computer wakes up, it returns to the state it was in when the screen saver started. The user who was logged on remains logged on.

3. **When you're happy with your screen saver settings, click OK.**

In previous versions of Windows, bypassing the screen saver password protection scheme was relatively easy. Not so in Windows XP. If the On Resume, Display Welcome Screen check box is checked, a potential cracker has to crack the Windows XP password itself — not an easy task.

If you want to get rid of your current screen saver, right-click an empty spot on the desktop, click Properties, click Screen Saver, and select None in the Screen Saver drop-down list. Click OK, and your screen will never be saved again.

Here's the trick you've been waiting for — the reason why you read this chapter in the first place. You can use screen savers to create a Super Boss Key — a key combination, such as Alt+F10, that you can press to make the PC immediately switch over to running the screen saver. The Super Boss Key runs independently of the usual Windows screen saver stuff: The Super Boss Key doesn't affect the screen saver you set up to run on your computer when it's idle. The screen saver is just a handy program that won't look the least bit suspicious if your boss glances at your PC's monitor.

Setting up the Super Boss Key is really quite simple:

1. **Make sure that Windows is showing filename extensions.**

   I rant about that in the section on showing filename extensions in Book I, Chapter 3. You need to see filename extensions in order to find your screen saver programs.

2. **Bring up the Search Companion by choosing Start⇨Search; then click All Files and Folders.**

3. **Run a search for all `.scr` files — which are your screen savers.**

   To do so, type ***.scr** in the All or Part of the File Name text box, and then click the Search button. You end up with a dozen or more `.scr` files that correspond to the screen savers listed in the Display Properties dialog box (see Figure 1-9).

4. **Decide on a screen saver that you want to use and look up the associated program's filename, as described in Table 1-3.**

Table 1-3 Screen Savers and Their Program Files

Screen Saver	*File*
3D Flower Box	`ssflwbox.scr`
3D Flying Objects	`ss3dfo.scr`
3D Pipes	`sspipes.scr`
3D Text	`sstext3d.scr`
Beziers	`ssbezier.scr`
Blank	`scrnsave.scr`
Marquee	`ssmarque.scr`
My Pictures Slideshow	`ssmypics.scr`
Mystify	`ssmyst.scr`
Starfield	`ssstars.scr`
Windows XP	`logon.scr`

5. **In the Search Results window, right-click the program's filename and choose Create Shortcut.**

   Windows displays this message: `Windows cannot create a shortcut here. Do you want the shortcut to be placed on the desktop instead?`

6. **Click Yes.**

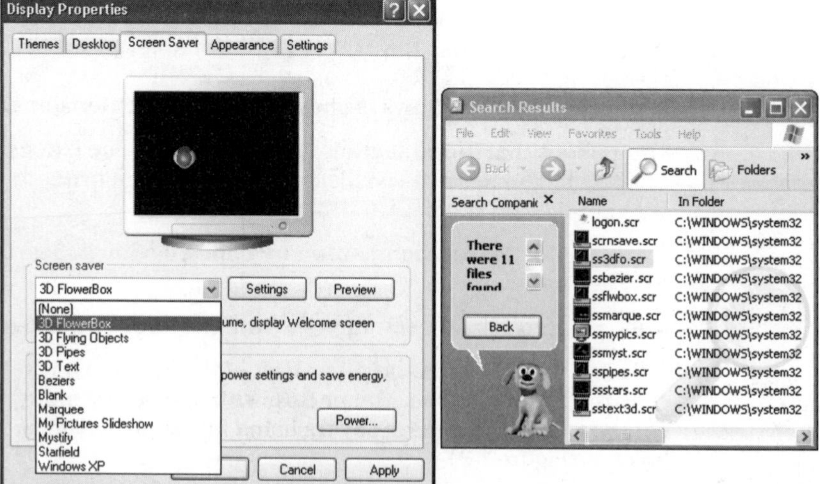

Figure 1-9: Screen savers in the Display Properties dialog box correspond to .scr program files.

7. **Go to the desktop, right-click the new shortcut, and choose Properties (see Figure 1-10).**
8. **Click once inside the box that says Shortcut Key, and then press the key combination you want to use to activate the Super Boss Key, uh, screen saver.**

   In Figure 1-10, I chose Alt+F10 (that is, I held down the Alt key, and then pressed F10).
9. **Click OK and your Super Boss Key is complete.**

A few programs "swallow" certain odd key combinations — if such a program is running, it grabs the key combinations and doesn't hand them over to Windows, so Windows won't know that you want to run your Super Boss Key screen saver. I haven't found many programs that swallow Alt+F10, but some undoubtedly exist. So test your Super Boss Key in all of your favorite clandestine situations before you really need to use it, okay? If you find that your chosen key combination doesn't work with an important program (the worst offenders are games), try different key combinations until you find one that makes the Super Boss Key work.

Figure 1-10: The properties for the shortcut to the screen saver that's on your desktop.

If you want to gussy up your Super Boss Key screen saver, right-click the shortcut and click Configure. You can change all of the screen saver's settings.

Seeing Desktop Text

If the characters you see on the Windows screen aren't good enough, Windows XP includes several options for improving the legibility of text on your desktop. The five main options are as follows:

- ✦ Activate ClearType, which can make some text easier to read, especially on portable computers and flat-panel displays.
- ✦ Have Windows show Large Fonts, which increases the size of the font used for icon labels, window titles, Windows Explorer text, and menus (but nothing else).
- ✦ Change the "dpi" setting, an arcane zoom setting that's poorly documented and best avoided, particularly because, once changed, the new zoom factor applies to everyone who uses the PC, in all of their applications.

Although you can find a few references to changing the dpi setting in the Windows XP Help and Support Center, only three people at Microsoft really understand the setting, and two of them are on sabbatical. (Okay, so I exaggerated a little bit. Not much.) Stay away from the dialog box (Display Properties⇨Advanced⇨General) and don't change the setting unless you're instructed to do so by someone who's willing to pay for all the therapy you'll need to cope with the aftermath.

- ✦ Use Magnification, which puts a strip on the screen that shows a highly magnified portion of the desktop.
- ✦ Try High Contrast, where Windows uses a coloring method that decreases details, but improves legibility, particularly at a distance, or for those with visual challenges.

Windows, per se, doesn't control many of the font settings that you may imagine. For example, if you want to increase the size of the fonts in the Help and Support Center, Windows Large Fonts support doesn't do a thing. You have to bring up the Help and Support Center, click Options, and adjust the Font Size Used for Help setting.

Activating ClearType

Microsoft's ClearType technology uses a very strange color-shading scheme — invented years ago (see `http://grc.com/cleartype.htm`) — to make fonts look better on certain kinds of displays. If you choose to have Windows use ClearType, Windows employs the technology everywhere for showing text on the screen — on the Windows desktop, inside your spreadsheet program, even inside Internet Explorer. Conventional wisdom says that ClearType works great on portable computers and flat-panel monitors.

My UWD (Unconventional Wisdom For Dummies) says that ClearType helps a bit with the labels under icons and small amounts of text scattered here and there on a flat-panel screen, but I'd rather hang my eyeballs out to dry than force them to stare at a word-processing screen that's been "enhanced" with ClearType. Yes, ClearType works much better on flat-panel displays than on traditional computer screens. No, I don't use it.

If you want to experiment with ClearType, *don't use Windows XP's settings*. Instead, follow these steps:

1. **Go to** `http://offroadsearch.com/software/cleartweak` **and download the latest version of ClearTweak.**

   ClearTweak is a ClearType tweaking utility from iolsland.com.

2. **Reset your monitor to its default settings.**

   If you have an "Auto" button on your monitor, push it. That should give ClearType settings the widest possible latitude.

3. **Double-click the ClearTweakSetup file to run it.**

   You see the ClearTweak main window, as in Figure 1-11.

4. **Select the ClearType Font Smoothing option button.**

   That turns on ClearType and shows you a sample of the effect in the Sample Text box near the bottom of the window.

5. **Click and drag on the slider or use the left and right arrow keys to fine-tune the effect.**

6. **When you find the setting that works best on your monitor (or if you just decide to turn the whole thing off by selecting the No Font Smoothing option button), click Close to save your settings.**

Figure 1-11: ClearTweak gives you full control over your ClearType settings and runs rings around anything available from Microsoft.

Showing large fonts

If you use the standard Windows Desktop Theme, you have an easy way to change the size of the fonts that Windows shows. Before you rush to your mouse, though, you should be aware of the limitations:

- ✦ The font size you select applies only to window title bars, labels for icons on the desktop, in Windows Explorer, and in menus. It doesn't change anything else.
- ✦ When you apply a new Desktop Theme (see "Using Desktop Themes" in this chapter), your old font size settings are thrown away.
- ✦ Not all Desktop Themes support multiple font sizes. The only way to know for sure is to try to change the size and see whether it works.

Nope, I don't know how to change the size of the fonts in the Windows Explorer task panes.

To change to larger fonts, follow these steps:

1. **Right-click any blank area on the desktop and click Properties.**
2. **Click the Appearance tab.**
3. **Choose the font size you want in the Font Size drop-down list.**

Using magnification and high contrast

I won't belabor the point here, but two Accessibilities settings can come in handy, even if you don't normally think of Accessibility as a code name for "seeing text on the desktop." The Magnifier puts a magnified strip along the top of the screen, which follows your mouse as you move it. High Contrast uses a modified color scheme to increase legibility of text.

Follow these steps to check out Magnification and High Contrast:

1. **Choose Start⇨Control Panel⇨Accessibility Options.**
2. **To work with High Contrast, choose Adjust the Contrast for Text and Colors on Your Screen under Pick a Task.**
3. **To start the Magnifier, choose Magnifier in the See Also section of the task pane.**

Using Desktop Themes

Windows XP Desktop Themes incorporate many settings in one easy-to-choose package. The themes revolve around specific topics that frequently (and refreshingly) have nothing to do with Windows — say, cars with carapaces, cavorting carnivores, or carnal caruncles. A theme includes six of the seven desktop levels I discuss in this chapter — a base color for the desktop, background, settings for fonts and colors of the working windows, pictures for the reserved Windows icons (Recycle Bin, My Documents, and so on), a set of mouse pointers, and a screen saver. A theme also includes a set of custom sounds that are associated with various Windows events. I've never seen a desktop theme that includes Active Desktop items.

To bring in a new theme, follow these steps:

1. **Right-click any open spot on the desktop and choose Properties.**
2. **Click the Themes tab.**
3. **Choose a theme from the Themes drop-down list.**

REMEMBER

When you bring in a theme, it replaces all seven of the desktop levels I discuss in this chapter, plus the sound scheme you may have had in place. The old background, icon pictures, mouse pointers, and screen savers all remain on your PC — the theme doesn't delete them — but if you want any of them back, you have to go through the customization steps you used earlier to reinstate them.

From time to time, Microsoft releases various packages that include new Windows XP themes. (The various Plus! packs for example, contain lots of themes.) If you want to spend your money that way, by all means help yourself. But be aware of the fact that there are zillions of Windows desktop themes available on the Web, and many of them are quite good. Simply instruct any half-sentient Web search engine to find *Windows desktop theme* or try `www.themeworld.com` for thousands of free themes.

Customizing Folders

In some cases, Windows Explorer lets you change a folder's thumbnail by modifying the picture that's superimposed on a picture of a folder. You may have seen that startling capability if you used Windows Media Player to "rip" a CD — the cover art for the CD probably appeared on the folder that contains the CD. If you ripped more than one album by a single artist, chances are good up to four album covers appear on the folder that contains all of the albums.

Simply follow these steps to change the picture superimposed on a folder:

1. **Start Windows Explorer by choosing Start⇨My Documents; Start⇨My Pictures, My Music, My Computer, or My Network Places; or by running a search by choosing Start⇨Search.**

2. **Navigate to the folder that you want to change.**
3. **Make sure that you're viewing thumbnails by choosing View➪Thumbnails.**

   Superimposed pictures appear only in Thumbnail View.
4. **Right-click on the folder.**
5. **If you want Windows to scan all the picture files inside the folder (including album cover art inside music folders) and place the four most-recently modified pictures on top of the folder, choose Refresh Thumbnail.**
6. **If you want to pick your own picture to superimpose on the folder, choose Properties and click the Customize tab.**

   You see the Properties dialog box shown in Figure 1-12.

   If you can't see the Customize tab, chances are good that you're trying to change the picture on a shortcut folder. Unfortunately, Windows won't let you change the picture superimposed on a shortcut folder.
7. **Click Choose Picture and choose any picture file — it need not be inside the indicated folder.**
8. **Click OK and the chosen picture appears superimposed on the folder while in Windows Explorer.**

   Although Windows can put up to four pictures on top of a folder, you are allowed to put only one on top.

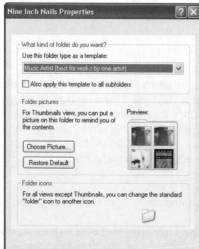

Figure 1-12: Choose the pictures to be superimposed on the folder in this dialog box.

Chapter 2: Organizing Your Windows XP Interface

In This Chapter

- **Harnessing the power of the Windows XP Start menu**
- **Getting at your most recently used documents quickly**
- **Starting your favorite programs with just a click**
- **Making workhorse programs start automatically**

Windows XP contains an enormous variety of self-help tools that can make your working (and playing!) day go faster. As you get more comfortable with the Windows inner world, you will find shortcuts and simplifications that really do make a difference.

This chapter shows you how to take off the training wheels.

Customizing the Start Menu

I gave you a brief overview of the Start menu in Book I, Chapter 2. In this chapter, I take a look at the beast in far greater detail.

Your screen may not look exactly like the one shown in Figure 2-1. If you bought your PC with Windows XP preinstalled, chances are very good that the PC manufacturer stuck some programs on the Start menu that didn't originate with Microsoft. If you want to take control of your Start menu, follow the steps in this chapter to get rid of the stuff you don't want or need. It's your Start menu. You won't break anything. Take the, uh, bull by the horns.

In order to change the Start menu for everyone who uses your computer, you need to be a designated Administrator. Find out more about becoming an Administrator in the section on using account types in Book I, Chapter 2.

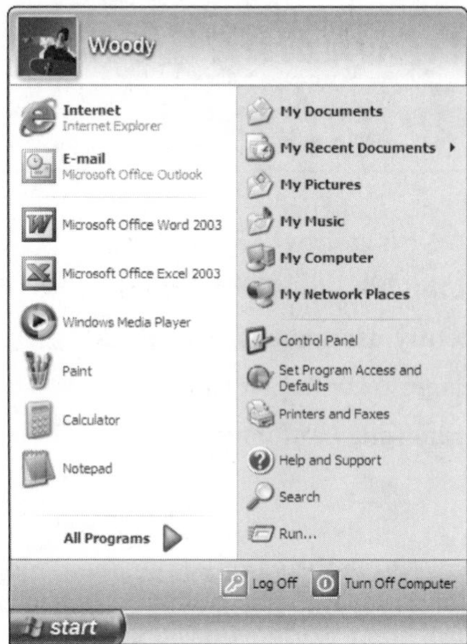

Figure 2-1: Woody's Start menu.

Genesis of the Start menu

Although the Start menu looks like it sprang fully formed from the head of some malevolent Windows god, in fact Windows creates the left side of the Start menu on the fly, every time you click the Start button. That's why your computer takes a little while between the time you click Start and the time you see the Start menu on the screen. Here's where the various pieces come from, looking from top to bottom:

- ✦ The name and picture at the top are taken from the Windows sign on screen. You can change them by following the procedure described in the section on changing user settings in Book I, Chapter 2.
- ✦ You can *pin* a program to the upper-left corner of the Start menu. Once pinned, it stays there until you remove it. Unfortunately, you can't pin a file. I go into details in the section, "Pinning to the Start menu," later in this chapter.
- ✦ The *recently used programs* list maintained by Windows goes in the lower left of the Start menu. Although you have a little bit of control over this list, Windows (or your PC manufacturer) may stack the deck, loading favored programs first, whether you use them or not. Most of the time, you'll probably let Windows take control of the list — after you've figured out how to unstack the deck. I talk about the way Windows maintains this list in the section, "Reclaiming most recently used programs."

✦ Down at the bottom, *All Programs* actually connects to two folders on your hard drive. This is the part of the Start menu that was designed by Microsoft to be easy to modify. You can add fly-out menus and change and delete items to your heart's content — all of which is really pretty easy. I talk about these features in the section, "Changing all programs."

Although you can make many little changes to the items on the right side of the Start menu (see the "Making minor tweaks to the Start menu" section) — and you should definitely spend a few minutes deciding whether any of the changes are worthwhile for you — the one big change on the right side is the inclusion of a Most Recently Used Documents list. Some people love it. Some people hate it. Read the "Showing recent documents" section and decide for yourself.

Pinning to the Start menu

Do you have one or two programs that run your life?

Yeah. Me, too. Word and Outlook. I use them day in and day out. I dream in Word. Sad but true.

Windows XP enables you to easily put programs of your choice way up at the top, in the upper-left corner of the Start menu. That's the high-rent district, the place my mouse gravitates to every time I click Start.

I don't know why, but Microsoft calls this "pinning" — kind of a wimpy name for the most powerful feature on the Start menu, eh? If you have Office on your computer, chances are good that the Office installer pinned Outlook on your Start menu as your e-mail program.

Here's how you pin Word 2002 (the word-processing program from Microsoft Office XP) or Word 2003 (in Office 2003) on your Start menu. The procedure for any other program works similarly:

1. **Both Word and Outlook are on the All Programs menu, so pinning them is easy. Choose Start⇨All Programs; then right-click the program and choose Pin to Start Menu.**

   In Figure 2-2, I'm choosing to pin Word 2003.

   TECHNICAL STUFF

   If the program you want to pin isn't on the Start menu already, you can use Windows Explorer or Search to find it. That isn't as easy as it sounds because many program filenames don't bear much resemblance to the program itself. For example, you can easily find `Outlook.exe`, Outlook's program file, with a standard Windows Search, but you may be hard-pressed to identify `Winword.exe` as the progenitor of Word. You can find many programs by choosing Start⇨My Computer, double-clicking the main hard drive, and digging into the folder called Program Files. After you find the program file, simply right-click it and choose Pin to Start Menu.

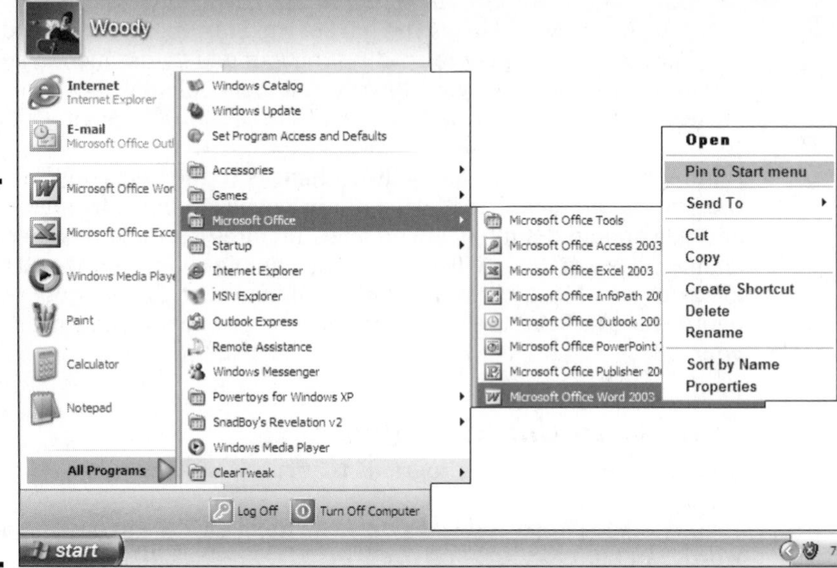

Figure 2-2: Right-click any program, anywhere on the Start menu, and pin it to the upper-left corner, in the high-rent district.

If you pin a program on the Start menu by right-clicking it and choosing Pin to Start Menu, Windows creates a second entry in the Start menu for the pinned copy. Your original — the program you right-clicked — stays where it was.

You can also drag and drop a program from anywhere in Windows onto the pinned list.

When the program gets pinned, it appears at the bottom of the pinned pile — which is to say, below your Web browser and e-mail program. You can click the program and drag it to any other spot in the pinned list that you like.

2. **Right-click the program and click Rename; then give the program a name that you can live with. Figure 2-3 shows Word at the top of the pinned list, with the name Word 2003.**

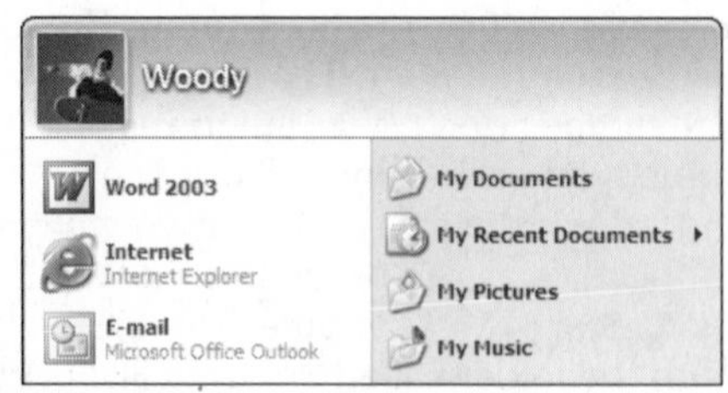

Figure 2-3: Word appears pinned at the top of the list.

If you pin a program on the Start menu by right-clicking it and choosing Pin to Start Menu, both the original Start menu entry and the new pinned entry are linked. If you change the name on one (right-click and click Rename), the other copy is changed as well.

You can remove any program in the pinned part of the Start menu. If you right-click either of the built-in pinned programs (marked Internet and E-mail) and click Remove from This List, the program is removed. If you right-click any other pinned programs (presumably ones that you put up in the high-rent district, or ones that your computer's manufacturer so graciously added to the list), click Unpin from Start Menu and the item goes away.

Note that unpinning a program removes it from only the pinned list in the upper-left corner of the Start menu. The program itself stays right where it is. So do any other shortcuts to the program, whether they're elsewhere on the Start menu or somewhere else in your computer, such as on your desktop. Unpin with impunity, sez I.

You can change the Internet and e-mail programs listed at the beginning of the pinned list if you have more than one Web browser or e-mail program installed. (You probably do because Windows XP installs MSN Explorer for both.) To change the Internet or e-mail program, follow these steps:

1. **Right-click Start and click Properties.**
2. **On the Start Menu tab, make sure that the Start Menu check box is selected, and then click the Customize button.**
3. **At the bottom, choose your favorite Web browser and/or e-mail program from the drop-down lists.**
4. **Click OK twice.**

Reclaiming most recently used programs

Directly above the Start button, in the lower-left corner of the Start menu, you find a list of the programs that you've used most recently. This list is really handy: It is updated dynamically as you use programs, so you always have a very good chance to see the program you need right there on the list.

When you run a program that's pinned to the upper-left corner of the Start menu (see the preceding section), it doesn't count: The most recently used list includes only programs that aren't up at the top of the Start menu.

At least, that's the theory. In fact, the Most Recently Used Programs list — like so many things in Windows XP — does a little bit more (or less?) than first meets the eye. Unless your hardware manufacturer has jiggered things, the first time you start Windows XP, you see these programs in the Most Recently Used area:

- Windows Media Player
- MSN Explorer
- Windows Movie Maker
- Tour Windows XP
- File and Settings Transfer Wizard

That's an extraordinarily weird arrangement of most recently used programs, until you realize that Windows Media Player gives you, uh, lots of opportunities to purchase goodies from Microsoft; the folks in Redmond stand to make a lot of bucks if you sign up for MSN; and the Windows XP Tour and the File and Settings Transfer Wizard greatly reduce the number of calls to Microsoft's Product Support Center. Make sense now?

In fact, the most recently used counter that controls what shows up in the most recently used programs box isn't quite kosher. If you play with the list for a while, you discover that the programs higher up in the list tend to stay on the list longer — whether you've used them or not. So Windows Media Player and MSN Explorer tend to hang around a whole lot longer than the Files and Settings Transfer Wizard (which you would expect), and many programs that you happen to run (which you probably wouldn't expect). I had to run one program a dozen times before it bumped the Media Player off the top of the list.

There's no reason on earth why you should keep Microsoft's advertising (or your PC manufacturer's either, for that matter, if your list varies from the standard one) on your Start menu. Fortunately, you can easily get rid of all the built-in most recently used programs and start out with a clean slate:

1. **Right-click the Start button and click Properties.**
2. **On the Start Menu tab, make sure that the Start Menu check box is selected, and then click the Customize button.**
3. **On the General tab, in the middle of the Customize Start Menu dialog box (see Figure 2-4), click the Clear List button.**
4. **While you're here, consider switching to smaller icons — which puts more programs on the Start menu in a smaller slice of real estate, although they'll be smaller and thus harder to hit with your mouse — and adding to the Number of Programs on the Start menu.**

   The Windows Customize Start Menu dialog box says that you can set the Number of Programs on Start menu (refer to Figure 2-4). That isn't true. In fact, the number shown is actually the number of programs that appear in the most recently used box, in the lower-left corner of the Start menu.
5. **Click OK twice, and your most recently used program list starts to reflect the programs that, uh, you have most recently used.**

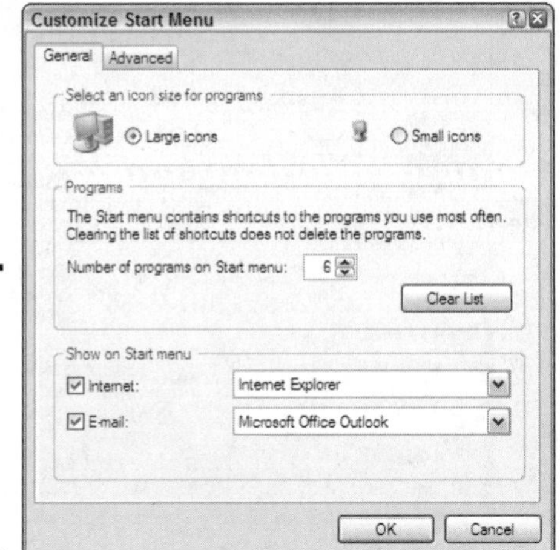

Figure 2-4: Control the most recently used program list from here.

Windows maintains the most recently used program list on its own: You cannot drag and drop items on the list. You can, however, remove programs from the list. Just right-click an offending program, and choose Remove from This List.

Changing all programs

When you choose Start⇨All Programs, Windows assembles the list of "all" programs by combining two separate folders on your hard drive: the Start Menu\Programs folder for you, and the Start Menu\Programs folder for All Users.

The programs that appear above the faint horizontal line on the All Programs menu actually live in the Start Menu folder. Programs below the line come from Start Menu\Programs and folders under there.

If you look at Figure 2-5, you see how the two folders get melded into the All Programs list: The All Users Start Menu\Programs folder is on the top; my Start Menu\Programs folder is on the bottom of Figure 2-5. Folders inside the Start Menu\Programs folders turn into fly-out menus on the All Programs list. Files inside the folders turn into menu entries. If you squint hard enough, you can see how Accessories shows up as a fly-out menu, with (among many others) the Calculator coming from the All Users side, and the Utilities folder coming from the Woody side.

The following rule has no exceptions: Everything on the All Programs menu comes from one or the other of the two Start Menu\Programs folders.

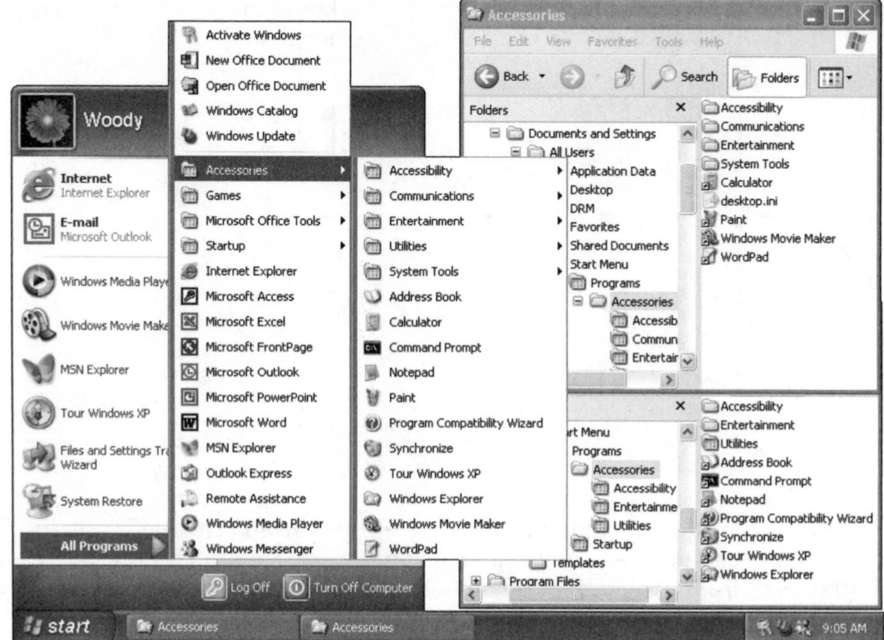

Figure 2-5: The All Programs menu is assembled from the Start Menu\Programs folders for All Users and for the logged-on user.

Because all All Programs programs (say that ten times real fast) come from one of the two folders, you can easily change things around. For example, I've been complaining for years about the way Microsoft Office bullies its way onto the Start⇨All Programs menu. Microsoft finally changed the way Office 2003 behaves, but if you have any earlier version, you see the bullying behavior. Every other set of programs from every other manufacturer has the good sense (and common decency) to install itself farther down on the All Programs line.

Take HP scanner software, for example. To run HP scanner programs, you choose Start⇨All Programs⇨HP ScanJet Software, and then you pick one of the scanner programs. That's great: The programs are grouped together, they're easy to find, and they don't take up a lot of space on the All Programs menu.

Not Office XP, Office 2000, or any earlier version.

If you have Microsoft Office XP installed on your PC, and you choose Start⇨All Programs, you immediately see all of the Office programs. Splat. Even if you use Microsoft Access once every 200 years, it still sits on your All Programs list, taking up space that could be better used by, oh, say EverQuest, Warcraft, or the latest incarnation of Doom. When you toss in New Office Document and Open Office Document — which I, for one, never use — and throw in the Office Tools fly-out menu for good measure, good ol'

Microsoft Office XP (and earlier) takes up nine slots on the main All Programs menu (see Figure 2-6), when it should take one.

Figure 2-6: Microsoft Office, bless its pointed little head, takes up nine slots on the main All Programs menu.

Got Office XP? Time to get out your scalpel and dissect your All Programs menu:

1. **Navigate to the** `C:\Documents and Settings\All Users\Start Menu\Programs` **folder.**

   You can do that by choosing Start⇨My Computer and double-clicking your way down, but a much faster method is to right-click the Start button, choose Explore All Users, and double-click Programs (see Figure 2-7).

   Next you want to create a fly-out menu called, simply, Office. It's easy.

2. **On the right side (which is to say, anywhere but in the task pane), right-click any open spot and choose New⇨Folder. Then type** Office **and press Enter.**

   You now have a new folder called Office, and it shows up on the All Programs menu as an empty fly-out (see Figure 2-8).

3. **Click the Microsoft Access menu line and drag it into the Office fly-out menu — over the text (Empty). Release the mouse button and Microsoft Access moves to the Office fly-out menu.**

4. **One by one, click and drag all the rest of the Office XP programs to the Office fly-out menu.**

Don't forget the New Office Document and Open Office Document entries at the top.

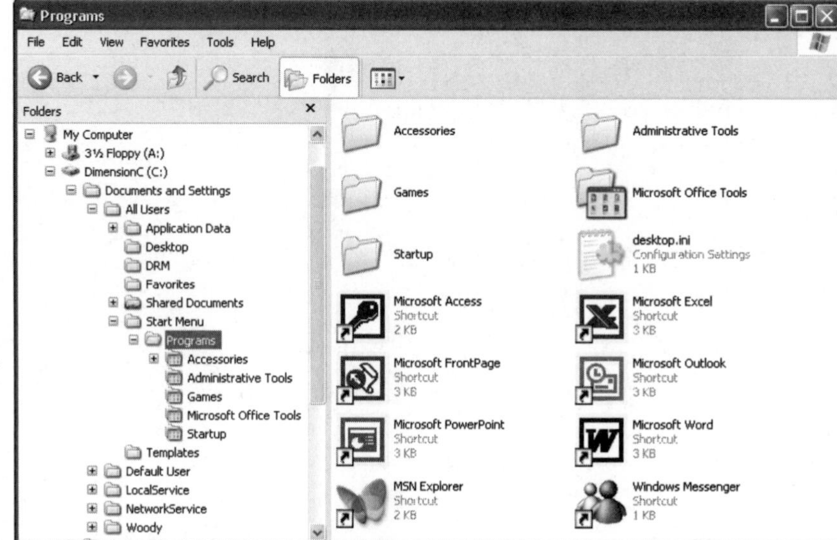

Figure 2-7: The All Programs menu entries.

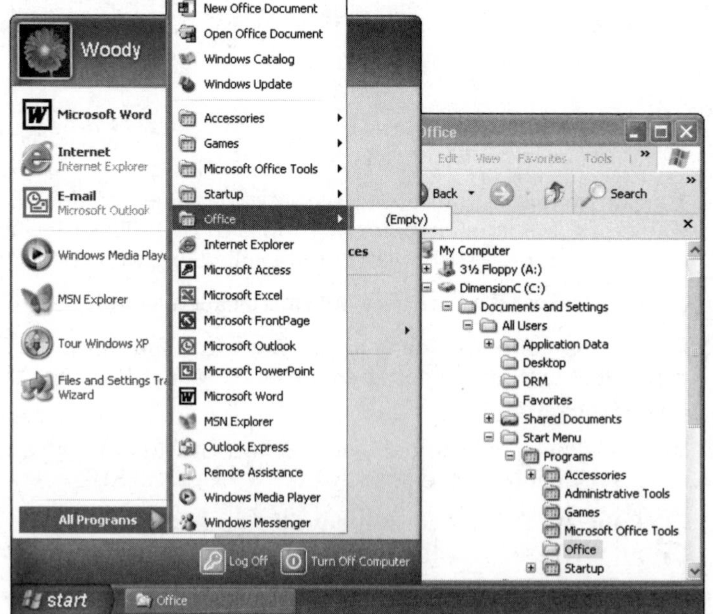

Figure 2-8: The new folder called Office appears as a fly-out on the All Programs menu.

5. Click Microsoft Office Tools and drag the entire fly-out menu over to Office. Release the mouse button and you have put Office in its place (see Figure 2-9).

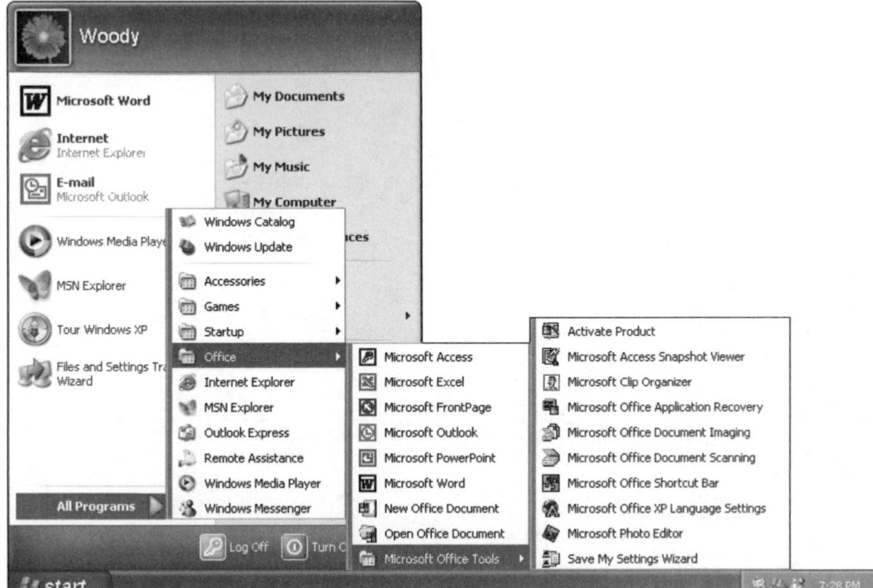

Figure 2-9: Office relegated to its own fly-out menu, where it belongs.

Showing recent documents

Some people love the recent documents feature. Most people hate it. That's why Microsoft turned it off in the final, shipping version of Windows XP/Home. Heaven only knows why it's present in Windows XP/Pro.

In most normal circumstances — with well-behaved programs that don't crash — Windows keeps track of which documents you've opened. You can have Windows show a list of those documents on the Start menu, just under My Documents (see Figure 2-10).

Folks who like the feature appreciate being able to retrieve documents quickly and easily, without spelunking for the program that created them: Click a Word document in the My Recent Documents folder, and Word comes to life, with the document open and ready to rumble.

Folks who hate the feature would just as soon open the application and use the application's most recently opened file list (typically on the File menu) to retrieve their documents. Some of the curmudgeons — present company definitely included — don't particularly want to leave (yet another) record of what they've been doing lying around for prying eyes.

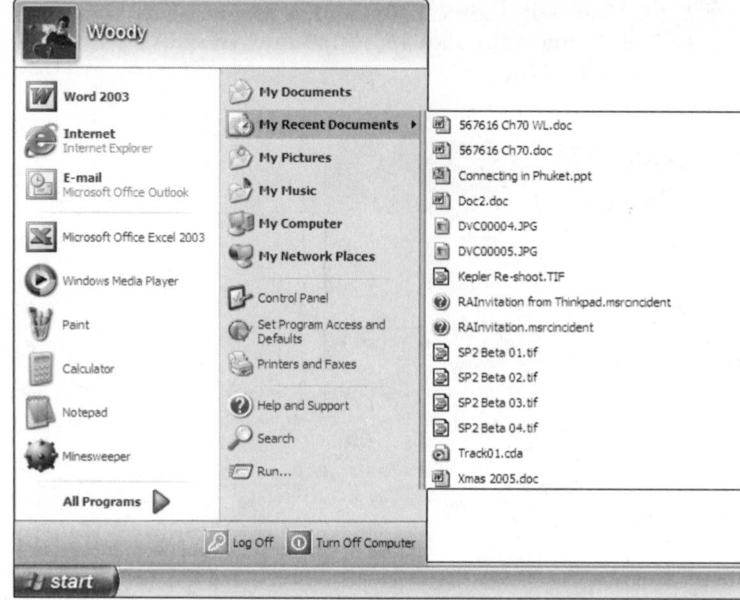

Figure 2-10: The My Recent Documents fly-out menu.

Follow these steps if you want to turn on My Recent Documents:

1. **Right-click Start and click Properties.**
2. **On the Start Menu tab, make sure that the Start Menu check box is selected, and then click the Customize button.**
3. **On the Advanced tab, select the List My Most Recently Opened Documents check box (see Figure 2-11).**

   Note that you can return to this location to clear out the list. But clearing the list here does *not* clear similar lists in your applications, such as Word or Internet Explorer. For those, you have to refer to the application itself.

Making minor tweaks to the Start menu

You can make a number of additional changes to the Start menu. Some of them are actually useful, particularly if you go into your computer fairly frequently to jiggle things. To tweak, follow these steps:

1. **Right-click Start and click Properties.**
2. **On the Start Menu tab, make sure that the Start Menu check box is selected, and then click the Customize button.**
3. **Click the Advanced tab and select the features you want to enable, based on the following list. Click OK twice.**

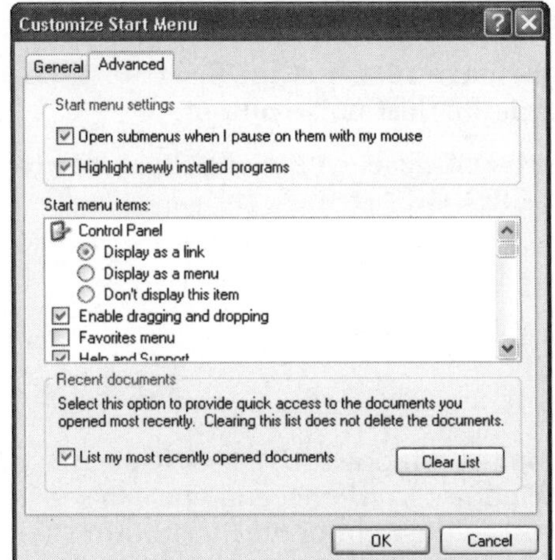

Figure 2-11: Enable My Recent Documents in the Customize Start Menu dialog box.

The following six Start menu items can be turned into fly-out menus:

✦ **Control Panel:** This item can show all of the "classic applets" (read: all of the individual Control Panel applications) in a fly-out. That's the Display As a Menu option in the Start Menu Items list.

✦ **Favorites:** This item creates a menu that can appear above My Computer, with Favorites (primarily from Internet Explorer) listed on a fly-out menu. To show Favorites, select the Favorites check box in the Start Menu Items list.

✦ **My Computer:** This item can have its own fly-out, listing your drives, as well as the Control Panel (which now appears twice on the Start menu), My Documents (again), and Shared Documents. Enable the fly-out by selecting the Display As a Menu option on the Start Menu Items list.

✦ **My Documents, My Music, and My Pictures:** These items can all have their own fly-outs, listing files, and folders in each. Select the Display As a Menu option on the relevant Start Menu Items list.

If you're an inveterate twiddler (or twiddler in training), in the Start Menu Items list, select the System Administrative Tools/Display on the All Programs Menu check box. The programs there will keep you occupied for years.

Do you install new programs rather frequently? Do you get really tired of Windows popping up its little yellow boxes, informing you that you've just installed a new program, when you know darn good and well that you just installed a new program? Here's a way to turn it off:

1. **Right-click Start and click Properties.**
2. **On the Start Menu tab, make sure that the Start Menu check box is selected, and then click the Customize button.**
3. **Click the Advanced tab and deselect the Highlight Newly Installed Programs check box. Click OK twice.**

I call it the D'OH switch.

Quick Launch Toolbar

Windows XP/Home turns on the Windows XP Quick Launch Toolbar automatically. If you're using Windows XP/Home, and you can see your Quick Launch Toolbar immediately to the right of the Start button, you can skip the following section on "Activating" and jump directly to the "Customizing" section.

Activating

Windows XP's Quick Launch Toolbar is a little tray of icons that sits next to the Start button, where you can stick shortcuts to start all of your favorite programs (see Figure 2-12). It's one of the handiest features in Windows — and if you are running Windows XP/Pro, you may not even know that it exists.

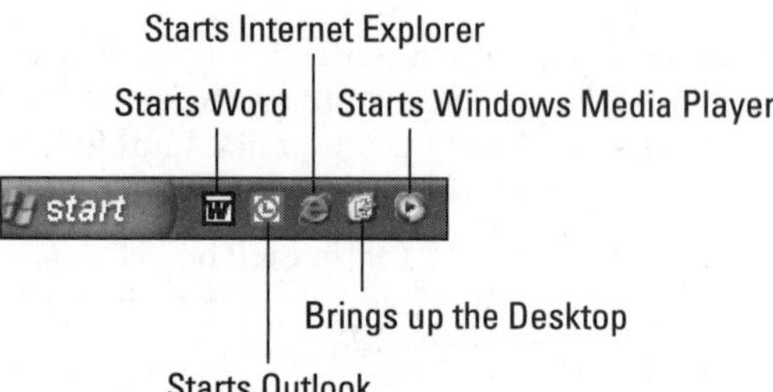

Figure 2-12: The Quick Launch Toolbar I use every day.

To start the Quick Launch Toolbar, right-click any open spot down on the Windows taskbar, and choose Toolbars⇨Quick Launch. That's all there is to it. Your initial Quick Launch Toolbar includes icons for Internet Explorer, the desktop, and the Windows Media Player.

Customizing

Adding your own icons to the Quick Launch Toolbar is very simple, too, but you immediately run into problems trying to squeeze more icons into that teensy-tiny space. Here's how to avoid the problem in the first place:

1. **Make sure the Quick Launch Toolbar is showing (right-click any open spot down on the Windows taskbar and choose Toolbars➪Quick Launch).**
2. **Unlock the taskbar so that you can increase the size of the Quick Launch Toolbar.**

   To do so, right-click any open spot on the Windows taskbar, and click the line marked Lock the Taskbar to remove the check mark.

   Windows shows two small drag handles, one to the left and one to the right of the Quick Launch Toolbar.
3. **Grab the drag handle on the right and stretch it out (to the right) a bit.**
4. **Find a program that you want to put in the Quick Launch Toolbar.**

   For example, if you have Microsoft Office installed and you want to put Word down there, choose Start➪All Programs, and look for Microsoft Word.
5. **Right-click the program, and drag it down to the Quick Launch Toolbar.**

   You see a big, black I-Beam in the Quick Launch Toolbar that indicates where the icon will go. When you release the icon, choose Copy Here.

   When you drag icons to the Quick Launch Toolbar, right-click and choose Copy Here, so that the original program shortcut stays intact. If you left-click (or right-click and choose Move Here), the shortcut gets moved.
6. **Drag as many icons to the Quick Launch Toolbar as you like. When you're done, butt the right drag handle up against the rightmost icon, and then right-click the Windows taskbar and choose Lock the Taskbar.**

You have more "play" with the Quick Launch Toolbar's resizing drag handles than you think. Try squishing the Quick Launch Toolbar by setting the right drag handle on top of the rightmost icon, and then lock the taskbar. When you choose Lock the Taskbar, chances are good that all of the icons appear anyway. It never hurts to tighten things up a bit, so Windows can use as much of the taskbar as possible.

Custom Startup

Do you start a specific program just about every time you crank up Windows? Maybe you want to get the Windows Media Player going every time Windows wakes up. A friend of mine always starts the Windows Calculator. Of course, he's a hopeless drudge, so don't let him influence you.

You can easily tell Windows XP that you want to run a specific program every time Windows starts. You just have to put the program in the \Startup folder.

Say you want to start the Windows Calculator every time anybody logs on to Windows. You can make that happen if you put a shortcut to the Calculator into the All Users \Startup folder, like this:

1. **Right-click the Start button and choose Explore All Users.**
2. **Double-click your way down to the** `C:\Documents and Settings\All Users\Start Menu\Programs\Startup` **folder.**
3. **Go back to the Start button, and choose Start⇨All Programs⇨Accessories.**
4. **Right-click the Calculator, and drag it to the \Startup folder. When you release the Calculator, click Copy Here.**

   You see a shortcut to the Calculator go into the \Startup folder (see Figure 2-13).

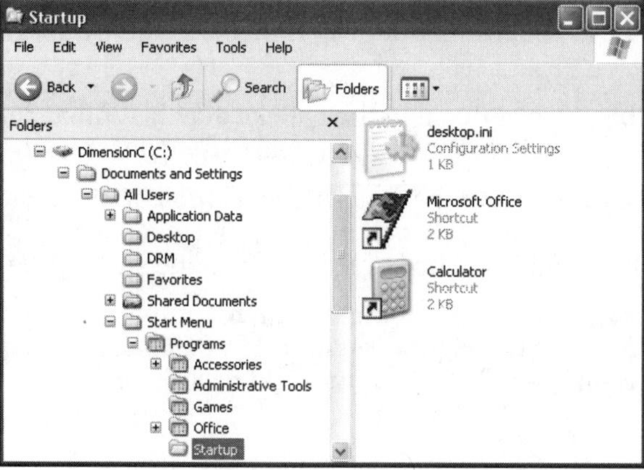

Figure 2-13: Put a shortcut to the Calculator in the \Startup folder, and it starts every time Windows does.

You're done. The next time anyone logs on to Windows, the Calculator will start.

If you want the Calculator to start for just one user, you need to put a shortcut to the calculator in that user's \Startup folder. The easy way: Have that user log on, right-click the Start button and click Explore. Then follow Steps 2 through 4 in the preceding list.

Chapter 3: Lock Down: Spies, Spams, Scams, and Slams

In This Chapter

- **Taking responsibility for your computer's security — proactively**
- **Discovering how and why you're vulnerable**
- **Avoiding the best-engineered traps: spyware, adware, and phishing trips**
- **Reducing your exposure to spam**
- **Using Windows' tools effectively**

The original version of Windows XP had more holes than a prairie dog field.

The current version of Windows XP ain't much better.

Windows XP isn't any more or less secure than any other operating system. (In fact, when it comes to security, all of them are prairie dog fields.) When Microsoft points out that Linux has more publicized security holes than Windows, it reminds me of the pot calling the kettle black. Windows owes its dubious distinction as the most penetrated program in history to one simple fact: It's a big, fat target.

The settings in Windows XP focus on keeping the software itself intact: Firewalls, automatic updates, and virus protection — the Windows Security Holy Trinity — are all meant to keep the bad guys out of your computer. But security goes deeper than that. Much deeper.

In this chapter, I take you through a brief overview of the Windows Security Center — more details follow in the next few chapters — but I also want to take you outside of the box, to see the kinds of problems we all face with our computer systems, and to look at a few key solutions.

Working the Security Center

If you go out looking for it, Windows XP's Security Center sits buried in an obscure corner of the Windows infrastructure: Choose Start➪All Programs➪Accessories➪System Tools➪Security Center. The Security Center itself, shown in Figure 3-1, consolidates a wide range of settings from many different parts of Windows — indeed, from places outside of Windows — all in one place:

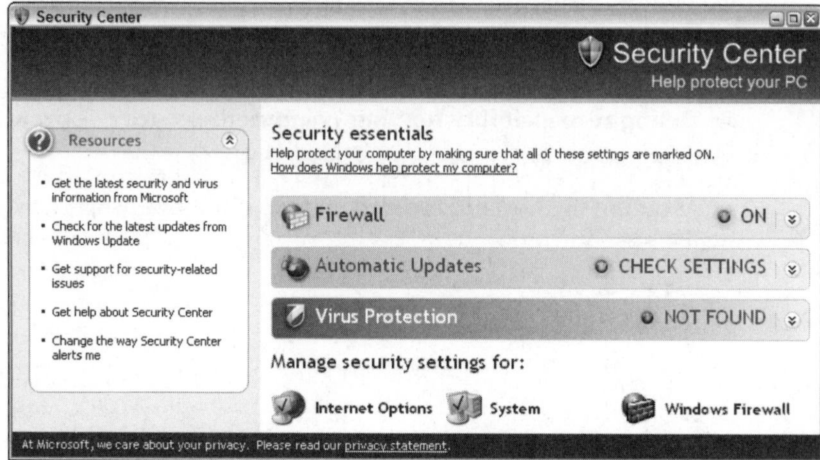

Figure 3-1: The Windows Security Center makes changing some security settings easy — but it's far from exhaustive.

* **Windows Firewall:** Blocks access to your computer from the Internet. I talk about Windows Firewall at length in Book II, Chapter 4.

A *firewall* is a program that insulates your PC (or network) from the Internet. At its heart, the firewall keeps track of requests that originate on your PC or network. When data from the Internet tries to make its way into your PC or network, the firewall checks to make sure that one of your programs requested the data. Unsolicited data gets dropped. Requested data comes through. That way, rogues on the Internet can't break in.

* **Automatic Updates:** Allows Windows to phone home and check for patches and patches to patches of patches. If you trust Microsoft (heh heh heh), you can even allow Windows to patch itself. Kinda like getting a license for self-administered lobotomies. See Book II, Chapter 5 for more about Automatic Updates.
* **Virus Protection:** Is supposed to look at your machine and see if you have a functional AV (antivirus) program, such as Norton AntiVirus. Unfortunately, it doesn't work all the time — and it doesn't prompt you to update the AV program religiously. You have to rely on the antivirus vendor for that. See Book II, Chapter 6 for more about virus protection.

All three of these functions focus on preventing attacks from outside — a noble goal, to be sure, but that's only part of the problem. In fact, the greatest danger comes from people who do something stupid and shoot themselves in the foot. And therein lies a story.

Understanding the Hazards

Not long ago, most PC viruses planted themselves on diskettes. People spread infections by passing around infected diskettes. Machines got infected when they started — booted — with infected diskettes in the drive. Infected machines subsequently put copies of the virus on every diskette that had the misfortune of being stuck in the PC's diskette drive. Although they had a bit of competition from other types of viruses, so-called Master Boot Record viruses ruled the PC roost for several years. The most famous — er, infamous — boot record virus, Michelangelo, received an enormous amount of media publicity in early 1992. If you were around at the time, you recall that Michelangelo fell flat on its face, putting egg on the face of more than a few self-appointed "experts" who predicted the Demise of Computing as We Know It.

You'll find that's a recurring theme.

One day in the summer of 1995, somebody wrote a little virus using WordBasic, the macro programming language that came embedded within Microsoft Word. The virus didn't work very well (see Figure 3-2). Matter of fact, it's a wonder it worked at all. But by the end of August 1995, a very large percentage of all the PCs on Microsoft's Redmond campus were infected with the Winword.Concept.A virus. Microsoft called it a "prank macro" at the time and downplayed its significance. Boy howdy, what a prank!

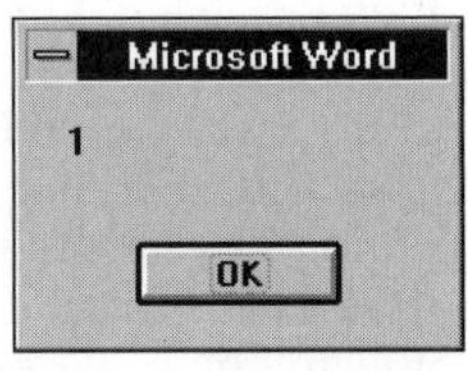

Figure 3-2: The Concept.A virus didn't do much more than show this uninspiring dialog box.

Winword.Concept.A spawned an entire industry. Two of them, in fact: the virus writers (whom I generally call "the guys in black hats" or, equivalently, "cretins"), and the antivirus software folks ("the guys in white hats"). Many of the best-known Internet-borne scares of today — the Bagles, the Netskys, the Melissas, the ILOVEYOUs, and their ilk — work by using the programmability built into the computer application itself, just like good ol' Concept.A.

The other big bunch of infectious baddies work all by themselves, with little or no user intervention required. Blaster and Slammer, for example, look for systems they can infect by scanning PCs connected to the Internet, checking for open doors (called "ports"). If you leave a door ajar, the program injects itself into your system, and then looks out on the Internet and tries to spread again. Sounds like the plot to a *Star Trek* episode, eh?

Infection only amounts to part of the story — quite possibly the most tractable part. Some harmful programs search for e-mail addresses and send them to spammers by the bit bucket full. Others watch as you type and shoot logs of your keystrokes to people who would love to know your bank account password. And then there's the phishing trips, where clever pieces of mail try to convince you to go to fake Web sites and enter confidential information.

Windows XP includes some very heavy-duty tools for protecting your PC and your network. It also includes some very heavy-duty capabilities — particularly related to networking — that make it all the more imperative that you protect yourself and the other people on your network.

We've come a long way, baby.

Dealing with Direct Attacks

I hear it every day. "Man, I just got hit with another virus. Had to scan all of my computers. It knocked me out for a week."

Viruses and worms *do* come looking for you. If you're using Windows XP and Office XP or Office 2003, you're a prime target — you and about 200 million other people have "Kick Me" signs hung out on the Information Highway. The trick is to put up enough barriers so the bad guys and their diabolical software go looking somewhere else. No self-respecting 18-year-old virus writer is going to bother with your system if it takes just a little bit of extra effort to crack. Why go to the trouble, when there are 200 million other systems waiting to get zapped?

Identifying types of attacks

People in the press tend to call every kind of software with malicious intent a *virus*. That's a bit like calling every TV personality Sam Donaldson. (No, Sam, I'm not making jokes about your hair again. Honest.)

In fact, there are many different kinds of bad software — *malware,* if you will — and no two antivirus experts agree completely on definitions. In general, and very loosely, the following definitions apply:

- **Virus:** A program that replicates itself. Usually it accomplishes its act of procreation by attaching itself onto another file, such as a Word document or Excel spreadsheet. The virus usually comes to life when the file is opened or run in some way. Viruses have a reputation for being destructive, but in fact very few viruses survive "in the wild" for any time at all, and not all of the ones that manage to keep themselves going have destructive payloads.
- **Worm:** A program that replicates itself like a virus, but it doesn't use another file as an intermediary: In effect, they're viruses that stand alone. Worms push themselves from PC to PC, almost always over a network. Bagle (see Figure 3-3) and Netsky are two well-known worms that can travel as programs attached to e-mail messages. Blaster and Sasser are worms that don't need e-mail: They go directly from jugular to jug . . . er, from machine to machine. Because they aren't held back by the need to be attached to a file, worms tend to travel much faster than viruses.

Figure 3-3: If you run a Bagle-infected attachment, you get this bogus message.

- **Trojan (or Trojan horse):** Like its namesake, a *Trojan* looks like a benign program that you want to run, but ends up doing something you don't expect. For example, a friend may send you a program that shows a fireworks display, without realizing that the same program is jiggering some of your Windows settings. Trojans don't replicate. That's the primary distinction between a Trojan and a worm or virus.
- **Blended Threat:** Increasingly, the bad programs that pose the biggest problems combine a multitude of infection paths (called *vectors,* just as biological viruses travel along vectors) with multiple infection methods: a *blended threat.* These suckers can spread their infections through shared hard drives on a home network, over the Internet to unprotected PCs via e-mail attachments, and through your child's report card. Okay, I'm exaggerating a little bit about the report card.

What's a buffer overflow?

If you've been following the progress of malware in general, and the beatings delivered to Windows XP in particular, you've no doubt run across the phrase *buffer overflow* or *buffer overrun* — a favorite tool in the arsenal of many virus writers. It may sound mysterious, but at its heart a buffer overflow is quite simple.

Programmers set aside small areas in their programs to transfer data from one program to another. Those places are called buffers. A problem arises when too much data gets put in a buffer (or, if you look at it from the other direction, when the buffer is too small to hold all the data that's being put in it). You might think that having ten pounds of offal in a five-pound bag would make the program scream bloody murder, but many programs aren't smart enough to look, much less cry uncle and give up.

When there's too much data in the buffer, some of it can spill out into the program itself. If the cretin who's stuffing too much data into the buffer is very clever, he/she/it may be able to convince the program that the extra data isn't data at all but, instead, is another part of the program, waiting to be run. The worm sticks a lot of data in a small space, and makes sure that the piece that flops out will perform whatever malicious deed the worm's creator wants. When the offal hits the fan, the program finds itself executing data that was stuffed into the buffer — running a program that was written by the worm's creator. That's how a buffer overrun can take control of your computer.

Every worm that uses a buffer overrun security hole in Windows takes advantage of a stupid programming error inside Windows. Programs inside Windows should be checking their buffers all the time. Sorry, Microsoft, but that's a stone cold fact, even if it means that Windows runs slower.

As far as I'm concerned, you can call a Trojan a virus, you can call a virus a worm, and you can call a worm a three-toed tree sloth. You can even call me late for dinner. But please, please, please don't call any of these ornery critters *bugs.* They aren't bugs. A *bug* is a mistake in a program. Many viruses and worms have bugs — the cretins who write them aren't always the brightest lights on the tree, know what I mean? — but that doesn't mean that they *are* bugs. Got it?

Rather than splitting hairs about whether a particular piece of malware is really a virus or a worm, I think it's more important for you to understand how malicious software can attack you and your system:

- Old-fashioned viruses still make the rounds attached to Word documents, Excel spreadsheets, even PowerPoint presentations and Adobe Acrobat documents. The virus typically starts spreading when you open an infected file.
- Destructive software often arrives in the form of a file attached to an e-mail message. You open the file and the malware kicks in, sending out

hundreds of messages with infected attachments to people in your e-mail contacts list and burying some sort of payload that will hurt you at some point in the future.

You don't stand a snowball's chance of protecting yourself from bad e-mail file attachments if Windows XP hides filename extensions from you. Those three little letters at the end of a filename, after the period, make all the difference. Read and follow the advice on showing filename extensions in Book I, Chapter 3.

- More and more cretins are finding ways to put bad programs inside Web pages and formatted e-mail messages. Once upon a time, conventional wisdom had it that merely looking at a Web page or viewing (or previewing) a formatted e-mail message couldn't get you infected. Conventional wisdom has been knocked down a notch or two.
- Direct network infectors are getting more sophisticated. If one PC on your Windows XP network gets infected, these bloodthirsty worms reach out to all the PCs on the network to infect them, too. Protection against malware is a group effort. Everybody on your network has to be careful.
- Your Windows XP machine can be turned into a zombie. That sounds like voodoo, I know, but it's true. The basic idea is pretty simple: People (actually, their automated henchmen) roam the Internet, looking for PCs that are easy to break into. When they find a PC with its front door unlocked, they stick a program on the PC and then move on without leaving much of a trace. At the appointed hour, all of the PCs — hundreds or even thousands of them with their zombifying programs — start bombarding a single Web site. The Web site can't handle all the traffic, and it's brought to its knees. The process is called a *Distributed Denial of Service*, or DDoS, attack.

Blaster is a prime example of a worm that set up a DDoS attack — and it struck out against Microsoft's Windows Update site. Microsoft didn't like that. Many people believe that the massive security upgrade to Windows XP known as Service Pack 2 was a direct result of the Blaster worm.

- Of course, if your front door is unlocked, DDoS may be the least of your worries. Anybody smart enough to turn your PC into a zombie can figure out how to wreak havoc on you, directly.

If you are using a dial-up Internet account, your exposure to the last two types of attacks — zombie and simple break-in — is minimal: Every time you dial into your Internet Service Provider, you get a different address, so would-be attackers won't be able to track you for very long. But if you have a persistent Internet connection — DSL or cable modem — the latter two types of attacks present a very real threat.

Where do worms hide?

Blended threat worms can transmit themselves in a number of ways, but individual computer users like you and me usually come face to face with the snarly little guys most frequently when they arrive attached to e-mail messages, or when they get deposited on our machines via a file sharing program. In order for the worm to propagate, somebody somehow has to open the infected file or run the program.

E-mail programs like Outlook and Outlook Express are generally set up to block certain kinds of files that are attached to incoming messages: Basically, the file gets stored away on your computer, but the program makes it almost impossible to even see the file, much less open it or run it. The latest version of Outlook blocks dozens and dozens of different kinds of files, based on the filename extension: Outlook won't show you a file attached to an e-mail message if the filename extension is EXE or BAT or COM or SCR — or any of a couple dozen others (see Book I, Chapter 3).

On the other hand, Outlook and Outlook Express allow ZIP files to pass through with glee. The cretins who write worms discovered that sending a destructive program — say, an EXE file — attached to an e-mail message isn't very effective anymore: Even if the recipient was running an older version of Outlook, or some other mail program that doesn't block attachments, most users' antivirus programs would set off alarms like crazy if an EXE came in on the back of a message. The percentage of people who clicked and let the worms procreate decreased dramatically, and the worm died on the vine. As it were.

So the cretins got smarter. Instead of attaching an EXE file to their infected messages, they would compress the file, and send the ZIP. Lo and behold, the Outlooks and the antivirus programs weren't smart enough to find the infected EXE inside the ZIP, and millions of hapless Windows users simply double-clicked the ZIP file to open it, and then clicked the EXE file inside to run it. Ka-boom.

So the antivirus software companies got smarter, and started scanning inside ZIP files to see if ZIP files attached to messages contained bad programs. The antivirus software started working again, alarms started going off again, and the worm-writing cretins went back to the drawing board.

Next, the cretins discovered that they could create ZIP files with passwords, and the password protection would disguise the infected program. They sent messages to people with infected attachments, and the password was included as text in the message itself. Lots of people thought they were getting secret files. They double-clicked the ZIP, entered the password in the message to unlock the ZIP, and then double-clicked the file inside the ZIP . . . and got zapped. That worked for a while — until the antivirus software companies figured out that they could scan the message, pick up the password, and then use the password to scan the protected ZIP files for bad programs.

Back to the drawing board once again, the malware writers discovered that they could ZIP their evil programs, use a password, and put the password in the message itself — but this time, they turned the password into a picture. A hapless soul looking at the message can read the password, no sweat. But the antivirus software scanners can't — the AV companies don't have programs sophisticated enough to look at a picture and extract the password. The cretins win again.

Protecting against attacks

With all the threats floating around, you may be tempted to toss Windows XP in the trash. All that great networking and Internet connectivity comes at a price, eh?

Nawwww. Yes, you need to be cautious. No, you don't need to throw the baby out with the XP bathwater. Here's a very short checklist of all the protection that you really require:

- Buy, install, update, and religiously use one of the major antivirus software packages. It doesn't matter which one — they all work well. As long as you update the signature files regularly by connecting to the manufacturer's Web site, and you use the product precisely the way the manufacturer recommends, you'll be protected from most nasties.

  You may think that antivirus packages target viruses, viruses, viruses, and that's the extent of it. Not so. All of the major antivirus packages these days protect against many different kinds of malware, from traditional viruses (and worms and Trojans) to bad Web pages (see Figure 3-4) to infected e-mail message attachments.

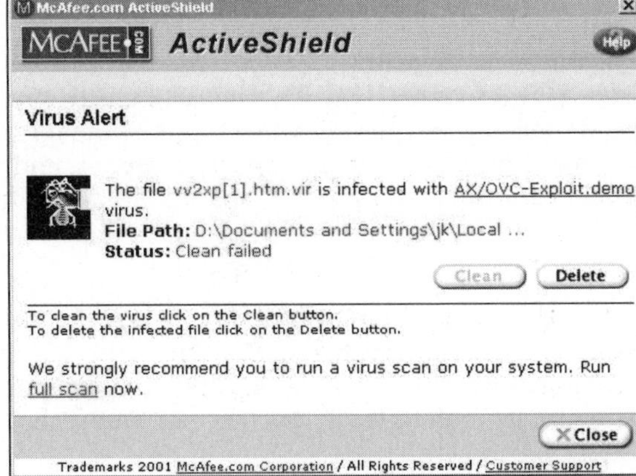

Figure 3-4: McAfee ActiveShield hiccups on a Web page that harbors a malicious program.

- Don't open files attached to e-mail messages until you do the following:
  - Contact the person who sent you the file and verify that he did, indeed, mean to send you the file.
  - After you verify that the sender actually sent the file, save the file on your hard drive and run your antivirus software on it to make absolutely certain that it passes muster.

Open the file only after you've jumped through both of those hoops.

- Update Windows XP regularly, but cautiously. See Book II, Chapter 5 for more information.
- Run a good firewall — Windows XP's Firewall will work fine — on any PC that's directly connected to the Internet.

If one of your PCs uses Internet Connection Sharing, make sure that it's using the Windows Firewall. If any other PC connects directly to the Internet — perhaps you have a portable that usually gets to the Internet via your Windows XP network using Internet Connection Sharing, but occasionally uses a dial-up connection — make sure that connection gets protected by Windows Firewall as well.

Recovering from an attack

Every day I get e-mail messages from people who are convinced that their PC has been clobbered by a virus. Most of the time the problems have nothing to do with viruses — intermittently bad hardware, an aberrant program, maybe a flaky Internet connection can cause all sorts of grief, and malware has nothing to do with it.

If you think a virus or worm has hit you, you should do three things immediately. Actually, this is one thing you *shouldn't* do, and two things you should do:

- **DON'T REBOOT YOUR COMPUTER.** This is particularly important advice with Windows XP because of the way it takes snapshots of "last known good" system configurations. If you get infected, reboot, and Windows XP mistakenly thinks your infected system is "good," it may update the "last known good" configuration information incorrectly. Resist the urge to hit the Reset button until you exhaust all possibilities.
- **Follow your antivirus software manufacturer's instructions.** If you threw away your copy of the manual, beg, borrow, or steal another PC and log onto the manufacturer's Web site. All the major antivirus software manufacturers have detailed steps on their Web sites to take you through the scary parts.
- **If you aren't running antivirus software, kick yourself.** No, kick yourself twice. Then pick one of the major antivirus software sites (such as McAfee at `www.mcafee.com` or Norton at `www.symantec.com/avcenter`) and follow the instructions there to download a demo version of their software.

The days of self-diagnosing and manually removing viruses and other malware have long past. Nowadays that's akin to do-it-yourself brain surgery. Rely on the professionals. Get help.

Keeping Spies and Ads at Bay

Viruses and worms can bring your system or your network to its knees.

By contrast, spyware and adware live like parasites inside your computer. *Spyware* sends information about your activities to unscrupulous companies, frequently without your knowledge. *Adware* bombards you with advertising that just won't let go. If you've ever had your Internet Explorer home page — the place IE goes when it starts — hijacked, you've been the victim of a specific type of adware called a *homepage hijacker*.

The terms "spyware" and "adware" have taken on more-or-less legal definitions. At least one company has been sued for using the term "spyware" to describe the offerings from a truly offensive software vendor. (See the notice from my good friend Dave Methvin at www.pcpitstop.com/dmvision.asp.) For that reason, I use the term *slimeware* — slime being in the eye of the beholder — to refer to sleazy programs that either phone home with information about your behavior or keep offering you garbage that you obviously don't want. For example, to me, Microsoft's spy-by-default Windows Media Player 8 rates as slimeware. You can make up your own mind.

Almost always, slimeware doesn't install itself. It comes along for the ride when you install a program that you think you want. Usually, you're advised of the presence of slimeware before you install it — buried somewhere on line 396 of a 527-line End User License Agreement.

Every Windows XP user should

- **Avoid installing programs that are notorious for including spyware and adware.** There's an abbreviated list of the worst offenders (and alternative programs that aren't slime-laden) at www.safer-networking.org/index.php?page=articles&detail=infected_and_clean.
- **Just say NO when a Web site asks you to install a program.** Unless you really need the program, you understand what it does, and you trust the Web site that's offering to put it on your computer, move on and don't look back.
- **Run a Registry Blocker/StartupMonitor.** Many programs — good, bad, slimy, and indifferent — stick themselves in the Windows Registry or in the Windows Startup folder so they run automatically when you restart your machine. There's a nifty, tiny program from MIT student Mike Lin that keeps watch over the appropriate parts of the Registry and Startup folder and warns you when a program tries to set itself to run automatically. Download StartupMonitor from www.mlin.net/StartupMonitor.shtml, install it, and keep track of programs that try to let

themselves in by the back door, as shown in Figure 3-5. If you click No when confronted with a Startup Blocker dialog box like the one shown in Figure 3-5, you'll take a giant step toward avoiding spyware, adware, and other kinds of slime.

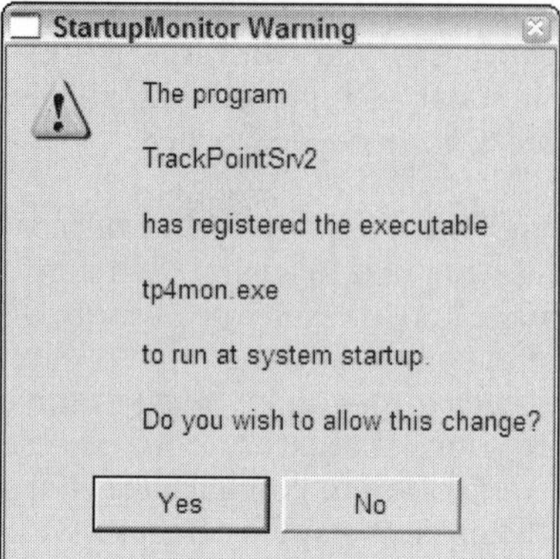

StartupMonitor Warning
The program
TrackPointSrv2
has registered the executable
tp4mon.exe
to run at system startup.
Do you wish to allow this change?
Yes
No

Figure 3-5: Startup Blocker lets you know if a program is trying to set itself up to run automatically every time you start Windows.

- **Download, install, update, and periodically run both Ad-Aware and Spybot Search & Destroy (see the following).** Both products are free for personal use, and each can detect and remove slimeware that the other one misses. Best to use both.

PCPitStop (`www.pcpitstop.com/pcpitstop/default.asp`) is an excellent source of spyware information. It also has a free scanner that runs over the Internet. Well worth checking.

I recommend that you install Ad-Aware first, and then Spybot S&D. The Spybot installer detects the presence of Ad-Aware, and warns you that Ad-Aware can find slimeware that's been "quarantined" by Spybot.

Ad-Aware, from Lavasoft in Sweden, picks up the vast majority of adware and spyware programs and, with your permission, zaps the offensive critters. It's one of the most frequently downloaded programs on the Internet, with 40 million copies downloaded as of this writing. To get the free version of Ad-Aware — which can be a bit hard to find — go to the Lavasoft Web site `www.lavasoft.de`, and on the left, click the line that says Ad-aware (see Figure 3-6). From that point, click the Download.com picture, and download the installation file (which is probably called `aaw6181.exe`, or something similar). When the file's downloaded, click Open and the installer will put Ad-Aware on your computer.

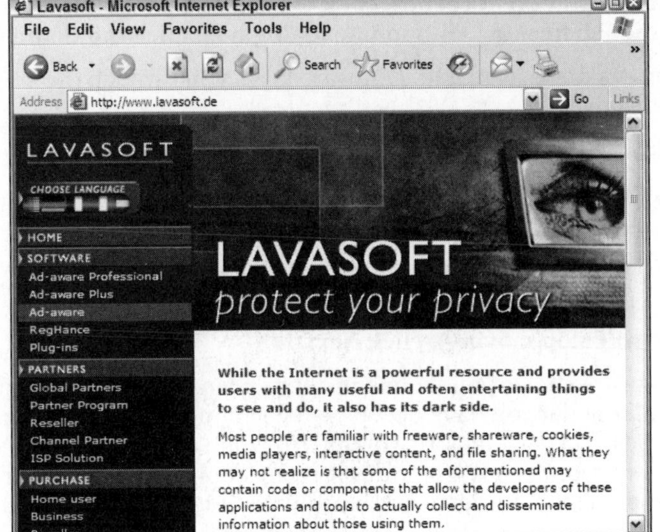

Figure 3-6: Finding the free version of Ad-Aware can be a bit difficult.

Personally, I run Ad-Aware every week. Here's the smart way to do it:

1. **Make sure you're connected to the Internet.**

   You should always update Ad-Aware to the most recent version before you run it, and you have to be connected to the Internet in order to get the update.

2. **Choose Start➪All Programs➪Lavasoft Ad-Aware➪Ad-Aware.**

   You see the Ad-Aware Status screen, shown in Figure 3-7.

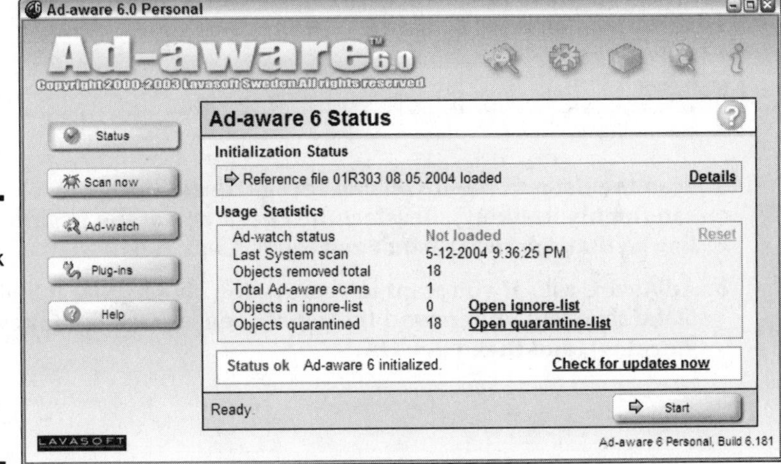

Figure 3-7: Always click the Check for Updates Now link prior to running Ad-Aware.

3. **In the lower-right corner, click the Check For Updates Now link. Then, in the Performing Webupdate dialog box, click the Connect button.**

   If an update is available, Ad-Aware takes you through the steps necessary to install it.

4. **Click OK, and then click Finish to return to the Status screen.**

5. **On the left, click the Scan Now button. Choose Perform Smart System-Scan, and then click Next.**

   Go out for a latte. This can take a long, long time.

6. **When the scan is done (you'll hear a funny sound and the progress bar will stop moving), click Next.**

   Ad-Aware shows you the results of its scan, as shown in Figure 3-8. Don't be alarmed if you have dozens — even hundreds, or thousands — of entries. The vast majority of the problems Ad-Aware encounters are minor irritants, not major disasters — cookies used to track your Web surfing habits, Registry entries that don't look kosher, and the like.

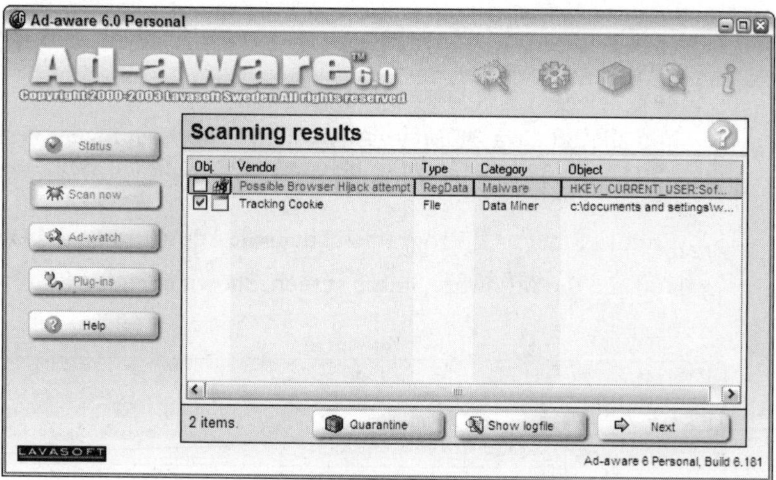

Figure 3-8: Ad-Aware detected that I set up Internet Explorer to start with a blank page and flagged that as a Possible Browser Hijack Attempt. Urp.

7. **Scan the list and see if you can recognize anything that's okay. If you can (highly unlikely), deselect the check box at the beginning of the line so that Ad-Aware won't zap it out. Click Next.**

8. **Ad-Aware asks if you want to remove the objects that it has identified. Make sure you understand the consequences (see the following Warning), and then click OK.**

Some programs, and I won't mention Kazaa by name, will die if you remove the slimeware that's built into the program. (That should tell you something about how completely Kazaa has sold out to the slime-meisters.) If you tell Ad-Aware to get rid of the infuriating scum that comes with recent versions of the file-and-music sharing program Kazaa, you won't be able to run Kazaa again. Good riddance, as far as I'm concerned, but your opinion may vary.

9. **Click the X button in the upper-right corner to close Ad-Aware.**

Spybot S&D works similarly. Download your free copy from `www.safer-networking.org`, and then run the installer (which is probably called `spybotsd12.exe` or something similar.

Every time you run Spybot S&D, avoid the temptation to start the scan immediately. Instead, click the Online button on the left (see Figure 3-9), and then click Search For Updates and install the latest version of the software.

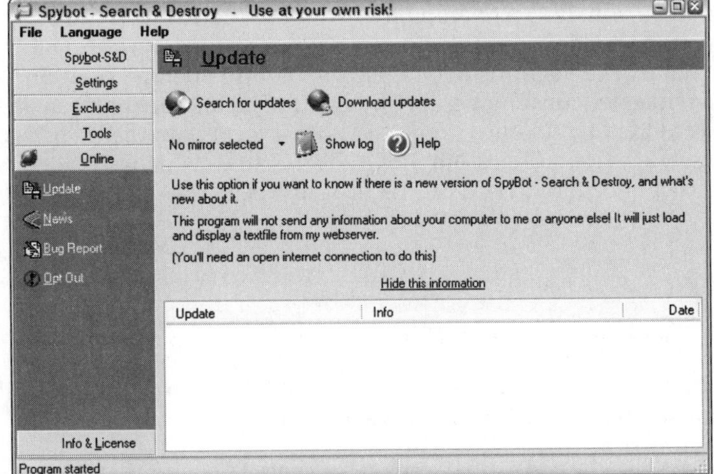

Figure 3-9: Make sure you update Spybot S&D before running it.

After you know you have the latest version, click the Spybot S&D button on the left, and then click Search & Destroy. Spybot scans your computer and, like Ad-Aware, the results can be overwhelming (see Figure 3-10). Spybot S&D frequently picks up programs that Ad-Aware misses, and vice versa. Don't be overly alarmed if you get a lot of hits. Most of the items Spybot finds are nuisances, not imminent threats.

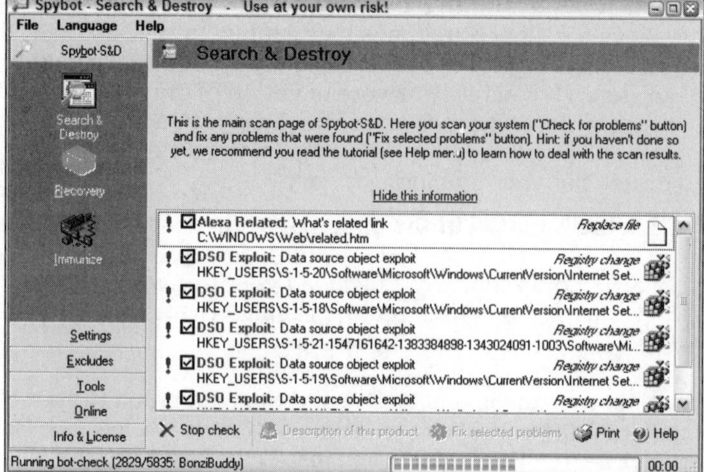

Figure 3-10: Like Ad-Aware, Spybot S&D scans and removes slimeware.

Steve Gibson, long a champion of Windows consumers (and a thorn in Microsoft's side!), has taken a special interest in spyware. Quoth Steve: "I consider the actions of companies that hide behind their fine print, take advantage of consumer trust and ignorance, and deliberately leverage complex hidden technology, to be the lowest form of personal privacy exploitation." He's right. Check out Steve's Web site — which is loaded with slime-busting information and products — at `http://grc.com/optout.htm`.

Spamming

Everybody hates spam.

Nobody has any idea how to stop it. Not the government. Not Bill Gates. Not your sainted aunt's podiatrist's second cousin.

By and large, Windows is only tangentially involved in the spam game — it's the messenger, as it were. But every Windows user I know receives e-mail. And every e-mail user I know gets spam. Lots of it.

I talk about spam, its causes and prevention — specifically by using Microsoft Outlook — in Technique 30 of *Office 2003 Timesaving Techniques For Dummies* (Wiley Publishing, Inc.). Some of the advice I give there is applicable to all Windows users, everywhere:

- **Don't encourage 'em.** Don't buy anything that's offered via spam (or any other e-mail that you didn't specifically request). Don't click through to the Web site. Simply delete the message. If you see something that might be interesting, use Google or some other Web browser to look for other companies that sell the same thing.

✦ **Only "opt out" if you know and trust the company that's sending you messages.** If you're on the Costco mailing list and you're not interested in its e-mail anymore, click the Opt Out button at the bottom. But don't "opt out" with a company you don't trust: They may just be trying to verify your e-mail address.

✦ **Never post your e-mail address on a Web site or a newsgroup.** Spammers have spiders that devour Web pages by the gazillion. If you post something in a newsgroup and want to let people respond, use a name that's hard for spiders to swallow: `woody (at) askwoody (dot) com`, for example.

✦ **Never open an attachment to an e-mail message.** Unless you know the person who sent it to you, you've verified with her that she intended to send you the attachment, and you trust the sender to be running an up-to-date antivirus package, it's not wise to open that attachment.

✦ **Never trust a Web site that you arrive at by "clicking through" a hot link in an e-mail message.** Be cautious about Web sites that you get to from other Web sites. If you don't personally type the address in Internet Explorer's address bar, you might not be in Kansas anymore.

✦ **If your e-mail program allows it, block automatic downloading of pictures inside e-mail messages.** That reduces the sender's ability to verify your e-mail address using a method called Web Beacons. Web Beacons are tiny pictures (or other components of a message) that "phone home" when you view the message. Some e-mail programs allow you to sever the link by not downloading pictures unless you specifically, manually request them. (For details, see *Office 2003 Timesaving Techniques For Dummies*).

Yes, the rumors you've heard are true. Microsoft used to put Web Beacons in their newsletters. Another one of those dirty facts the Redmondians would rather sweep under the table.

Ultimately, the only long-lasting solution to spam is to change your e-mail address and only give out your address to close friends and business associates. Even *that* won't solve the problem, but it should reduce the level of spam significantly. Helluva note, ain't it?

Phishing

Think that message from Wells Fargo (or eBay, PayPal, Citibank, whatever) asking to verify your account password (social security number, account number, address, telephone number, mother's maiden name, whatever) looks official?

Think again.

Phishing — sending e-mail that attempts to extract personal information from you, usually through a bogus Web site — has in many cases reached levels of sophistication that exceed the standards of the financial institutions themselves. (See Figure 3-11.)

Why spam filters get ulcers

There are 1,300,925,111,156,286,160,896 ways to spell *Viagra*. No, really. If you use all the tricks that spammers use — from simple swaps such as using the letter "I" instead of "i" or inserting e x t r a s p a c e s in the word, to tricky ones like substituting accented characters — there's more than one sextillion different ways to spell Viagra. (If I can use that word in print.)

Hard to believe? See `http://cockeyed.com/lessons/viagra/viagra.html` for an eye-opening analysis.

Spam scanners look at e-mail messages and try to determine if the contents of the potentially offensive message match certain criteria. Details vary depending on the type of spam scanner you (or your Internet Service Provider) use, but in general, the scanner has to match the contents of the message with certain words and phrases stored in its database. If you've seen a lot of messages with odd spellings come through your spam scanner, you know how hard it is to see through all of those sextillion variations.

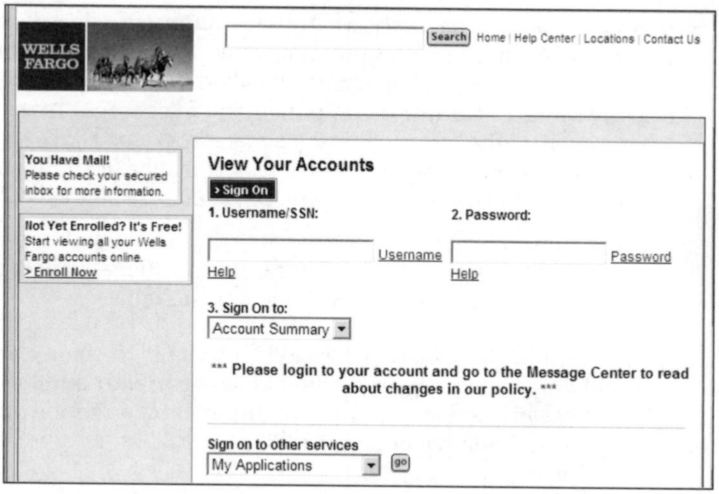

Figure 3-11: This message looks like it's from Wells Fargo, but it isn't.

Here's how it works.

1. Some scammer, often using a fake name and a stolen credit card, sets up a Web site. Usually it's a very professional-looking Web site — in some cases, indistinguishable from the "real" site. The fake Web sites can be so convincing that they show you a real-looking address in the address bar (see Figure 3-12), or the little "locked" secure site icon in the lower-right corner of Internet Explorer.

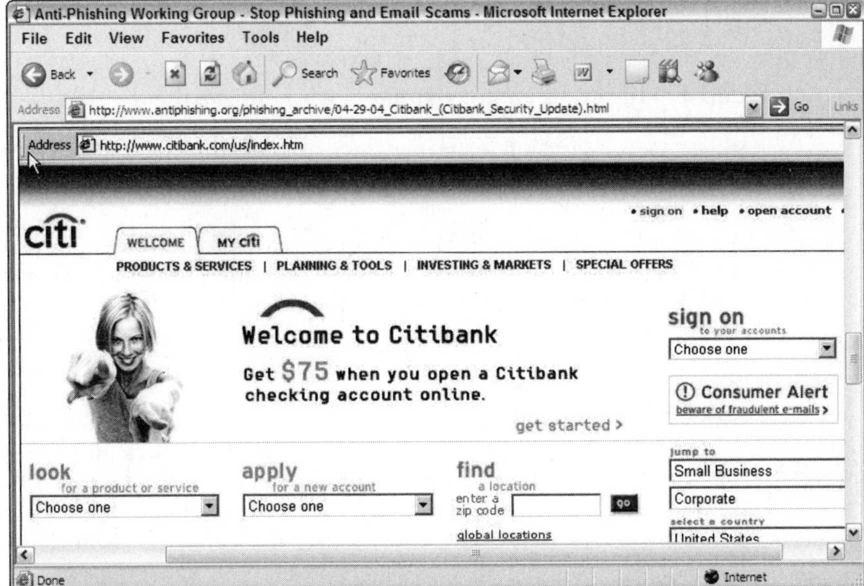

Figure 3-12: Example of a fake Citibank Web site from the Antiphishing tutorial at `www.antiphishing.org`.

2. The Web site asks you for personal information — most commonly your account number and password, or the PIN number for your ATM card. If you enter that information, many times you're transported to the real site — but the information you entered is sent directly to the scammer.

3. The scammer turns spammer and sends out hundreds of thousands of bogus messages. The messages include a clickable link to the fake Web site and a plausible story about how you must go to the Web site, log on, and do something to avoid dire consequences. The "from" address on the messages is *spoofed* so the message appears to come from the company in question. The message usually includes official logos — many even include links to the "real" Web site, even though they encourage you to click through to the fake site.

4. The scammer watches incoming traffic from the fake Web site, gathers the information typed in by gullible people, and uses it quickly — typically by logging on to the bank's Web site and attempting a transfer, or by burning a fake ATM card and using the PIN. Within a day or two — sometimes just hours — the Web site is shut down, and everything disappears into thin ether.

Phishing has become so popular because of the sheer numbers involved. Say a scammer sends out 1 million e-mail messages advising Wells Fargo customers to log on to their accounts. Only a small percentage of all the people who receive the phishing message will be Wells Fargo customers, but if the hit rate is just 1 percent, that's 10,000 customers.

Most of the Wells Fargo customers who receive the message will be smart enough to ignore it. But a sizable percentage — maybe 10 percent, maybe just 1 percent — will click through. That's somewhere between 100 and 1,000 suckers, er, customers.

If half of the people who click through provide their account details, the scammer gets 50 to 500 account numbers and passwords. If most of those arrive within a day of sending out the phishing message, the scammer stands to make a pretty penny indeed — and he or she can disappear with hardly a trace.

Note that I'm *not* talking about using your credit card online. Credit card transactions online are as safe as they are face to face; more so, actually, because if you use a U.S.-based credit card, you aren't liable for any loss due to somebody snatching your card information or any other form of fraud. I use my credit cards online all the time. You should, too.

The following advice will help you to protect yourself against phishing:

✦ If you get an e-mail message that contains any links to the Web, don't click the links. Nowadays, almost all messages with links to commercial sites are phishing come-ons. Financial institutions, in particular, don't send out messages with links anymore — and few other companies would dare. If you feel motivated to check out a dire message, go into Internet Explorer and type the address of the company by hand.

✦ Don't ever type information into an e-mail message and click to send it. (Refer to Figure 3-11 for an example of this kind of message.) Don't give out any of your personal information unless you've manually logged onto the company's Web site.

✦ If you get a phishing message that may be new or different, send copies to the U.S. Federal Trade Commission (`uce@ftc.gov`), the Anti-Phishing Working Group (`reportphishing@antiphishing.com`), and the company being phished (Citibank, eBay, PayPal, whatever). You need to include headers with the message. To grab a message header in Outlook, open the message, and then choose View➪Headers. Copy everything in the Internet Headers text box, and include that information in the forwarded copy of the message.

The Anti-Phishing Working Group, `www.antiphishing.org`, has a wealth of information on phishing, including an invaluable description of the steps you should take if you accidentally gave your personal information to a phisher.

Avoiding Hoaxes

Tell me if you've heard this one:

- A virus will hit your computer if you read any message that includes the phrase "Good Times" in the subject (that was a biggie in late 1994). Ditto for any message titled "It Takes Guts to Say 'Jesus'" or "Win a Holiday" or "Help a poor dog win a holiday" or "Join the Crew" or "pool party" or "A Moment of Silence" or "an Internet flower for you" or "a virtual card for you" or "Valentine's Greetings," and so on.
- A deadly virus is on the Microsoft [or put your favorite company name here] home page. Don't go there or your system will die.
- If you have a file called [put a filename here] on your PC, it contains a virus. Delete it immediately!

They're all hoaxes. Not a breath of truth in any of them.

The hoaxes hurt. Sometimes when real worms hit, so much e-mail traffic is generated from warning people to avoid the worm, that the well-intentioned watchdogs do more damage than the worm itself! Strange but true.

Do yourself a favor. Me, too. If somebody sends you a message that sounds like the following examples, just delete it, eh?

- A horrible virus is on the loose that's going to bring down the Internet.
- Send a copy of this message to ten of your best friends and for every copy that's forwarded, Bill Gates will give [pick your favorite charity] $10.
- Forward a copy of this message to ten of your friends, and put your name at the bottom of the list. In [pick a random amount of time] you will receive $10,000 in the mail, or your luck will change for the better. Your eyelids will fall off if you don't forward this message.
- Microsoft [Intel, McAfee, Norton, Compaq, whatever] says you need to download something, or not download something, or go to a specific place, or avoid a specific place, and on and on.

If you think you've stumbled on the world's most important virus alert, via your uncle's sister-in-law's roommate's hairdresser's soon-to-be-ex-boyfriend, (remember, he's the one who's a *really smart* computer guy, but kind of smelly?), count to ten twice, and keep three important points in mind:

- Chances are very good — I'd say, oh, 99.9999 percent or more — that you're looking at a half-baked hoax that's documented on Rob Rosenberger's Virus Myths site, `www.vmyths.com`. Check it out.

- If it's a real virus, all of the major news agencies will carry reports that (even if they're inaccurate!) are far, far more reliable than anything you get in e-mail. Check out `www.cnn.com`, `www.cnet.com`, or your favorite news site before you go way off the deep end.
- If the Internet world is about to collapse, clogged with gazillions of e-mail worms, the worst possible way to notify friends and family is via e-mail. D'OH! Pick up the phone, walk over to the water cooler, or send out a carrier pigeon, and give your intended recipients a reliable Web address to check for updates. Betcha they've already heard about it anyway.

Try hard to be part of the solution, not part of the problem, okay?

Chapter 4: Security Center: Windows Firewall

In This Chapter

- Discovering what Windows Firewall can — and can't — do
- Knowing when Windows Firewall causes problems — and how to get around them
- Making Windows Firewall work the way you want

A *firewall* is a program that sits between your computer (or your network) and the Internet, protecting you from the big, mean, nasty gorillas riding around on the Information Highway. A good firewall is a traffic cop that, in the best of all possible worlds, only allows "good" stuff into your computer (or network), and keeps all the "bad" stuff out on the Internet, where it belongs. A *great* firewall not only keeps the bad stuff out, it also prevents your computer (or network) from sending bad stuff to the Internet, if your computer gets infected with a virus or other security problem.

Nowadays, everybody who's connected to the Internet needs a firewall.

The original version of Windows XP included a 98-pound weakling of a firewall called *Internet Connection Firewall.* ICF intentionally slacked off on its duties as traffic cop, specifically so that Windows XP users wouldn't be inconvenienced or confused by the firewall's actions. Imagine, if you will, a traffic cop in New York City who was just too polite to stop cars. That's ICF's fatal flaw.

ICF had another major problem: It was buried five levels deep inside an arcane series of Windows dialog boxes. In the first edition of *Windows XP All-In-One Desk Reference For Dummies,* it took a full page just to show you how to turn ICF on. Most people who needed ICF never did figure out how to turn it on. The procedure for making slight changes to the firewall was so complex that Microsoft's official documentation (Knowledge Base article 308127) didn't get it right until version 2.1. That's version 2.1 of the *documentation,* for heaven's sake.

Full-fledged firewall companies faced even stiffer challenges, particularly in making firewalls for Windows XP. Symantec, for example — purveyor of Norton Personal Firewall — went through three major bug patches, covering at least six significant security holes, in the first five months of 2004.

Understanding Windows Firewall

Starting with Service Pack 2, Windows XP includes a decent, capable — but not foolproof — stateful firewall called *Windows Firewall* (see the sidebar, "What's a stateful firewall?"). Windows Firewall (WF, for short) has several characteristics that make it very different from the old ICF:

✦ **WF is on by default.** Unless you change something, Windows Firewall is turned on for all of the connections on your PC. (So, for example, if you have a LAN network cable, a wireless networking card, and a modem on a specific PC, WF is turned on for all of them.) The only way Windows Firewall gets turned off is if you deliberately turn it off, or if the Network Administrator on your Big Corporate Network decides to install Windows Service Packs with Windows Firewall turned off (which may be a good choice, in some cases).

✦ **WF settings can be changed relatively easily.** When you make changes, they apply to all of the connections on your PC.

✦ **WF kicks in before the computer is connected to the network.** With ICF, believe it or not, there was a time lag between the PC being connected to the network and when the firewall became active. A lot of PCs got infected between the time they were connected and when the firewall came up.

✦ **WF has a new "lockdown" mode.** By selecting one easy-to-find Don't Allow Exceptions check box (see Figure 4-1), you can lock down your computer so that it only accepts incoming data from "safe" locations. (I show you how to find this check box in the section, "Remote Assistance," later in this chapter.) In practice, that means you can use Internet Explorer to look at Web sites, and you can send and receive e-mail, as well as using printers and folders on your local network if you have one, but most other online functions are locked out. For example, if you use the Internet to play games with other folks who are online, or you connect to your computer at work, locking down your PC will prevent you from connecting. A lockdown even shuts down any connection to other computers or printers (or other shared devices) on the network. That's great if you're connecting in an airport and don't want other travelers to get at your Shared Documents folder. But it's a real pain in the neck in your home or office.

If you hear about a new worm making the rounds, you can easily lock down your computer for a day or two, and then go back to normal operation when the worm stops ping-ponging over the Internet. You might need to turn off the Don't Allow Exceptions setting long enough to print on a shared printer, or get at some data on your network, but you'll be essentially impenetrable whenever the Don't Allow Exceptions check box is selected. If you're connecting to a strange network (say, using a wireless connection at a coffee shop or in a hotel), you can lock down while logged on and sip your latte with confidence.

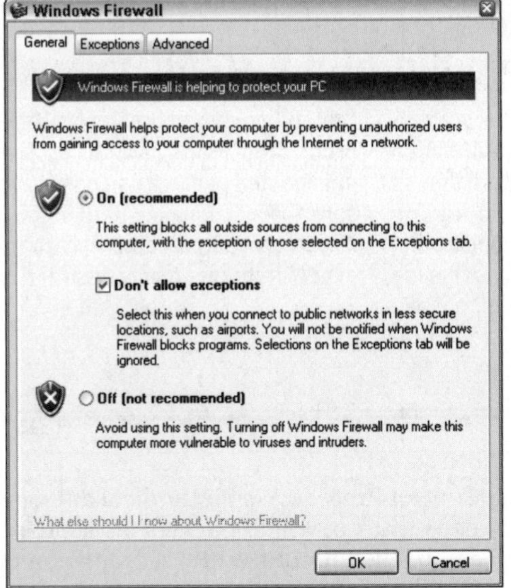

Figure 4-1: The Don't Allow Exceptions check box allows you to lock down your computer with a couple of simple clicks.

WF watches over data coming in from the Internet. Unfortunately, it isn't smart enough to monitor what you're sending out. So if your machine gets infected and suddenly starts spewing out 100,000 infected messages an hour, or sending one ping per second to `www.microsoft.com`, WF won't tell you a thing.

At this point, I need to inundate you with a bunch of jargon so that you can take control of Windows Firewall. Hold your nose and dive in. The concepts aren't that difficult, although the lousy terminology sounds like it was invented by a first-year advertising student. Refer to this section if you get bewildered when wading through the WF dialog boxes.

As you no doubt realize, the amount of data that can be sent from one computer to another over a network can be tiny or it can be huge. Computers communicate with each other by breaking the data up into *packets* — small chunks of data with a wrapper that identifies where the data came from and where it's going.

On the Internet, packets can be sent two different ways:

✦ **UDP** (User Datagram Protocol) is fast and sloppy. The computer sending the packets doesn't keep track of which packets were sent, and the computer receiving the packets doesn't make any attempt to get the sender to resend packets that vanish mysteriously in the bowels of the Internet. UDP is the kind of *protocol* (transmission method) that can work with live broadcasts, where short gaps wouldn't be nearly as disruptive as long pauses, while the computers wait to resend a dropped packet.

What's a stateful firewall?

At the risk of oversimplifying a bit, a *stateful firewall* keeps track of packets of information coming out of your computer and where they're headed. When a packet arrives and tries to get in, the firewall matches the originating address of the incoming packet against the log of addresses of the outgoing packets to make sure that any packet allowed through the firewall comes from an expected location.

Stateful packet filtering isn't 100 percent foolproof. And there have to be exceptions, so unexpected packets can come through for reasons discussed elsewhere in this chapter. But it's a very fast, reliable way to minimize your exposure to potentially destructive packets.

- **TCP** (Transmission Control Protocol) is methodical and complete. The sending computer keeps track of which packets it's sent. If the receiving computer doesn't get a packet, it notifies the sending computer, which resends the packet. Almost all communication over the Internet these days goes via TCP.

Every computer on a network has an *IP address*. The IP address is a collection of four sets of numbers, each between 0 and 255. For example, 192.168.0.1 is a common IP address for computers connected to a local network; the computer that handles the Dummies.com Web site is at 208.215.179.139. I tend to think of the IP address as analogous to a telephone number.

When two computers communicate, they not only need each others' IP address, they need a specific entry point called a *port* — I think of it as a telephone extension number — to talk to each other. For example, most Web sites respond to requests sent to port 80. There's nothing magical about the number 80: It's just the port number that people have agreed to use when trying to get onto a Web site's computer. If your Web browser wants to look at the Dummies.com Web site, it'll send a packet to 208.215.179.139, port 80.

Windows Firewall works by handling all of these duties simultaneously:

- It keeps track of outgoing packets and allows incoming packets to go through the firewall if they can be matched with an outgoing packet. (In other words, WF works as a stateful firewall.)
- If your computer is attached to a local network, Windows Firewall allows packets to come and go on ports 139 and 445, but only if they came from another computer on your local network, and only if they're using the TCP protocol. Windows Firewall needs to open up those ports for file and printer sharing.

- Similarly, if you're attached to a local network, Windows Firewall automatically opens ports 137 and 138 for the UDP protocol, but only for packets that originate on your local network.
- If you've specifically told Windows Firewall that you want it to allow packets to come in on a specific port and the Don't Allow Exceptions check box isn't selected, WF follows your orders.
- Windows Firewall allows packets to come into your computer if they're sent to the Remote Assistance program (unless the Don't Allow Exceptions check box is selected). Remote Assistance (see Book I, Chapter 3) allows other users to take control of your PC, but it has its own security settings and strong password protection. Still, it's a known security hole that's enabled unless you turn it off.
- You can tell Windows Firewall to accept packets that are directed at specific programs. Usually, any company that makes a program designed to listen for incoming Internet traffic will add their program to the list of designated exceptions when the program gets installed.
- Unless an inbound packet meets one of the preceding criteria, it's simply ignored. Windows Firewall swallows it without a peep.

Starting, Stopping, and Goosing WF

Windows Firewall is on by default, but if it gets turned off, the little Windows Security Alert icon in the System Notification area (next to the clock in the lower-right corner of your monitor) should start pestering you relentlessly with warnings. It doesn't hurt to periodically check and be sure that your firewall is working:

1. **Choose Start⇨Control Panel⇨Security Center.**

   You see the Security Center window shown in Figure 4-2.

2. **In the lower-right corner, click Windows Firewall.**

   The Windows Firewall dialog box appears with the General tab showing (refer to Figure 4-1).

3. **Following the recommendations in Table 4-1, choose the setting you need.**

4. **Click OK, and then click the X (Close) button to exit of the Security Center window.**

The settings in Table 4-1 apply to all of your connections — your local network connections, wireless connections, modem, VPN connection, and anything else that is, or can be, connected to a network. Any network.

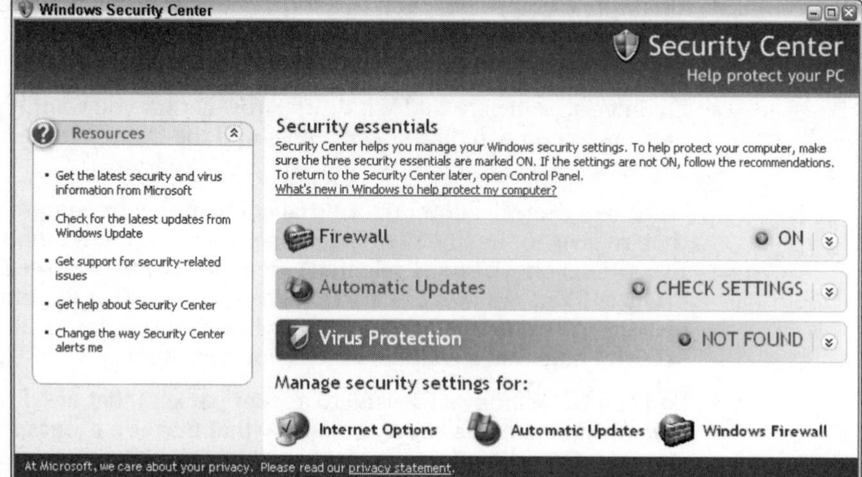

Figure 4-2: Windows XP Security Center.

Table 4-1 Windows Firewall General Settings

Setting	*Means*	*Recommendation*
On (Recommended)	Allow incoming packets that conform to the "stateful" criteria, plus any specified on the Exceptions tab.	Use this setting except when you're on the road, or when you're in dire circumstances.
Don't Allow Exceptions	Only allow packets that conform to the "stateful" criteria.	Use this setting if you have a portable connected to a network other than your "normal" network. Other people on the network won't be able to get into your machine, but you won't be able to use printers or shared files on the "foreign" network.
Off (Not Recommended)	All incoming packets are allowed in.	If you absolutely have to get your computer talking to another computer, you may be forced to use this setting. But if you do, be very mindful of the fact that you've let your guard down completely — and turn Windows Firewall back on the moment you can.

Making Exceptions

Firewalls can be absolutely infuriating. You may have a program that's worked for a hundred years, but the minute you install or activate a firewall, it just stops working, for absolutely no apparent reason.

You can get mad at Microsoft and scream at Windows Firewall, but when you do, realize that at least part of the problem lies in the way the firewall *has* to work. It has to block packets that are trying to get in, unless you explicitly tell it to allow them to get in. And — perhaps most infuriatingly — WF has to block those packets by simply swallowing them, not notifying the computer that sent the packet. Windows Firewall has to remain "stealthy" because if it sends back a packet that says, "Hey, I got your packet but I can't let it through," the bad guys will have an acknowledgement that your computer exists, they'll probably be able to figure out what firewall you're using, and they may be able to combine these two pieces of information to give you a headache.

Far better for Windows Firewall to act like a black hole.

You can tell WF to let through packets according to three separate criteria (see Figure 4-3):

- ✦ There's a short list of four predefined "services" that you can allow or disallow — File and Printer Sharing; Remote Assistance; Remote Desktop; and the UPnP Framework. Select the corresponding check box on the Exceptions tab to allow a service.
- ✦ You can tell WF to let through any TCP or UDP packets on a specific port by clicking the Add Port button (see the "Adding a port" section, later in this chapter). You type the port number, tell WF if you want to allow TCP or UDP, click OK, and Windows Firewall adds the port to the exception list.
- ✦ You can tell WF to let through any packet that's destined to a specific program by clicking the Add Program button (see the "Adding a program" section, later in this chapter). You pick the program, and tell WF if you want to allow communication from any address on the Internet, from specific addresses on the Internet, or only from your local network. Click OK and the firewall allows packets destined for that specific program.

File and printer sharing

When you run the Network Setup Wizard, it selects the File and Printer Sharing check box on the Exceptions tab. Enabling file and printer sharing allows your computer to get access to all the folders, printers, and other shared hardware devices (such as, oh, a CD drive) on your local network.

File and printer sharing works by opening up ports 139 and 445 for TCP over the local network and by opening ports 137 and 138 for UDP on the local network. (See the section, "Understanding Windows Firewall," earlier in this chapter, for an explanation of TCP and UDP.)

If you deselect the File and Printer Sharing check box on the Exceptions tab (refer to Figure 4-3), you keep other computers on your local network from getting at your shared folders and shared hardware devices. But you also keep your computer from getting at shared folders and devices on the network.

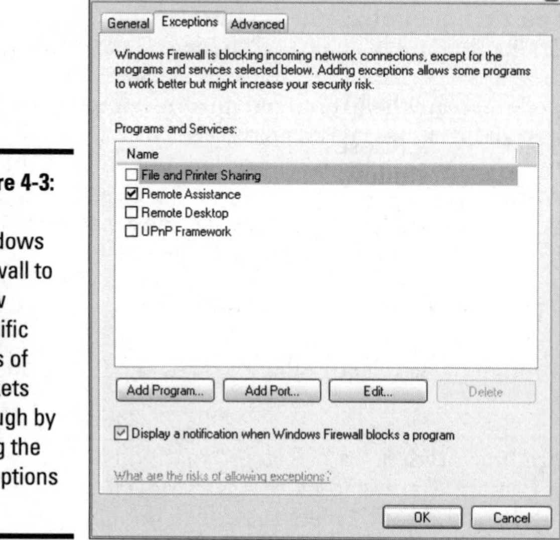

Figure 4-3: Tell Windows Firewall to allow specific kinds of packets through by using the Exceptions tab.

Remote Assistance

Remote Assistance enables a "guru" to take control of a novice's computer remotely to help solve a problem or show the novice how to do something. If you're the guru and you're trying to get a Remote Assistance session going, and the novice has deselected the Remote Assistance check box on the Exceptions tab (refer to Figure 4-3), you get the terse message shown in Figure 4-4.

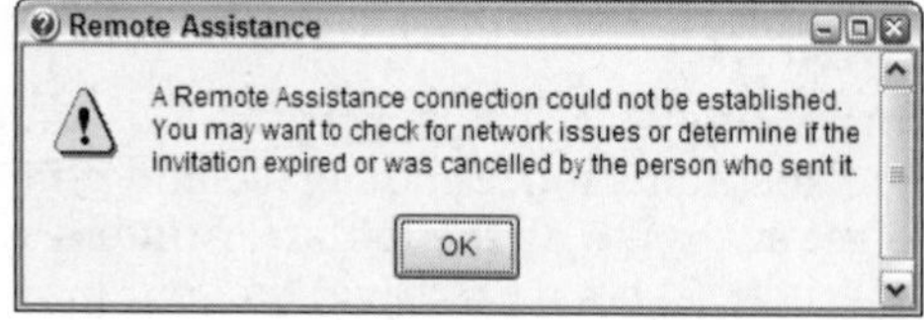

Figure 4-4: The novice's firewall is blocking the Remote Assistance request.

If that happens to you, get on the phone to your novice, and tell him or her to follow these simple steps:

1. **Choose Start⇨Control Panel⇨Security Center.**
2. **In the lower-right corner, click Windows Firewall.**

3. **On the General tab, make sure that the On option button is selected.**

   If the novice has the Don't Allow Exceptions check box selected, you won't be able to get in.

4. **Click the Exceptions tab and select the Remote Assistance check box.**

5. **Click OK, and then click the X (Close) button in the upper-right corner to close the Security Center window.**

Remote Desktop

Remote Desktop only works with Windows XP/Professional.

If you use Remote Desktop to get at a computer while you're on the road, you have to go in and manually change Windows Firewall to allow Remote Desktop. On the Exceptions tab of the Windows Firewall dialog box, select the Remote Desktop check box, and Windows Firewall won't get in the way when you try to connect.

Just remember to change WF *before* you leave on your trip, okay?

UPnP framework

UPnP — Universal Plug 'n Play — was once the source of a major security hole in Windows XP and a series of botched patches from Microsoft. I like to call it "Windows for refrigerators and toasters" but UPnP's a little more complicated than that. UPnP is the protocol used by Windows to talk to all sorts of different kinds of devices on a network. I guess that means it's Windows for refrigerators and toasters and heaters and stereos and remote-controlled window blinds. (Not to mention those way-cool water fountains and mood lights. But I digress.)

If you need UPnP support, you'll know it — the toaster won't toast under Windows control unless UPnP is activated. You tell your firewall to keep its hands off the toaster interface here, on the Exceptions tab of the Windows Firewall dialog box.

Adding a program

Some programs need to "listen" to incoming traffic from the Internet; they wait until they're contacted, and then respond. Usually, you'll know if you have such a program because the installer tells you that you need to tell your firewall to back off. If you want to tell Windows Firewall that it should let packets through if they're destined for a specific program, follow these steps:

1. **Choose Start⇨Control Panel⇨Security Center.**

   You see the Security Center window (refer to Figure 4-2).

2. **In the lower-right corner, click Windows Firewall.**

   Windows Firewall opens with the General tab selected (refer to Figure 4-1).

3. **Click the Exceptions tab, and then click the Add Program button.**

   Windows Firewall displays the Add a Program dialog box, as shown in Figure 4-5.

4. **Pick the program that's designed to receive unsolicited packets from the Internet.**

   Realize that you're opening up a potential, albeit small, security hole. The program you choose better be quite capable of handling packets from unknown sources.

5. **Click OK twice to go back to the Security Center window.**

Figure 4-5: Choose the program that's the designated receiver for inbound packets.

Adding a port

Adding a port to the Exceptions list is inherently less secure than adding a program. Why? Because the bad guys have a hard time guessing which programs you've left open — there are a whole lot of programs to choose from — but probing all of the ports on a machine to see if any of them let packets go through is comparatively easy.

Still, you may need to open a port to enable a specific application. When you select the check box to allow Remote Desktop, for example, you're opening up port 3389. That's the security price you pay for enabling programs to talk to each other.

How do you know when you need a port?

Most first-time firewallers are overwhelmed by the idea of opening up a port. Although it's true that you need to treat ports with care — an open port is a security threat, no matter how you look at it — sometimes you really need to open one. How do you know when you absolutely have to open a port? Usually, you get a phone call like this:

"Dude. My game won't hook up with your game. You got a firewall or somethin'?"

"Uh, yeah. I'm running Windows Firewall."

"Shaw, man. You want to play Frumious Bandersnatch, you gotta open up ports 418, 419, 420, an' 421."

"Does Frumious use UDP or TCP?"

"What's TeeCeePee, some kinda disease? I dunno, man. I just read in the instruction book that ya gotta have 418, 419, 420, an' 421 open. Doncha ever read the freakin' manual, dude?"

At which point, you guess that Frumious Bandersnatch uses the TCP protocol (that's the most common choice), you run through the Security Center to liberate the four ports, and you've got the game working in 30 seconds flat.

Follow these steps to open a port:

1. **Choose Start➪Control Panel➪Security Center.**

   The Security Center window appears (refer to Figure 4-2).

2. **In the lower-right corner, click Windows Firewall.**

   You see the Windows Firewall dialog box, General tab (refer to Figure 4-1).

3. **Click the Exceptions tab, and then click the Add Port button.**

   Windows Firewall displays the Add a Port dialog box, as shown in Figure 4-6.

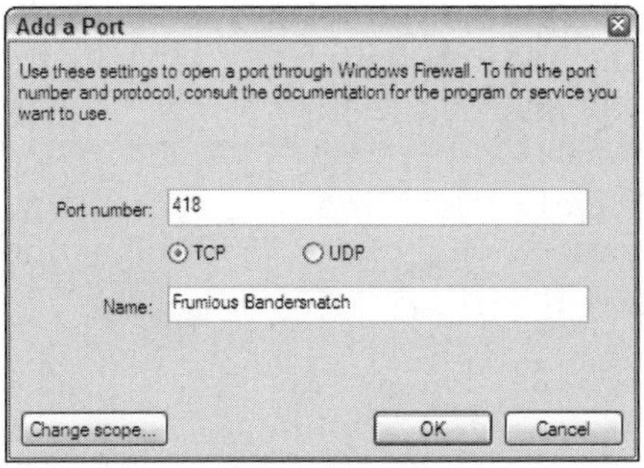

Add a Port

Use these settings to open a port through Windows Firewall. To find the port number and protocol, consult the documentation for the program or service you want to use.

Port number: 418

TCP UDP

Name: Frumious Bandersnatch

Change scope... OK Cancel

Figure 4-6: To open a port to any packet attempting to use it, type the port number and select TCP or UDP.

4. **Type the port number that you want to open. Select TCP or UDP as the protocol (if in doubt, stick with TCP), give the exception a name, and click OK.**

   See the section, "Understanding Windows Firewall," earlier in this chapter, for a description of TCP and UDP.

5. **The Windows Firewall dialog box includes an Exception entry for the port you just entered (see Figure 4-7). Select the check box next to the new entry, and then click OK to go back to the Security Center window.**

Every port that you open to the outside world is a potential location for an attack. Open ports sparingly, and when you're done, close them by deselecting the check box in the Programs and Services list.

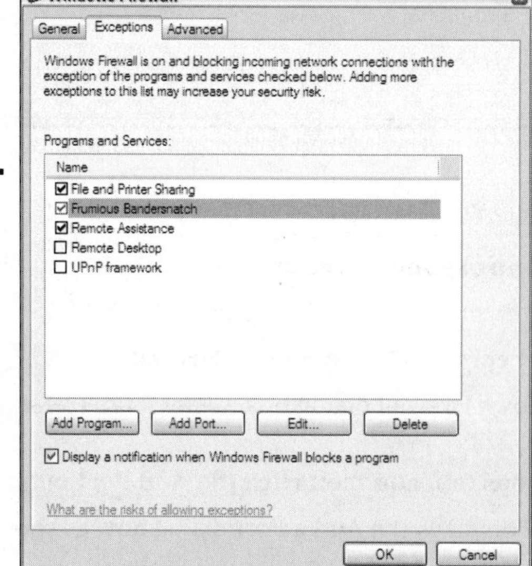

Figure 4-7: Individual ports that you add manually appear as check boxes in the Programs and Services list.

You can add only one port at a time. If you need to add ports 418, 419, 420, and 421, you have to click the Add Port button four separate times, type in the pertinent information four separate times, and select four separate check boxes in the Programs and Services list every time you want to block or unblock the ports. Dude.

Chapter 5: Security Center: Automatic Updates

In This Chapter

- Getting the whole story about Windows Update
- Deciding what level of automatic update (if any!) is right for you
- Making Windows Update work the way you want

Windows Update stinks. Massively.

Permit me to elaborate.

Both the security patches that Microsoft dribbles out to users *and* the method by which Microsoft delivers those patches to users stinks. Massively.

It's been a mess since the day Windows XP first shipped. It's still a mess now. Microsoft promises that Windows Update will be fixed Real Soon Now. I'll believe it when I see it.

To Patch or Not to Patch

Microsoft periodically releases security patches for Windows XP. Most of the time, on most machines, the patches perform as advertised — they fix a defect in the product. Fair enough. Beats a product recall, I guess.

Sometimes, though, the patches don't work right. A couple of my favorites:

- The infamous UPnP patch debacle, starting in November 2001 (details at `www.woodyswatch.com/winxp/archtemplate.asp?2-n03`), saw Microsoft patching, re-patching and re-re-patching a hole in the part of Windows that listens for new items as they're attached to a network. (I call it "Windows for toasters and refrigerators" because home automation equipment leads the pack of possible uses.) The FBI's National Infrastructure Protection Center followed along after Microsoft like a kid cleaning up after his dog: NIPC issued a warning about the security hole, an update, another update, and ultimately an advisory that Microsoft had finally solved the problem.

What's a "critical" update?

Microsoft has very strict definitions for its various levels of security patches. The official "severity level system" defines these levels of security holes:

* A *critical* security hole is "A vulnerability whose exploitation could allow the propagation of an Internet worm without user action."
* An *important* hole is "A vulnerability whose exploitation could result in compromise of the confidentiality, integrity, or availability of users' data, or of the integrity or availability of processing resources."
* A *moderate* security rating signifies that "Exploitability is mitigated to a significant degree by factors such as default configuration, auditing, or difficulty of exploitation."
* And a *low* hole is "A vulnerability whose exploitation is extremely difficult, or whose impact is minimal."

Lest you really believe that you should install critical updates before you install important updates — or that you can, say, ignore moderate updates entirely — you need to realize that Microsoft's use of the terms is, in fact, quite arbitrary and at times highly debatable. Several recent "critical" patches don't address unassisted worm propagation. In at least one instance, the severity level of a security hole was changed after enough people complained. The assignment of a security level seems to reflect internal Microsoft politics more than anything else. So take the severity level rating with a grain of salt, okay?

✦ In April 2004, Microsoft released a slew of patches, one of which, dubbed "MS04-014" locked up some Windows 2000 machines tighter than a drum (see Knowledge Base article 841382). If you installed the patch on a Windows 2000 machine, and you were unlucky, you couldn't boot the machine. The only solution was to haul out your installation CD and perform major brain surgery.

If you used the old Windows Update for any amount of time at all, you've no doubt witnessed first-hand how the old Update program would fail to find important updates, or urge you to install the same updates twice, lock up, quit mysteriously, or insist on installing such "critical" updates as the one that removed the swastika symbol from a wayward Microsoft Office 2003 font. *Critical?*

Worse, many of those updates can't be uninstalled, so the old bugs in the Windows Update installer left you with unstable patches that were inconsistently applied.

Microsoft's new Windows Update doesn't suffer from the most egregious problems of its (many) predecessors. Microsoft spent tens — maybe hundreds — of millions of dollars to make sure that's so. But those of us who lived through the earlier versions won't soon forget the nightmares.

I've been at this business a long time — been using Windows since the days of Windows 286, which shipped on a single diskette, and I wrangled with DOS long before that. Of all the Microsoft features that I don't trust, and there are many, Windows Automatic Update rates as the single Microsoft feature that I trust the least. Microsoft has gone to extraordinary lengths over the past couple of years to reinforce my distrust and to demonstrate plainly and unambiguously that when it comes to updating Windows, Microsoft doesn't have a clue.

Understanding the Patching Process

When Microsoft patches a security hole in Windows, it issues a Security Bulletin (see Figure 5-1). Security Bulletins get sequential numbers, such as MS04-015, denoting the 15th Security Bulletin issued in year 2004.

Microsoft Security Bulletin MS04-015

Vulnerability in Help and Support Center Could Allow Remote Code Execution (840374)

Issued: May 11, 2004
Updated: May 11, 2004
Version: 1.1

Summary

Who should read this document: Customers who use Microsoft® Windows®

Impact of Vulnerability: Remote Code Execution

Maximum Severity Rating: Important

Recommendation: Customers should install the update at the earliest opportunity.

Security Update Replacement: None

Caveats: Microsoft Knowledge Base Article 841996 documents a known issue that customers may experience when they install t on a system where the Help and Support Center service is disabled. For the installation of this security update to be successful, th Support Center service cannot be disabled. The article also documents recommended solutions for this issue. For more informatio Knowledge Base Article 841996.

Figure 5-1: Security Bulletin MS04-015, complete with a warning about unintended side effects of the patch.

You might think that Bulletin MS04-015 would talk about the 15th security patch in year 2004, but you'd be wrong. Microsoft bunches up security patches, sometimes releasing several completely unrelated patches in one Security Bulletin. Why? Because Microsoft knows that the world at large correlates the number of Security Bulletins with the relative "holiness" of its software. If Windows releases only 30 patches in a year, and Linux releases 48, which operating system is more secure?

Each Security Bulletin refers to one or more Knowledge Base articles, which give further details about the patch. The six-digit KB article number appears at the end of the description of the patch (see Figure 5-1, which refers to Knowledge Base article 840374).

Unfortunately, the Knowledge Base article number is important because it's frequently the only way you have to identify the patch. If you need to remove the patch because, say, it clobbers an important part of Windows, you'll need the KB article number to work with the Control Panel's Add or Remove Programs.

While you can use Windows Update to identify patches that your computer requires, download, and even install them, it's important to realize that you can download the patch manually and run it without Windows Update's interference, er, assistance. That can come in handy if you need to apply the same patch to many PCs, or if you want to download the patch when your Internet connection is not busy, but wait to install the patch later.

To download and install a Security Bulletin patch manually, follow these steps:

1. **Go to the Security Bulletin and click the link to download the update.**

   Use the address `www.microsoft.com/technet/security/bulletin/MSxx-xxx.mspx` where MSxx-xxx is the Security Bulletin number. In this example, I'm tracking down the patch associated with Security Bulletin MS04-015, so I go to `www.microsoft.com/technet/security/bulletin/MS04-015.mspx` and click the Download the Update for Windows XP link (see Figure 5-2).

   The site doesn't even mention the Security Bulletin. No wonder people get so confused.

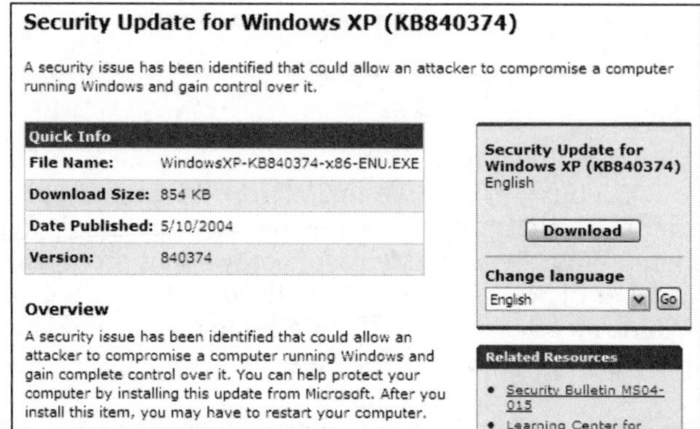

Figure 5-2: The download site for Security Bulletin MS04-015.

2. **Make sure that you're getting the right patch for your system, and then click the Download button.**

Windows Security Center gives you the dire warning shown in Figure 5-3. Presumably, the patch will do more good than harm. (I know, I know, but hope springs eternal.)

Figure 5-3: Windows Security warns you about installing a Windows security patch from the Windows Web site. Oy.

3. **Click Save and save the file someplace convenient.**

   It's always easier to save the patch, and then come back and run it later.

4. **When Internet Explorer tells you that it's finished downloading the patch, click Open.**

   That patch should unzip itself, run, and finish normally.

5. **If necessary, restart your computer.**

   No, not all patches require you to restart your computer. But some do — and if you don't restart your PC when it's required, the patch won't "take" and you'll still be exposed to whatever security hole the patch was supposed to fix.

Generally, it's much simpler to have Windows keep track of which patches are required and to download them automatically, but if you need to apply the same patch to multiple machines, a manual download can save hours of trouble.

Choosing an Update Method

I describe how to manually download and install Windows security patches in the preceding section. In this section, I explain how Windows can automate part or all of that procedure, and point out the shortcomings (and benefits!) of letting Windows do the heavy lifting.

Before you adjust Windows Automatic Update, it's worth taking a few minutes to think through what Windows has to offer, and decide which approach works best for you.

You can choose from four different levels of Windows Automatic Update:

- **Let Windows determine when new updates are available, download them, and install them automatically for you — typically in the middle of the night.**

  This is a good option for people who get easily confused by the process of telling Windows that it's okay to install new updates. It's also a good option if you don't have the time or inclination to look online to see if a specific update has major problems. At the same time, though, it leaves your PC vulnerable to Microsoft's spotty patch record. In the worst case, you may come in one morning, turn on your PC, and not be able to use it at all. Microsoft recommends this setting for all PC users. I only recommend it for people who are too intimidated to take control of their computer's fate.

- **Let Windows determine when new updates are available, download them, and then ask your permission to install them.**

  For folks who are willing to wait a day or two to install a new patch, and check online to see if a patch is causing more harm than good, this is the best approach. While it's true that the gestation period for new worms is shrinking — the bad guys are picking up on Microsoft's security patches and figuring out how to exploit the holes shortly after the patches are announced — it's rare that a freshly patched security hole turns into an active exploit in a few days. And, generally, word of botched security patches surfaces within a few days.

- **Let Windows determine when new updates are available, and then notify you.**

  This option makes sense for people who want to manually download a patch (using the method in the preceding section), so they can apply the same patch to multiple machines.

- **Turn off Windows Automatic Update entirely.**

  It's hard to imagine any situation where this makes sense.

When Windows Update reaches into your computer to see what you have installed, which patches have been applied, and the like, it doesn't retrieve any personally identifiable information. It doesn't even retrieve your activation key. As far as I've been able to tell, Microsoft doesn't attempt to spy on your machine via the Automatic Update program. So don't turn it off entirely unless you're really, really paranoid.

Adjusting Windows Update

After you decide on an update approach, as outlined in the preceding section, you have to wade through Windows' jury-rigged interface to make your decision take effect. Here's how:

1. **Choose Start⇨Control Panel⇨Security Center to bring up the Windows Security Center.**
2. **If you can't see the Automatic Updates panel (see Figure 5-4), click the down-arrow button to the right of Check Settings.**

   Windows tells you if you're currently using full automatic updating; automatic downloading (shown in Figure 5-4); automatic notification of new updates only; or if automatic updates is turned off (which neither Microsoft nor I recommend).
3. **If you want to change your Automatic Updates setting, click the icon marked System, and then click the Automatic Updates tab.**

   Do NOT click the Turn on Automatic Updates button. (Microsoft has rigged that button so it turns on full Automatic Updating — and you probably don't want that.)

   Windows shows you the System Properties dialog shown in Figure 5-5.

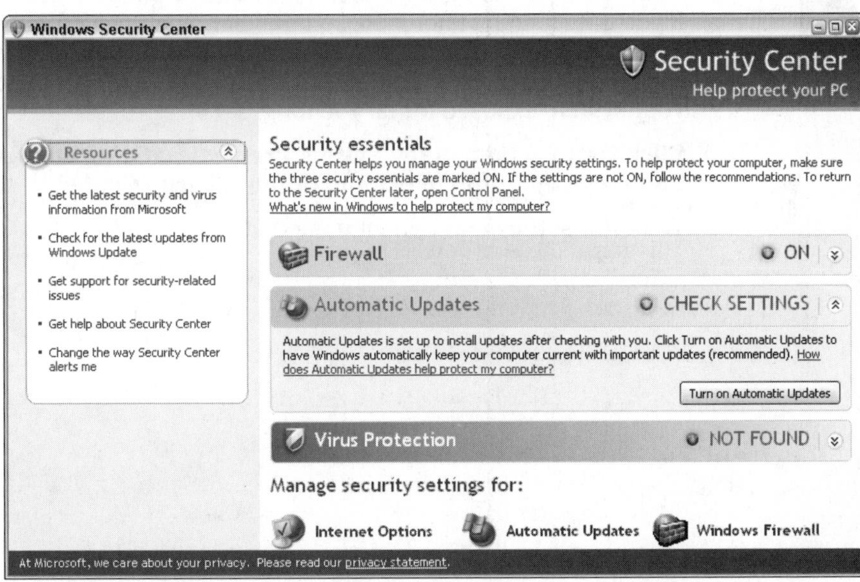

Figure 5-4: The Security Center gives you a short description of your current Automatic Update setting, and what it means.

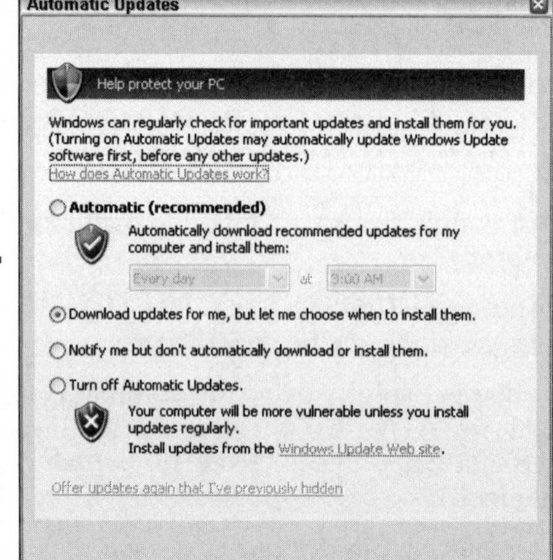

Figure 5-5: Automatic Updates settings are buried in this System Properties dialog box.

4. **Select the option button that corresponds to the automatic update setting you want (see the preceding section of this book for details and recommendations).**

   If you choose the Automatic option, you can also specify whether you want Windows Update to check every day or once a week for updates. If you decide to let Microsoft update your machine without your knowledge or consent, I strongly recommend that you have Windows check for updates every day. Going a full week without an update can leave your system exposed for far too long.

5. **Click OK to get out of the System Properties dialog box, and then click the X (Close) button to exit out of the Security Center.**

   Your new settings take effect immediately.

Chapter 6: Security Center: Virus Protection

In This Chapter

- **Understanding how antivirus products work with Windows**
- **Caring for your antivirus program**
- **Downloading and installing AVG-Free, a free-for-personal-use antivirus program**

Every single Windows user should install, update, and religiously use an antivirus program. No exceptions, no excuses.

One question I hear all the time is, "Which antivirus program is the best?" My answer: They all work great. Pick one of the major packages and *just do it*. While you're worrying about whether this package scans better or that package blocks better, or that another package costs a few bucks more or less, your system is at risk. Flip a coin if you have to. But get your computer protected.

Now, with the advent of a product called AVG-Free, first-class antivirus software is available at no cost for personal use. You don't have an excuse anymore. I show you how to install and use AVG-Free in this chapter.

Understanding Antivirus Software

Antivirus software protects your computer from viruses, right?

Well, yes and no.

Most antivirus software packages these days work in two very different ways:

- **Signature matching:** The antivirus software looks inside files to see if any portion of the file matches a big database of known "bad" snippets of data. When a new virus or worm is discovered, characteristic parts of the infecting program are added to the signature database. Signature matching still forms the backbone of the antivirus industry, but the black-hat cretins are getting better and better at writing malware that modifies itself, rendering signatures useless.

Worms that don't need e-mail

All e-mail users come in contact with infected attachments to e-mail messages — sadly, they've become a way of life, even with the most sophisticated and up-to-date virus removal tools. Antivirus programs catch infected attachments, most frequently via signature matching.

But there's an entire class of worms that don't use e-mail at all. As of this writing, Slammer, Blaster, and Sasser are the best known, but there are many others. These worms find ways to get into a computer, typically through a port that isn't protected by a firewall (see Book II, Chapter 4). Then the worm uses a previously known hole in Windows to run a simple, small program. Blaster and Sasser would then contact a Web site and download a bigger, nasty program, which in turn goes out on the Internet and looks for unprotected ports and unpatched Windows systems. Slammer did all its dirty work with the original, tiny (376 byte) program.

Because many systems don't have firewalls — or their firewalls leak like sieves — and many systems aren't regularly patched with Windows Update (see Book II, Chapter 5), a fair percentage of all the computers connected to the Internet can get zapped.

The lessons are obvious — patch Windows, use a firewall — but a good antivirus program may also help by detecting abnormal activity. In this case, a prescient AV program could detect a blast of probes going out of an infected PC to look for unprotected ports. That kind of heuristic analysis is more fiction than fact at this point, but it's definitely the way of the future.

Some industry pundits (rightly) observe that a steady flow of updated signature files drives revenue for the antivirus industry: If you drop your subscription, you don't get any new signatures. The antivirus software industry has one of the few software products that becomes nearly obsolete every few days. There are powerful economic incentives to stick with the signature-matching model — which, by its very nature, only works *after* a new virus has been released.

✦ **Heuristic analysis:** The antivirus software relies on the behavior (or the expected behavior) of a program to catch the destructive software before it has a chance to run. Although an enormous amount of research has gone into heuristic analysis, a black box that takes a file and determines if it's going mess up a PC is still a long way off. In fact, there are sound theoretical reasons why a perfect black box of that ilk can never exist.

When a bad piece of software is identified, the antivirus program offers to remove the infection. In the case of viruses attached to other files, in most cases the offensive program can be removed without destroying the "host" file. Some AV packages have the ability to shut down a PC's links to the outside world if a particularly virulent worm is detected.

Antivirus software typically watches for infections in one of three ways, and each of the ways hooks into Windows in a different manner:

- **A complete scan.** Typically, you schedule full scans of all your files in the middle of the night, or shortly after you download a new signature file. Windows runs a full scan the same way as any other program.
- **On the fly.** When you open a file or run a program, Windows alerts your antivirus software, and the AV software kicks in to scan the file before it gets run or opened. Similarly, if you download a program from the Internet, or run a program on a Web page, Windows has your AV software check before you have a chance to shoot yourself in the foot.
- **Lurking.** Good antivirus software runs in the background, looking for specific events that may be indicative of an infection. Some AV packages include firewalls, spam blockers, and other components that take lurking to a higher level, but almost all AV software watches while you work, running as a separate Windows task in the background.

In addition, all AV software scans e-mail messages and attachments for infected files; some scan before the mail gets to the e-mail program, others scan as attachments get opened.

Antivirus software manufacturers face many pressures, but aside from detecting all known viruses (and trying to catch some that aren't yet known), one of the top priorities is performance. It takes time to scan a file, and computer folks, being impatient by nature, don't like the idea of waiting while the AV software does its thing. The next time your computer goes out to lunch while you're trying to open a file, take heart. The PC you save may be your own.

What's a false positive?

The bane of antivirus software's existence, a *false positive* occurs when a perfectly good file is identified as infected. Most frequently, simply by chance, part of an uninfected file may contain the same sequence of characters as a virus, which triggers a signature match.

This all sounds like a gentlemanly mix up, old chap, stiff upper lip and all that, until you start getting inundated with angry messages from people who accuse you of posting an infected file on the Internet. When you write back and tell them that the antivirus software is at fault, many people won't believe you, and some will accuse you of trying to spread an infection for personal gain.

Oh yeah. It happens all the time.

Be aware of the fact that antivirus software isn't absolutely foolproof. Sometimes the identified bogeymen only exist as a figment of some pattern-matching program's imagination.

Ground Zero

As of this writing, every major Windows worm outbreak — including the Slammer worm, which infected at least 75,000 computers within 10 minutes of its release in January 2003 — relies on a known, already-patched security hole in Windows. Systems that get infected are only vulnerable because the people who run the systems didn't apply a patch that was readily available from Microsoft. The cretins who write worms watch Microsoft's patches closely and try to create programs that exploit the patched holes, knowing full well that a large percentage of all the systems connected to the Internet aren't updated very often.

Some day soon, that will change. And not for the better.

A so-called "Ground Zero" or "Zero Day" worm would use a previously unknown, and therefore unpatched, hole in Windows. If the really clever guys in black hats ever get smart enough to find a wide-open hole in Windows (and, particularly, Windows Firewall) before Microsoft patches it, we're all in a world of hurt.

There's a precedent. Way back in November 1988, Robert Morris, Jr., a grad student at MIT, released a worm that brought down 6,000 UNIX machines — a very large percentage of all the computers connected to the Internet, such as it was. By all accounts, Morris wasn't trying to hurt anything. He only wanted to see what would happen if a program could move from machine to machine. The "version 1.0" worm that got out had bugs that made it clog up every infected machine, and the rest is history. The Computer Emergency Response Team, CERT, was created in response to Morris's worm.

Virus and worm writers can go to great lengths to hide their malicious creations. The *polymorphic* virus illustrates the point. A polymorphic virus changes every time it infects, so signature matching doesn't work very well, if at all. One favored method for making a virus polymorphic: Encrypt it using a key that changes every time the virus infects. When the virus runs, its first job is to decrypt the main part of the virus. After it's decrypted, the main part goes out and infects, but the malicious code it passes on is encrypted with a different password. Thus, no two copies of the virus look the same, and signature matching on anything but the (typically very small) decrypting part of the virus won't work.

Heuristic analysis of files to try to detect malware suffers from one near-fatal flaw. By its nature, heuristic analysis looks at a program's behavior or expected behavior and draws conclusions about the program based on what it looks like it'll do. There's no black-and-white, no signature matching "AHA! I got a real one!" finality to the analysis. Instead, heuristic programs live in a world of shades of gray, where there's a 60 percent chance this type of behavior is wormlike and a 78 percent chance that behavior is wormlike. Antivirus software analysts have to turn that kind of soft data into an up-or-down "This is a virus" or "That isn't a virus" result. Frequently, they (or, more correctly, their programs) don't guess right.

For an interesting, insightful — and very controversial — analysis of the situation, see Rob Rosenberger's "Rantings" at `http://vmyths.com/rant.cfm?id=605&page=4`.

Taking Care of Your AV Program

McAfee calls them "DAT files." Symantec (Norton) calls them "Virus Definitions." F-Secure and Kaspersky both use the term "Antivirus Database," while Grisoft (AVG) goes the other way, with "Virus Database." Trend Micro (PC-cillin) says "Pattern File." Panda uses "Signature Files," and CA has "Virus Signatures." For Sophos, they're "IDEs."

No matter what you call them, the signature-matching database file lies at the center of every antivirus product's capabilities.

In normal use, you should update your antivirus software's signature file daily. I suggest you do it in the morning, just before you start to work. I know that some manufacturers suggest you only update once a week, but I think that's shortsighted, particularly given the current level of malware activity.

Here's the security schedule I recommend for most Windows XP users:

- **Keep an eye on Microsoft's updates to Windows XP, but don't install them automatically.** (See Book II, Chapter 5.) Instead, wait until the other pioneers have arrows in *their* backs, and then make sure that your system won't end up in worse condition after the patch.
- **Download antivirus signature files daily.** Your first job each morning should be to verify that your AV software has been updated properly, and that the program's icon is visible in your system tray, next to the clock.
- **Check for massive new outbreaks daily.** Most AV software companies have e-mail newsletters that will warn you of major new problems. Checking your AV software manufacturer's home page every day to see if any news is breaking is also worthwhile. Just keep in mind that your AV manufacturer has a vested interest in getting you to buy more software. Of course, AskWoody.com will give you the straight scoop, round the clock.

Be leery of mainstream press reports of new, pending, or possible infections. The folks who write those breathless newspaper articles frequently don't know what they're talking about — they get the details wrong and hype nonexistent problems. Far better to rely on more, uh, trustworthy news sources.

How to report a virus

Antivirus software manufacturers are constantly looking for new viruses, worms, Trojans, and other forms of malware.

Unfortunately, at least 90 percent (and probably more like 99 percent) of what they receive is junk — requests for technical support, old hoaxes, viruses that have been around for a hundred years, and stuff that doesn't bear any resemblance to real, infectious programs.

If you have a new virus, your AV software manufacturer wants to hear from you. The instructions vary depending on the manufacturer (see the following table), but if you're sure you've found a new creepy-crawly, by all means submit it.

There's no need to submit a new virus to more than one manufacturer. They all talk to each other, regularly, vociferously, and new viruses make their way rapidly from company to company. It's a credit to the AV industry that the lines of communication have been kept open, even among fierce competitors, and that samples of "real" viruses are made available to legitimate researchers, usually within hours of being identified.

Antivirus Company	Submission Instructions
F-Secure	`http://support.f-secure.com/enu/home/virusproblem/sample`
Frisk F-PROT	`www.f-prot.com/virusinfo/submission_form.html`
Kaspersky	`www.kaspersky.com/support.asp?chapter=26`
McAfee	`www.mcafee.com/anti-virus/report_virus.asp?`
Symantec (Norton)	`www.symantec.com/avcenter/submit.html`

- **If you think you have a virus, report it to your antivirus software manufacturer.** See the "How to report a virus" sidebar in this chapter for instructions.
- **If there's a major outbreak, don't — I repeat, *don't* — send e-mails to all your friends.** That only makes the problem worse. Pick up the phone and call anyone who needs to know. Don't worry. If it's a big virus outbreak, they'll probably know already.
- **Run a complete scan of your system once a month.** If you have your signatures updated, and your antivirus software is working properly, you don't need to do a full scan very often.

Antivirus software manufacturers create new versions of their programs from time to time and, of course, they'll try to sell you the latest and greatest. In my experience, "old" AV programs with properly updated signature files are still effective six months or even a year after the "new" version comes out. You may get zapped by a completely new piece of malware, but then again, you might get zapped even if you're running the absolutely latest version of the antivirus software with up-to-the-second signature files.

Downloading and Installing AVG-Free

What? You don't have an antivirus program? Are you tired of the Windows Security Center icon telling you "Your computer might be at risk/Antivirus software might not be installed"?

Hey, if it takes some nagging to get you with the program, so be it.

If you want a full-featured antivirus package, run down to your nearest software shop (or hit one of the AV software sites on the Internet) and get one of the packages. They all work well. The top-rated package this week will probably be different from the top-rated package next week. Flip a coin, read a review, and dive in.

Or if you're very cheap, like me, you can download and install a perfectly usable free-for-personal-use antivirus program — AVG-Free from Grisoft. It goes in like a champ, co-exists peacefully with Windows, and you can't beat the price: free for a home user.

Here's how to do it:

1. **Go to Grisoft's Web site, `www.grisoft.com`.**
2. **On the main page (see Figure 6-1), click the link on the left side for the AVG Free Edition.**
3. **At the bottom of the AVG Free Edition page, click the Download AVG Free Edition button. Read the license agreement and if you agree, click Yes, I Agree.**
4. **Fill out the registration form. You must provide a valid e-mail address so that the AVG download routine can send you an installation key.**
5. **Follow the instructions to download the software. When the download finishes, run the file and click the Setup button (see Figure 6-2).**
6. **Check your incoming e-mail for a message from the downloader. The message includes your registration code.**
7. **Type the registration code in the indicated text box during installation, follow the wizard, restart your computer, and you're protected.**

   AVG-Free registers itself to start automatically each time your computer starts. It also automatically installs scanners for Office documents and Outlook e-mail messages.

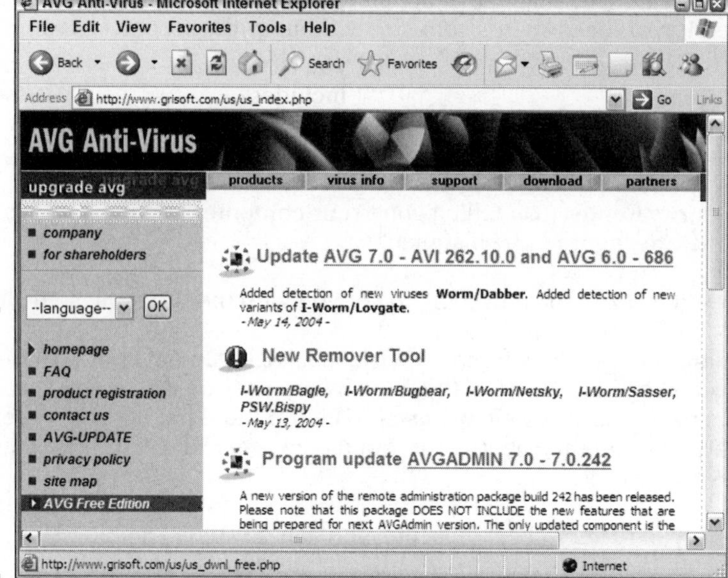

Figure 6-1: Quality antivirus software for personal home use doesn't cost a thing.

AVG 6.0 Anti-Virus System Setup

AVG 6.0 Anti-Virus System Free Edition SETUP

This is a fully functional free version.
AVG offers powerful and reliable protection against computer viruses.

Setup

Cancel

About

WinZip® Self-Extractor © Nico Mak Computing, Inc. http://www.winzip.com

Figure 6-2: AVG-Free arrives in a file called `avg6665fu_free.exe` (or something similar). Double-click the file to run it.

8. **AVG-Free steps you through downloading the latest virus signature file, creating an emergency boot disk, and running a full scan of your computer, as shown in Figure 6-3.**

9. **If you're connected to the Internet, the First Run Wizard downloads and updates the signature file, as shown in Figure 6-4.**

10. **The First Run Wizard takes you through a complete scan of your system, as shown in Figure 6-5.**

    Sit back and relax. It'll take a while.

11. When the wizard's done, your system's protected.

AVG-Free is actually version 6.0. If you're willing to pay a few dollars, you can upgrade to version 7.0, which includes many more features, and a less-congested signature file download site.

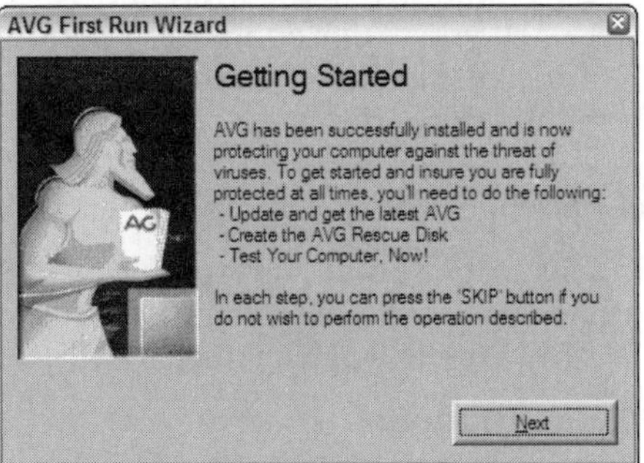

Figure 6-3: AVG-Free steps you through the necessary initial runs.

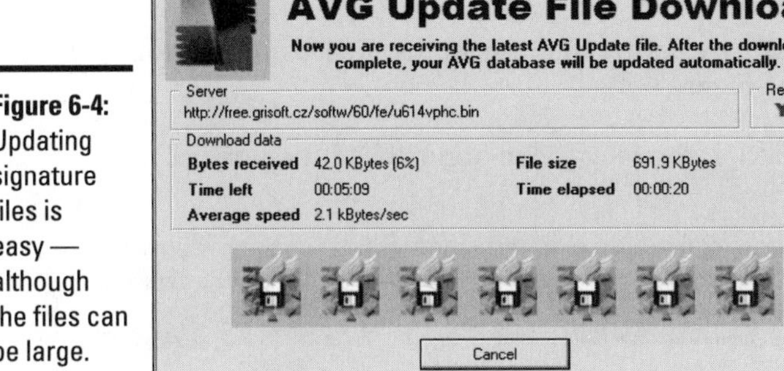

Figure 6-4: Updating signature files is easy — although the files can be large.

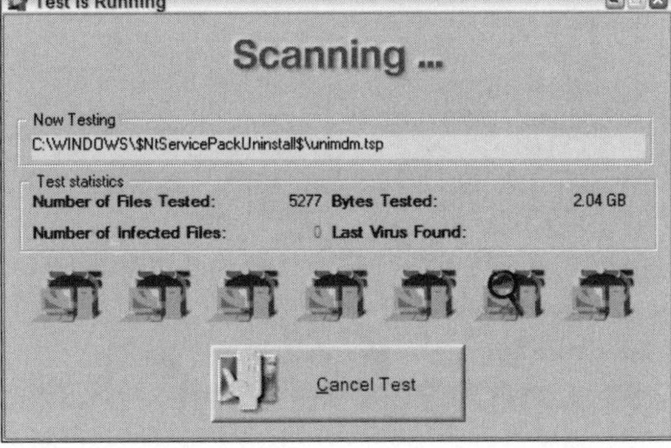

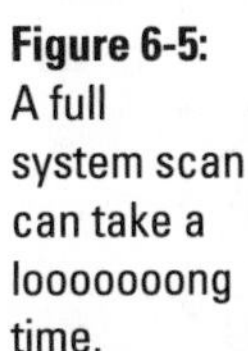

Figure 6-5: A full system scan can take a looooooong time.

Making Windows Acknowledge Your AV Program

The Windows Security Center has an infuriating habit of not properly identifying installed software. In the specific case of AVG-Free, Windows may or may not realize that it's running properly.

If the Windows Security Center icon down in the system tray, next to the clock, continues to incorrectly tell you "Your computer might be at risk/Antivirus software might not be installed," even after your AV program is up and running, you can tell Windows to put a cork in it:

1. **Choose Start⇨Control Panel⇨Security Center.**

   Windows shows you the Security Center. In Figure 6-6, the Security Center tells me that Virus Protection Is Not Found, even though I know dern good and well that AVG-Free is working fine.

2. **Click the Recommendations button.**

   Windows brings up the Recommendation dialog box, as shown in Figure 6-7.

3. **Select the I Have an Antivirus Program That I'll Monitor Myself check box, and then click OK.**

   Windows obliges by noting that the status of virus protection is Not Monitored (see Figure 6-8).

At least Windows stops showing those obnoxious little boxes.

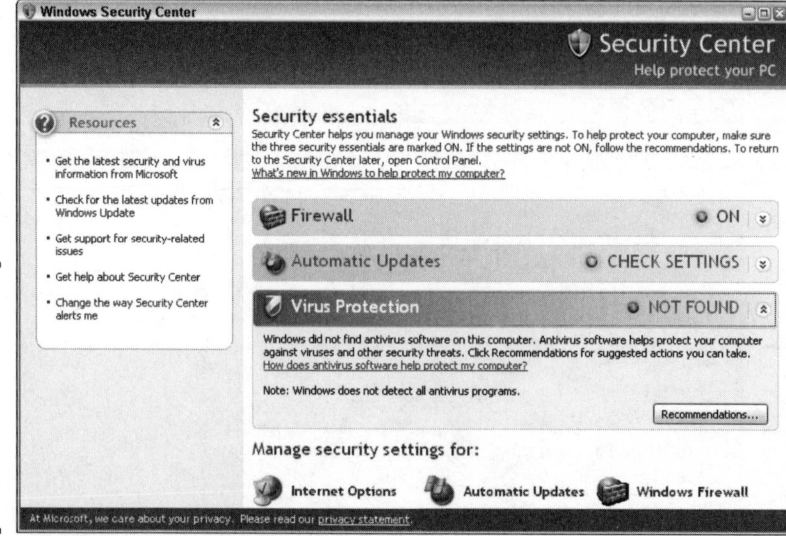

Figure 6-6: The Windows Security Center doesn't detect AVG-Free.

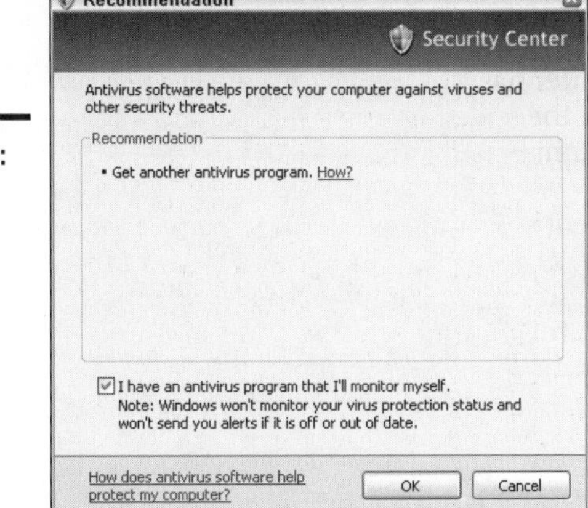

Figure 6-7: Tell Windows to back off if it doesn't recognize your antivirus software.

Figure 6-8: The best you can do is to have the Windows Security Center acknowledge that the state of your antivirus protection is Not Monitored.

Book III

Windows XP and the Internet

The 5th Wave
By Rich Tennant
DATA MINING
©RICHTENNANT
Hold on, Brad - I forgot the canary.
DOWN

Contents at a Glance

Chapter 1: Expanding Your Reach through the Internet

In This Chapter

- **Introducing the Internet**
- **Going through a quick rundown on getting connected to the Internet**
- **Finding out how much it will cost**
- **Discovering the truth behind all the bad things you've heard**

Internet this. Web that. E-mail today. Hair (or at least spam about hair products) tomorrow.

Windows XP makes it easy to get online. That means you can dash off a quick message to your daughter, send a birthday card to your mom, pick up the latest baseball scores and news headlines, glance at the stock market, look up show times and locations at a dozen local theaters, compare features and prices on the latest mobile phones, and check out the weather in Phuket (pronounced *Poo-KET*, by the way), Thailand, all in a matter of minutes — if your Internet connection is fast enough.

On the other hand, you probably have heard that the Internet is full of viruses, it isn't safe to use your credit card to order stuff from a Web site, pornographers lurk on every corner, and everything you do on the Internet is being monitored.

That's what the guy who works in the computer shop told you, isn't it?

What Is the Internet?

You know those stories about computer jocks who come up with great ideas, develop them in their basements (or garages or dorm rooms), release their product to the public, change the world, and make a gazillion bucks?

This isn't one of them.

The Internet started in the mid-1960s as an academic exercise — primarily with the RAND Corporation, MIT, and the National Physical Laboratory in England — and rapidly evolved into a military project, under the U.S. Department of Defense's Advanced Research Project Agency, designed to string together research groups working on ARPA projects.

By the end of the 1960s, ARPA had four computers hooked together — at UCLA, SRI (Stanford), UC Santa Barbara, and the University of Utah — using systems developed by Bolt Beranek and Newman, Inc. By the time Windows XP hit the stands in October 2001, well over 100 million computers were registered permanently on the Internet, and half a billion people could connect to the Internet with computers in their homes.

Today, there are so many computers connected directly to the Internet (including all of you who run DSL or cable modems) that the Internet's addressing system is running out of numbers, just like your local phone company is running out of telephone numbers. The current numbering system — called IPv4 — can handle about four billion addresses. The next version, called IPv6, can handle 340,000,000,000,000,000,000,000,000,000,000,000,000 addresses, which should last us for a while, doncha think?

Ever wonder why you rarely see hard statistics about the Internet? I've found two big reasons: Defining terms related to the Internet is devilishly difficult these days. (What do you mean when you say "X number of computers are connected to the Internet"? Is that the number of computers up and running at any given moment? The number of different addresses that are active? The number that *could be* connected if everybody dialed up at the same time? The number of different computers that get connected in a typical day or week or month?) The other reason is that the Internet is growing so fast that any number you publish today will be meaningless tomorrow.

Inside the Internet

Some observers claim that the Internet works so well because it was designed to survive a nuclear attack. Not so. The people who built the Internet insist that they weren't nearly as concerned about nukes as they were about making communication among researchers reliable, even when a backhoe severed an underground phone line or one of the key computers ground to a halt.

As far as I'm concerned, the Internet works so well because the engineers who laid the groundwork were utter geniuses. Their original ideas from 40 years ago have been through the wringer a few times, but they're still pretty much intact. Here's what they decided:

- **No single computer should be in charge:** All the big computers connected directly to the Internet are equal (although, admittedly, some are more equal than others). By and large, computers on the Internet move data around like kids playing hot potato — catch it, figure out where you're going to throw it, and let it fly quickly. They don't need to check with some uber-computer before doing their work; they just catch, look, throw.

- **Break the data into fixed-size packets:** No matter how much data you're moving — an e-mail message that just says "Hi" or a full-color, life-size photograph of the Andromeda galaxy — the data is broken up into packets. Each packet gets routed to the appropriate computer. The receiving computer assembles all the packets and notifies the sending computer that everything came through okay.
- **Deliver each packet quickly:** If you want to send data from Computer A to Computer B, break the data into packets and route each packet to Computer B using the fastest connection possible — even if that means some packets go through Bangor and others go through Bangkok.

Taken together, those three rules ensure that the Internet can take a lickin' and keep on tickin'. If a chipmunk eats through a telephone line, any big computer that's using the gnawed line can start rerouting packets over a different telephone line. If the Cumbersome Computer Company in Cupertino, California loses power, computers that were sending packets through Cumbersome can switch to other connected computers. It all works quickly and reliably, although the techniques used internally by the Internet computers get a bit hairy at times.

Using the Internet

Big computers are hooked together with high-speed communication lines: the Internet *backbone*. If you want to use the Internet from your business or your house, you have to connect to one of the big computers first. Companies that own the big computers (Internet Service Providers) get to charge you for the privilege of getting onto the Internet through their big computers.

If you have a dial-up modem, here's how your connection to the Internet works:

1. **You pay.**

   You may find an Internet Service Provider (ISP) by using one of the Windows XP sign-up options; you may receive a prepaid ISP account with AOL, MSN, or one of the other biggies when you buy your PC; you may talk to that kid in the computer shop; you may even see a "free three months" deal of some sort. In any case, you have to plunk down your credit card or write a check and pay the piper.

What's a modem?

Your computer really, really wants to talk to other computers. If you hook your computer up to another computer with a fairly short cable, they can talk digitally, sending 1s and 0s over the cable to each other. Cool. But if your computer has to talk over the telephone line, that's another story entirely.

Back in the early days of telephones, all connections were analog: You talked into a mouthpiece; that caused a varying amount of electricity to travel through the telephone line; the earpiece on the other end of the telephone line picked up the electrical changes and converted the impulses back into sound. Those phones were a bit like tying a piece of string to two paper cups — the sound pulses in the cup on one end made the string vibrate, and the cup on the other end converted the vibrations back to sound.

Nowadays, telephone systems are entirely digital. (Well, almost entirely digital. I'll come back to that in a second.)

Computers are digital beasts — they talk in 1s and 0s. Telephones are analog beasts — they want varying pulses. Modems bridge the gap. They convert digits into pulses and vice versa. Think of it this way: Your computer has a string of 1s and 0s that it wants to send to your friend Moe's computer — let's say, 11001. You and Moe, being game Dummies, decide to play modem. (Bear with me, okay?)

You call Moe and exchange pleasantries. When you're both ready, you both tell your computers to have at it. Your computer starts flashing the 1s and 0s on the screen that it wants to send to Moe's computer. You see a 1 on your computer's screen and yell into the telephone, "ONE!" Moe hears you say "one," and types a 1 into his computer. You shout "ONE" again, and Moe types another 1. Then you shout "ZERO," and Moe types a 0. "ZERO" again, 0 again. Then "ONE," and Moe types a 1. When your computer is finished, it flashes a message on the screen. You yell, "I'm done Moe, did you get it?" Moe yells back, "Yep, I got it!"

That's what a modem does. When it's sending data, it takes the 1s and 0s that the computer wants to send and shouts into the phone "ONE" or "ZERO." When it's receiving data, it listens for "ONE" and "ZERO" and relays the appropriate number to the computer. Some extra work is involved — exchanging pleasantries and making sure that all the data came through — but at its heart, a modem alternately yells and listens.

Here's the ironic part: Although the telephone system used to be entirely analog, these days it's almost entirely digital. The only analog part is the short distance — called the *local loop* — from your house to the closest telephone switch. Nowadays, when you talk into the telephone, a varying amount of electricity (an analog signal) is sent on the phone line that only goes as far as the switch — typically a few hundred yards. When your voice hits the switch, it's digitized and sent to the receiving switch, where it's converted back to analog so that it can travel the final few hundred yards to Moe's house. In essence, your slow-as-a-snail modem exists only to make the trip from your house to your local telephone switch. Everything else travels at blazing speeds.

DSL technology simply leap-frogs that final few hundred yards. Instead of converting your PC's digital 1s and 0s to analog ONEs and ZEROs, the DSL box makes sure that the digital data that your PC generates gets patched directly into the already-digital network. Cable modems hook into the already-digital cable TV line that probably goes to your house. Easy, eh?

2. **Your Internet Service Provider may hand you some software with instructions attached.**

   At the very least, your ISP gives you an I.D., a password, and a telephone number. Follow the ISP's instructions — using whatever software the ISP requires — to connect. (Windows XP's standard connection dialog box is shown in Figure 1-1.)

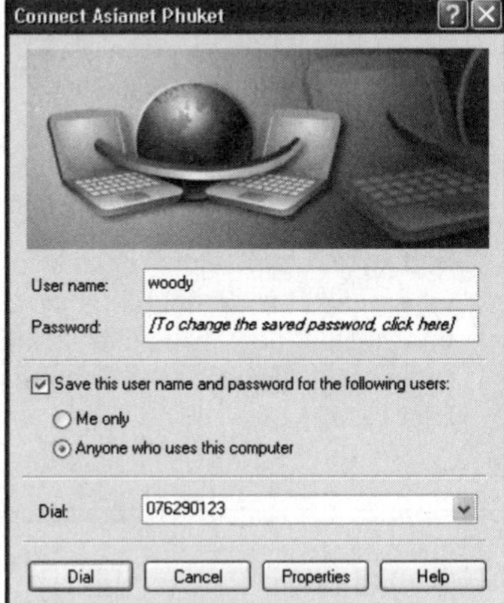

Figure 1-1: If you connect directly to the Internet, you use a dialog box like this one.

3. **When you connect, your computer dials your ISP's telephone number.**

   That pinging sound you probably hear ("ping-ping-pong-ssssssss") is the sound of your computer trying to talk to the ISP's computer over your modem. (See the sidebar, "What's a modem?")

4. **As soon as the modems are talking to each other, your computer sends your I.D. and password.**

   The ISP's computer makes sure that you have a valid account (which is to say, the computer makes sure you paid your bill).

5. **If the ISP's computer gives the okay, the connection is opened up, and you can start using your software — Internet Explorer, AOL, Outlook, Outlook Express, or one of the many others.**

6. **When you're done, you tell the computer to hang up the modem.**

I have an extensive list of ISP sign-up options and the myriad ways you can spend your ISP bucks in Book III, Chapter 2.

Hooking up

Some Internet Service Providers specifically forbid using a fast Internet connection on more than one computer. They have a right to make whatever absurd demands they like — and if push comes to shove, you have to abide by their rules of service. But the simple fact is that they have no way of knowing that you're sharing a fast Internet connection among several computers, short of looking at the settings on computers connected to your network . . .

. . . Unless you have a wireless network. If you've set up a wireless network, your ISP may get upset if you allow any scruffy old computer to use the network to get on the Internet. That's an emotionally charged topic these days, particularly because folks in New York City used anonymous "free" wireless systems to get the word out about the 9-11 aftermath. Granted, your ISP probably won't find out unless somebody posts access information for your network in a highly visible place, or somebody reports your random act of kindness to the ISP. But is it their business? See the Electronic Frontier Foundation's Web site, `www.eff.org/Infrastructure/Wireless_cellular_radio/wireless_friendly_isp_list.html`, for details and a list of ISPs that don't have corncobs lodged in their thinking orifices.

Putting together a home or small office network where all the computers use a single fast Internet connection is like falling off a log if you're using Windows XP. See Book IX, Chapter 2 for details.

If you have a DSL or cable modem connection, here's how your Internet connection works:

1. **You pay.**

   Funny how that's the first step, no matter what you do, eh?

   If you're thinking about springing for DSL or cable Internet access, don't waste another second. You need it. With rare exceptions, the price of fast Internet is so low these days that throwing away your dial-up modem is a no-brainer.

2. **If you're using DSL, the telephone company has to flip a switch that turns your phone line into a DSL line. The cable modem guys may have to come out and wire something, too.**

   You can use a regular telephone (fax machine, answering machine) on a DSL line at the same time that you're using it for your computer. But when you're blabbing on the phone, the computer connection gets slower, so consider getting a new phone line primarily for the Internet.

3. **Your Internet Service Provider may install a box — a cable modem, DSL router, or something similar — that's about the size and shape of a CD player, and they may come out and hook you up. Or they may just give you the sign-up information and let you buy and install your own box.**

Those of you with networks take note: Some Internet Service Providers get all excited and want to charge you extra money if you connect the cable modem or DSL router to a network hub. If you get a Neanderthal cable guy who starts blustering about extra charges, smile and have the installer attach the cable modem or router to your main computer, and promise-with-your-pinkie-finger that you won't let the other computers on your network use the fast Internet connection. As long as your main computer has Windows XP, it's easy to tell all the PCs on your network to use the fast connection — see the sidebar on "Hooking up" — and there's no way the DSL or cable company will ever know of your intransigence, short of an inspection of your computers' settings.

4. **If your ISP installs the box, you should be connected before the installer leaves your premises. If you install the box yourself, follow the router/modem manufacturer's instructions — usually you have to go in with Internet Explorer and set your ID and password — and connect to the Web site of your choice.**
5. **Make sure your firewall is working.**

   See Book II, Chapter 4 for more about the Windows Firewall.
6. **If you have other computers on your network, follow the instructions in Book IX, Chapter 2 to run the Windows XP Network Installation Wizard and get all of them to use your new fast Internet connection.**
7. **There's no need to turn off the modem/router, disconnect, or reconnect. Ever. You former dial-up modem users may applaud.**

What Is the World Wide Web?

People tend to confuse the World Wide Web with the Internet, which is a lot like confusing the dessert table with the buffet line. I'd be the first to admit that desserts are mighty darn important. Life-critical, in fact, if the truth be told. But they aren't the same as the buffet line.

In order to get to the dessert table, you have to stand in the buffet line. In order to get to the Web, you have to be running on the Internet.

Make sense?

The World Wide Web owes its existence to Tim Berners-Lee and a few co-conspirators at a research institute called CERN in Geneva, Switzerland. In 1990, Berners-Lee demonstrated a way to store and link information on the Internet so that all it took was a click to jump from one place — one Web page — to another. By the time Windows XP shipped in October 2001, almost two billion pages were on the Web.

Like the Internet itself, the World Wide Web owes much of its success to the brilliance of the people who brought it to life. The following are the ground rules:

- **Web pages, stored on the Internet, are identified by an address such as** `www.dummies.com`**.** Although you're probably accustomed to seeing addresses that start with `www` and end with `com`, `org`, or `edu`, plenty of addresses don't.
- **Web pages are written in a funny kind of language called HTML.** HTML is sort of a programming language, sort of a formatting language, and sort of a floor wax, all rolled into one. Many products claim to make it easy for novices to create powerful, efficient HTML. None of them do.
- **In order to read a Web page, you have to use something called a Web browser.** A Web browser is a program that runs on your computer and is responsible for converting HTML into something you can read and use. The vast majority of people who view Web pages use Internet Explorer as their Web browser. Unless you live under a rock in the Gobi Desert, you know that Internet Explorer is part of Windows XP. Today, anyway. Heaven only knows what the courts will do.

One unwritten rule for the World Wide Web: All Web acronyms have to be completely, utterly inscrutable. For example, a Web address is called an URL, or Uniform Resource Locator, pronounced *earl*. HTML is short for Hypertext Markup Language. On the Web, a gorgeous, sunny, palm-lined beach with the scent of frangipani wafting through the air would no doubt be called SHS — Smelly Hot Sand. Sheeesh.

The best part of the Web is how easily you can jump from one place to another — and how easily you can create Web pages with hot links (also called hyperlinks or just links) that transport the viewer wherever the author intends. That's the "H" in "HTML," and the original reason for creating the Web so many years ago.

Who Pays for All This Stuff?

That's the $64 billion question, isn't it?

The Internet is one of the true bargains of the 21st century. When you're online — for which you probably have to pay AOL, MSN, your cable company, or some other Internet Service Provider a monthly fee — the Internet itself is free.

Web sites

Most Web sites don't charge a cent. They pay for themselves in any of several ways:

- **By reducing a company's operating costs:** Banks and brokerage firms, for example, have Web sites that routinely handle customer inquiries at a fraction of the cost of H2H (er, human-to-human) interactions.
- **By increasing a company's visibility:** This means that the Web site gives you a good excuse to buy more of the company's products. That's why architectural firms show you pictures of their buildings and food companies post recipes.
- **By drawing in new business:** Ask any real estate agent.
- **By contracting advertising:** Some popular sites like `www.newyorktimes.com` sell ad spots outright.
- **By using bounty advertising:** Smaller sites run ads, usually selected from a pool of advertisers. The advertiser pays a bounty for each person who clicks on the ad and views its Web site — a so-called *click through*.
- **By affiliate programs:** Smaller sites may also participate in a retailer's affiliate program. If a customer clicks through and orders something, the Web site that originated the transaction gets a percentage of the amount ordered. Amazon.com is well known for its affiliate program, but many others exist.

Some Web sites have an entrance fee. For example, if you want to use the Oxford English Dictionary on the Web (see Figure 1-2), you have to part with some substantial coin — $295 (U.S.) per year for individuals, the last time I looked. Guess that beats schlepping around 20 volumes.

E-mail

E-mail frequently comes free from your ISP. Keep these points in mind:

- Most ISPs limit the amount of mail that you can store for free.
- Most ISPs limit the size of individual e-mail messages, coming and going — you can't send or receive really big file attachments.
- When your friends have your I.D., it's difficult to switch ISPs because you have to tell all your friends about your new I.D.
- Plenty of free e-mail services exist on the Internet. `http://mail.google.com`, `www.hotmail.com` and `http://mail.yahoo.com` are among the more popular, but you can find hundreds of alternatives at `www.emailaddresses.com`.

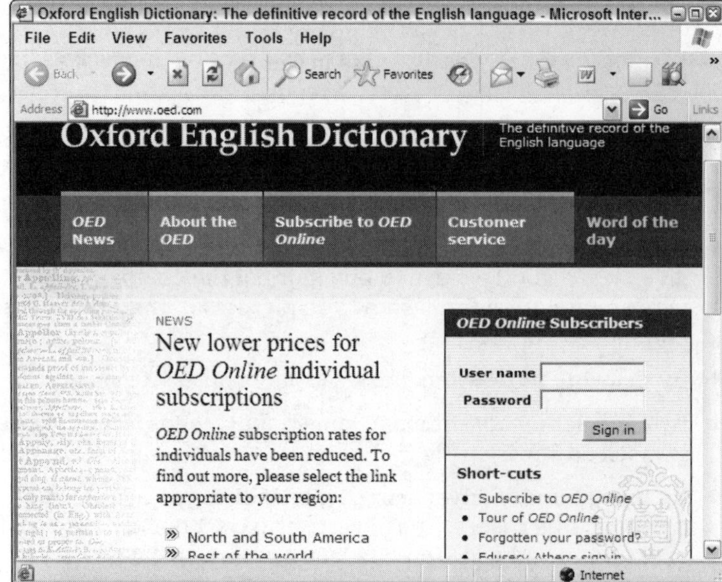

Figure 1-2: The Oxford English Dictionary: Venerable resource, pricey Web site.

Other Internet products

E-mail newsletters are usually free, although an increasing number charge a small annual fee to help defray costs. Generally, the cost of creating and distributing a newsletter is not great — many newsletters rely almost solely on volunteer contributions — so newsletter publishers get by on small fees charged to advertisers. Many newsletters advertise products, services, or Web sites connected to the publisher.

Newsgroups are almost always free, providing that your Internet Service Provider offers a news service. Unmoderated Usenet newsgroups — the kind of Internet newsgroup that has no human involved in filtering out the drivel — run themselves. Moderated newsgroups have volunteers who go over the postings before they get sent on to newsgroup members, removing the offal.

Internet Myths Exploded

The Internet is wild and woolly and wonderful — and, by and large, it's unregulated, in a Wild West sort of way. Some would say it's unregulatable, and I'd have to agree. Although some central bodies control basic Internet coordination questions — how the computers talk to each other, who doles out domain names such as `dummies.com`, what a Web browser should do when it encounters a particular piece of HTML — no central authority or Web Fashion Police exists.

Being on the Internet doesn't absolve an individual or company of all restrictions, of course. An American company has to abide by American laws. An American company doing business in Germany has to abide by German laws, as well. Individuals can run afoul of regulations in one location while conforming to rules in another location. It's very confusing.

Most of the bad things you hear about the Internet, though, don't hold water. I wanted to put a bunch of them together, here in one place, so that you can grab your brother-in-law by the ear, whip out this book, and say, "There! I told you so!"

Viruses

"Everybody" knows that the Internet breeds viruses. "Everybody" knows that really bad viruses can drain your bank account, break your hard drive, and give you terminal halitosis — just by looking at an e-mail message with "Good Times" in the Subject line.

Right.

In fact, viruses (I use the term loosely) can hurt you, but hoaxes and lousy advice abound. Every Windows XP user should take these seven steps:

1. **Use a firewall.**

   Windows Firewall, which was installed automatically if you have a sufficiently new version of Windows XP (see `http://windowsupdate.microsoft.com`), will suffice, as long as you don't open up any ports (see Book II, Chapter 4).

2. **Don't install programs that look fishy (see Figure 1-3).**

   Unless the downloadable software comes from a major manufacturer, and you know precisely *why* you need it, you probably don't want it.

Figure 1-3: Programs that install directly from the Internet trigger warning boxes like this.

You may think that you absolutely have to synchronize the Windows clock (which Windows XP does amazingly well, no extra program needed), tune up your computer (gimme a break), use those cute little smiley icons (gimme a bigger break), install a popup blocker (the version of Internet Explorer in Service Pack 2 does great; so does the Google toolbar), or get an automatic e-mail signer (your e-mail program already can — read the manual, pilgrim!). What you'll end up with is an unending barrage of hassles and hustles.

If you click on the Name link (refer to Figure 1-3), you can read about all the wonderful software that will be installed on your computer in addition to the stuff that you thought you would get, as shown in Figure 1-4. Avoid the slime. Click the Don't Install button.

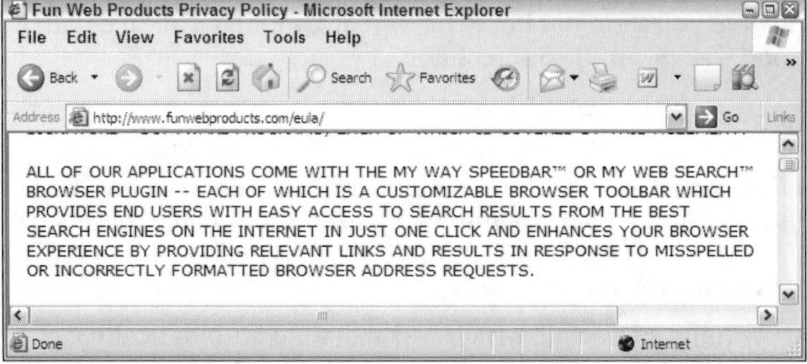

Figure 1-4: Click Don't Install to skip getting slimed with stuff like this.

3. **Buy, install, update, and religiously use one of the major antivirus software packages.**

   It doesn't matter which one — all of them are good. See Book II, Chapter 6 for more on antivirus software.

4. **Never, ever, ever open a file attached to an e-mail message until you do the following:**

   - Contact the person who sent you the file and verify that he or she did, in fact, send you the file intentionally. The most virulent and destructive attacks these days come in the form of files attached to e-mail messages that are automatically sent out by an infected system.

   - After you contact the person who sent you the file, don't open the file directly. Save it to your hard drive and run your antivirus software on it before you open it.

5. **Follow the instructions in Book I, Chapter 3 to force Windows XP to show you the full name of all the files that are on your computer.**

   That way, if you see a file called `something.cpl` or `iloveyou.vbs`, you stand a fighting chance of understanding that it could be an infectious program waiting for your itchy finger.

6. **If you get a virus warning in e-mail, take it with a grain of salt.**

   Check Rob Rosenberger's Virus Myths page, `www.vmyths.com`, to see whether it's a known hoax, or look at the hoax listing on your antivirus software manufacturer's Web site. Most of all, realize that if a killer virus is on the loose and attempting to overload the Internet and bring it to its knees, the worst possible way for you to notify your family and friends is by sending them e-mail!

7. **Flip to the very end of this book — Book IX, Chapter 4 — for information about protecting yourself against virus attacks.**

You have to be careful. But your uncle's sister-in-law's roommate's hairdresser's soon-to-be-ex boyfriend, who's a really smart computer guy (but kinda smelly) may not be the best source of unbiased information.

Don't send that virus warning

Every time a new virus appears, millions and millions of people take it upon themselves to forward virus warning messages to all of their friends, who dutifully forward the warnings to all of their friends, and so on. In several recent cases, the amount of damage done by well-intentioned people sending out warning messages to their friends actually exceeded the amount of damage done by the virus itself — the drain on systems around the world was so great.

To top if off, some of the warning messages are full of bogus information. Two recent bogus warnings advised people to delete perfectly legitimate files from their PCs, claiming the files were infected! A friend tells ten of her friends, who each tell ten of their friends, and all of a sudden people are self-inflicting far more damage than any mere virus could've done. Makes me wonder what would happen if you started a chain letter advising people to stick a wad of chewing gum in their CD drives to prevent the spread of the dread CD virus.

If you feel a real urge to warn all of your friends about the latest virus, don't forward a message to them, no matter how authoritative it may seem. Instead, pick up the phone or walk over to their cubicles, point them to a reputable news organization's Web site, and let them read the latest news for themselves.

And if a friend forwards you a virus warning in e-mail, do all of us a big favor. Send him the preceding paragraph, ask him to print it out and tape it to the side of his computer, and beg him to refer to it the next time he gets the forwarding urge.

Thank you.

We regularly cover viruses and other kinds of destructive software — with a rather jaundiced eye, quite frankly — at www.AskWoody.com.

Credit card fraud

A very large percentage of people who use the World Wide Web refuse to order anything online because they're afraid that their credit card number will be stolen and they'll be liable for enormous bills. Or they think that the products will never arrive, and they won't get their money back.

If your credit card was issued in the U.S. and you're ordering from a company in the U.S., that's simply not the case:

- The Fair Credit Billing Act protects you from being charged by a company for an item you don't receive. It's the same law that governs orders placed over the telephone or by mail. A vendor generally has 30 days to send the merchandise, or they have to give you a formal, written chance to cancel your order. For details, go to the Federal Trade Commission's Web site, www.ftc.gov/bcp/conline/pubs/buying/mail.htm.
- Your maximum liability for charges fraudulently made on the card is $50 per card. The minute you notify the credit card company that somebody else is using your card, you have no further liability. If you have any questions, the Federal Trade Commission will help. See www.ftc.gov/bcp/conline/pubs/credit/cards.htm.

Some online vendors, such as Amazon.com, absolutely guarantee that your shopping will be safe. The Fair Credit Billing Act protects any charges fraudulently made in excess of $50. Amazon says it will reimburse any fraudulent charges *under* $50 that occurred as a result of using its Web site. For details, see www.amazon.com. Many credit card companies now offer similar assurances.

That said, you should still take a few simple precautions to make sure that you aren't giving away your credit card information:

- **When you place an order online, make sure that you're dealing with a company you know.** In particular, *don't* click on a link in an e-mail message and expect that you'll go to the company's Web site. Type the company's address into Internet Explorer, or use a link that you stored in IE's Favorites list.
- **Only type in your credit card number when you're sure that you've arrived at the company's site, and when the site is using a secure Web page.** The easy way to tell whether a Web page is secure is to look at the address, and look for the lock icon at the bottom of Internet Explorer (see Figure 1-5). Secure Web sites scramble data, so anything that you type on the Web page is encrypted before it's sent to the vendor's computer.

The address changes from http:/ to https://

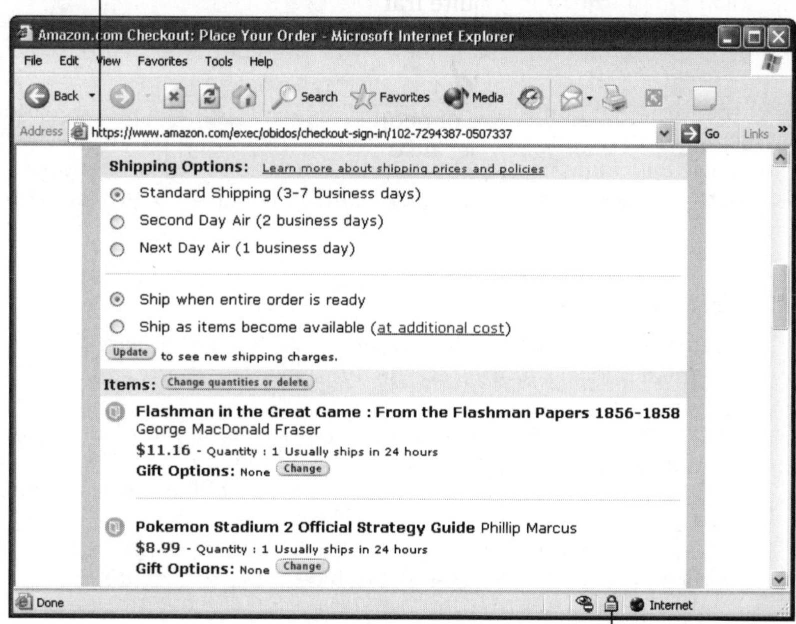

Figure 1-5: A secure Web site.

The lock icon signifies that the page is secure

Beware of the fact that crafty Web programmers can fake the lock icon and show an `https://` address to try to lull you into thinking that you're on a secure Web page. In order to be safe, you need to make sure you're using a reputable company's Web site — and the only way to do that is to type the address into Internet Explorer's address bar or use a Favorites link that you've set up.

- **Don't send your credit card number in an ordinary e-mail message.** E-mail is just too easy to intercept. And for heaven's sake, don't give out any personal information when you're chatting online.
- **If you receive an e-mail message requesting credit card information that seems to be from your bank, credit card company, Internet Service Provider, or even your sainted Aunt Martha, don't send sensitive information back via e-mail.** Insist on using a secure Web site and type the company's address into Internet Explorer.
- **You may be tempted to put your credit card information in a monster database such as Microsoft's Passport.** Make sure that you understand the consequences of your actions before you type in your credit card number. See Book IX, Chapter 4.

The rules are different if you're not dealing with a U.S. company and using a U.S. credit card. For example, if you buy something in an online auction from an individual, you don't have the same level of protection. Make sure that you understand the rules before you hand out credit card information.

Identity theft continues to be a problem all over the world. Widespread availability of personal information online only adds fuel to the flame. If you think someone may be posing as you — to run up debts in your name, for example — see the U.S. government's main Web site on the topic at `www.consumer.gov/idtheft`.

Just pass a law

Online pornography is big business — billions of dollars a year. It's one of the great success stories on the Internet.

Online gambling is big business, too — billions more. According to the *Miami Herald* (`www.miami.com/mld/miamiherald/business/international/8268545.htm?1c`), online gambling is a $6.1 billion per year business.

If there's a vice to be mined and a buck to be made, you can bet that somebody on the Internet is going at it, full-tilt boogie, right now.

I wish I had a nickel for every time I've heard some well-meaning person tell me that the U.S. Congress is at fault. If Washington would only pass a law, the sentiment goes, we could crush these pornographers (or bookies, quacks, hatemongers, pill pushers, insert your favorite whipping boy here) overnight.

Uh, yeah. Sure.

Here's how the Internet works. Say the government of Moronovia decides that Internet sites shouldn't be allowed to show pictures of Minnie Mouse. There's a hue and cry in Parliament, a bill gets passed, and all the Moronovian Web sites featuring poor little Minnie are crushed into silicon dust, their Webmeisters marched off to serve 20 years at hard labor.

Halfway around the world in Enterprizistan, a Web designer is scanning the headlines and discovers that the Moronovian Web sites featuring Minnie Mouse are all down. He rummages around the Web for a day or two, dredges up some grainy pics of our favorite subversive mouse, throws together a Web page (`www.minniemouse.ezn`, anybody?), and he's suddenly in business.

That's how it works.

Forward this message and save a poor child

Yes, it's true. Bill Gates will send you $10 for every copy of this e-mail message that you forward to a friend. I know. I asked Bill over coffee this morning. You can help a poor child survive a horrendous operation, because Intel will send ten cents to her for each copy of this message that you forward. I know. I asked Intel over coffee this morning. A bunch of hackers are going to start a riot on AOL next week, and they'll come after you if you don't send this message to ten of your AOL friends. I know. I scalded a hacker with hot coffee this morning. The President is about to impose a federal tax for every e-mail message you open. I know. I asked George Washington over coffee this morning. Your computer will die if you open any e-mail message with "It takes guts to say 'Jesus'" in the subject line. I know. I asked Jesus over coffee this morning. For the record, he likes low-fat lattes, half caffeine, extra foam, with a light dash of cinnamon.

Gimme a break, folks.

Virus myths and chain letters flood the ether. If you send messages like those, you're only contributing to the problem. Bill Gates isn't going to fork over ten bucks for mailing a message. George, er, the President doesn't have any way of counting how many e-mail messages you read. It takes guts to ignore the chain letters, even when they come from people you know and otherwise respect.

Before you forward that improbable message and add to the deluge of bogus bits ricocheting around the information highway, drop by Rob Rosenberger's Virus Myths home page, `www.vmyths.com`. Rob doesn't have any particular axes to grind. He doesn't sell antivirus software or spam scanners. He didn't make a mint from Code Red. He's a refreshing voice of sanity in this truly bizarre world. And he could keep you from making a really big fool of yourself.

If you want to control where your kids can and can't go, consider using AOL. I've had very mixed success with Net Nanny (`www.netnanny.com`) and Cyber Patrol (`www.surfcontrol.com`). The problem, of course, is that the packages don't block some sites that should be blocked — and at the same time, the packages shut out some perfectly good, even educational, sites.

Yes, some things can — and should — be done to curb Internet excesses. In some cases, legislation can make a difference. In many cases, it's just expectorating in the wind.

Since the U.S. CAN-SPAM act (`www.spamlaws.com/federal/108s877.html`) was enacted on January 7, 2003, has the volume of spam you've received increased or decreased?

This legislation stuff cuts both ways. The Internet provides a hotbed of activity for subversive groups that oppose authoritarian regimes in many countries. In the end, widespread availability of Internet access may well end up being the most democratizing influence of our generation. Watch the People's Republic of China. Watch Burma, er, Myanmar.

Big Brother is watching

You can easily get caught up in the Big Brother hysteria. After all, the Net has reached into everyone's lives, and it's easy to get paranoid about something so big and so important. Still, you have to use a little common sense.

Some of the stuff that sounds like science fiction is true! Case in point: the FBI's Carnivore program, which monitors e-mail. Although the program was renamed DCS1000 more than a year ago (now *that* makes me feel more secure), the fact remains that the FBI is fully capable of monitoring e-mail, methodically and thoroughly.

Keep these facts in mind:

- No way exists for a person or company to monitor who receives copies of a text e-mail message (although a method called Web Bugs can be used in certain circumstances to monitor the destination of formatted e-mail messages; see `www.eff.org/Privacy/Marketing/web_bug.html`).
- No way exists for a company or the government to tell which telephone calls that you place originate from your computer's modem.
- Nobody (except the Internet Service Provider who handles your e-mail) can count how many e-mail messages you send or receive.
- If you use a program such as Outlook or Outlook Express, nobody can tell whether you've read an e-mail message or just deleted it.
- When it comes to large online data collection agencies accumulating personal information about you, as an individual, your worst enemy is . . . you. Don't give out any information that makes you uncomfortable.

The Internet is still a rather chaotic, anarchic place. A lot of people are fighting hard to keep it that way.

Chapter 2: Connecting to the Internet

In This Chapter

- Deciding whether to use a dial-up or broadband Internet connection
- Doing the dial-up dirty deed
- Working around trouble spots
- Connecting to the Internet with DSL and cable

This chapter explains how to get connected to the Internet. Of course, the easiest way to do that is with Internet Explorer (IE), the Web browser that comes (surprise, surprise) packaged with your version of Windows XP — at least until a federal judge says otherwise.

Connecting with IE is, thankfully, a pretty straightforward process. You aren't likely to encounter many superhuman challenges along the way — perhaps an unrecognized modem or a misplaced password, or you might need to kick your cable guy, but nothing insurmountable. This chapter walks you through the basics of making that initial IE connection and helps you anticipate and hopefully avoid any potential trouble spots on your path.

You may already be an old hand at making Internet connections. If that's the case, go to the head of the class and move along to the next chapter.

Dial-Up or Broadband?

While my ultimate goal is to get you running on the Information Highway, the details vary greatly depending on whether you use a dial-up modem or a fast Internet connection (typically via DSL service, a cable TV modem, or ISDN).

DSL, ADSL, ISDN, cable, and the like are called *broadband* connections because they're faster than a dial-up modem. At least, theoretically. *(Definition: A broadband connection is any Internet connection that's faster than the one you have. Heh heh heh.)* For an overview of how modems and DSL/cable lines work, see Book III, Chapter 1. ***Hint:*** The only real difference between DSL and a regular old dial-up connection is in the "last mile" between your house or office and the telephone switch.

What's the big deal about bandwidth? If you're just now learning about the phenomena of pushing pictures, words, and sound through your phone lines into your PC, you may not understand the fuss over bandwidth issues. Put simply, *bandwidth* is the size of the channel through which the data can flow. The larger the channel, the more data can flow through at the same time. When you hear people talking at parties about "increasing bandwidth" and dropping terms like "broadband connections," "ISDN," and "T-1 lines," realize that what they really want is more data, sent (and received) faster.

You plug a regular, old-fashioned, everyday telephone line into a dial-up modem. Unless you paid the phone company, your cable TV company, or an Internet Service Provider extra money to have broadband service installed, you're using a regular, old-fashioned, everyday telephone line, and you'll use it with a dial-up modem.

If you have a dial-up modem, follow the directions in the next section, "Dialing with Dollars," to get connected. If you are using a DSL router/modem or a cable modem, smile and follow the directions later in this chapter, "Connecting with DSL or Cable."

If you have a portable computer that's normally connected to a network, and the network has its own fast DSL or cable Internet access, you may want to configure the portable to use its dial-up modem while you're on the road. In that case, you may have to follow the instructions in both sections. Just make sure you unplug the portable from the network *before* you work on the modem so that the different settings don't drive you nuts.

Dialing with Dollars

So you're trying to get connected using a dial-up modem and a boring (yet cheap!) telephone line? This section shows you how to find your modem and ensure that you have what you need before connecting.

Finding your modem

If you want to see what Windows XP thinks your modem of choice is, you can get a quick glimpse by getting into the Control Panel, like this:

1. **Choose Start➪Control Panel➪Printers and Other Hardware➪Phone and Modem Options.**
2. **Click the Modems tab in the dialog box that appears.**

   Is a modem listed (as in, oh, Figure 2-1)? Eureka! You're ready to rumble.

Figure 2-1: A typical internal modem on a portable PC.

If you want to install drivers for another modem, you can click the Add button in the Modems tab of the Phone and Modem Options dialog box to start the process. Simply have the disk or CD that came with your modem handy (or know where the driver files are stored on your hard drive), and Windows XP prompts you for the information that it needs as the drivers are installed.

Do you have an ISP?

An ISP, or Internet Service Provider, is the mysterious link between you and all of the Internet world. This kindly, elderly person — er, large, hulking mainframe computer — is the presence that accepts your computer's incoming calls and passes the necessary data to and from the sites you visit and the e-mail accounts you use.

Before you begin to explore the Internet, you need to establish a relationship with an ISP. If you're using a dial-up modem, the Internet Service Provider will most likely give you the following:

- ✦ A phone number to use to dial in to the ISP's system
- ✦ A user name (also called a user ID) that you use to identify yourself
- ✦ A password to ensure that other people can't use your user name

If you're going to use your ISP for e-mail, you should receive some more information:

- ✦ Your e-mail address, like `woody@askwoody.com` or `billg@microsoft.com`

- The names of the computers that are used to send and receive mail (so-called POP3 and SMTP servers), such as `pop3.email.msn.com` or `secure.smtp.email.msn.com`
- Any special user names, passwords, or other instructions that you need to get connected to the computers that send and receive your mail

Frequently, ISPs give you even more information — designed to help people running Macs or old versions of Windows — but you probably won't need it:

- The numeric IP addresses you need in order to log on to your ISP's server
- The domain name and DNS address
- A CD or disk with any software needed to log on to the ISP site

Some CDs are packed with junk. No, you don't need a seven-year-old version of Eudora, thank you very much. Other CDs, though, are designed to help you through Windows XP's setup options, as detailed in the next section. That's the kind of CD worth having.

Many ISPs also give you a certain amount of Web storage space, in case you want to create your own Web site.

If you don't already have an account with an ISP, you can establish one through Windows — and give Bill Gates the bounty — or you can go shopping for an account that you select yourself. You see how in the section, "Creating a new connection," later in this chapter.

One of the best ways to find a reputable ISP is to ask friends, family, and coworkers what ISP they use. Stay away from the ISPs everyone complains about — no matter how low their rates or how great their "free access" offers may sound. Remember: A day without Internet access is a day without sunshine.

Creating a new connection

Ah, if only Windows were smart enough to apply plug-and-play technology to phone lines, you'd never need to mess with setting up another Internet account. You could just plug in the phone line and let Windows figure the rest out for you. Windows XP doesn't make it quite that easy, but it does include a New Connection Wizard that takes care of most of the dirty work. You simply follow the prompts on-screen, answer a few questions, click a few buttons, and you're online. Here's the process in a nutshell:

1. **Choose Start⇨My Network Places.**

   If you can't find My Network Places on your Start menu, click Start⇨Control Panel⇨Network and Internet Connections and on the left, click My Network Places.

2. **In the Network Tasks pane, choose View Network Connections.**

   The Network Connections window appears, showing existing dial-up and network connections on the current computer (see Figure 2-2).

3. **Click Create a New Connection.**

   This launches the New Connection Wizard.

At first glance, you may think that the choice you want in My Network Places is Add Network Place, but don't be fooled: The option you're looking for is Create New Connection. Add Network Place launches a wizard that signs you up for an online storage service — but it's not your doorway to the Internet.

The opening screen appears, telling you that the wizard will lead you through the steps necessary to connect to the Internet, connect to a private network, or set up a network in your home or small office. Click Next to get started with the fun stuff.

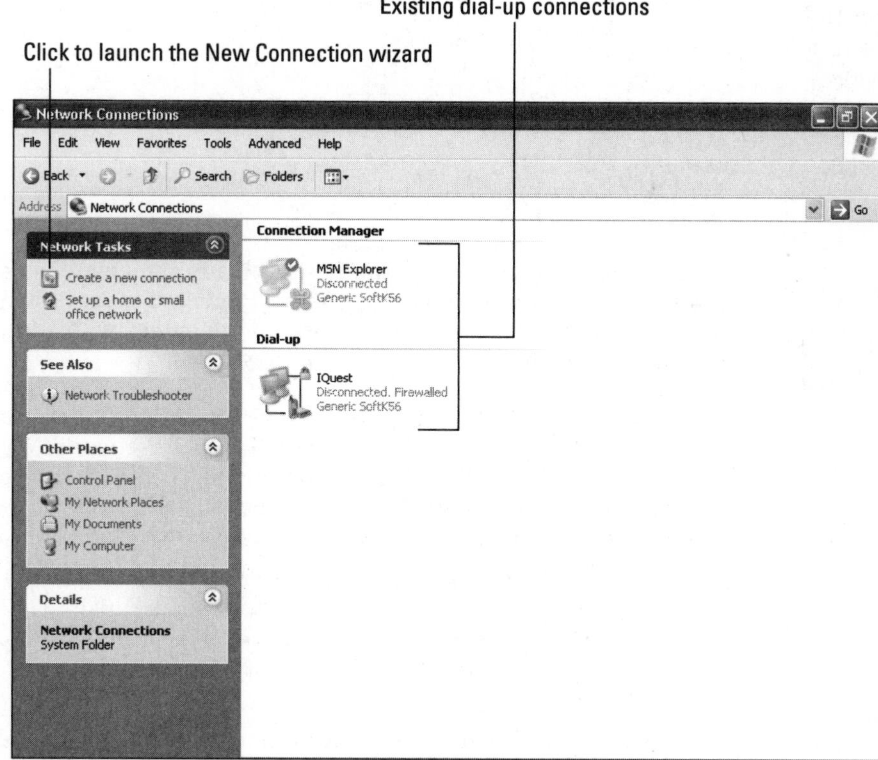

Figure 2-2: Launch the New Connection Wizard from the Network Tasks pane.

Four choices then greet you on the next page of the wizard. The first one is the one you want: Connect to the Internet. When you click it and click Next, the screen shown in Figure 2-3 appears.

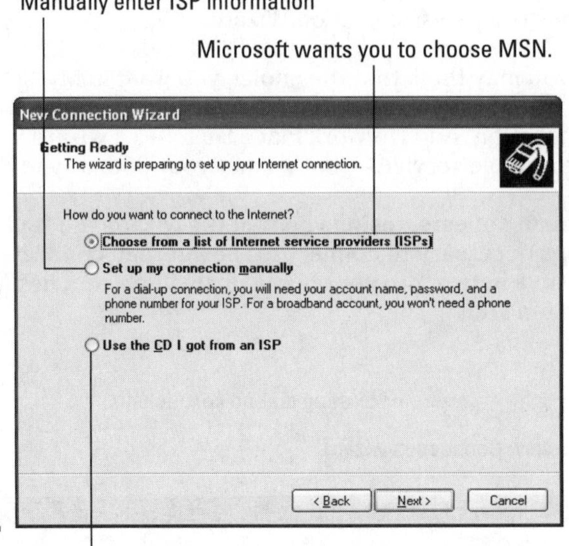

Figure 2-3: Choose the way in which you want to set up your connection.

The three different choices on the Getting Ready screen are important because they each launch different paths. Predictably, the first choice — the default choice — steers you to spend more money with Microsoft. Make your choice and click Next. Here's how they differ:

- **Choose from a List of Internet Service Providers (ISPs):** This option gives you the opportunity to choose Microsoft Network (MSN) (not that you're in a captive audience or anything), or to Select from a List of Other ISPs (see Figure 2-4). If you choose Select from a List of Other ISPs, Microsoft steps you through a referral process.

  If you have no problem paying Mother Microsoft for Internet access, you can leave the first option selected and click Finish to complete the wizard. MSN then steps in with a message box asking whether you want to get on the Internet with MSN Explorer, as shown in Figure 2-5. Click Continue and establish your account.

  Microsoft wants you to download and use MSN Explorer (see Book V, Chapter 1). You can think of MSN Explorer as a helpful program that eases your way onto the Internet. Or you can think of it as an extended advertisement for Microsoft products and services.

Figure 2-4: Microsoft stacks the deck — but if you want MSN, it's easy.

✦ **Set Up My Connection Manually:** This option takes you to a screen that gives you the choice of creating a standard dial-up connection (like the one you use if you have a regular-old modem in a plain-old PC). You can also elect to connect to a broadband (DSL, cable, or ISDN) connection or use a broadband connection that is always active (no sign-in required — by far the most common kind of broadband connection). The rest of this section describes specifics on completing this step.

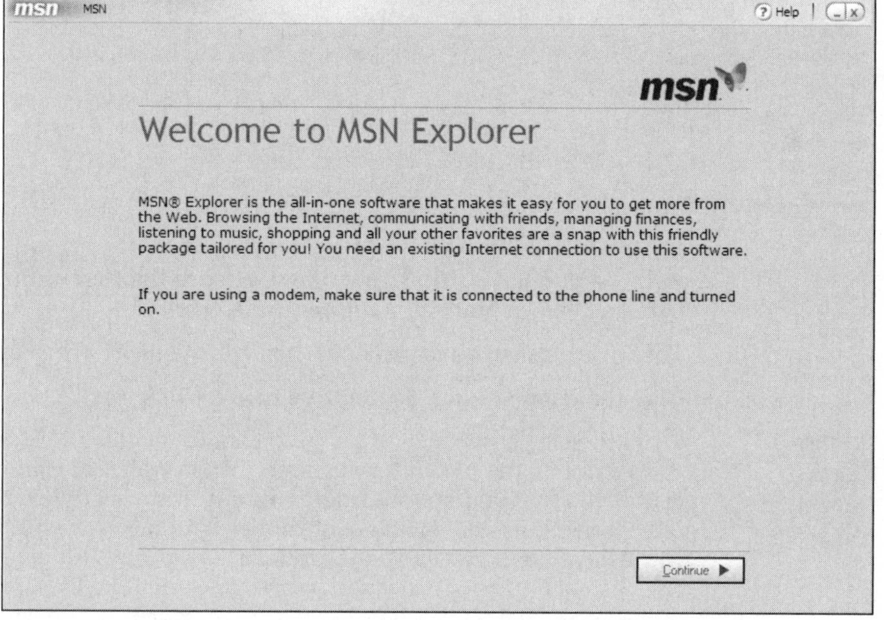

Figure 2-5: Microsoft makes it easy (maybe a little too easy) to sign up with MSN Explorer.

✦ **Use the CD I Got from an ISP:** This option displays a screen that prompts you to insert the CD and click Finish; the setup program then launches and leads you through the connection process. This is so simple that your cat can do it — no further explanation necessary.

Depending on the configuration of your particular system, you may not see these three options. If not, don't sweat it — the process will take you right on into the next step.

If you have an existing Internet dial-up account and you want to use that information on this computer, choose Set Up My Connection Manually. Don't sweat it — it's simple. Here are the steps:

1. **In the Getting Ready screen of the New Connection Wizard (refer to Figure 2-3), click Set Up My Connection Manually; then click Next.**

   The Internet Connection screen appears, as shown in Figure 2-6.

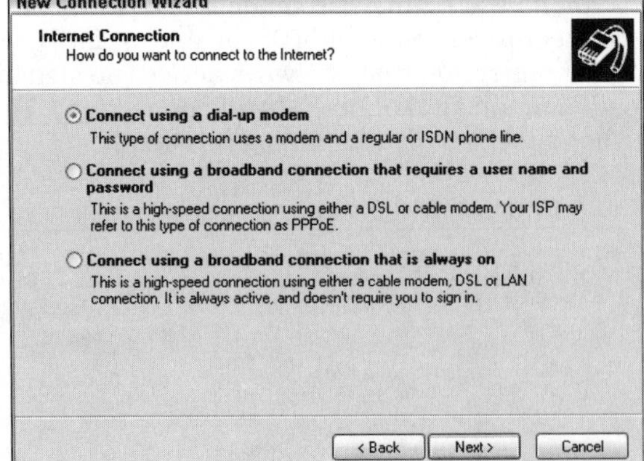

Figure 2-6: If you use a plain, old-fashioned, dial-up modem, the first choice works.

2. **Because you have a dial-up modem, choose the first option, Connect Using a Dial-Up Modem, and then click Next.**

   The wizard asks you to provide a name for your ISP (see Figure 2-7).

3. **Give the connection a descriptive name. Click Next.**

   If you're using a portable, it's a good idea to include the location of the connection in the name (for example, "Walla Walla" in Figure 2-7). That way, if you find yourself returning to a city, it's easy to leaf through your old connections and switch over to the right one — even if your flight was delayed and you can't see straight.

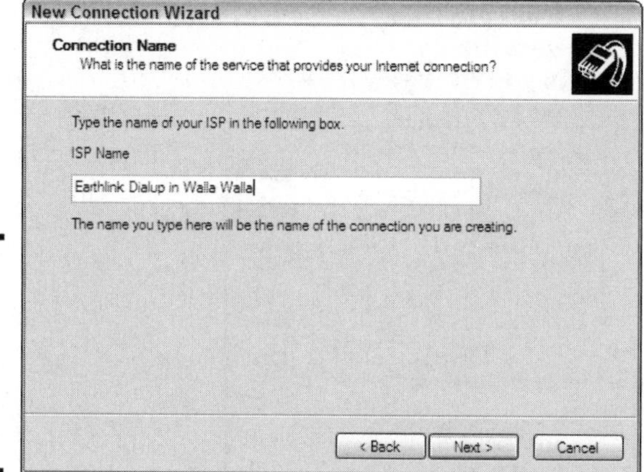

Figure 2-7: Each "connectoid" has a name that you choose.

4. **Enter the phone number that your modem will dial to access the ISP, as shown in Figure 2-8. Click Next.**

New Connection Wizard

Phone Number to Dial

What is your ISP's phone number?

Type the phone number below.

Phone number:

5551212

You might need to include a "1" or the area code, or both. If you are not sure you need the extra numbers, dial the phone number on your telephone. If you hear a modem sound, the number dialed is correct.

< Back Next > Cancel

Figure 2-8: Enter the phone number for the ISP only.

If you commonly dial this connection from a hotel room, do not include the "9 to get out" here, or any other number that you have to dial in order to get an outside line. That's handled in the Phone and Modem Options dialog box, which you can see if you choose Start⇨Control Panel⇨Network and Internet Connections, and then choose Phone and Modem Options in the pane on the right. Click the Location from the list, and then click Edit.

5. **In the Internet Account Information screen (see Figure 2-9), enter the user name for your account and the password you were given. Retype the password in the Confirm Password text box.**

Enter the user name provided by your ISP

Type your assigned password

New Connection Wizard

Internet Account Information
You will need an account name and password to sign in to your Internet account.

Type an ISP account name and password, then write down this information and store it in a safe place. (If you have forgotten an existing account name or password, contact your ISP.)

User name:

Password:

Confirm password:

☑ Use this account name and password when anyone connects to the Internet from this computer

☑ Make this the default Internet connection

< Back | Next > | Cancel

Retype your password

Figure 2-9: When creating a new dial-up connection, enter the user name and password provided by the ISP.

You may want to deselect one or both of the options selected by default in the Internet Account Information screen. If you need flexible settings for your connections that allow multiple users to use your system or that enable users to select from various ISPs, you may find these options more of a hindrance than a help. If you leave the options selected, the account name and password you entered will be used automatically for all users of your computer, and the current Internet connection will be the one used for all connections.

Click Next to move to the last screen of the wizard. Here you have the option to create an Internet shortcut on your desktop. If you want to create the shortcut, select the check box, and then click Finish.

This completes the New Connection Wizard, and Windows XP begins the process of actually getting connected to the Internet.

Getting connected

Okay, now you've finished the techie part. It's all downhill from here. At the end of the New Connection Wizard, Windows XP automatically displays the Connect Dialup Connection dialog box so that you can enter the information that you need in order to make the connection (see Figure 2-10).

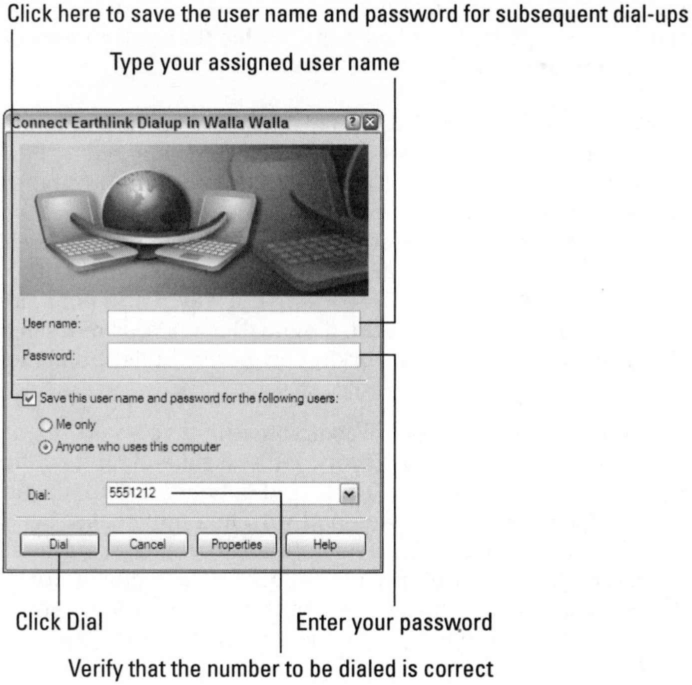

Click here to save the user name and password for subsequent dial-ups

Type your assigned user name

Connect Earthlink Dialup in Walla Walla

User name:

Password:

Save this user name and password for the following users:

Me only

Anyone who uses this computer

Dial: 5551212

Dial Cancel Properties Help

Click Dial

Enter your password

Verify that the number to be dialed is correct

Figure 2-10: To make the connection, just fill in the info and click the Dial button.

Enter the user name and password that your ISP provided, if Windows doesn't fill it in for you. If you want the information to be retained so that you don't have to type it each time you go online, select the Save This User Name and Password for the Following Users check box. After you click the option, the suboptions become available; now you can choose whether you want the information to be saved for only you or for anyone who may use your computer.

Double-check the number in the Dial drop-down list to make sure that your modem will dial the right number. You can click the Dial drop-down list to see any other available access numbers; click the one you want.

Finally, click the Dial button. Your modem dials the number shown and establishes the connection to the Internet. Time to celebrate! Get up, walk around, tell your neighbor, open a Snapple — but don't forget to come back. The fun is just beginning!

Uh-ohs and their answers

Even with all the best-laid plans in the world, sometimes unexpected glitches crop up. If your connection doesn't go smoothly the first time, don't despair.

With a little trial and error, you'll be able to get around the difficulty and get online in no time. Here are a few possibilities that you can check out if things aren't going your way:

- **"I'm not getting a dial tone."** This is a scary problem but usually something simple, such as a not-quite-connected phone line. First, check your hardware connections. Is the phone line plugged into the wall and all the way into the computer? Next, make sure you're using a functioning phone cord. Phone cords sometimes get a small stress break somewhere near the middle. You can also try plugging a phone into the connector to make sure the phone line is working the way it should. If none of those things is the problem, run the diagnostics on your modem (see the "I don't think my modem is working properly" bullet point) to sleuth out the problem.
- **"My ISP isn't answering."** Was it something you said? If not, check the clock. If you are dialing into your ISP at a time of high traffic — usually between 8:00 a.m. and 11:00 a.m. and between 1:00 p.m. and 5:00 p.m. — your ISP may simply be swamped with incoming calls. Get yourself a cup of coffee and try again in a few minutes. If you try continually and are unable to get a rise out of your ISP, give their tech support line a call. The server may be down or — worst-case scenario — your modem could be failing and not giving the ISP's server the "handshake" it's looking for.
- **"I can't connect."** Make sure that you've entered your user name and password correctly. (Most common source of problems: Caps Lock is turned on when you type your password.) Also, double-check the telephone number that your modem is dialing. Finally, check your ISP information, including the IP address or DNS, if your ISP insisted that you enter those numbers manually. When all else fails, call your ISP and ask them to walk you through the connection process. That's what tech support is for.
- **"I don't think my modem is working properly."** If you fail to get a dial tone and your modem shows no signs of life, you can run diagnostics to take your modem's pulse and check its overall health. To test your modem, choose Start➪Control Panel➪Printers and Other Hardware. Next, click Phone and Modem Options. When the Phone and Modem Options dialog box appears, click the Modems tab. Your installed modem should be displayed in the Modem box. Double-click it to have Windows XP quickly run diagnostics. The results are displayed in the Device Status area of the General tab (see Figure 2-11). If you have continuing problems, click the Troubleshoot button to have Windows help you explore further solutions.

  If you click the Troubleshoot button, it's easy to run a quick psychoanalysis of your modem's problems:

  1. **Select the Modem tab.**

2. **Double-click the modem to start the test.**
3. **Windows XP displays the results of the test.**
4. **Click Troubleshoot to see more suggestions.**

✦ **"My connection suddenly disconnects."** If you lose your connection repeatedly, the problem may be between your modem and your ISP. Check with your modem manufacturer to see whether software updates exist that would improve the consistency of the connection.

Figure 2-11: You can easily run diagnostics if your modem is misbehaving.

Connecting with DSL or Cable

So you have a broadband connection, do you? Congratulations. I can't live without mine.

Most of the time, your Internet Service Provider or the cable TV company or the telephone tech comes out and sets up your broadband connection just well enough to get one computer connected to the Internet. That's cool — in fact, that's all you need. If you have a network that you need to get connected, *don't turn off the PC that's connected* until you've run the Internet Connection Wizard on all the PCs on the network (see Book IX, Chapter 2).

In some cases, particularly with DSL (or ADSL), you have to set up the broadband connection yourself, and that's when things can get dicey: You have to dig into the belly of the DSL router/modem, the cable TV box, or the ISDN box. No two routers work exactly the same way, but most of them — at least, most of the more modern routers — share a few characteristics.

Here's how to break into your router:

1. **Only dive into your router if you need to set it up for the first time, or if the power goes out for so long that the router's lost all of its settings.**

   This is brain surgery. If you can bring up Internet Explorer and it connects to any Web page, your router/modem is working fine. If your computer used to get connected to the Internet, but it stopped all of a sudden, chances are good your ISP's computer went down, or your phone line is broken — the router probably works just fine. Only dig into the router if you've exhausted all other possibilities. Ain't broke, don't fix. Got it?

2. **Most routers use a simple Web-based interface. Read your router's manual and find out what address the router uses for itself.**

   In this example, my router uses the address 192.168.1.1.

3. **Start Internet Explorer and type the router's address in the address bar.**

   In this case, I type **http://192.168.1.1** and press Enter.

   My router responds by requesting a password (see Figure 2-12). Yours probably will, too.

4. **Look in your router's documentation and find what to enter in the User Name and the Password text boxes. Type the default user name and password into the Connect dialog box, and then click OK.**

   Your router's main configuration page appears (see Figure 2-13).

Figure 2-12: Most DSL modem/routers require you to provide a user name and password.

Home | LAN | WAN | Bridging | Routing | Services | Admin

home | System Mode | Quick Configuration

S/W Version:	3.959AVT1.8124A/138030917a2	DSL Version:	Y1.16.3		
Serial Number:	abcd	Standard:	Multimode		
Mode:	Routing	Up		Down	
Up Time:	5:40:46	Speed	Latency	Speed	Latency
Time:	Thu Jan 01 07:15:25 1970	896 Kbps	Interleaved	2048 Kbps	Interleaved
Time Zone:	GMT				
Daylight Saving Time:	OFF				
Name:	-				
Domain Name:	-				

WAN Interfaces

nterface	Encapsulation	IP Address	Mask	Gateway	Lower Interface	VPI/VCI	Status
pp-0	PPPoE	172.16.10.216	255.255.255.255	172.16.10.216	aal5-0	0/66	
oa-0	Routed	192.168.255.1	255.255.255.252	0.0.0.0	aal5-7	0/40	

Figure 2-13: Your router's main page will look different from this one, but the kinds of configuration information you need to provide will be similar.

If you can't get your router to accept the user name and password that were provided at the factory, somebody changed either or both. If you got the router from your ISP, call them and ask for the user name and password. If your son's been messing with the router, well, you know who to ask. If all else fails, the router has a reset button. *Call your ISP* and ask them if it's okay to reset your router.

In router-speak, the *LAN* refers to the computer that the router's connected to, or it may refer to your home or office network; the *WAN* refers to the DSL or cable connection to the Internet Service Provider.

5. **Find the place where the router expects you to enter the ISP's user name and password.**

home | System Mode | Quick Configuration

Default Route:	Enabled
Gateway IP Address:	0 0 0 0
PPP	
Username:	076290167@hinet.
Password:	••••••••
Use DNS:	Enable / Disable
DNS	
Primary DNS Server:	0 0 0 0
Secondary DNS Server:	0 0 0 0

Figure 2-14: Type in the user name and password for your router to connect to the ISP.

Most routers have an easily accessible area that contains the user name and password that are assigned by the ISP — that is, the user name and password that your router has to use to connect to the ISP. You may need to read the manual, or you may be lucky enough to have a Quick Configuration option, as does this router (see Figure 2-14).

6. **Type the user name and password in the provided location, and then click Submit (or Update or Refresh or Commit or Commit and Reboot — the terminology varies depending on the manufacturer).**

7. **Choose File⇨Close to leave Internet Explorer.**

   Your modem/router should reset itself and automatically connect to your ISP.

If all else fails, call your ISP. Be sure you have the name and model number of your router/modem handy, and also be sure that you're sitting next to the computer that's supposed to be connected to the Internet. Good luck and keep cool.

Chapter 3: Managing E-Mail and Newsgroups with Outlook Express

In This Chapter

- **Using Windows XP's free e-mail program — Outlook Express**
- **Putting together decent e-mail messages with a minimum of hassle**
- **Keeping on top of your contacts**
- **Using Microsoft's only newsgroup reader — Outlook Express**

Who was it that said the best things in life are free? Whoever said it may have been thinking about Outlook Express. (Of course, you can't really say it's *free* if you consider it part of the price you paid for Windows XP.) Outlook Express is a surprisingly full-featured e-mail program that enables you to send messages in just about any form you want, receive messages from multiple accounts, and even work with newsgroups to find out what the buzz is on topics that are most interesting to you.

Outlook Express may sound like Outlook — part of Microsoft Office — but the two have very little in common. Outlook is the 800-pound gorilla of the personal information management game, with e-mail, task manager, calendar, scheduler, and more. Outlook Express focuses on e-mail and newsgroups — the two features that you're likely to want most in a daily e-mail program.

Microsoft doesn't update Outlook Express very often. Why? Outlook Express doesn't make Microsoft any money: The development budget goes to Microsoft Office, Hind Udder on Da Big Cash Cow. In fact, that lack of big-budget tinkering may be one of OE's most endearing features: Benign neglect means OE is easy to use, reasonably full-featured, and less prone to glitter-grades. Outlook Express works well enough for many folks, and it doesn't creak under all the built-in folderol that festoons Outlook.

Getting Started with Outlook Express

Outlook Express is a great little program if you don't have any other way to get your e-mail. But if you use AOL or MSN for e-mail, or you're already hooked up to Outlook itself in Microsoft Office, you can skip this chapter (do not pass go, do not collect $200).

Even if you use the big Outlook (from Microsoft Office), you need Outlook Express to get into the Internet's newsgroups. Don't ask me why, but Microsoft still hasn't put newsgroup support in Outlook.

All you need in order to start Outlook Express is a connection to the Internet. When you're online, just click the little Outlook Express icon in the Windows taskbar at the bottom of your screen, or choose Start⇨E-mail/Outlook Express. The Outlook Express window appears, as shown in Figure 3-1.

The Outlook Express window is pretty easy to figure out. At the top of the window, you find the familiar title bar and menus; beneath that, you find the Outlook Express toolbar. Table 3-1 provides an overview of the Outlook Express tools. The screen is divided into four different panels:

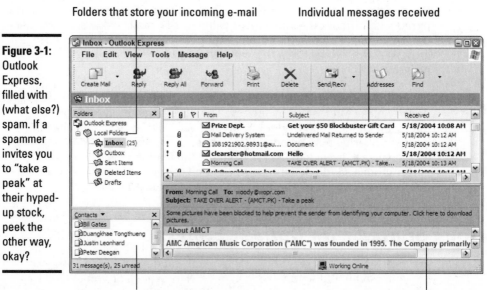

- ✦ The Folders panel displays all the folders you've created in Outlook Express and some you have not created — the Inbox, Outbox, Sent Items, Deleted Items, and Drafts folders have been created automatically for you.
- ✦ The Contacts panel shows the contacts in the selected Address Book (which may include contacts you've established in Windows or MSN Messenger).
- ✦ The messages list in the top-right panel shows all the messages in the currently selected folder.

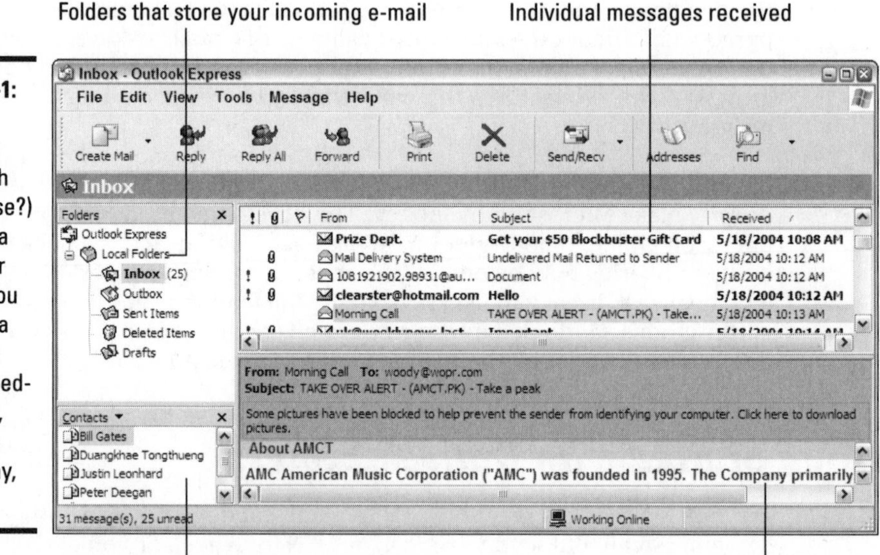

Figure 3-1: Outlook Express, filled with (what else?) spam. If a spammer invites you to "take a peak" at their hyped-up stock, peek the other way, okay?

✦ The individual message panel shows the contents of the message that is highlighted in the messages list.

Table 3-1 Outlook Express Tools

Button	*Name*	*Description*
Create Mail	Create Mail	Displays the Create Mail window so that you can compose a new message
Reply	Reply	Enables you to respond to the current message
Reply All	Reply All	Lets you respond to all the recipients of the current message
Forward	Forward	Forwards the current message to the new recipient(s) that you choose
Print	Print	Displays the Print dialog box so that you can print the current message
Delete	Delete	Deletes the current e-mail message
Send/Recv	Send/Recv	Sends any mail you've created and checks your mail server to see whether you have any new mail
Addresses	Addresses	Displays the Address Book so that you can add, edit, or delete contacts
Find	Find	Enables you to search for a message that you've sent or received, people on the Web, or specific text phrases

Conversing with E-Mail

When you originally go through the "connecting to the Internet" stage of Windows XP installation, you are asked for the ISP information and e-mail account information. This info is plugged into Outlook Express automatically so that the first time you launch the program, the program should check your mail without any action from you.

The process of setting up mail accounts — and you can set up dozens, if you choose — is a simple one. Then you're free to create, send, and receive mail messages at will.

Setting up mail accounts

How many e-mail accounts do you need? Many people have several e-mail addresses — perhaps one for work, one for school, one for personal use. And then let's not forget the kids' e-mail addresses.

If you want to add other e-mail accounts or modify your existing one, follow these steps:

1. **Start Outlook Express.**
2. **Choose Tools⇨Accounts, and then click the Mail tab.**

   The Internet Accounts dialog box appears, as shown in Figure 3-2.

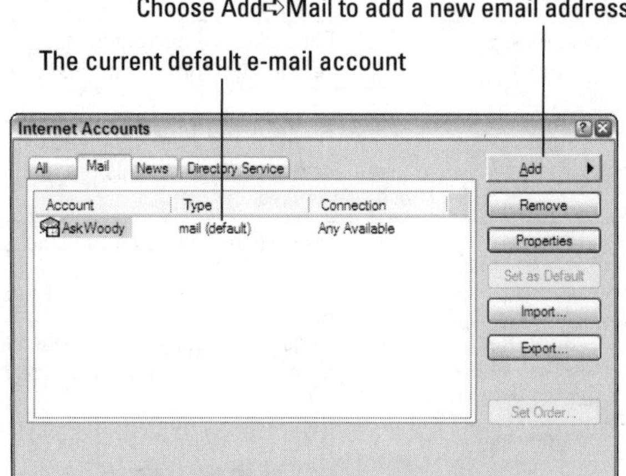

Figure 3-2: Adding an account.

3. **Click Add, and then choose Mail.**

   This act launches the Internet Connection Wizard, which walks you through the steps involved in specifying your e-mail connection information and e-mail address. The POP and SMTP Server entries (which is to say, the name of the computer that handles your incoming mail, and the name of the computer that handles your outgoing mail, respectively) should come directly from your Internet Service Provider.

Later in this chapter, you find out how to work with newsgroups. When you want to add a newsgroup to Outlook Express, you use this same procedure to add the newsgroups that you want to work with.

Retrieving messages and attachments

When you want to check your e-mail, click the Send/Recv button on the Outlook Express toolbar. A dialog box opens, showing you the status as Outlook Express checks each e-mail account you use for new messages. If you want to only receive messages, you can click the down-arrow to the right of the Send/Recv button and choose Receive All from the menu.

That's the easy part.

The hard part lies in retrieving files attached to your e-mail messages. The latest version of Outlook Express blocks certain kinds of files, based on the filename extension of the attached file (see Book I, Chapter 3 for a discussion of filename extensions). If Outlook Express receives a message with a file attached to it, and the filename extension of the attachment is on the list in Table 3-2, you receive the message, "OE removed access to the following unsafe attachments in your mail," as shown in Figure 3-3.

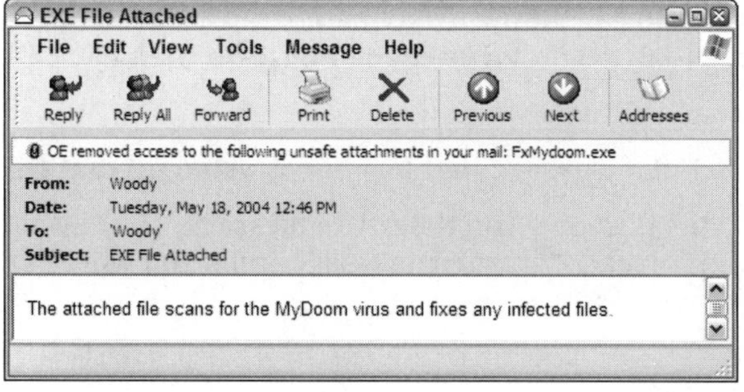

Figure 3-3: When Outlook Express receives a file that has any of the filename extensions listed in Table 3-2, it blocks the file.

Table 3-2 Blocked "Unsafe" Attachments in Outlook Express

Attachments with These Filename Extensions May Contain Viruses								
.ad	.adp	.asp	.bas	.bat	.chm	.cmd	.com	.cpl
.crt	.exe	.hlp	.hta	.inf	.ins	.isp	.js	.jse
.lnk	.mdb	.mde	.msc	.msi	.msp	.mst	.pcd	.pif
.reg	.scr	.sct	.shb	.shs	.url	.vb	.vbe	.vbs
.vsd	.vss	.vst	.vsw	.ws	.wsc	.wsf	.wsh	

If you receive an e-mail message and you need to get at a blocked file attached to the message, here's how to do it:

1. **By far the safest, fastest, easiest way to get the attachment is to e-mail the person who sent you the message and ask him or her to zip the file and send it to you again.**

   If your friend is using Windows XP, have him or her click Start➪My Computer and navigate to the file, right-click on the file and choose Send To➪Compressed (zipped) Folder. Windows will create a compressed file with a `.zip` filename extension, which you will be able to open immediately when you get it.

2. **If you can't get the file resent to you, or you're in a big hurry, use Steps 3 through 7 following, but be careful to *finish all the steps*.**

   In particular, make sure you turn security on again when you're done, as described in Step 7.

3. **In the main Outlook window (refer to Figure 3-1), choose Tools➪Options, and then click the Security tab.**

   Outlook Express shows you the Options dialog box shown in Figure 3-4.

4. **Deselect the Do Not Allow Attachments to Be Saved or Opened That Could Potentially Be a Virus check box, and then click OK.**

   OE returns to the main window.

5. **Double-click the message that has the attachment that OE blocked.**

   Outlook Express shows you the entire message, as shown in Figure 3-5, without the "blocked" warning message (refer to Figure 3-3).

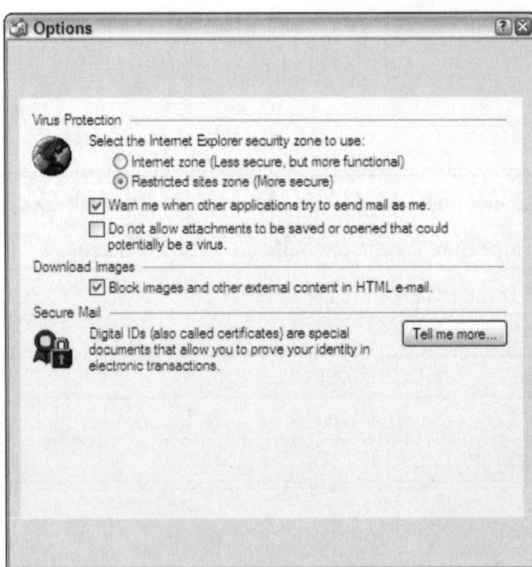

Figure 3-4: Turn off attachment scanning here.

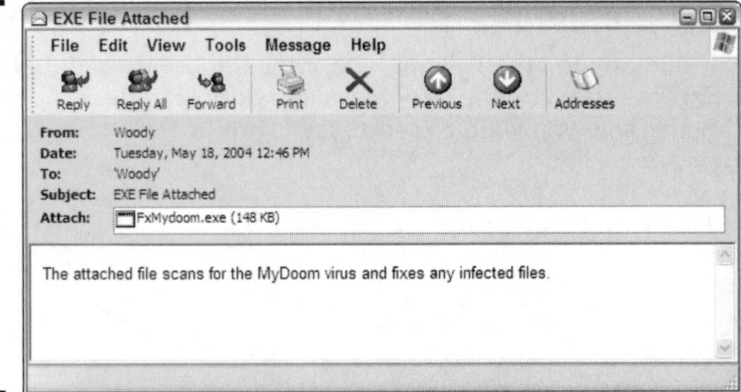

Figure 3-5: With attachment security turned off, Outlook Express lets you get at any file attached to a message.

6. **At this point, you can double-click on the file to run it (see Figure 3-6), right-click on the file and save it, or choose File➪Save Attachments and save the file.**

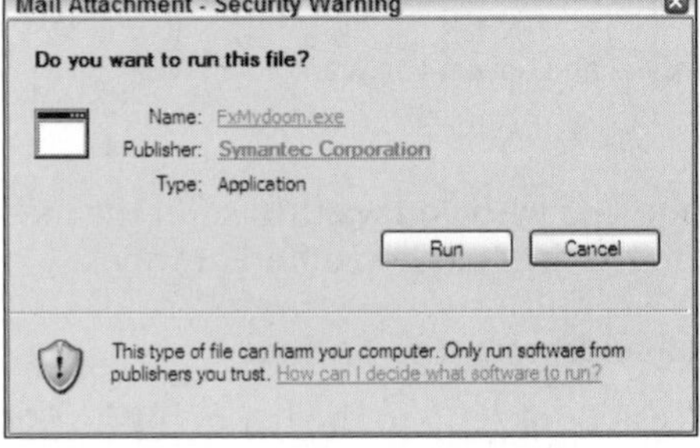

Figure 3-6: If you try to run an attached file by double-clicking on it, OE tests your sanity with this final warning.

Be very, very cautious if you run the file by double-clicking on it, okay? That's how machines get infected with viruses. Far better to save the file and use your (recently updated!) antivirus program to scan the file, individually, before you open or run it. *I warned you. . . .*

7. **Turn attachment security back on. Back in the OE main window, choose Tools➪Options➪Security, select the Do Not Allow Attachments to Be Saved or Opened That Could Potentially Be a Virus check box, and then click OK.**

Don't forget the last step. It's important.

Creating a message

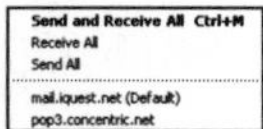

When you're ready to create a message, click the Create Mail button in the Outlook Express toolbar. The New Message window appears so that you can create the message you want to send (see Figure 3-7).

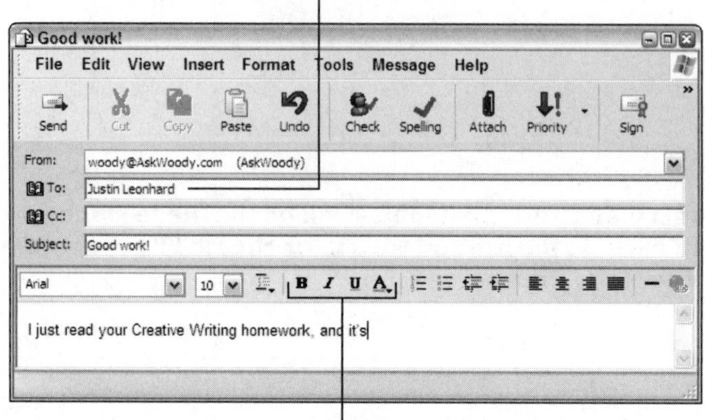

Figure 3-7: Writing a new message.

Your first step involves choosing who you want to send the message to. You can enter the person's e-mail address in two different ways:

- ✦ You can type the e-mail address in the To line.
- ✦ You can click the Address Book icon to the left of the To line and select the recipient you want from the Address Book. (To select a recipient, click the contact from the list on the left, click To, and then click OK.)

Outlook Express then adds the contact name or e-mail address in the To line.

Next, enter a Subject for your message. For best results, keep it fairly short and make it descriptive.

Finally, type the body of your message. You've got a wide open space to do just that. You can enter the words the way you want them without any fancy formatting, or you can change the look of the text by choosing a different font and size, changing colors, indenting information, and more.

Why does OE block pictures?

Unless you specifically tell Outlook Express that you want it to download and show you pictures inside e-mail messages, it won't. There's a reason why — and it has nothing to do with all the, uh, shall we say, er, creative pictures floating around on the Internet these days.

Pictures can be put inside e-mail messages in one of two ways. Either the whole picture goes in the message, or a *link to* the picture goes inside the message. The link points to a place on the Internet where OE can retrieve the picture, if you ask it to. If the whole picture is inside the message, OE shows it. But if there's a link, OE won't retrieve the picture unless you tell it to.

Why? Something called a "Web beacon." Spammers learned long ago that they could put unique pointers inside e-mail messages, referring back to a picture on their Web site. When OE reaches out and grabs the picture, it leaves behind a trace of where it came from — and that trace can be linked to the e-mail address of the person who received the message. Spammers send out millions of messages with Web beacons, and they're rewarded with a list of all the e-mail addresses of the people who opened the messages.

OE doesn't follow the picture links — and thus it doesn't confirm the validity of your e-mail address to spammers — unless you click Tools⇨Options, click on the Security tab, and deselect the Block Images and Other External Content in HTML E-mail check box.

Formatting your text

If you've ever used a word-processing program, you won't have any trouble figuring out Outlook Express's formatting tools. Just above the text area of the New Message window, you see a formatting toolbar with all the look-and-feel tools you'll ever need. Table 3-3 lists the various formatting tools and their functions.

Table 3-3 Formatting Tools for Your E-Mail Messages

Button	*Name*	*Description*
Arial	Font	Allows you to choose the font for your message
10	Size	Determines the size of the font used
	Paragraph Style	Lets you assign a style to selected text
B	Bold	Boldfaces selected text

(continued)

Table 3-3 *(continued)*

Button	*Name*	*Description*
	Italic	Italicizes selected text
	Underline	Underlines selected text
	Font Color	Enables you to choose a new color for text
	Formatting Numbers	Creates a numbered list
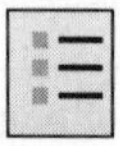	Formatting Bullets	Creates a bulleted list
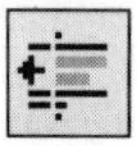	Decrease Indentation	Reduces the amount of space in the left margin
	Increase Indentation	Increases the spacing of the left margin
	Align Left	Left-aligns selected text
	Center	Centers selected text
	Align Right	Right-aligns selected text
	Justify	Justifies selected text
	Insert Horizontal Line	Adds a horizontal line at the cursor position
	Create a Hyperlink	Enables you to add a hyperlink in the message
	Insert Picture	Lets you add an image at the cursor position

Adding a signature automatically

Many people have little catch-phrases, business mottos, *bon mots,* snips of *bathos,* kinky double entendres, explicit . . . well, you get the idea . . . and more that they like to stick on the end of their e-mail messages. If you're into these kinds of signatures, you can let Outlook Express add a signature for you automatically. Here are the steps for adding a signature:

1. **Choose Tools➪Options.**
2. **Click the Signatures tab, and then click the New button.**
3. **Enter your signature in the Edit Signature box or add the file that you want to attach by selecting the File option button and browsing to the file that you want to use (see Figure 3-8).**

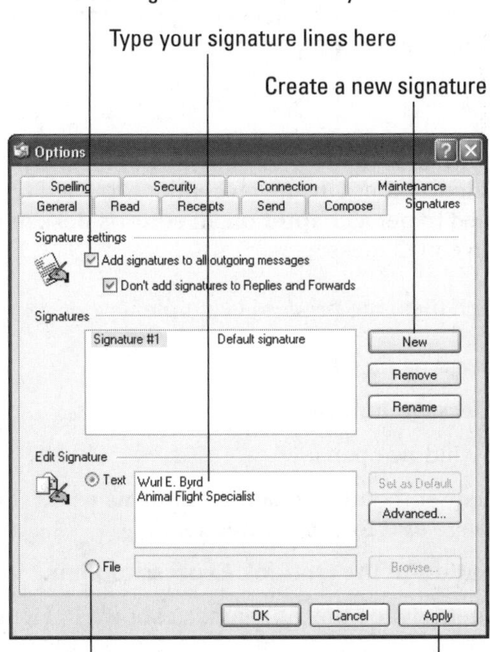

Figure 3-8: Adding a signature to outgoing e-mail.

4. **Select the Add Signatures to All Outgoing Messages check box to add the signature to all outgoing messages.**
5. **Click OK.**

Checking spelling

Have you ever dashed off a quick e-mail message, only to discover later that you misspelled a critical word? You can avoid embarrassing moments like that by running Outlook Express's spelling checker before you send your messages. To check spelling, simply complete your message and then click the Spelling button (in the center of the Outlook Express toolbar) before you click the Send button. If the program suspects a misspelling, the Spelling dialog box appears and you can choose the spelling that you want or enter a new spelling. Click Cancel to close the dialog box.

Outlook Express doesn't have its own built-in dictionary. Instead, it hijacks the dictionary used by Microsoft Office. You can run a spell check only if you have Word, Excel, or PowerPoint installed.

If youre spulling is as louzy as mine, you probbly want OE to chek it every time you put togethr a mesage. To do so, back on the main Outlook Express toolbar, choose Tools⇨Options, click the Spelling tab, and select the check box called Alwayz Chck Spullng Befour Snding. Or something like that.

Attaching files

A common operation for e-mail is the piggy-backing of files. When you need to get a report to an office in Vancouver, you send it attached to an e-mail message. When you need to get a chapter on an editor's desk in Indianapolis, you attach the file to an e-mail message.

When you want to attach files, the process is simple:

1. **Start Outlook Express as usual.**
2. **Click the Create Message button.**

   The New Message window opens.
3. **Choose the recipient and enter the subject line as usual. Type the body of your message and format as needed.**
4. **Click the Attach button in the Outlook Express toolbar.**

   The Insert Attachment dialog box appears, as shown in Figure 3-9.
5. **Navigate to the folder where the file is stored.**
6. **Click the file that you want to attach.**
7. **Click the Attach button to add the file.**

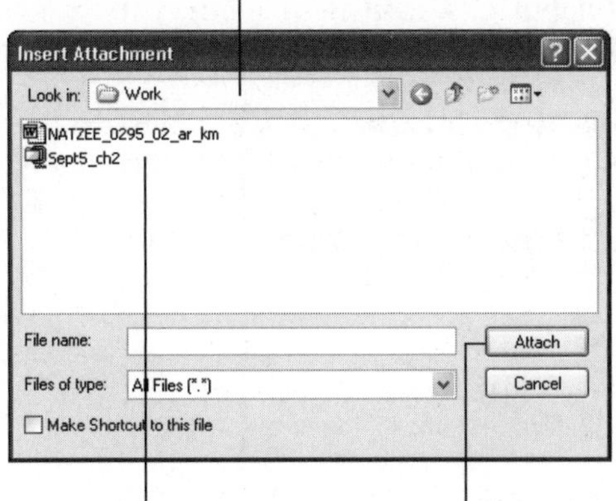

Figure 3-9: Attaching a file to your message.

Note that Outlook Express allows you to attach any file you like to an outbound message. Problems may arise on the receiving end, though, if the person you're sending the message to has an e-mail program (like Outlook Express) that blocks certain kinds of files.

You can easily add more than one file to your e-mail message. If you want to select multiple files in the same folder, press and hold Ctrl while you click.

Sending a message

Okay, ready, set, send! Just click the Send button in the Outlook Express window. If you want to save the message that you created and send it later, choose File➪Send Later. Outlook Express tells you that it is saving the message in your Outbox folder and you can send it when ready.

If you want to save a message and work on it again before you send it, choose File➪Save. This places the message in your Drafts folder. When you want to continue working on it, simply open the Drafts folder and double-click the message.

Maintaining Your Contacts

You may already know about the Windows Address Book. It's that magical place that stores all your e-mail contact information — and then some. The Address Book stores not only e-mail addresses; it also includes mailing addresses, telephone numbers, and much more (see Figure 3-10).

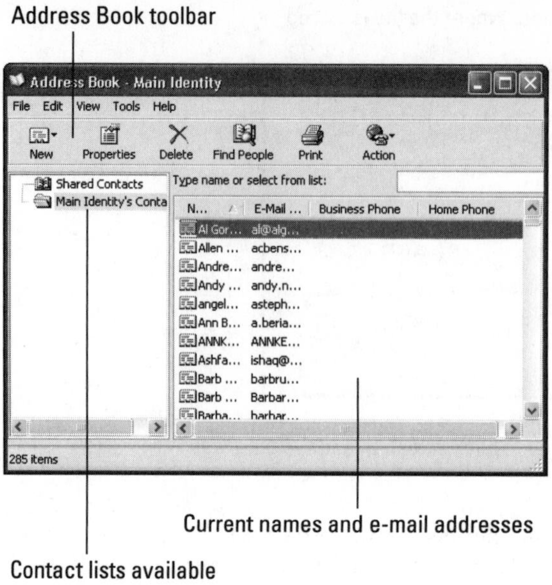

Address Book toolbar

Current names and e-mail addresses

Contact lists available

Figure 3-10: Address Book.

Adding a contact

If you're a really popular person and you need to be able to add a new contact, you're in luck. The process is easy. Here are the steps:

1. **Start Outlook Express. Click the Addresses button to bring up the Address Book.**
2. **Click New.**
3. **Choose your option:**
   - **New Contact:** An individual or organization.
   - **New Group:** A bunch of contacts, usually grouped together so that you can easily send one e-mail message to a whole group of people.
   - **New Folder:** Appears in the folder list.
4. **Click New Contact.**

   The Properties dialog box appears (see Figure 3-11).
5. **When you've entered all the pertinent information about your contact, click OK to add the contact to the Address Book and to close the Properties dialog box.**

Type the contact name

Select additional tabs to enter more contact info

Properties

Name | Home | Business | Personal | Other | NetMeeting | Digital IDs

Enter name and e-mail information about this contact here.

First: Middle: Last:

Title: Display: Nickname:

E-Mail Addresses: Add

Edit

Remove

Set as Default

Send E-Mail using plain text only.

OK Cancel

Enter the e-mail address here

Figure 3-11: Entering a new contact.

Importing a contact list

One of the neat features of Outlook Express is how easily you can import contact lists that you've used in other applications or other programs. This means that if you've been growing a HUGE contact list on your other computer, you can now use the same contact list in Outlook Express. To import a contact list, follow these steps:

1. **Start Outlook Express. Click the Addresses button to bring up the Address Book.**
2. **Choose File⇨Import and select one of the following options:**
   - Address Book (WAB)
   - Business Card (vCard)
   - Other Address Book
3. **Pick the Address Book File to Import From; then click Open.**

When you choose Other Address Book, the Address Book Import Tool dialog box comes up. Choose the program or file type that you used to create the contact list; then click Import. Outlook Express then imports your contacts.

Searching for contacts

You can search for people — either in your own Address Book or out there somewhere on the Internet.

To search for contacts, follow these steps:

1. **Start Outlook Express. Click the Addresses button to bring up the Address Book.**
2. **In the Address Book window, click the Find People button.**

   The Find People dialog box appears, as shown in Figure 3-12.

Click here to choose where you want to look

Type the name of the person you're looking for

Click to start the search

Figure 3-12: Finding people near and far.

3. **If you want to locate a user in your existing Address Book, click the down arrow at the top and choose Address Book. If you're connected to a Big Corporate Network and the corporate address book is available, choose Active Directory.**

   Don't bother with the Directory Services choice in the drop-down list. They're ridiculously limited. If you really want to look for somebody on the Internet, use `www.anywho.com` or `http://people.yahoo.com` — or just go to `www.google.com` and run a search on the person's name.
4. **Enter any information about the person you want to find in the Name, E-mail, Address, Phone, or Other text boxes.**
5. **Click the Find Now button to start the search.**

Creating groups

If you often want to send e-mail to large groups of people at once, you can create a group in Outlook Express. For example, suppose that you want to send the latest *Dilbert* cartoon to all the people on your international sales staff. You would follow these steps:

1. **Display the Address Book by clicking Address Book in the Outlook Express toolbar.**
2. **Click the New button.**

   A submenu appears.
3. **Click the New Group option.**

   The Properties dialog box opens with the Group tab displayed (see Figure 3-13).
4. **Enter the name of the group that you want to create.**
5. **Click the Select Members button to choose the people that you want to include in your group.**

   The Select Group Members dialog box appears.
6. **Select names by clicking the ones you want in the window on the left, and then click the Select button to add the names to the Members list on the right.**

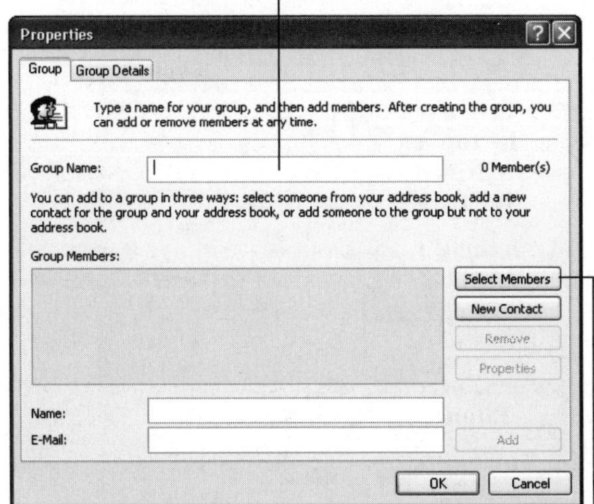

Figure 3-13: You can easily create a group to handle bulk e-mail.

If you want to select multiple names, press and hold Ctrl while you click additional names. When you click Select, all the highlighted names are copied to the list on the right.

7. **Click OK when you're finished.**

   Your group is created.

Romping through Newsgroups

Outlook Express is also a newsreader, which means you can subscribe to and post to Internet newsgroups without ever leaving your e-mail program. A newsgroup is a bulletin-board-like list that may be organized around any number of different topics. Newsgroups are often unmoderated, which means that anybody can essentially say anything (and often they do).

Although the Outlook Express approach to Internet newsgroups has a lot to recommend it, some people find the Google approach superior. See for yourself: Go to `http://groups.google.com` (shown in Figure 3-14) and see if you can read, respond to, and absorb newsgroup information better there than in OE.

Don't believe anything you hear and only half of what you see. And don't believe anything at all that you see posted on a newsgroup until you've had a chance to verify it ten ways from Tuesday.

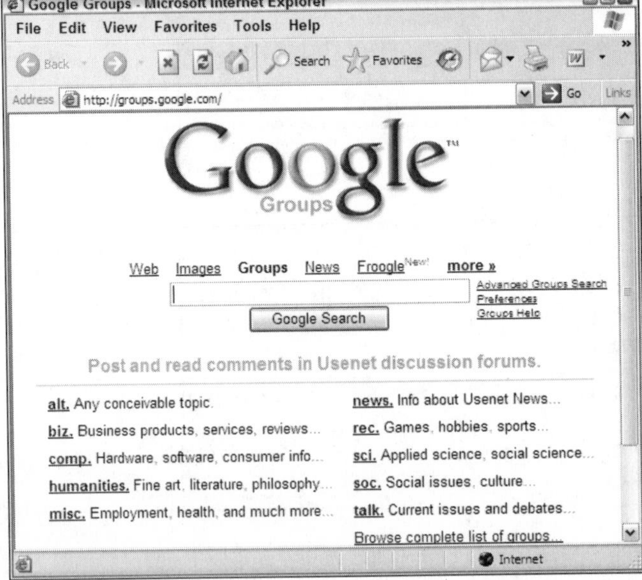

Figure 3-14: The Google interface can be much easier than that of OE, especially if you want to scan many newsgroups for information.

Still, you can find some good information in newsgroups. You may be able to find a topic that interests you — professionally or personally. The following sections explain various ways to set up and work with newsgroups in Outlook Express.

Setting up Outlook Express News

When you first begin working with Outlook Express, the newsreader is not installed by default. You have to tell Windows XP that you want to use the newsreader before it is made available to you. Here are the steps to get things set up:

1. **Start Outlook Express.**
2. **Choose Tools⇨Accounts.**

   The Internet Accounts dialog box appears.
3. **Click the News tab.**
4. **Click the Add button and choose News.**

   This launches the Internet Connection Wizard.
5. **When prompted, enter the name of your news server (you may need to get this from your Internet Service Provider), and click Finish.**

   The news server is added to the News tab of the Internet Accounts dialog box.

   To stay on top of the latest on Windows XP and other Microsoft products, you may want to make sure that you have the "official" Microsoft newsgroups available. If your ISP doesn't have you covered already, add the news server called `msnews.microsoft.com`.
6. **Click Close to complete the operation.**

   A message appears asking whether you would like to download newsgroups from the news account you added. If you want to add newsgroups, click OK; otherwise, click No.

Downloading all the newsgroups takes a few minutes, but it's worth the wait. You get the list that Outlook Express uses to let you know what's available, so you have to download it sooner or later if you want to subscribe to newsgroups.

Subscribing to newsgroups

After you set up Outlook Express to work with newsgroups, the name of your news server appears at the bottom of the Outlook Express list in the Folders panel. When you're ready to subscribe to newsgroups, click the news server name.

Outlook Express displays a message telling you that you have not yet subscribed to any newsgroups for this account. If you want to see a list of newsgroups, click Yes. The Newsgroup Subscriptions dialog box is displayed (see Figure 3-15).

You can use two different ways to find the newsgroups that you're interested in:

- ✦ Type a word or phrase in the Display Newsgroups Which Contain text box at the top of the dialog box.
- ✦ Scroll through the list and hope that something catches your eye.

When you find a group that you want to join, click Subscribe. You can repeat the process for as many newsgroups as you want to add. When you're finished subscribing to newsgroups, click OK to close the dialog box.

Looking at messages

After you've set up the newsreader and subscribed to groups, you can read messages whenever you want. The newsgroups are listed in the Outlook Express Folders panel, as shown in Figure 3-16.

To have Outlook Express check for new messages on your subscribed newsgroup, click the Synchronize Account button. The newsreader searches the newsgroups for new messages and lets you know which ones are unread.

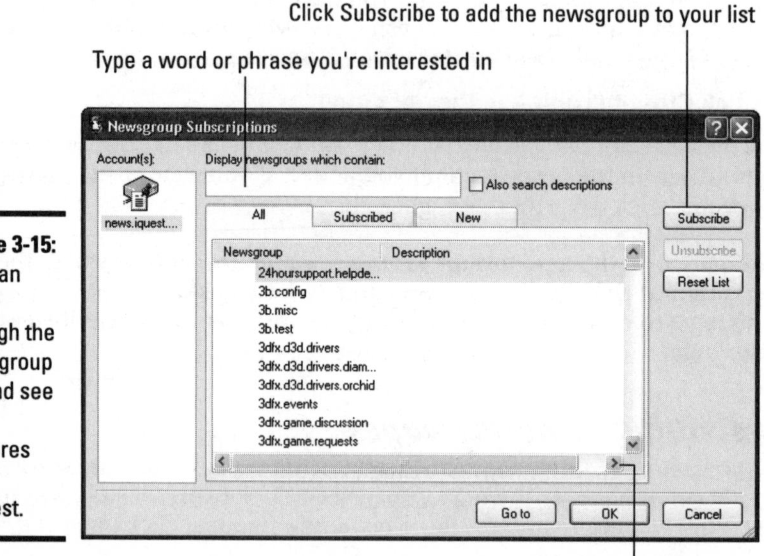

Figure 3-15: You can scroll through the newsgroup list and see what captures your interest.

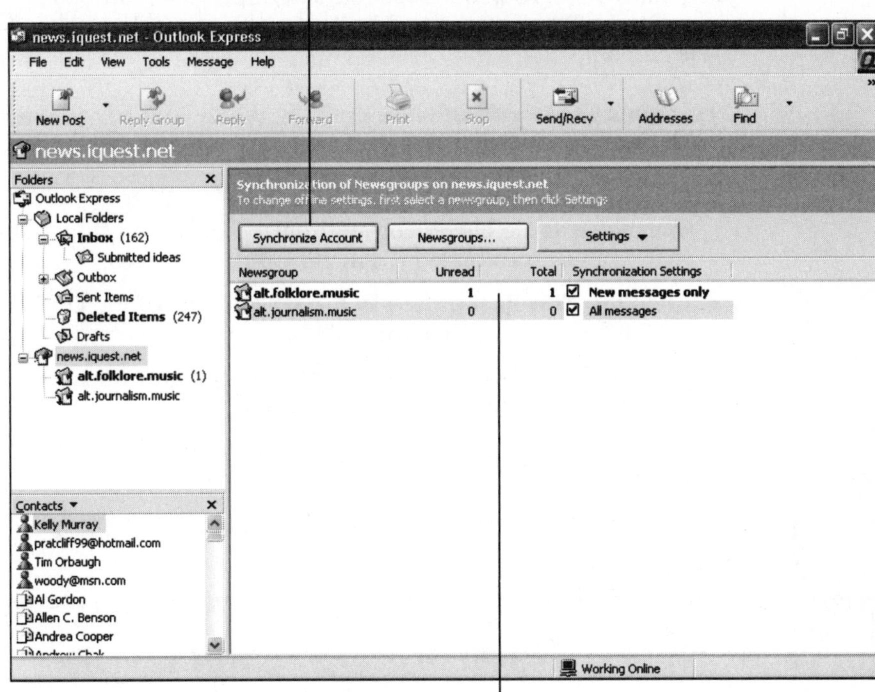

Figure 3-16: Working with the newly subscribed newsgroups.

To search for messages on specific topics, take advantage of the enormous database maintained by on the Web by Google at `http://groups.google.com`. It's one of the Internet's best-kept secrets.

To choose a newsgroup, double-click the newsgroup name. The messages appear in the panel on the top right of the newsgroup window.

To view a message in a newsgroup, double-click it. The message opens in a message window. You can then reply to the group, reply to the individual, forward the message to another person, print the message, move to the previous or next message, or display your Address Book.

Posting your own messages

After you've lurked for a while (which is to say, after you've watched what's happening for a bit, making like a fly on the wall), you may decide to jump in the fray and cast your wisdom upon the waters. Just remember that when you post a newsgroup message to the group, anyone who logs on to the newsgroup will be able to read it. To create a newsgroup message, follow these steps:

1. **Launch the newsreader by clicking the newsreader name in the Outlook Express Folders panel.**
2. **Select the newsgroup that you want to post to.**

   You may want to click the Synchronize Account button first to make sure that you've downloaded the most recent messages.
3. **Click the New Post button in the far left side of the Outlook Express toolbar.**

   What looks like a typical e-mail message window opens with the name of the newsgroup displayed in the top line.
4. **Enter a subject for the message and then type the body of the message.**
5. **Click the Send button to post the message to the group.**

Newsgroup manners

Some newsgroups are moderated (meaning that somebody's watching and sifting through the messages before they're made available at large), but most are not. As a result, newsgroups can get rude, raunchy, and downright mean. If you want to participate in helpful, respectful newsgroups, you can do your part by following these simple newsgroup rules:

* **Don't flame.** A *flame* is an inappropriately angry message directed at a specific person. Take a walk around the block. Do some push-ups. Don't flame.
* **DON'T SHOUT!** Typing in all uppercase is the same as shouting in the online world.
* **Don't answer inflammatory or obscene messages.** If your group has a case of the nasties, avoid making even sarcastic comments back. The less said to those kinds of postings, the better.
* **Don't get fancy.** Nobody wants to see decorative fonts, colorful backgrounds, or HTML messages in a newsgroup posting. Why? Because of the time they take the download (and the differences in people's personal tastes). To stay on everybody's good side (which often isn't easy to do in newsgroups), keep it plain and simple with straight text.

Chapter 4: Chatting with Windows Messenger

In This Chapter

- **Getting the right Messenger — Windows, MSN, .NET, or ???**
- **Using Messenger effectively**
- **Disabling Messenger completely if you don't want it**

No doubt you know that Windows Messenger, uh, MSN Messenger, er, .NET Messenger instant messaging service, lets you interact with other people instantly — usually by typing, but also by talking (if your computer is equipped with speakers and a microphone and your Internet connection can handle the load), or even with live video.

I hear three questions about Messenger, over and over again:

- What's the difference between all the Messengers?

  and/or

- Why won't it work on my (or my mom's) machine?

  and/or

- How do I get rid of it?

This chapter gives you some real world answers.

Choosing the Right Messenger

Microsoft has two different programs called Messenger and, in addition, two completely different services called Messenger, one of which has absolutely nothing to do with Windows Messenger. That's why you're confused.

The two programs you're wondering about

- **Windows Messenger:** The old workhorse that comes free with Windows XP. Most of the Office 2003 applications (Word, Excel and Outlook), Outlook Express, and Windows' own Remote Assistance (see Book I, Chapter 3) all hook into Windows Messenger. Figure 4-1 shows you how

Outlook 2003 can alert you if someone who sent you a message is currently online and logged on to Windows Messenger: If a person in your Windows Messenger Contact list sends you an e-mail message, hover your cursor over his name, and Outlook 2003 will look to see if he's currently logged on. If you're on a Big Corporate Network, Exchange only works with Windows Messenger.

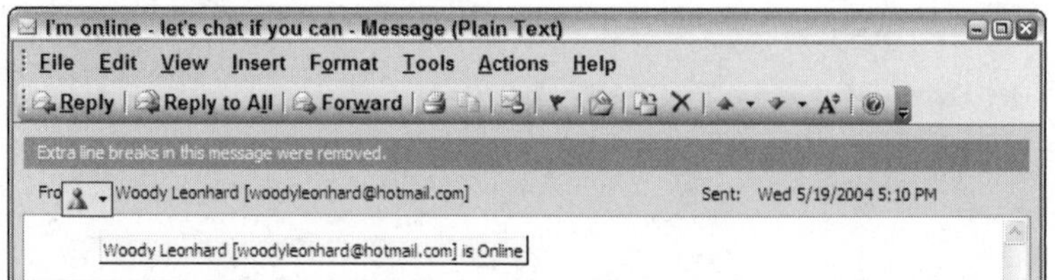

Figure 4-1: Outlook 2003 shows you if a contact is currently logged on.

- **MSN Messenger:** The flashier upstart that shows off Microsoft's latest instant messaging technology. It doesn't work with Office 2003 applications, Outlook Express, or Remote Assistance. It isn't part of Windows; you have to install it separately. Download it from `http://messenger.msn.com`; it'll take half an hour over a fast dial-up modem, but it is free.

Microsoft doesn't make any money from Windows Messenger, so it isn't as cool — or updated as frequently — as MSN Messenger. MSN Messenger's *raison d'etre,* of course, is to convince you to get your buddies to use MSN Messenger, buy Microsoft products, use Microsoft services, and maybe even subscribe to MSN. Makes all the difference.

Fortunately, you don't have to choose between Windows Messenger and MSN Messenger — you can have both: Install MSN Messenger, and Windows Messenger is still there, sitting forlorn on your Start menu. A few points to keep in mind:

- Windows Messenger and MSN Messenger play together pretty well — if you're using Windows Messenger, you can send messages to a buddy who's using MSN Messenger, and vice versa — with one stupid exception. If you're using Windows Messenger with Outlook, Outlook Express, or Remote Assistance, your buddies running MSN Messenger may not be able to contact you. MSN Messenger may not even realize that you're logged on — and there's nothing you can do to escape the cloak of invisibility.
- You can run Windows Messenger and MSN Messenger at the same time, but if you do, you have to be using two different Passport accounts. Yes, that means you can talk to yourself. Sheesh.

✦ When you install MSN Messenger, it usually sets itself up to run automatically each time you start Windows. Windows Messenger isn't quite so brazen: You have to change a setting to make it start automatically. If you set up Windows Messenger to start automatically, MSN Messenger will *not* start automatically.

If you're really into instant messaging, go ahead and install MSN Messenger. It won't hurt. But if instant messaging feels more like an intrusion than an ally, and you only use it occasionally — or in conjunction with Office or Remote Assistance — stick with Windows Messenger. You won't be missing much.

You can always use AOL's Instant Messenger (`www.aim.com`), or Yahoo!'s (`http://messenger.yahoo.com`). As of this writing, none of the three — Microsoft's, AOL's, and Yahoo!'s Messengers — talk to each other, so if you have a buddy who's using Yahoo! and you want to send messages to her, you have to run Yahoo! too.

Two more Microsoft products bear the name "Messenger" and neither of them is an instant messaging program:

✦ *.NET Messenger Service* is the glue that binds together the legions of Windows Messenger and MSN Messenger users. It isn't a program that you can run. It's more like plumbing. .NET Messenger Service is tied in to *.NET Passport,* Microsoft's giant database of Windows users, which validates user names and passwords for Windows Messenger, MSN Messenger, and Hotmail.

Microsoft has a love/hate relationship with the word ".NET". One day, the 'Softies declare that everything is .NET — "Nothing but .NET" reverberates like frog grunts from the soggy Redmond campus. The next day it's more like ".NET? What's that? Our customers don't understand the term .NET so we're going to quit using the word." If you're confused, you aren't alone. *I* never got the big picture behind .NET. It always struck me as another way for Microsoft to put its fingers in the Internet pie and to try to make a buck as middleman.

✦ The poorly-named *Messenger Service* in Windows XP and Windows 2000 (sometimes called *Windows Messenger Service*) got a whole lot of publicity a couple of years ago when some cretins figured out how to hijack this internal Windows communication "feature" and put popup ads on unsuspecting user's computers. (See Figure 4-2; details at `http://grc.com/stm/ShootTheMessenger.htm`.)

Windows Messenger Service has absolutely nothing to do with Windows Messenger or MSN Messenger. The latest update to Windows XP shuts off Messenger Service, so you don't have to worry about it anymore. Unless the spammers figure out a way to turn it back on again. . . .

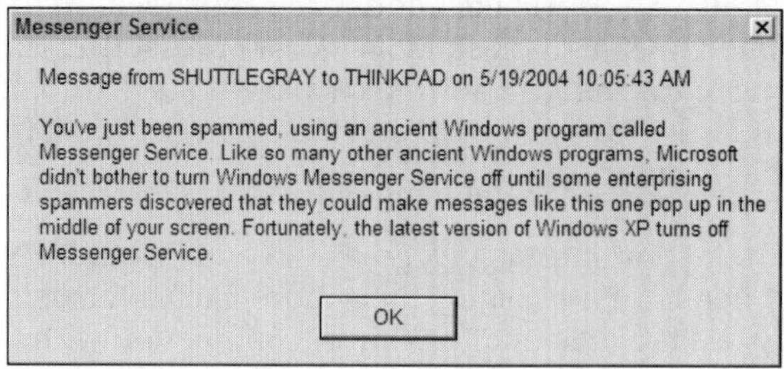

Figure 4-2: Windows Messenger Service produces weird boxy messages like this one.

In the rest of this chapter, I talk about Windows Messenger. For the lowdown on MSN Messenger, see Book V, Chapter 5.

Making Messenger Work

Using Windows Messenger is remarkably easy — providing the person you're trying to chat with isn't running a firewall, or his firewall has been set up to let Windows Messenger (and MSN Messenger) through.

Here's the way I use Windows Messenger:

1. **Sign up for a new, free Hotmail account at** `www.hotmail.com` **by clicking the Don't Have a .NET Passport? Get One Now link.**

   The dialog box shown in Figure 4-3 appears.

Profile Information

Help

First Name: William

Last Name: Gates

Your first and last names will be sent with all outgoing e-mail messages.

Language: English

Country/Region: United States

State: Washington

ZIP Code: 98572

Time Zone: Pacific Time - PST

Gender: Male Female

Birth Date: February 29 1985 (ex. 1999)

Occupation: Unemployed/between jobs

Account Information

E-mail Address: woodychat @hotmail.com

Figure 4-3: Sign up for a new Hotmail account with a bogus name so that you have a .NET Passport account for Windows Messenger.

That will give you a new i.d. like `woodychat@hotmail.com`, which you can use for Windows Messenger, MSN Messenger, and any other .NET Passport-related product.

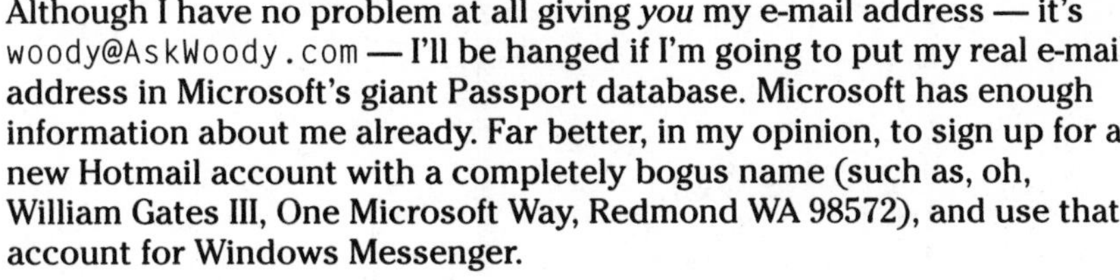

Although I have no problem at all giving *you* my e-mail address — it's `woody@AskWoody.com` — I'll be hanged if I'm going to put my real e-mail address in Microsoft's giant Passport database. Microsoft has enough information about me already. Far better, in my opinion, to sign up for a new Hotmail account with a completely bogus name (such as, oh, William Gates III, One Microsoft Way, Redmond WA 98572), and use that account for Windows Messenger.

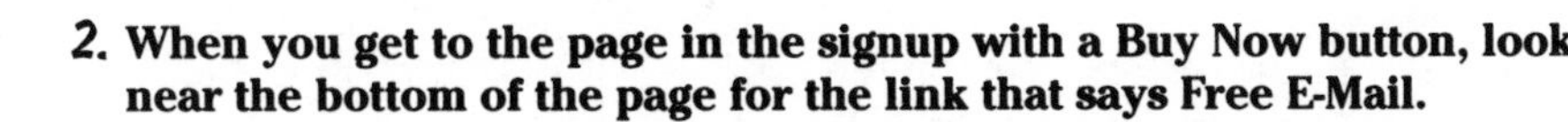

2. **When you get to the page in the signup with a Buy Now button, look near the bottom of the page for the link that says Free E-Mail.**

   If you want a free account, you have to click the well-hidden Free link.

3. **Choose Start➪All Programs➪Windows Messenger.**

   Windows Messenger greets you with an invitation to poke a hole through your firewall, as shown in Figure 4-4.

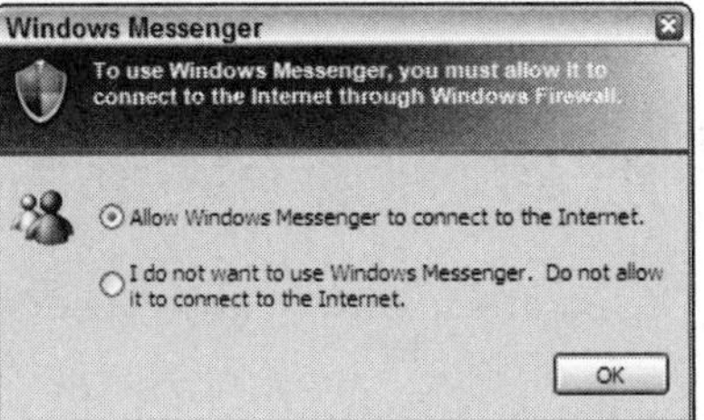

Figure 4-4: In order for Windows Messenger to work, it has to be allowed out of your firewall.

4. **Select the Allow Windows Messenger to Connect to the Internet option button, and then click OK.**

   Windows Messenger invites you to sign in (see Figure 4-5).

5. **Click the Click Here to Sign In link.**

   Microsoft wants you to associate your .NET Passport (and thus your e-mail I.D.) with your computer and Windows user name (see Figure 4-6).

Keep in mind that the big Passport database can (and probably does) keep track of the Internet address that you use to log in — the IP address — but Passport doesn't have any way of positively identifying the computer that you're using. Sounds like a small detail, but plenty of fur flew among privacy advocates when Microsoft tried to make each PC individually identifiable.

Figure 4-5: Sign in for the first time.

6. **If you have a bogus Hotmail I.D. handy (see Step 1), or if you really don't mind adding your real e-mail address to Microsoft's Passport database, click Next.**

   The wizard wants to know if you already have an e-mail address.

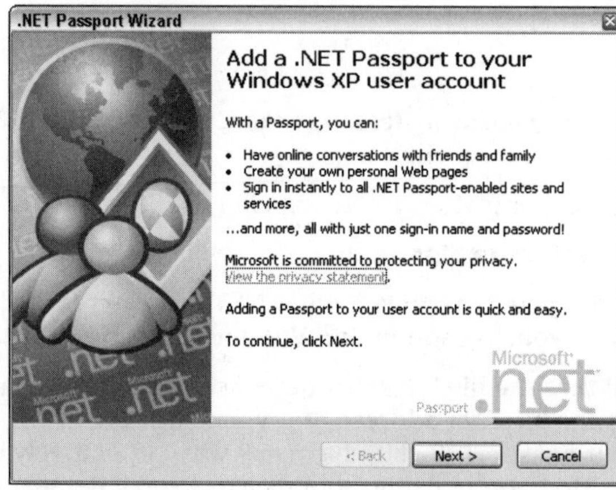

Figure 4-6: This wizard steps you through the process of getting a .NET Passport.

7. **Select the Yes (you do have an e-mail address) option button, and then click Next.**

   The wizard asks if you already have a .NET Passport, as shown in Figure 4-7.

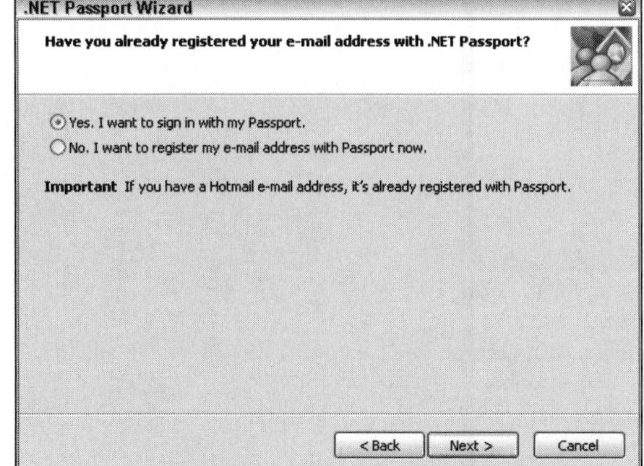
.NET Passport Wizard
Have you already registered your e-mail address with .NET Passport?
Yes. I want to sign in with my Passport.
No. I want to register my e-mail address with Passport now.
Important If you have a Hotmail e-mail address, it's already registered with Passport.
< Back
Next >
Cancel

Figure 4-7: If you have a Hotmail account, you already have a .NET Passport.

8. **If you have a .NET Passport (or a Hotmail account), select Yes, I Want to Sign In with My Passport, and then click Next.**
9. **Fill in your .NET Passport e-mail address (don't forget to include the @hotmail.com if you're using a Hotmail account), and your password. Select the Associate My Passport with My Windows User Account check box if you want Windows Messenger to log on automatically. Click Next.**

   The wizard tells you that you're done.
10. **Click Finish.**

    Windows Messenger tells you to Add a Contact, as shown in Figure 4-8.
11. **Click Add a Contact.**

    Windows Messenger steps you through the process of adding a Contact (see Figure 4-9). All you need is your buddy's e-mail address — the one that she uses to log on to Windows Messenger.
12. **When you add a Contact, and that Contact doesn't yet have you on her buddy list, *she* gets a message like the one shown in Figure 4-10. The Contact gets to choose if she want you to "see" her or not.**

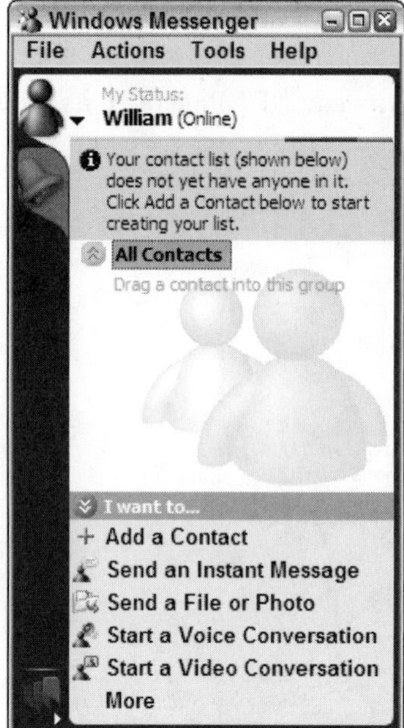

Figure 4-8: Time to add buddies, er, Contacts to your list.

That means you can add someone to your Contacts, do everything properly, have her show up on your Contacts list — but never be able to connect to her because she told Messenger that she didn't want to be visible to you. Tough luck, eh?

Figure 4-9: Add buddies by typing in the e-mail addresses they use when they log on to Windows Messenger.

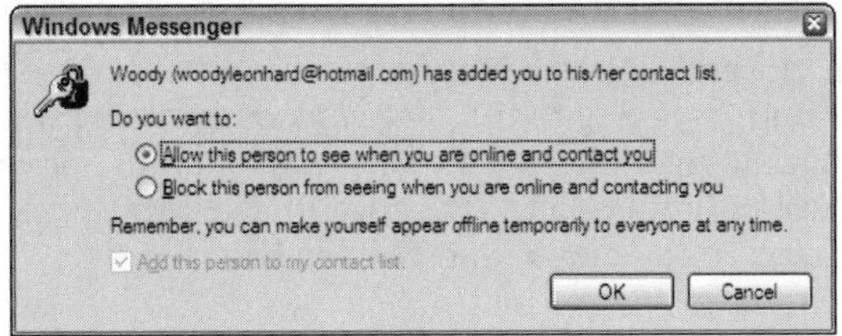

Figure 4-10: Your erstwhile buddies have to give their okay before you can see them.

13. **To start a conversation, click the Send an Instant Message link.**

    Windows Messenger sets up a Conversation window, as shown in Figure 4-11.

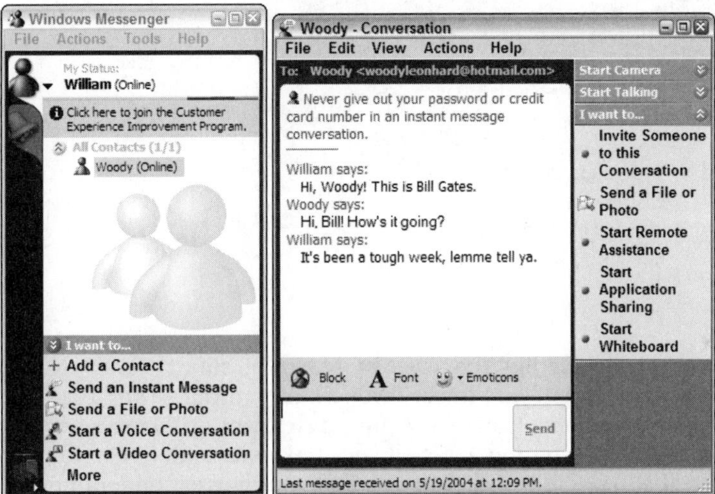

Figure 4-11: Bill and I have a little chat.

14. **Type your message in the box at the bottom of the Conversation window. When you press Enter or click the Send button, the message gets sent to the designated recipient(s).**

    While you're limited on the amount of text you can type in the message box, if you press Enter, you can keep on typing. You can copy text from just about anywhere and paste it into the message box: Windows Messenger treats it as if you typed it all out.

15. **When you're done chatting with this Contact, choose File⇨Exit or click the X (Close) button to exit out of the Conversation window.**

16. **When you're done with Windows Messenger, choose File➪Close or click the X button to close the main Windows Messenger window.**

Even if you've closed Windows Messenger, it's still active — still lurking in the background, listening for incoming messages, still waiting to interrupt what you're doing with a ripply *garururump* sound. If you want to *really* turn the bloody thing off, right-click on the Messenger icon in the System Tray (next to the clock) and choose Exit.

Both Windows Messenger and MSN Messenger get all tripped up in firewalls. For example, if you try to use the Start Application Sharing feature of Windows Messenger (as shown on the right in Figure 4-11), the other PC may get a message like the one shown in Figure 4-12.

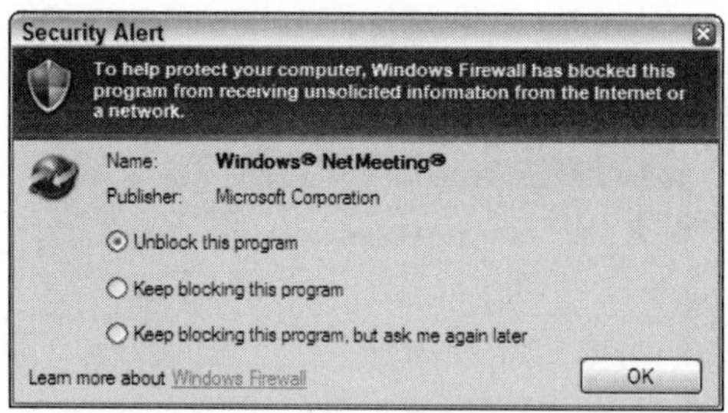

Figure 4-12: To initiate Application Sharing, the person you're chatting with has to blast another hole through her firewall.

The person running the other PC has to be smart enough to figure out that you're the one trying to get through the firewall — and that the application that you're using is called Windows NetMeeting (there's no mention of "Application Sharing"). It's all very hokey and full of version 1.0 potholes, but if you persist, and both you and your correspondent have full control over your firewalls, you'll probably get it to work. Sooner or later.

In case you were wondering, allowing Messenger to go through your Windows Firewall establishes an Exception for the program `C:\Program Files\messenger\msmsgs.exe`. Allowing NetMeeting through sets up an Exception for `C:\Program Files\NetMeeting\conf.exe`. That means Windows Firewall (see Figure 4-13) will allow packets through the firewall that are addressed to either of those programs.

Windows Messenger comes with smileys and fonts and instant pictures and voice — and a whole bunch of additional features, many of which are similar to the ones in MSN Messenger. See Book V, Chapter 5 for details.

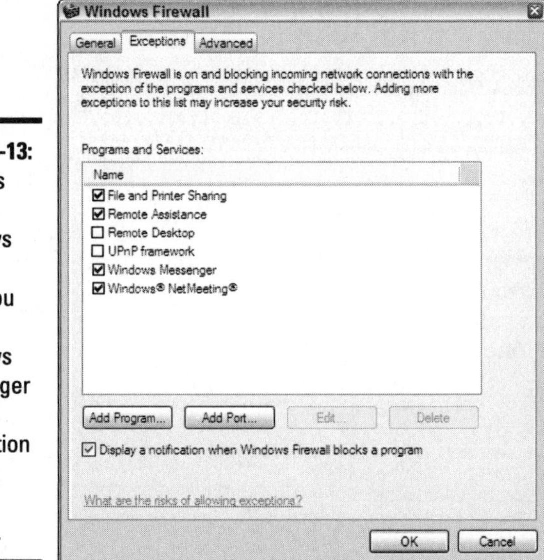

Figure 4-13: Changes made to Windows Firewall when you allow Windows Messenger and Application Sharing to bust through.

Killing the Messenger

Sorry about the heading. Couldn't resist.

Many people think of Windows Messenger as an intrusive time sink, only marginally more annoying than having a swarm of killer bees take up residence on a motherboard. Bosses hate it because somewhere between 70 and 99 percent of all the Windows Messenger traffic on business computers consists of vapid personal time-wasting conversations.

Which leads me to one of the most frequently asked questions about Windows XP: How do you get rid of Windows Messenger, completely, so that it doesn't start itself automatically, announce to the world at large when you're online, and start going *garururump* at the most annoying times?

Although it's true that you can turn off most of Windows Messenger's most annoying attributes by choosing Tools➪Options and deselecting most of the check boxes on the Preferences tab (see Figure 4-14), many people want to get rid of Windows Messenger completely.

While you can't get rid of Windows Messenger entirely — Windows XP keeps vestiges of it around no matter how hard you try — it's easy to take the program off your Start menu and basically drive a stake through its heart:

1. **Choose Start➪Control Panel➪Add or Remove Programs. Then click the icon marked Add/Remove Windows Components.**

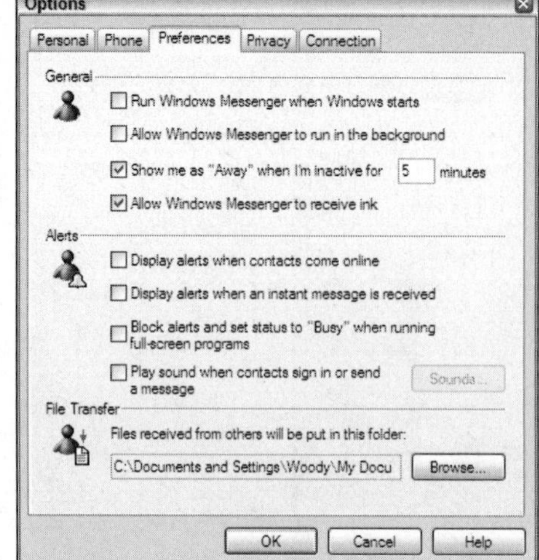

Figure 4-14: Deselect all of these check boxes and Windows Messenger will usually behave itself.

You see the Windows Component Wizard, as shown in Figure 4-15.

2. **Deselect the Windows Messenger check box, and then click Next.**
3. **When the wizard is done, click Finish.**

   All visible evidence of Windows Messenger should be well and truly gone.

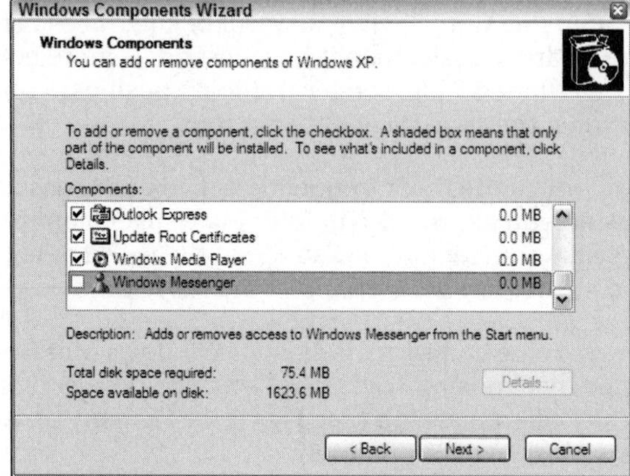

Figure 4-15: This is where you bury Windows Messenger so deeply it should never darken your door again.

If you change your mind and want Windows Messenger back, follow the same three steps, but in Step 2, *select* the Windows Messenger check box.

Book IV

Adventures with Internet Explorer

"Good news, honey! No one's registered our last name as a domain name yet! Hellooo Haffassoralsurgery.com!"

Contents at a Glance

Chapter 1: Finding Your Way around the Internet Explorer Window

In This Chapter

- ✔ **Getting ready to browse the Web**
- ✔ **Touring the IE window**
- ✔ **Finding your way around the Web**
- ✔ **Doing stuff with Web pages**
- ✔ **Playing hide and seek with IE**

This chapter explains how to find your way around the Web using Internet Explorer (IE). Book III shows you how to make contact with your ISP's computer. After that connection is made, you're ready to make your computer actually *do* something. If that "something" involves browsing the Web, your next step is to launch Internet Explorer.

Ready, Set, Browse!

As soon as you've made the connection with your ISP, you can begin your browsing session. You use Internet Explorer to do this. You have two different ways to launch IE:

- ✦ Click the Internet Explorer icon on the taskbar.
- ✦ Choose Start⇨Internet (see Figure 1-1). Internet Explorer launches and fills your Windows work area.

Internet Explorer launches, and after a relatively brief moment (primarily depending on the speed of your Internet connection), a Web page appears. What that page contains depends on whether your computer is set up to begin with a specific page, called a home page. Microsoft sets up `www.msn.com` as the home page by default, if you installed Windows from the original CD. Most PC manufacturers set the home page display to something related to their systems.

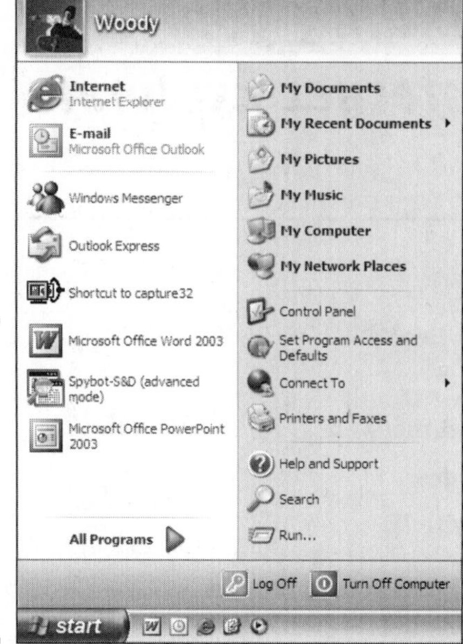

Figure 1-1: Launch Microsoft Internet Explorer from the Start menu or the taskbar.

A Walk around the IE Window

One of the great things about Internet Explorer is that you can be an absolute no-clue beginner, and with just a few hints about tools and such, you can find your way around the Web like a pro. Figure 1-2 gives you a diagram of the basic layout of the Internet Explorer window. As you can see, IE packs lots of possibilities in that small space. The items you'll use most often are these:

- **Menu bar:** Contains six menus: File, Edit, View, Favorites, Tools, and Help. Each menu includes a different set of commands related to working with Web sites. (See Table 1-1 for a description of the various menus.)
- **Standard toolbar:** Includes tools you use to find your way around on the Web and work with the Web pages that you find. (See Table 1-2 for an overview of the tools on the Standard toolbar.)
- **Address bar:** Enables you to type the Web address of a page that you want to move to directly.
- **Browse window:** The part of the window that displays the Web pages you visit. In Figure 1-2, Microsoft's preferred home page, `www.msn.com`, appears.
- **Status bar:** Displays information about Web pages, links, or actions that you can take while visiting a site.

The Web works — use it!

I'm constantly amazed at how *in*frequently some people use the Internet. A friend of mine wanted to find a Realtor in a small town in Colorado. So she picked up the phone and called the Colorado Association of Realtors. After a few minutes on hold, she dutifully transcribed the names, addresses, and telephone numbers of three Realtors — and she only made a couple of mistakes.

If she had used Google to find the Colorado Association of Realtors Web site, and typed the small town's zip code on the Find a Realtor page, she would've been able to print out a complete list of all the Realtors in that town, accompanied by addresses, phone numbers, contact names, Web sites, and e-mail addresses — and it would've taken half the time and one-tenth the hassle of working on the phone.

The Web is a wonderful invention: It's the best, most complete reference in the history of humanity. And it's free. Use it!

Figure 1-2: The IE window includes everything you need to work the Web.

Checking out IE menus

So who needs menus anymore? With all the buttons and links and clickable things on the screen, you may wonder why you need to spend time opening menus and selecting commands. Even though you can do many of the most common Web tasks right from the IE window — such as printing, adding Web pages to your Favorites folders, searching for information, and moving to new pages — you can carry out a number of operations only by using the IE menus. Table 1-1 gives you an introduction to the various menus, so that you know what to use when.

Table 1-1 The Fare on Internet Explorer Menus

Menu	*Description*
File	Open, edit, save, print, and send Web pages; import and export "Favorites" and cookies to and from other browsers and other computers.
Edit	Select, cut, copy, paste, and find text on the current Web page.
View	Control the display of the IE window. You can display and hide toolbars, change the text size, display the browser window in full-screen size, move to another page, and refresh the current page.
Favorites	Add shortcuts to your own favorite pages and organize or remove the favorites that Microsoft and/or your PC manufacturer provided.
Tools	Adjust the built-in popup blocker, synchronize your data if you're working offline, update Windows, show links, and more.
Help	Provides help in the traditional contents and index display, as a tip of the day, or as online help.

Unpacking the Standard toolbar

That bar of buttons stretching across the width of the IE window (just beneath the menu bar) isn't just a pretty, colorful collection of decorative items: They are tools that you can use to accomplish things on the Web. Check out Table 1-2 to see what those colorful little buttons can do for you.

Table 1-2 The Right Tools for the Job

Tool	*Name*	*Description*
Back	Back	Moves to the previous Web page.
	Forward	Moves to the page following the current one in the sequence you have selected.
	Stop	Stops the loading of the current page.
	Refresh	Updates the display of the current page.

Tool	Name	Description
	Home	Returns to the page you have set as the home page.
Search	Search	Displays the Search Companion so that you can look for specific information.
Favorites	Favorites	Opens the Favorites panel so that you can choose, add to, or organize your favorite Web sites.
	History	Opens the History panel so that you can select Web pages you've visited previously.
	Mail	Enables you to send and receive e-mail and to send Web pages and links from IE.
	Print	Prints the current Web page.
	Edit	Launches an editor (such as Notepad or Microsoft Word).
	Discuss	Lets you attach notes to a Web page, if the person who created the page allows it.
	Research	Brings up a Research pane on the left to make it easy to look up words in the Encarta Dictionary or to search for topics in the Encarta Encyclopedia. (Or you can go to `http://encarta.msn.com`.)
	Messenger	Launches Windows Messenger (see Book III, Chapter 4).

Right now you may just be learning to use IE, but later on, you may be in the mood for a toolbar change. You can create your own custom toolbar buttons and rearrange the toolbars to appear the way you want them. To find out more, see Book IV, Chapter 3.

Displaying the Tip of the Day

If you're new to this whole browsing thing and you want to have a little help along the way, you can turn on IE's Tip of the Day feature. The tips appear in the bottom portion of your screen, which takes up a little real estate, but they provide simple suggestions that you can try as you work.

To display the Tip of the Day, follow these steps:

1. **Choose Help in the menu bar.**

   The Help menu opens.

2. **Click Tip of the Day.**

   A new pane opens just above the status bar at the bottom of the Internet Explorer window. You may get a security warning. If so, click the warning message and choose Allow This Page to Access My Computer (see Figure 1-3).

3. **Review the tip and then, if you want to see another tip, click Next Tip.**

   If you want to close the tip box, click the X (Close) button to the left of the tip area.

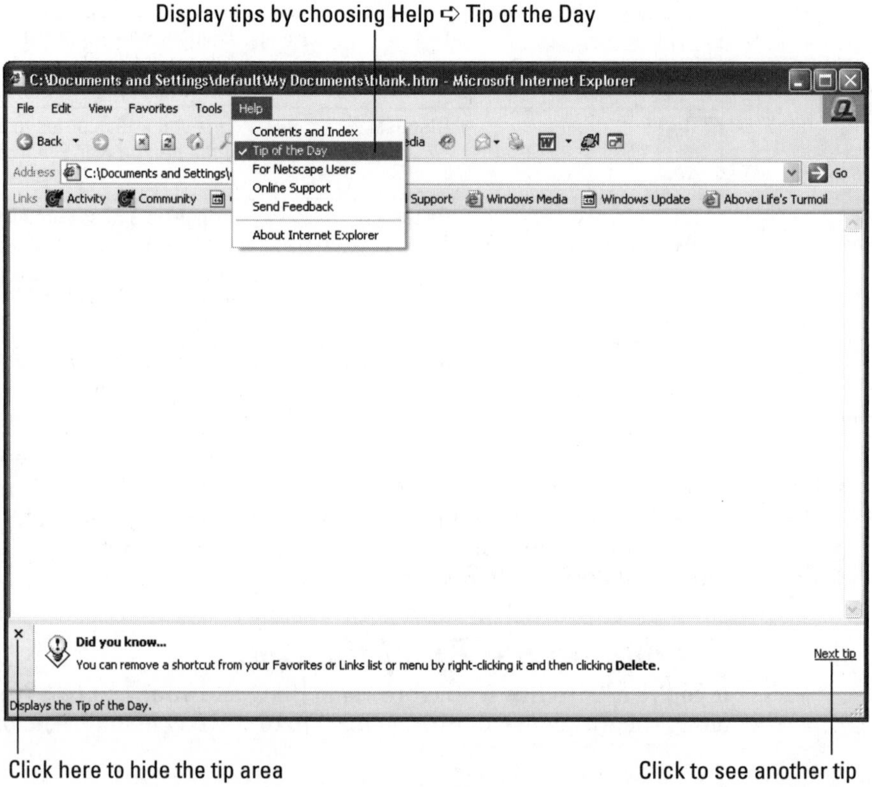

Display tips by choosing Help ➪ Tip of the Day

Click here to hide the tip area

Click to see another tip

Figure 1-3: You can display tips to help you find your way around IE faster.

Exploring Web Pages

Everybody wants to be on the Web, and chances are — unless you've been living in a remote corner of the world somewhere — you've already had at least some experience with Web surfing. I see Web page addresses, called URLs (a geeky acronym for Uniform Resource Locator) plastered all over everything — from bumper stickers and mud flaps to billboards and gum labels. And this proliferation is the same all over the world. Web sites give us the ability to find out more about a company, a product, a person, or a place. We can find out about health issues, read news stories, make travel arrangements, and more. When you first begin to surf the Web, the possibilities seem limitless. And, believe me, unless you start out with a plan, you can float around out there in Massive Information Overload Land until the dog, the kids, or the alarm clock brings you back to reality.

So your best bet is to start with a plan. Where do you want to go and what do you want to find? You may want to do one (or all) of the following things:

- **Go to a specific site:** Want to check out the online presence of a new employer you're considering? Or perhaps you want to enter the Go-to-Greece! contest being offered by your local grocery store.
- **Search for information:** You can use various search engines to enter a word or a phrase and get the addresses of dozens — or hundreds — of Web sites with the information you seek.
- **Listen to Internet radio while you work:** A number of sites — some of them traditional on-air radio stations — now use Internet technology to broadcast radio programs through streaming audio.
- **Make travel arrangements:** All the major airlines — and numerous other travel companies — now offer travel packages online.
- **Check your stocks:** Again, you have your choice of brokerage firms — from the largest to the smallest — available online. Some Web sites offer you a stock ticker as a downloadable option, which enables you to check how your stocks are doing while you work (assuming, of course, that you *are* working . . .).
- **Hold a business meeting:** Web conferencing has made real the opportunity to meet with people in a virtual conference room and share ideas, review presentations, and even have private conversations that the rest of the group doesn't hear. All it takes is a hefty Internet connection and a couple of cheap cameras.
- **Watch a preview of a new movie:** Not sure that you want to spend the exorbitant price on movie tickets without an ironclad guarantee that the movie will be worth the price of admission? You can now go to movie sites galore to watch trailers and behind-the-scenes clips of popular movies. (Check out `www.catsanddogsmovie.com` for a site that's *better* than a movie!)

- **Check up on your competitors:** Oh come on, admit it. That's the first site you visited, right? You have to keep tabs on the mom-and-pop store down the block that undercuts your price on lip balm.
- **Find new math games for your kids:** Who wants to sit and go through math drills with third graders all day long? Free, downloadable math games are out there on the Web for your choosing. Check them out, and load them up. Your kids will think they're fun — and they may even learn something.

Web page basics

Depending on the sites you visit, you may be greeted by a variety of things: pictures, text, advertisements, and more. Those various elements enable you to interact with the sites in different ways: Some Web sites are there for your entertainment; others want to sell you something; others give you the opportunity to chat or play games; and still others offer links to additional information and services.

Figure 1-4 shows the main screen for MSN.com. As you can see, this page offers lots of different experiences. Other general-interest portals — `www.yahoo.com`, `www.cnn.com`, `www.espn.com`, `www.time.com`, `www.businessweek.com`, `www.sciam.com`, `www.howstuffworks.com`, and thousands of others — try to lure you to their sites by providing candy for your eyes (and in some cases, *mirabile dictu* for your brain).

Understanding links

Clicking any of the items highlighted in Figure 1-4 causes an action to happen because each of those items are *links* — connections that take you to another page or carry out a programmed event (such as starting your e-mail program). You may notice a number of links that look different on Web pages that you visit, but most fall into one of two categories: text links or graphics links.

- A text link can be a word, phrase, tag, or menu item.
- A graphics link can be a picture, button, map, photo, drawing, or some other art item.

How can you tell a text link from regular text? Text links usually appear in a color different from the surrounding text, and in many cases, the linked text is underlined. You can prove that a text phrase or an image is in fact a link by positioning the mouse pointer over the phrase or image. If the pointer changes to the hand pointer, you know you're hovering over a link. In Figure 1-5, a number of text links — both underlined and not underlined — appear. Additionally, several graphics links are used to take you to additional pages in the site.

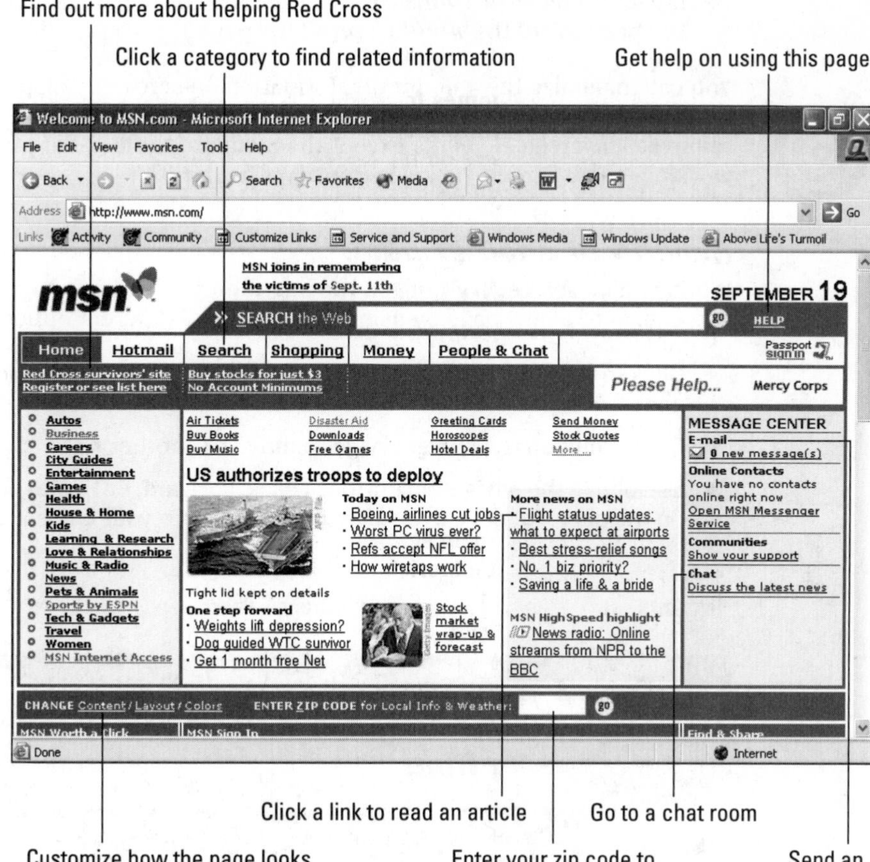

Figure 1-4: Internet Explorer starts by displaying the default page, MSN.

Scroll around the town

If you've used computers for any length of time at all, you've made your peace with the fact that everything doesn't fit on the screen at one time. If you're creating a letter, you have to scroll down to add your signature line. If you've been working on an Excel spreadsheet, you're accustomed to paging down to create a chart in an open area of the workbook. You also find that more often than not, you have to scroll down to the bottom of a Web page in order to see all the text and graphics displayed there.

So how do you scroll? Three different ways

- Press the PgDn (Page Down) key or the down-arrow key.
- Drag the scroll box in the vertical scrollbar (along the right edge of the IE window) downward, toward the bottom of the window.

- ✦ If your mouse has a wheel, roll it. (You may have to click a blank spot on the page to get the wheel to scroll the page.)

You can maximize the amount of information on-screen by displaying IE in Full Screen view. To do this, choose View➪Full Screen or press F11. This removes all screen elements except the Standard toolbar. For more about working in Full Screen view, see Book IV, Chapter 3.

Moving to another page

When you've seen everything on the page and you're ready to move along, you can go to a new page by using one of several different options:

- ✦ Click in the Address text box and type the new Web page address; then click Go or press Enter.
- ✦ Click a link on the current page to move to another page.
- ✦ Use one of the navigation buttons (Back, Forward, or Home), if they appear on the page, to move to another page relative to your current position.

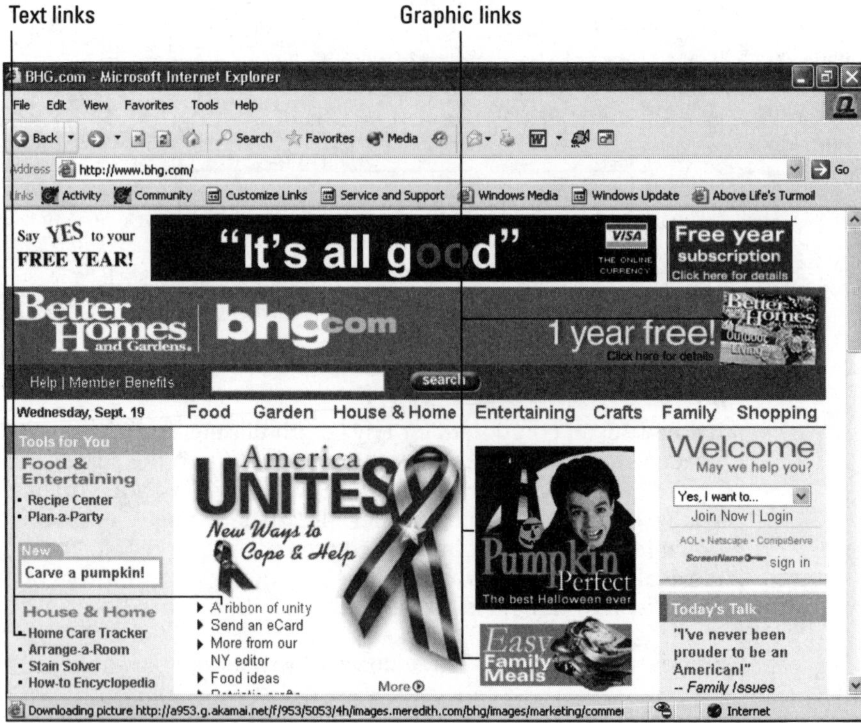

Figure 1-5: This site, which is included in the Favorites with Windows XP, includes a number of different types of links.

Did you go to the wrong page? If you find that you entered the wrong address or you went to a page that wasn't where you meant to go, you can cancel the load operation by clicking the Stop button on the Standard toolbar. This halts the download process, during which IE transmits the text and graphics to your computer. As soon as you click Stop, you can re-enter the address of the Web page that you want to see.

Want to make the new page appear in a new window — so you don't "lose your place" on the current page? Easy. Just hold down the Shift key while you click or press Enter.

Returning to a previous page

While you move from page to page, Internet Explorer remembers where you've been. Similar to dropping breadcrumbs, you can return to a page you saw previously by clicking the Back button on the Standard toolbar (which takes you to the last page displayed before the current one).

If you want to return to a page that is further back in your memory than the most recent page, follow these steps:

1. **Click the Address down arrow.**

   A listing of previous sites appears.

2. **Click the site that you want to see.**

   The site appears in the browser window.

Some really ornery Web pages hijack IE's Back button — when you click Back, they keep you trapped on the current page. But they can't hijack the list of previous sites that's available if you click the down arrow to the right of the Back button. Choose from the list, and Internet Explorer will get you off even the most intransigent page.

When you search for past sites, you have another easy way to sift through pages that you saw weeks ago. You use the History button on the Standard toolbar to display folders storing the various pages from your recent history. For more about working with History folders, see Book IV, Chapter 2.

Going Home

Clicking Home on the Standard toolbar takes you back to the site that you entered as your home page — the page that appears automatically when you first launch Internet Explorer. If you didn't even know you *entered* a home page, you may still have the default configuration set up in your system. Want to take a look? The steps are simple:

1. **Use Internet Explorer to go to the page that you want to establish as your home page.**
2. **Choose Tools⇨Internet Options.**

   The Internet Options dialog box appears, as shown in Figure 1-6.
3. **On the General tab, choose one of three options:**
   - Click the Use Current button if you want to make the current Web page — the one currently showing in Internet Explorer — your home page.
   - Click the Use Default button if you want to return the home page selection to the page that was set on your computer when you first purchased it. (Boo! Hiss!)
   - Click the Use Blank button if you want Internet Explorer to display no Web page at all.
4. **Click OK to close the Internet Options dialog box and return to the Web.**

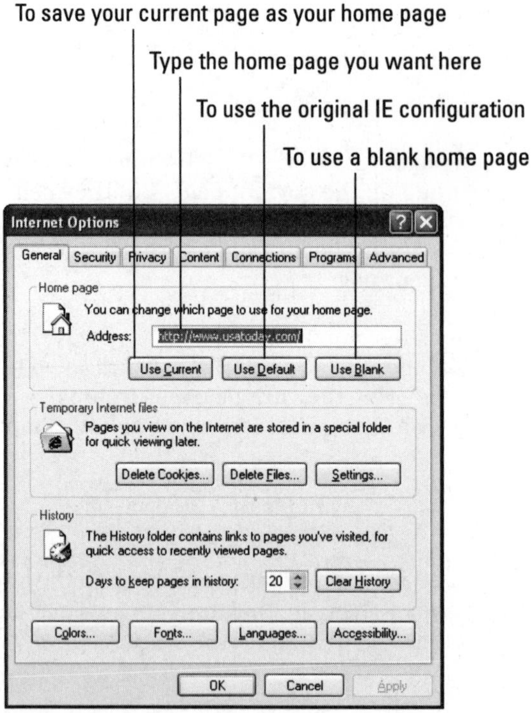

To save your current page as your home page

Type the home page you want here

To use the original IE configuration

To use a blank home page

Figure 1-6: You can choose any site on the Web as your home page.

Why would somebody want to load a blank page every time they started Internet Explorer? At first glance, it doesn't appear to make much sense to have IE show you a screen full of nothing when you start it. Personally, I always use a blank page. Why? It lets Internet Explorer start faster: No futzing around, waiting for the Internet to catch up with you. When IE is going, I move quickly and easily to the place I want to go.

Doing Stuff with Web Pages

Now that you're beginning to find the pages you want to explore, you need to know what to do with them after you find them. When you find a page that you just can't let go — Aunt Edna in Des Moines just *has* to see that new gazpacho recipe! — you can do one of three different things with the page to make sure Aunt Edna enjoys the treasure you've found:

- ✦ E-mail the Web page to another person.
- ✦ Save the Web page for your own use.
- ✦ Print the Web page and mail, fax, or file it.

The sections that follow take a closer look at each of these worthy goals.

E-mailing Web pages

What a boon — having e-mail capability right there on the IE Standard toolbar. When you've found a page you particularly like, you can e-mail the page to another user by clicking the Mail button and choosing Send Page from the drop-down list. This action launches your e-mail utility (which is most likely Outlook or Outlook Express, unless you've chosen something different). You can then select the To: recipient and click Send to send the page.

Instead of sending the whole page as an e-mail message, why not send a link to the page? It's much more efficient and generally faster. Either click the Mail button and choose Send a Link, or copy the address from the Address box and paste it into an e-mail message.

Saving Web pages

If you find one of those invaluable articles that backs up every argument you've ever made about buying quality running shoes (ammunition guaranteed to convince your mate), by all means, save it! Or — if you finally find that sparkling New! icon you've seen on other peoples' sites, you can capture it to use on your own pages by saving the image to a file. This section explains how to save pages — and graphics items — for your own use later.

Saving to a file

There's no mystery to saving a Web page. It's not a whole lot different from saving any document in any program anywhere. Ready for the process? Don't blink — you may miss it:

1. **Navigate to the Web page you want to save.**
2. **Choose File➪Save As.**

   The Save Web Page dialog box appears, as shown in Figure 1-7.

3. **Navigate to the folder in which you want to save the page.**
4. **In the Save As Type drop-down list, choose Web Archive, Single File (*.mht).**

   That forces Internet Explorer to save all the pieces of the Web page — including the graphics — in a single file. If you stick the whole page in one file, it's easy to move the file around without losing the pieces.

5. **Enter a name for the file if you want to change it.**
6. **Click Save.**

   Internet Explorer saves the file in the folder you specified.

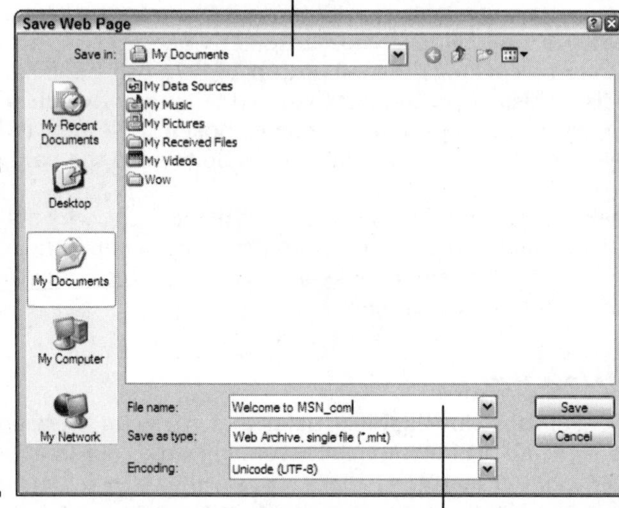

Figure 1-7: If you find a page that's particularly fetching, you can save it to your hard drive to look at later.

Saving an image

Suppose that you run across a picture that you really love, or an icon that you must have, or a banner that you want to remember. You can save the image to your own hard drive by following these steps:

1. **Right-click on the image that you want to save.**

   A shortcut menu appears (see Figure 1-8).

2. **Click Save Picture As.**

   Windows brings up the display the Save As dialog box.

3. **Navigate to the folder in which you want to save the file.**

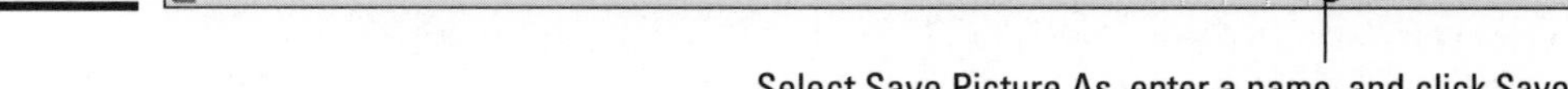
Right-click the image you want to save
Select Save Picture As, enter a name, and click Save

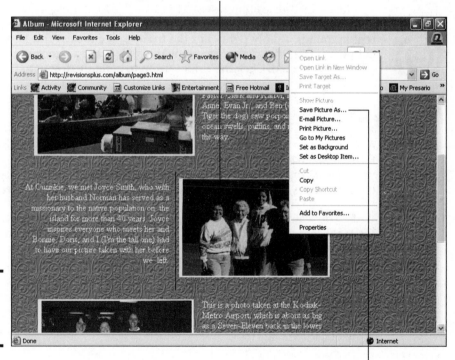

Figure 1-8: Saving an image from a site.

4. **Enter a name for the file, if needed.**
5. **Click Save to save the file.**

A word about copyright: If you didn't create the picture yourself, it doesn't belong to you. Taking images from the Web may be fine for your own personal use (sending a recipe to Aunt Edna is probably okay as well), but if you use images, text, ideas, pages, diagrams, music, or more as part of your business or as part of something you intend to make money on, you may be in danger of copyright violation. When in doubt, check it out: `www.benedict.com/info/info.aspx` is a great place to find more information on copyrights.

Printing Web pages

Here's another simple one: When you display a page that you want to print, just click the Print icon on the IE Standard toolbar, and Internet Explorer sends the current Web page to the printer. If you don't have a printer installed or connected, the program sends the file to the print queue where it sits, captive, until you connect the printer.

If you want to print only the current frame in a Web page that displays content in frames, simply right-click the frame and choose Print from the shortcut menu. The Print dialog box appears, and you can choose your printing options as needed. Click the Print button to send the frame to the printer.

Leaving and Returning to IE

Another great thing about working online is that you can easily move back and forth between applications in Windows XP. To minimize Internet Explorer while you go work on something else, click the Minimize button in the upper-right corner of the window. Internet Explorer reduces to an item on the taskbar.

When you want to restore the display of Internet Explorer, click the item in the taskbar. If you have more than one Web page open, a shortcut menu of available pages appears. Click the page that you want to see, and the IE window is restored to the screen. If you had only one page open, Internet Explorer opens as soon as you click its item in the taskbar.

Chapter 2: Advanced Browsing and Searching with Internet Explorer

In This Chapter

- Reliving your past browses
- Saving sites for later
- Collecting your favorite things
- Searching the Web with Google

This chapter explains how to expand your Web horizons by capturing and organizing the sites you find and want to keep. You also discover how to look back over where you've been on the Web and find out how to search for your next leaps forward. The History and Favorites tools are the focus of this chapter, and I also take you through the basics of using the Google search engine. So get ready to take one step backward and two steps forward as you build up your IE muscles.

Going Back to the Past

Did you know that Internet Explorer knows where you've been on the Web? Depending on the sites you visit, this may be good or bad news for you (or for your kids). In its History folders, Internet Explorer keeps track of the pages you've landed on. If that makes you curious — or nervous — follow these steps so that you can check out your past visits for yourself:

1. **Connect to the Internet if you're not already connected.**

   Don't know how to connect to the Internet? See Book III, Chapter 2 for details.

2. **Click the IE icon in the taskbar or choose Start⇨Internet to launch Internet Explorer.**

   Internet Explorer opens.

3. **Click the History button in the IE toolbar.**

   The History pane opens along the left side of the IE window (see Figure 2-1).

Click the folder of the day of week you want to display

Click the history tool in the IE toolbar

Choose the page you want to see

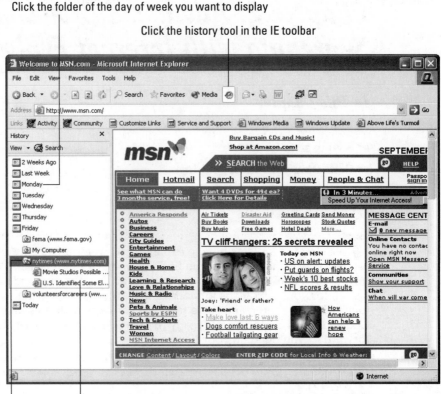

Select the site to visit

Figure 2-1: Click History in the IE toolbar to display your choices of sites to revisit.

4. **Choose the date(s) that you want to view.**

   If you want to see the sites that you visited last week, for example, click the Last Week selection. A list of visited sites appears.

5. **Click the site that you want to view.**

   Available pages within that site are displayed in the list.

6. **Click the page you want.**

   The selected page is displayed in the IE window.

If you're hoping to find a site that you visited more than two weeks ago, you're out of luck with History, although you can still search — most likely with Google — to find the site you seek. See the section, "The Secrets of Web Searching," later in this chapter, for more info on that.

History in the making

Some parents (okay, and maybe spouses) use the History files to make sure that other family members are surfing on the straight and narrow. Chances are, your employer is doing the same thing at work (but probably with a piece of software designed to spot policy infractions).

Whether your weakness is *Dilbert,* sports stats, or Ru Paul's fashion advice (oy!), remember that sneaking always shows up in the wash. The moral? Big Brother is watching. You're safest to stick with the sites that you would visit even if your mother were looking over your shoulder. And for those times when the temptation is just too great (everybody needs a good David Letterman fix once in a while), at least shred the evidence in your History folders. (See the "Clearing your History folder" section to find out how.) That won't necessarily keep your boss from finding where you've been surfing, but it'll probably stall your teenage son.

Changing your view

Internet Explorer initially stores the pages you visit in nice, neat little time capsules, but you may want to change the view to something you're more comfortable with. You can organize past sites four different ways:

- **By date:** Arranges pages according to *when* you visited them. (Yes, you already saw this, unless you slept through the first part of this chapter.)
- **By site:** Displays a strict alphabetical listing of site names (which may or may not be helpful, considering that not all site names — the part before the ".com" or ".org" — sort in a sensible way).
- **By most visited:** Lists your past sites according to how many times you visited them. Have you checked out *Dilbert* more often than you've read *The New York Times*? The list shows you the answer (don't worry — I won't tell).
- **By order visited today:** Gives you a listing of the sites you visited today, in the order you visited them (with the most recent sites listed at the top).

You can also click My Computer in the History panel to view Web pages and documents you've accessed on your computer system.

To change the view displayed in the History pane, click the View button and choose the option you want to use. After you make your selection, IE redisplays the pages accordingly. Select the site that you want to see by clicking it; choose a specific page within a site by clicking that page. The page is displayed in the IE window, and you're free to move on to other things.

When you want to close the History pane and recover the full display of the IE window, simply click the X (Close) button in the upper-right corner of the History pane.

Moving to another page

I know what you're saying to yourself: "There must be a better way. Do I have to mess with all of these folders and sites?" Until we, like our American Express cards, are endowed with smart card technology, we won't be able to simply remember all the sites we like — no matter how much ginkgo we take. But if you're looking for a faster, easier way to return to a site you've already typed in — oh, just a day or so ago — the answer is right under your mouse pointer:

1. **Make sure Internet Explorer is working (still or again).**
2. **Click the down-arrow on the right side of the Address bar.**

   Surprise! A list of previously viewed sites appears, as shown in Figure 2-2.
3. **Click the site that you're looking for and you move there. Smooth, eh?**

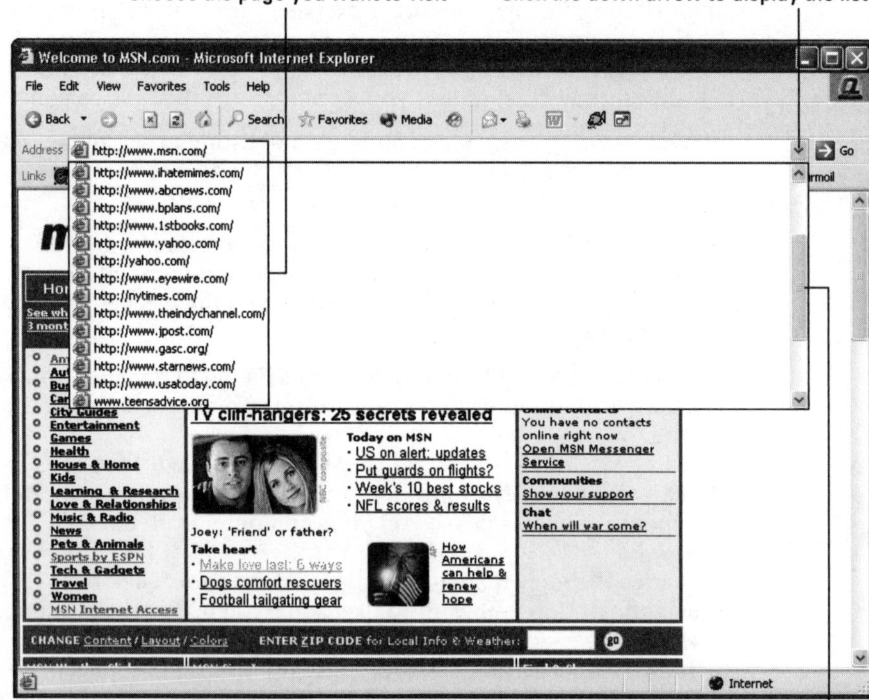

Figure 2-2: Click the Address down-arrow to display a list of recently viewed files.

One of the downsides of using the Address listing is that you don't know when you last visited the site or how high it ranks in your "most visited" category. (You don't even know *who* visited it, if several people in your home or office use your computer and you haven't set up different user accounts.) But if fast is what you want, this recall method is your best bet.

IE uses the same list for a kind of automatic completion by watching what you type in the Address bar and trying to match Web sites that you've already visited with the stuff you type. If you've been to MSN.com recently, for example, simply typing **m** in the Address bar will likely bring up `http://www.msn.com` as one of the automatic completion options. To go to a displayed Web site, hit the down-arrow key until you get to the site you want, and then press Enter.

Increasing long-term memory

So how long does IE keep your past browsings stored away on your hard drive? By default, 20 days' worth of wanderings are available to you through the History pane. If you want to up that number, you can increase your hold on the past all the way up to 99 days. If you want to reduce the amount of past baggage you carry, you can decrease the number all the way down to 0.

To make the change, follow these steps:

1. **Start Internet Explorer.**
2. **Choose Tools⇨Internet Options.**

   The Internet Options dialog box appears (see Figure 2-3). Click the General tab, if necessary.
3. **In the History area, change the setting for number of days in one of three ways:**
   - Click the up arrow to increase the number of days stored on the hard drive.
   - Click the down arrow to decrease the days.
   - Click in the text box and type the number of days you want to use.
4. **After you make the change, click the Apply button.**

   IE records your change and tracks the sites accordingly.
5. **Click OK to close the Internet Options dialog box and return to IE.**

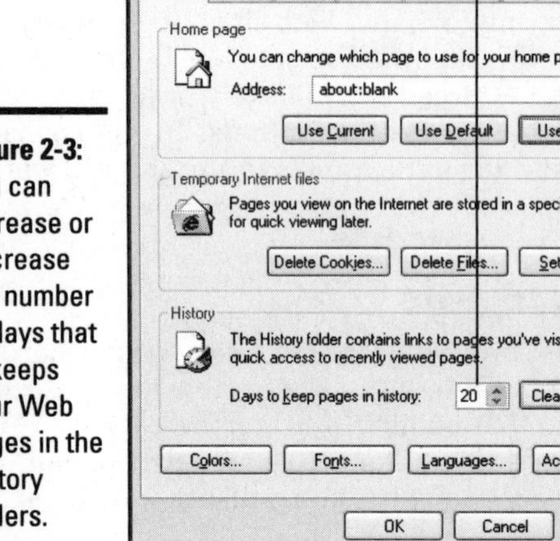

Figure 2-3: You can increase or decrease the number of days that IE keeps your Web pages in the History folders.

Clearing your History folder

Clearing out your Internet Explorer History folder won't speed up your computer, make Web pages load faster, or cure your terminal case of halitosis: All IE stores is a tiny bit of data, little more than the addresses of the pages you've seen. (If you need more space, clear your Temporary Internet Files — see the sidebar, "Saving space — Losing time.")

You should clear your History folder when you don't want anybody to be able to look at the list of Web pages that you've gone to. It's really that simple.

Here are the steps:

1. **Launch Internet Explorer by, say, choosing Start⇨Internet Explorer.**

   You don't have to be connected to the Internet to perform these steps.

2. **Choose Tools⇨Internet Options.**

   The Internet Options dialog box appears (refer to Figure 2-3).

3. **In the History area, click the button marked Clear History.**

   A message box appears, asking, "Er . . . are you sure you want to do this?"

Saving space — Losing time

Increasing or decreasing the number of days of History that IE stores doesn't have much effect on the amount of data stored on the hard drive — even a hyperactive surfer will have a hard time cranking up a History folder that's much larger than 1MB. By contrast, Temporary Internet Files on your computer can take up 10, 50, even a 100 *times* that much.

Those Temporary Internet Files only exist to speed up your Internet access: when IE hits a Web page that it's seen before, if a copy of the page's contents appears in the Temporary Internet Files folder, IE grabs the stuff on the hard drive instead of waiting for a download. That can make a huge difference in IE's responsiveness (particularly if you use a dial-up modem), but the speed comes at a price: the 10, 50, or 100MB of space you have to give to IE's brain.

If you want to clear out IE's Temporary Internet Files, in Internet Explorer choose Tools➪Internet Options. On the General tab, in the middle of the dialog box, click the Delete Files button. You won't hurt anything, but revisited Web pages will take longer to appear.

4. **Click Yes to continue.**

   Depending on how many files and days are stored, your computer may be busy deleting files for several minutes. But when you're clean, you're clean.

5. **Click OK to close the dialog box and go on your merry way.**

Clearing your History is a bit like a lobotomy: You have no "oops!" factor giving you a chance to easily recover from a mistake. When those pages are gone, they're gone. So think twice or thrice about what you're clearing before you click that shiny button.

"Those who forget the past are condemned to repeat it." — George Santayana, *Life of Reason*, 1905

Playing Favorites

As your surfing savvy increases, you'll begin to find pages that are keepers — Web sites with information that you know you'll want to be able to find later. Internet Explorer gives you an easy way to collect and organize those sites in a feature called Favorites.

Window's preselected Favorites

When you start Internet Explorer for the first time and click the Favorites button, you may notice that Microsoft (or the company that sold you the computer) splays a whole slew of folders covering a variety of topics, from home and health to banking and sports (see Figure 2-4, which lists the Favorites found in an MSN online service installation). You also see a number of strategic alliances represented there: Many third-party vendors involved in "partnering" with Microsoft and hardware manufacturers get their links built right in to the default Favorites folders. And they pay dearly for the privilege.

The Favorites displayed on your system will be different from the ones shown in Figure 2-4 — after all, this real estate is unabashedly for sale, your PC manufacturer will no doubt wish to cash in, and Microsoft isn't quite so aggressive in selling screen real estate on a monopoly operating system. But the steps for displaying, selecting, adding, and organizing Favorites all work the same way no matter how many preset Favorites you find in your folders.

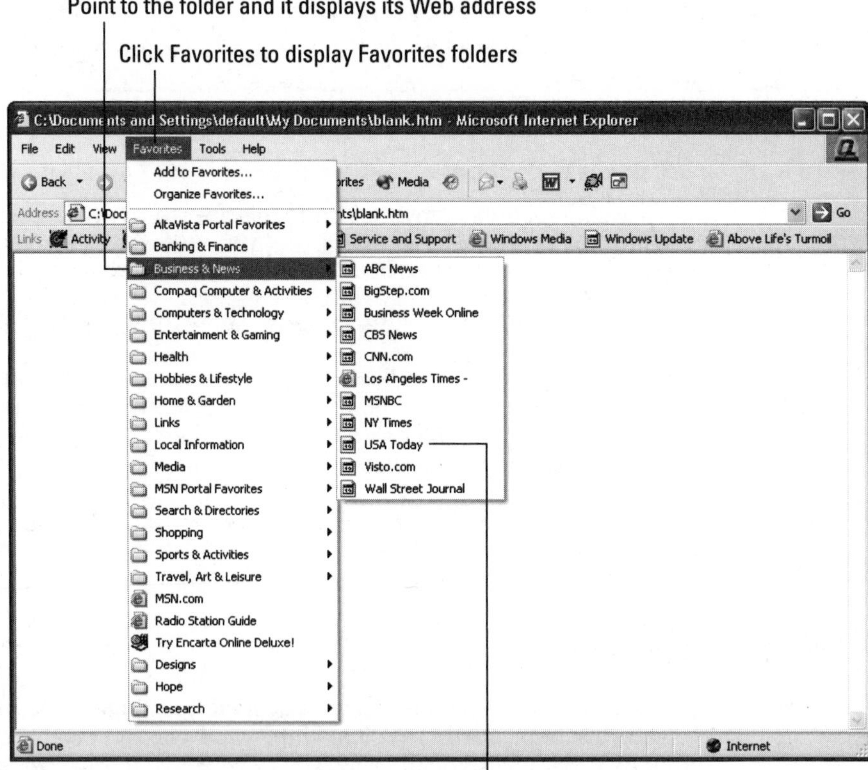

Figure 2-4: IE comes with folders full of preset favorites, ready for exploring.

To explore the Favorites Microsoft has, uh, thoughtfully arranged for you, follow these steps:

1. **Start Internet Explorer.**
2. **Click Favorites on the main menu.**

   A list of Microsoft-and-your-hardware-manufacturer's Favorites folders appears.
3. **Right-click on any of *their* Favorites that aren't *your* Favorites, and choose Delete.**

   It's your Favorites menu. Give all the slimy advertisers the boot.
4. **Click any folder that interests you.**

   A submenu of sites appears. Right-click on any of them that deserve to go into the bit bucket, and choose Delete for them, too.
5. **If you see any sites that you think might be useful, click on its name in the Favorites list.**

   Internet Explorer goes to the site.

Adding Favorites of your own

When you find yourself viewing a site that you want to go back to later, you can add the site to your own Favorites folder. Internet Explorer enables you to add sites to the preset folders, or you can create a new folder that is specific to your own needs. These are the steps to add a Favorite of your own:

1. **Go to the Web site that you want to stick in your Favorites list.**
2. **Choose Favorites⇨Add to Favorites.**

   If you can't see the full Add Favorite dialog box, shown in Figure 2-5, click the Create In button.
3. **Navigate to the folder in which you want to store the site, or create a new folder by clicking the New Folder button.**

   If you want to create a new folder to store the Web page you're adding, click the New Folder button in the Add Favorite dialog box. The Create New Folder dialog box opens. Type a name for the folder (spaces and punctuation characters are okay) and click OK. IE adds the folder to the Create In list in the Add Favorite dialog box, and you can select it as you would any of the existing folders.
4. **Click OK to save the link and close the dialog box.**

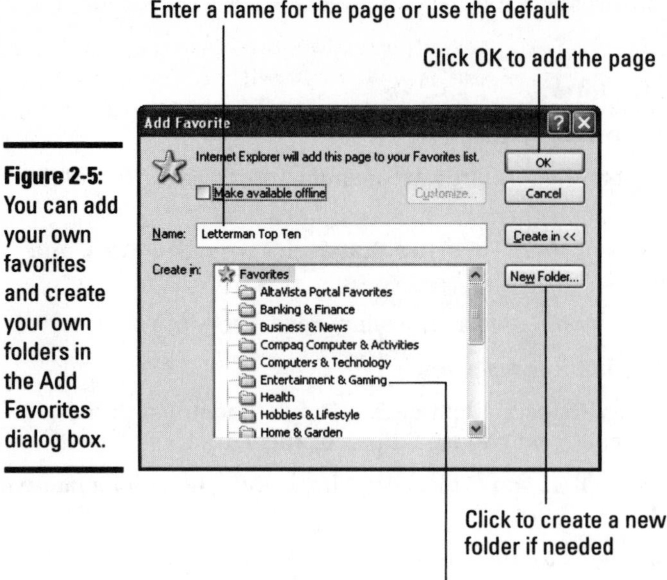

Figure 2-5: You can add your own favorites and create your own folders in the Add Favorites dialog box.

Making a site available offline

If you have a notebook computer, or if your main computer isn't connected to the Internet all the time, you may find that you want to save some sites for later reference. You can make a site *available offline* — that is, store it on your computer to make it available to you, in Internet Explorer, even when you aren't connected to the Internet. You can also control how much of the site you store on your computer by using the Offline Favorite Wizard. Here's how:

1. **Make sure that the site that you want to add appears in the IE window (which means that you must be connected to the Internet).**
2. **Choose Favorites⇨Add to Favorites.**

   The Add Favorite dialog box appears.
3. **Choose the name and folder for the page, as usual.**
4. **Select the Make Available Offline check box.**

   The Customize button becomes available.
5. **Click the Customize button.**

   The Offline Favorite Wizard starts.

6. **Click Next to start the process.**

   The wizard's first question is whether you want to make pages linked to the current one available offline as well. If you select the Yes option button, you can choose how many pages deep you want to download (see Figure 2-6).

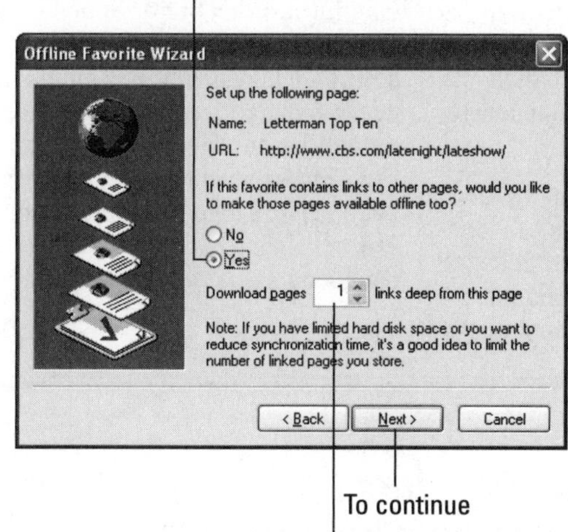
To make linked pages available offline
Offline Favorite Wizard
Set up the following page:
Name: Letterman Top Ten
URL: http://www.cbs.com/latenight/lateshow/
If this favorite contains links to other pages, would you like to make those pages available offline too?
No
Yes
Download pages 1 links deep from this page
Note: If you have limited hard disk space or you want to reduce synchronization time, it's a good idea to limit the number of linked pages you store.
< Back
Next >
Cancel
To continue
Tell IE the number of links to follow

Figure 2-6: Use the Offline Favorite Wizard to tell IE how much information you want to store in your favorite pages.

WARNING!

Downloaded pages — especially those with photos, animation, and sound — can take up a huge amount of hard drive space. If you're trying to conserve space on your system, download only the pages you need.

7. **Choose when you want IE to synchronize the page you are adding, and click Next.**

   You can opt to do it manually (by choosing Tools⇨Synchronize), or you can set up a schedule to do automatic synchronizing.

8. **If the site you added needs a password, select Yes in the next page of the wizard and enter your user name and then your password twice.**

9. **Click Finish to complete the wizard and return to the Add Favorite dialog box.**

10. **Click OK to close the dialog box and continue surfing.**

    Later, when you're offline, you can work with the page that you saved.

Synchronized (Web) swimming

One of the problems of working with Web pages offline is that they can change without you knowing it. For that reason, Internet Explorer provides a synchronizing feature that enables you to make sure that you have the most recent content from the site. One of the stops in the Offline Favorite Wizard asks you to choose when you want to synchronize your pages. You can choose to synchronize pages manually or automatically.

To synchronize your pages manually, click Tools⇨Synchronize whenever you are connected to the Internet. The Synchronize dialog box appears, and you can simply choose the page and click Synchronize to start the process.

To synchronize your pages automatically, you create a schedule that takes care of it for you. You can create the schedule while you're working with the Offline Favorite Wizard (select the option I Would Like to Create a New Schedule when it is presented). Specify how often (in days) you want the pages to be synchronized, select the time of day, and enter a name for the event if you choose. (You can simply leave the default name, My Scheduled Update, if you like.) Finally, select the check box in the wizard page to force IE to connect automatically if you are not online when your scheduled update time occurs.

Organizing your Favorites

Sometimes surfing presents you with so many exciting things to look at that you may simply save pages right and left without taking the time to put them in folders. Over time, this creates a mess of pages in your Favorites menu and means you have to go scrolling through many pages in order to find the page you want.

To straighten your folders and your life, follow these steps:

1. **On the IE toolbar, click the Favorites button, and in the Favorites pane that appears, click the Organize button.**

   Alternatively, choose Favorites⇨Organize Favorites.

   The Organize Favorites dialog box appears, as shown in Figure 2-7.

2. **In the folder list, select the folder containing the link(s) that you want to change.**

3. **Select the link that you want, and then click one of the following command buttons:**

   - **Create Folder:** Creates a new folder to store the page. A new folder appears in the list; you type the name for the folder and press Enter.

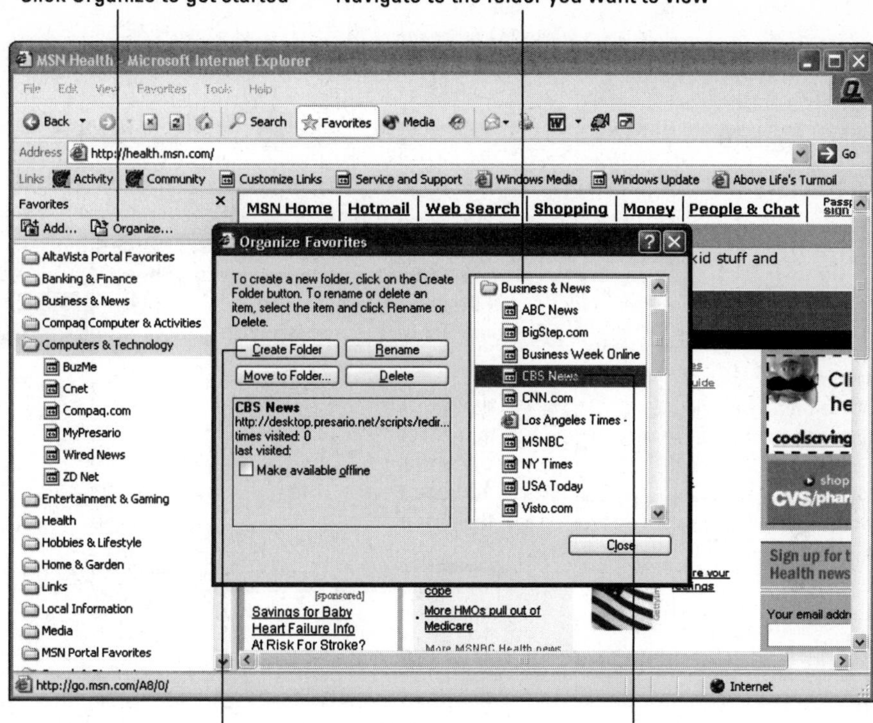

Figure 2-7: Click the Organize button to display the Organize Favorites dialog box.

- **Move to Folder:** Allows you to choose a new location for the link. The Browse for Folder dialog box opens so that you can select the folder to which you want to move the link (see Figure 2-8).
- **Rename:** Allows you to enter a new name for the link (or folder). The link that you selected appears with the name highlighted; you simply type the new name and press Enter.
- **Delete:** Removes the link (or folder). The Confirm Folder Delete message box appears so that you can confirm that you want to delete the selected link. Click Yes to continue.

4. **Click OK to close the Browse for Folder dialog box, and then click Close to close the Organize Favorites dialog box.**

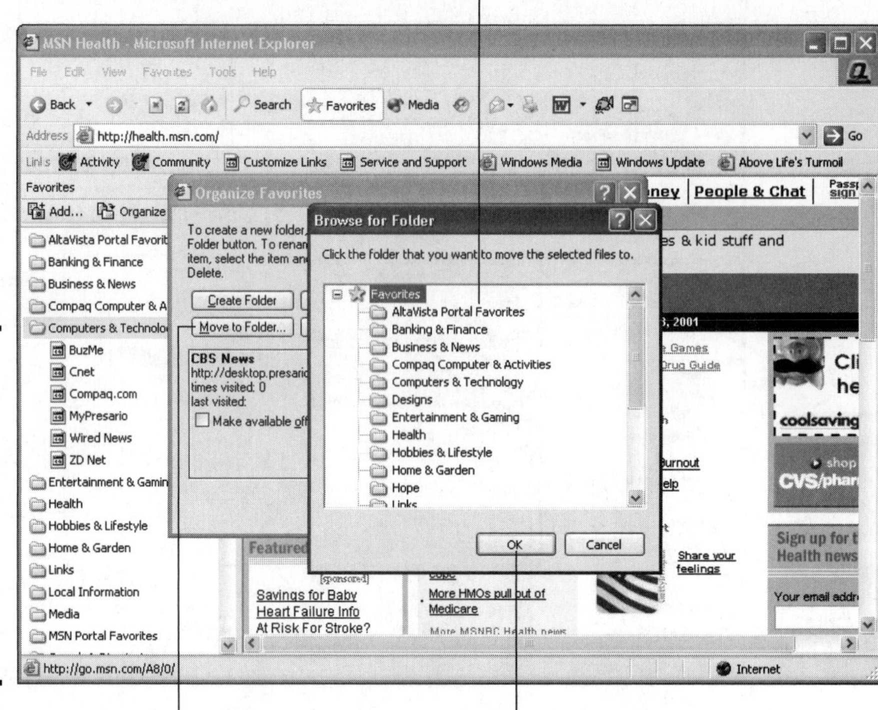

Figure 2-8: Move the links to your favorite Web pages to a new location by using the Browse for Folder dialog box.

The Secrets of Web Searching

Internet searching can be a lonely business. You're out there, on the Internet range, with nothing but gleaming banner ads and text links to guide you. What happens when you want to find information on a specific subject but you're not sure where to start? IE has a helper to assist you with just this dilemma: the IE Search Companion, which lurks beneath the Search button on the Standard toolbar. But there's a better way: Google.

As this book went to press, Microsoft was about to release a new search engine that's squarely aimed at Google. Microsoft President Steve Ballmer says that failing to keep up with Internet search technology is Microsoft's "biggest mistake in years." While anyone who has a nodding acquaintance with Microsoft's predatory monopolistic practices might take issue with Steve B's sense of priorities, the fact remains that alternatives to Google abound. There's no need to develop a religious attachment to a single search engine. Look around, and go with what works best for you. We cover search engines with, uh, religious fervor at AskWoody.com.

Googling

It ain't easy being the biggest, baddest search engine around. A decade or so ago, Google (then called BackRub) amounted to little more than a simple idea: If a lot of Web sites point to a particular Web page, chances are good that the page being pointed to contains information that many people would find interesting.

Stanford grad students Larry Page and Sergey Brinn, BackRub's founders, scrimped together enough money to build a working prototype in a Stanford dorm room. By 1998, the (ahem!) PageRank system was generating a lot of interest on campus: Students could actually find the stuff they wanted without slogging through endless lists of categories. In September 1998, Page and Brinn adopted the name Google, opened a real office with a cool U.S. $1,000,000 initial capital. Truth be told, the "office" was in a garage, which came with a washing machine, dryer, and hot tub. They blew all the money on computers. My kind of people.

Google has gone from one of the most admired companies on the Web to one of the most vilified, and the PageRank system, which tries to assign a number predicting the relevance of a page to a specific query, has been demonized in terms rarely heard since the Spanish Inquisition. Few people now believe that PageRank objectively rates the "importance" of a Web page — millions of dollars and thousands of months have been spent trying to jigger the results. But, like it or not, Google just works. Google's spiders, which crawl all over the Web night and day looking for pages, have indexed billions of pages, feeding hundreds of millions searches a day.

Using the Google Toolbar

When all is said and done, I use Google dozens of times a day. If you've never given it a try, you should — and the easiest way is through the Google Toolbar. Here's how to get it installed:

1. **Start Internet Explorer and go to** `http://toolbar.google.com`**.**

   Google's Toolbar download page appears, as shown in Figure 2-9.

2. **Choose your preferred language, and then click the Download Google Toolbar button. When the Windows Security Center asks if you want to run or save the file, go ahead and run it. (You may have to click Run twice.)**

   Google has the usual 278-page End User License Agreement, to which you must click Agree.

   The most important decision you need to make about Google is the privacy question, which (much to their credit) Google describes completely and accurately in its Choose Your Configuration window (see Figure 2-10).

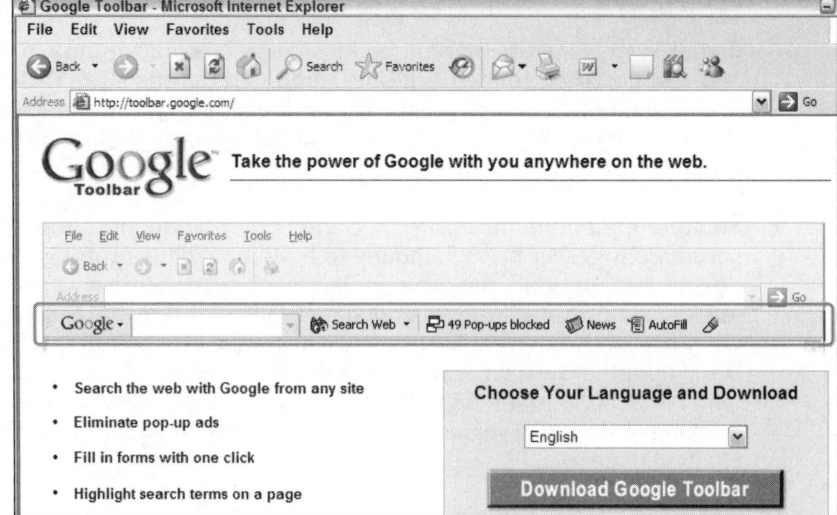

Figure 2-9: The Google Toolbar, by far the easiest way to use the Google search engine.

Google Toolbar Installer for Windows NT/2000/XP - English (2.0.111-big/en)

Google Toolbar

Choose Your Configuration

PLEASE READ THIS CAREFULLY
IT'S NOT THE USUAL YADA YADA

By using the advanced features of the Google toolbar, you may be sending information about the sites you visit to Google. This is needed to make some features of the Toolbar available to you.

In order to show you more information about a site, the Google Toolbar has to tell us what site you're visiting, which it does by sending us the URL.

This does NOT tell us who YOU are (your name or email address), but does tell us that a user has requested the PageRank for a given site.

Google will not sell or provide personally identifiable information to any third parties. To learn more about the privacy protections we have built into this system, read our Toolbar Privacy Policy, located here: http://toolbar.google.com/privacy.html

You must select one of these options before clicking Next:

◉ Enable advanced features (anonymous information will be sent to Google)
○ Disable advanced features (no information will be sent to Google)

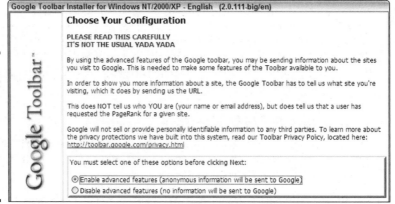

Figure 2-10: Do you want to send information about your surfing to Google? Tough question.

3. **Choose between the Advanced version of the toolbar and the, uh, Unadvanced version, and then click Next.**

   Although I have more than a little trepidation about allowing multi-billion-dollar companies to track my Web surfing behavior, I, personally, use the Advanced version of the toolbar. The Advanced version shows you a Web page's PageRank when you surf to it — a useful, if not infallible, indication of the page's prominence in the Web's pecking order. In exchange for receiving that information, though, your computer sends a message to Google's big database, telling the Googlies which page you're looking at — something of a Neilsen Rating in real time. I've never heard of Google abusing its massive database, but I suppose it's at least theoretically possible.

4. **Click Next one more time and Google downloads and installs the toolbar automatically.**
5. **Give the Google Toolbar a whirl by typing a topic of interest and hitting Enter (or clicking the Search Web button).**

   In Figure 2-11, I searched for my own name. You might want to try the same. Could be interesting.

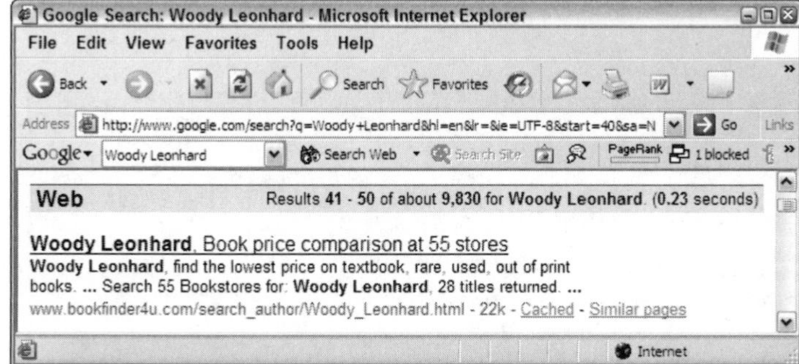

Figure 2-11: Have you ever Googled yourself?

6. **Click the down arrow next to the word Google on the toolbar, and choose Options. Modify the toolbar to fit the way you want to work.**

   On the Options tab, I deselect the BlogThis! check box (if you aren't a blogger, you probably will, too), the News button (it's just as easy to choose Google⇨Google Links⇨Google News), and the Options button (who needs ya, baby?). On the More tab, I select the Search Site, Search Images, and Search Groups check boxes. But that's just me. Play with it a bit and see what you like.

Googling tricks

Google searches more than mere Web pages. If you click the down arrow on the Google button and then select Google Links (shown in Figure 2-12), you find that

- Google maintains an enormous database of pictures, called *Google Images*. If you're looking for a picture of almost any imaginable description (say, Lon Chaney in *The Hunchback of Notre Dame,* or a graph of the global propagation of the Slammer worm, or a candid pic of the giant gecko called Tokay), it's here. In spades.

- Google owns newsgroups. If you're looking for Internet newsgroups — the largely unmonitored postings of millions of Internet users, on every topic under the sun — don't bother with Outlook or Outlook Express, go straight to *Google Groups*. Google literally owns the newsgroup archive, to a first approximation, anyway. Google's newsgroup tools and interface run rings around anything Outlook Express can deliver.

- ✦ Google has a directory of Web pages. (A Web *directory* is a lot like the Yellow Pages: If you know the kind of information you're looking for, you can leaf through the directory to find a site that might provide what you need.) Although Yahoo! has traditionally maintained the most complete directory of Web pages on the Internet, Google's effort ain't half bad.
- ✦ Google news competes with CNN.com and other newsy sites. Froogle tries to sell you things. Blogger blogs the blogs. And so on.

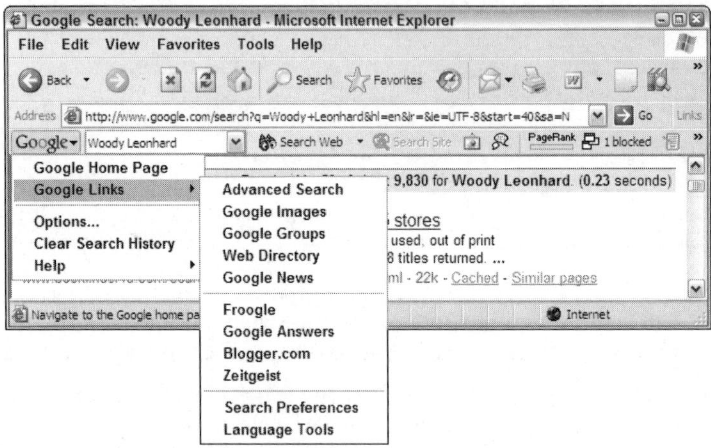

Figure 2-12: Jump to different pages on the Google Web site through the Google Links submenu on the Google Toolbar.

Google has many tricks up its sleeve. For example

- ✦ If you want to find the status of your UPS or FedEx delivery, just type the package number (digits only) in the Google search bar and hit Enter.
- ✦ The search bar's a stock ticker: Type a symbol such as **MSFT** or **SCBSET**.
- ✦ It's a calculator: Type **123*456** in the Google bar and your answer appears.
- ✦ It converts: Try entering **26 inches in centimeters** or **5 liters in gallons** or **3 oz in kg**.

To get a feel for some of the esoteric services Google provides, click the "more" button on the main page. ***Hint:*** Check out the Google store (`www.googlestore.com`) for the cool black T-shirt that everybody loves.

I cover Google tricks extensively in *Windows XP Timesaving Techniques For Dummies* (Wiley Publishing, Inc.).

Chapter 3: Making Internet Explorer Your Own

In This Chapter

- Making IE work your way
- Rearranging tools and toolbars
- Turbocharging your surfing
- Digging up the truth about cookies
- Saying goodbye to IE's Content Advisor: RIP

I hear the same questions over and over again about making Internet Explorer run faster (there isn't much you can do), bypassing some of IE's more, uh, idiosyncratic behavior (there are a few solutions), and whether certain IE features really work (in general, if you have to ask, the answer is probably no).

In this chapter, I take you through the tricks that will help you get the most out of IE, even if you have to drag it kicking and screaming into the 21st century. I tell you the truth about cookies. I show you how to customize IE. And — if all else fails and you've made a mess of things — you can return your IE settings to the way they were before you made all the modifications. At the end of this chapter, I tell you how.

Getting the Most from IE

A small handful of Internet Explorer tricks can make all the difference in your productivity and sanity.

Every IE user should know the following shortcuts:

- IE will automatically stick `http://www.` on the front of an address that you type and `.com` on the end if you hit Ctrl+Enter. So if you want to go to the site `http://www.dummies.com`, simply type **dummies** in the Address bar and press Ctrl+Enter.

- Sometimes you really want IE to open a new window, and leave your current window where it is, so you can easily refer back to it. Usually, the Web page you're on has control over whether clicking on a link will open a new window or not, but you can override the page's setting. To make IE open the linked page in a new window, hold down the Shift key when you click a link. Alternatively, you can right-click a link and choose Open in New Window.
- Getting IE to open new windows in a specific size and location can be problematic. In general, if you arrange an IE window so it's in the location that you want, and then choose File⇨Close to get out of Internet Explorer, IE is smart enough to remember the size of the window: The next time you open IE, the window should appear at the same size, in the same place. Unfortunately, on some machines, and under some circumstances, IE "forgets." If you want IE to always open new pages "maximized" to fit the whole screen, download and install the free program called IE Maximizer, from jiiSoft, `www.jiisoft.com/iemaximizer` (see Figure 3-1).

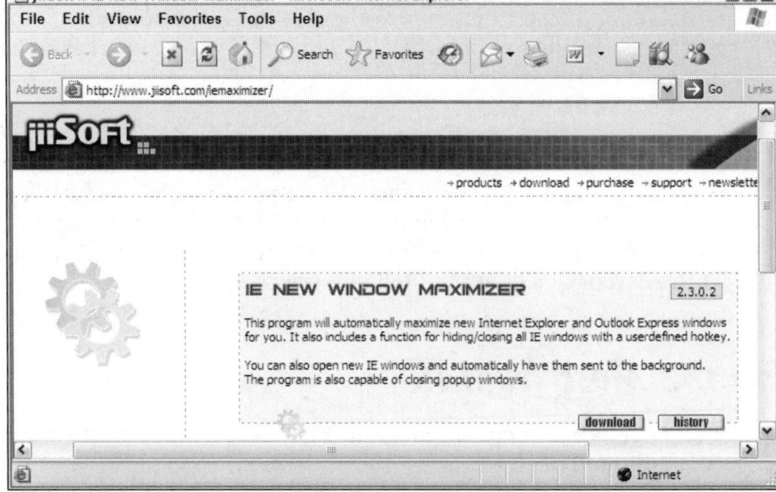

Figure 3-1: Make IE open new windows maximized by running IE Maximizer, a free program from jiiSoft.

- If your PC manufacturer, or some piece of hijacking scumware, replaces the logo in the upper-right corner of the Internet Explorer window, you can get the original back:

  1. **Choose Start⇨Run.**
  2. **Type the following in the text box:**

     ```
     rundll32 iedkcs32.dll,clear
     ```

3. **Press Enter.**

   IE reverts to its usual logo.

Making IE Run Faster

In general, if you want IE to run faster, you need to get a faster Internet connection. Beefing up your computer, adding more memory, getting a larger hard drive — none of that stuff really does much to make Web surfing faster. The bottleneck is your Internet connection.

If you're stuck with a slow connection, and you're a bit desperate, there's one trick that will speed up IE — but at a price. You can turn off graphics. When you tell IE to load a page without the graphics, the browser displays an empty box where the image would be. That's a bit like going to the Louvre and seeing only empty picture frames, but if you want to get through quickly, it may help.

Here's how:

1. **Choose Tools⇨Internet Options.**

   The Internet Options dialog box opens.

2. **Click the Advanced tab.**
3. **Scroll down to the Multimedia section (shown in Figure 3-2), and deselect the Show Pictures check box.**
4. **Click OK to close the dialog box.**

Just the facts, ma'am! If you're interested only in information, you can further reduce download times by clearing the check boxes for Play Animations in Web Pages, Play Videos in Web Pages, and Play Sounds in Web Pages. This reduces your Web pages to straight text information, which may not be much fun but makes surfing much faster.

Even after you turn off the display of pictures, you can still view a picture if you choose. When the Web page appears, simply right-click the image placeholder (which usually is a small box surrounding a red X). When the shortcut menu appears, click Show Picture, and the image appears on the page.

You turned the display of graphics back on, but they still aren't appearing. What gives? Press F5 to refresh the display and IE reloads the page, which includes downloading the graphics as expected.

Choose Tools Internet ⇨ Options to display the dialog box

Click the Advanced tab and scroll to the Multimedia section

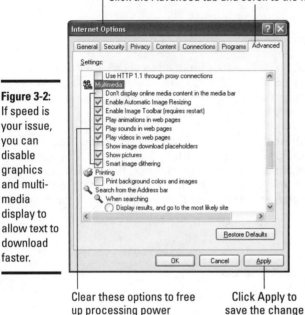

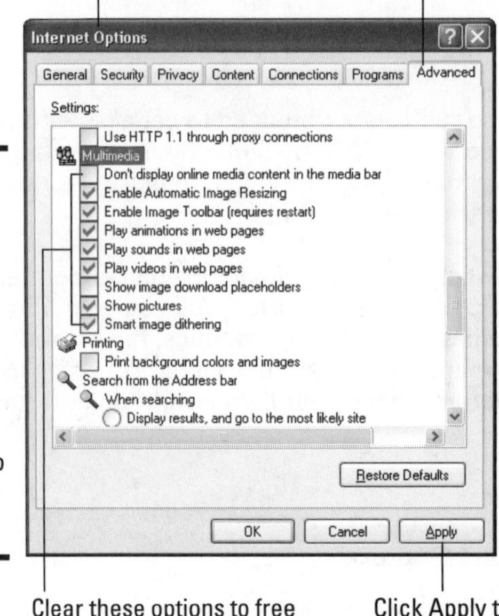

Clear these options to free up processing power

Click Apply to save the change

Figure 3-2: If speed is your issue, you can disable graphics and multimedia display to allow text to download faster.

One other way to boost IE performance is to increase the amount of storage space allowed for those temporary Internet files. I, personally, have never been able to *feel* a difference when I jack up the space — that's my criteria for a good performance boost — but your results may vary. Here's how:

1. **In Internet Explorer, choose Tools⇨Internet Options, and on the middle of the General tab, where it says Temporary Internet Files, click the Settings button.**

   You see the Settings dialog box shown in Figure 3-3.

2. **Move the slider marked Amount of Disk Space to Use to the right.**

   If you have a lot of room on your hard drive, you can afford to let IE get a little sloppy. But remember that the gains you'll experience, day to day, aren't really that great.

3. **When you're happy with your choice, click OK.**

Figure 3-3: More room for temporary files means IE doesn't have to download Web pages as frequently, thus saving you a (small) bit of time.

A New Look for IE

Any marketing person at Microsoft will tell you: All users are not created equal. Some want a system that's fully customizable; others want everything done for them. If you're one of those people who like to play around with things to get them just right, you'll like the amount of flexibility IE gives you in deciding the way you want things to look.

Reading the fine print

Depending on the size of your monitor and the quality of the display, the Web content that you see may be a bit of a strain to read. Some site designers try to cram as much information as possible on a page, crushing paragraphs of text into a 13-inch diagonal space. You can control this to some degree by making the size of the text larger and easier to read. Here are the steps:

1. **In Internet Explorer, choose View➪Text Size.**
2. **Select a new size for the text (see Figure 3-4).**

   The display changes immediately. Don't like it? Change it again.

One trade-off when you enlarge the text size is that less information fits on the screen, which means that you have to do more scrolling to read through articles that capture (and hold) your interest.

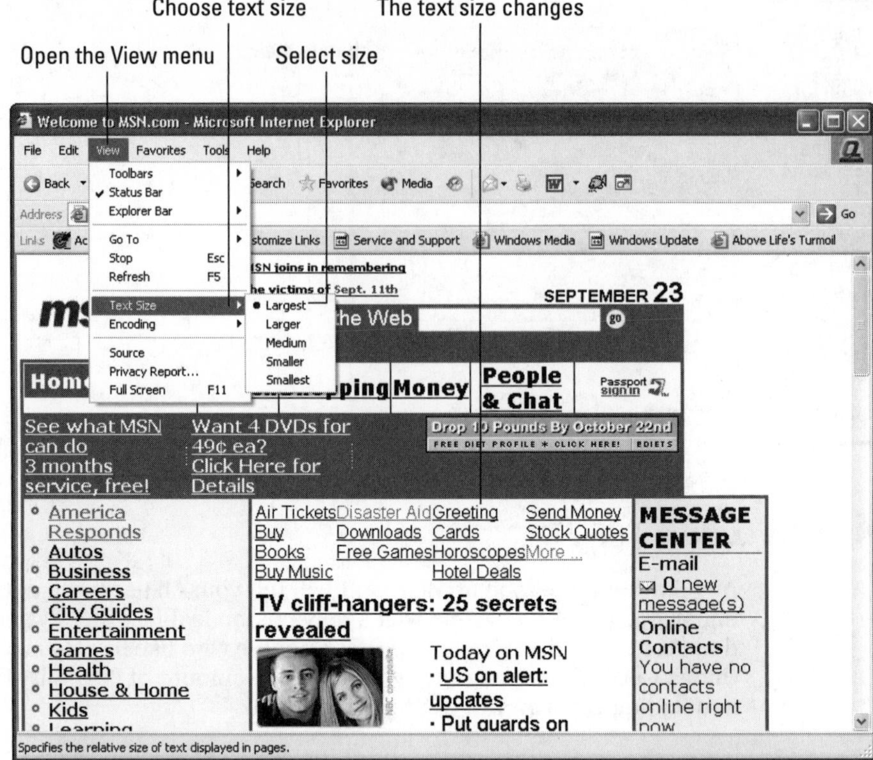

Figure 3-4: You can choose five different sizes of text for IE's display.

Coloring IE

Another way to make IE your own involves changing the colors displayed in the browser window. For those pages that don't have any color preset in the coding of the page, you can change the color of the text or the background; you can also change the link colors used on the pages you visit, if those pages do not have link colors specified.

Here are the steps to change the colors IE displays:

1. **Choose Tools⇨Internet Options.**

   The Internet Options dialog box appears.

2. **In the lower-left corner, click the Colors button.**

   The Colors dialog box appears, as shown in Figure 3-5. Here you can select two different kinds of color controls:

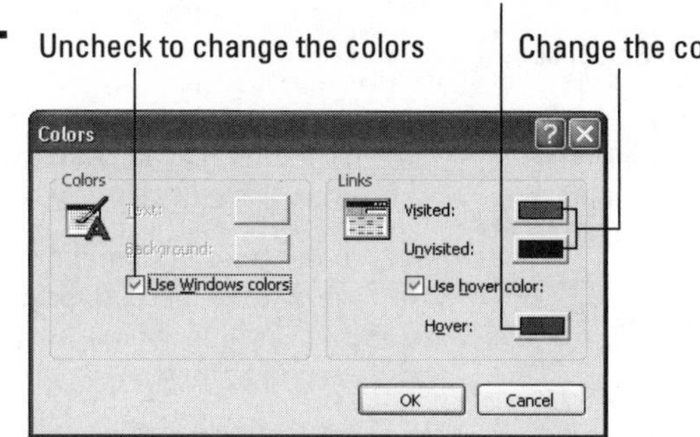

Figure 3-5: Put your crayons away — you can color your screen any hue you want using IE's color options.

- On the Colors side of the dialog box, you can choose whether you want to use the standard Windows colors (which is the default selection); or you can select the Text and Background colors yourself. If you want to set your own Text and Background colors, deselect the Use Windows Colors check box. The Text and Background choices then become available and you can modify the colors by clicking the selection and choosing the new color from the displayed palette.
- On the Links side of the dialog box, you specify the colors of the links you have visited, the links you have yet to visit, and the color used to highlight the link when you "hover" over it with the mouse. Click the color selection that you want to change and choose the color from the displayed palette.

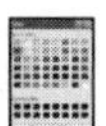

3. **Click the new color from the displayed Color palette.**

   If you want to create your own color, click the Define Custom Colors button and enter the specifications for the color you want to use.

4. **Click OK to close the palette, and then click OK again to close the Colors dialog box and make the changes to your browser settings.**

If you're convinced that your color scheme will work better than the color combinations other Web designers have put together, you can override the colors selected by other Web designers by clicking the Accessibility button in the Internet Options dialog box. When the Accessibility dialog box appears, select the Ignore Colors Specified on Web Pages check box to disable the Web colors specified by the Web page designers. Click OK to close the dialog box, and then return to the Colors dialog box and choose the colors you want.

What colors work?

Granted, not all Web page designers know what they're doing. Some companies and individuals seem to have a knack for online display — they seem to know how to balance pictures, text, headlines, colors, and animation to give users a page that's easy to read and delivers the information they're looking for. But often the design is intended to shock. Users are met by an overabundance of special swirling effects, clashing characters, animated text, and flashing buttons.

If you're a brave enough soul to want to make your own color improvements on the top of this visual cacophony, by all means give it a shot. But if your intent is to create a display that is easy (or at least not impossible) to read, remember these simple color guidelines:

- **The higher the contrast, the better the readability.** The contrast between the text and the background colors is important in helping the reader decipher the text. Use dark text on a light background whenever possible (or the reverse, light text on a dark background).
- **Stay away from background colors that may overwhelm the text.** Bright red for a page background would be glaring and hard to stare at for long.
- **Use dark colors for skinny text.** If the font used on the site is small and thin, letters may disappear (especially for those in the over-40 crowd) if the color selected for text is too light. If your background is light, stick with black, dark blue, deep green, or brown lettering for smaller text.
- **Remember that they're *your* preferences.** If other people will be using your computer, you may want to confer with other users before changing all backgrounds to pea green and all text to apricot. After all, one person's "pretty" is another's "egad!"

Getting the big picture with Full Screen view

As you get more comfortable surfing the Web (and more opinionated about what you do and don't like), you may want to do away with some of the toolbars in lieu of more screen real estate. Especially if you are working the Web primarily on a fact-finding mission (meaning you are finding and reading articles on various topics), having a maximum amount of space on-screen means you do less scrolling.

You can choose from two easy ways to display your Web browser in full screen view: Press F11 or click the Full Screen button in the toolbar. Everything except the navigation tools disappears, as shown in Figure 3-6.

When you want to jump to a new page, don't panic. You can restore IE to its traditional display by pressing F11 a second time.

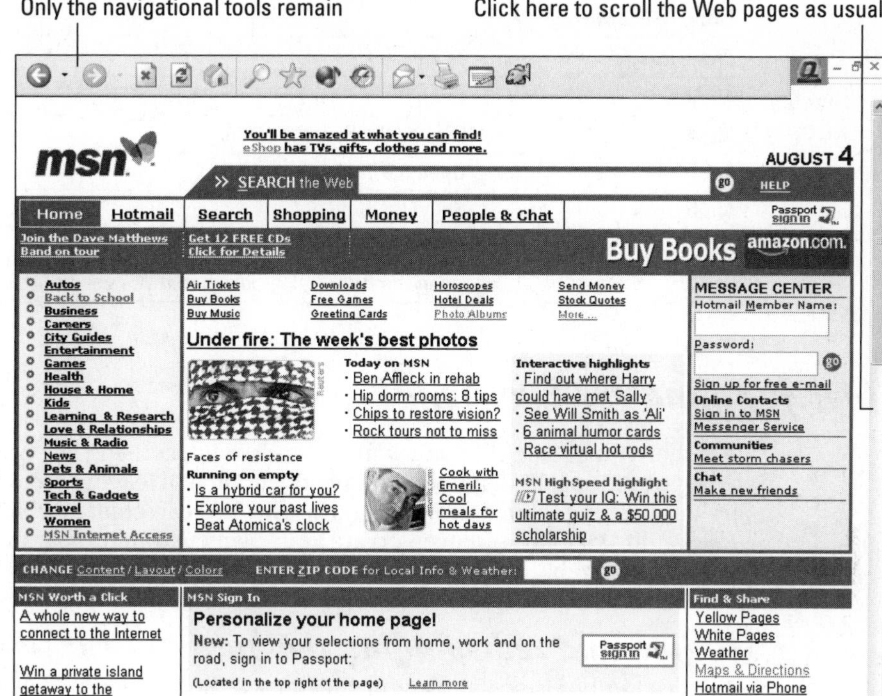

Figure 3-6: Using Full Screen view gives you maximum screen real estate.

If you want to display only the address bar in full screen view (so that you can jump from page to page while getting the greatest possible amount of room on-screen), press Alt+V to display the View menu, point to Toolbars, and select Address Bar. The address bar appears to the right of the navigational tools, as you see here:

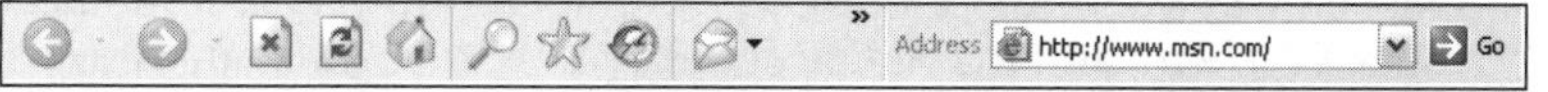

Table 4-1 lists some keys you can use to quickly navigate a full screen.

Table 4-1 Quick Keys for Full Screen Navigating

Press This	*To Do This*
Alt+F	Open the File menu
Alt+E	Display the Edit menu

(continued)

Table 4-1 *(continued)*	
Press This	***To Do This***
Alt+V	Open the View menu
Alt+A	Display the Favorites menu
Alt+T	Open the Tools menu
Alt+H	Show the Help options
Ctrl+F	Display the Find dialog box
Ctrl+P	Open the Print dialog box so that you can print the current page

Tool Juggling for Everyone!

Whether you decide that you want to work in full screen view or you return to the traditional IE display, you have the choice of leaving the tools as they are or changing them around as you see fit. You can control which toolbars you want to display and even create your own custom toolbars while you're working the Web.

Hiding and redisplaying toolbars

Hiding a toolbar is so simple you may miss it. Ready? Right-click the toolbar you want to hide. When the shortcut menu appears, click the name of the toolbar, removing the check mark, the toolbar is removed from the IE display.

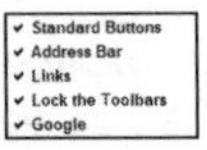

When you want to redisplay the toolbar, simply right-click on another toolbar. The shortcut menu appears, complete with the name (but no checkmark) of the hidden toolbar. Click the name to redisplay it.

Note how the Google Toolbar appears as an option on this list. This is the easiest way to hide the Google Toolbar, should you feel the need to push it out of the way and maximize screen real estate for your Web pages.

Changing the tool display

Want to go a step further? As your experience with IE grows, you notice that you use some tools to do lots of things and rarely use other tools at all. You may decide that you want to reorganize the tools so that the ones you use most are in the easiest-to-reach places on your toolbar. Use the Customize option to make these kinds of changes.

Right-click the IE toolbar and choose Customize. The Customize Toolbar dialog box appears, as shown in Figure 3-7. This dialog box displays the full list of available toolbar buttons on the left side and shows on the right the buttons used for the current toolbar. At the bottom of the dialog box, you see that you can change the placement of text and the size of the icons, if that floats your boat.

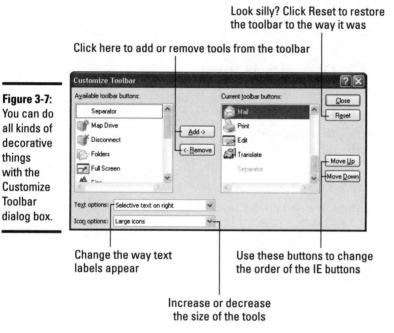

Look silly? Click Reset to restore the toolbar to the way it was

Click here to add or remove tools from the toolbar

Change the way text labels appear

Use these buttons to change the order of the IE buttons

Increase or decrease the size of the tools

Figure 3-7: You can do all kinds of decorative things with the Customize Toolbar dialog box.

To add a new button to the toolbar, select it in the Available Toolbar Buttons list and click Add. The button is added to the IE toolbar list.

To move the button to the place on the toolbar where you want it (or to move other tools around), make sure that the tool is selected and then click the Move Up or the Move Down button to put the button in the correct position. Click Close to save the change and return to the IE window.

Have you noticed the little divider line between the Home and Search buttons on the IE toolbar? That little line is called a *separator,* and it simply helps divide up different kinds of tools so that you can find them more easily. You can add separators to your toolbars, too. Just click Separator (at the top of the Available Toolbar Buttons list in the Customize Toolbar dialog box) and then click Add. This adds the separator to the current IE toolbar. You can then put the separator where you want it by clicking the Move Up or the Move Down button.

What's in a text label?

How important is it to see the little labels that tell you what the button does? To some of us, labels are annoyances; to others, they're lifesavers. IE gives you the option of hiding text labels altogether or changing their position. Here are the steps:

1. **Right-click the IE toolbar and choose Customize to display the Customize Toolbar dialog box (refer to Figure 3-7).**
2. **Click the Text Options down arrow.**

   You have three choices:

   - **Show Text Labels:** Displays all the text labels beneath the buttons.
   - **Selective Text on Right:** The default selection that shows only some text labels to the right of the button.
   - **No Text Labels:** Hides all text labels and displays only the buttons themselves.
3. **Click your choice and click Close.**

If you overhaul everything, moving buttons around and changing the text and size of the icons, and then you decide that you were just running on low blood sugar and made an error in judgment, you can undo all your changes by clicking the Reset button in the Customize Toolbar dialog box.

Changing button size

You can change the size of *icons, buttons, thingies* — whatever you want to call them — in the Customize Toolbar dialog box. Display the dialog box by right-clicking the IE toolbar and clicking Customize; then click the Icon Options down arrow. Your options are

- **Large Icons:** Displayed by default
- **Small Icons:** Reduce the size of the icons by half

Why would you want to reduce the size of the IE tool icons? Making the buttons smaller means that you can fit additional tools on the IE toolbar but still keep the toolbar as small as possible, giving you more screen space. This also helps if you intend to display the toolbar in Full Screen view — by adding buttons, you can load the toolbar with as much functionality as possible.

Linking your way

One special toolbar — the Links toolbar — lets you get to your most favorite sites with just one click. If you've never used the Links toolbar, it's probably because Microsoft preloads the Links toolbar with a lot of advertising. But you can take control of it for your own devices. And sites.

To do so, follow these steps:

1. **Make sure you can see the Links toolbar by right-clicking on any Internet Explorer toolbar and making sure Links is checked.**
2. **If the Links toolbar is way off to the right (and it probably is), right-click on any IE toolbar and uncheck the line marked Lock the Toolbars. Then click and drag the word Links, rearranging the toolbars so you can see them all.**
3. **When you get Links out in the open, right-click on any IE toolbar and check the line marked Lock the Toolbars.**
4. **To add a Web page to the Links toolbar, navigate to the Web site you want to add, and then click the icon in the Address bar to the left of the site's address and drag it onto the Links toolbar.**

   Alternatively, you can choose Favorites⇨Add to Favorites, and in the Add Favorite dialog box that appears, click the Links folder icon to add the site to the Links toolbar. Rename the site as necessary, and then click OK.
5. **To rename a link, right-click on it, choose Rename, type in a new name, and click OK.**

   Make the names short 'n' sweet so that you can fit more pages on the Links bar.
6. **To rearrange links on the Links toolbar, click and drag to the new location.**
7. **To get rid of a link, right-click on it and choose Delete.**

Dealing with Cookies

Cookies are small text files that Web pages store on your computer to keep information about your choices and preferences. Cookies are small files but, depending on the number of sites you visit (and the way in which you've set your preferences to allow cookies), they can quickly accumulate in the space reserved for your temporary Internet files.

Do you need cookies? Mostly, no. If you subscribed to a site (such as *The New York Times*) and provided a user name and password, that information may be stored in a cookie on your computer. When you go to the site, the site reads the cookie and you are able to log on without entering your user name and password each time. But the majority of cookies are simply files that Web pages put on your computer that have nothing to do with making things more convenient for you — and everything to do with marketing, marketing, and more marketing. Those are the ones you can delete without a second thought.

Cookies don't have anything to do with spam — you'll get the same junk e-mail even if you tell your computer to reject every cookie that darkens your door. Cookies don't spy on your PC, go sniffing for bank accounts, or keep a log of those, ahem, artistic Web sites you visit. They do serve a useful purpose but, like so many other concepts in the computer industry, cookies are exploited by a few companies in questionable ways. And, unfortunately, Microsoft's implementation of cookies has left much to be desired — particularly because of security holes that made cookies from one site available to rogue Web pages. That hole has been plugged, but it certainly should give you pause.

I talk about cookies extensively in Book IX, Chapter 4. If you're worried about cookies and want to know what's really happening, that's a great place to start.

Deleting cookies

You can delete cookies individually or as a group. To delete all cookies, choose Tools⇨Internet Options. In the Temporary Internet Files section in the middle of the General tab, click Delete Cookies. A message box appears, asking whether you want to proceed. Click OK to clear all cookies.

If you want to delete individual cookies, follow these steps:

1. **In Internet Explorer, choose Tools⇨Internet Options.**

   The Internet Options dialog box appears.

2. **In the Temporary Internet Files area of the General tab, click the Settings button.**

   The Settings dialog box appears (refer to Figure 3-3).

3. **Click the View Files button to display the Temporary Internet Files window, in which all cookies and files are listed (see Figure 3-8).**

4. **Select the cookie that you want to delete and press Delete. Repeat as needed; then click the Close (X) button to return to the Settings dialog box.**

5. **Click OK to close the dialog box, and click OK again to return to IE.**

IE stores files as well as cookies in temporary storage. You can delete all files at once by clicking Delete Files in the General tab of the Internet Options dialog box.

Controlling cookies

You can call the shots when it comes to accepting cookies in IE. Depending on your settings, Internet Explorer may alert you when a Web page starts to put a cookie on your system (see Figure 3-9). You can click the More Info button to display help information on cookies.

Select the cookie and press delete

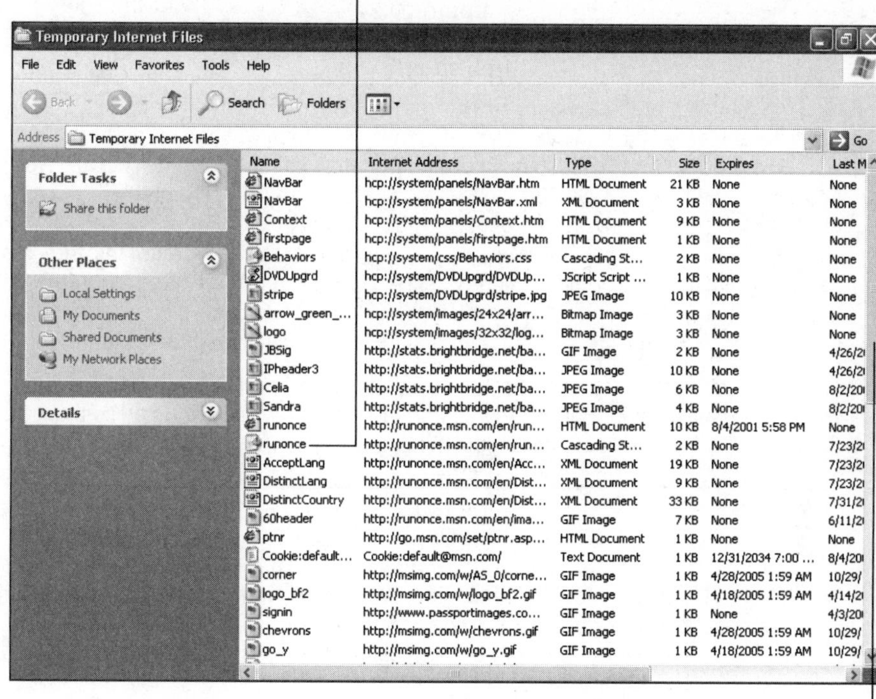

Scroll to the cookie or file you want to delete

Figure 3-8: Deleting cookies one by one by one.

Figure 3-9: This message appears when a site attempts to drop a cookie on your hard drive.

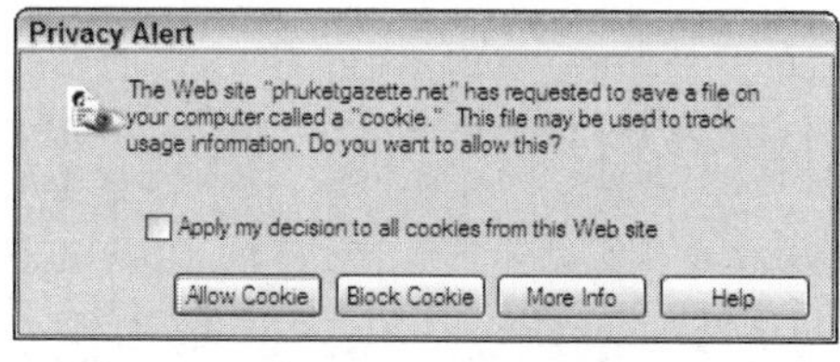

If you want to raise the bar on your privacy so that IE accepts fewer cookies, you can change your privacy settings. Here's how:

1. **Choose Tools➪Internet Options.**
2. **Click the Privacy tab.**

Banish a site

Some pesky sites keep track of your activities by piggy-backing on the cookies of "partner" sites. (Doubleclick is a prime example — many sites allow Doubleclick to gather information about people who visit their sites; see Book IX, Chapter 4). Other sites are Web friends and you want to allow their content, no matter what. You can be the one to make these choices by telling IE which sites to block and which to allow. You do this in the Per Site Privacy Actions dialog box.

To get to this dialog box, choose Tools⇨Internet Options. Click the Privacy tab and, at the bottom of the page, click the Edit button. This action takes you to the Per Site Privacy Actions page, in which you can enter the address of the sites that you want to block (simply type the URL and click the Block button) or allow (type the URL and click the Allow button). After you enter the address of the site, the site moves to the Managed Web Sites list in the bottom of the page. If you want to remove the site later, click it and click the Remove button.

After you finish entering the sites you want to manage, click OK to close the dialog box.

The Settings area displays a slider that you can use to raise or lower the settings for cookies. The default setting is Medium, but the range goes from Accept All Cookies to Block All Cookies. Each time you choose a new setting, a full description of the setting appears in the right side of the dialog box.

3. **Drag the slider to the setting that you want.**

   If you want greater control over your cookies, click the Advanced button and have IE always ask before accepting a cookie (see Figure 3-10).

4. **Click OK to close the dialog box and return to the IE window.**

Figure 3-10: For maximum control over cookies, have IE ask you every time a site tries to put a cookie on your computer.

If you try a new setting and decide later that you don't like it, you can return the setting to the default by choosing Tools⇨Internet Option, clicking the Privacy tab, and clicking the Default button.

Overriding the Content Advisor

Once upon a time, Microsoft thought it could rule the world.

Er. Uh. Well, some things never change, but never mind.

Back in the not-so-good old days, Microsoft decided that it would put a hook in Internet Explorer that would block access to "questionable" sites. The initial push was full of sound and marketing fury — and signified nothing. The first effort fell flat on its face. RSAC, the independent, Microsoft-funded organization entrusted with maintaining the RSACi rating system, went out of business in 1999. Internet Explorer's Content Advisor dialog box (click Tools⇨Internet Options, pick the Content tab, click the Enable button under Content Advisor) talks about RSACi, although the organization that implemented it no longer exists (see Figure 3-11).

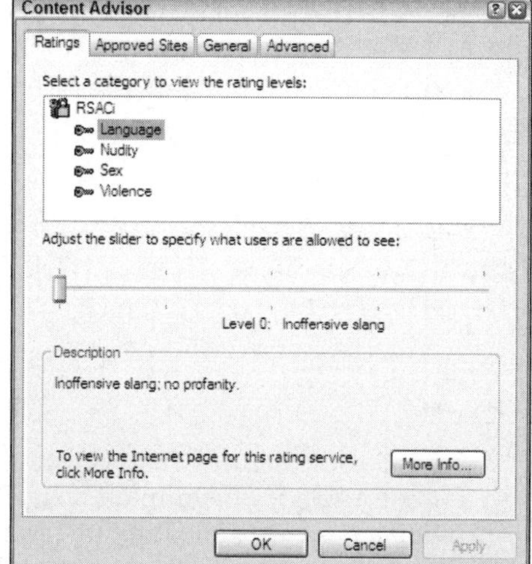

Figure 3-11: The Content Advisor continues to refer to an organization that doesn't exist.

In place of RSAC, a new organization called the Internet Content Rating Association has come along. Based in Brighton, UK, with an office in Washington D.C., the ICRA (`www.icra.org`) maintains a completely voluntary rating system, which is backward compatible with RSACi, but works very differently: Web site developers answer a questionnaire and, based on their responses, the Internet Explorer Content Advisor can block access to specific sites. Alternatively, the IE Content Advisor can block access to all sites that don't have an ICRA rating. That's a bit like looking at the Pacific Ocean and restricting your swimming to an area of one square foot.

The problems with this approach are manifold, but two in particular stand out:

- Self-rating invites no end of problems: No matter how well ICRA constructs its questionnaire, and no matter how objectively Web site authors answer the questions, there will always be differences of opinion.
- Blocking sites doesn't really work unless a very significant percentage of all sites are rated. In this case, the ICRA doesn't publish figures, but I think it's fair to say that a truly minuscule percentage of all Web sites have ICRA ratings. While the organization's goals are laudable, of course, the results have been dismal.

The number-one question I get about the IE Content Advisor goes like this: I forgot my password, and the Hint I typed (see Figure 3-12) doesn't help; *how do I turn the %$#@! thing off?*

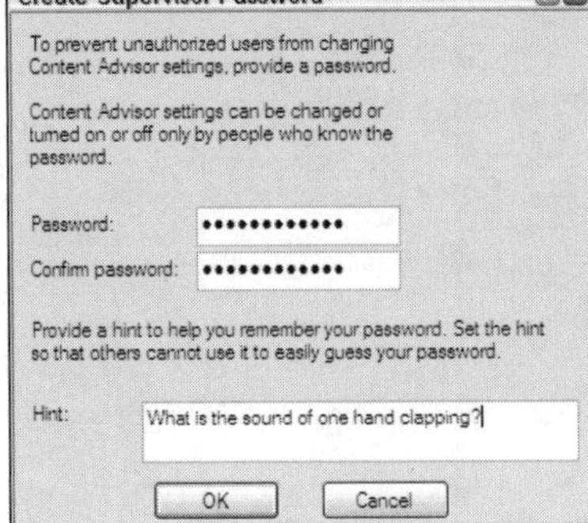

Figure 3-12: Setting a password for the Content Advisor.

Turns out that you can turn Content Advisor off completely in a few minutes. In the process, you have to provide a password that will be required if you ever want to enable the Content Advisor again. That's to keep your kids from disabling Content Advisor without leaving a trace.

If there are any wiseacre kids in the audience — my son went through a spell like that — listen up! This series of steps will take off the password, but it won't put the password back: Your parents will know that you disabled it. They may not know how you did it, but when they try to enable the Content Advisor again, they'll have to enter the password *that you typed*. Gotcha.

Disabling Content Advisor when you've forgotten the password takes a short trip into the Windows Registry.

The Registry isn't nearly as scary a place as you think — but you do have to be careful. Don't go changing any settings willy-nilly, and stick to the instructions you see here. It's true that making a bad change to the Registry can crash Windows, but you really have to try hard to mess things up that badly.

Here's how to get rid of the Content Advisor password:

1. **Make sure you are not running Internet Explorer.**
2. **Click Start➪Run.**

   Windows XP's Run dialog box appears.
3. **Type** regedit **and press Enter.**

   The Windows Registry editor comes up and shows you your Registry.
4. **Click the plus signs on the left to navigate down to HKEY_LOCAL_MACHINE\SOFTWARE\Microsoft\Windows\CurrentVersion\policies\Ratings.**

   The Registry Editor should look like Figure 3-13.

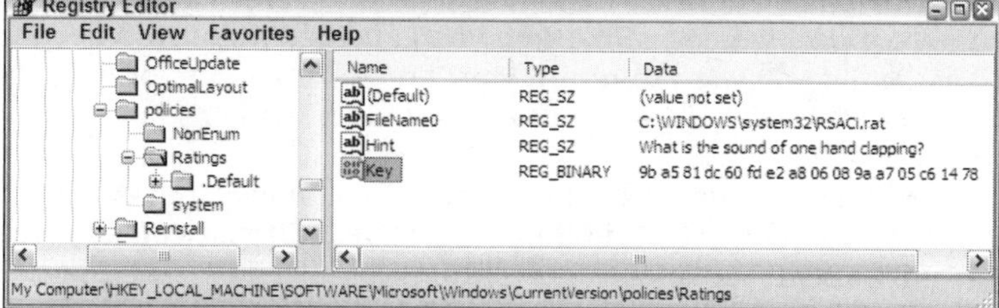

Figure 3-13: Where the Content Advisor password lives in the Registry.

5. **On the right, click the entry marked Key once, and then press the Delete key.**

   That gets rid of the password, but you aren't done yet.
6. **Click File➪Exit to get out of the Registry Editor.**
7. **Restart your computer.**

   Yep, you have to restart Windows XP so that Internet Explorer will catch on to the fact that it doesn't have a Content Advisor password anymore.
8. **Get Internet Explorer going. In IE, choose Tools➪Internet Options, and then click on the Content tab.**

9. **Up at the top, under Content Advisor, click the Disable button.**

   IE shows you the Create Supervisor Password dialog box (refer to Figure 3-12).

   Some places on the Internet will tell you that you can click OK at this point and the Content Advisor will be disabled. Not so. In Windows XP, you have to enter a new password.

10. **Enter a new password and hint, and then click OK.**

    Content Advisor tells you that it has been turned off.

    If you ever want to Enable Content Advisor again, you have to provide the *new* password. Kids, you've been warned.

Going Back to Zero

Throughout this chapter, you've discovered how to make all kinds of changes — changes in the way things look, the way they operate, even the types of sites you're allowed to view. But what if you make all these changes and then decide that you liked the way things were in the good old days, way back before you added all these crazy colors and enlarged the text? Simple. Ready? Choose Tools➪Reset Web Settings.

The Reset Web Settings dialog box offers to return all your Web settings to the way they were the first time you launched IE. All you need to do is click Yes. And if you want to return your home page to the original default, just leave the check box selected. What could be easier?

Resetting works great for those aesthetic changes, but getting rid of the Content Advisor takes another step, providing that you know your password. Choose Tools➪Internet Options and click the Content tab. In the Content Advisor area, click the Disable button. IE prompts you for your password. A small popup box tells you that the Advisor has been disabled. Click OK to complete the process and then click OK again to close the Internet Options dialog box and return to the IE window. If you've forgotten your password, see the preceding section.

Book V

Connecting with Microsoft Network

Contents at a Glance

Chapter 1: MSN: Who Needs Ya, Baby?

In This Chapter

- Getting to know Microsoft Network and its pieces
- Finding out how much it costs
- Comparing MSN Explorer to Internet Explorer
- Switching from AOL to MSN

Of all the products that Microsoft has foisted on an unsuspecting public over the past ten years, Microsoft Network has gone through the most changes.

I was one of the original alpha testers for Microsoft Network. Back then, MSN was a proprietary network, an online island isolated from the outside world, competing with the old CompuServe. Badly. The first test version of MSN came on two floppies, one of which resolutely refused to install on any machine I could find. Microsoft sent me fresh diskettes. They didn't work either.

Some things never change.

MSN itself has been rebranded and re-re-rebranded so many times that it doesn't bear any resemblance to its original form. Nowadays, MSN competes against AOL, of course, for the hearts and minds (and checkbooks) of Windows users who want to get on the Internet but don't want the hassles. At least, that's the marketing thrust. More than an AOL clone, though, MSN is Microsoft's catch-all division for anything Internet related that doesn't fall into the other divisions. I won't mention MSNBC by name. Or Encarta.

MSN is a hodgepodge of software, services, and products that in many cases bear little resemblance to each other except for the name. If you start to feel overwhelmed by MSN This, MSN That, and MSN Something Else, remember that it's just marketing hype: no substance, all flash. Microsoft has stitched the pieces together in some cases, but in other cases, they're just kind of stuffed into this big five-pound bag called MSN.

As a smart Dummy, you need to know what MSN has to offer that you might want. You also need to know about the pitfalls, of which there are many.

Home of the Free and the Not-So-Free

The parts of MSN that concern you and your PC can be roughly divided into two groups: the free stuff and the, uh, not-so-free stuff.

Microsoft doesn't give away the free MSN stuff as a civic duty, for the good of the computer community, or to atone for its monopolistic sins. No way. Every single piece of MSN is designed to heap feeelthy lucre into Microsoft's coffers. Although Hotmail, for example, has a free version, you're constantly hounded to pay for the premium version, and nearly half of every screen you see will contain advertising. MSN Explorer is a cool-enough answer to AOL's gaudy interface, er, "experience," but MSN Explorer hits you with ads at every turn. Microsoft gives away the software. But in turn it gets a captive audience — your eyeballs. There ain't no such thing as a free lunch. At least, not in Microsoft Land.

Here are the free parts of MSN:

- ✦ **Hotmail:** By far the largest free e-mail service on the Internet (see Figure 1-1; see the sidebar, "A brief history of Hotmail"), Hotmail's free version comes with an ever-changing amount of free storage space, limits placed on the size of individual messages (which can cause problems if you send photographs or other large files), a policy of wiping out your old messages if you don't log on for 30 days, a lot of spam blocking, and even more advertising, which is only marginally less annoying than the spam.

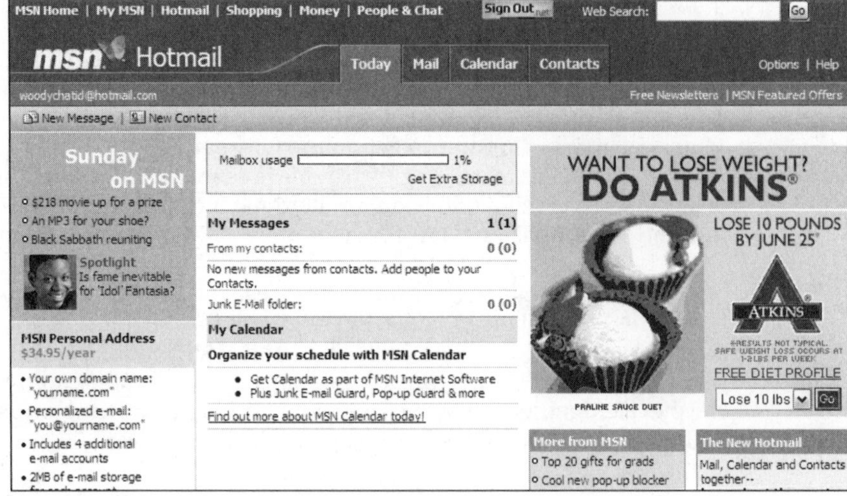

Figure 1-1: Ads, ads and more ads — today's MSN Hotmail out-spams the spammers.

A brief history of Hotmail

Hotmail blazed new ground as the first free Web based e-mail service when Sabeer Bhatia (a native of Bangalore and graduate of both Caltech and Stanford) spent $300,000 (U.S. dollars) to launch it in 1996. On December 31, 1997, Microsoft bought Hotmail for $400,000,000, and the service has never been the same. Microsoft struggled with Hotmail for many years, adding new users like flies, but always suffering with severe performance problems and crashes heard round the world. Ultimately, Hotmail (`www.hotmail.com`) was shuffled under the MSN (Microsoft Network) wing of the corporate umbrella, its free services clipped, its user interface subjected to more facelifts than Dick Clark. Which is saying something.

Hotmail is currently under siege by both Yahoo! Mail (`http://mail.yahoo.com`) and Google's GMail (`http://mail.google.com`), not to mention AOL "You've Got" Mail. There's very little reason to stick with Hotmail unless you have an @hotmail.com I.D. that many people use. Take a look around.

When you sign up for Hotmail, you automatically sign up for a .NET Passport: no Passport, no Hotmail. You'll also need a Passport to install MSN Explorer or use MSN Messenger. If you decide to add your soul to that great Microsoft database in the sky, make sure you follow the instructions in Book III, Chapter 4, in the section called "Making Messenger Work," to get a Passport that's at least partially anonymous.

- **MSN Explorer**: An arguably kinder, gentler version of Internet Explorer, MSN Explorer puts a "high touch" picture-frame around your Web pages (see Figure 1-2; `http://messenger.msn.com/install`). Built to compete head-on with AOL, MSN Explorer is designed for people who want to send and receive e-mail, surf the Web, send and receive instant messages, and . . . spend money. On Microsoft and Microsoft "Partner" products, of course.

Surprisingly, MSN Explorer and Internet Explorer get along with each other quite well: You can switch back and forth between the two with no ill effect. MSN Explorer doesn't have anywhere near the configurability or other options that Internet Explorer users take for granted, but it's entirely usable and even cute — in a Ru Paul sort of way. Too much fashion sense for one program, to my mind, but if you're coming off AOL, MSN Explorer might help you get through withdrawal symptoms.

Looking at the toolbar in MSN Explorer, you might think that you could chat by clicking the People & Chat button. Ain't so. Clicking that button sends you to the MSN Chat farm, but you can't get in unless you pay. See the not-so-free entry for Chat later in this list.

Figure 1-2: MSN Explorer lets you surf the Web with a big frame across the top and down the left side. Oh, and a few ads. Fancy that.

✦ **MSN Messenger:** A far-more-advanced version of Windows Messenger, MSN Messenger (shown in Figure 1-3; `http://messenger.msn.com`) is notable for its use of the latest instant messaging technology — and its near-complete disregard for backward compatibility, both with Microsoft Office applications, and (surprise!) MSN Explorer itself.

Because of unending problems that I've encountered using MSN Messenger with Office and MSN Explorer, I recommend that you use MSN Messenger only if you don't need or want to use the Messenger-enabled portions of Office (such as the ability to tell whether a person who sent you an e-mail message is online at the moment; see Book III, Chapter 4, or you need to use the application sharing whiteboard features; see Book V, Chapter 5). I also recommend that you *not* use MSN Messenger if you want to use MSN Explorer — I've had no end of hassles with bad interactions between the two.

✦ **The MSN Toolbar:** A nearly pixel-perfect rip-off of the Google toolbar (Figure 1-4; `http://toolbar.msn.com`), this toolbar only hooks into Internet Explorer — it doesn't work with MSN Explorer. As you might expect, the MSN toolbar takes you to the MSN search engine, Hotmail, and whichever version of Messenger (Windows or MSN) you have set up as your default instant messenger program.

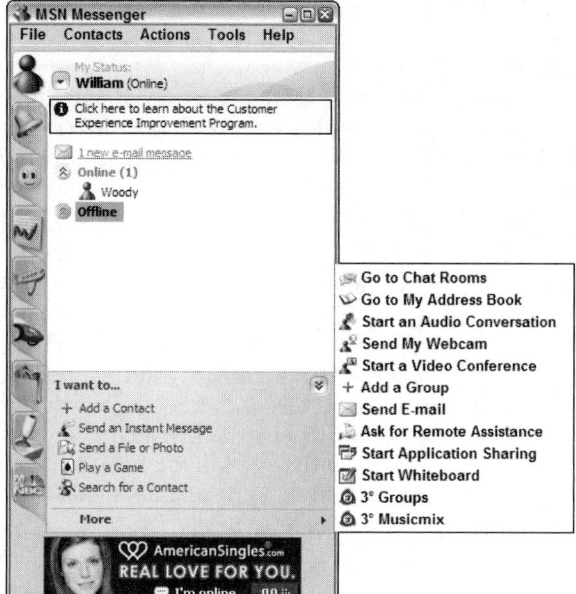

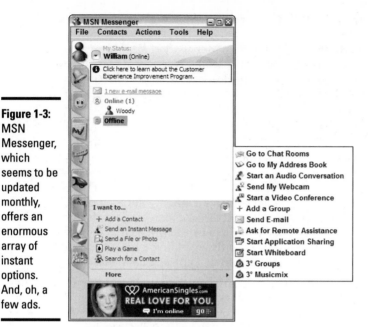

Figure 1-3: MSN Messenger, which seems to be updated monthly, offers an enormous array of instant options. And, oh, a few ads.

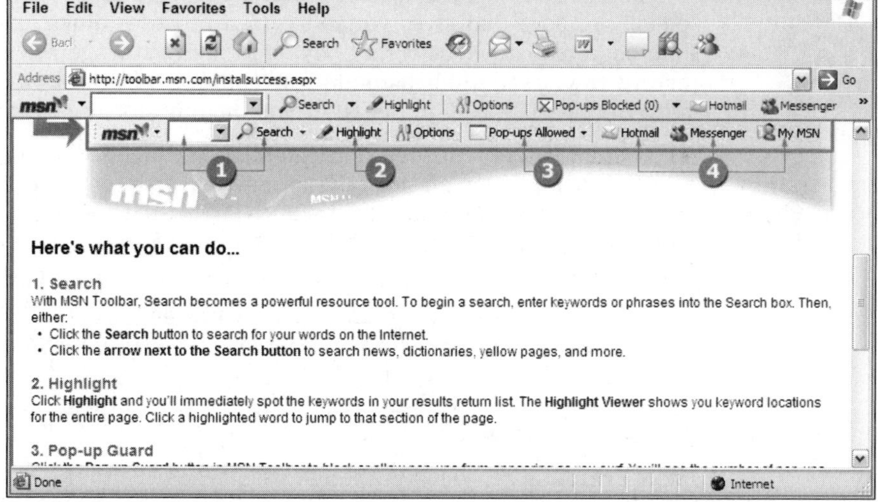

Figure 1-4: Google's toolbar in MSN clothing — it only works with Internet Explorer. Pity there isn't enough room for any ads.

So much for the free stuff. These parts of MSN cost you money:

- **MSN as an Internet Service Provider (called MSN Internet Access):** If you don't already have an ISP — which is to say, if you don't already pay $20 or $30 or $40 per month for Internet access — MSN will gladly connect you to the Internet. You simply sign up and pay the monthly fee. MSN offers more than 7,000 dial-up phone numbers, and one of the largest DSL/Broadband networks in the world. They ain't the cheapest, but their coverage rates among the best.

  No matter what you do, ultimately you have to pay full retail for the MSN ISP service. But if you're smart, you may be able to get your first month or two or three free, or at a greatly reduced price. The cheapest way to sign up for MSN ISP service is to get it when you buy a new PC. Failing that, if you have an MSN Internet Access icon on your desktop (most new computers do), click it and check the price. You should also check the Web site `www.msn.com` directly, even if you have to get to it from an Internet café, to see if MSN is running any special deals.

- **Hotmail Extra Storage:** For a fairly small annual fee, MSN will let you store more Hotmail message data on their servers. They'll also remove the 30-day logon requirement (where you have to log on every 30 days or lose all your old e-mail), allow you to send and receive larger e-mail attachments, and let you into the MSN Chat areas (see the next point).

  That's a rather ho-hum development: If you need more space, go with an e-mail provider that gives you more, for free or for much less money. Microsoft also advertises that paying for extra storage will give you access to your Hotmail account from Outlook, but Outlook 2003 comes with that feature built in, whether you pay for more space or not.

- **MSN Chat:** You might think that installing MSN Explorer and/or going to the MSN Chat site main page (`http://chat.msn.com`) would be all it takes to get chatting away in one of the MSN Chat rooms. Not so. Before you can chat, you have to sign up for Hotmail Extra Storage (see the previous bullet). No, it doesn't make sense. Yes, it works that way.

  MSN Chat also has a nasty habit of installing an "Avenue A" tracking cookie on your computer. Avenue A (which recently renamed itself "aQuantive, Inc.") tracks your Web browsing by using cookies in privacy-busting ways. See the sidebar, "The Doubleclick shtick," in Book IX, Chapter 4 for more information.

- **MSN Premium Services:** Although the packages and their details vary from day to day, MSN offers additional features for $5 to $10 per month. Some of the features you already have — Windows Firewall, an antivirus program (you *do* have an antivirus program, don't you?), a popup blocker. Some of them may be of interest, depending on your situation: a Parental Control module (see `www.kidsnet.com/chart.asp` for a competitor's analysis of MSN Parental Controls, or Google *MSN Parental*

Control); a version of Microsoft Money that you use online; a few add-ons to MSN Encarta (much of which is available free at `www.encarta.com`); Photos Plus editing software; and a connector that allows you to get at your MSN mail from Outlook (which looks suspiciously like the connector that comes with Outlook 2003 for retrieving Hotmail).

Everyone's situation is different, but you should make sure you understand what you're buying before you type in your credit card number.

Getting the Best of All Worlds

So which components of MSN should you get?

Tough question. Here's what I recommend:

- **Get MSN Messenger.** If you use Microsoft Office's instant messaging features, you can't use MSN Messenger. In most cases, that really doesn't make much difference. In my experience, about 0.0001 percent of all Microsoft Office users even know about the program's hooks into Windows Messenger, and substantially fewer ever use the features productively. But the other 99.999 percent of us could benefit from MSN Messenger's newer (admittedly occasionally less-than-stable) technology.
- **If you have to use Passport — and you must if you install MSN Messenger — tie it to a free Hotmail account.** Hotmail isn't considerably better or worse than its competitors, and you may find it useful for low-volume e-mail. Use the trick I describe in Book III, Chapter 4, in the section about making Messenger work, to keep from entering your personal information in Microsoft's big database.
- **Only install MSN Explorer if you're an AOL junkie.** For most people, Internet Explorer does much more, and it's much less intrusive.
- **Consider MSN Internet Access if you travel a lot.** MSN isn't the only game in town, but it's reasonably priced, available everywhere, and quite reliable.
- **Think twice — three times — before spending your money on MSN's other features.**

Moving from AOL to MSN

If you currently use AOL, read this chapter and the next chapter to see if MSN would give you more. If you decide to move from AOL to MSN, follow these steps:

1. **Realize that you aren't the first person who has changed from AOL to MSN.**

   In fact, Microsoft devotes a big piece of its MSN marketing and support effort to getting people to switch — and it shows.

2. **Use MSN's TrueSwitch software.**

   TrueSwitch automatically transfers e-mail messages, contact information, and calendar entries from AOL to MSN. Then it will send messages to everyone in your Address Book, advising them of your new MSN address. Finally, it will help you cancel your AOL account, and will forward messages sent to your old address to your new address for one month free of charge.

   You can preview the steps at `www.trueswitch.com/msn`.

3. **Make sure AOL cancelled your account according to your instructions.**

   Check your credit card bill closely. If AOL doesn't do what you ask, call 1-888-265-8008 and don't take no for an answer.

Chapter 2: MSN Explorer

In This Chapter

- Exploring MSN Explorer
- Installing MSN Explorer
- Finding out the tips and tricks for using it

This chapter explains how to set up and get moving with MSN Explorer, the free Microsoft Network-centric version of Internet Explorer. Designed as a kind of Internet Explorer with a less intimidating interface — and borrowing more than a few pages from AOL's playbook — MSN Explorer includes all kinds of bells and whistles to play with, as well as friends to chat with along the way.

MSN Explorer originated as Microsoft's answer to the AOL Leviathan: Flashy — some would say gaudy — and unabashedly directed at novices, MSN Explorer emphasizes fun over function, with a design that's meant to suck you in and keep you in the Microsoft fold, spending your bucks and shekels on products whose sales line the 'Softie coffers. Experienced Netties sniff at the pretty face and deeply hidden plumbing in MSN Explorer. But for tens of millions of PC users, MSN Explorer *is* the Internet — and those nerds with pocket protectors are missing out on the cool stuff.

What Is MSN Explorer?

Everybody wants an online community to belong to, don't they? After all, we humans are social animals. We want to chat, and learn, and laugh, and share. We want to buy and sell stocks in a way that makes us rich. We want to find games for our kids that don't cost us anything. We want to trade stories with other parents that make us feel better about the crazy things our kids did last night.

MSN Explorer provides an instant online community, complete with e-mail, calendars, chat rooms, and more. It offers customizable news (the news you're interested in, delivered to the MSN Explorer browser); local weather; simple search capabilities; shopping; music — whatever your interests and activities are, MSN provides some mind fodder for an hour or ten.

And, except for the chat rooms, MSN Explorer is free.

On the other hand, MSN Explorer abounds with advertising; it's very difficult — indeed, in some cases impossible — to customize; if you don't have a big monitor or turn off the bar on the left, MSN Explorer gets in the way of every Web page; and many people find all those clunky buttons distracting.

Is it a floor wax? Is it a breath mint? Fortunately, you don't need to decide once and for all. You can run both MSN Explorer and Internet Explorer on the same machine, no sweat. Pick MSN Explorer when you feel gregarious. Run IE when you have to get some work done. Nothing to it.

Introducing MSN Explorer

MSN Explorer is similar to AOL, packaged in kinder, gentler colors; presented with softer edges; and focused on *you,* which, depending on your trust level with Microsoft, may be either a good or a bad thing. For example, you have the option of creating an online calendar that tells you where to be and when to be there. Your Online Contacts List collects the names and addresses of your favorite people. Your mail is convenient and Web based, which means you can read it from a friend's computer or an Internet kiosk at the mall. But it also means that all of these things are stored online and not on the hard drive of your own safe little system. No biggie? Maybe not. But giving away too much information makes some people nervous.

That said, MSN Explorer is visually inviting and pretty easy to figure out. The buttons at the top of the window are large, colorful, and obvious. The names underneath save you from having to wonder what you're clicking (see Figure 2-1).

Click the first button, Home, and MSN Explorer goes to the page displayed by default when you log on. You have a little bit of control over what appears on your home page — although most of it will always look like `www.msn.com`. To personalize your home page, in the upper-right corner, click Help & Settings, and then click Customize Content on Your Home Page. MSN gives you all of the options shown in Figure 2-2 and many more.

Click the E-mail icon in MSN Explorer and you go straight to Hotmail, Microsoft's ubiquitous free e-mail program (shown in Figure 2-3). Hotmail lives on the Web, which means that you can read your mail online from anywhere — Kalamazoo, the *Queen Mary,* the surface of Mars. As usual, you can send and receive messages with attachments, pictures, and more. You also keep your Address Book online. And to keep those embarrassing errors to a minimum ("Looking forward to seeing you tomarrow!"), you can run the spelling checker automatically before you send — providing that you have Microsoft Office installed on your PC.

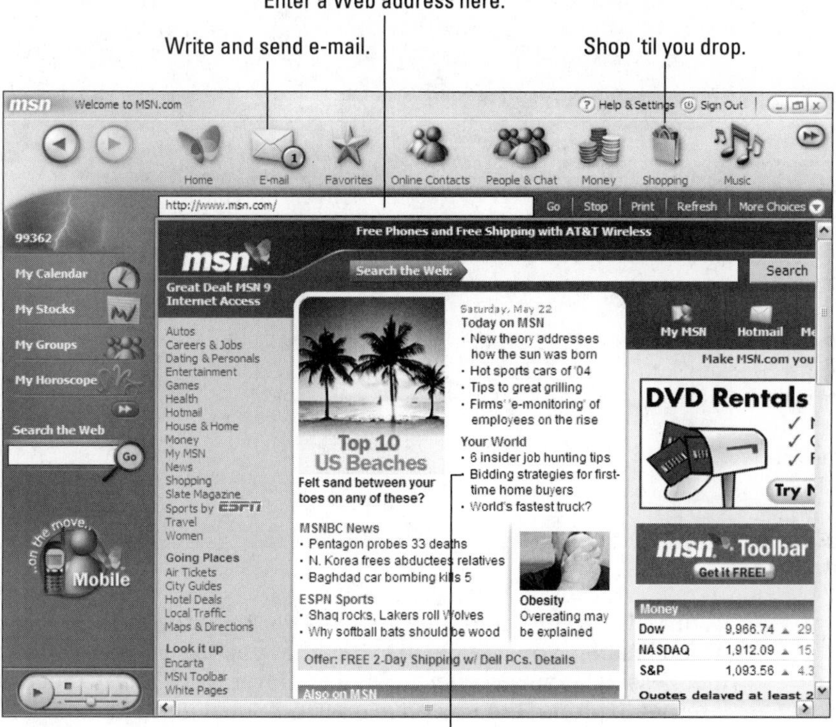
Enter a Web address here.
Write and send e-mail.
Shop 'til you drop.
Read about topics that interest you.

Figure 2-1: A smooth, sedate look and feel for MSN Explorer.

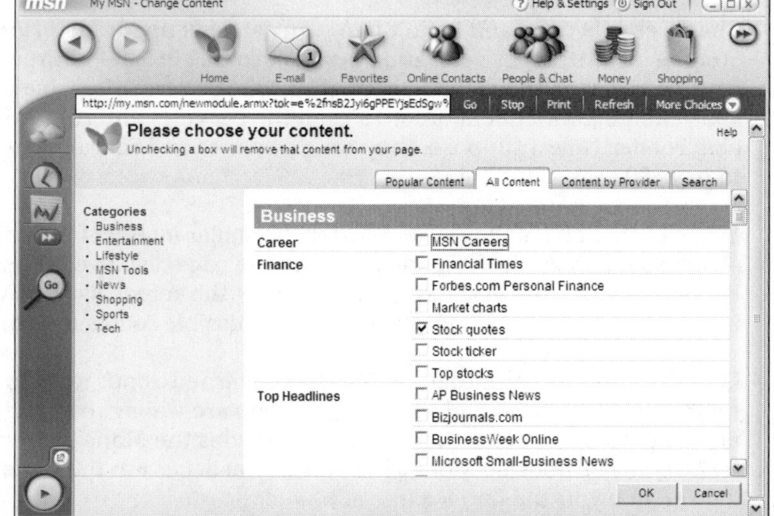

Figure 2-2: MSN Explorer lets you customize your home page, to some extent.

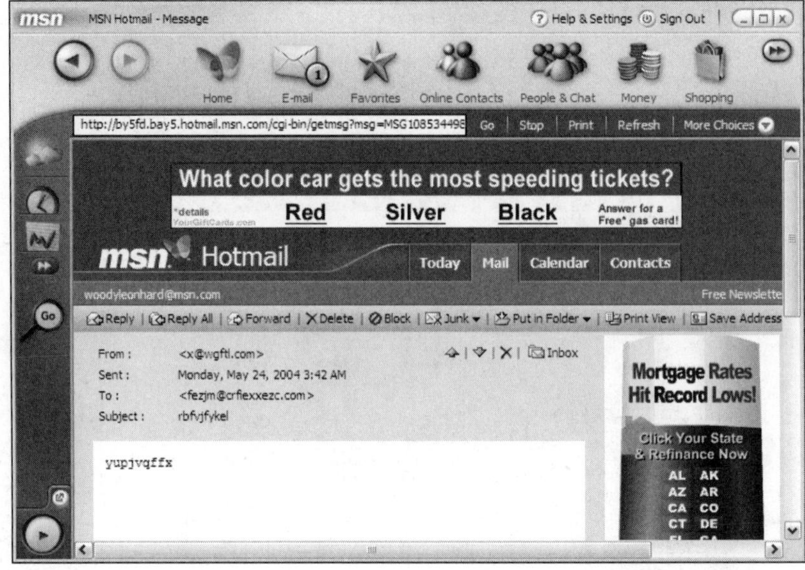

Figure 2-3: My first piece of Hotmail spam. The message is that little thing in the lower-left corner, next to all the advertising.

Both MSN Explorer and Internet Explorer have the familiar Favorites feature, which enables you to save the sites that you like so that you can return to them easily later. Favorites in MSN Explorer work pretty much the same as in Internet Explorer, but you have one additional perk: MSN makes it easy for you to copy your Favorites from Internet Explorer into MSN Explorer.

Online Contacts hooks directly into Windows Messenger or MSN Messenger, if you have it installed (see Book V, Chapter 5).

Chat is chat is chat, and it ain't free. You can sign up for MSN Hotmail Extra Storage for $19.95 per year, and Microsoft tosses in Chat for free — but the days of free chat ended in October 2003, when Microsoft claimed it had to start charging for chat in order to keep the perverts and riff-raff out of free chat rooms. Now, I suppose, they have perverts and riff-raff who can afford to pay $20.

You know the chat shtick — find people of similar interests, strike up a conversation, and party online. Figure 2-4 shows the page displayed when you click People & Chat in the MSN Explorer toolbar — the screen lists the various interests you may have and suggests some possible routes for exploration.

MSN Explorer assumes that people are concerned about ways to manage their money online — and seeks people who are willing to spend their money online — and for that reason, it includes the Money tool right on the MSN toolbar. Choosing Money here gives you access to the same financial information you can find for free at `www.cnbc.com`.

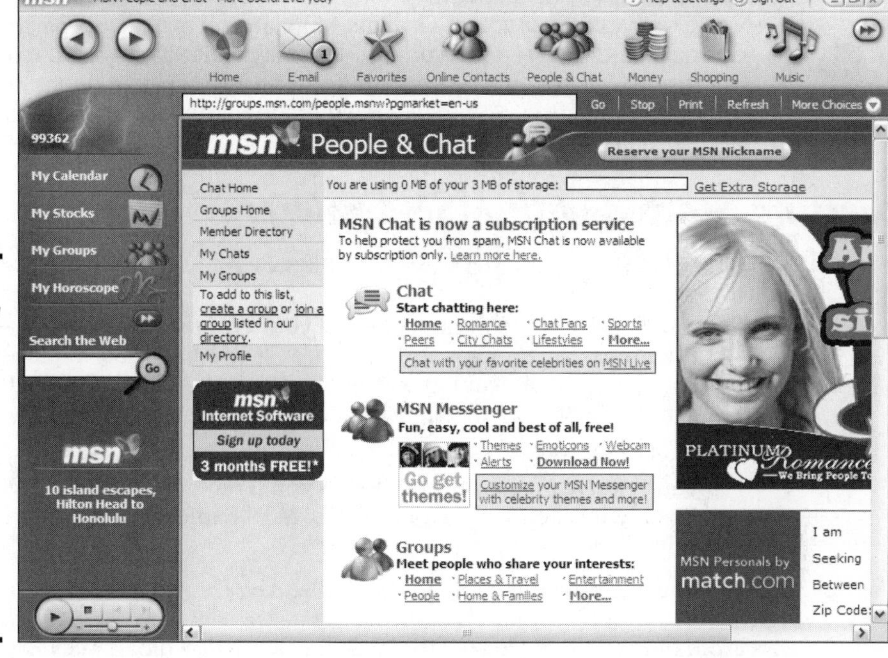

Figure 2-4: I am a *biped* seeking a *sexagenarian* with interests in *fungal cultivation, prattle crossings,* and *hyperketosis.*

Microsoft *really* wants you to sign up for MSN Money Plus, which is functionally a small subset of Microsoft Money, the comprehensive money management program from Microsoft. Money Plus enables you to manage your finances through MSN. You can pay bills online, find a mortgage, track stocks, and more. But you have to pay every month for Microsoft's Premium services to get at Money Plus, and . . . do you *really* want to put all of your financial information on Microsoft's computers?

A Shopping tool on the toolbar takes you right into a page with all sorts of Microsoft-sponsored purchasing possibilities. The Music tool launches `www.windowsmedia.com` — the same Web page that you see in Windows XP's Media Player — so that you can download songs, listen to streaming music, and generally avoid the after-lunch doldrums.

Finally, clicking the Games icon (you may have to click the > arrows on the right to see this icon) in MSN Explorer connects you directly to `www.zone.com`, the 100 percent Microsoft owned and operated Web front end to Microsoft's interactive games. And, oh, did I mention, you also have an opportunity to download the full versions of the games for just $24.95! Or is it $19.95? Seriously, the free online versions — dubbed MSN Games — can provide a bit of respite, although nobody would mistake them for recent best-sellers.

S . . . L . . . O . . . W. One of my first experiences with MSN Explorer took a while to manifest. If you click a link to an article from the MSN home page during prime time (early evening), you may wait almost a full minute to see the results. Microsoft's beefing up its servers, but if you don't have a fast Internet connection, you may get gangrene in the interstitial pauses.

Getting Started with MSN Explorer

There are three common ways to get MSN Explorer:

- ✦ It may have come preinstalled on your computer. Choose Start⇨All Programs and look for MSN Explorer. If you find MSN Explorer is already listed, Microsoft wants you to jump through some hoops before you can run it: See Steps 7 through 12 later in this section.
- ✦ If you sign up to use MSN for Internet Access — where MSN becomes your Internet Service Provider — you'll receive a CD with MSN Explorer included. When you install the CD, MSN Explorer comes along for the ride.
- ✦ You can download and install it directly.

From time to time, Microsoft makes it easy to download MSN Explorer — links have been known to appear at `http://explorer.msn.com` and elsewhere on the MSN site. Unfortunately, those links seem to come and go. At this point, I've only found one reliable way to get a copy of MSN Explorer, and it's a bit, uh, strange, but here goes.

This is also a nifty way to get a free @msn.com e-mail address. Amaze your friends. Intimidate your enemies. Collect them all before they're gone. . . .

Here's how to get MSN Explorer:

1. **Choose Start⇨Control Panel⇨Network and Internet Connections.**

   The Network and Internet Connections window appears.

2. **Under Pick a Task, click Set Up or Change Your Internet Connection.**

   The Internet Properties dialog box appears, with the Connections tab displayed.

3. **Click the Setup button.**

   This launches the New Connection Wizard. You see a Welcome screen. Ho-hum. Click Next.

4. **On the Network Connection Type page of the wizard, leave the default setting, Connect to the Internet, selected. Click Next.**

5. **In the Getting Ready page of the wizard, leave the default set at Choose from a List of Internet Service Providers (ISPs). Click Next.**
6. **On the Completing the New Connection page of the wizard, choose the line marked Get Online with MSN, and click Finish.**

   The MSN Explorer installer appears with one of the most obscurely worded dialog boxes in all of Windows XP (see Figure 2-5). Believe it or not, this dialog box is asking you if you want to replace Internet Explorer on your Start menu (up in the upper-left corner) with MSN Explorer.

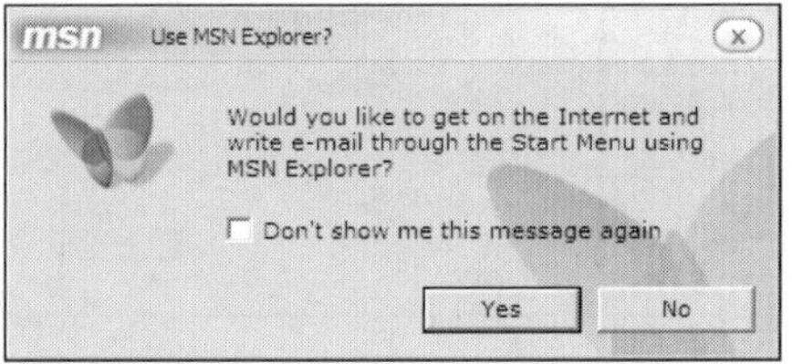

Figure 2-5: MSN Explorer is asking if you want to have Internet Explorer on your Start menu replaced by MSN Explorer.

7. **Unless you're absolutely sure that you will want to use MSN Explorer all the time, click No.**

   The MSN Explorer installer greets you with another obscurely worded screen (see Figure 2-6).
8. **Click Continue.**

   The installer wants to know if you want to sign up to use MSN as your Internet Service Provider (see Figure 2-7). If you're downloading MSN Explorer to try it out, you probably don't.
9. **Select the No, I Already Have Internet Access option button, and then click Continue.**

   The installer asks if you already have an MSN Internet Access account (you probably don't), and then it connects to the Internet using your current Internet connection (D'oh!). Next, the installer wants to know if you already have a Hotmail or MSN.com e-mail address, as shown in Figure 2-8.

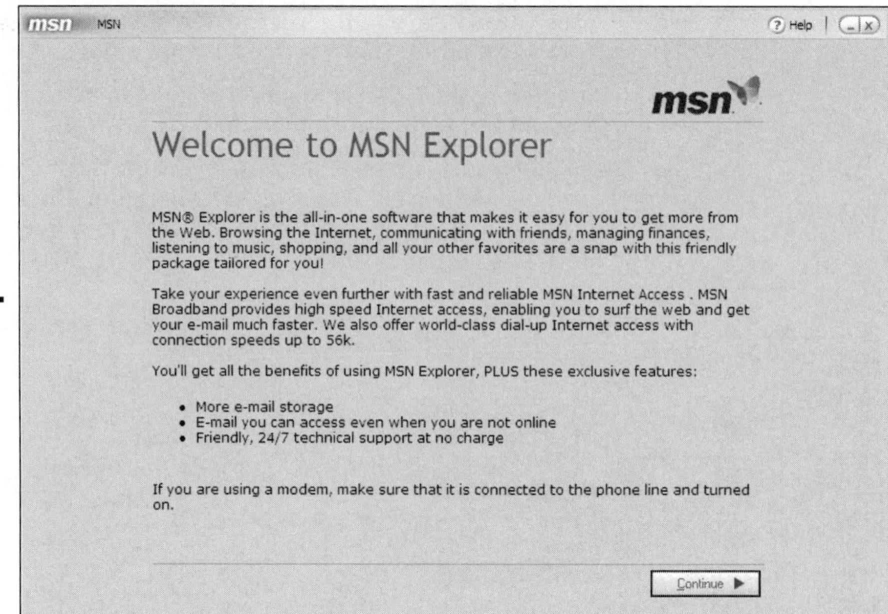

Figure 2-6: "MSN Explorer is the all-in-one software" Funny. I thought it was a program.

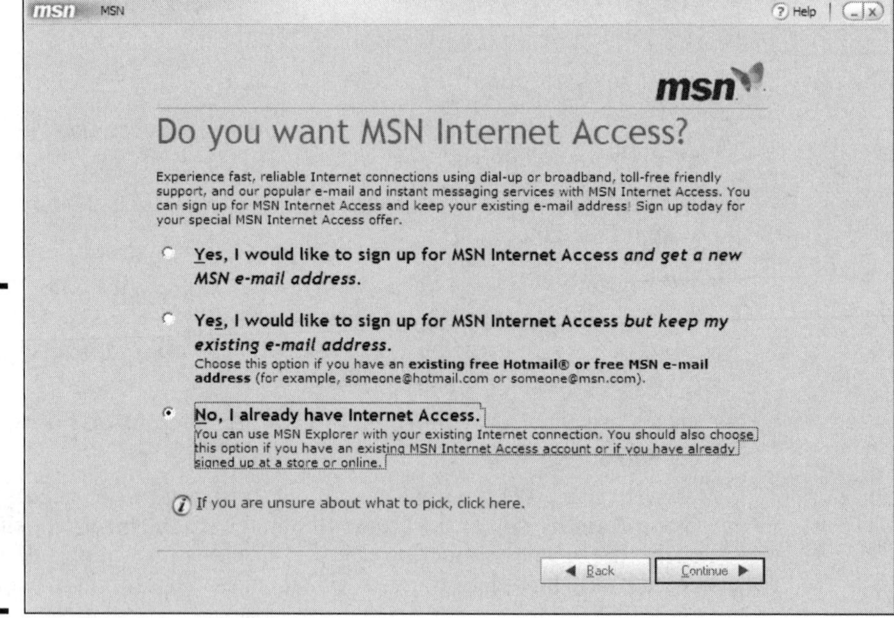

Figure 2-7: If you're already using the Internet, you don't want to pay for MSN Internet Access too.

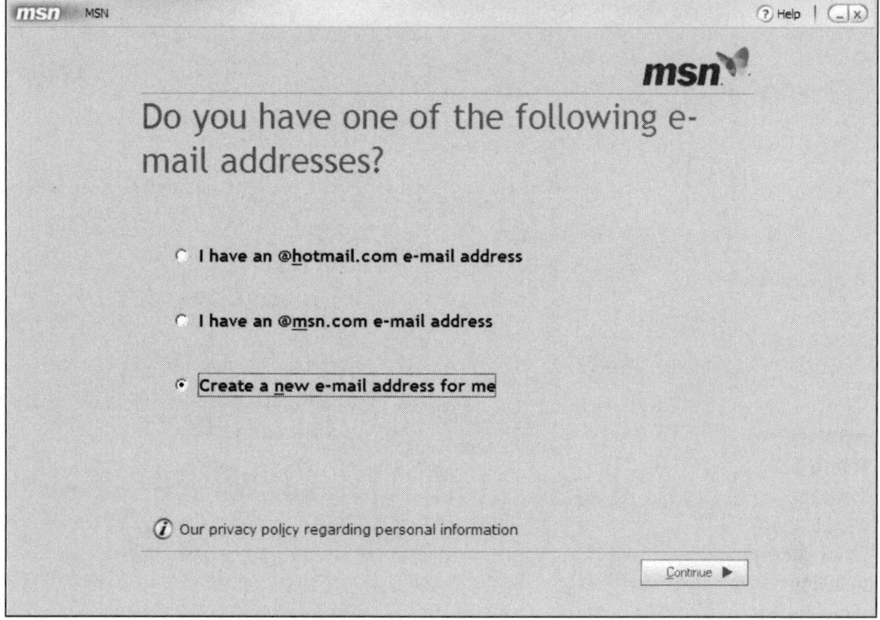

Figure 2-8: Select this option button and you'll get a *free* @msn.com e-mail address.

10. **If you want a free @msn.com e-mail address, select the Create a New Email Address for Me option button, and then click Continue.**

    You have to fill in your name (Mr. William Gates), your location (Washington, USA, 99362), your birthday, and your occupation (Unemployed/Between Jobs and McNealy). You have to accept the 431-page Terms of Use Agreement, and then the installer asks for a password and secret question (see Figure 2-9).

11. **Finish going through the rest of the questions.**

    You'll know that MSN Explorer is installed and ready to roll when you see the Welcome to MSN box shown in Figure 2-10.

12. **Click Sign In, provide your password, and MSN Explorer is up and running (see Figure 2-11).**

MSN Explorer lets you set up as many as nine different user accounts so that you can have different accounts for each of your family members and your pets. Each account can have its own home page, e-mail account, favorites list, and Online Contacts List, too. MSN Explorer allows only one person to be the manager or administrator, however — so only that person is given the power to delete existing accounts. To add more user accounts, click Help & Settings in the upper-right corner, and then choose Add Additional Users.

msn MSN
Help

msn

Please create a private password

You need a password to log on with MSN Explorer. You should memorize your password. Your password must be at least eight (8) characters long

Password ••••••••••••
Retype your password ••••••••••••

Note: To help protect your privacy, your password will always show on the screen as ********

If you forget your password, we will simply ask you your secret question. When you provide the correct answer, you'll be able to create a new password for yourself.

Secret Question What is your favorite pet's name?
Answer to Secret Question Chia

Tips for creating a good password

Back Continue

Figure 2-9: Choose from a short list of secret questions.

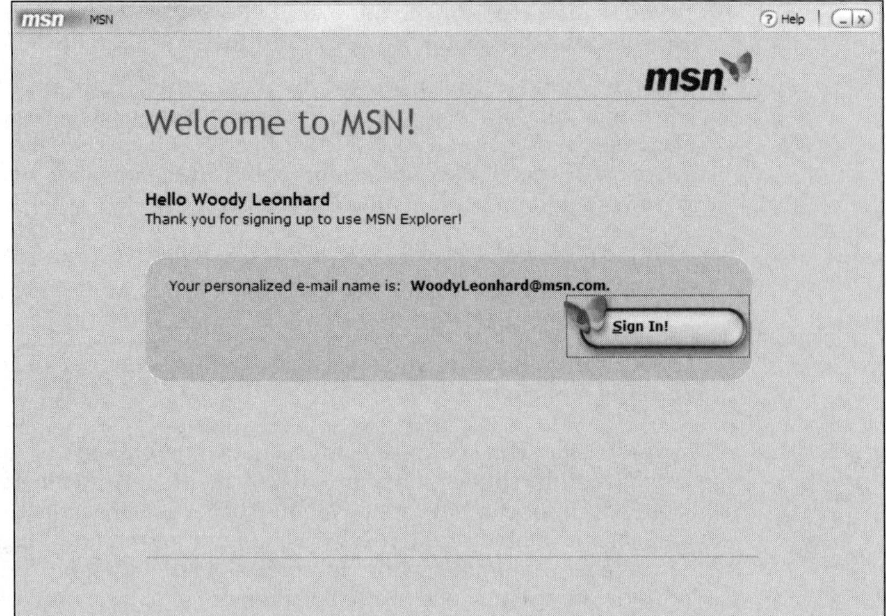

Figure 2-10: MSN is locked and loaded.

What's with these "secret questions"?

Okay, so most of us forget a password or two during our online life span. Knowing that you might forget the password you've chosen, software manufacturers like Microsoft (and sometimes credit card companies) ask you to choose hints that will jog your memories. MSN Explorer asks you, as part of the setup process, to choose a "secret question" that will give you a suggestion about the password you've entered. These secret questions are anything but secret. They include ho-hum prompts like these:

- What is your mother's maiden name?
- What is your favorite pet's name?
- What is your anniversary (mm/dd/yy)?
- What is your father's middle name?
- What is your favorite sports team?

If someone asked me (and nobody did), I'd give them some double-secret, nobody-can-answer-these questions. I'd choose things like, "In which side of the dresser drawer do I keep my socks?" or "What is my favorite snack?" or "How many accountants does it take to buy a pack of light bulbs?" or — my favorite — "What is the sound of one hand clapping?"

Figure 2-11: You're ready to take the tour.

You can leave MSN Explorer by clicking Sign Out, or by clicking the X (Close) button in the upper-right corner. To start MSN Explorer again, choose Start➪All Programs➪MSN Explorer. I bet that if you start MSN Explorer once or twice, you'll find that Windows keeps it on your Start menu's most-used list for a long, long time.

Chapter 3: Taking MSN Explorer for a Spin

In This Chapter

- Checking out the MSN Explorer window
- Getting ready to surf
- Getting your passport to a better world
- Changing that password
- Personalizing your home page, your way

This chapter explains how to chart your Web course with MSN Explorer. You discover what the Web landscape looks like, and you find out about the pros and cons of Microsoft Passport. You also see how to do important, functional, and fun things such as change your password, choose security settings, and customize your MSN home page.

MSN Explorer is completely, utterly dependent on the Internet being up. You can't change even the smallest setting without a working connection. If your Internet connection goes up and down, don't even try to use MSN Explorer — stick with Internet Explorer.

Checking Out MSN Explorer

Ready to take a spin with MSN Explorer? Good. Here's how:

1. **Choose Start⇨All Programs⇨MSN Explorer.**
2. **If you're paying MSN for Internet service, your computer should connect directly.**

   If not, and you have a dial-up modem, you may have to type in a user I.D. and password for your Internet Service Provider. The MSN login window appears.
3. **If you have created multiple accounts on your computer, choose your account, enter your password, and click the Sign In button.**
4. **MSN Explorer displays your home page.**

Figure 3-1 shows you the basic elements on the MSN Explorer window that you use to surf, e-mail, chat, and jam on the Web.

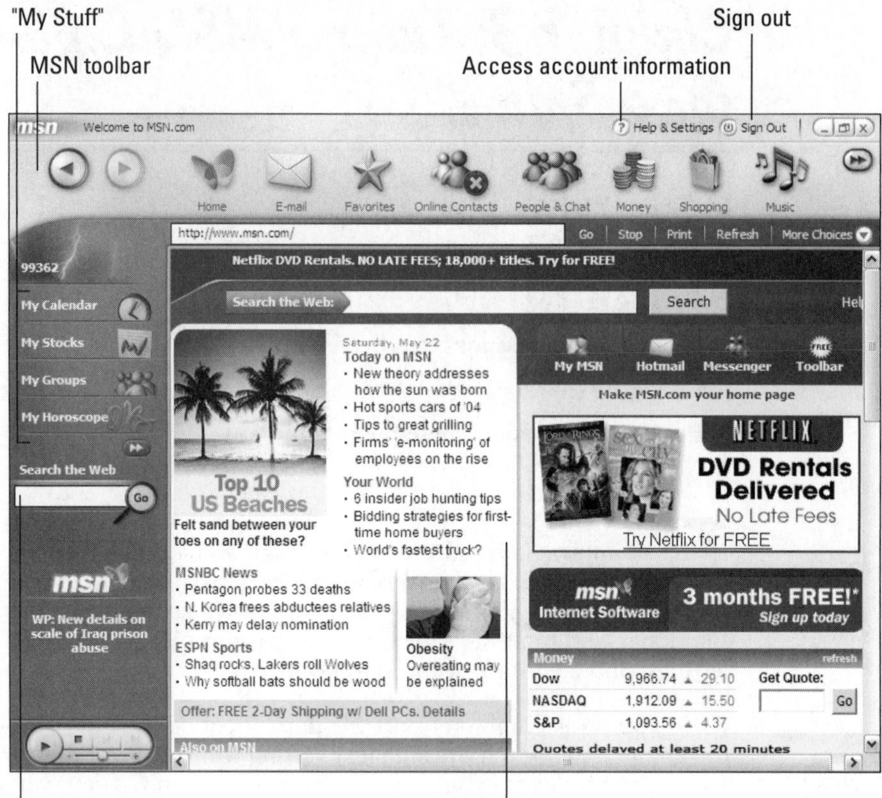

Figure 3-1: Scoping the MSN Explorer windows.

If you've previously made a few trips around the Web using Internet Explorer, AOL, or other online services, you'll be able to find your way around easily in MSN Explorer. Here are the most important features:

- **Toolbar:** The MSN toolbar includes tools that give you quick access to the various features and communities in MSN Explorer. Table 3-1 introduces you to each of the tools.
- **Address bar:** The Address bar enables you to navigate around the Web, find what you're looking for, and control your MSN account settings.
- **Web window:** This is the area in which the content of the Web page appears — you find text, images, links, and more as you move from page to page.
- **Activities area:** As part of your home page, MSN Explorer tells you what's going on in your other areas of interest. If you have created a Buddy List, MSN Explorer tells you whether any of your buddies are

currently online. Additionally, this area shows you whether you have any new e-mail and gives you the option to write a new e-mail message.

- **My Stuff:** This column on the left provides links to four areas that MSN thinks you'll want easy access to, including two that may be useful: My Calendar and My Stocks. It also includes icons for My Groups (which you can only get to if you subscribe) and My Horoscope (which . . . oh, don't get me started). Fortunately, you can get rid of icons you don't want by clicking the double-right arrows at the bottom of the list and choosing Personalize My Stuff.
- **Search:** No big surprise here — use the Search text box to enter the topic that you want to find on the Web, and Microsoft's search engine will tackle it. Microsoft has been changing (and improving!) its search engine over the years. At some point, you may find that it's as good as Google. Give it a try with your real-world problems, and see if you like it better than the alternatives.
- **Media Player:** Your very own built-in sound system, placed conveniently in the bottom-left corner of the MSN Explorer window. When you click Play, you are taken to the Entertainment.MSN.com Music page so that you can select the type of music that you want to hear. And maybe do a little shopping while you're there.
- **Help & Settings:** This selection, in the upper-right corner of the MSN window, takes you to the Member Center, where you can customize your MSN Explorer settings.

Table 3-1 MSN Explorer Tools

Button	*Name*	*Description*
	Back	Displays the previous Web page.
	Forward	Displays the next Web page in the sequence.
	Home	Displays the home page you've set for MSN Explorer display.
	E-mail	Launches Hotmail so that you can write, send, and read e-mail.
	Favorites	Displays the sites that you have saved to your Favorites list.
	Online Contacts	Starts MSN Messenger so you can add, view, or talk with buddies through instant messaging.

(continued)

Table 3-1 *(continued)*

Button	*Name*	*Description*
	People & Chat	Takes you to the People & Chat page so that you can start chatting (after signing up and paying a fee).
	Money	Launches the Money page, giving you all kinds of resources including My Money, Investing, Banking, Planning, Taxes, and Community areas. If you want more, Money Plus will give you a wide range of financial services — for a fee.
	Shopping	Takes you to a page with lots of shopping opportunities. Fancy that.
	Music	Displays the Entertainment.MSN.com Music site so that you can listen to Internet radio stations — if you want to listen to clips from albums, you'll probably have to pay for the Radio Plus service.

Surfing the Web with MSN Explorer

One of the features that distinguishes MSN Explorer from some of the other online services is something that you can easily miss — the way in which the Web is built into all the activities in the service. You can see no real division between Web surfing and e-mail, Web work and chat, Web pages and shopping, managing your money, or listening to music. It all works together transparently, without requiring much conscious thought.

Following links

Links on MSN Explorer look similar to the links that you see in other browsers. You find the following types of links in MSN:

- Text links appear underlined, often in a color different from regular text
- Buttons provide quick-click access to other pages
- Image links can be pictures of products, photos, or icons

How can you tell what's a link and what's just text or pictures? When you position the mouse pointer over a link, the arrow changes to a pointing hand. To follow the link, simply click the mouse button.

Navigating Web pages

Two of the primary navigational tools that you use to move around in MSN Explorer are actually part of the MSN Explorer toolbar:

- Click the Back button to return to the Web page that you were viewing previous to the current page.
- Click the Forward button to move to the next Web page in the current sequence. (***Note:*** You have to go back before you can go forward. Er, if you have not previously used the Back button, the Forward button will not be available.)

You can find the rest of the tools and buttons that you use for working with Web pages in the Address bar. Table 3-2 gives you an overview of those tools.

Table 3-2 Deciphering the Address Bar

Button	*Name*	*Description*
	Address	Type the Web address of the page that you want to visit in this text box; and then press Enter or click Go.
Go	Go	Click this button to go to the page that you entered in the Address text box.
Stop	Stop	Interrupts the loading of the current page.
Print	Print	Prints the current page.
Refresh	Refresh	Updates the display of the current page.
More Choices	More Choices	Displays a menu of choices that you can use to work with the current page, including New Window, E-mail This Page, Find on Page, View Privacy Report, Cut, Copy, Paste, Select All, Help, Settings, and About MSN Explorer.

When you find a page that you want to keep, click the Favorites tool on the MSN Explorer toolbar. A menu appears, giving you two options: Add to Favorites and Organize Favorites. When you click Add to Favorites, a dialog box appears. Type a name for the page and click OK. MSN Explorer saves the page so that you can later access it by simply clicking the Favorites button.

How MSN Explorer Works with Passport

.NET Passport, first widely used with Windows XP, has caused big reactions — some positive, most negative. Passport (or so the corporate rhetoric goes) is meant to give you the utmost in online convenience, storing all your passwords, user names, and so on, in one handy location that you have with you whenever you surf the Web. In theory, carrying this Passport enables you to log into all Passport-compatible sites with your single e-mail address and password.

The big benefits that Passport advertises are these:

- **Convenience:** Enter information once; use it many times.
- **Control:** The Kids Passport enables you to set parental controls.

Microsoft used to collect credit card information and store it in a separate database called the Passport Wallet. This "Express Purchase," uh, feature was roundly criticized and rarely used. Microsoft finally gave up on collecting financial data after about two years. It never really got off the ground.

Microsoft promises that Passport is protected by cutting-edge security technology and a "strict privacy policy" (enforced by frowning Web matrons). However, many people feel slightly queasy at the thought of giving a large corporate entity any more personal information than absolutely necessary, and Passport in particular is a mighty big target that's had more than its fair share of cracking attempts.

How does Passport work? When you sign into a "Passport participating site," you enter your e-mail address and password (the same information that you enter when signing into MSN Explorer) and the site checks the login information to verify it. When you're in, you're in — and you can surf, shop, and more, knowing that you don't have to stop and get additional information.

Want to find out more? The people at www.passport.com are glad to tell you all about it. Just be sure to check your wallet before you leave.

Signing up for a Passport

If you want a Passport, I generally recommend that you sign up for a free Hotmail account using a fictitious name, using the method explained in Book III, Chapter 4, in the section about making Messenger work. In the process of signing up for a Hotmail account, you get a .NET Passport — whether you want one or not.

You can sign up for a Passport directly, or find out more about Passports, by doing one of two things:

- Go to www.passport.com.
- .net Passport Click the Microsoft Passport icon anywhere you see it.

The Microsoft Passport site appears, giving you lots of information about the passport idea and enabling you to sign right up (see Figure 3-2).

Figure 3-2: Want to store all those pesky numbers in one place?

Getting a Kids Passport

One of AOL's strengths is a well-developed parental controls system. One of the features totally missing in MSN Explorer is a parent's choice feature that enables parents to set controls to keep their kids safe: For that, you have to pay more money and get the MSN Premium service.

Perhaps Kids Passport is one attempt to provide a bit of a safety net for kids, but in my opinion, it's a bit lame. The idea is based on the regular Passport — collecting information so that you can use it when, where, and how you want. With Kids Passport, kids can't share information unless they have consent from a parent. Working through the Kids Passport system, permission is requested if a child starts to visit a site that requests more information than they have "clearance" to give.

If you're interested in finding out more about Kids Passport, take a look at its site (`https://kids.passport.net`). You can find out which sites are participating in the Kids Site Directory, visit the Parent area, or read through the Kids Passport FAQ (see Figure 3-3).

Go to kids.passport.net

Click to get to the Microsoft Passport page

Figure 3-3: Kids Passport helps you set up parental controls.

Setting and Changing Passwords

After you grow accustomed to MSN Explorer, you may decide that you want to change the password you originally selected. Piece of cake. Here's the process:

1. **Start MSN Explorer as usual.**
2. **Click Help & Settings.**

   The Member Center window appears (see Figure 3-4).
3. **Click Change Your Password.**

   The window appears so that you can enter the new password you want.
4. **Type the password that you currently use in the Type In Your Current Password text box.**
5. **Type the new password once in the Type In Your New Password text box and again in the Type In Your New Password Again text box.**
6. **Click the Change Now button to save your changes.**

MSN Explorer enables you to create up to nine different accounts — with nine different passwords — on your system.

Figure 3-4: Modifying your password just takes a trip to the Member Center.

Your Home Page, Your Way

As you probably noticed, the MSN Explorer screen does not have a lot of room. If you want to control what kind of information is displayed in that limited space, you can call on MSN Explorer's personalization features. To customize your home page, follow these steps:

1. **Start MSN Explorer as usual.**
2. **Click Help & Settings.**

   The Member Center window appears (refer to Figure 3-4).
3. **Click Item 3, Customize Content on Your Home Page.**

   The Personalization window for My MSN jumps into view, as shown in Figure 3-5.
4. **Select any of the major providers, and then click the All Content tab to see a more complete listing.**

   The All Content tab has more than 100 options for your viewing pleasure.
5. **Select the topics in the left column that you want to see on your home page.**

   Descriptions of online content choices appear in the Web window. Scan through the list and select the check box to add the content.
6. **Click the OK button to update your home page.**

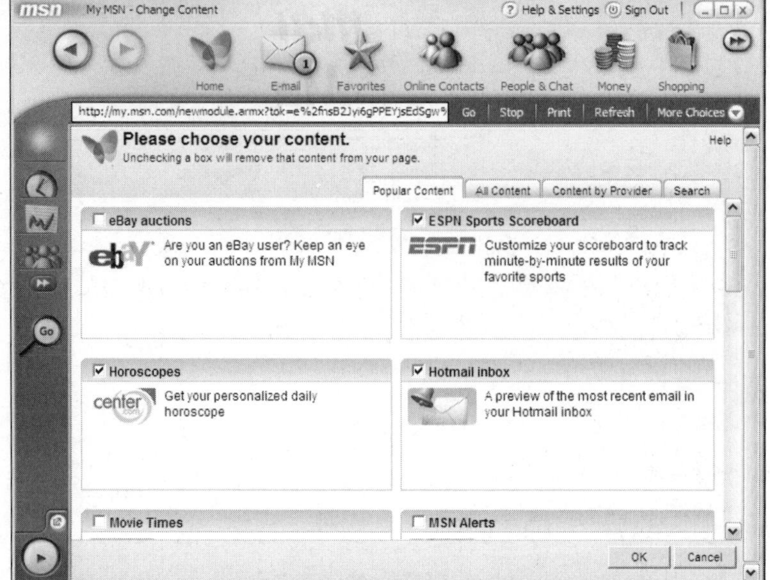

Figure 3-5: The display ads for big-name providers appear on the Popular Content tab.

Chapter 4: Hotmail (a.k.a. MSN E-Mail)

In This Chapter

- Using e-mail in MSN Explorer
- Putting Hotmail, er, MSN Explorer E-mail through its paces
- Using your Contacts list

This chapter explains how to receive, write, and send e-mail with Hotmail, er, MSN Explorer E-mail. And after you read your e-mail, what are you going to do about it? This chapter gives you the ins and outs for organizing the mail you want to keep and tossing the mail you don't want. And as you add to your bevy of online friends, you will no doubt want to add them to your Contacts list (which Microsoft used to call the MSN Address Book).

Sending and Receiving E-Mail

The e-mail program that you use in MSN Explorer may be different from other e-mail programs that you have used. When you click the E-mail icon in MSN Explorer, it goes straight to Hotmail. In almost every respect, MSN Explorer acts just like any other Web browser by giving you access to Hotmail. Compare the MSN E-mail in MSN Explorer (shown in Figure 4-1) to Hotmail in Internet Explorer (shown in Figure 4-2).

MSN E-mail, which is to say, Hotmail, remains the world's most popular Web-based e-mail service. *Web-based* means that the mail isn't delivered to an Inbox on your computer; you don't have copies of any messages sitting around on your PC. Instead, the mail stays online, on Microsoft's big computers, waiting for you to open, view, and file it away when you're ready.

This chapter shows you how to work your mail with MSN Explorer, but the techniques are identical in Hotmail itself. If you ever find yourself on the road and wanting to check your mail, if you can get online with any Web browser — whether MSN Explorer is available or not — simply go to `http://hotmail.com` and see what's waiting. That's the beauty of Web-based mail:

- You can access your e-mail anytime you can get to the Web.
- You can send and receive file attachments in precisely the same fashion from MSN Explorer, Internet Explorer, Netscape, Mozilla, or any other Web browser.
- You don't have to use your own hard drive storage space for downloaded mail.

The downside of Web-based e-mail? Beyond the normal questions (such as "Do I want Microsoft to store my Contacts list?"), the main problems I hear

- If Microsoft's servers are slow (or down), mail runs like molasses (or not at all).
- Storing more than a tiny bit of mail can be expensive.
- Unless you save a message on your PC, you don't have anything to go back to if you accidentally or intentionally delete an old message.

In earlier versions of Hotmail, you couldn't save and store a message-in-progress; but in MSN Explorer's e-mail (which is to say, in the current version of Hotmail), you can park a message in your Drafts folder and come back to it whenever the urge strikes.

Reading your mail

You know right away when you start MSN Explorer whether you have unread e-mail or not. The E-mail button in the MSN Explorer toolbar shows a small number if new mail awaits your attention.

To read your mail, click the E-mail icon on the toolbar. As shown in Figure 4-1, the Hotmail window opens, displaying seven different icons:

- **New:** Lets you create new e-mail messages, of course, but it also allows you to put your own custom folders on the left side of the screen. It also lets you create new Contacts and Groups of Contacts. If you're paying extra for the Hotmail/MSN Explorer Calendar and To-Do List features, you also have the option of creating new Appointments (which is to say, Calendar entries) and Tasks (those are in your To-Do list).
- **Delete:** Sends any checked messages to the Trash Can.
- **Block:** Sends any checked messages to the Trash Can, and adds the sender to your blocked senders list (see the sidebar, "On blocking senders").
- **Junk:** Reports any checked messages to the Hotmail authorities and, optionally, adds the sender to your blocked sender's list.

Figure 4-1: MSN Explorer's mail, as viewed from MSN Explorer.

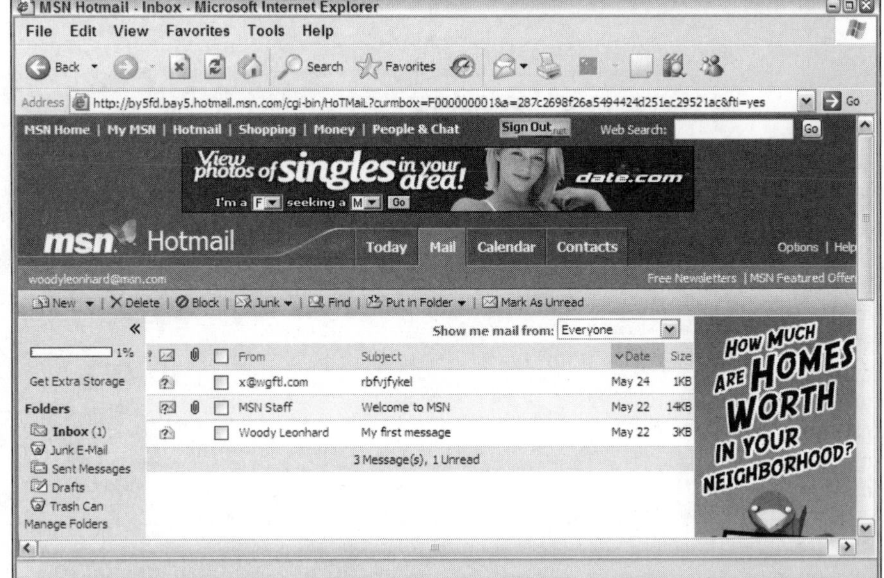

Figure 4-2: Hotmail, as viewed from Internet Explorer. With a few very subtle exceptions, only the ads change.

In May 2003, Microsoft claimed that it blocked 2.4 billion pieces of spam a day. By now, that number has doubled or tripled or more. You can report incoming junk e-mail, but with volumes like that, you aren't even spitting in the wind.

- **Find:** Brings up Hotmail's underaspirated Find function, which lets you search for messages based on words in the message, or the From/To/Subject fields.
- **Put in Folder:** Moves any checked messages to the folder you choose. No, you can't drag and drop messages. You have to click in the box in front of the From field, click Put in Folder, and choose the folder.
- **Mark as Unread:** Marks any checked messages as unread.

If you've never read a specific message, Hotmail puts a light color behind the line with the message. The total number of unread messages appears in parentheses next to the Inbox folder over on the left side of the screen, and it's also on the E-mail icon on the MSN Explorer toolbar. After you read the message, the light color highlight goes away, and the number in parentheses goes down by one. Marking a message as unread simply replaces the highlight and increases the counter, in case you want to pretend that you never saw the message.

To read a new message, simply click the text in the From or Subject column. The message opens in the Hotmail window, as shown in Figure 4-3.

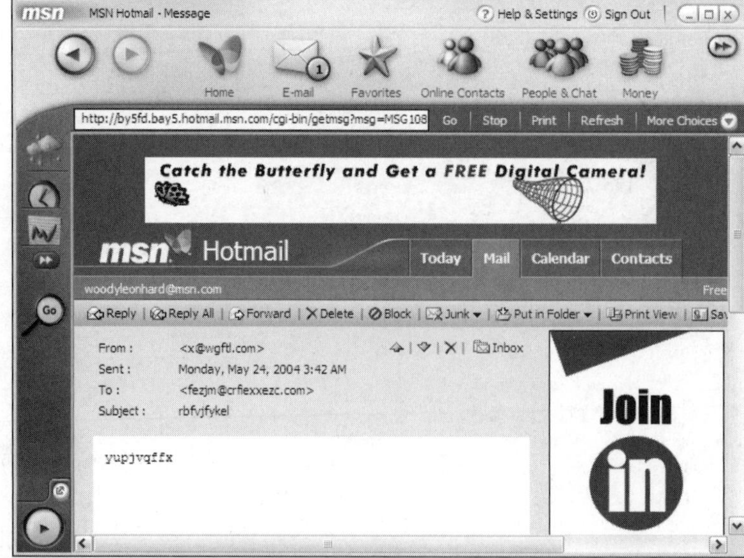

Figure 4-3: The first "real" message in my new @msn.com account was — you guessed it — a piece of spam.

What to do with your mail

After you open and read an e-mail message, what are you going to do with it? You have several options — you can print it, file it, reply to it, forward it to someone else, or delete it. Hotmail includes handy-dandy little buttons to help you finish off those tasks. Table 4-1 gives you an overview of the various tools in the Hotmail window. Here's a quick rundown of the steps involved in carrying out the various procedures:

- To reply to a message, click Reply, type your message, and click Send. (Yes, it's really that simple.) If your message was sent to multiple recipients, click Reply All to send the same response to everyone on the recipient list.
- To forward a message to another person, click Forward, and enter the recipient's e-mail address or choose the recipient from your Contacts list. Type any message that you want to insert at the top of the forwarded message and click Send.
- To send the message to the Trash Can, click Delete.
- The Block, Junk, and Put in Folder buttons work the same way as in the main window; see the preceding section for details.
- To print a message, click Print View. Hotmail displays the message in a new window, in a form — a *view* — that's suitable for printing, as shown in Figure 4-4. If you still want to print the page, click the Print button in that new window. To close the new window, click the X (Close) button in the upper-right corner.

  ASKWOODY.COM

  While it's true that you can print the whole screen, including any visible portion of the message, by clicking the Print button to the right of the Address bar (underneath the People & Chat icon), you'll get a lot of extraneous junk on the printed page. Far better to use the Print View button, down in the message itself.
- To save the address of the sender or any recipients in your Contacts list, click Save Address. Hotmail responds with the New Contacts page, as shown in Figure 4-5. Fill out the form and click OK.

On blocking senders

Once upon a time, e-mail "black lists" or "blocked sender's lists" were an effective tool against spam: If you kept getting spam from an address, you put it on the black list, and your e-mail program would automatically stick mail from that address in your Junk E-mail folder.

Nowadays, life isn't so simple. Spammers rarely use the same return address twice — and in many cases they "spoof" their addresses, so you have no idea who really sent the message. Black lists do have their uses, though, as Bozo filters. (And I mean no disrespect, Bozo!) If you keep getting annoying mail from a person who simply won't take a clue, stick him or her on your blocked sender's list. All of the mail from that person's e-mail address will go straight to the Junk E-mail folder, with nary a whimper.

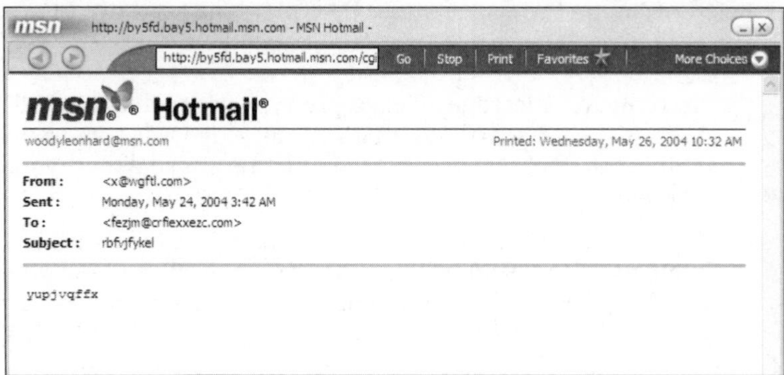

Figure 4-4: Click the Print View button and Hotmail creates a new window with a copy of the message that prints very well.

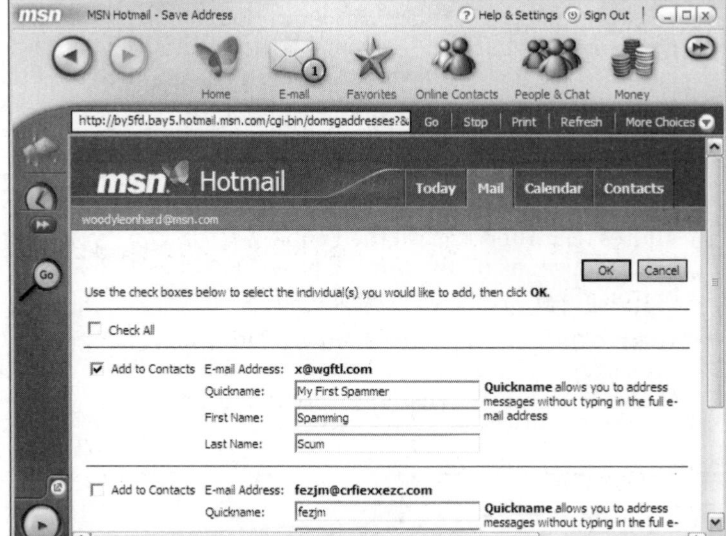

Figure 4-5: Fill out the Contacts form and click OK.

Table 4-1 E-Mail Options

Button	*Name*	*Description*
Reply	Reply	Opens a message so that you can reply to the current message.
Reply All	Reply All	Opens a message so that you can send a reply to all the people listed on the current message.
Forward	Forward	Enables you to send the current message on to someone else.

Button	Name	Description
X Delete	Delete	Puts the current message in the Trash Can folder.
Block	Block	Puts the e-mail address of the sender in the blocked sender's list, so that you won't get any more mail from that e-mail address.
Junk	Junk	Notifies the Hotmail folks that this is a piece of spam; optionally, adds the sender to the blocked senders list.
Put in Folder	Put in Folder	Displays a folder list so that you can save the message where you want it.
Print View	Print View	Creates a copy of the current message in a form that's suitable for printing.
Save Address	Save Address	Lets you put the address of anyone in the From: or To: list in your Contacts list.
Inbox	Shortcuts	Lets you, respectively, see the previous message, the next message, move the message to the Trash Can folder, and go back to the Inbox.

Writing e-mail

Ready to compose a message? By now, you can probably guess the process. It's simple when you know what you want to say. Here are the steps:

1. **Start MSN Explorer as usual.**
2. **Click the E-mail icon on the toolbar. If you aren't in the Mail section, click the Mail tab.**

   Sometimes MSN Explorer sticks you in Hotmail's Today section. When you're in the Mail section, you can see the contents of your Inbox (refer to Figure 4-1).
3. **Click New.**

   A blank e-mail window appears, listing your Contacts list entries on the right side of the screen (see Figure 4-6).
4. **Click an entry in your Contacts list to add the name to the To text box or type the e-mail address directly in the text box.**
5. **Click in the Subject text box and type a heading or topic for your message.**
6. **Type the message in the blank part of the message window.**

   If you want to change the look of the text, you have to start Hotmail's Rich Text Editor. To do so, choose Tools⇨Rich Text Editor ON. Hotmail shows you a formatting toolbar (see Figure 4-7), from which you can change the font, size, color, style, alignment, add emoticons, and so on.

The usual text-editing rules apply: Select the text you want to format, and then click the appropriate button.

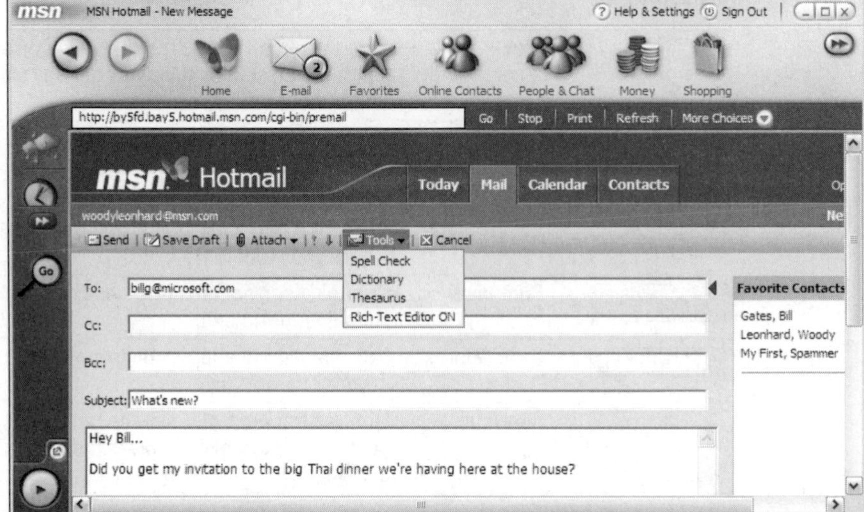

Figure 4-6: Hotmail makes it easy to write and send e-mail online.

Figure 4-7: Hotmail lets you add smileys and other emoticons, as well as formatted text, if you know where to find the Rich Text Editor.

7. **If you want to save a copy of your outbound message in your Sent Messages folder, you MUST select the Copy Message to Sent Folder check box (you find it at the bottom of the message), as shown in Figure 4-8.**

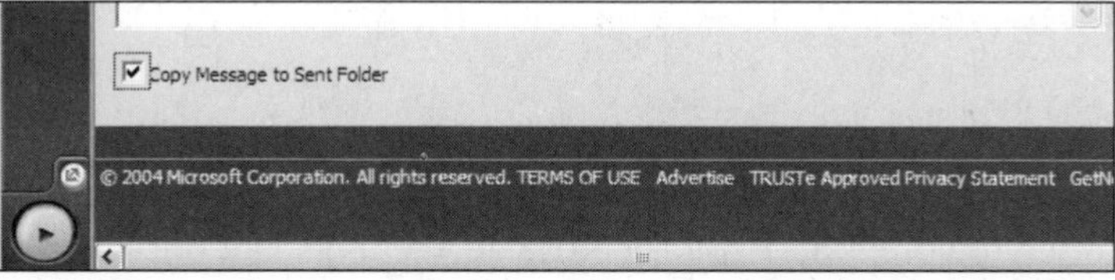

Figure 4-8: To keep a copy of your outgoing message in the Sent folder, you must select this check box.

If you forget to select the Copy Message to Sent Folder check box, you can only retrieve a copy of your sent message by writing to someone who received it and asking them to send a copy back.

8. **When your message is ready, click Send.**

   MSN Explorer tells you that your message is being sent. When the operation is complete, you hear a chime, indicating that the task is completed.

Many people — especially busy people — open an e-mail message only if they know what the message is about. So make sure that your Subject line is short, clear, and to the point. This helps to ensure that your message gets read.

Managing Your Contacts List

Unfortunately, MSN Explorer doesn't come with the names and addresses of your 5,000 closest friends already entered. That's up to you to do. Luckily, the Contacts list feature is simple to use, and it's handy, too, if you don't mind storing all your information on Microsoft's big computers.

In earlier versions of MSN Explorer and Hotmail, the Contacts list was called the *Address Book*. Microsoft changed the name because it found that a lot of people were wondering why the Address Book in Outlook Express (and Windows in general) didn't match the one in MSN Explorer/Hotmail. (I wonder, too, but that's another story.)

To further complicate matters, Outlook (the big Outlook, in Microsoft Office) has a Contacts folder, too, but that one doesn't connect to Outlook Express, Windows, MSN Explorer, or Hotmail, except via a very hokey, error-prone text-based import/export capability. If you see a reference to an "Address Book" in MSN Explorer or Hotmail (and you will — see, for example, the dialog box for adding new Online Contacts in MSN Messenger), realize that they're talking about the Contacts list. Also realize that the Contacts list in MSN Explorer/Hotmail isn't the same as similar-sounding lists in any other product.

It gets worse.

MSN Explorer uses two different Contacts lists — one for e-mail (called, simply, Contacts), the other for MSN Messenger (called, confusingly, Online Contacts). If you add an Online Contact to MSN Messenger, it's automatically added to your MSN Explorer/Hotmail Contacts list. But if you add someone to MSN Explorer/Hotmail Contacts, you have to manually add them to the MSN Messenger Online Contacts. If you delete someone from your MSN Explorer/Hotmail Contacts list, they aren't automatically removed from your Online Contacts. Oy. What a mess.

To view the Contacts list, simply click E-mail on the toolbar, and then click the Contacts tab. The screen shown in Figure 4-9 appears.

The easiest way to add a new entry to your Contacts list is by picking off the e-mail address of someone who sent you a message, or someone who was copied on a message sent to you. I explain how to do that in the section, "Reading your mail," earlier in this chapter.

If you want to add a new Contact to your list manually, follow these steps:

1. **Start MSN Explorer, click the E-mail icon on the toolbar, and then click the Contacts tab.**

   You see your current Contacts list (see Figure 4-9).

2. **Click New.**

   The Add New Contact dialog box appears, as shown in Figure 4-10.

3. **Fill out the information for the person you want to add.**

4. **If you want this Hotmail Contact to be available in your MSN Explorer Favorites short list of Contacts, select the Mark This Contact As a Favorite check box.**

   When you select the Mark This Contact As a Favorite check box, MSN Explorer shows the Contact on its short list of favorites when you click the Favorites line on the left side of the main Contacts window (refer to Figure 4-9). There's nothing particularly magical about Favorites. It's just a convenient way to reduce the amount of wading you have to do to find a Contact that you need in a hurry.

5. Click Save to save the entry.

Hotmail adds the name to your Contacts list, and the name is available the next time you begin to write a message or click the Contacts tab.

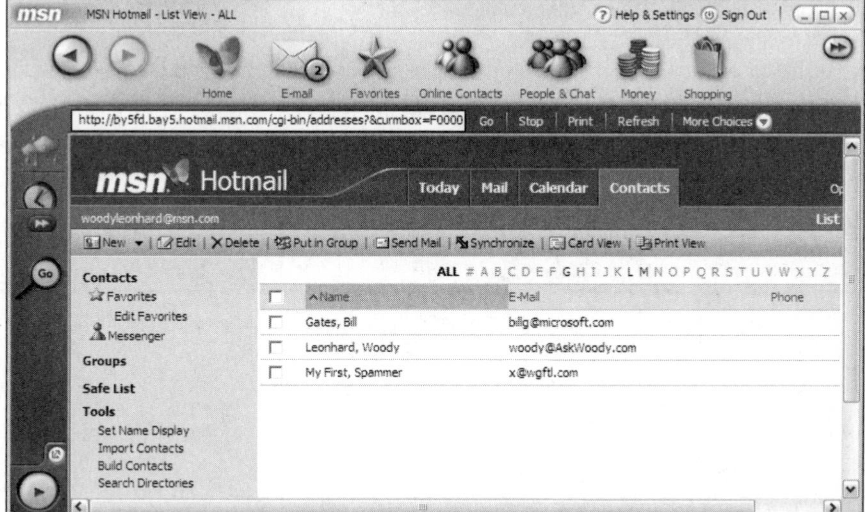

Figure 4-9: My Hotmail/ MSN Explorer Contacts list.

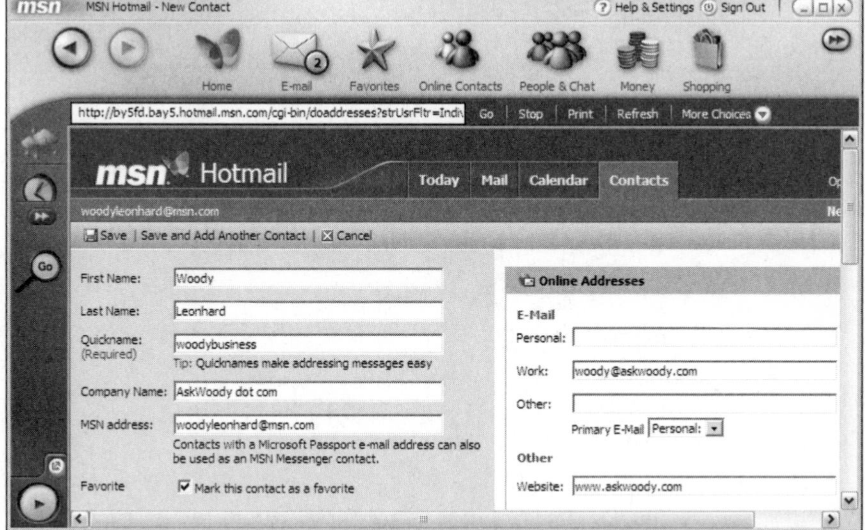

Figure 4-10: New MSN Explorer/ Hotmail Contacts are entered here.

Importing addresses

At least in theory, MSN Explorer lets you import entries from Outlook Contacts list and Outlook Express Address Book, adding them to your MSN Explorer/Hotmail Contacts list. To import an Address Book, follow these steps:

1. **Go into Outlook 2000, 2002 (the version in Office XP), 2003, or Outlook Express and export your address list as a "Comma Separated Value" (CSV) file.**
2. **Start MSN Explorer as usual.**
3. **Click the Contacts tab (refer to Figure 4-9).**
4. **On the left, under Tools, click the Import Contacts link.**
5. **Choose whether you want to import addresses from Outlook or Outlook Express. Click Next.**

   Follow the instructions to import a CSV Contacts list.

Chapter 5: MSN Messenger

In This Chapter

- Finding out what MSN Messenger does — and doesn't do
- Installing MSN Messenger
- Staying safe in a virus-ridden IM world

Most industry observers credit AOL with inventing instant messaging (or IM), back in the early 1990s, when nobody knew exactly what "instant messaging" meant — it was just a handy, if clumsy, way for AOL members to chat with each other.

1996 marked a major turning point in instant messaging, when AOL introduced "Buddy Lists" — stored lists of AOL members' I.D.s that made it much simpler to connect — and an Israeli company called Mirablis released ICQ, the first messaging program that worked for anybody on the Internet, whether they paid for AOL or not. AOL coined the term AOL Instant Messenger (AIM), and turned it into A Big Deal — and then they bought Mirablis, cornering the IM market.

Yahoo! and Microsoft entered the fray not long after, each with its own incompatible IM program. Microsoft tried to make MSN Messenger compatible with AIM, but AOL tweaked a few bits and suddenly MSN Messenger users couldn't talk to AIM users anymore. Yahoo! has actively kept other IM programs from getting onto its network. And so on. Lawsuits piled on top of lawsuits. Users got lost in the crush. Many polyglot alternatives to AIM, Yahoo! Messenger, and MSN Messenger exist — several manage to converse with one, two, or (at times) all three of the big programs. That is, until one of the 800-pound gorillas rolls over and scratches itself — and *poof!* the small companies get squished again.

Terminology is everything, particularly when the lawyers get added to the mix. "Instant Messenger" is a Service Mark of Time Warner (formerly AOL Time Warner), so you won't see that phrase used anywhere but in AOL-related material. AOL invented the term Buddy List. MSN Messenger used to have Online Buddies, but now they're called Online Contacts. I wonder why?

As things stand, if you use AIM, you can send instant messages to anyone who uses AIM or subscribes to AOL. If you use Yahoo! Messenger, you can talk to other people who use Yahoo! Messenger. And if you use MSN Messenger, you can talk to others with MSN Messenger, and (most of the time, anyway) anybody who's using Windows Messenger.

As this book went to press, Microsoft announced that it was going to make it easier for big business to commingle MSN Messenger, AIM, and Yahoo Messenger. I remain skeptical, but stranger things have happened. If you need to communicate with people using different instant messaging programs, look into Trillian, `www.trillian.cc`, which can talk with all three, albeit one service at a time.

MSN Messenger versus AOL and Yahoo!

Taken together, the three big players in instant messaging — AOL, Yahoo!, and Microsoft — release at least one new version of their instant messaging programs a month. The best IM program today may be tomorrow's toast.

Instant messaging allows people who are actively on the Internet to exchange written messages and, increasingly

- Talk to each other, using microphones and speakers/headphones, or even with a conventional-looking telephone that plugs into a computer's USB port. Some telephone applications require both parties to be attached to their computers at the same time, and the phone call goes from computer to computer. Others are smart enough to allow someone connected to his or her computer to dial a plain, old, everyday telephone. The so-called *VoIP* (Voice over IP/Internet connection) applications are getting smarter all the time.
- Look at each other using live Webcams, either one on one, or in multi-user video conferences.
- Interact with each other by, for example, drawing on a shared whiteboard.
- Send files to each other, including pictures, data files, programs, and other potentially hazardous nuclear waste.
- Listen to music together. No, I'm not joking.
- Play games.

Each ensuing version of the three major IM programs add a little glitz, some cool new icons, maybe a twist on the picture sending theme, or a new way to choose music. But major changes are few and far between, and none of the IM vendors has been consistently first to market with important new features.

So how do you choose which IM program to use? Easy. Ask your friends what they use. If you want to talk to them via IM, you need to use the same program they're using. Sad state of affairs, but that's how it works.

MSN Messenger versus Windows Messenger

Every Windows XP user has Windows Messenger installed. It comes along for the ride with Windows itself.

MSN Messenger has to be downloaded and installed separately (unless you got it with your PC, or you installed it as part of the MSN Internet Access CD).

Windows Messenger and MSN Messenger look a lot alike, but they don't work the same way, and sometimes they won't talk to each other: A person using MSN Messenger may not be able to "see" someone who's logged on with Windows Messenger, and vice versa.

I go into details on the differences between Windows Messenger and MSN Messenger in Book III, Chapter 4. In general

- If you use the Messenger features in any of the Microsoft Office applications, you're pretty much stuck with Windows Messenger.
- If you use MSN Explorer very much, there are some conflicts with MSN Messenger. Personally, I've encountered enough problems that I wouldn't run both MSN Explorer and MSN Messenger at the same time.
- You *can* install and use both Windows Messenger and MSN Messenger on the same machine. But you shouldn't run both of them at the same time.
- MSN Messenger has a lot of new features that are pretty cool.

Given all of that, I personally use MSN Messenger, and I recommend that you do, too, if you can.

Installing MSN Messenger

MSN Messenger is free. It'll run on any Windows XP computer. You can install it without harming Windows Messenger. What's not to like?

Here's how to get it:

1. **Using Internet Explorer or MSN Explorer, go to** `http://messenger.msn.com` **(see Figure 5-1).**
2. **Click the Download button.**

   Windows XP puts up a Security Warning dialog box, as shown in Figure 5-2.

Figure 5-1: Download MSN Messenger from the Messenger home page.

Figure 5-2: This dialog box is particularly confusing, but you want to click the Run button.

3. **In spite of what the Web site says, click the Run button in the Security Warning dialog box.**

   Sit back and have a latte. Even with a fast broadband connection, downloading MSN Messenger can take three or four minutes. When Windows finishes the download, you see yet another Security Warning dialog box, as shown in Figure 5-3.

4. **Click the Run button on the second Security Warning dialog box.**

   The MSN Messenger installer kicks in (see Figure 5-4).

Figure 5-3: Windows tosses up a second security warning.

Figure 5-4: You finally arrive at a normal installer dialog box. Just follow the instructions.

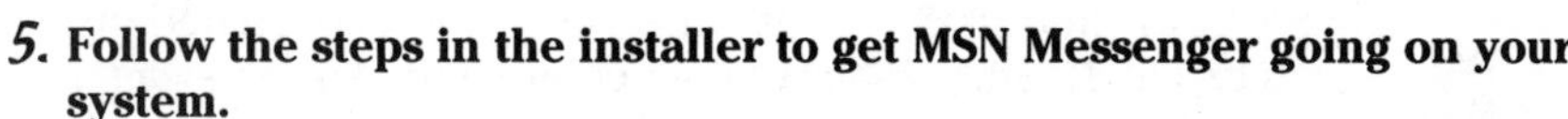

5. **Follow the steps in the installer to get MSN Messenger going on your system.**

   The installer tries to put the MSN toolbar (a cheap rip-off of the Google toolbar) on your machine, and make MSN Search your default search engine (puh-lease). If you're gullible enough, go right ahead.

6. **When the installer is done, choose Start⇨All Programs⇨MSN Messenger to run MSN Messenger.**

Starting with Online Contacts

Before you can start sending messages to your Online Contacts, you have to set up some Online Contacts, eh?

When you first connect to MSN Messenger, the program goes out to Hotmail and imports your Contacts list into MSN Messenger's Online Contacts (see Book V, Chapter 4 for a description of the interactions between MSN

Explorer Mail/Hotmail's Contacts list and MSN Messenger's Online Contacts list). If you've used Hotmail much at all, that should give you a running start on filling up your Online Contacts.

You can (and will!) add other people to your Online Contacts, but keep these points in mind:

- You can only add a person to your Online Contacts list if he or she has an e-mail address that's been registered with Passport.

  In fact, in a very real sense, you don't add *people* to your Online Contacts list. You add e-mail addresses. The e-mail address is the key to communicating with another person: You can try to send a message to John Doe till the cows come home, but unless you have John Doe's e-mail address in your Online Contacts list, *and* John Doe is logged on to MSN Messenger (or Windows Messenger) using that specific e-mail address, you won't be able to do Jack with John. Er, you won't be able to communicate with him.
- When you add a person to your Online Contacts list, that person has an opportunity to decline your offer — and you'll never know that he or she opted to stay quiet. The person appears on your Online Contacts list just like any other Contact. But MSN's connecting software will never notify you when that person is online.
- Don't put too many people in your Online Contacts. Why? The clatter of the alerts when they log on and off the Internet will drive you nuts. It's like listening to ten different conversations at once. Yes, you can turn off the *alerts* — the bleeps and bloops that notify you when a Contact logs on or off of the Internet. Yes, you can tell MSN Messenger to pretend that you're offline. But in the end, do you really want to talk with all of those people?

If you know someone who has an MSN.com or Hotmail e-mail address — or if you know the e-mail address of somebody who's signed up for Passport — you can invite him or her to participate in instant messaging by following these steps:

1. **Start MSN Messenger.**

   You can do that by choosing Start➪All Programs➪MSN Messenger. Alternatively, start MSN Explorer, click the Online Contacts icon at the top, and then choose View My Online Contacts.

   In either case, you may have to log on to MSN Messenger. Once you've done so, you see the MSN Messenger main screen, as shown in Figure 5-5.

2. **At the bottom, click Add a Contact.**

   MSN Messenger responds with the Add a Contact dialog box (see Figure 5-6).

   This dialog box refers to the Address Book, which Microsoft has renamed Contacts. It's the Contact list for your MSN Explorer Mail/Hotmail account.

Figure 5-5: MSN Messenger's command center.

Figure 5-6: You can add anyone with a Passport-registered e-mail address.

3. **Choose between bringing in an Online Contact from your MSN Explorer Mail/Hotmail Contacts list or typing in a new Online Contact's e-mail address by hand. Then click Next.**

   If you choose to type in an address, MSN Messenger asks you to type in the address, as shown in Figure 5-7. Note that MSN Messenger is looking for an e-mail address that's been registered with Passport. (By definition, any address ending in `@hotmail.com`, `@msn.com`, or `@microsoft.com` has been registered with Passport.)

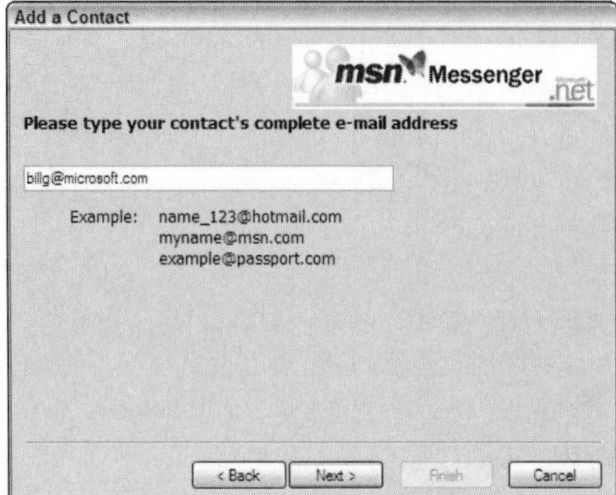

Figure 5-7: To add an Online Contact, type his or her e-mail address directly into this box.

If you enter an e-mail address that isn't registered with Passport, MSN Messenger offers to "help" by sending the person an e-mail message extolling the virtues of Passport, asking him or her to sign up, as shown in Figure 5-8. That message includes your name in the Subject line, and your e-mail address buried in the body of the message. You can't change the text in the body of the message.

4. **Keep following the directions to add as many Online Contacts as you like. When you're done, click Finish.**

After you have your Online Contacts in order, you're ready to start talking.

Figure 5-8: If an e-mail address isn't registered with Passport, Messenger sends this to get the other person to register.

Sending an Instant Message

When you're ready to send an instant message to an Online Contact, follow these steps:

1. **Start MSN Messenger.**
2. **Double-click the name of the Contact you want to, uh, contact.**

   The message window appears, as shown in Figure 5-9.
3. **Type your message (it appears at the bottom) and press Enter or click the Send button.**

   The message appears in the top portion of the window. When the recipient begins entering a message, you see a descriptor telling you so in the bottom portion of the message window.
4. **Your correspondent may respond. If so, the conversation appears in the top window (see Figure 5-10). Type until you get bored. When you're done, choose File⇨Close (or click the X/Close button).**

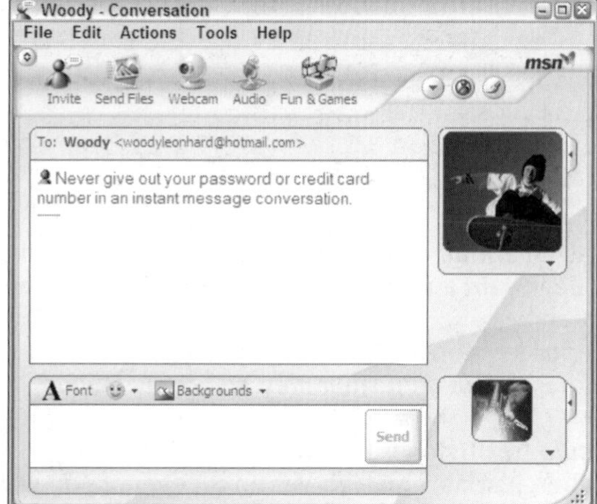

Figure 5-9: Start a conversation with just a couple of clicks.

The conversation can continue as long as you wish, and you can spice it up with emoticons (smiley faces and more) and acronyms if you wish.

That's just the beginning, of course. MSN Messenger's feature set changes with each new version. The best way to figure out what's available and how to use it is to simply start clicking. In my experience, the audio conferencing capabilities (if all participants have fast Internet connections) are well worth exploring, and the Webcam/video conferencing may be. Some folks like the games (click the icon of a joystick in the lower-left corner), but I tired of them quickly.

As with most computer things, the best way to learn is to try something new. Go for it. You won't break anything.

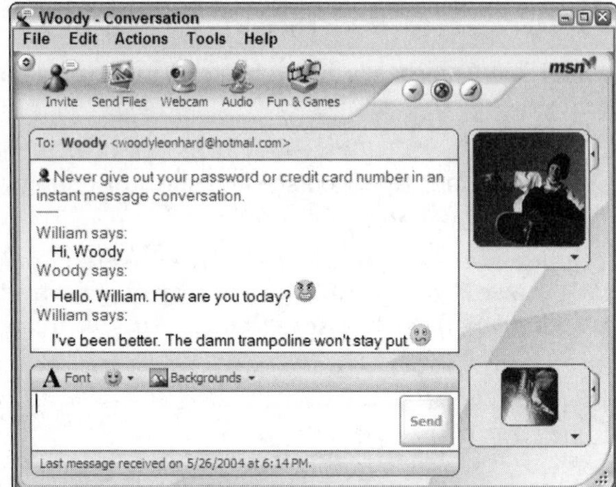

Figure 5-10: It's easy to maintain an instant conversation — and difficult to carry on a meaningful one.

Instant Messaging Safety

Much has been written about viruses and worms, firewalls and servers. Precious little has been said about security problems with instant messaging.

Every MSN Messenger session starts with the words *Never give out your password or credit card number in an instant message conversation.*

Of course, that *should* be obvious. *You* would never give out your password or credit card number, just as a matter of course, even if you were conversing with someone who claimed to be an MSN Administrator or your ISP's Security Coordinator or the First Half Brother of the Man in the Moon ("See? His e-mail address is `FirstHalfBrother@ManInTheMoon.com`! So he *must* be the First Half Brother . . .")

One of the first IM-related viruses was called `buddypicture.net`. (Actually it was a Trojan — you had to run the program before it would infect you.) Buddypicture roamed through infected AOL Instant Messenger systems, scanning the AIM Buddy List, sending instant messages to people saying, "I can't believe I found (the person's name) picture here. HAHAHA." The

Smileys and BTWs

As you get really good at this online communications thing, you'll want faster methods of letting people know what you think and feel.

Emoticons, or smileys, are small icons that you can use to communicate feelings to an online buddy or to people in a chat room. To produce smiley faces and other items in your instant communications, try these:

:)	Smiling face
:0	Yawn
:P	Tongue out
;)	Wink
:(	Frown
:S	Uncertain
:|	Bored

Acronyms are shorthand methods of saying often-used phrases. Here are some acronyms that you may want to use:

<G>	Grin
<EG>	Evil grin
AFK	Away from keyboard
BRB	Be right back
BTW	By the way
FWIW	For what it's worth
GMTA	Great minds think alike
IMHO	In my humble opinion
LOL	Laughing out loud
ROFL	Rolling on the floor laughing
TMI	Too much information
TTFN	Ta ta for now

message included a hyperlink which, when clicked, transported the hapless IMer to the `buddypicture.net` Web site. There, with appropriate but obscured warnings, a couple of clicks would install the BuddyPicture "adware" — scarcely discernable from a virus, in my opinion — which scanned the AIM Buddy List and sent out more inviting messages.

That's only the tip of the iceberg. My advice

- Don't ever run or open a file that's sent via an instant message, no matter who seems to be sending it to you. Save the file, and run it through your antivirus program's recently-updated scanner before you do anything. Even if it passes muster, make sure the person sending it to you will vouch for it. If you have any doubt whatsoever, the safest thing to do: Delete it.
- Be careful chasing down links, and never download anything on a Web site that you reach via an IM link. There are plenty of bad Web sites out there, and most of them have very convincing facades.
- Remember that everything you type into an instant message can be recorded. The latest IM software saves everything.
- The person you're sending an instant message to may not be the person you thought you were talking with. Wish I had a nickel for every time a kid posed as his parent in an IM exchange. And vice versa.

- ✦ Remember that everything you type into an instant message can, conceivably, be read by anybody who's sufficiently interested. Sending an instant message is not unlike sending a postcard. If you want your privacy, use message encrypting (which is only now becoming available), and remember that even an encrypted message can be cracked.
- ✦ Watch your antivirus software manufacturer to see when IM protection becomes available. If you use IM much at all, it's probably worth the extra cost.

Book VI

Adding and Using Other Hardware

"... and Bobby here found a way to extend our data transmission an additional 3000 meters using coax cable. How'd you do that, Bobby – repeaters?"

Contents at a Glance

Chapter 1: Finding and Installing the Hardware You Want

In This Chapter

- **Finding out what hardware is available**
- **Figuring out how it works**
- **Upgrading hardware**
- **Adding audio**
- **Installing and using new hardware**

Let's face facts: You don't need all of the fastest, most expensive gadgets to get value out of your computer.

On the other hand, equipment that fits your needs can help you do more and better work in less time.

This chapter reviews the common computer accessories currently available to help you decide whether any of them would be valuable to you.

Understanding Hardware Types

Before you can make an informed decision about adding a new piece of hardware to your computer or network, you have to understand how hardware connects to your PC and what you need to make that sparkly new toy work.

Juggling internal and external devices

An *internal device* is one that goes inside your computer's case. An *external device* has its own case and is connected to your computer by a cable.

An internal device is more convenient to use. If you have to move your computer, the internal device goes right with it. There's no cable or separate power cord to get tangled and catch dust. But you have a physical limit on the number of internal devices you can cram into a box.

On the other hand, an external device is often more flexible — and it's almost always more expensive. If you have more than one computer, you can move an external device from one to another as the need arises.

An internal device may be an *adapter card* that plugs into one of the *slots* on your computer's motherboard, or it may be connected to a *controller* by an internal cable. All external devices are connected to a controller.

The type of *interface* that a device has determines the type of controller it needs. (The next section explains interfaces.) A single controller can operate several devices with the same type of interface. Some types of controllers are built into the motherboard; others must be added as adapter cards.

Choosing an interface

Any device connected to your computer uses some type of *interface* to move data back and forth. The interface is just a physical connection — a plug, if you will. Many types of devices are sold with a choice of interfaces, and you need to know enough about the different interfaces to choose the right one for your needs.

Interfaces for adapter cards

Adapter cards (computer cards that plug straight into the PC's motherboard) use one of three types of interfaces, corresponding to the three types of slots on the motherboard. The names of the slots are pretty weird, but don't let the terminology put you off. There were reasons for the names, once upon a time, but they don't really mean much nowadays. Like, oh, "New York." Know what I mean?

The *PCI interface* gets the nod for most adapter cards. It's physically strong (so you'll have a hard time breaking the sucker when you stick a card in the slot), and lots of electrical contacts are inside. PCI supports *Plug and Play* operation, which means that Windows XP can detect the properties of an adapter card and do much or all of the software installation automatically. Most Windows computers have three, four, or five PCI slots.

The *AGP interface* is for video adapter cards only — that is, cards that slap stuff up on your screen. An AGP slot is shorter than a PCI slot. Some AGP slots have a little lever that flips up on the back to hold the card in tighter. Video adapters with the AGP interface can offer better performance than those with the PCI interface. AGP is also a plug-and-play interface.

Not all Windows PCs have separate AGP slots, so check before you buy an AGP card, okay? An AGP card without an AGP slot is about as useless as a kite without a string.

As this book went to press, the *PCI Express* (sometimes called *PCI-2*) *interface* was just starting to hit the market. It remains to be seen if the new technology will supplant both PCI and AGP. While PCI Express runs much faster than traditional PCI (say, 10 to 20 times as fast), it isn't all that much faster than AGP. You can only use PCI Express cards in a PCI Express computer. Will PCI Express take over the industry? Hard to tell. But if you bought a fancy AGP video card for your old PC, don't blithely assume that it will work in a new PC.

The *ISA interface* is a much older interface, and it's not Plug and Play. Most modern Windows computers have just one ISA slot or none at all.

Do not buy an adapter card with an ISA interface unless you need something unusual that is only made that way. If you buy an ISA card, expect to spend lots of hours wrestling with arcane topics such as IRQs, DMA channels, and base I/O addresses — all three of which were government plots designed to keep computers out of the hands of "normal" people. You have a hard time finding ISA cards nowadays for a reason. Let them die a well-deserved death.

IDE and EIDE interfaces

The *EIDE interface* controls the hard drive on most Windows computers. Often it controls the CD-ROM drive or DVD drive as well. All modern Windows computers have a built-in EIDE controller or two, sitting on the motherboard, usually attached with wide ribbon cables to all the hard drives and CD drives in the PC.

The *IDE interface* is an ancestor of EIDE, and you still find hard drives that are designed to run with IDE. If your computer has an EIDE interface, you can probably plug an IDE hard drive into it, but you're talking slug city.

IDE and EIDE interfaces are rarely used for external devices because the length of the cable connecting the controller to the device is quite limited.

Serial ATA interface

If you've ever poked around the innards of your computer, no doubt you've noticed those long, not-so-flexible "ribbon cables" that connect hard drives, CD drives, floppies, and the like to the motherboard. As this book went to press, a number of companies had introduced new technology that would make ribbon cables obsolete.

The *Serial ATA* approach replaces those 40- or 80-wire ribbons with a single cable that looks like a stereo patch cord. Of course, Serial ATA is faster, smarter, better than its predecessor. Of course, it's completely incompatible — you need Serial ATA hard drives, CD drives, and the like to go on one end of the cable; and your PC has to have Serial ATA sockets on its motherboard. At this point, it's anyone's guess whether Serial ATA will roll over the market or turn into another dodo.

SCSI interface

The *SCSI* interface (pronounced *scuzzy*) is for fast devices such as high-performance disk drives and tape drives. It is used for both internal and external devices, although USB and FireWire (see the following two sections) have largely taken over external connections.

Very few Windows computers have a SCSI controller built in. A controller must be installed in one of the slots on the computer's motherboard. Here's the reason why: Although SCSI is theoretically faster than EIDE, in practice very few people recognize much of a speed improvement when moving "up" from EIDE to SCSI. But SCSI is almost always (and sometimes quite considerably) more expensive than EIDE. Unless you have a crying need for SCSI speed, stick with EIDE.

USB interface

The *USB interface* ranks as the closest you can get to a universal controller. The original USB 1.0/1.1 was slow as a slug, but USB 2.0 (also known as "hi-speed USB") runs at 480 megabits per second — which is as fast as most of the connections *inside* your computer. All modern Windows computers have a built-in USB controller, and any PC made in the past couple of years has USB 2.0.

The latest versions of Windows XP contain rock-solid USB drivers: If you're having trouble getting USB to work on your computer, update Windows!

If you get a new computer, it will undoubtedly include a couple of USB 2.0 slots. But if you have an older computer, how can you tell if you have USB 1.1 or USB 2.0? It's easy — if you know the trick:

1. **Click Start, right-click on My Computer, and choose Properties.**
2. **Click the Hardware tab.**

   Windows XP shows you the System Properties dialog box shown in Figure 1-1.
3. **Click the Device Manager button.**

   Windows XP shows you a list of all the devices on your system, as shown in Figure 1-2.
4. **At the bottom of the device list, click the + sign next to Universal Serial Bus Controllers.**

   Look for the word "Enhanced." USB 2.0 controllers are called "Enhanced controllers." If you can't find the word *Enhanced* (as is the case in Figure 1-2), you have an older USB controller — most likely USB 1.1 (USB 1.0 is quite uncommon).

5. **Click the X (Close) button in the upper-right corner of the Device Manager window to close it, and then click Cancel to get out of the System Properties dialog box.**

Figure 1-1: To find out if you have USB 1.1 or 2.0, look in the Device Manager.

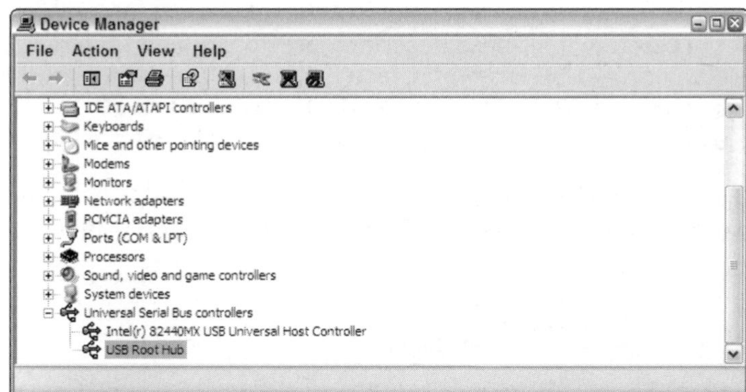

Figure 1-2: This USB controller is not USB 2.0 — it's an older USB 1.1.

There's no problem at all plugging USB 1.1 devices (such as a printer or a scanner or a camera) into USB 2.0 ports: The devices just go at the slow USB 1.1 rate. On rare occasion, you may have trouble with a USB 2.0 device plugged into a USB 1.1 slot. If that happens to you, and you can't get your computer to recognize the USB 2.0 device, take the device back to the store and get a refund. Life's too short.

The USB interface is used only for external devices. It is the most flexible interface for such devices, and the easiest to use. You can plug in or remove a USB device without restarting your computer: Just click the icon in the system tray (down near the clock) that says Safely Remove Hardware. Windows XP simply notices the device's presence or absence and adjusts itself accordingly. You can't do that with most other types of interfaces. In fact, you may damage the device or your computer if you try.

FireWire/1394

FireWire slots — sometimes called "1394" slots because they're based on a standard number IEEE 1394 — used to look like the wave of the future. With the emergence of USB 2.0, though, few manufacturers do much with FireWire: It runs about the same speed as USB 2.0, it's Plug and Play like USB, but it doesn't appear that FireWire holds many advantages over USB 2.0.

FireWire grew up around the camera/video industry, and that appears to be the extent of its support, although you'll find it in widespread use on Macs. You may find yourself someday with a digital video camera or digital camcorder that demands FireWire. If so, you can buy a FireWire-to-USB 2.0 converter box that should solve the problem.

Serial and parallel external interfaces

These two types of external interfaces are used mainly for printers, scanners, and external dial-up modems. Both of them are much older than the other types of external interfaces described previously, and they're becoming much less common — USB is simpler, faster, cheaper, and better. Parallel interfaces are 25-pin plugs, typically used to attach a printer to a PC. Serial interfaces are 9-pin plugs; you frequently see them used with external dial-up modems.

Almost all Windows computers have a parallel interface (good for one device), and most have one or two serial interfaces (good for one device each).

Upgrading the Basic Stuff

You probably have a printer, but it may not suit your needs — heck, photo-quality printers are so good nowadays that I'm frequently tempted to throw my old printer out the window. Your monitor may have died — or you might've fallen in love with that gorgeous 21-inch flat hussy at your local Comput-O-Rama. Perhaps that giant 20GB hard drive that you bought two years ago doesn't look so gigantic anymore — particularly since the kids discovered how easy it is to transfer pictures taken on the digital camera.

Be of good cheer.

For the most part, basic upgrades under Windows XP go slick as can be.

Dealing with drivers

Most types of devices raise the question of compatibility: Will this gadget work with Windows XP? You can dissect that question a thousand different ways, but the real acid test is a simple one: Is a good driver available for the hardware? (A *driver* is a program that allows Windows XP to interact with the hardware.)

In most cases, the answer is yes simply because Microsoft now hounds hardware manufacturers who have the temerity to distribute bad drivers. (Video board manufacturers seem to be immune to this rule, however — I *still* have no end of trouble with video drivers.)

A high-level 'Softie I know once told me that 50 percent of all the tech support calls Microsoft had to answer dealt with bad drivers. That's powerful incentive — and the main reason why Windows XP wants to "phone home" when it crashes (see the following figure).

Most Windows XP crashes, and a big part of Microsoft Product Support's workload, stems from bad device drivers — which Microsoft didn't write!

Hard as it may be to believe, that new piece of hardware you just bought may require no driver at all because its interface to the computer is completely standardized, so that Windows XP can operate any device of the same type. Most (but not all!) keyboards, monitors, and mice work like that. Any such device may have unique features that are available only with an appropriate driver, though.

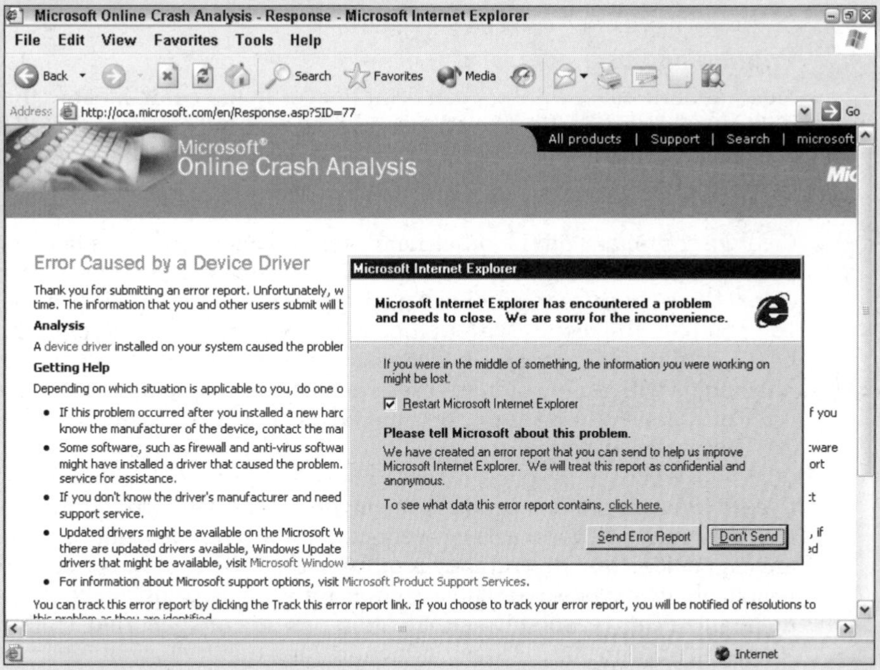

Evaluating printers

Most modern printers come in one of two types:

- **Inkjet printers:** These work by spraying tiny droplets of ink on paper. Inkjet printers tend to be small, light, and inexpensive. They make less noise than laser printers and consume far less power. Photo-quality printers need expensive paper, but they produce pictures that rival quickie photo labs.
- **Laser printers:** These work by fusing powdered toner onto the paper, essentially the same way a photocopier works. Laser printers tend to be larger and heavier than their inkjet cousins, and they cost more too. On the other hand, laser printers tend to be faster than inkjet printers, and any laser printer worth its salt produces much sharper results than an inkjet, at least on normal paper.

Choosing between inkjet and laser would be a reasonably simple chore, if it weren't for one big, fat variable: the cost of consumables.

Inkjet ink costs considerably more per page than laser toner does. This can make an inkjet printer cost more than a laser printer when you consider the cost of supplies over time.

Printing photos

Most modern inkjet printers can print images in full color. Most of them print photographs well, and some are designed specifically for that task. They're cheap to buy (but not so cheap to run — color ink cartridges cost a fortune!), and easy to use.

Color laser printers, on the other hand, are still expensive. The laser printing process does not deal well with areas of even tone or subtle variations in color. A few color laser printers claim to produce photo-quality output, but if you compare the results with that of an inkjet photo printer, you're bound to be disappointed. The majority of color lasers are intended only for printing documents with solid-color features such as headings and charts. Like other laser printers, color laser printers are faster than color inkjet printers and are cheaper to operate.

Dye sublimation printers produce the highest-quality photographic output, yielding results as good as a conventional photographic print or better. They are expensive, though, and they require special paper and dye/ink, both of which are also expensive. The materials for a single print can cost several dollars. For this reason, dye sublimation printers are generally suitable only for photo printing, or for low-production, high-quality brochures and the like, not for general printing.

Considering multifunction devices

Several companies sell *multifunction devices* that can do two or more functions, such as printing, photocopying, faxing, and scanning.

A multifunction device saves space and usually costs less than several separate devices. On the other hand, it is a compromise; it can't be designed to perform any of its functions as well as a single-purpose device would. Also, you must deal with the inconvenience of not being able to use more than one of the device's functions at a time, and you run the risk that a breakdown will take away your ability to do several things.

A multifunction device can be a real convenience if you use each of its functions lightly. If you use one function frequently, you're better off buying a dedicated device to perform that function. On the other hand, if you need to print, copy, and scan, getting one machine to cover all the bases makes a great deal of sense.

Exploring exotic features

You can get printers that accept paper up to 11 inches wide. Wide-carriage inkjet printers cost a few hundred dollars extra; wide-format laser printers cost a thousand dollars or more extra. Even larger format printers are available from specialized suppliers (at specialized prices).

Many laser printers and some inkjet printers can print a page and then turn it over and print the other side. This is called *duplex printing.* It's a valuable feature if you print proposals or reports whose appearance is important, or if you mail a lot of documents and would like to save postage by reducing weight.

Some applications, notably Microsoft Word, include rudimentary support for duplex printing on a standard printer — if you don't mind taking a stack of printed pages out of the printer, flipping it over, and feeding it back in. The trick lies in figuring out which pages to print first (odd or even), whether they should be printed in normal order (pages 1, 3, 5, and so on) or reverse order (pages 5, 3, 1), and exactly how the stack needs to be flipped (face up, face down, rotated or not). With a bit of experimenting and a bit of time spent on the File➪Print dialog box (see Figure 1-3), you can undoubtedly coax your standard printer into doing duplex.

An almost endless list of printers exists to meet specialized needs. For example, banner printers print on wide rolls of paper; drafting printers can print architectural drawings and similar documents on paper up to several feet wide; label printers can produce mailing labels one at a time; and more. If you need something unusual, look for it on the Web or ask people who deal with equipment for your business or hobby. Chances are that if you can imagine a printer with some specialized feature, somebody sells one.

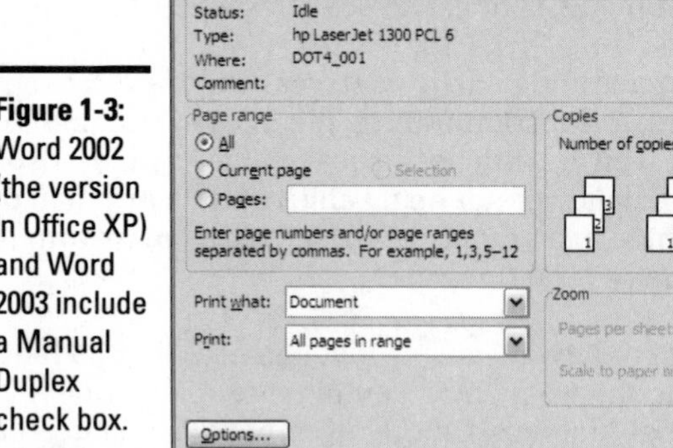

Figure 1-3: Word 2002 (the version in Office XP) and Word 2003 include a Manual Duplex check box.

Making a final decision

After a lot of years advising people and companies about printers, I've come to a handful of very simple conclusions:

- ✦ If you don't print a lot, get a good color inkjet printer from one of the major manufacturers. You won't go wrong with any of them.
- ✦ If you do print a lot — say, more than a dozen pages a day — get a laser. It costs less in the long run, although the initial expense is higher. For the occasional color print, find a company nearby that lets you run your pictures through their color inkjet.
- ✦ If you really, really need a color laser (or dye sub) printer, you'll know it as soon as you see a printout. Do the math, and hold onto your pocketbook.
- ✦ If you need to print color *and* a lot of black-and-white documents, consider getting both an inkjet printer and a laser printer. The laser printer still can pay for itself, and you won't have to compromise the quality of one type of output in order to get both.

No matter what you do, go with USB (unless you need to plug a very high volume printer directly into your network hub). USB is faster, cheaper, and easier to use than any other alternative.

Choosing a new monitor

Once upon a time, CRT (cathode ray tube) screens ruled the roost: They were hot enough to fry an egg; prone to flicker and wavy lines; and the big ones weighed as much as an elephant. A big elephant. Nowadays, CRTs have one big advantage over flat-panel *LCD* (liquid crystal display) screens: They're cheap.

Evaluating CRT versus flat-panel monitors

Flat-panel LCD displays, the kind you see on laptop computers, have become more popular than desktop CRT monitors in the last few years. They have several inherent advantages over conventional CRT monitors:

- ✦ With no bulky CRT inside, they are much lighter and occupy less space.
- ✦ They use less power.
- ✦ The image is very sharp, straight lines always look perfectly straight, and color convergence is perfect.
- ✦ Because their images persist longer than those of a CRT, they don't flicker.

They also have some disadvantages, many of which aren't obvious at first blush:

- ✦ Although the prices keep coming down, LCD monitors cost considerably more than comparable CRT monitors, and the price discrepancy will probably be with us for a long time to come.
- ✦ Few LCDs have screens larger than 17 inches or resolutions greater than 1280 x 1024 (for details on screen resolution, see the next section). Bigger screens cost a lot more.
- ✦ If you play games or work with fast-moving images, make sure that you can put up with a specific LCD's refresh rate before you buy it. LCDs are notorious for not keeping pace with some games, turning crisp images of, oh, smashing taxi cabs into mushy blobs of smashing taxi cabs. Come to think of it, maybe there isn't all that much difference.
- ✦ The manufacturing process frequently produces screens with *dead pixels.* A dead pixel shows up as a black spot (or some other nonmatching color) in the image. Most manufacturers consider an LCD display functional if it has no more than three dead pixels, but a single dead pixel may drive you crazy, especially if it sits near the middle of the screen. If you look at a screen and immediately notice its dead pixel(s), pass it by.

  If you buy a flat-panel monitor and one or two or three pixels suddenly die, you can do precious little about it.
- ✦ An LCD can be difficult to read from certain angles, particularly far off the screen's axis. This can be a problem if several people have to watch the computer screen at once.
- ✦ LCDs tend to reproduce colors less accurately than CRTs, which makes them less suitable for working on photographs and movies.
- ✦ The longer image persistence that makes LCDs flicker-free has a down side: If you use applications that produce rapidly moving images, such as games and Windows Movie Maker, the movement tends to blur.

Digital Video Interface

CRT monitors live in an analog world: They're controlled by signals that vary in strength, much as a television attached to a Nintendo gets driven by three cables controlling the Red, Green, and Blue colors.

LCD monitors, on the other hand, are all digital, all the time. Internally, they control each dot on the screen with 1s and 0s, on and off, just like your computer.

The video card was invented specifically because the bits inside your computer needed to drive an analog monitor. The video card translated 1s and 0s inside the computer into varying-intensity red, green, and blue dots on the screen. In short, video cards served as digital-to-analog converters, feeding signals to CRT monitors.

Times have changed. It doesn't make any sense at all for the video card to translate bits into an analog signal, only to have an LCD monitor translate the analog signal back into bits. That's the crux of the Digital Video Interface plugs: Eliminate the video card middleman.

More and more LCD monitors come equipped with DVI plugs. More and more video cards come equipped with DVI ports. Unlike the old D-shaped VGA plugs, which have 15 round pins arranged in 3 rows of 5 each, the much larger and more rectangular DVI plugs have a single flat pin and (usually) 24 round ones, in an asymmetrical pattern.

If you have a choice, go with DVI. It's faster, more reliable — and the pins are less likely to get crunched when your ham-fisted cousin starts switching around monitors.

Picking the right screen size

The most obvious characteristic of a monitor is its screen size. Standard CRT monitors are made with screens that are nominally 15, 17, 18, 19, and 21 inches across the diagonal. Flat-panel LCD screens are generally available in (nominal) 15 and 17 inches, with 19, 20, 21, and sky's-the-limit sizes for a pretty penny more.

Manufacturers of standard CRT monitors (and television sets, for that matter) have a funny way of measuring the diagonal size of the screen — they frequently measure the size of the CRT itself, without regard to the fact that some of the screen is hidden by the plastic case, and therefore can't be seen. On a standard CRT monitor, if you measure the diagonal of the visible screen, it's as much as an inch less than the rated size of the screen. Some manufacturers come clean and tell you the actual visible area. Far too many do not.

A monitor's maximum *resolution* is at least as important as its screen size.

Resolution is the number of image-forming dots, or *pixels,* that the monitor can display horizontally and vertically. Standard CRT screens can vary the number of pixels shown on-screen. Flat-panel displays cannot.

If you're working with flat-panel LCD screens, the resolution is fixed, typically at 1024 x 768 (for 15-inch screens) or 1280 x 1024 (for 17-inch screens). While it may be theoretically possible to change the resolution (from, say, 1024 x 768 down to 800 x 600), the results often leave much to be desired because the grid of dots in a flat-panel display is fixed — the modified screen resolution is a sleight of hand, performed by interpolating between dots on the grid.

Standard CRT monitors have specified maximum resolutions, advertised by the manufacturer. The following are typical:

- 1280 x 1024 for a 15, 17, or 18-inch monitor
- 1600 x 1200 for a 19-inch monitor
- 1600 x 1200 or 1800 x 1440 for a 21-inch monitor

Some, uh, Dummies think that screen resolution has something to do with how sharp a picture appears on the monitor. It doesn't. As the resolution increases, the amount of information shown on the screen increases. The picture itself may be sharp or fuzzy, depending on how well the monitor works — a good monitor shows a sharp picture at 1600 x 1200, for example, while a lousy monitor may be so fuzzy at 1024 x 768 that you're forced to run at 800 x 600.

I think the easiest way to understand the phenomenon is to consider the effect of screen resolution on a plain-vanilla Excel 2003 spreadsheet:

- At 800 x 600 resolution, you can see cells A1 through L25 — or 300 cells — on a completely virgin spreadsheet.
- At 1024 x 768, you can see cells A1 through O34, or a total of 510 cells. That's 70 percent more usable cells than at 800 x 600.
- At 1280 x 1024 — the practical limit for detailed text work on any standard CRT screen, and most flat-panel screens, unless your eyesight is a darn sight better than mine — Excel 2003 shows cells A1 through S50, for a grand total of 950 cells. That's 86 percent more cells than at 1024 x 768, and more than three times as many as at 800 x 600.

Although you probably won't spend most of your time sweating over thousand-cell spreadsheets, this little comparison combined with a lot of experience leads me to a few simple generalizations:

- Any monitor you buy nowadays (17-inch CRT monitor or 15-inch flat-panel) will handle 1024 x 768 resolution just fine. At 1024 x 768, you can see two-thirds of a page in Word or Excel. For most Windows users, that's good enough.

- Most 19-inch standard CRT monitors do well at 1280 x 1024. Flat-panel LCD monitors at 17 inches or larger run at 1280 x 1024, too. If you move up to 1280 x 1024, you can see almost an entire page in Word. In Excel, you almost double the number of cells that you can see in a spreadsheet, compared to 1024 x 768 resolution. Because of that, 1280 x 1024 makes sense for most people who use a monitor all day long.
- Resolutions above 1280 x 1024 come in handy if you commonly need to work on more than one Word document at a time or if you're struggling with really hairy spreadsheets. Unfortunately, the screens that can handle really high resolution (for ordinary eyes, anyway) tend to be quite expensive. Before you shell out the bucks to reach to the resolution stratosphere, make sure you try some real-live work on the monitor of your choice at the resolution of your choice, and let your eyes be the judge.

Fighting flicker

Some people can't stand screen flicker, no way, no how, especially under certain kinds of fluorescent lights. If screen flicker really bugs you, get a flat-screen LCD monitor. They don't flicker. End of story.

A standard CRT monitor's *refresh rate* is the number of times per second that it redraws the image on its screen. The refresh rate is measured in Hertz, abbreviated Hz, just like the frequency of a radio wave. At a refresh rate of 70 Hz, your monitor redraws the image 70 times per second.

No matter what kind of monitor you're considering, you have to ask yourself: Does anything about the monitor bother you, such as a shiny screen that casts reflections into your eyes? If you have niggling doubts now, they'll turn into major headaches (literally and figuratively) after you've spent a thousand or two hours in front of the beast.

If a CRT monitor's refresh rate is too low, the image flickers. Most people cease to notice flicker at about 72 Hz, but this can be influenced by the monitor's CRT (cathode ray tube, or picture tube), the ambient lighting, and the sensitivity of your eyes. A refresh rate of 75 Hz looks flicker-free to almost everybody, and higher rates generally give no advantage.

A standard CRT monitor's refresh rate is variable, just as its resolution is. The maximum refresh rate typically is lower at higher resolutions: You can run 80 Hz refresh at 1024 x 768 resolution, say, but only 72 Hz at 1280 x 1024. Before you buy a monitor, try it out at its highest resolution and see if the refresh rate is high enough to eliminate flicker. Be wary of really cheap monitors, which may have a maximum refresh rate as low as 60 Hz at their highest resolution.

Flat-panel refresh rates are often measured in milliseconds — a 30 ms refresh rate is pretty standard for an LCD screen. If you play games or watch movies (or other detailed animation) on your computer, though, you may want a faster screen: 16 ms seems to represent a decent compromise between price and blurs. But be aware of the fact that, with a flat-panel monitor, a good-quality picture and DVI connection are at least as important as fast refresh numbers, even for folks who have permanent joystick implants.

Resolution and refresh rate are both controlled by your computer's video adapter: Your monitor may be capable of 1280 x 1024 at 80 Hz, but your video adapter has to be able to pump out a signal at that rate. The monitor's specifications determine whether the monitor can display the image that the video adapter produces. Thus, if you upgrade your monitor, you may have to upgrade your video adapter to take advantage of your new monitor's capabilities.

Checking and setting the resolution and refresh rate

Fortunately, Windows enables you to easily check and set the resolution and refresh rate that your monitor uses:

1. **Right-click in any blank place on the Windows desktop and choose Properties.**

   Windows XP opens the Display Properties dialog box.

2. **Click the Settings tab.**

   Figure 1-4 shows this tab. The Screen Resolution slider shows the display's current resolution.

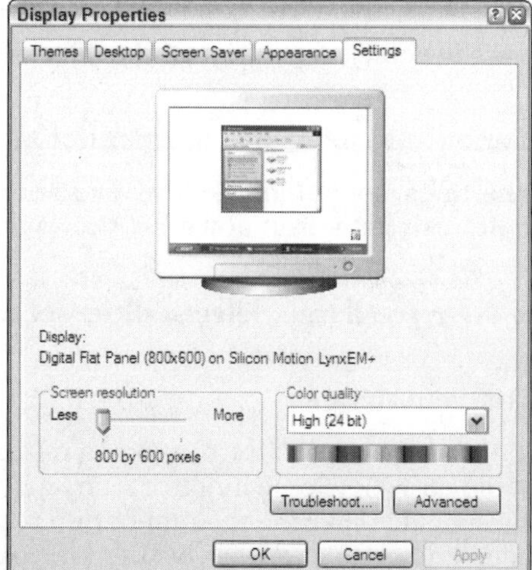

Figure 1-4: The Display Properties dialog box, Settings tab.

3. **If you want to change the resolution, move the slider to the setting you want. If you don't want to change the resolution, you may skip to Step 7.**
4. **Take a look at the Color Quality drop-down list.**

   If Windows XP set it to a lower value than you want when you moved the slider, you may have to upgrade or replace your display adapter. (See the section, "Picking a video adapter.")
5. **Click the Apply button.**

   Windows XP changes the display's resolution.
6. **If Windows XP opens a dialog box that asks if you want to keep the new settings, click Yes to keep the new settings or No to return to the old ones.**

   If the display disappears or becomes unreadable, press the Esc key to return to the old settings. (Or, if you wait 15 seconds, Windows XP returns to the old settings automatically.) This means that you chose a resolution that your monitor cannot display. You have to choose a lower resolution.
7. **When you're done, click OK to close the Properties dialog box.**

To check and set the refresh rate your monitor uses, follow these steps:

1. **Choose Start⇨Control Panel.**
2. **In the Control Panel, double-click Displays to open the Display Properties dialog box.**

   Equivalently, you can right-click in any blank place on the Windows desktop and choose Properties.
3. **Click the Settings tab.**

   Windows XP shows you the screen resolution and color depth, as shown in Figure 1-4.
4. **Click the Advanced button, and then click the Monitor tab.**

   You see your monitor settings, something like the ones shown in Figure 1-5. The Screen Refresh Rate drop-down list shows the display's current refresh rate.
5. **If you want to change the refresh rate, select a different rate and click Apply.**

   Windows XP changes the refresh rate.

   Make sure that you don't force the monitor to run at a refresh rate that's higher than the maximum allowed: Some monitors may get very upset and refuse to show anything if you swing the number up too high; older monitors have even been known to overheat. Make sure you don't go too far by either by selecting the Hide Modes That This Monitor Cannot Display check box or, if the check box is grayed out (as it is in Figure 1-6), by checking the documentation that came with your monitor to see what the manufacturer recommends for a maximum refresh rate. In any event, choosing a refresh rate that's lower than the one you're currently using won't hurt anything.

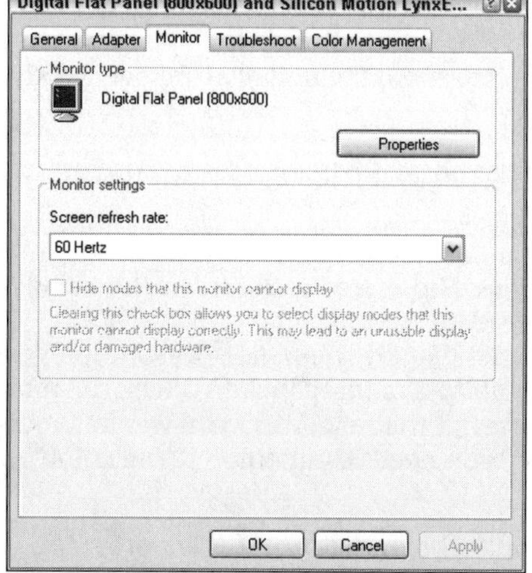

Figure 1-5: The Monitor and Graphics Card Property dialog box, Monitor tab.

6. **If Windows XP opens a dialog box that asks whether you want to keep the new settings, click Yes to keep the new refresh rate or No to return to the old one.**

   If the display disappears or becomes unreadable, press the Esc key to return to the old refresh rate (or wait for Windows XP to return automatically). This means that you chose a refresh rate that your monitor cannot display at the current resolution. You have to choose a lower refresh rate or a lower resolution.

7. **When you're done, click OK to close both properties dialog boxes and, if necessary, click the X (Close) button to get out of the Control Panel.**

Picking a video adapter

You may want to replace your video adapter card to get higher resolution and a higher refresh rate, better performance, or additional features. Some graphics cards promise faster rendering of three-dimensional objects in several popular games. Many graphics cards fail to live up to their promises.

Surprisingly, business users (which is to say, people who don't use their PCs for fast action games) may want to upgrade their video cards, particularly if they're still using the built-in on-board video that comes "free" with new computers. A decent video card — even a relatively cheap one — can make text look better and eliminate the distracting smears that frequently accompany scrolling through documents, e-mail messages, or spreadsheets.

To produce a display with a given combination of resolution and refresh rate (see the discussion in the preceding sections), both your monitor and your video adapter have to be up to the challenge. If you buy a monitor that can run at 1800 x 1600 with 92 Hz refresh, you may also have to buy a more capable video card to keep up with it.

Alternatively, you could consider refinancing a Third World country. This stuff doesn't come cheap, folks.

When you choose a new video adapter, consider the following points:

- Be sure that the card can display the highest resolution you want with a refresh rate high enough to eliminate flicker. Check the number of colors that the card can display at the resolution you want. If you work with video or photographs, you need 32-bit color ("true color") at the resolution you'll be working at.
- If your computer's motherboard has an AGP adapter slot, get an adapter with an AGP interface. (See the section, "Interfaces for adapter cards," earlier in this chapter.)

- If your monitor has a Digital Video Interface, get a video card with a DVI port. It's worth paying extra. Trust me.
- Get an adapter designed to perform well with the types of applications you run. If you play video games a lot, you should get a *3D adapter,* which has special hardware to display game images quickly; bonus points for an adapter with full DirectX support (that's the program inside Windows that makes video — and video games — run faster).
- If you want to watch TV on your computer, or use the computer to capture video from a TV signal or VCR, choose a card that supports TV input and output. (Generally you can use a USB port for copying pictures from a video camera; see Book VII, Chapter 2 for more information about video capture.) Many video board manufacturers have TV support that rivals Windows Media Center (see Book VIII).

  I've been particularly impressed by the ASUS line of video cards, which come with a very capable TV program, free, that's easier to use than Windows Media Center. See `http://usa.asus.com` for details.

In my experience, the single greatest source of frustration with Windows since its inception has been lousy video drivers. I've seen it happen year in and year out, in every version of Windows, with every video card manufacturer. Windows XP is no exception. Video card manufacturers take a long time to come out with decent drivers for their wares — and when they have a stable driver, the pressure to incorporate new features frequently leads to unstable newer versions. If you buy a new video card, make sure you check the manufacturer's Web site for the latest Windows XP driver prior to installing the card. And always keep your old video card, just in case the new one simply won't work.

Most video adapters have built-in *video memory,* which they use to hold the image displayed on the screen. Some adapters let you add more video memory to get higher resolutions with more colors. Check out this option before you replace your card. If you can reach your goal by adding video memory to your existing card, that can be a cheaper and easier way to go.

Getting enough memory (RAM)

Random Access Memory (RAM) is the type of memory that your computer uses to hold the programs it is running and the data they are working on. If a Windows XP system has too little RAM, it has to keep writing one piece of code or data to a *swap file* on your hard drive to make space to read in another. A little while later, it has to write something else to the swap file to make space to read the first item back in.

This situation can reduce your computer's overall performance, even to the point where the computer spends more time writing things to the swap file and reading them back than it spends doing useful work. Thus you may be able to increase your computer's performance by adding more RAM.

How much RAM you need depends on the types of applications you run, and to some extent on your working habits, such as how many different applications you tend to run at one time.

RAM is measured in *megabytes,* abbreviated MB. A megabyte is roughly a million bytes. A *kilobyte* (KB) is 1024 bytes. A *byte* is the basic unit of computer storage, commonly equated with one character, or eight bits. A *bit* is a one or a zero. If that has you confused, ask your eight-year-old niece. Trust me. She understands this stuff better than the guy at the computer shop.

As a rule, a Windows XP computer needs at least 128MB to run at all, particularly if you're using Microsoft Office. If you use more than one Office program at a time, or if you use Outlook in Office XP or Office 2003 (which automatically launches a hidden copy of Word), you need at least 256MB. Applications that work with graphics, such as movie editors and drawing programs, often require 256MB and do much better with 512MB.

To decide how much memory you need, look for recommendations in the documentation for the applications you run. Also observe your computer's behavior. If your computer tends to have fits of frantic disk activity while you're working with a file that's already open, more RAM may well be useful. The same is true if your computer uses the hard drive a lot when you switch from one open application to another.

Here's how to tell how much RAM your computer has now:

1. **Choose Start⇨Control Panel.**
2. **Click Performance and Maintenance and then click System.**

   Windows XP opens the System Properties dialog box.
3. **The General tab displays the amount of RAM in your system, as shown in Figure 1-6.**

Adding more RAM is reasonable if you just suspect you need it. RAM is not very expensive, and adding it can't hurt. If you do need it, it can help you a lot.

Different computers require different types of RAM. This is an issue of compatibility with the computer's motherboard, not with Windows XP. Be sure to buy memory that is compatible with your computer.

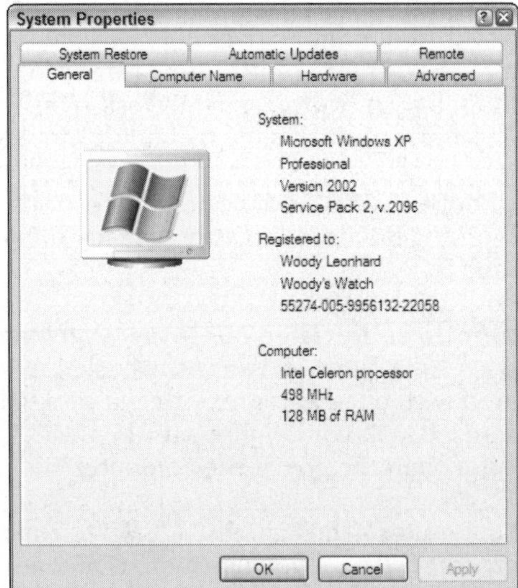

Figure 1-6: The System Properties dialog box displays the amount of RAM in your system.

Upgrading keyboards

Face it. The keyboard that came with your computer wouldn't even make a decent boat anchor. Don't get me wrong. Those mushy, squishy, tinker-toy keyboards would make fine Cracker Jack prizes, and casual computer users can get by with them for years. I wouldn't look down *my* nose at your flimsy, somnambulant, ludicrous excuse for a keyboard. Sniff.

Seriously, if you spend more than a few hours a day at the computer, you're probably wondering why your fingers hurt and why you make so many mistakes typing. There's a good reason why. That keyboard you're using probably cost a dollar. Maybe less. Getting a new one can make a big difference in how well you type and can speed up your computing enormously. You know. So you can get a life. . . .

Several companies now make *ergonomic* keyboards, which are contoured to let you type with your hands in a position that (supposedly) reduces the stress on them. These keyboards take some getting used to, but some users swear by them. Personally, I swear *at* them. You can get a wireless keyboard. You can also get a keyboard with a built-in pointing device to replace the mouse. Heck, you can probably get one that *looks* like Mickey Mouse.

If you're serious about replacing your tin-can keyboard, keep these points in mind:

- Look for a keyboard that feels right. Some folks like quiet keys. I like 'em loud. Some prefer keys with short throws — ones you don't have to push very far. I like long throws. Some prefer minimal tactile feedback — when you push the key, it doesn't push back. I like lots of tactile feedback. Most current keyboards have a row of function keys across the top. I like mine on the left. Everybody's different, and the only way you're going to find a keyboard that you like is to try dozens of them.

- If you've been using a "straight" keyboard, make sure you can get used to a split ergonomic keyboard before you buy one. I know a lot of people who have given up in disgust when their fingers couldn't adapt to the ergonomic split.
- Wireless keyboards have batteries that wear out. With regular wired keyboard, you don't have to worry about interference or blocked sensors. Sure, cables are ugly. But they're very reliable.
- Expensive keyboards aren't necessarily better than cheap ones. Big-name keyboards aren't necessarily better than generics.
- Heavy keyboards are better than light ones, unless you're going to schlep your keyboard with you on your travels through Asia. Heavy keyboards with rubber feet stay put.

What keyboard do I use? The Avant Stellar, `www.cvtinc.com`, which is surely the Sherman Tank of the keyboard biz. The beast weighs almost as much as a portable computer, and it costs just under two hundred bucks. It's ugly, it's retro, and it's decidedly un-hip. But it keeps goin' and goin' and goin' and goin'.

All keyboards designed for Windows computers are compatible with Windows XP. A keyboard may require a driver to operate its special features, though. Check its compatibility if this is a possible concern for you.

Choosing a mouse — or alternatives

Mice are probably available in more varieties than any other computer accessory. You can get mice with special ergonomic profiles, colored mice, transparent mice, special mice designed for kids, and on and on.

Optical mice now rule the roost. An *optical mouse* uses a light source and sensor to detect movement over a flat surface. It has no rolling ball to slip or stick, and it rarely needs to be cleaned. You may find this particularly helpful if you have furry pets, and your mouse tends to get clogged by their hair.

Some folks prefer a *trackball* to a mouse. A trackball is a stationary device with a large ball resting in a cup on the top. You operate it by turning the ball with your palm or thumb. I hate 'em.

Some folks like to use a *graphics tablet* instead of or in addition to a mouse. You control software with a graphics tablet by touching its surface with a special stylus. Unlike a mouse, the graphics tablet detects position, not motion, so you can literally point at the item you want. You can even write or draw with the stylus. Graphics tablets are popular with serious users of photo editors and other graphics software, and they're becoming more popular since Microsoft started producing "digital ink" programs like OneNote that can read what you write, to a first approximation anyway. Many of these applications have special graphics tablet support and can detect the amount of pressure you're applying to the stylus. Thus you can press hard to draw a wide line, for example, or lightly to draw a thin line.

Tablet PCs — the kind that are designed to be used with a stylus and (almost invariably) OneNote — aren't for everyone. Some people love them. Most people don't get used to them. I count myself among the latter. If you ever think about buying a Tablet PC specifically for its note-taking capabilities, try to borrow one for a day or two before you plunk down the cash. You may find that the reality doesn't live up to the glitz. Or you may find that you love it!

A *touchpad* is similar to a graphics tablet, but you control it with your fingertip instead of a stylus. You "click" by tapping the pad. A touchpad is very convenient for moving the pointer around the screen, but because most people's fingers are less pointy than a stylus, it's not very good for drawing or writing. Touchpads usually are just a few inches long and wide, and cost $20 to $50, whereas graphics tablets are larger and cost $100 or more.

Touchpads are available with a serial interface, a USB interface, or the funny round plug used by most keyboards and mice (called a *PS/2 connector*). You can also buy a keyboard that has a touchpad built in, and which needs only the keyboard's usual connector. And, of course, touchpads and belly buttons (er, pointer sticks) are common on notebook computers.

All mice designed for Windows computers are compatible with Windows XP. Specialized devices such as graphics tablets may require special drivers; make sure the device you buy is Windows XP compatible.

Adding storage devices

You can add several types of storage devices to your computer: hard drives, CD, and DVD drives, USB flash memory drives (or Memory Sticks, if you use a Sony product), other types of disk drives, memory card readers, and tape drives.

Choosing a second hard drive

All Windows XP computers have a hard drive, but you can add a second one if you need more storage space.

Hard drive capacity is measured in *gigabytes,* abbreviated GB. One gigabyte is 1,000 megabytes, or 1,000,000,000 bytes.

Once upon a time, removable storage was dominated by Zip disks and other contraptions with adapter kits that let you "plug in" a hard drive by sliding it into a slot in your computer's front panel. Fast USB has nearly made those beasts obsolete, although in a few cases *hot swappable* hard drives have their place.

Your second hard drive can go inside or outside your computer. Here's a quick guide:

- ✦ If you only need a gigabyte or so, don't get a hard drive. Look at USB flash drives or Memory Sticks (see the "Understanding flash memory and keydrives" section, later in this chapter). Also consider archiving your little-used data to CD or DVD (see the next section), or setting up a network and just transferring data you don't need very often to a different computer.
- ✦ If you decide to go with a second hard drive, get at least twice as much hard drive space as you think you'll need. If you're shooting and storing a lot of pictures and videos, get four times as much as you think you'll need.

- Don't overlook external hard drives. For a few dollars more, you can frequently get a drive that plugs into your USB port, runs almost as fast as a "normal" hard drive, requires basically zero effort to install — and it's completely portable. External hard drives have saved my tail more than once when my computer went belly-up and I needed to get at its data.

- There's always a "sweet spot" for hard drives, a point at which the cost per gigabyte is lowest. (The very largest hard drives always command a premium, and small hard drives don't give the best byte-fer-the-buck.) When comparing hard drives, always compare the cost per gigabyte, and go for the cheapest. Yes, I know the experts will tell you that the rotation speed is important, or rated Mean Time Between Failure rules, or that brand "X" is more reliable than brand "Y." In my experience, none of that really matters. Go for cheap.

It's also possible to replace your first hard drive with a larger one, but then you have to reinstall Windows XP, reinstall all of your applications, and transfer your data. (There are ways to transfer the operating system and applications intact, but they require special hardware or software.)

If you go with an internal hard drive, be sure to buy a hard drive with the same type of interface as the disk controller in your computer. For most current Windows computers, that means an EIDE interface.

Picking CD-RW or DVD-/+RW drives

If you don't have a CD or DVD writer, it's time you picked one up. I talk about CD-R and CD-RW in Book I, Chapter 6. DVD writing is a bit more complicated because of some conflicting standards, but these days almost all DVD burners support all the common formats. (See `www.pcmag.com/article2/0,1759,1592823,00.asp` for a good overview.)

If you're looking at buying a CD or DVD writer, keep these points in mind:

- DVDs hold six times as much data as CDs. Minimum. When you compare prices, keep that in mind — and also the fact that blank DVDs are considerably more expensive than blank CDs.
- DVD writers are much slower than CD writers, so it's going to take a long time to write all that data!
- CDs are almost universal: When you burn a CD, you can probably use it in just about any computer, and any modern CD player will play music on a burned CD. DVDs are a little more finicky. It may take a while to figure out just what kind of DVD you need to burn in order to get the right kind of DVD for a specific player.

✦ External CD and DVD writers (that is, writers that sit outside your main computer) with USB cables are almost always easy to install, and work with very few hassles. (See the "Installing New Hardware" section at the end of this chapter.) Given a choice, always go USB.

Don't take the speed ratings such as 64x, 8x, or 16x as gospel. They represent the maximum rotation speed of the drive in various modes (reading, writing, rewriting) compared to "1x" — the speed that audio CD players use — but there are no real standards in the industry, and what you see may not be what was promised.

Understanding flash memory and keydrives

Regular computer memory — RAM — needs a constant supply of power to keep going. *Flash memory* is a special kind of computer memory that doesn't self-destruct when the power goes out. Technically a type of EEPROM (Electronically Erasable Programmable Read Only Memory), flash memory comes in many different kinds of packages.

If you've spent any time with electronic cameras, you probably know about all about memory cards — SD (Secure Digital), CF (Compact Flash), and SM (Smart Media) cards — and if you've been around Sony equipment, you also know about Memory Sticks. All of them rely on flash memory.

For us computer types, flash memory comes in a little package — frequently the size and shape of half a pack of gum — with a USB connector on the end. You can call it a USB flash memory stick (that's my preference), a keydrive or a keychain drive (people really use them as keychains? I dunno — my favorite keychain looks like Watto from *Star Wars*), a pocket drive, a pen drive, a USB key, or a USB stick (that's what my cables do when they get old).

If you have your USB drivers up to date, here's how hard it is to use a USB flash memory stick:

1. **Plug the USB flash memory stick in a USB slot.**
2. **You're done.**

   The data on the drive looks like data on any other drive. Choose Start➪My Computer, and you can look at it. Or you can open a file on the stick with any program.

The salespeople would have you believe that it's cool to have color-coded sticks (I just put a sticker on mine), fancy encrypted memory (so if somebody steals the stick it takes him ten minutes to look at the data instead of ten seconds), designer outsides, and on and on. Here's what I say:

- Make sure you get USB 2.0 (or later) even if you don't think you need the transfer speed
- Buy twice the amount of memory that you think you need — you'll use it some day
- Go for price

If you need to read the other kinds of flash memory — memory cards, the kind normally used in cameras or MP3 players — buy a cheap generic USB multiformat memory card reader. Shouldn't set you back more than ten bucks, and they can come in very handy.

Backing up to tape

Tape is the medium of choice for backing up data on Web servers and other large computers. It's less popular on personal computers because tape drives tend to be expensive, but it has advantages that you shouldn't overlook. Tape is reliable, economical, and reusable, and it's the only backup medium with enough capacity to back up an entire hard drive at once — short of a second hard drive, anyway.

The low cost of tape makes it feasible to keep several generations of backups. If you need to refer to an old version of a file or recover a file that you deleted weeks or even months before, that can be a lifesaver.

When you choose a tape drive, look for one with enough capacity to back up your entire hard drive on one tape and enough speed to do it in a time that you consider reasonable.

As with disk drives, choose a tape drive with a type of interface that is appropriate for your computer. Drives are available with EIDE, USB, and SCSI interfaces.

If you decide to buy an external tape drive, your choice of interfaces is limited to USB and SCSI. There's a particular reason why you may prefer an external drive: If your computer needs repair, you can more easily move an external drive to a loaner system to restore your data and resume your work. Tape drives are not standardized, so you can't necessarily read your tape on any loaner that has a type drive — even assuming that you can find any loaner that has a tape drive!

Unlike the various types of disks, a tape drive must be read and written by a special utility program. Several software publishers sell such backup utilities. Check with a given utility's publisher for information about what devices it supports.

USB Hubs

Your Windows computer probably has two or four USB connectors, but you can attach many more USB devices to it than that. In theory, you can attach 127 USB devices to one computer. If you keep that many devices, you probably have no space left to sit down!

To attach additional devices, you need the USB equivalent of a power strip to turn one connector into several. That device is called a *USB hub.*

A USB hub has one USB connector to attach it to a computer and several connectors to attach it to devices. Hubs most often have either four or seven device connectors.

If you run out of USB ports, get a powered USB hub — one that draws electricity from a wall plug. That way, you protect against power drains on your computer's motherboard. If at all possible, plug your USB hub into a UPS so that a sudden loss of power doesn't cause a surge down the USB hub's power supply.

You can plug one USB hub into another — daisy chain them — to attach more devices than a single hub can support.

The maximum length of a USB cable is not precisely defined, but the figure of 5 meters (about 16 feet) is widely accepted. This is the maximum length of a cable from a computer or a hub to a hub or a device. The maximum total length between the computer and any device is about 25 meters or 80 feet.

Beefing Up Communication

No computer is an island unto its own. At least, not anymore. With Windows XP, you have no excuse to remain isolated. Networking is part and parcel of the eXPerience.

Establishing a network

The standard way to network several computers together is to put a network interface card, or *Ethernet adapter,* in each one. All of the Ethernet adapters are then cabled to a central *hub.* Other Ethernet-compatible devices, such as printers and high-speed modems, may also be attached to the hub — although you'll probably find it much easier to plug them into computers attached to the network.

If a network has only two devices, it doesn't need a hub; the devices may be connected directly to each other with a special cable, called a *cross-over LAN cable*. (The most common type of two-device system consists of one computer and one DSL or cable modem. See the "Running high-speed Internet access" section, later in this chapter.)

I talk about networking extensively in Book IX.

Wireless networking, commonly called Wi-Fi or 802.11g (or the older 802.11b), has finally come of age. With the latest Windows XP drivers, wireless networks almost always get up and going in a matter of minutes, and the signals hold up amazingly well, even through several layers of concrete walls. See Book IX for all you need to get going with wireless.

Many Ethernet adapters and hubs use a standard called *100BT* or *100BaseT* (pronounced *one hundred base T*), which theoretically can transfer data at 100 megabits (about 12 megabytes) of data per second (commonly abbreviated as 100 Mbps or 12 MBps). The latest Ethernet networks operate at gigabit, or even 10 gigabit speeds: One gigabit equals 1 Gbps, which is ten times faster than 100 Mbps. Realistically, networks never function at their fully rated speed, but some come close.

By contrast, older wireless networks work at 3 to 6 Mbps, and the new ones (the so-called 802.11g standard) go up to 100 Mbps. Wireless networks connect to hubs or routers — basically, radio receiving stations, which act like the base station of a portable phone — and the wireless base stations can, in turn, be plugged into Ethernet hubs.

Here's one way to put it in perspective. The text (not the pictures) of the 33-volume *Encyclopedia Britannica* would take

- ✦ A very long day to download over a fast dial-up modem. Maybe two, if your dial-up lines are as reliable as mine.
- ✦ 5 minutes to transmit over an older 802.11b wireless network.
- ✦ 30 seconds to go over a standard (100BaseT) Ethernet network, or a newer (802.11g) wireless network.
- ✦ 3 seconds to move over a gigabit network. Less than half a second on a 10 gigabit network. Or . . .
- ✦ About 200 years to print on my trusty little DeskJet.

That's a whole lotta data. You connect an Ethernet adapter to a nearby hub with a *LAN cable* that resembles the wire used to plug a telephone into the wall, although the LAN cable (called CAT-5) is thicker and the plugs on the end (called RJ-45) are wider. Over longer distances (up to 100 meters, or about 330 feet), you can use the same cable, but it needs to be installed with no kinks or bends — a job best left to an experienced CAT-5 or CAT-6 cable puller.

Ethernet networking is a mature technology, and the devices are highly standardized. With few exceptions, you can mix different brands of hardware without compatibility problems.

Running high-speed Internet access

If you use the Internet more than a few minutes a day, you really should look into getting a high speed line. Whether you go *DSL* (Digital Subscriber Line, which hooks into the telephone company's switches), *cable modem* (which uses the cable TV company's wire), or *satellite* (which bangs against that big bird in the sky), the difference in speed between a 56 Kbps dial-up connection and a 20-times-as-fast 1 Mbps broadband connection will leave your eyeballs flapping in their sockets. Run up to 6 Mbps and you may feel that you've found a new religion.

Which one should you get? Tough question — and there are no easy answers. But here's what I've found:

- ✦ There's very little difference, from a technical viewpoint, between DSL and cable. Both have pros and cons, and the effective transmission speed (typically measured in millions of bits per second, or Mbps) can be doubled or quadrupled at the provider's whim. The big differences that you need to take into account are the quality of the tech support from the company you choose and the net additional price, given what you already pay for cable TV or phone service.
- ✦ DSL and cable are (pretty much) weather-independent, but a bad rain or snowstorm will knock out satellite.
- ✦ If you play online games, you don't want a satellite connection. Although satellite can give you great "burst" data transfer speeds, and the scores on the speed tests look wonderful, the inherent time lag in getting a signal up to the satellite and back down again plays havoc on quick game moves.

Speeds, prices, and quality of service vary all over the place, and they change from week to week and city to city. Ask people you know and trust about the service, and check the newspaper ads for prices.

Upgrading Imaging

Windows XP includes many exciting new features that may lead you to install some new hardware that lets you capture and manipulate graphics.

Choosing a scanner

A scanner is a valuable accessory for many computer users. It works by scanning the image on a sheet of paper with a light sensor. The scanner then digitizes the image and transmits it to your computer.

You can use an image captured by a scanner in many ways: You can attach it to an e-mail message, include it in a document, publish it on a Web site, use it as a starting point for artwork, or print it for your daughter's Science Fair project.

Optical character recognition (OCR) software can "read" printed material from a scanner with some degree of accuracy and turn it into an editable document.

Scanners are available with USB, SCSI, and parallel interfaces. (See the section, "Choosing an interface," earlier in this chapter.) In most cases, the USB interface is preferred for its speed and ease of use.

Scanning paper items

Paper scanners for the consumer market fall into two categories. *Flatbed scanners* have a flat plate of glass covered by a hinged lid. You place the copy face down on the glass, close the lid, and the scanner moves the light sensor over the copy. *Path-through scanners* have a set of rollers that draws a sheet of copy past the sensor.

The two types of scanners cost about the same. Path-through scanners are more compact and convenient, but also more limited because they can scan only unbound sheets of paper. Flatbed scanners can handle books, magazines, and rigid material such as cardboard.

Most scanners do a creditable job of scanning black-and-white or color photographs or drawings as well as printed material.

A path-through scanner is sometimes called a *sheetfed scanner,* but that term also refers to a flatbed scanner with an automatic paper transport. The latter type is a relatively expensive gadget intended for high-volume work. There's an obvious potential for misunderstanding here.

Scanning photographic film

You can purchase an accessory for many flatbed scanners that enables you to scan photographic negatives and transparencies. This accessory goes by various names such as *transparency unit* or *transparency adapter*. Its essential purpose is to light negatives and transparencies from behind.

These units do an adequate job, but they have one big weakness: They can't increase a scanner's optical resolution. A resolution of 1200 DPI is plenty when you're scanning an 8½ x 11 inch page, but it doesn't go nearly as far when you're scanning a 1 x 1½ inch frame on a piece of film. If you enlarge that tiny image to a decent size, the results look pretty bad.

You have several solutions to this problem:

- ✦ If you expect to scan a lot of negatives and transparencies, buy a *film scanner* — a scanner designed just for this purpose. Film scanners have much higher optical resolution than flatbed scanners in the same price range.
- ✦ If you need high-quality photographic scans only occasionally, send your film out to a service bureau to be scanned.
- ✦ If you need occasional photographic scans and don't need really top quality, have prints made and scan the prints. That way you can do the job yourself without having to buy any additional gadgets.

Picking a digital or video camera

A digital camera captures images in electronic memory, from which you can transfer them to a computer. A digital video camera does the same thing for movies.

Digital cameras and digital video cameras are more convenient than conventional cameras because you can see their images without waiting for film processing. They are less expensive to use because they record on reusable media, and you don't have to pay for processing — but then again, the cost of batteries (if you don't quickly buy and use rechargeable batteries) can eat away at what you save on film.

An Internet camera, or *Webcam,* is a camera that connects directly to a computer and depends on computer processing to record an image. A computer can use one to capture either still pictures or video. Most Internet cameras use a USB interface.

I talk about digital cameras, video cameras, and Webcams in Book VII, Chapter 3.

Adding Audio

Windows XP's Media Player rocks 'n' rolls, but it doesn't do much unless your PC can play the tunes.

Choosing a sound card

A computer that can input and output sound has any number of interesting uses, such as

- ✦ Playing CDs and DVDs
- ✦ Recording and playing back music with Windows Media Player or other applications
- ✦ Recording, editing, and viewing movies with Windows Movie Maker or other applications
- ✦ Gaming
- ✦ Internet telephony (making telephone calls through the Internet) and teleconferencing
- ✦ Voice recognition (converting speech into text, as input to a word-processing application, for example)
- ✦ Composing electronic music

Many modern computers have sound hardware built into the motherboard. If your computer does not — or if the sound support on your motherboard makes Norah Jones sound like Fritz the Cat — you can add a sound card to bring your ears into the 22nd century. Here's what to look for:

- ✦ 5.1 channel surround sound. If you commonly play games that leave you on the edge of your seat, and you want to occasionally fall *off* your seat, go for 7.1 surround sound.
- ✦ For watching movies, get Dolby and THX certification.
- ✦ Full Windows Media 9 or 10 (or later) support.

The inside of a computer is a difficult place to process audio signals because it is awash with all sorts of electromagnetic signals. A sound card needs good shielding to avoid picking up noise. The card's *signal to noise ratio* (SNR) measures its noise immunity. An SNR of 70 dB is so-so. An SNR of 90 dB is quite good, and 100+ isn't, uh, unheard of.

When you price this stuff, remember that you're going to need good (if not particularly expensive) speakers, a subwoofer, possibly a control center, remote, and anything else that curls your toes. This stuff ain't cheap. So make sure you know what you're buying into when you get a good audio card. That said, even a cheap audio card from a major manufacturer can give you outstanding sound — much more than your current speakers can handle, guaranteed.

Voice recognition is a particularly demanding application. If you plan to use this type of software, you need a decent sound card and an excellent microphone. See the "Choosing a microphone" section, later in this chapter.

MIDI sound generation (a technology developed for synthesizing electronic music) used to be a big deal because many games used it to generate sound. Today, with CD-ROMs and big hard drives universally available, most games produce sound directly from digital soundtracks. MIDI is important only if you want to compose electronic music on your computer. In that case, look for a card with a large number of *voices;* that is, a card that can generate a large number of different sounds at the same time.

Hooking up speakers and headphones

To get sound out of your computer, you need either speakers or a set of headphones. Audiophiles spend a great deal of attention (and money) on these choices, but most folks do quite well with something considerably less, uh, precious. Here are a few pointers to help you choose something appropriate.

Decide how much quality you need. For casual gaming or music listening, almost any equipment will do. Yes, you can even haul out that old stereo and plug the "line out" output from your sound card into the AUX connector on the stereo. That's what I do on all my less-endowed systems.

If sound quality is important to you, you need to be more selective, and the inexpensive speakers packaged with many computer systems probably won't satisfy you.

Look for the following things in a good speaker system:

- **Broad, flat frequency response for reproducing high and low frequencies accurately.** (Your sound card must have a comparable response, or the best speakers in the world won't help!)
- **Low total harmonic distortion (THD).** If the THD figure is below 1 percent, you won't notice any distortion at all unless your hearing is unusually sensitive.
- **More than enough power to produce the amount of sound you want.** A healthy surplus of power lets you avoid turning the volume all the way up, minimizing distortion.
- **Magnetic shielding.** If you intend to place speakers near your CRT monitor, this prevents the speakers' magnets from distorting the monitor's image.

When you compare frequency response and harmonic distortion, try to get numbers from an impartial source — preferably all of the numbers from the same source. There are many ways to measure these things, so comparing measurements of different products that come from different places is not very useful.

A four-speaker or six-speaker system, augmented by a *subwoofer* (a separate speaker that reproduces very low frequencies), often called 5.1 or 7.1 surround sound, can give the sound a stronger feeling of coming from a particular place. Good games make extensive use of this. When a race car whizzes by on the screen, the game designers make sure that you can *hear* it coming up on your left and speeding away to your right.

Surround sound can also make a significant impact in rock music recordings and movies. For most other types of recordings, it makes less difference if it's used at all.

Headphones are a good alternative to speakers for some users. Not only do they let you enjoy your music without disturbing your friends and neighbors; they also let you get primo quality sound for a lot less money than a set of top-of-the-line speakers.

If you go with headphones, decide whether you want *open-back* headphones, which sit on your ears, or *closed-back* headphones, which enclose your ears in padded cups. Closed-back headphones shut out most ambient noise and tend to have better bass response, but they are heavier, and for some users, less comfortable. If you want surround sound, look for headphones that are closed-back.

Choosing a microphone

You need a microphone for Internet telephony, teleconferencing, or voice recognition software — software that translates what you say into the printed word.

Don't rush out and buy a voice recognition system just because a vendor (most especially Microsoft) tells you it's the best thing since sliced butter. While voice recognition has its niche uses — certainly many physically challenged people welcome it as a godsend, and for informal note-taking, it can work reasonably well — the fact remains that a 95 percent accuracy rate on voice recognition stinks. Why? Because you either have to send out a letter with loads of words misspelled (or a spreadsheet with one cell in five that's absolutely off the wall), or you have to spend loads of time correcting the stupid machine's errors. Usable voice recognition is still many years, possibly many decades, away.

For telephony or voice recognition, the distance from your mouth to the mike is crucial — varying the distance can screw up voice detection or make your phone conversations boom and peter out — so seriously consider buying a fairly expensive headphone/mike combination. It's the only way to maintain a consistent distance between your mouth and the mike.

Don't expect to find audiophile sound quality in a headset with a microphone. If you want that, buy one headset for listening to music and another for talking.

Picking a digital audio/video player

Call it an MP3 player if you like. Tack on a movie screen and call it a Portable Media Center. You can spend a pittance or a king's ransom, and the technology is changing at breathtaking pace.

When you choose a digital audio or video player, consider these factors:

- **What does it play?** If you're stuck with Microsoft-owned formats such as WMA (Windows Media Audio) and WMV (Windows Media Video), you have much less flexibility than you would with industry standards such as MP3 and MPG. If you can only play items downloaded from a single source, expect the price of downloads to escalate accordingly.
- **Total capacity:** How many hours of music or video does the player hold? At what level of quality?
- **Expansion:** Can you increase the player's capacity by adding a memory card? If so, what type of card? If you have other devices that use memory cards, does the player use the same type?
- **Convenience:** Is the player's design convenient for you? Can you understand the %$#@! controls? Some of these gizmos make the 747's cockpit control console look simple.
- **Features:** Does the player have any special features that you want?

Choosing a Personal Data Assistant

A *personal data assistant,* or PDA, is a small computer that runs on batteries and can be held in one hand.

PDAs come in two forms. One is small enough to fit in your pocket. You enter information by touching a stylus to the LCD display. This type of device typically can read handwritten printing, although you may have to learn a special stylized version of the alphabet to use it. You may be able to buy a separate compact keyboard for entering larger amounts of text.

The other type of PDA is larger and has a full keyboard. Typically, the keyboard is smaller than the standard size but is large enough to make touch typing possible, if a bit, uh, contorted.

You should view a PDA as an electronic device in its own right, not as a tiny, limited computer. From this point of view, the lack of a keyboard is not necessarily a great disadvantage. Your particular needs may make a device with a keyboard more useful than a device that fits in your pocket, though.

When you choose a PDA, consider these factors:

- ✦ Does it fit in a pocket or not? Does it have a keyboard or not? If not, do you need a plug-in keyboard, and can you add one?
- ✦ What applications are built in? What applications can you add?
- ✦ What operating system does it run?
  - Some PDAs run a version of Microsoft Windows called *Windows CE,* which runs special, highly stunted versions of applications such as Microsoft Word and Excel. These PDAs provide a familiar environment that is highly compatible with your Windows XP system. You can move Word and Excel documents from your computer to your PDA and back, although you lose a lot in the translation.
  - Other PDAs run an operating system designed for portable computing from the ground up, most often the *Palm OS* from Palm, Inc. These devices can run applications equivalent to Word and Excel, but the applications are different and their compatibility is more limited.
- ✦ What is the device's battery life?
- ✦ How much data can the device store? Does it have a slot for plugging in a memory card? If so, what type?
- ✦ What provisions does the device have for exchanging and synchronizing data with your Windows XP computer?
- ✦ What provisions does the device have for other types of communication? Does it have a built-in modem, or can you add a modem? What about wireless access?
- ✦ What special features or accessories do you need? Are they available?

Installing New Hardware

If you have a USB device — a printer, hard drive, scanner, camera, flash memory card, foot massager, water desalination plant, or demolition machine for a new intergalactic highway — just plug the device into a USB port, and you're ready to go.

Okay. I exaggerated a little bit.

Two fundamentally different approaches to installing new hardware exist. It amazes me that some people never even consider the possibility of doing it themselves, whereas other people wouldn't have the store install new hardware for them on a bet!

Have the store do it

When you buy a new hard drive or video card, or anything else that goes inside your computer, why sweat the installation? For a few extra bucks, most stores will install what they sell. This is the easy, safe way! Instead of messing around with unfamiliar gadgets, which may be complicated and delicate, let somebody experienced do the work for you.

Different types of hardware present different levels of difficulty. It may make plenty of sense for you to install one type of device but not another.

At one end of the scale, installing a new video card or hard drive can be rather difficult and is best done by an expert. At the other end, speakers don't need any installation; you just plug them in and they work. The store can show you where the connectors go, but you have to plug them in yourself when you get home.

Here are some guidelines to help you judge how difficult an installation is likely to be:

- ✦ Any device that goes inside your computer is best left to the store unless you have experience with that specific kind of computer hardware.
- ✦ Any device that has a SCSI interface is best left to the store.
- ✦ A device with a USB interface is usually easy; nine times out of ten, you just plug it in and it works.
- ✦ A device with a serial or parallel interface is likely to be in between.
- ✦ Most wireless networking systems nowadays go in with nary a hiccup.

A cable modem should be installed by the communication carrier's technician if at all possible. DSL modems are easier to install, but you have to know whether your phone line is ready. The modem just plugs in, but the telephone line or cable may require configuration or rewiring to deliver the signal properly.

If you're unsure whether to install something yourself, ask the store what's involved. If you decide to try it, but the instructions confuse you or scare you when you read them, don't be embarrassed to go back and ask for help.

I do.

Do it yourself

If you decide to install a device yourself, the job is more likely to go smoothly if you observe these guidelines:

- **Don't just dive in — read the instructions first!** Pay attention to any warnings they give. Look for steps where you may have trouble. Are any of the instructions unclear? Does the procedure require any software or parts that appear to be missing? Try to resolve these potential problems ahead of time.
- **Back up your system before you start.** It's unlikely that your attempt to install a new device will disturb your system if it fails, but a backup is a good insurance policy in case something bad happens. You need to back up your data files. Windows XP will create a system checkpoint and back up all the internal stuff.
- **Write down everything you do in case you need to undo it or ask for help.** This is particularly important if you're opening up your computer to install an internal device!
- **If the device comes with a Windows XP driver, check the manufacturer's Web site to see if you have the latest version.** A company usually keeps drivers in one or more Web pages that you can find by clicking a link for Drivers, Downloads, or Support. If you discover a version that is newer than the one packaged with the device, download it and install it instead.

If you can't tell whether the version on the Web site is newer because you can't tell what version came with the device, you have two choices:

- Download and install the Web site's version just in case. It's unlikely to be older than the one that came with the device!
- Install the one that came with the device. Then check its date and version number. (See the "Checking a driver's version" section, coming up next.) If the one on the Web site proves to be newer, download the newer one and install it. Read the instructions; you may need to uninstall the original driver first.

Checking a driver's version

To check the version number of a driver, follow these steps:

1. **Choose Start⇨Control Panel.**
2. **Click System.**

   Windows XP opens the System Properties dialog box.
3. **Click the Hardware tab.**

4. **Click the Device Manager button.**

   Windows XP opens the Device Manager window, as shown in Figure 1-7.

5. **Click the plus sign next to the heading that contains the device you want to check.**

   Windows XP expands that heading to show its devices, as shown in Figure 1-8.

   You may have to try several headings to find the right one. If you guess wrong, just click again to collapse the heading you expanded.

6. **Double-click the device to open the Device Properties dialog box.**
7. **Click the Driver tab to display details about the driver, as shown in Figure 1-9.**

   You should be able to identify the latest driver by its date, its version number, or both.

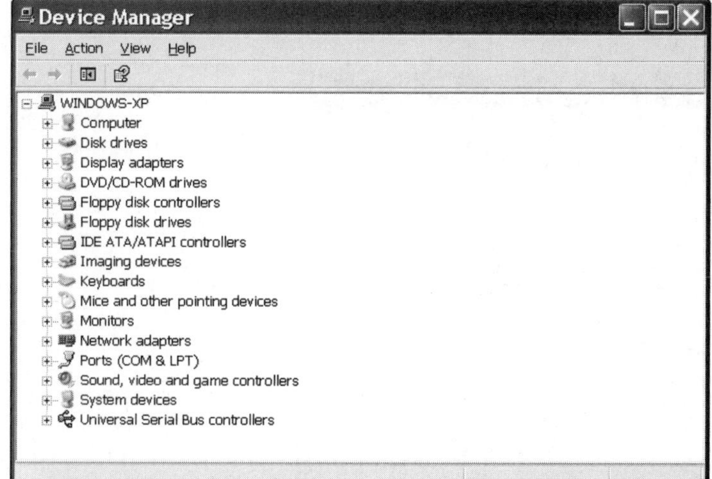

Figure 1-7: The Device Manager window.

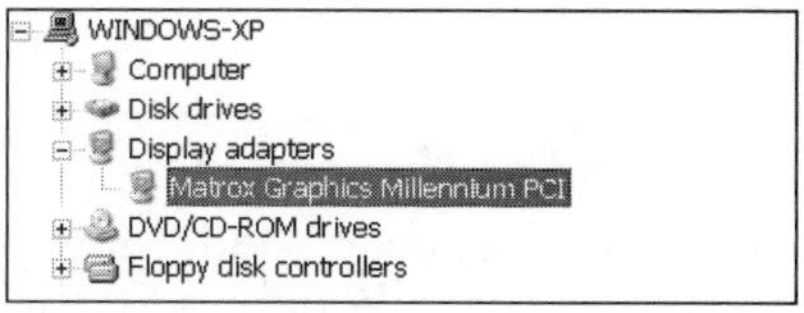

Figure 1-8: Click the plus sign to expand a heading.

If anything goes wrong

If your installation is unsuccessful, try these things in any order that makes sense to you:

- ✦ Review the instructions. Look for a section with a title such as "Troubleshooting" for suggestions on how to proceed.
- ✦ Call or e-mail the manufacturer's technical support service for help. The manual or the Web site will tell you how.
- ✦ Call the store, or pack everything up and take it in. If you happen to have a seven-foot-tall friend named Guido who drags his hairy knuckles on the ground, take him along with you. Moral support, eh?

If your computer no longer works correctly, restart Windows XP with the last known good configuration. (See the instructions in the next section.)

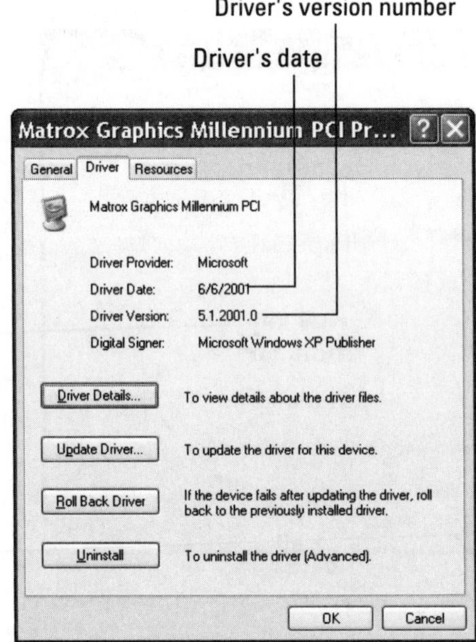

Figure 1-9: The Driver tab of the Device Properties dialog box.

Restarting with the last known good configuration

When you install a new device driver, you change Windows XP's *configuration*. The next time you restart your computer, Windows XP tries to use the new configuration. If it succeeds, it discards the old configuration and makes the new one current.

Sometimes you install a new device driver, and everything goes to heck in a handbasket. If that happens to you, you need to restart Windows XP and tell it to use the "last known good configuration" — which is to say, Windows should ignore the changes you made that screwed everything up and return to the state it was in the last time it started. That effectively removes the new driver from Windows XP.

To start Windows with the last known good configuration, follow these steps:

1. **If your computer is operating, choose Start⇨Turn Off Computer.**

   Windows XP opens the Turn Off Computer dialog box. Click the Restart button. Then skip to Step 3.

2. **If your computer isn't operating at all, press the power button to turn it off.**

   If that doesn't work, try pressing the button again and holding it in for several seconds. If that doesn't work either, pull the power cord out of the back of the computer; wait a few seconds, and then plug it in again. If you're working with a portable, you may have to remove the battery. Yes, it happens.

   Press the power button again to turn the computer back on.

3. **Watch the display while your computer restarts. When the message** `Please select the operating system to start` **appears, press F8.**

   Windows XP displays a menu of special start-up options that you can choose.

4. **Use the up-arrow and down-arrow keys to move the menu's highlight to Last Known Good Configuration, and then press Enter.**
5. **Finish the start-up procedure as usual.**

If this procedure restarts your computer successfully, Windows XP discards the "new" screwed-up configuration and returns permanently to the last known good configuration.

Installing USB hardware

Nine times out of ten, when you install a new USB device in a Windows XP computer that has all the latest fixes, everything works easily. The general procedure

1. **Read the manual.**

   Some hardware installs automatically: Plug it in, and it works. Most hardware needs a little help: You have to put a CD in the CD drive shortly after you plug it in, and let Windows pull the driver off the CD. Some hardware, though, takes a little extra help, and you have to run an installation program on the product's CD before you plug it in.

The only way to know for sure which approach works for the specific piece of hardware that you bought is to read the furshlinger manual! Look for the section with instructions on installing the hardware on a Windows XP computer. Follow the instructions.

2. **After you've read the manual and done what it says, plug the USB device into any handy USB slot.**

   Windows realizes that you've just installed a new USB device, and cranks up the Found New Hardware Wizard (see Figure 1-10).

Figure 1-10: Windows found your USB device.

3. **Select Yes, This Time Only radio button to let Microsoft see if it has a new driver for the hardware, and then click Next.**
4. **Follow the rest of the steps in the wizard, and at least nine times out of ten, you'll end up with a functioning device.**
5. **If you can't get the device working, check Microsoft's Knowledge Base article for troubleshooting USB devices.**

   It's at `http://support.microsoft.com/?kbid=310575`.

Chapter 2: Working with Printers

In This Chapter

- Attaching a new printer to your PC or network
- Choosing the default printer
- Solving out print queue problems
- Troubleshooting other problems with printers

Ah, the paperless office. What a wonderful concept! No more file cabinets bulging with misfiled flotsam. No more hernias hauling cartons of copy paper, dumping the sheets 500 at a time into a thankless plastic maw. No more trees dying in agony, relinquishing their last gasps to provide pulp as a substrate for heat-fused carbon toner. No more coffee-stained reports. No more paper cuts.

No more . . . oh, who the heck am I trying to kid? No way.

Industry prognosticators have been telling us for more than a decade that the paperless office is right around the corner. Yeah, sure. Maybe around your corner. Around my corner, I predict that PC printers will disappear about the same time that *Star Trek* reruns go off the air. We're talking geologic time here, folks.

Windows XP has great printer support. It's easy once you grasp a few basic skills. (For information about choosing a printer, see Book VI, Chapter 1.)

Installing a Printer

You have three ways to make a printer available to your computer:

- ✦ You can attach it directly to the computer.
- ✦ You can connect your computer to a network and attach the printer to another computer on the same network.
- ✦ You can connect your computer to a network and attach the printer directly to the network's hub.

Connecting a computer directly to a network hub isn't difficult, if you have the right hardware. Each printer controller is different, though, so you have to follow the manufacturer's instructions.

At the time this book was written, a fourth method of attaching a printer to your PC was starting to emerge from the primordial Windows ooze. It involves printing directly over the Internet, to a printer attached to the Internet. As you may imagine, there are a few, uh, logistical problems with this approach — I mean, if you think you get junk faxes now, wait till the spammers figure out how to shanghai your office printer to the tune of 40 pages per minute! Still, the technology may take hold, and you should keep your ear to the ground for it.

Attaching a local printer

So you have a new printer, and you want to use it. Attaching it locally — which is to say, plugging it in directly to your PC — is the simplest way to install a printer, and the only option if you haven't got a network.

First, physically connect the printer to your computer. If the printer uses a USB connector, simply plug the connector into your PC's USB port. If the printer uses a serial or parallel connector, turn your computer off, plug in the connector, and turn the computer back on.

After you connect your printer to the computer, you must make Windows XP recognize it. This is what "installing the printer" means.

If you have a USB printer, Windows XP will almost always detect it and install it automatically when you turn the printer on. You may need to put the CD that came with the printer in the CD drive — but then again, you should probably check and see if there's a newer driver available for the printer. Table 2-1 has the Web addresses you should visit to search for new printer drivers. You're welcome.

Table 2-1 Driver Sites for the Major Printer Manufacturers

Printer Manufacturer	*Find Drivers at This URL*
Brother	`www.brother.com/E-ftp/info/index.html`
Canon	`www.usa.canon.com/html/conCprSupport.jsp?type=xp`
Dell	`http://support.dell.com/filelib/criteria.aspx?c=us`
Epson	`www.epson.com/cgi-bin/Store/support/SupportIndex.jsp`
HP	`http://welcome.hp.com/country/us/en/support.html`
Lexmark	`http://support.lexmark.com/cgi-perl/selections.cgi`

If you have a parallel or serial printer — one that connects with a large D-shaped plug to your computer — Windows XP may detect and install it automatically when you restart the computer. If that doesn't happen, you have to haul out the big guns.

If you have a printer that lets you choose between USB and parallel connections, always use the USB connection, even if you have to buy a USB hub to get another USB port (see Book VI, Chapter 1). USB is faster, easier to set up, and easier to maintain than a parallel port connection.

Use this procedure to install a parallel or serial printer:

1. **Click Start. If you see an entry on the right that says Printers and Faxes, click on it. If you don't see a Printers and Faxes entry, click Control Panel⇨Printers and Other Hardware⇨Printers and Faxes.**

   No matter how far you have to travel, Windows ends up in the Printers and Faxes dialog box shown in Figure 2-1.

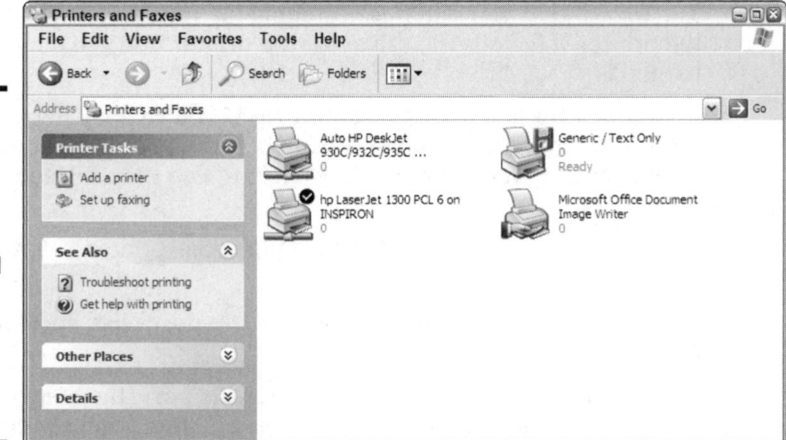

Figure 2-1: A typical network containing two real printers and two ersatz "printers" installed by Microsoft Office.

2. **In the Printer Tasks list, click Add a Printer.**

   This starts the Add Printer Wizard and displays a Welcome page.

3. **Click Next.**

   The wizard displays the page shown in Figure 2-2. Select the Local Printer Attached to This Computer radio button.

   All USB printers are Plug and Play. Serial and parallel interface printers generally are not, although the printer's documentation may claim otherwise.

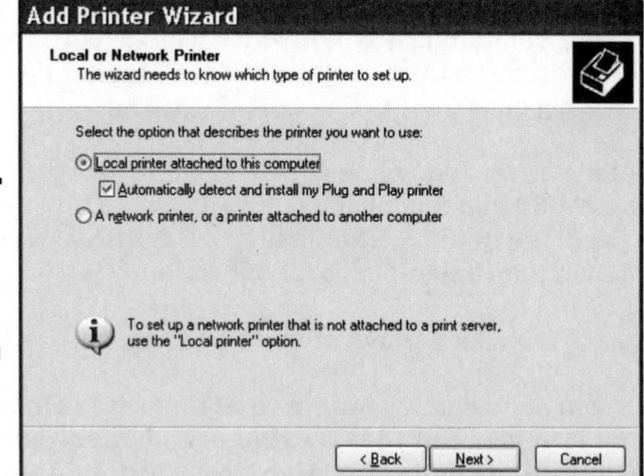

Figure 2-2: The Add Printer Wizard asks if you have a local or network printer.

4. **If you have a Plug and Play printer, select the Automatically Detect and Install My Plug and Play Printer check box and click Next.**

   The wizard tells you that it is searching for your printer. When it finds the printer, it installs the driver for the printer. You can jump all the way to Step 9.

5. **If your printer is not Plug and Play (or if you're back here because Windows XP couldn't automatically identify your printer), clear the Automatically Detect and Install My Plug and Play Printer check box. Click Next.**

   Windows asks you to identify which port your printer is connected to (see Figure 2-3).

6. **Select the appropriate port from the drop-down list, and then click Next.**

   Most Windows computers have one parallel port (the long oval one) and one or two serial ports (short oval ones). If your printer is connected to a parallel port, it is almost undoubtedly connected to the port named LPT1. If it is connected to a serial port, you must determine whether it is connected to the port named COM1 or COM2. The back of your computer may be stamped or etched with the names of the serial ports, but if you can't tell, tell the wizard that it's connected to COM1. If that doesn't work, shut down your computer, turn it off, and move the cable to the other serial port connector. Then you know it's in COM1. Probably.

7. **The wizard displays a page that prompts you to select your printer's brand and model, as shown in Figure 2-4. Select the brand and the model, and then click Next.**

If your printer's brand and model aren't in the lists, you can still install your printer if you have a diskette or CD-ROM with a Windows XP driver for it or if you can snag the driver on the printer manufacturer's Web site (see Table 2-1). Click the Have Disk button and follow the wizard's prompts.

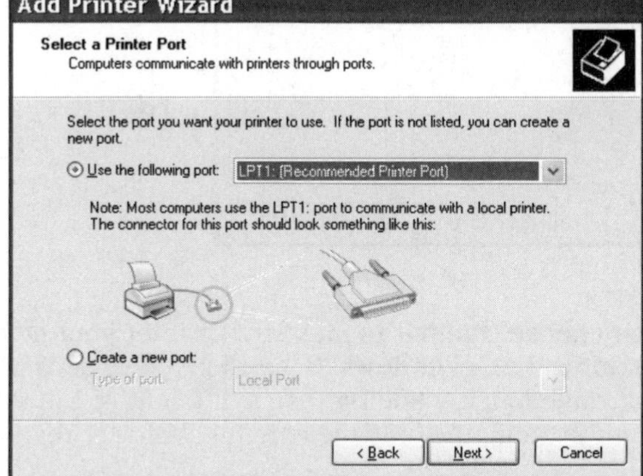

Figure 2-3: The Add Printer Wizard wants you to select a printer port.

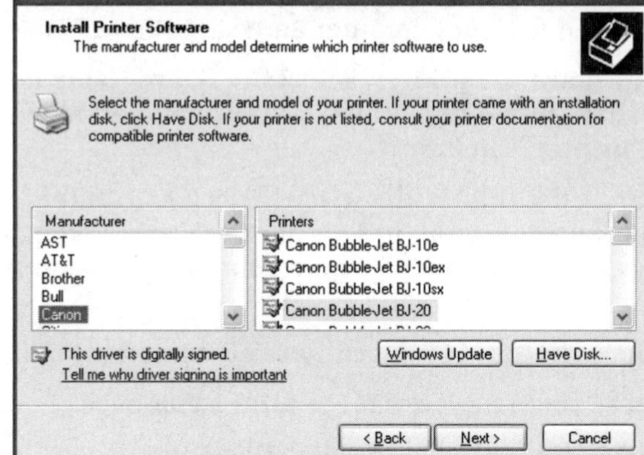

Figure 2-4: Tell the Add Printer Wizard to install the printer software.

8. **The wizard prompts you to enter a name that Windows XP may use to identify this printer (see Figure 2-5). Accept the default name or enter another name that is short but meaningful to you.**

Short printer names (such as LJ4 or DJ930C) are easier to remember and harder to mistype.

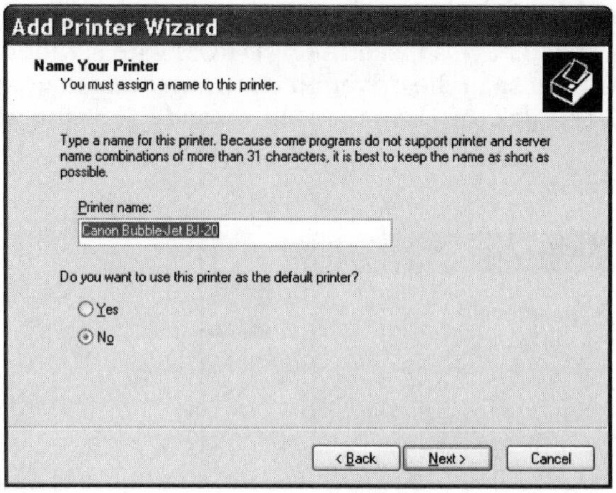

Figure 2-5: Give your printer a name in the Add Printer Wizard.

You also must choose whether to make this printer your *default printer* — that is, the printer that a Windows XP application uses to print documents unless you explicitly tell it to use a different one. If this is the only printer on your system, the only meaningful choice is Yes.

If your computer is attached to a network and you have configured a network with the Home Networking wizard, the wizard asks whether you want to share the printer, as shown in Figure 2-6. *Sharing the printer* means that users of other computers on the network can see that this printer is attached to your computer and can print documents on it.

9. **If you want to share the printer, select the Share Name radio button and enter a share name that other network computers may use to identify this printer. Click Next.**

   If you are sharing the printer, the wizard asks you to enter the printer's location and comments about it. This information is optional, but it helps other network users understand where your printer is and how it ought to be used.

10. **Enter the appropriate printer location and comments and click Next.**

    The wizard asks whether you want to print a test page.

11. **Select the Yes radio button, and then click Next.**

    The wizard displays a summary of information about your printer.

12. **Click the Finish button to print the test page.**

    The wizard displays a dialog box that asks whether the test page was printed correctly.

13. **If the test page was printed correctly, click OK to end the wizard. If it was not, click the Troubleshoot button and follow the instructions that the wizard displays.**

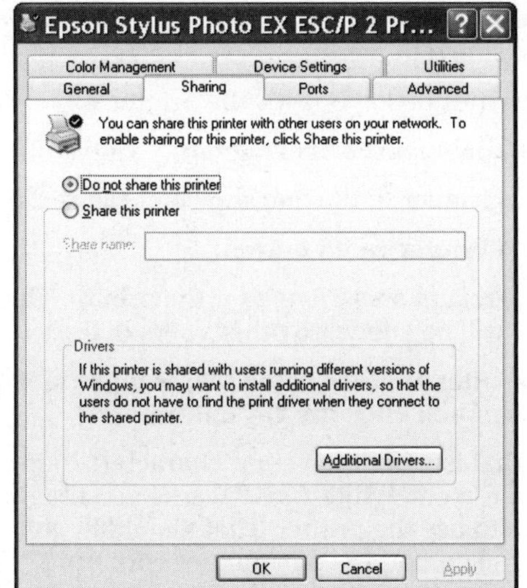

Figure 2-6: A printer's Properties dialog box, Sharing tab.

Using a network printer

Windows XP networks work wonders. I talk (and talk and talk) about them in Book IX. If you have a network, you can attach a printer to any computer on the network and have it accessible to all the users on all the computers in the network. You can also attach different printers to different computers, and let the network users pick and choose the printer that they want to use as the need arises.

Sharing a printer

Before other computers on a network can use a printer, the printer must be officially shared. In order to share a printer, an Administrator has to go onto the *host* PC — that is, the PC to which the printer is physically attached — and tell Windows that the printer should be shared.

I talk about Administrators in Book I, Chapter 2. If you are using Windows XP Home, chances are good that you are an Administrator.

The procedure for sharing a printer depends on the operating system running on the host computer — that is, the computer that the printer is attached to. The following steps describe the procedure for a host that runs Windows XP (other versions of Windows use very similar procedures):

1. **On the printer's host computer, choose Start⇨Control Panel.**
2. **In the Control Panel, click Printers and Other Hardware.**

   This opens the Printers and Faxes dialog box (refer to Figure 2-1).

3. **Right-click the icon for the printer that you want to share and choose Properties from the shortcut menu.**

   This displays a Properties dialog box for the printer.

4. **Click the Properties dialog box's Sharing tab.**

   The Sharing tab looks similar to the one shown in Figure 2-6.

5. **Select the Share This Printer radio button.**

   Windows XP fills in a default share name for the printer. This is a name by which the printer will be known to other users of the network.

6. **If you like, you may enter another name that is more meaningful to your network's users. Then click the OK button.**

   If you enter a name that is more than eight characters long or contains spaces or special characters, Windows XP warns you that MS-DOS computers will be unable to use the printer. That shouldn't give you any gray hair unless some of the computers on your network run MS-DOS instead of Microsoft Windows, or you plan on using some esoteric, ancient species of network administration software.

Installing a shared printer

Sometimes Windows XP is smart enough to identify printers attached to your network and install them right on the spot, and you don't have to lift a finger. When you look at a list of printers in Windows XP, it identifies these automatically recognized printers as "Auto" printers — `Auto HP DeskJet on Shuttlegray`, for example. Slick.

Sometimes (and for the life of me, I don't know why), Windows XP doesn't automatically recognize all the printers on a network. For those special occasions, you need to install the printer manually on any PC that wants to use it:

1. **Make sure that the printer is installed on the host PC — that is, go over to the PC that the printer is attached to, and make sure that you can use it.**

   Try firing up a word processor and print a page, or something along those lines. If the printer doesn't work on the host PC, start at the beginning of this chapter, and get the printer going.

2. **Follow the steps in the preceding section to make sure that the printer is officially designated a shared printer.**

   At least 90 percent of the time, if you can't get a PC to recognize a printer attached to the network, either the printer itself isn't working on the host (see Step 1) or the printer isn't properly designated as a shared printer (see Step 2).

3. **On the computer that doesn't automatically recognize the printer, choose Start⇨Control Panel.**

4. **In the Control Panel, click Printers and Other Hardware.**

   This opens the Printers and Faxes dialog box (refer to Figure 2-1).

5. **Click Add a Printer to start the Add Printer Wizard and display the Welcome page. Ho-hum.**

6. **Click Next.**

   The wizard displays the Local or Network Printer page (refer to Figure 2-2).

7. **Select the A Network Printer, or a Printer Attached to Another Computer radio button. Then click Next.**

   The wizard displays the page shown in Figure 2-7.

8. **Select the Connect to This Printer radio button (the middle button). Leave the Name text box empty. Click Next.**

   The wizard displays the Browse for Printer page, as shown in Figure 2-8. The Shared Printers dialog box displays the printers and computers in your workgroup.

9. **Click the printer you want. Then click Next.**

   If the wizard does not display the printer that you want to install, you can install it anyway, but you must type its name into the Printer text box above the Shared Printers dialog box. The name has this form:

   ```
   \\host\printer
   ```

   For *host,* substitute the name of the host computer as it appears in the Shared Printers dialog box. For *printer,* substitute the share name of the shared printer. You get something like `\\Dimension\LJ4`. The section, "Finding names of shared printers," later in this chapter, explains how to find the printer's share name.

Figure 2-7: The Add Printer Wizard asks you to specify a printer.

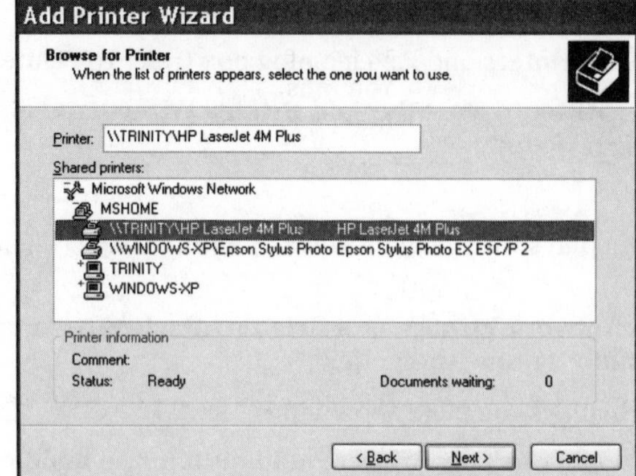

Figure 2-8: Browse for a printer in the Add Printer Wizard.

10. If the host computer requires you to log in to use its resources, the wizard displays a Connect dialog box, as shown in Figure 2-9. Enter a user name and password that are valid on the host computer, and then click OK.

If you connect successfully, the wizard asks whether you want to make this printer your default printer, that is, the one that an application uses unless you explicitly tell it otherwise.

11. Select the Yes or No radio button, as appropriate, and then click Next to finish off the wizard.

Figure 2-9: The Connect dialog box.

Breaking through Windows Firewall

If you can't find the computer or the printer that you're looking for, the most likely culprit is Windows Firewall. You must allow File and Printer Sharing on both of the computers, and the Windows Firewall on both computers has to be notified of your choice.

To make sure that File and Printer Sharing is allowed on a specific machine, follow these steps:

1. **Choose Start⇨Control Panel; in the lower-right corner, click Security Center.**

   Windows brings up the Security Center (see the full discussion in Book II, Chapter 4).

2. **In the lower-right corner, click the icon marked Windows Firewall, and then click the Exceptions tab.**

   You see the Windows Firewall Exceptions list, as shown in Figure 2-10.

3. **Make sure the File and Printer Sharing check box is checked.**

4. **Click OK, and then click the X (Close) button in the upper-right corner of the Security Center to get back to Windows.**

Remember that File and Printer Sharing has to be allowed on both the "host" computer — the one with the printer physically attached to it — and on the computer that you want to be able to use the printer from.

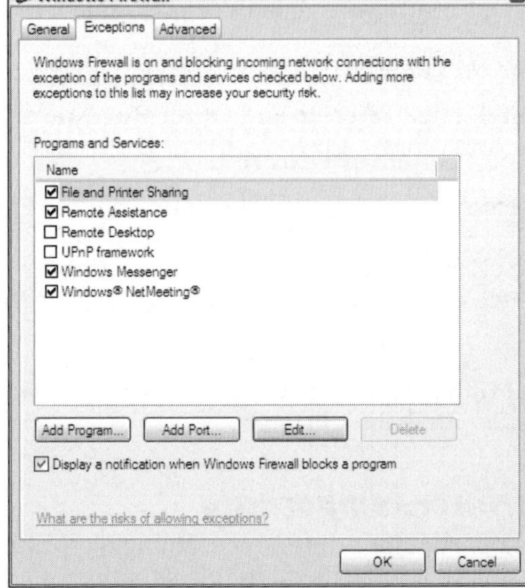

Figure 2-10: Allow File and Printer Sharing through your firewall here.

Finding names of shared printers

Occasionally, finding out the share names of shared printers on your local area network is useful, whether you have installed the printers on your own computer or not. Follow these steps:

1. **Choose Start⇨My Network Places, and in the task pane, click View Network Computers.**
2. **Double-click any host computer that you think may harbor a recalcitrant printer.**

   If an officially designated shared printer is attached to the host computer, it shows up with a printer icon. The share name appears immediately to the right of the printer icon.

Selecting a Printer

If more than one printer is installed on your computer, either directly or through a network, you want to be able to choose different printers for different jobs. You may print ordinary documents to a laser printer, for example, and photographs to a color inkjet printer.

Changing the default printer

At any time, one of the installed printers is Windows XP's *default printer.* The default printer is the one that any application uses unless you tell it to use some other printer.

To see which printer is currently your default printer, follow these steps:

1. **Choose Start⇨Control Panel.**
2. **In the Control Panel, click Printers and Other Hardware.**
3. **Click View Installed Printers or Fax Printers.**

   A check mark appears next to the default printer (refer to Figure 2-1).

If the icon is small, the check mark may be hard to see. Choose a view that displays large icons, such as Icons or Thumbnails, by clicking View on the menu bar.

To change the default printer, right-click the printer that you want to make the default. Then click Set As Default Printer.

Changing the printer temporarily

If you want to print to a particular printer once, changing the default printer and then changing it back is inconvenient. In this situation, you can change the printer temporarily.

To print a document with a different printer than the default one, follow these steps:

1. **Choose your application's Print command as you ordinarily would, usually by choosing File➪Print.**

   The application opens a Print dialog box, as shown in Figure 2-11. The dialog box lists the printers installed on your computer. The default printer is highlighted.

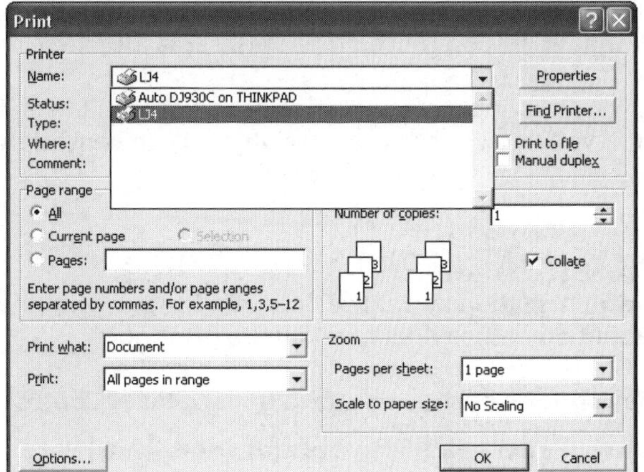

Figure 2-11: The Word 2002 Print dialog box.

2. **Click the printer that you want to use.**
3. **Print as usual.**

   The application uses the printer that you've just chosen.

A temporary printer change affects only the application in which you make the change; so if you switch printers in Word, for example, it won't change the printer in Excel or Photoshop. Some applications use the printer that you select for only one print operation; others remember it until you change it again.

If you're using an application that remembers the temporary printer, you can change it back the next time you print something. If you don't use the printer again for a while, though, you may easily forget to do so. It's a good idea to change back to the default printer as soon as you're done printing, while you're thinking about it. This Tip is brought to you by a guy who once accidentally printed a 50-page black-and-white brochure on a fancy, expensive color printer.

Using the Print Queue

You may have noticed that when you print a document from an application, the application reports that it is done before the printer finishes printing. If the document is long enough, you can print several more documents from one or more applications while the printer works on the first one. This is possible because Windows XP saves printed documents in a *print queue* until it can print them.

If more than one printer is installed on your computer or on your network, each one has its own independent print queue. The queue is maintained on the host PC — that is, the PC to which the printer is attached.

Windows XP uses print queues automatically, so you don't even have to know that they exist. If you know the tricks, though, you can control them in several useful ways.

Displaying a print queue

You can display information about the document that a printer is currently printing and about any other documents in its print queue:

1. **Get on the printer's host computer. Choose Start⇨Control Panel.**
2. **In the Control Panel, click Printers and Other Hardware.**
3. **Click the printer whose queue you want to display.**
4. **In the list of Printer Tasks over on the left, click See What's Printing.**

   The Control Panel opens a printer queue window, as shown in Figure 2-12.

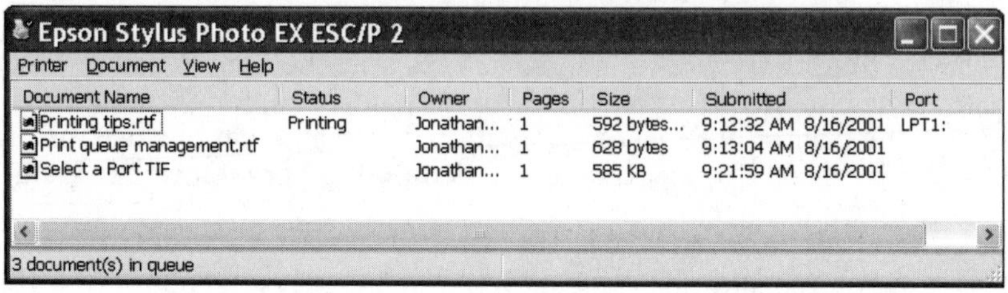

Figure 2-12: A printer queue window.

The jobs in the print queue are listed from the oldest at the top to the newest at the bottom. The Status column shows which job is printing.

You can close the Control Panel window and keep the print queue window open for later use. You can minimize the print queue window and keep it in the taskbar. That can be very handy if you're running a particularly long or complex print job — Word mail merges are particularly notorious for requiring close supervision.

Controlling a print queue

You can use the print queue window, described in the preceding section, to exercise several types of control over the print queue.

If several users are printing documents to the same printer, Windows XP does not let them interfere with each other's work. Thus, you can control the documents that *you* placed in the queue; you cannot control other users' documents, nor can they control yours.

Pausing and resuming a print queue

When you *pause* a print queue, Windows XP stops printing documents from that print queue. If a document is printing when you pause the queue, Windows XP tries to finish printing that document and then stops.

Why would you want to pause the print queue? Say you want to print a page for later reference, but you don't want to bother turning your printer on to print just one page. Pause the printer's queue, and then print the page. The next time you turn the printer on, resume the queue, and the page prints.

Sometimes Windows has a hard time finishing the document — for example, you may be getting print buffer overruns (see the "Troubleshooting" section, later in this chapter), and every time you clear the printer, it may try to reprint the overrun pages. If that happens to you, pause the print queue, and then turn off the printer. As soon as the printer comes back online, Windows is smart enough to pick up where it left off.

When you *resume* a print queue, Windows XP starts printing documents from the queue again.

To pause a print queue, choose the print queue window's File menu, and then click the Pause Printing command. To resume the print queue, choose the same command again. The Pause Printing command has a check mark next to it when the queue is paused.

Depending on how your network is set up, you may or may not be able to pause and resume a print queue on a printer attached to another user's computer.

You can pause and resume the print queue in another way: Right-click the printer in the Control Panel's Printers and Faxes display, and then click the Pause Printing or Resume Printing command. Only one of these commands appears in the shortcut menu at a time, depending on whether or not the print queue is paused.

Pausing, restarting, and resuming a document

Why would you want to pause a document? Say you're printing a Web page that documents an online order you just placed, and the printer jams. You've already finished entering the order, and you have no way to display the page again to reprint it. Pause the document, clear the printer, and restart the document.

Here's another common situation where pausing comes in handy. You're printing a long document, and the phone rings. To make the printer be quiet while you talk, pause the document. When you're done talking, resume the document.

When you *pause a document*, Windows XP is prevented from printing that document. Windows XP skips the document and prints later documents in the queue. If you pause a document while Windows XP is printing it, Windows XP halts in the middle of the document and prints nothing on that printer until you take further action.

To pause a document, select that document. Choose the print queue window's Document menu, and then click the Pause command. The window shows the document's status as Paused.

When you *restart a document,* Windows XP is again allowed to print it. If the document is at the top of the queue, Windows XP prints it as soon as it finishes the document that it is now printing. If the document was being printed when it was paused, Windows XP stops printing it and starts again at the beginning.

Resuming a document is meaningful only if you paused it while Windows XP was printing it. When you *resume a document,* Windows XP resumes printing it where it paused.

To resume or restart the print document, select that document and choose the print queue window's Document menu, and then click the Resume or Restart command.

You have another way to pause a document: Right-click that document in the print queue window and choose the Pause command. To restart or resume the document, right-click the document and click the Resume or Restart command. (These commands appear in the menu only when the document is paused.)

Canceling a document

When you *cancel a document,* Windows XP removes it from the print queue without printing it. You may have heard computer jocks use the term *purged* or *zapped* or something totally unprintable.

Here's a common situation when document canceling comes in handy. You start printing a long document, and as soon as the first page comes out, you realize that you forgot to set the heading. Cancel the document, change the heading, and print the document again.

To cancel a document, select that document. Choose the print queue window's Document menu, and then click the Cancel command. Or right-click the document in the print queue window and click the Cancel command. Or select the document and press the Delete key.

When a document is gone, it's gone. There's no Recycle Bin for the print queue.

Setting Printer Properties

Windows XP provides two means of controlling the properties of a printer: through the printer's Properties dialog box and through its Preferences dialog box. Both of these dialog boxes are accessible through the Control Panel. The Preferences dialog box is also accessible through an application's Print command.

In general, the Properties dialog box controls the printer's overall properties, and the Preferences dialog box controls properties that affect an individual document. The two groups of properties are not cleanly separated, though, and some properties may appear in both.

Using the Properties dialog box

To open a printer's Properties dialog box, follow these steps:

1. **Choose Start⇨Control Panel.**
2. **In the Control Panel, click Printers and Other Hardware.**

   This opens the Printers and Faxes dialog box (refer to Figure 2-1).
3. **Right-click the icon for the printer and select Properties from the shortcut menu.**

   This displays a Properties dialog box for the printer, as shown in Figure 2-13.

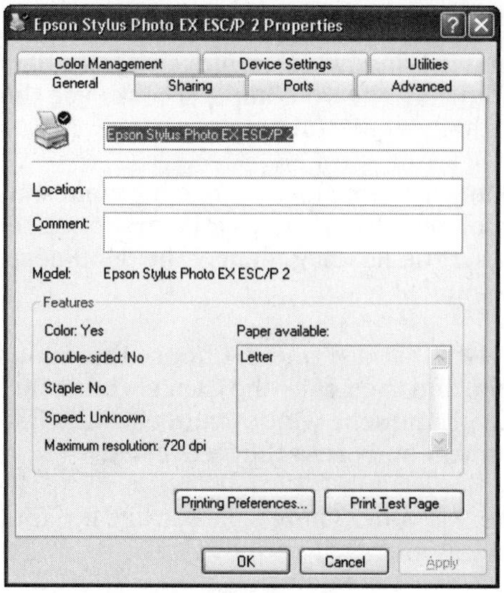

Figure 2-13: The General tab in a typical printer's Properties dialog box.

The Properties dialog box has several tabs. The set of tabs, and in some cases their contents, depends on the features of your printer. Most of the tabs control technical aspects of printer operation and are best left at their default values. The following tabs contain information that you may want to inspect or change:

- **General tab:** Describes the printer's name, location, comments (see the "Attaching a local printer" section, earlier in this chapter), and basic characteristics such as its color-printing capability and its resolution. You can change the name, location, and comments only.
- **Sharing tab:** Controls the printer's shared status and share name. (See the section, "Sharing a printer," earlier in this chapter.)
- **Device Settings tab:** Controls features specific to this type of printer. (See Figure 2-14.)

  On most printers, this tab lets you specify the size of paper, such as letter size, legal size, envelopes, and so on. If the printer can select among two or more paper sources, you can specify the size of paper for each. This allows Windows XP to select the right paper source for the paper size that you request when you print a document.
- **Utilities tab:** Gives you access to special operations that the printer can perform, such as nozzle cleaning for an inkjet printer.

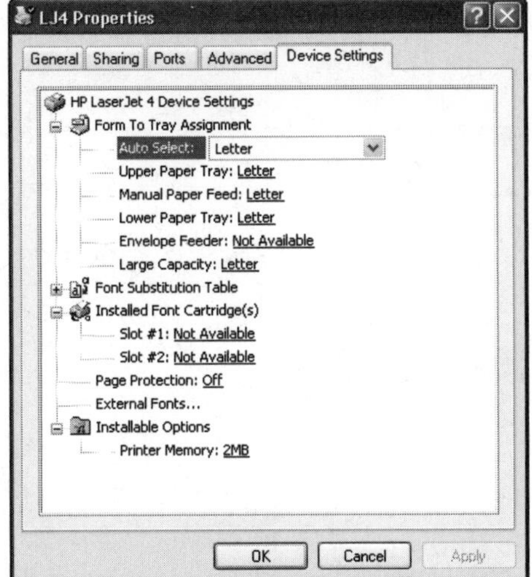

Figure 2-14: The Device Settings tab in a typical printer's Properties dialog box.

Using the Preferences dialog box

Are you confused by all of this Properties/Preferences bull? Yeah, me too. I know the reason why you're so confused. Microsoft and the printer manufacturers aren't the least bit consistent in how they identify all of these printer settings. If you're using Windows XP and Office 2003, and you play around with them a bit, you find all sorts of annoying anomalies.

My favorite: the HP LaserJet driver. If you right-click a LaserJet printer in Windows XP's Printers and Faxes list and pick Printing Preferences, you get the Preferences dialog box (which happens to be the subject of this section). Fair 'nuff. But if you go into an Office application, choose File➪Print, and click the Properties dialog box — note that I said *Properties,* not *Preferences* — you get a nearly identical Preferences dialog box. The only difference (see Figure 2-15) is that the Office dialog box sets preferences for one particular document, not default preferences for the printer in general.

Anyway, here's how you open the Printing Preferences dialog box:

1. **Choose Start➪Control Panel.**
2. **In the Control Panel, click Printers and Other Hardware.**
3. **Right-click the icon for printer and choose Printing Preferences from the shortcut menu.**

   You get a dialog box similar to the ones shown in Figure 2-15.

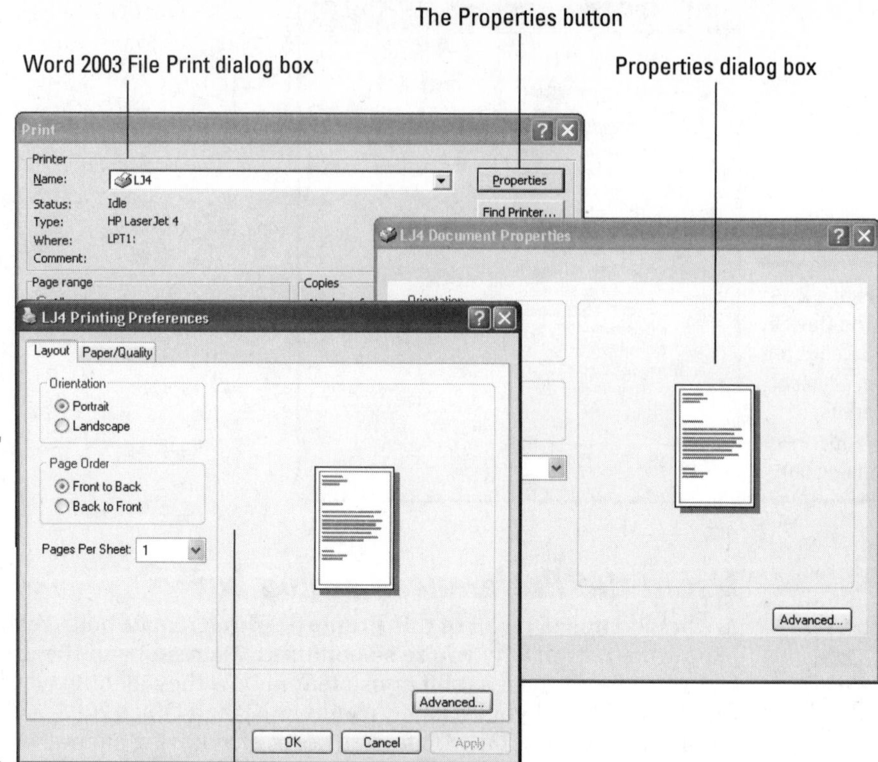

Figure 2-15: Properties? Preferences? What's the difference? Microsoft doesn't seem to know.

Like the Properties dialog box, the Preferences dialog box has several tabs, and the set of tabs and their contents depend on the features of your printer. The most common tabs are the Layout tab, the Paper/Quality tab, and the Utilities tab.

The Layout tab controls the following options:

- **The orientation of printed output:** In *portrait* orientation, the document is printed so that the top and bottom of each page run along the short dimension of the paper. In *landscape* orientation, the top and bottom of each page run along the long dimension of the paper.
- **The page order of printed output:** Whether the document is printed from the first page to the last or from the last to the first. If you're tired of resequencing printout pages when they emerge from your printer, change this option.

- **The number of pages per sheet:** If you select a number larger than 1, Windows XP reduces the size of each printed page in order to place more than one page on each sheet of paper.
- **The Advanced button:** Displays a dialog box of advanced properties that depend on the features of your printer.

The Paper/Quality tab, shown in Figure 2-16, controls one or more of the following options, depending on your printer's features:

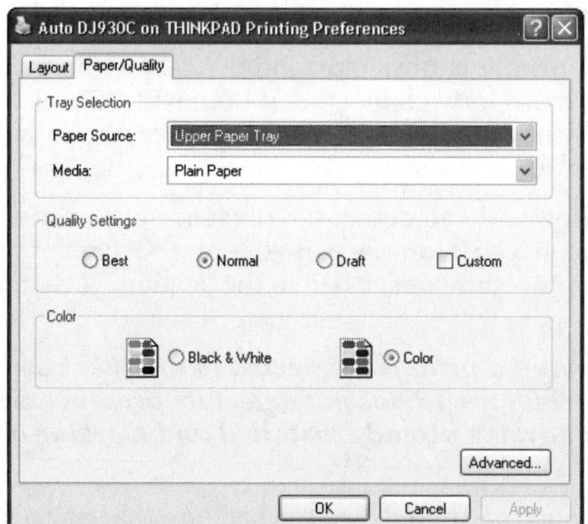

Figure 2-16: The Paper/Quality tab in a typical printer's Preferences dialog box.

- **The paper source to be used:** In most cases, it's best to keep the default, Automatically select, and use the Print dialog box to choose the size of paper you want. Windows XP then selects the paper source that contains the right size, according to the settings you entered in the Properties dialog box.
- **The type of paper or other media in the printer:** Other media include copier paper, photo-quality paper, or overhead projector transparency film. (Some printers can adjust to produce optimum results on different types of media.)
- **The quality setting to use:** If your printer supports a choice of quality settings, you can choose among values such as Best, Normal, and Draft. Lower-quality settings generally speed up printing and save ink but may look grainy.
- **Whether to print in color or black and white:** When you print documents that contain color but don't need it to be useful, you may choose black and white to conserve the relatively expensive color ink.

The Utilities tab presents the same utilities as the Utilities tab in the Properties dialog box.

Troubleshooting

The following list gives some typical problems with printers and the solutions to those sticky spots:

✦ ***I'm trying to install a printer. I connected it to my computer, and Windows XP doesn't detect its presence.***

  Be sure that the printer is turned on and the cable from the printer to your computer is properly connected at both ends. Check the printer's manual; you may have to follow a procedure (like push a button) to make the printer ready for use.

  In general, Windows XP can detect the presence of a printer only if it is connected through a USB interface. If Windows XP cannot detect your printer, use the procedure described in the section, "Attaching a local printer."

✦ ***I'm trying to install a printer connected to another computer on my network, and Windows XP doesn't detect its presence. I know that the printer is okay; it's already installed and working as a local printer on that system!***

  The printer may not be shared. See the section, "Sharing a printer," earlier in this chapter.

  If the host PC reports that the printer is shared, look at the computers attached to your network by choosing Start⇨My Network Places. If no computers show up, something is wrong with your network connection. If computers are shown but the printer's host is not among them, something is wrong with *its* network connection.

  If the printer's host is visible on the network, you should be able to install the printer by typing in its name. The section, "Installing a shared printer," explains how to do this.

  Finally, you may have disabled File and Printer Sharing on one of the PCs or both. See the section, "Breaking through Windows Firewall," earlier in this chapter, for help.

✦ ***I can't use a shared printer that I've used successfully in the past. Windows XP says it isn't available when I try to use it, or Windows XP doesn't even show it as an installed printer anymore.***

  This can happen if something interferes with your connection to the network or the connection of the printer's host computer. It can also happen if something interferes with the availability of the printer; for example, if the host computer's user has turned off sharing.

If you can't find a problem, or if you find and correct a problem (such as File and Printer Sharing being turned off) but you still can't use the printer, try restarting Windows XP on your own system. If that doesn't help, remove the printer from your system and then reinstall it.

To remove the printer from your system, open the Control Panel's Printers and Faxes window, and then right-click the printer and choose the Delete command from the shortcut menu. Windows XP asks if you're sure you want to delete this printer. Click the Yes button.

To reinstall the printer on your system, use the same procedure that you used to install it originally. See the "Installing a shared printer" section, earlier in this chapter.

✦ ***I printed a document, but it never came out of the printer.***

Check the printer's print queue, over on the host PC (the one directly attached to the printer). Is the document there? If not, investigate several possible reasons:

- The printer isn't turned on. In some cases, Windows XP can't distinguish a printer that is connected but not turned on from a printer that is ready, and it sends documents to a printer that isn't operating.
- You accidentally sent the document to some other printer.
- Some other user unintentionally picked up your document and walked off with it.
- The printer is turned on but not ready to print, and the printer (as opposed to the host PC) is holding your whole document in its internal memory until it can start printing. A printer can hold as much as several dozen pages of output internally, depending on the size of its internal memory and the complexity of the pages.

If your document is in the print queue but isn't printing, check the following:

- The printer may not be ready to print. See whether it is plugged in, turned on, and properly connected to your computer or its host computer.
- Your document may be paused.
- The print queue itself may be paused.
- The printer may be printing another document that is paused.
- The printer may be "thinking." If it is a laser printer or some other type of printer that composes an entire page in internal memory before it starts to print, it will appear to be doing nothing while it processes photographs or other complex graphics. Processing may take as long as several minutes.

Look at the printer and study its manual. The printer may have a blinking light or a status display that tells you it is really doing something. As you become familiar with the printer, you get a feel for how long various types of jobs should take.

- On the other hand, the printer's status display may tell you that the printer is offline, out of paper, jammed, or unready to print for some other reason.

✦ ***I tried to print a complex document, and only part of it came out. I got an error message that said something like "Printer Overrun," either on the last printed page or on the printer's status display.***

This can happen on laser printers and other printers that compose a whole page at a time in internal memory. The error occurs if a page is too complex for the amount of memory in the printer.

The following procedure corrects the problem in most cases, although details may vary with the type of printer you use:

1. **Press the printer's Reset control, or turn the printer off and then back on.**
2. **In Windows XP, open the printer's Properties dialog box and click the Device Settings tab. (See the section, "Setting Printer Properties," earlier in this chapter.)**
3. **Look for a property named Page Protection. Its setting should be OFF for this problem to have occurred.**
4. **Click the Page Protection property.**

   The setting OFF is replaced by a drop-down list. Use the list to change the item's setting to ON. With Page Protection turned ON, the printer assembles each page in the printer's memory before printing it. With Page Protection OFF, the printer can start printing a page and get halfway through before discovering that it doesn't have enough memory to print the whole page. It happens, from time to time, with complex graphics.

Chapter 3: Getting the Scoop on Scanners

In This Chapter

- Installing a scanner in one — or two or three — easy steps
- Using a scanner
- Using scanners over your network
- Troubleshooting common problems with scanners

A *scanner* is a device that "reads" an image from paper and creates a digital version of the image. It's like a copier that produces an image inside your computer instead of on another sheet of paper.

I've singled out scanners for special treatment because scanners have so many potential uses. Combine a scanner and a printer to create a multi-talented, powerful copier. Team a scanner with e-mail and a service like J2 (`www.j2.com`), and you can send and receive faxes to or from anywhere in the world at a fraction of the cost — without an extra phone line. You can use scanners with *optical character recognition* (OCR) software to convert printed text into editable document files. You can sit on the scanner's glass and create immoral, er, immortal images to send in e-mail or to post on your Web page for posterior, er, posterity. Scanners certainly rate as versatile critters.

Book VI, Chapter 1 discusses how to choose a scanner. This chapter discusses how to set up and use a scanner.

Installing a Scanner

No doubt your new scanner comes with a fancy, big, printed sheet with step-by-step instructions for installing the beast and getting it running. I'd like to add a couple of points of emphasis, particularly for flat-bed scanners, compliments of the Dummies School of Hard Knocks. To wit:

1. **Find a place for your scanner that's going to work for you.**

   Scanners need extra room around the sides. You're going to try to scan a copy of the *Encyclopedia Britannica* someday, and it's gonna droop way over on the left, and then it's gonna droop way over on the right. If you cram your scanner into a teensy-tiny spot, you'll swear at it every time you want to scan anything bigger than a postage stamp.

2. **After you put your scanner in its place and remove all the plastic wrapping paper, cardboard, foam, and packing tape, and then clean off the sticky goo and heaven-knows-what, *you have to unlock the lamp.***

   Look for the little sliding gizmo on the side or the back, probably with a picture of a lock on it. When you move the scanner around, you want to lock the lamp — that keeps it from getting knocked around and smashing up the insides of the machine. But before you can use the scanner, the lamp has to be unlocked.

3. **Plug in the power cord.**

   Yeah, I've forgotten to do that, too.

4. **If your scanner uses a USB interface, plug the data cable in to the scanner at one end, and plug the other end into the USB port on your PC. Turn the scanner on.**

   Windows XP should detect the scanner's presence and install it. Small popup windows describe the progress of the installation, as shown in Figure 3-1. At the end of the installation, you have a fully functional scanner. If Windows XP doesn't detect the scanner, mutter a few words of supplication to the WinGods, and skip to Step 6.

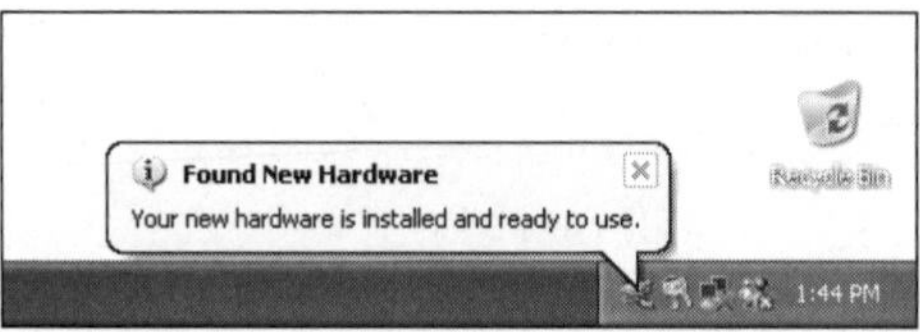

Figure 3-1: Progress of the installation for a Plug and Play scanner.

5. **If your scanner doesn't use a USB port, you have to turn off your PC and turn off the scanner before you connect the data cable. When the cable's connected, turn the PC back on.**

After the cable's connected, Windows XP turns on your scanner when it comes back to life. If the scanner's mechanism moves when you turn it on, making a humming noise, wait until the noise stops. Then turn on your PC. If you're lucky, Windows XP detects the scanner, installs everything you need, and you're ready to roll. If you're unlucky, you end up at Step 6, too.

6. **So now that you know Windows XP didn't autoinstall your scanner, don't worry. Happens to the best of us. You need to get the Add New Hardware Wizard running, thusly: Choose Start⇨Control Panel⇨ Printers and Other Hardware. In the left pane, click Add Hardware.**

   Windows XP starts the Add New Hardware Wizard and displays a "welcome" page. Ho-Hum.

7. **Click Next.**

   The wizard searches for hardware that has not yet been installed. If the wizard finds your scanner, it installs the scanner and tells you it is done.

8. **Click the Finish button to close the wizard, which ends the procedure.**

   If the wizard doesn't find your scanner, it asks whether the hardware has been connected.

9. **Select the Yes, I Have Already Connected the Hardware radio button, and then click the Next button.**

   The wizard displays a list of the installed devices that it recognizes.

10. **Check to see whether your scanner is in the list. If it is, click the Cancel button to close the wizard.**

    Your scanner is connected and working, even if you didn't think it was.

11. **If your scanner is not in the list of installed devices, scroll to the end of the list, select Add a New Hardware Device, and then click the Next button.**

    The wizard asks whether you want to search for new hardware and install it automatically. Sheesh. If you get to this point, the wizard has already tried to find it and didn't succeed! Gimme a break.

12. **Select the radio button labeled Install the Hardware That I Manually Select, and then click the Next button.**

    The wizard displays a list of common types of devices.

13. **Click Imaging Devices, and then click the Next button.**

    The wizard displays a list of brands on the left and scanners on the right.

14. **Click your scanner's brand, click the model, and then click the Next button. Answer any additional questions the wizard asks.**

    When you have answered all of the questions, the wizard installs the scanner and tells you it is done.

If your brand and model of scanner aren't in the Add New Hardware Wizard lists, you can still install your scanner if you have a Windows XP driver for it. The driver may come with the scanner on a floppy diskette or CD-ROM, or you may be able to download it from the manufacturer's Web site. To install a scanner by supplying a driver, click the Have Disk button in the Add New Hardware Wizard and follow the wizard's prompts.

Sometimes a scanner's Windows 2000 driver works in Windows XP; sometimes it doesn't work. If no Windows XP driver is available, try the Windows 2000 driver, if it exists — and if that's not possible, try a Windows NT driver.

Hewlett-Packard's ScanJet software, called HP Precision Scan, includes a driver that makes installing and using a scanner over a Windows XP network easy. To make an HP ScanJet scanner work on any computer on your network

1. **Make sure you have the latest version of HP Precision Scan by checking the HP Web site at** `www.hp.com`**.**
2. **Attach the scanner to a PC on the network (called the "host" PC); then install the scanner on the host PC normally, using the instructions for the Precision Scan software.**
3. **Make sure that the HP Precision Scan LAN Host program is running. If it is, you see an icon shaped like a scanner in the notification area of the Windows taskbar — down near the clock. If it isn't there, choose Start⇨Programs⇨HP ScanJet Software⇨HP ScanJet Utilities⇨Share Scanner.**
4. **Install the HP Precision Scan software on any PCs on the network that you want to be able to use the scanner. The PCs automatically detect the shared scanner on the scanner's host computer.**

When the HP Precision Scan LAN Host program is running, and Precision Scan is installed on a networked PC, scanning from that networked PC is as simple as scanning on the host.

Getting the Most from a Scanner

Windows XP's Scanner and Camera Wizard performs basic scanning tasks with any type of scanner.

Your scanner may come with software that has features the wizard lacks. Check your scanner's manual for information. Unless the manufacturer's scanning software has a feature that you really, really need — such as network sharing, discussed in the preceding section — you're probably much better off to stick with the Windows XP native software.

Scanning with the wizard

To use the Scanner and Camera Wizard, follow these steps:

1. **Choose Start⇨Control Panel.**

   Windows XP opens the Control Panel window.

2. **Click Printers and Other Hardware, and then click Scanners and Cameras.**

   Windows XP opens the Scanners and Cameras window.

3. **Double-click the icon that represents your scanner.**

   Windows XP opens the wizard and displays a "welcome" page.

4. **Click the Next button.**

   You may find it easier and faster to get at the scanner by starting Paint (choose Start⇨All Programs⇨Accessories⇨Paint), and then scanning directly into a Paint document (File⇨From Scanner or Camera).

   The wizard displays the Choose Scanning Preferences dialog box, as shown in Figure 3-2.

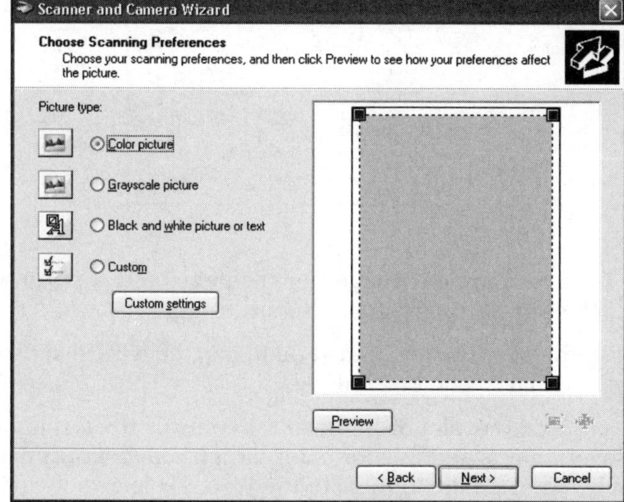

Figure 3-2: The wizard's Choose Scanning Preferences dialog box.

5. **Click the radio button for the type of copy you are scanning.**

   In the Choose Scanning Preferences dialog box, note that the Black and White Picture or Text option button applies to line drawings, which do *not* have shades of gray. They are, quite literally, black and white.

The Preview button lets you zoom in to a specific portion of the picture. See the section, "Using the Preview button," later in this chapter, for details.

The Custom Settings button enables you to control brightness, contrast, and resolution. See the section, "Using the Custom Settings button," for details.

6. **Click Next.**

   The wizard displays the Picture Name and Destination dialog box, as shown in Figure 3-3.

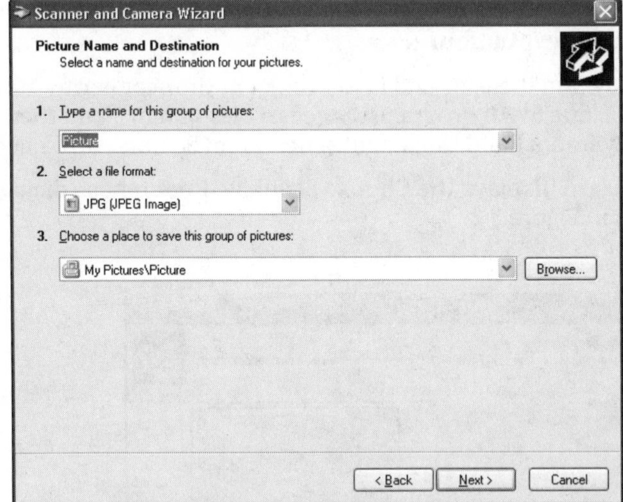

Figure 3-3: The wizard's Picture Name and Destination dialog box.

7. **In the Type a Name text box, enter the name you want to give the file to be created from the item you're scanning.**

   If you use the same name for several items, the wizard adds numbers to the name to make each one unique.

   The Select a File Format drop-down list controls the format in which the file is saved. JPG is suitable for color pictures, and works particularly well for pictures destined to go to the Web. TIF is a good choice for grayscale and black and white.

   The wizard automatically stores the scanned images in the My Pictures folder, in a subfolder with the name you entered. If you entered "Meeting notes," for example, it stores the images in *My Pictures\Meeting notes*. If you want a different folder, you can choose one by clicking the Browse button or from the Choose a Place drop-down list.

8. **Click Next.**

   The wizard displays the Scanning Picture dialog box, shown in Figure 3-4, while it scans. When the wizard finishes scanning, it displays a dialog box that asks you what you want to do next. This dialog box is designed for pictures downloaded from a digital camera and isn't very useful for scanner copy.

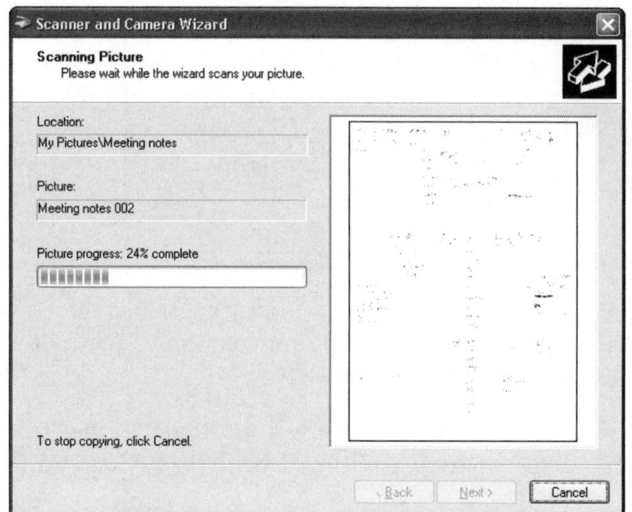

Figure 3-4: The wizard's Scanning Picture dialog box.

9. **Click the Cancel button to close the wizard.**

Using the Preview button

In the section, "Scanning with the wizard," Step 4 of the Scanner and Camera Wizard brings up the Choose Scanning Preferences dialog box (refer to Figure 3-2). If you click the Preview button, your scanner performs a quick preview scan of the copy and displays the image in the preview pane, as shown in Figure 3-5.

Notice the rectangle composed of dotted lines with little solid squares in the corners. That dotted line outlines the area that will be included in the scan. Initially, the dotted line covers the entire image area of the scanner.

If you need only part of the image, you can move the selection's borders to contain just the part you need. Drag each of the selection's corner boxes to the place where you want that corner to be. You can also move a single side of the selection by dragging the dotted line that marks that side.

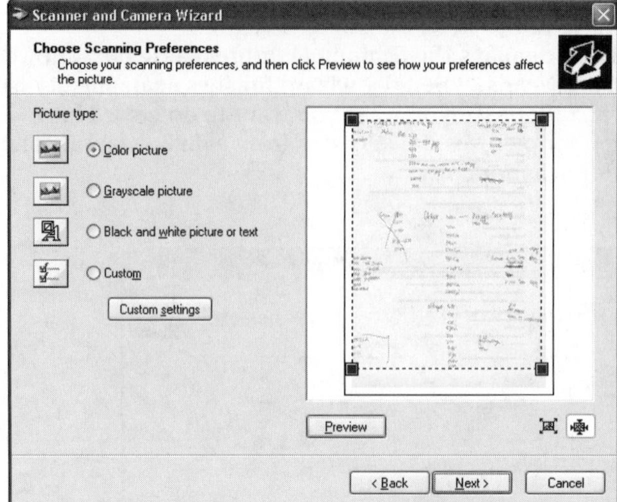

Figure 3-5: Effect of the Preview button.

Why is it useful to scan a selected part of your copy? Why not just scan the whole thing? Here are a couple of reasons:

- ✦ The size of an image file is roughly proportional to the area being scanned. You can save hard drive space by scanning only the area you need.
- ✦ The time required to complete a scan depends on how far the scanning lamp must move while scanning. That is, it depends on the height of the scan area you have chosen. Even if the scanner must move down the page to the start of the selection, it can do that faster than it would if it had to scan the whole way.

Both of these factors become more significant when you increase the resolution of the scan. For details, see the "Using the Custom Settings button" section, later in this chapter.

After you set up the scan area, you can make the wizard show an enlargement by clicking the "enlarge" button. This lets you see more detail so that you can be sure that you set the scan area correctly.

To reduce the preview image so that the entire image area is shown again, click the "entire page" button.

When the selection is set the way you want it, click the Next button. The wizard scans only the part of the image that you have chosen.

Using the Custom Settings button

In the section, "Scanning with the wizard," Step 4 of the Scanner and Camera Wizard brings up the Choose Scanning Preferences dialog box (refer to Figure 3-2). If you click the Custom Settings button, you have a chance to control the details of the scan.

Click Custom Settings, and the wizard displays a Properties dialog box like the one shown in Figure 3-6.

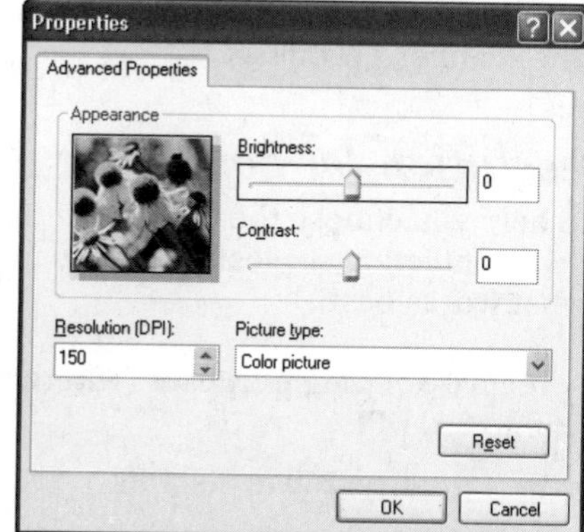

Figure 3-6: The Custom Settings properties dialog box.

This dialog box lets you adjust the appearance of the scanned image. Within limits, you can correct shortcomings in the copy you're scanning as follows:

✦ **Brightness control:** Adjusts the brightness of the image. Move the control to the right to brighten the image; move it to the left to darken the image.

In a black-and-white image (a line drawing or text without grays), darkening the image is helpful if the copy is very light, making letters and lines appear thin and broken. Lightening the image is helpful if the background is not clean, creating dark speckles all over the image.

✦ **Contrast control:** (Present only for color and grayscale images.) Adjusts the contrast of the image — that is, changes the image to increase or decrease the sharpness of the transition between bright and dark parts of the picture. Move the slider right to increase the contrast (to sharpen the transition between light and dark); move it left to decrease the contrast.

✦ **Picture Type list:** Lets you choose the type of scanned image to create color, grayscale, or black and white.

- **Resolution field:** Lets you set the resolution of the scan in dots per inch (DPI). The default value is suitable for medium-resolution images with most types of copy. A higher value yields an image with more detail but makes the scan go more slowly and produces a larger image file. A lower value yields an image with less detail but makes the scan go faster and produces a smaller image file. See the sections, "Choosing the best resolution for your work" and "Choosing the best resolution for your scanner."
- **Reset button:** Resets all of the Custom Settings to their default values.

Depending on the manufacturer and the model of scanner you're using, there may be additional options available in the dialog box. Don't be scared. Give them a try. You won't break the scanner. I promise.

Choosing the best resolution for your work

Here are some suggestions to help you choose the best resolution for scanning a given type of work. If two conflicting suggestions apply to your work, try a range of values to see what works best:

- **Scanning documents for record-keeping purposes (where reasonable legibility is sufficient):** 150 to 200 DPI.
- **Scanning documents for best quality:** 250 to 300 DPI.
- **Scanning documents for optical character recognition (OCR):** 400 to 500 DPI, or as recommended by the OCR application.
- **Scanning printed text:** 400 to 500 DPI.
- **Scanning text and photographs in glossy magazines:** 250 to 300 DPI.
- **Scanning photographic prints:** 250 to 300 DPI.
- **Scanning line art (black-and-white images):** 250 to 300 DPI.
- **Images to be printed:** Choose a value no more than one-third of the resolution of the printer. For example, if the printer's resolution is 600 DPI, scan at no more than 200 DPI. A setting higher than 300 DPI generally does not improve the results in any case.
- **Images to be displayed on a monitor:** 72 DPI.

In each case, if the image will be enlarged, increase the resolution in proportion. For example, if the image will be printed or displayed three times the size of the original, multiply the recommended resolution by three. ***Remember:*** The one exception to this rule is for text and photographs in glossy magazines — the recommendation of 250 to 300 DPI is based on the size of the dots that form in images in the original copy. Increasing the resolution generally does not improve the results of the scan.

Choosing the best resolution for your scanner

To get the best results, you must not only consider the resolution that's best for your work, you also need to pick a resolution that your scanner will treat with some care. You are best off choosing a resolution that divides evenly into your scanner's optical resolution. For example, if your scanner's optical resolution is 1000 DPI, 200, 250, or 500 DPI is a good resolution to use. If your scanner's optical resolution is 1200 DPI, use 200, 240, 300, 400, or 600 DPI.

If your scanner's optical resolution is different in the horizontal and vertical dimensions, use the lower number.

You can find your scanner's optical resolution by consulting its manual or by displaying its Properties dialog box like this:

1. **Choose Start⇨Control Panel.**

   Windows XP opens the Control Panel window.
2. **Click Printers and Other Hardware, and then click Scanners and Cameras.**

   Windows XP opens the Scanners and Cameras window.
3. **Right-click the icon that represents your scanner and choose Properties.**

   Windows XP displays the scanner's Properties dialog box, as shown in Figure 3-7. In this example, the Properties dialog box shows that the scanner's optical resolution is 1000 DPI.

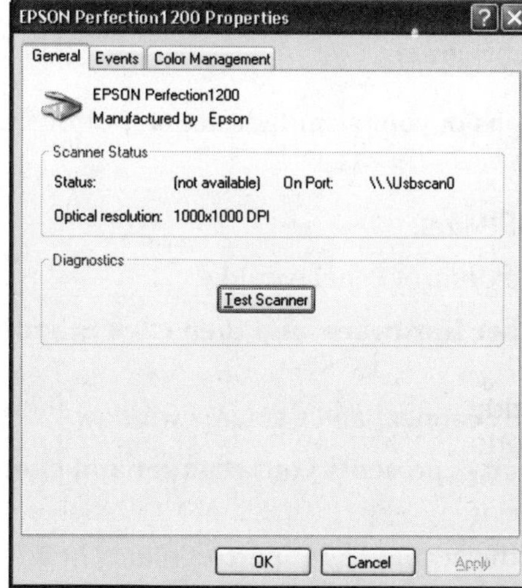

Figure 3-7: A scanner's Properties dialog box.

If you check the manual, look for the scanner's *optical resolution* or *hardware resolution*. Don't be misled by the "maximum resolution" or "interpolated resolution" — marketing bafflegab of the first degree — which is usually much higher. Using a resolution greater than the scanner's optical resolution generally does not improve the results of scans.

Scanner Skullduggery and Useful Tricks

The following couple of sections go over some handy things to know when it comes to the art of scanning.

Printing a scanned image

One way to print a scanned image is to open it with Windows Paint, and then choose File⇨Print.

Another way is to use the Photo Printing Wizard, which is described in Book VII, Chapter 3.

Many scanners come with a photocopier utility that scans and prints an image in one step. This is a more efficient way to make a paper copy with a scanner. Some photocopier utilities have features that are available on only very expensive copiers.

Programming your scanner's action buttons

Many scanners have buttons to perform specific actions, such as starting a scan and making a photocopy. These buttons are a convenience; after you put copy in the scanner, you can simply press a button instead of going back to your computer to run a program.

You can control the functions of your scanner's action buttons with the scanner's Properties dialog box:

1. **Choose Start⇨Control Panel.**

   Windows XP opens the Control Panel window.

2. **Click Printers and Other Hardware, and then click Scanners and Cameras.**

   Windows XP opens the Scanners and Cameras window.

3. **Right-click the icon that represents your scanner and choose Properties.**

   Windows XP displays the scanner's Properties dialog box.

4. **Click the Events tab (see Figure 3-8).**

Figure 3-8: The Properties dialog box, Events tab.

The Select an Event drop-down list names the events that your scanner can generate (that is, the action buttons it has). To see the function of an action button, select that button from the list.

To change the function of the action button, click one of the radio buttons in the Properties dialog box's Actions group:

- **Start This Program:** Enables you to select a program to run when the button is pushed.
- **Prompt for Which Program to Run:** Tells Windows XP to prompt you to select a program when you push the button.
- **Take No Action:** Disables the button.

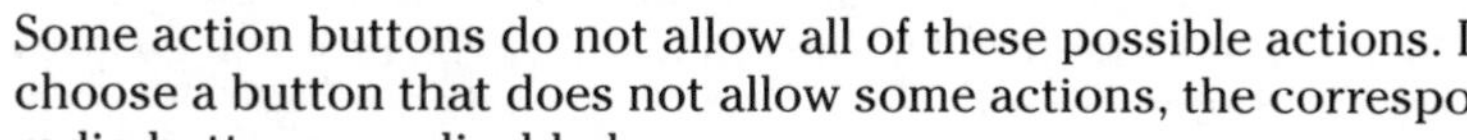

REMEMBER

Some action buttons do not allow all of these possible actions. If you choose a button that does not allow some actions, the corresponding radio buttons are disabled.

5. **Click the OK button to apply your changes and close the Properties dialog box, or click the Apply button to apply your changes and leave the dialog box open.**

Troubleshooting

Here's a quick list of things that can go wrong with scanners and what you can do about them:

- ***My scan came out blank!***

  Make sure you remembered to put the document in the scanner, facing the right way. Repeat after me: D'OH!

- ***My scanned document is dark gray on light gray, instead of black on white.***

  The image type is probably set to Color or Grayscale. Set it to Black and White.

- ***My scanned photograph is all black and white; no grays, no color.***

  The image type is probably set to Black and White. Set it to Color or Grayscale.

- ***My scans always seem to come out a little crooked.***

  When you put the copy on the scanner's glass plate, align the edges of the copy with the frame around the plate. This is easiest if you push the copy right into a corner of the frame. On most scanners, the upper-right corner is the one to use.

  Aligning copy is particularly hard when you're scanning a newspaper article. You usually have to fold the newspaper to make it fit in the scanner, and then the copy has no edges that are likely to be square with the text. In this case, you should try to fold the newspaper back on itself so that you can see at least one edge of the individual page you're scanning.

- ***I tried to scan, but the wizard said that "the current picture could not be copied."***

  To test the scanner's electronics and its connection to the computer, close the Scanner and Camera Wizard; then right-click the icon for the scanner and choose Properties. In the Properties dialog box (refer to Figure 3-7), click the Test Scanner button. If Windows XP reports that the scanner failed the test, look for a problem in the connection. If the connection appears to be okay, look for a problem with the scanner.

  If Windows XP reports that the scanner passed the test, try to scan again. Be sure to click the Preview button before performing the scan. For some reason, this often makes the problem go away. (At least, it does for me.)

- ***I tried to scan a picture from a magazine, and it came out with light and dark bands all over the surface.***

  This effect is called a *moiré pattern*. It happens when one pattern of image elements is superimposed on another, and the two patterns are almost (but not quite) aligned. In this case, the first pattern consists of the dots that make up the picture you're scanning, and the second pattern consists of the pixels in the scanned image.

  Try again with a slightly lower resolution. Keep reducing the resolution a little at a time until the moiré pattern disappears.

Book VII

Joining the Multimedia Mix

"Ironically, he went out there looking for a 'hot spot.'"

Contents at a Glance

Chapter 1: Jammin' with Windows Media Player

In This Chapter

- **Getting the latest version of Windows Media Player**
- **Media Guide: The worldwide program schedule**
- **Copying music from a CD**
- **The Media Library: Where your music is kept**
- **Copying music to a CD or digital audio player**
- **Changing Media Player's appearance**
- **Customizing Media Player**

Windows Media Player is da *MAN*. Er, uh. Wait a sec. Let me start over. WMP *sucks*. No that's not what I meant. Hold on. I've got this loud thud coming from my speakers, the Water Ambience visualization looks like smoke in Godzilla's eye, and Trent Reznor is screaming "You can't take it away from me." Lemme turn the volume down. There. Yeah. That's better.

What I meant to say is that Windows Media Player (or WMP) *sucks you in* from the moment you start it. As Windows XP's built-in boom box, it plays CDs, of course, but it also lets you play, organize, and generally enjoy any kind of music stored on your computer, whether the tunes came from CDs, the Internet, or your buddy down the hall. It also plays video and lets you tune into the nascent Internet radio market.

If you have a CD writer, Windows Media Player creates CDs that contain any combination of tracks you want. If you have a digital audio player, WMP copies music to the player so that you can hip and/or hop, as circumstances dictate, wherever you go.

Windows Media Player can even do a chameleon act, changing its *skin* — its appearance on your screen — to suit your whims.

Windows Media Player's normal appearance is a little unusual. If you use skins, it can get downright weird. You've been warned.

The competition

Windows Media Player isn't the only game in town. Although WMP excels in some respects, at least three other competitors deserve your attention — if not your ears.

Lots of folks swear by Winamp, a mercifully compact, surprisingly capable player from Nullsoft (www.winamp.com). The basic player is free. If you want to add MP3 ripping and CD burning, it costs all of $14.95 — and you won't be pestered until the day you die to buy and download songs from a proprietary library.

RealOne (www.realone.com) offers a limited feature, free version of its RealPlayer multimedia program, or a 14-day free trial of its $19.95 version, which has more features than you can shake a stick at. I'm not a fan of RealOne — over many years of experience, I've seen it crash and lock up, left and right, on a dozen different PCs, and I think it's unconscionable how often it phones home, for no apparent reason — but your results may vary.

On the other hand, Apple's truly compelling media player, called iTunes, deserves a look. (No, I'm not an Apple fan either; I've had older versions of Apple's QuickTime freeze on Windows machines so often that I could scream — and iTunes uses QuickTime.) I really like the clean, accessible interface of iTunes, and the fact that it handles MP3 files from the get-go.

Unlike WMP, iTunes doesn't try to sell you something every minute of the day, and it doesn't try to steer you toward "Digital Rights Management" — the copy protection scheme that will drive you nuts. Yes, Apple wants to sell you music. Yes, they want you to buy an iPod. But if you install iTunes correctly (no need to select it as the default player for your audio files; also, deselect the check box in the installer that says Show iTunes Music Store), it's considerably less annoying than Windows Media Player — and more versatile, too, although the audio quality isn't as good.

Oh. And it's free: Check it out at www.itunes.com.

Getting the Latest WiMP

If you haven't specifically gone fishing for the latest version of Windows Media Player (affectionately known as *WiMP* to it fans), you should take a look and see what Microsoft has available. Drop by www.microsoft.com/windows/windowsmedia and make sure that you have the latest and greatest.

The download is free — you already paid for Windows Media Player when you bought Windows. More to the point, Microsoft keeps adding new "features" to WiMP that try to sell you something, so the upgrades come frequently, and invariably at no charge.

To see what version of WMP you currently use, start Windows Media Player, choose Help➪About Windows Media Player (you may have to hover your mouse cursor above the Windows Media Player window to see the menu bar). The version number will say something like 10.00.12345. That's

Microsoft-speak for version 10. If you have version 8 or 9, it's well worth upgrading to version 10.

If you find a newer version of WMP, download the file and run it. When you install WMP, take special care with the dialog box shown in Figure 1-1. Make sure you deselect the Acquire Licenses Automatically for Protected Content check box (and make sure you *don't* select the last three check boxes) before clicking Next to complete the installation. Leaving the last three check boxes deselected prevents Microsoft from filling its database with details of your playing habits.

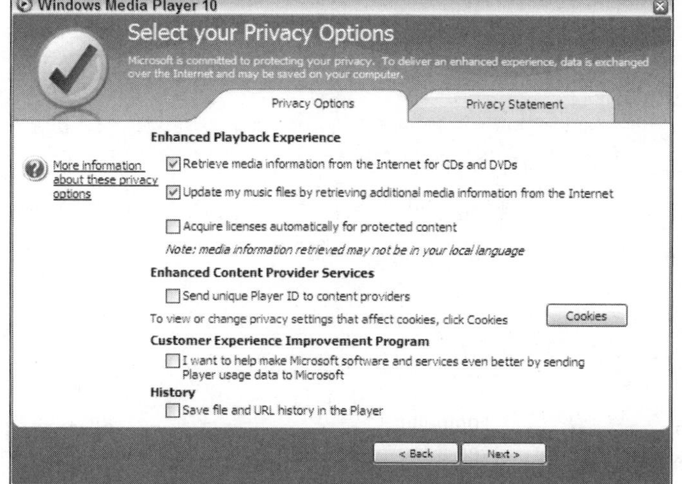

Figure 1-1: To minimize headaches, deselect the Acquire Licenses Automatically check box and keep the last three items deselected.

If you keep the Acquire Licenses Automatically for Protected Content check box selected, each time that you add a protected file (typically a song in Microsoft's proprietary WMA format, or a video in WMV format) to your computer, Windows Media Player will go out to the company that owns the copyright on the file and ask for a license. (See the section, "Understanding Digital Licenses," later in this chapter for details.) It's none of Microsoft's business when you copy a file onto your computer or download one; nor is it the business of the copyright holder. If you need to buy a license in order to play a song or watch a video, you can do that when you're good and ready to play the song. Harumph.

If you've already installed WMP, or the latest version came preinstalled on your PC, take a moment now to turn the $#@! Acquire Licenses setting off. To do so

1. **Start Windows Media Player.**
2. **Choose Tools➪Options. (You may have to hover your mouse cursor above the Windows Media Player window to see the menu bar.) In the Options dialog box that appears, click the Privacy tab (see Figure 1-2).**

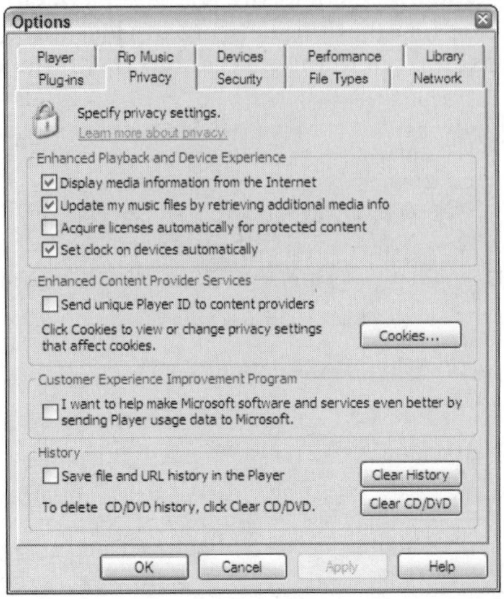

Figure 1-2: If you already have WMP installed, deselect the Acquire Licenses Automatically check box on the Privacy tab.

3. **Deselect the Acquire Licenses Automatically for Protected Content check box.**
4. **Click OK.**

   Clear the check box, and WMP will not automatically phone home to Microsoft and/or the copyright holder when you copy or download a digitally protected WMA file onto your computer.

The rest of the installation is pretty innocuous, particularly if you're willing to associate WMP with all of your media files. (When you *associate* a file with Windows Media Player, double-clicking that kind of file — such as an `.mp3` or an `.avi` file — automatically starts playing the file in Windows Media Player.)

Starting with the Media Guide

To start Windows Media Player, choose Start➪All Programs➪Windows Media Player. (If you have the Quick Launch toolbar enabled — see Book I, Chapter 2 — there's probably an icon for WMP down in the toolbar, too.) If the Media Guide isn't showing, click the Guide button at the top of the WMP window. The application now should look something like the version shown in Figure 1-3.

Figure 1-3: Windows Media Player's main page is just `www.WindowsMedia.com`, shown with the WMP surrounding box.

Windows Media Player looks like Figure 1-3 if you have a continuous connection to the Internet, or if the application can make a connection. That is because the Guide is actually a Web page — `www.WindowsMedia.com`, which you can view with any Web browser.

If Windows Media Player can't connect to the Internet, it shows a warning that says `The page cannot be displayed`. This warning looks just like the message that Internet Explorer would display in this situation because this part of Windows Media Player really *is* Internet Explorer, with an odd-looking border around the edges, and without the navigation tools you're accustomed to.

The Media Guide hooks into `www.WindowsMedia.com`, which is owned and operated by — you guessed it — a little company in Redmond, Washington, that also makes PC operating systems. The `www.WindowsMedia.com` site features clips from new music and videos, entertainment news, and other information that may interest users of WMP. Many of the pages have links that allow you to buy the products described.

Windows Media Player really, really, really wants to be connected to the Internet whenever it runs. If it can't connect, you can still use it to perform offline operations, such as playing stored music and writing CDs, but be ready to put up with constant complaints about Web sites that Windows Media Player can't access. Microsoft Web sites, of course.

Notice that Windows Media Player has no menu bar. Well, actually it does, but often the menu bar is hidden. Most of the time, you can use the application just fine without the menu bar, but when you need an operation that is accessible only through the menu bar, you can make it visible. Simply click the up and down arrow button shown near the upper-left corner of the window in Figure 1-3. Click the button again to make the menu bar go away.

When the menu bar is hidden, a Windows application's Minimize and Close boxes appear in the upper-right corner of the Windows Media Player window. They work just as they do when they appear in their usual places.

You control Windows Media Player with the row of buttons that runs across the top of the window.

Playing with Now Playing

The first control button on the WMP control bar is named Now Playing. When you click it, if you've never used WMP before, you get an offer to scan your computer and add any discovered songs or videos to WMP's Media Library (see Figure 1-4).

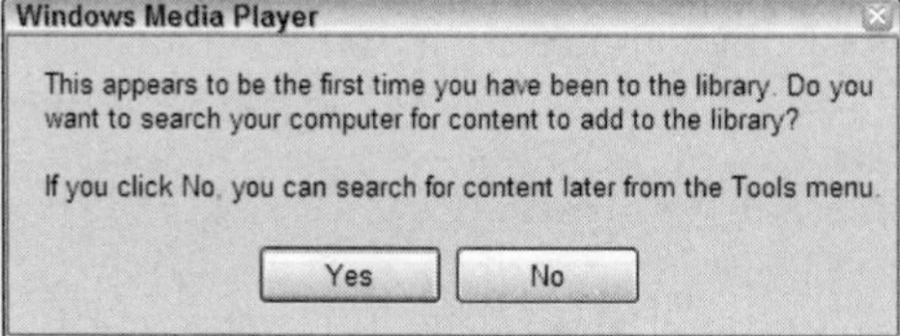

Figure 1-4: WMP offers to scan your drives for songs and videos.

No doubt you're wondering why WMP needs to scan your computer to set up the Media Library — after all, Windows Media Player is part of Windows, and Windows should know which songs and videos are already on your hard drive, right? Well, no. Although WMP tries to convince you otherwise, the Media Library isn't a separate place on your hard drive where the media files are stored. In fact, the Library is an ad-hoc catalog of media files that may reside anywhere on any hard drive. The Media Library may or may not accurately reflect which files are actually on the hard drive at any given moment. See the section, "Organizing Your Media Library," later in this chapter for details.

It's a good idea to have WMP scan your hard drive for songs and videos, so if you see the dialog box shown in Figure 1-4, click Yes. You will then get a dialog box like the one shown in Figure 1-5.

Figure 1-5: Turn the Media Library scanner loose on all of your drives.

To make sure all of your drives (including removable drives) get scanned, select All Drives in the Search On drop-down list, click Search, and then go get a latte. Depending on how many files you have, it can take a long, long time to scan every one. When the scan is finished, you have to click Close on the terminal dialog box.

If you ever want WMP to rescan your hard drives, choose Tools⇨Search for Media Files (or press F3) to start the scan (refer to Figure 1-4).

When WMP comes back up for air, you should see the Now Playing panes, as shown in Figure 1-6.

Figure 1-6: Now Playing shows you which songs have been queued up to play.

If you see a message on the left that says "Feature Not Available," you're lucky — it means you haven't shelled out extra bucks to Microsoft to see album information that you can find anywhere on the Internet. For example, the information on the Nine Inch Nails' album *Pretty Hate Machine* shown in Figure 1-6 can be retrieved, free, from `www.allmusic.com` (see Figure 1-7).

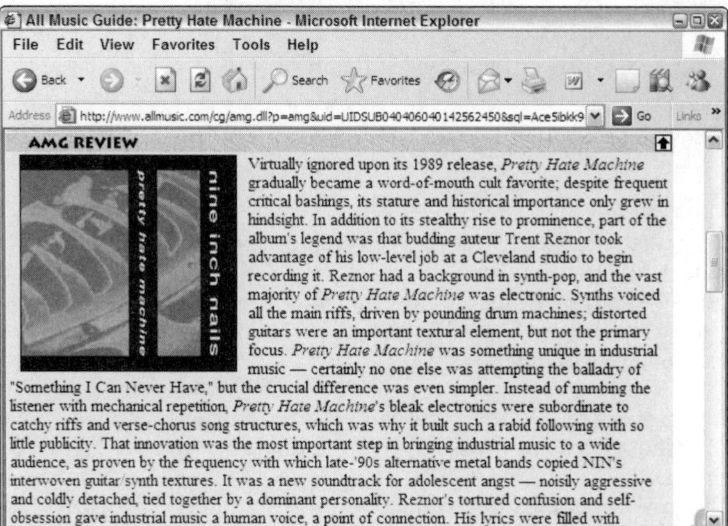

Figure 1-7: If you see a Feature Not Available notice in WMP, remember that album information is just a click away at `www.allmusic.com`.

If you've paid for Microsoft's premium service, the left side of the Now Playing window shows you all sorts of boring information about the album. If you're accustomed to the groovy visual effects changing to music that became WMP's hallmark, you have to click the button marked Info Center View and pick Visualizations. From that point, you can pick any of dozens of different pictures that move with the groove, as shown in Figure 1-8 — or download new ones.

You can make your visualization expand to fill the entire screen by clicking the button to the left of the Buy CD bar.

The right side of the Now Playing window displays a *playlist,* which is just a sequence of tracks. This particular playlist, the Now Playing playlist, is the list of tracks that are currently queued up to play, one after the other. To play a different track from the current playlist, double-click the track down in the list of playlist contents.

Playback buttons

The buttons along the bottom of the window control Now Playing. As shown in Table 1-1, they are very similar to the buttons on a conventional CD player.

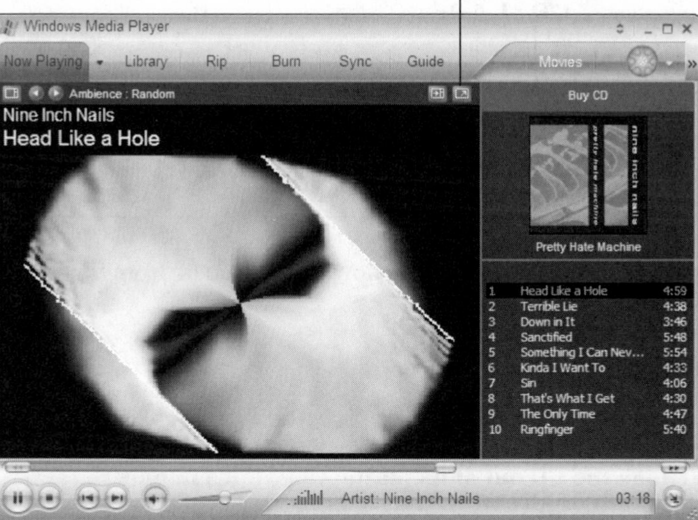

Figure 1-8: The 30 visualizations that ship with WMP are free. You can find many more on the Web by Googling "wmp visualization."

Table 1-1 Playback Buttons for Windows Media Player

Button	*What It Does*
	The Pause button pauses the playing.
	When playing is paused, the Pause button toggles to a Play button. Click it again to make playing resume.
	The Stop button stops the playing.
	Click the first button to start playing again. Unlike Pause/Resume, Stop/Start returns to the start of the track. To start a different track, double-click that track over in the playlist.
	The Previous Track button skips to the start of the previous track. From the first track in the playlist, it skips to the beginning of the last track on the playlist.
	The Next Track skips to the start of the next track. From the last track in the playlist, it skips to the first.
	The Mute button silences the sound. Click the button again to restore the sound. Unlike the Pause button, the Mute button does not halt playing. If you mute the sound for ten seconds, you miss hearing ten seconds of the track. If you mute Eminem for ten seconds, you get unwrapped (hardy har har).

(continued)

Table 1-1 *(continued)*

Button	*What It Does*
	The little slider to the right of the buttons controls volume.
	The big slider above the buttons shows WMP's position in the current track. As the track progresses from beginning to end, the slider moves from the left to the right. While WMP is playing a track, you can shift it to any point in the track by clicking that point on the track or by dragging the slider control to that point.

That's about all you need to know to play music from a playlist. Rocket science.

Playing a CD

Want to play a CD? That's hard, too. Here's how:

1. **Take the CD out of its plastic case, if it's in one.**
2. **Wipe the pizza stains off the shiny side (don't worry about the other side).**
3. **Stick the CD in the PC's drive and close it.**
4. **If Windows asks whether you want to Play Audio CD Using Windows Media Player (see Figure 1-9), click No I'd Rather Clip My Toenails What Did You Think I Wanted To Do? and then click OK.**

Figure 1-9: Windows may ask if you want to play the CD you just stuck in your CD drive. Yes, you probably do.

If WMP isn't running already, it starts all by itself. Then you wait a few seconds, and WMP starts playing the first track, using the Now Playing window, showing you the last visualization you chose. If the album is in Microsoft's big database in the sky, album info appears magically in the Now Playing screen, as shown in Figure 1-10.

Figure 1-10: Windows Media Player correctly identifies Nathan & the Zydeco Cha Chas. Hey, I'm impressed.

You can use the control buttons the same way for a CD as you do for a playlist — to pause and resume playing, select different tracks, and so on.

To WMP, the CD *is* a playlist. The tracks on the CD appear in the playlist area on the right side of the window. Look at the drop-down list of playlists in the upper-right corner of the window; the name of the CD appears as the selected item.

How does WMP know what's on the CD? After it identifies the CD from information encoded along with the recorded tracks, it gets the CD's description and track titles through the Web, from a database maintained for that purpose.

You music gearheads may be surprised to hear that the WMP database isn't maintained at `www.WindowsMedia.com`. The album shown in Figure 1-10 is described fully at `www.allmusic.com` — but it isn't even mentioned on Microsoft's Windows Media site.

If a CD is quite obscure — or really good — it may not be in Microsoft's database. Then WMP can display only the information it finds on the CD itself: the number of tracks and the playtime of each track (see Figure 1-11). If a CD isn't in Microsoft's database, you can enter the names of the songs manually. (To do so, right-click any song and choose Edit, and then type in a new name.)

Changing the size of the window

In its initial form, WMP occupies a substantial chunk of real estate on the desktop. To make it smaller, drag a corner of the window to the desired location, as you do with any other window. But note that when the menu bar is not visible, the only corner you can drag is the lower-right one.

Figure 1-11: This CD is not in the Windows Media Player database, although it's a best-selling Asian classic.

Copying from a CD: Also Known as Ripping

Before you copy music from a CD onto your computer, take a few minutes to find out more about MP3 and the reason why Windows Media Player may not have MP3 as an option for copying.

The MP3 conundrum

When you copy music from a CD to your computer — a process called *ripping* — you have to juggle a number of competing goals:

- You want to get the best-quality music possible, of course.
- You don't want the music to take up a lot of space. That isn't such a big deal with today's gargantuan hard drives. But if you're going to transfer your music to a portable audio player, every megabyte counts — the smaller the files, the more music you can fit on a player.
- You want to obey the copyright law, but you sure as shootin' don't want an obnoxious copy protection scheme to get in the way of making legal copies, or copying songs to other PCs or portable players for your own use.

- I'm just guessing here, but I'd be willing to bet that you really don't want Microsoft to take control over the internal workings of digital music and video. If you accept WMP's default settings, you're helping Microsoft in its quest to dominate the way music and videos are stored and played.

You can record music in many different *formats* — think of them as different methods for converting sound into bits. The formats are all different, and translating a song from one format to another can really put a crimp on the quality of the recording.

I have a detailed explanation of the various recording formats, their pros and cons, and recommendations for recording bit rates, in Technique 46 of *Windows XP Timesaving Techniques For Dummies* (Wiley Publishing, Inc.). If you're an audiophile (or a mini-phile, or even a de-phile), that Technique is well worth reading. If music doesn't drive your life, though, there are some general guidelines that apply in most cases, which I repeat here.

Back in the dark ages, if you wanted to record music on a computer, you used the MP3 format. It wasn't (and isn't) the fanciest format on the street; it makes files that are bigger than they need to be; and it doesn't support some really cool capabilities found with newer formats (such as Dolby-style 5.1 channel recording). With all its shortcomings, MP3 took off, and became the universal language of digital music. If you have something that plays digital music — whether it's an old PC, an ancient portable audio player (there's a reason why they're called "MP3 players"), or a 200GB iPod — it'll understand MP3.

MP3 has one additional, crucial saving grace: It ain't Microsoft.

Everybody and his brother has tried to introduce a format that's better than MP3, and almost all of them have succeeded, technically. But none of them have even approached MP3's colossal share of the market and minds of the world's music consumers — until Microsoft launched its WMA (and WMV) format.

WMA (for audio files) and WMV (for video files) are proprietary formats: Microsoft owns them, lock, stock, and digital barrel. Microsoft wants you to use WMA format. It wants to see WMA supplant MP3 as the audio file format of choice, for all computer users, everywhere.

There are plenty of reasons why Microsoft wants to control the format of digital media — and almost all of them are spelled with dollar ign.

When Microsoft first shipped Windows XP, it decided to refrain from including a program that would allow you to turn your audio CDs into MP3 files. (The program is called an MP3 *codec* — *co*der/*dec*oder — but don't let the techie talk throw you.)

Back at the dawn of Windows XP time, Microsoft howled that it couldn't afford to pay the royalties for an MP3 codec — ah, the irony of hindsight! — but all of us jaded Microsoft observers knew that the company's primary aim was to convince consumers to use the WMA format. Guess what? It worked. WMA now competes head-to-head with MP3, not just because of its technical superiority (and, yes, WMA makes smaller, better-sounding files), but also because WMA was good enough, and folks didn't want to go the extra mile to use MP3s.

Now many of those same consumers wonder why they can't copy their WMA files more than once or twice, or get them to play on a second computer (Hint: Think about the "Digital Rights Management" that Microsoft is selling to the recording labels), and why they can't get the CDs they created from their audio CD collections to work on older audio CD players. (Hint: MP3 is still the only universal format.)

There are three ways to get an *MP3 codec* (that is, a program that lets you turn audio CDs into MP3 files):

- ✦ You may already have it. Many new PCs ship with MP3 codecs because the PC manufacturers want you to be able to use the MP3 format.
- ✦ You can download and use it for free, if you get and use Apple's iTunes (see the sidebar, "The competition," earlier in this chapter).
- ✦ You can download and install an independent manufacturer's MP3 codec for use in Windows Media Player. Usually, you have to pay a bit. But it's money well spent, in my opinion.

To see if your computer already has an MP3 codec, follow these steps:

1. **In Windows Media Player, choose Tools⇨Options. (You may need to click the up and down arrow in the upper-right corner to see the menu bar.)**

   The Options dialog box appears.

2. **Click the Rip Music tab.**

   WMP shows you the dialog box shown in Figure 1-12.

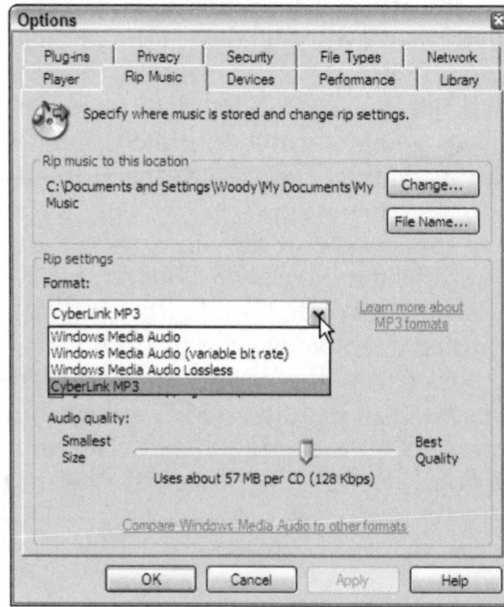

Figure 1-12: The Rip Music tab tells you if you have the ability to "rip" tracks off your audio CDs and turn them into MP3 files.

3. **Under Rip Settings, click the down-arrow to see the contents of the Format drop-down list.**

   If you have MP3 available, and you want to record in MP3 format, choose it, leave the slider at 128 Kbps recording quality (which is good for most people; see Technique 46 of *Windows XP Timesaving Techniques For Dummies*), and then click OK to go back to Windows Media Player.

   You may notice that when you choose to record in MP3 format, the Copy Protect Music check box grays out. Most excellent. That's because you *can't* copy protect an MP3 file.

   If MP3 is not on the list, and you want to record in MP3 format, you have to download and install an MP3 codec. (Or you can install iTunes and rip your CDs with it instead.)

4. **To buy an MP3 codec, click the Learn More About MP3 Formats link. Follow the instructions to buy, install, and activate the codec.**

   That link takes you to a page with offers from the three largest MP3 codec manufacturers. All three work well. I, personally, have used the CyberLink MP3 codec and DVD codec, without a single hiccup, since the earliest days of the Windows XP beta test.

If you have an MP3 codec that was created for an earlier version of Windows Media Player, it will almost undoubtedly work with WMP 10. No need to buy a new one. Just install the old one.

Ripping away

Here's how to *rip* a CD — that is, convert the audio tracks on the CD into files that your computer can work with:

1. **Using the steps at the end of the preceding section, tell WMP what format you want for your computer files, and how "good" you want the sound to be.**

   In Figure 1-12, I chose MP3 format — which I will continue to use until Microsoft beats the industry into submission — and 128 Kbps recording quality — which is plenty good enough for all but top-end stereo equipment. You can fit about 60 songs recorded this way on a 256MB MP3 player, or 5,000 songs onto a 20GB iPod.

2. **Put the audio CD that you want to copy into the CD drive.**

   If Windows Media Player isn't running, Windows asks if you want to start it (refer to Figure 1-9).

3. **Click the Rip tab at the top of the WMP screen.**

   WMP shows you a list of the tracks, as shown in Figure 1-13.

Figure 1-13: Ripping music couldn't be simpler.

4. **If you want to rip all of the tracks (er, copy all of the songs) on the CD, you don't need to do anything. But if you want to select specific songs to copy, select the check boxes to the left of each track that you want to copy, and deselect the check boxes next to the ones you want to leave behind.**

   In Figure 1-13, I decided to copy all of Nathan's Zydeco songs. Great stuff.

5. **Click the Rip Music button, near the middle up at the top.**

   Windows Media Player dutifully copies the tracks you've selected, placing the "ripped" files in the default folder, which is most likely your My Music folder.

   Earlier versions of Windows Media Player tried to shame you into applying copy protection at this point. If you're still running WMP 9 or earlier, and you get a message box that asks if you want to add copy protection to your music, tell WMP to stuff it, okay?

   WMP makes a folder for each artist, and inside the artist's folder, it makes a subfolder for each album. The music tracks go into the album's folder. If you're connected to the Internet, WMP grabs all the associated album information — track titles, album cover art, artist — and sticks it in the folder along with the music. Very sweet.

6. **Copying can take a while, so sit back and listen to the music, or go grab a latte or two.**

   When WMP's done, all of the tracks will be marked Ripped to Library, as in Figure 1-14.

Your newly ripped album appears in the Media Library list.

Figure 1-14: As songs get converted to a form that Windows can understand, WMP moves them to your My Music folder.

Organizing Your Media Library

WMP uses the Media Library to organize soundtracks. When you understand how the Media Library works, you can organize your music just the way you want.

Where the Media Library comes from

It's easy to get confused about the relationship between tracks — files on your computer — the Media Library, and playlists. Here's my favorite analogy, with books and libraries (I'm kinda partial to books, ya know):

- ✦ Say that a track is roughly analogous to a book.
- ✦ Your computer is like a library. A big library.
- ✦ The Media Library corresponds to the library's card catalog.
- ✦ Each playlist is like a special-purpose card catalog.

If you keep that analogy in mind, it's easy to understand that

- ✦ When the world's perfect, every track (audio, video, or TV recording) on your computer (or network) is in the Media Library, every track in the Media Library and every track in every playlist is on your computer (or network). But the best laid plans o' mice 'n men gang aft agley. . . .
- ✦ It's entirely possible to have a track on your computer that isn't in the Media Library. (That's analogous to the situation where you have a book in the library that isn't in the card catalog.)

- You can remove a track from the Media Library without taking it off your computer. (In analogy, you can yank a card out of the catalog without pulling the book out of the library.)
- It's possible to have entries in the Media Library that refer to tracks that have been deleted or aren't available because, for example, they may refer to a folder that's offline. (Analogously, you can have card in the card catalog that refers to a book that's been checked out — or chucked out.)
- Surprisingly, it's also possible to have tracks in a playlist that aren't in the Media Library. (Analogously, you can have a card in a special-purpose card catalog that refers to a book in the library — but the book doesn't have a card in the main catalog.)

To put it succinctly, Windows Media Player isn't smart enough to keep everything in synch. It tries — in particular, it monitors certain folders, watching to see if you add or remove audio and video files. But sometimes WMP gets very, very confused.

If you ever have a few minutes (or hours!) to spare, and you want to synchronize your Media Library with all the tracks that are on your PC (or network), try this:

1. **In Windows Media Player, choose Tools➪Search for Media Files. (You may need to click the up and down arrow in the upper-right corner to see the main menu.)**
2. **If you can't see the Advanced Search Options at the bottom, click the button that says Advanced Options.**

   WMP shows you the Add to Library by Searching Computer dialog box, as shown in Figure 1-15.

Figure 1-15: Rescan all of your drives to rebuild the Media Library.

3. **In the Search On drop-down list, select All Drives.**
4. **Make sure the Add Files Previously Deleted from Library check box is selected.**
5. **Click the Search button and go out for lunch.**

   When you come back, the Media Library should be rebuilt.
6. **Click Close, and Windows Media Player comes back, good as new.**

Leafing through the Media Library

Click the Library button up at the top to display the Media Library. WMP displays a window split into three panes, with the Media Library's structure on the left, the contents of the selected item in the middle, and the current Now Playing playlist on the right, as shown in Figure 1-16.

Figure 1-16: My Media Library (or at least a tiny part of it).

The Media Library is organized into folders, just like the Windows XP file system. Unlike the file system, the Media Library has a fixed set of folders:

- **All Music:** Contains all the audio tracks that are in your Media Library, such as those you have ripped from CDs. You can get at audio tracks by artist, composer, album, genre (rock, classical, comedy, folk, jazz, dance, Cajun, and so on), year released, or the star rating that you've assigned to individual tracks. There's also a, uh, special place for music that you've bought using WMP's connection to Napster or other online stores.

An album is "in" the Media Library if you have copied at least one track from that album with the Copy from CD operation, or if you have dragged a folder containing music into the My Music folder.

- **All TV:** Includes all TV shows that you've recorded using Windows Media Center Edition, as Book VIII, Chapter 2 explains. Shows are listed by title, series, genre, date recorded, actors, or your star ratings.

Windows Media Center Edition uses a weird file format called DVR-MS for recorded television programs. (So-called `*.dvr-ms` files.) As of this writing, several companies are trying to crack the format, and/or make "official" translators that change DVR-MS files into other kinds of files that the rest of the computer industry can work with. Until that happens, the only programs that can play your DVR-MS files are Windows Media Player and Windows Media Center (which actually uses WMP to do the playing). You can't even use Windows Movie Maker — Movie Maker doesn't understand DVR-MS files.

- **Video:** Video recordings, discussed in Book VII, Chapter 2. WMP can play video files in almost any format, including MPG, AVI, ASF, WMV, and many others.
- **My Playlists:** Playlists that you create or that come with Windows XP. Click the plus sign to expand the item into a list of playlists, and then select a playlist to see the audio tracks or video clips that it contains.
- **Auto Playlists:** WMP maintains an extensive collection of playlists, based on the ratings you've assigned to songs, when you last listened to the songs, if you've recently added the tracks to the Media Library, and much more.

Finding the tracks you want

The Media Library folders are powerful tools for keeping your recordings organized because they offer so many different ways of looking at the same information.

Want to know what albums contain recordings by a given artist? That artist's entry in the Artist folder tells you. Want to look at one of those albums to see what else is on it? The album's entry in the Album folder tells you.

It behooves you to keep your data clean. Misfiled and misidentified songs lead to endless frustration when you can't find a song that you know should be in the Media Library. If you want to change the data associated with a bunch of songs, find them in the Media Library, select the songs (Ctrl+click to select individual songs, or Shift+click to select a group of songs), right-click on one of fields (for example, the Album or the Artist) and choose Edit. Type in the new value, press Enter, and all of the selected songs are changed at the same time.

WMP also provides a tool to edit data works on one song at a time (Figure 1-17). It's slow, but it works. To use it, right-click on a misidentified track, and choose Advanced Tag Editor.

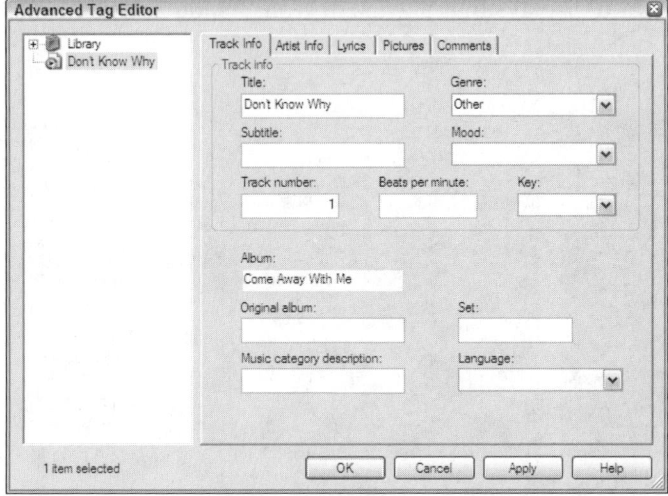

Figure 1-17: Windows Media Player's tool for editing "Tag" information about songs is rudimentary, but it works.

One of WMP's most powerful capabilities, the ability to create and manipulate playlists based on your own ratings of individual songs (or movies or TV shows), only works if you take the time to rate your songs! To rate any track at any time, right-click on it, choose Rate, and give it a rating from 1 to 5 stars.

Sorting

You can sort a list in the middle pane of the Media Library by the contents of any column. For example, click the All Music⇨Album Artist folder to display a list of all the artists, and then click an artist's name. Now click the heading of the Title column to sort the list of tracks by the title of the song. Click the heading of the Album column to sort the list by album. Click a heading twice in a row to sort the list backward on that column. If your collection of recordings is large, sorting the list in different ways can help you find items you want.

Searching

You can search the Media Library for items that have certain words in their titles or for artist names, album names, or genres. When your collection of recordings becomes too large to inspect easily, this is a convenient way to find things in it.

To search the Media Library, click in the box to the left of the Search button (directly underneath the Now Playing button). Enter a word that appears in at least one track title, artist name, or album name in the Media Library. Click the Search button. WMP searches the library, constructs a new playlist named Search Results that contains all the tracks that match the search criteria, and displays that playlist in WMP's middle window, as shown in Figure 1-18.

Figure 1-18: Searching for all the songs with "Queen" in the title, artist name, or album name fields is a snap.

The Search Results playlist is just like any other playlist, except that the contents of the list — the matching tracks — change every time you conduct a new search. You can keep a Search Results playlist around for a long time, or you can right-click on Search Results, choose Save as New Playlist, and save it for posterity.

Playing tracks in the Media Library

You can play a track directly from the Media Library. Just select the track and click the Play button at the bottom of the WMP window — or double-click on the track and WMP cuts straight to it.

You can even play a group of tracks by selecting the group. To play all of the songs by a given artist, for example, select that artist under the Artist folder and click Play, or double-click on an album under the Artist's name.

Nailing Track 6, Unknown Artist, Unknown Album

You probably already know that if you rip a CD while your PC isn't connected to the Internet, the Windows Media Web site may not be able to provide the track name, artist, and so on. In that case, the Media Library lists the track number as the track name and shows the artist, album, and genre as "Unknown" (see Figure 1-19).

Blech.

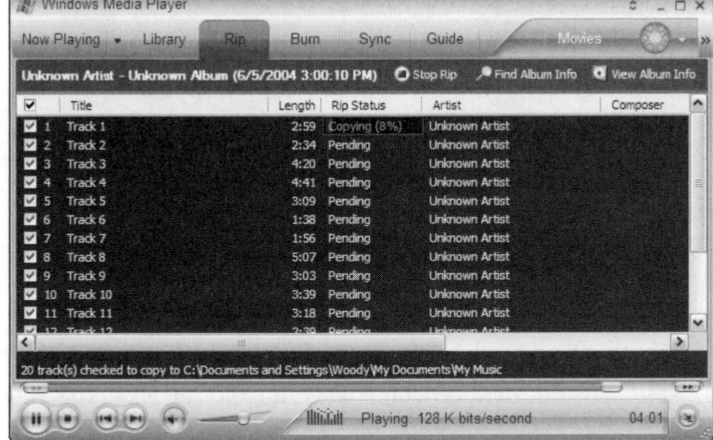

Figure 1-19: If you're offline when you rip a CD, WMP can't find the album's information.

Although many CDs these days include album cover art and other identifying information, Windows Media Player may or may not be able to pick up that information when it's ripping — and if you have an Internet connection that's, uh, less than 100 percent reliable, you may soon find yourself with a bunch of songs that claim to be "Track 6, Unknown Artist, Unknown Album." Fortunately, with WMP 10, if you can get connected to the Internet, you can probably retrieve the information — unless you have a very obscure CD that isn't in the WMP database.

Follow these steps to retrieve data for an "Unknown" album:

1. **Make sure you're connected to the Internet, and then start Windows Media Player.**
2. **Find the album in the Library.**

   Hint: It's listed among the albums under "U" for "Unknown."
3. **Double-click on the album, or the first track, to start playing the album.**
4. **Click Now Playing.**

   WMP shows you the Now Playing view. "Unknown Album" appears in the upper-right corner (see Figure 1-20). There may or may not be a picture of the album cover.

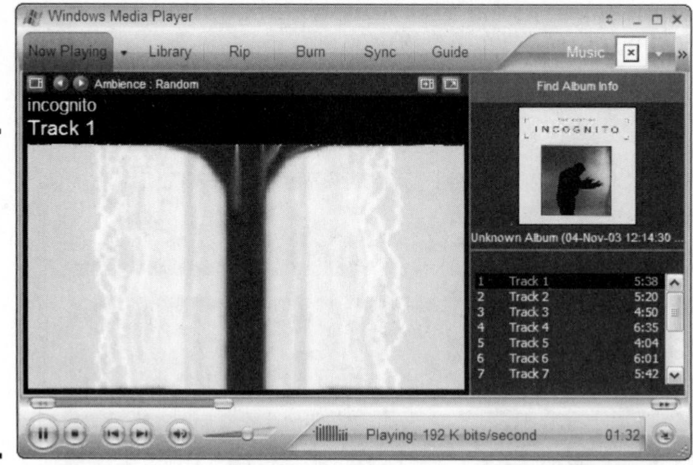

Figure 1-20: Albums that were ripped while WMP was offline may not have all of their pieces properly identified.

5. **Click the line Find Album Info above the Unknown Album box.**

   WMP runs out to Microsoft's Web site and retrieves the album information, if it can find the info (see Figure 1-21).

Figure 1-21: WMP finds the closest match for an "unknown" album from the AMG database (`www.allmusic.com`).

6. **If WMP found the correct album, click Finish.**

   WMP automatically updates the file information, replaces any information stored in the Media Library, and generally repairs all the broken pieces, without any further instruction.

Managing playlists

Er, maybe that should be *mangling* playlists.

WMP gives you all sorts of control over which songs you hear, and it does so through playlists. Did you ever want to rearrange the order of the songs on the Beatles' *White Album*? My son just about croaked when he found out he could burn a CD that plays Britney Spears' "Oops! . . . I Did It Again" immediately after Eminem's homage "Oops! . . . The Real Slim Shady Did It Again." You've got the power. Hmmm. That's a catchy tag line, isn't it?

Media Library enables you to create your own playlists, and you can modify them to your heart's content.

Creating a new playlist

If you have a favorite set of tracks that you like to hear in a particular order, and the tracks are in the Media Library, you can build a playlist that gives you precisely what you want. It's like being able to create your own custom CD.

In fact, you can use a playlist to *make* your own custom CD, if you have a CD burner (er, recorder). Nothing to it. The section, "Burning a CD," later in this chapter, explains how.

To make your own playlist, follow these steps:

1. **Click the New button on the right side of the Media Library window and choose Playlist.**

   Windows Media Player invites you to drag items to the new playlist, as shown in Figure 1-22.

Figure 1-22: Build a new playlist by dragging tracks into the area on the right.

2. **On the left, choose the way you want to look at your Media Library (by artist, by album, by genre, and so on), navigate to each song that you want on the playlist, and then drag it to your preferred location on the right.**

   Alternatively, you can just click a track, and then click the Add to "New Playlist" line at the top of the playlist pane.

   WMP adds the track to the playlist. In Figure 1-23, I build a playlist of recordings of the *Adhan* — the Islamic Call to Prayer.

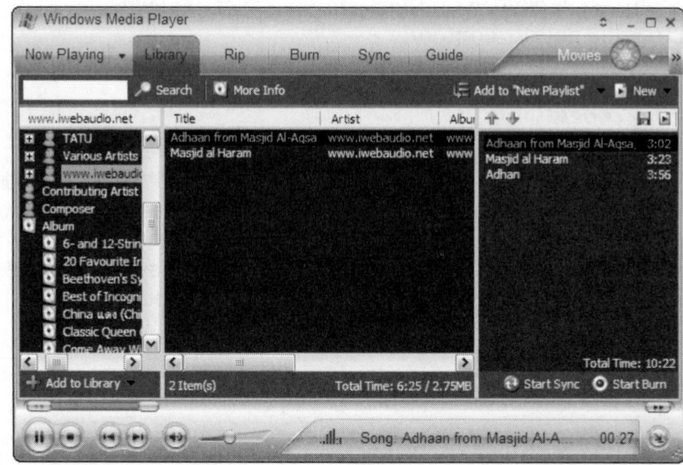

Figure 1-23: Create a new playlist by dragging, or by clicking on a track and then clicking Add to "New Playlist."

3. **If you decide that you don't want a specific song on the playlist, right-click it, and choose Remove from List. You can move the songs up and down on the playlist by clicking the up and down arrows.**

4. **When you're happy with your playlist, click the icon that looks like a diskette at the top of the playlist.**

   WMP responds with a Save As dialog box, as shown in Figure 1-24.

5. **Type a name for your new playlist in the File Name text box and click Save.**

   WMP saves your new playlist. It appears anywhere playlists appear, anywhere in Windows Media Player.

That's how hard it is to create a new playlist.

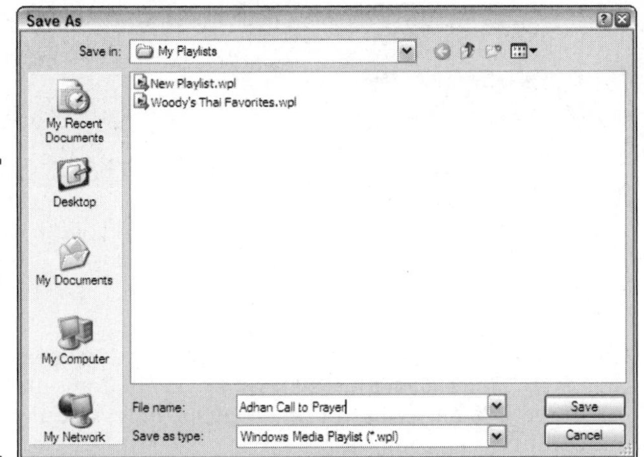

Figure 1-24: Give your new playlist a name, and it's saved the same way as any other playlist.

Adding a track to a playlist

In the Media Library, you can add a track to any playlist, at any time:

1. **Select any folder or folder item that contains that track, so that the track appears in the right pane of the window.**
2. **Right-click on the track and choose Add To, and then choose the playlist.**

   It's that easy.

Alternatively, you can bring up a playlist so that it appears on the right (say, by navigating to My Playlists on the left), and then drag new tracks into the playlist. Just remember to save the playlist by clicking the icon that looks like a diskette when you're done.

You can add the same track to any number of playlists. Just right-click it again, pick Add To, and choose a different playlist.

Don't worry about using up storage space. Playlists take almost no room. No matter how many playlists you add a track to, the Media Library maintains just one copy of the track. Playlists are like headings in a library catalog: No matter how many headings a particular book is indexed under, there's still just one copy of the book.

Renaming and deleting playlists

To delete a playlist, right-click the playlist in the My Playlists list and choose Delete. Or just click the playlist and press the Delete key. WMP responds with a confusing dialog box, as shown in Figure 1-25. Deleting the playlist only deletes the playlist itself, not the actual songs in the playlist.

Figure 1-25: Don't worry. Removing a playlist does not remove the songs from your computer.

When working with playlists, you can safely choose to either Delete from Media Library or to Delete from Media Library and My Computer. There's essentially no difference between the two choices, unless you want to copy playlists from computer to computer.

To change a playlist's name, right-click the playlist and choose Rename.

Managing the contents of playlists

Just as you can manage playlists, you can manage the contents of a playlist.

To make any type of change to a playlist, first select the playlist in the left pane of the Media Library to display its contents in the right pane.

To delete a track from the playlist, right-click the track and choose Delete from Playlist, or select the track and press Delete.

To change a track's position in the playlist, just drag the track to the position you want, or use the up and down arrows above the list.

Deleting tracks from the Media Library

No matter how many playlists a track is added to, your hard drive still contains just one copy of the track. The reverse is just as true: Even if you delete a track from every playlist that contains it, the track is still on your hard drive, and the Media Library still has a record of the track.

It's possible to remove a track from the Media Library, though.

If you right-click on a track, an album, or even an artist or genre, and pick Delete, WMP asks if you want to delete the track (album, whatever) from the Media Library only, or if you want to delete it from both the Media Library and your computer (refer to Figure 1-25).

It's rare that you want to delete a track from your computer — although if you have 200GB of tracks (and I won't mention a certain contributor to this book by name), you might want to free up hard drive space by working from inside Windows Media Player. In general, choose to delete the track from the Media Player (so it doesn't clutter up things when you're looking for stuff you really want to play), but don't delete the track from your computer. That way, if you change your mind and want to get the track back, you can just press F3 and have WMP rescan all your computer's hard drives.

Take care not to delete a track from the Media Library when you intend to remove it only from a playlist. When you right-click a track in a playlist, the Delete command and the Remove from List command are right next to each other! It's easy to choose the wrong one.

Working with files and Web sites

WMP can play more than tracks from CDs or the Media Library. It can play any sound recording or video clip that is accessible to you from a file on your computer, through your local area network, or through the Internet.

This opens up all sorts of possibilities. You can trade soundtracks with your friends through e-mail. You can download tracks from multitudes of Web sites. Or you can buy, buy, buy using the (many!) conveniently located links to Microsoft-partner Online Stores — Napster and CinemaNow being the poster children of the Microsoft Online Store generation.

If you feel compelled to enrich Microsoft in yet another way, click the Movie button in the upper right of the screen, or click the down arrow next to it, to be whisked away to Microsoft's partners. Hold onto your pocketbook. Shopping through WMP may be convenient, but it certainly ain't cheap.

Playing a file

The easiest way to play a file that contains a sound recording is to double-click on it. Failing that, you can start WMP, make sure that WMP's menu bar is visible (you may have to click on the up and down arrow in the upper-right corner). Choose File➪Open. Use the Open dialog box to find and open the file. When you click the Open button, WMP plays the file.

If you don't have any sound recordings outside the Media Library, you can try this with a bunch of sound recordings that come with Windows XP. These files contain the sounds that you hear when you log on, log off, and so on. Go to `C:\Windows\Media` and try opening any of the media files you find there.

Playing a Web site

To play a Web site, choose File➪Open URL. Type the Web site's address (a URL such as `www.templesholom.com/audio/cantor/friday_night/shma.mp3`) and click OK.

Because the addresses of files on the Web are often long and difficult to type, copying the address is easier than typing it. Here's one way to do it:

1. **Use Internet Explorer to navigate to a Web page that contains a link to the sound recording.**
2. **If you clicked the link, Internet Explorer would play the recording. Don't do that now; instead, right-click the link and choose Copy Shortcut.**
3. **Return to WMP, click the File/Open URL command, and paste the URL (the *shortcut*) into the dialog box.**

Adding a file or Web site to the Media Library

This process is very similar to playing a file or a Web site, as I discuss in the preceding section. To add a file to the Media Library, follow these steps:

1. **Show the menu bar (if it isn't visible) by clicking the up and down arrow in the upper-right corner of the WMP screen.**
2. **Choose File⇨Add to Library⇨Add File or Playlist.**

   WMP shows you a standard Windows File Open dialog box.
3. **Click the file you want to add to the Media Library, and then click the Open button.**

   WMP adds the file to the Media Library as an entry in the All Music folder.

To add a Web address to the Media Library, follow the preceding steps, but in Step 3 choose Add URL.

Note that when you add a file or a Web site to the Media Library, you're not storing a copy of the sound recording in the library; you're just storing a *reference* to it. When you play the recording through the Media Library, WMP actually plays the original copy, wherever it happens to be stored.

If you add a file to the Media Library and later delete or move the original file, the entry for the file still appears in the Media Library, but WMP can't play the file. The same is true if you add a Web site to the Media Library and the Web site moves it, deletes it, or goes out of service.

In many cases, you have a choice between downloading a file from a Web site and adding it to the Media Library or simply adding its address to the Media Library. Each approach has advantages.

Advantages of downloading the file and adding it to the Media Library are

- You have your own copy of the recording. You don't risk losing access to it if it becomes unavailable through the Web.
- You don't have to be concerned about whether you can download the recording fast enough to play it without pauses. If your Internet connection is slow or the Internet is busy, the download may take a long time, but when it is over, you can play the file continuously.

Advantages of adding a Web site address are

- It consumes virtually no space on your hard drive. Sound recordings, on the other hand, tend to be large. So if you download a lot of files, they consume a lot of hard drive space.
- Adding the Web site address may be your only option. Many Web sites let you play music directly from their site but won't let you download files because they don't want to distribute free copies of their intellectual property.

Some sound recordings are stored in formats that WMP can't read. These may be proprietary formats for which you are legally required to purchase a special player from an independent source. If you try to play a file or Web site that is recorded in one of these formats, WMP displays a message that says it cannot play the file.

Burning CDs

If your computer has a CD writer, you can create an audio CD by using tracks in the Media Library. Windows Media Player makes it easy.

Of course, you can also burn CDs and DVDs by using Windows XP itself — I talk about that in Book I, Chapter 5. The procedure is quite simple: In Windows Explorer, drag the files you want to put on the CD into the CD's folder, and then work with a wizard to transfer the files to CD. That method works great for copying, say, MP3 files (or WAV files) onto a CD. As long as you have another computer, or a player that works with MP3 or WAV files, using Windows itself and copying plain old computer files makes a lot of sense.

But if you want to make an audio CD — that is, a CD that you can stick into any old CD player — you need to use Windows Media Player. Just as ripping (see the section, "Copying from a CD: Also Known as Ripping," earlier in this chapter) changes audio sound tracks into files that the computer can understand, burning with Windows Media Player transforms those files back into audio sound tracks that any CD player can play.

Burning DVDs — that is, transferring movies to a DVD writer — is an entirely different can of worms. Microsoft doesn't support burning movies (as of the time this book went to press, anyway). If you want to get a movie onto a DVD, you have to use a program from some other company. The technology and the legalities seem to change from day to day, so your best bet for getting the latest is to run a Google search for "Windows XP burn DVD."

In any case, you can't copy live feeds such as programs from radio stations. Such programs are broadcast for listening only, so recording them would often violate the intellectual property rights of the radio station or of others.

Understanding CD-Rs and CD-RWs

There are two types of writeable CDs: CD-Rs and CD-RWs.

CD-R is short for *CD readable*. This is a CD that you can write to one time. After a CD-R has been written to, you cannot add to it or erase it.

CD-RW is short for *CD read-write*. This is a CD that you can erase and rewrite many times.

A CD-R writer can write only CD-Rs. A CD-RW writer generally can write either CD-Rs or CD-RWs. Most CD writers sold today are CD-RW.

You generally can play a CD-R on a conventional CD player or on a computer's CD-ROM drive (or a CD-R drive, or a CD-RW drive). But CD-RWs don't work all the time: Many modern CD players take CD-RW discs, no problem, but older CD players almost universally demand simple CD-Rs.

You can find a detailed discussion of CD-Rs and CD-RWs in Book I, Chapter 5.

WMP cannot add data to a partially recorded CD-RW. Before you can reuse a CD-RW, you must erase it, like this:

1. **Put the CD-RW in the CD writer.**
2. **Choose Start⇨My Computer.**
3. **Select the CD writer.**
4. **Click Erase CD-RW.**

Burning a CD

In this section, "CD" refers to both CD-Rs and CD-RWs.

The process of writing data to a CD is called *burning*. WMP enables you to burn a plain, old-fashioned, everyday audio CD very, very easily. Here's the quickest way I know to put together a dynamite audio CD:

1. **Start Windows Media Player.**

   You can click on the WMP icon in your Quick Launch toolbar, or choose Start⇨Windows Media Player, or (if you can't see Windows Media Player) choose Start⇨All Programs⇨Windows Media Player.

2. **Click the Library button to go to the Media Library, and then create a playlist that contains all of the tracks you want to burn on the CD.**

   Follow the instructions in the section, "Creating a new playlist," earlier in this chapter. In Figure 1-26, I build just such a list for some of my favorites.

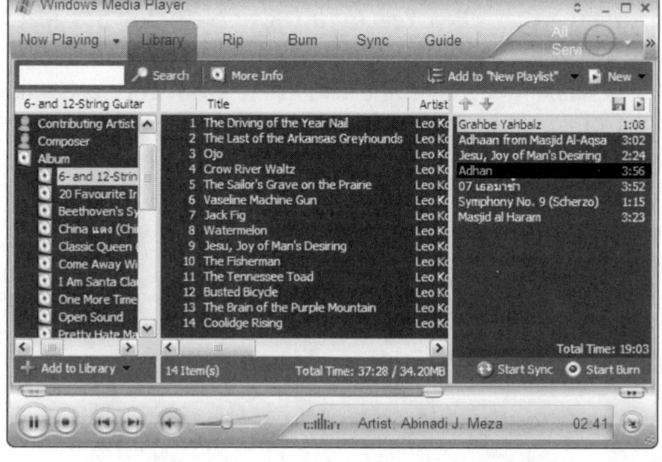

Figure 1-26: The fast way to create an audio CD: Start by building a playlist with the tracks you want to burn.

The 30-second version: Click the New button in the upper-right corner and choose Playlist. Then click and drag the tracks that you want to burn over to the right-hand side. Move the tracks around to put them in the order you like by clicking and dragging. If you decide you don't want a particular track, right-click on it and choose Remove from Playlist.

Keep an eye on the Total Time number at the bottom of the list. If you get up to 70 minutes, you're pushing the theoretical limit of a single CD (which can vary between 74 and 80 minutes, depending on the type of CD you're using and the phase of the moon).

3. **Make sure your CD burner (er, CD-R or CD-RW drive) is working, and put a blank CD in the burner.**

4. **In WMP's lower-right corner, click Start Burn.**

Windows Media Player warns you that you haven't saved your new playlist with the dialog box shown in Figure 1-27.

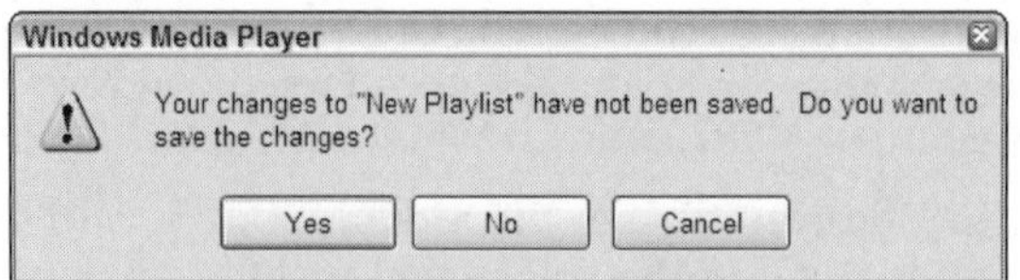

Figure 1-27: WMP urges you to save your new playlist — always a good idea.

5. **If you want to save your playlist (it may help if you have problems burning the CD), click Yes. In the Save As dialog box (see Figure 1-24), type in a name for the playlist, and click Save.**

   WMP starts converting the tracks (that's the process of changing each track from a computer-readable form like MP3 or WMA into the native audio CD format), as shown in Figure 1-28.

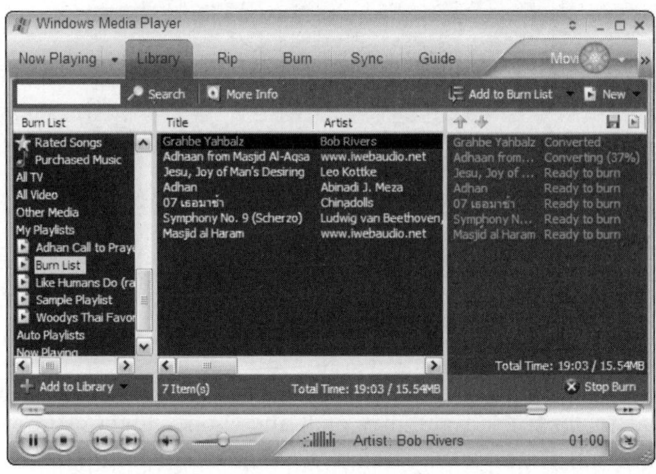

Figure 1-28: Before writing the tracks to a CD, WMP converts them to a format that plays on a CD player.

After all the tracks are converted, WMP burns each one to the CD. It's really that simple. When WMP's done, pull the CD out of the CD burner and plop the CD into any CD player. The magic's the music.

The copying process takes a substantial fraction of the time it would take to play the copied tracks, the exact time depending on the speed of your CD writer.

It is best not to use your computer for other tasks while writing a CD. If another task's activity prevents WMP from writing a continuous stream of data, the CD will be spoiled.

If you interrupt the writing process by clicking the Cancel button or by removing the CD from the writer before it is complete, WMP goes bananas, and the whole process stops. If you screw up a CD-RW, you must erase it before you can reuse it. A fried CD-R ain't good for anything but a coaster.

Syncing with a Portable Player

Call it an MP3 player, if you will. (The folks at Microsoft do.) Or call it an iPod, a jukebox, or a portable digital audio player. Moving your songs from your computer to an MP3 player has never been simpler.

Audio is only part of the story, though. The new generation of portable video machines — whether you call the device a Portable Media Center (a term trademarked by Microsoft, of course), video jukebox, digital video player, or that dern MTV thingy — seems poised to take over the toy market.

Windows Media Player handles both audio and video (including recorded TV) with aplomb. In fact, when WMP works right, transferring files to your portable player is every bit as easy as burning a CD. Easier, actually, because you don't have to put a blank CD in the drive.

Here's how to get your tunes and flicks onto your MP3 or video player:

1. **Attach your player to one of your computer's USB ports and turn it on.**

   Windows XP should identify the player with the Found New Hardware Wizard. If all else fails, read the player's instruction manual and run the program on the CD that came with the player to get the drivers working. You may need to visit the manufacturer's Web site to download the latest drivers. This technology is changing fast, and drivers become obsolete overnight.

2. **Start Windows Media Player.**
3. **Click the Library button to go to the Media Library, and then create a playlist that contains all of the tracks you want to burn on the CD.**

   See the preceding section of this book for details.

4. **In WMP's lower-right corner, click Start Synch.**

   Windows Media Player may warn you that you haven't saved your new playlist (refer to Figure 1-27).

5. **To save your new playlist (and you should), click Yes, type the name of the playlist in the Save As dialog box, and then click Save.**

   WMP copies the files in your playlist onto your portable player.

6. **When the copying is done, unplug your portable player, and have at it.**

   Transferring songs, video, and TV shows is really that simple.

If you click the Start Synch button and WMP warns you that it cannot detect a connected portable device, a couple of things could be wrong:

- ✦ WMP may not have noticed that you have attached the player to the computer. To fix this problem, quit WMP, unplug your device, plug it back in, wait for Windows XP to recognize it, and then restart WMP.
- ✦ You may not have the right driver. Go to the manufacturer's Web page, click your heels three times, and pray that you can find a driver that works right with the current version of Windows Media Player.
- ✦ Windows XP may not support your particular player. To fix this problem, you may need a new bank account.

Choosing a Skin

A *skin* is a little file that changes WMP's appearance. I'm not talking subtle changes here; I'm talking complete transformation. A skin can make WMP look like a 1950's juke box, a *Star Trek* phaser, a funny face, or Bill G's trampoline room.

If you like intriguing visual effects, skins are for you.

Skins have a practical advantage, too: Most of them make WMP occupy less screen space in *skin mode* than it does in its normal *full mode*. Skins do this by presenting only WMP's most frequently used functions; but if those are the only functions you need, why should you mind? You can always switch back to full mode when you need a function that your preferred skin doesn't provide.

Switching skin modes

Getting WMP into skin mode is easy. Click the Switch to Skin Mode button in the bottom frame, to the right of the volume control slider. Or use the shortcut Ctrl+2.

What does skin mode look like? Well, that depends on the skin. The skin that WMP displays out of the box looks like the one shown in Figure 1-29.

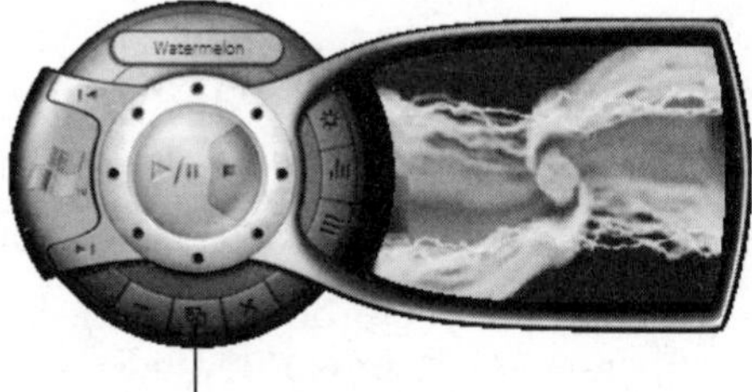

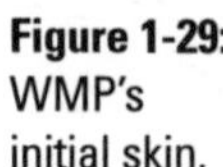

Figure 1-29: WMP's initial skin.

To get out of skin mode, each of the skins has a Return to Full Mode button. The buttons move all around; no two skins seem to have the same button in the same place, but that's part of the fun, eh?

Controlling WMP's functions in skin mode can be a, uh, challenge. Who woulda thought that clicking on Toothy's tooth (see Figure 1-30) would move fast forward and fast back in the current track?

Figure 1-30: The Toothy skin's tooth performs WMP's "seek" function, moving backward and forward in the current track.

When in doubt (or if you don't find these games amusing anymore — where have I heard that phrase?), right-click on the skin and you will see a more-or-less normal selection of functions, including the option to Switch to Full Mode.

You can also switch WMP back to full mode with the shortcut Ctrl+1. That should be easy to remember: Ctrl+2 for skin mode, Ctrl+1 for full mode.

The volume control is usually on the graphic equalizer or in the audio controls.

More skins!

Choosing a new skin while you're in "normal" full mode requires some gymnastics. Here's how:

1. **In Windows Media Player, choose View⇨Go To⇨Skin Chooser.**

   If you can't see the View menu (and you probably can't), click the up and down arrow in the upper-right corner of the window.

   WMP shows you a handful of built-in skins, as shown in Figure 1-31.

Figure 1-31: Choose a brainy skin. I call this one the Hannibal Lecter Special.

2. **If you want to find more Microsoft-approved skins, click the More Skins button. You'll be transported to Microsoft's skin collection, which has some truly remarkable skins, ready to download for free.**

   Or you can hit one of the thousands of sites on the Web that have skins, almost all of which are completely free. Try `http://skinz.org` or `http://customize.org`.

3. **Double-click on a skin you want to try.**

   WMP flips into skin mode, with your chosen skin.

Customizing WMP

You can customize WMP in a large number of ways. You get to most of the settings by choosing Tools⇨Options. This command displays a dialog box with a bunch of tabs for customizing many aspects of WMP's behavior:

- **The Player tab:** Controls general aspects of WMP's behavior, such as checking for automatic updates.
- **The Rip Music tab:** Controls aspects of the copying process, such as the amount of data compression to apply when copying a CD. (More compression makes the copied tracks occupy less space, but reduces sound quality.) It also controls the folder to which music is copied (by default the My Music folder, which is the folder that the Media Library uses).
- **The Devices tab:** Lists available devices that WMP can use (such as CD drives and portable players) and enables you to control certain aspects of their behavior.
- **The Performance tab:** Lets you control how WMP handles streaming media.
- **The Library tab:** Controls access to the Media Library by other applications and other sites on the Internet. It also tells WMP which folders to monitor for additions to, and deletions from, the Media Library.
- **The Privacy and Security tabs:** Primarily control how much information you send to Microsoft every time you use WMP.
- **The File Types tab:** Lets you select file types, such as `.wav` and `.mp3`, for which you want WMP to be the default player. (Double-click one of these files in a folder and its default player — whatever application that may be — plays it.)
- **The Network tab:** Lets you select the network protocols that WMP may use to receive streaming media. It also lets you control *proxy settings,* which you may have to change if your computer is on a local area network protected by a firewall.

My privacy settings are shown in Figure 1-32. If you decide to give Microsoft more information than the amount shown in that figure, I strongly recommend that you click the Learn More About Privacy link and read the information with a thoroughly jaundiced eye.

It'll take an advanced degree in Computer Science to even begin to understand many of these settings. Come to think of it, I have an advanced degree in Computer Science, and *I* don't understand some of those settings. It's a good policy to change one of the options only if you understand it well and keep careful notes so that you can restore the original setting if anything goes wrong.

There's no harm in *looking* at the options, though. You can discover a lot by clicking the Help button on each tab of the Options dialog box.

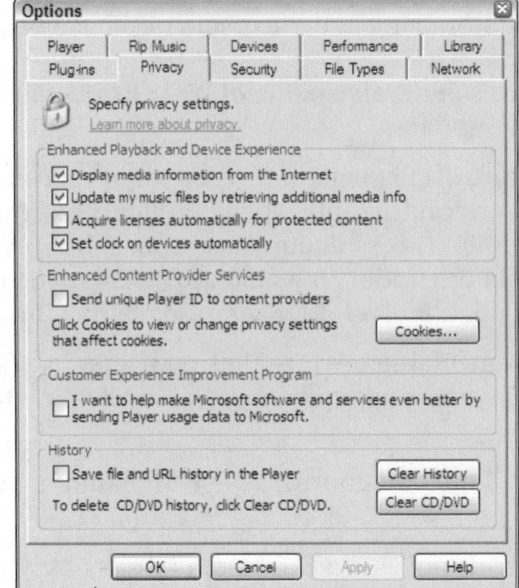

Figure 1-32: The most information I'll give to Microsoft.

Understanding Digital Licenses

You know about copyrights. The law says that the creator of a written work (including a sound recording or a video) has a right to fair compensation for the copying and use of the work. With some very limited exceptions, it's illegal to deprive the copyright owner of these rights . . . for example, by e-mailing copies of the work to 50 of your closest friends.

Copyright has always been difficult to enforce where computers are involved because copying data is so easy. WMP supports a concept called *digital licensing,* which helps to protect the rights of copyright owners.

If you ever wonder if a particular track on your computer has a digital license, use Windows Media Player to find the track, right-click on it and choose Properties. Details about the license appear on the License tab.

Acquiring a license

Here's how digital licensing works. The owner of the copyright in a sound recording or a video clip (or even an entire TV show or movie) can encode the recording in a Windows Media Audio (`.wma`) file or a Windows Media Video (`.wmv`) file for video clips and lock the file so that no one can play it without a digital license. Then the owner (called a *content provider* in this context) can publish the file in any manner, such as putting it on a public Web site. Anyone can download the file, but no one can use it without first obtaining a license.

How do you get a license? That's entirely up to the content provider! If the content provider is a record company, it typically sells you a license. Thus the content provider gets its money and you get a useable copy of the recording, just as if you bought one in a store.

What can you do with a licensed file after you get the license? Not, as you may suppose, anything you want. In particular, you can't e-mail copies of the file and the license to 50 of your closest friends. If you try, your friends will get a useless file because your license is good only on your computer. (Your friends are free to get their own licenses, of course, and then they can play the file.)

Microsoft keeps tweaking the restrictions and capabilities of its licensing regime. For example, some audio files may be downloaded to an MP3 player (oops, a portable audio player), and the license may specify that you can listen to the songs. You may get the right to listen to the song on several MP3 (there's that word again) players, or on several PCs.

MP3 players — that is, machines that play MP3 files — don't get caught up in the licensing game. MP3 files aren't licensed. Can't be licensed. No way, no how. Nor can MPG video files. Only some proprietary formats — foremost among them Microsoft's WMA and WMV files — can even *have* licenses.

Here are some important restrictions that a digital license may carry:

- The license is valid only on your computer.
- The license may expire at some point, requiring you to obtain another. (Whether a license expires, and when, is up to the content provider.)
- The license may prevent you from using the file in certain ways (for example, you might not be allowed to copy it to a digital audio player).

Using digital licenses

It's important to back up your computer's digital licenses. If you ever have to restore your copy of Windows XP because of a hardware or software failure, you have to restore your digital license backup to use your licensed files — yes, the files you paid for. If you have no backup, you would have to obtain each license again from its issuer. That would be troublesome, time consuming, and probably expensive.

Of course, it isn't enough to back up your digital licenses to your PC's hard drive. You have to make (or keep) a separate copy elsewhere, specifically in the event that your hard drive dies. Licensing is a slippery slope.

Similarly, if you move your operations to a new computer, you must restore your digital license backup to the new computer to use your licensed files.

Windows XP allows you to restore backed-up digital licenses a total of four times.

Backing up a license

To back up your digital licenses:

1. **In Windows Media Player, choose Tools➪Manage Licenses (if you can't see the Tools menu, click the up and down arrow in the upper-right corner).**

   This displays the Manage Licenses dialog box, as shown in Figure 1-33.

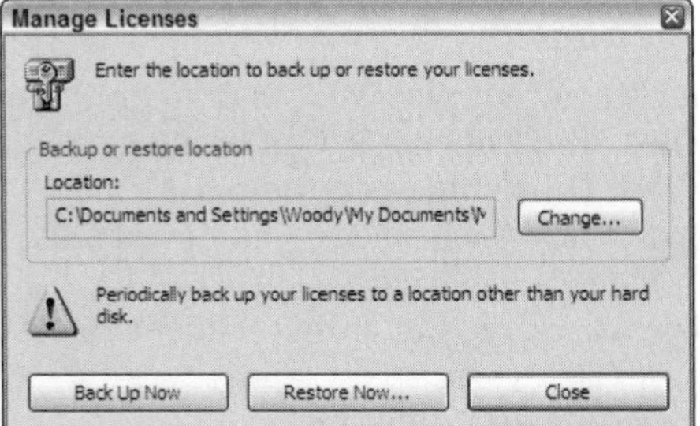

Figure 1-33: Windows XP allows you to back up or restore your digital licenses for your WMA and WMV files.

2. **Click the Change button. Select the device or folder in which you want to store the backup, and then click OK.**
3. **After you choose a location for the backup, click the Back Up Now button.**

   WMP backs up your licenses in the specified location and then displays the message `Transfer complete`. Click OK.

Microsoft recommends backing up the licenses to a diskette. This has the advantage of preserving the licenses if your computer's hard drive crashes, or if the computer itself is lost or damaged. Diskettes are not a very reliable storage medium, though, so if you use this option, always back up in duplicate. A safer medium for backups would be a second hard drive on your computer, a hard drive on your network (if you have one), a flash memory device, or CD.

How often should you create an updated backup of your licenses? Ideally, you should do it whenever you acquire a new license. Realistically, you should do it on a regular schedule, the frequency depending on how often you tend to acquire digital licenses.

Restoring the licenses

The procedure for restoring the licenses is very similar to the procedure for backing them up:

1. **Ensure that your latest backup is available to your computer.**

   If it is on a CD, for example, put the CD in your computer's CD drive.

2. **In Windows Media Player, choose Tools⇨Manage Licenses.**
3. **Click the Change button and select the device or folder in which the backup is located. Click OK.**
4. **Click the Restore Now button.**

   WMP restores your licenses from the specified location.

If you try this process just to see how it works, *don't click Restore Now.* Remember that Windows XP allows you to restore your license backup only four times.

Making your songs unusable

One of the most hare-brained options in all of Windows-dumb, the Copy Protect Music check box on the Rip Music tab (see Figure 1-34) only exists to trip the unwary. I talk about that check box in the earlier section, "Copying from a CD: Also Known as Ripping." Now that you know about digital licensing, you're ready for the details.

If you select the Copy Protect Music check box, every time you rip a song into WMA format — that is, every time you copy a song from an audio CD and turn it into a WMA file, which your computer can understand — Windows Media Player invents a digital license for the track and locks down the WMA file with that specific license.

Yes, you read that right. Windows Media Player creates a music track that can be played only on your computer. If you copy the WMA file to another computer, Windows Media Player can't play it. The file is essentially useless.

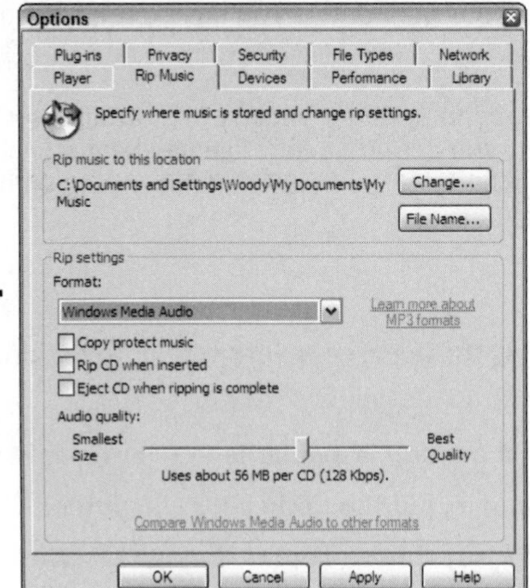

Figure 1-34: Only a fool would select the Copy Protect Music check box.

Do yourself a favor. Don't select that check box. Better, go buy an MP3 codec and rip into MP3 format, so you *can't* get gouged by Microsoft's latest copy protection scheme.

Chapter 2: Lights! Action! Windows Movie Maker

In This Chapter

- **Recording and editing video**
- **Using still pictures as titles**
- **Bringing in narration and background sounds**
- **Organizing your clips**

Windows Movie Maker brings a full-featured video-editing workshop to your PC. You can use it to create anything from a few seconds of action — say, to dress up an e-mail message — to a full-length documentary about your kid's first birthday party. Get the sound synchronization right, and you could even toss together a decent music video, sell it to Hollywood, and turn into an overnight sensation.

Just remember where you got the idea, huh?

Windows Movie Maker (WMM) isn't going to drive George Lucas out of business any time soon, although the current version runs rings around the "version 1.0" that originally shipped with Windows XP. You don't want to bet your company or your reputation on WMM — in the course of writing this chapter, it froze several times, and WMM steadfastly refused to open a movie file created by . . . Windows Movie Maker. WMM may not be the best entry-level movie-editing product on the market, but you can't beat the price.

What You Need to Create Movies

Movie making requires a lot of hardware. Obviously, unless you're editing footage someone else has shot, you need some type of video camera, although a cheap Webcam suffices if you don't mind limiting yourself to pictures that can be shot with a Webcam tethered to a computer. You need a lot of computer, too, to handle big video files.

The competition

So what's not to like about a free video-editing tool that's guaranteed to be 100 percent Windows XP compatible? Windows Movie Maker covers most of the bases, but you may want to plunk out a few more pesetas for a couple of specific features.

The most common complaint I hear about WMM? It creates movie files only in Microsoft's proprietary WMV or DV-AVI format (you can put a copy of the movie in DV-AVI format back on your digital video recorder). If you want to create a DVD, you're outta luck. As long as you're only going to put movies back on your video camera, or if you'll be viewing them on a Windows XP computer, the limitation doesn't matter much. But if you want to create MPEG-2 files for DVDs (or MPEG-1 files for VCDs), you're better off with Sony Screenblast Movie Studio (less than $100 from `http://mediasoftware.sonypictures.com`) or the professional level Adobe Premiere (around $700 from `http://adobe.com/products/premiere`).

Both Movie Studio and Adobe Premiere support *chroma key,* the blue screen picture-on-picture method for cutting one video into another, and panning/zooming in on still pictures that Apple calls the Ken Burns Effect (*à la* Ken Burns of PBS's *Civil War, Jazz,* and *Baseball* fame).

Are these programs worth the money? Up to you.

As a practical minimum, you want

- A 1.2 GHz Pentium or faster.
- At least 256MB of RAM. Try to get 512MB or more. Run WMM on a machine with less than 256MB, and you'll spend more time waiting than editing.
- A FireWire (IEEE-1394) or USB 2.0 port to attach your camera.
- At least 2GB of free hard drive space. Windows Movie Maker uses Microsoft's WMV format, which does a good job of compressing video, but as a general rule, video goes through hard drive space like Orville Redenbacher goes through corn.

If you suffer from analog video, not to worry! Your old VCR or Hi-8 camcorder can send pictures to your computer, although the results won't hold a candle to all-digital capture. All you need is a converter that plugs into the VCR or movie camera's video jack (preferably S-Video) and audio jacks, and connects to your computer's USB port. Pinnacle and Belkin, among many other manufacturers, make such a beast.

Introducing Windows Movie Maker

Windows Movie Maker doesn't look much like other Microsoft applications: It's specially built for the task at hand and doesn't make many bones about that fact. If you start Windows Movie Maker (choose Start⇨All Programs⇨ Accessories⇨Windows Movie Maker), you see the window shown in Figure 2-1.

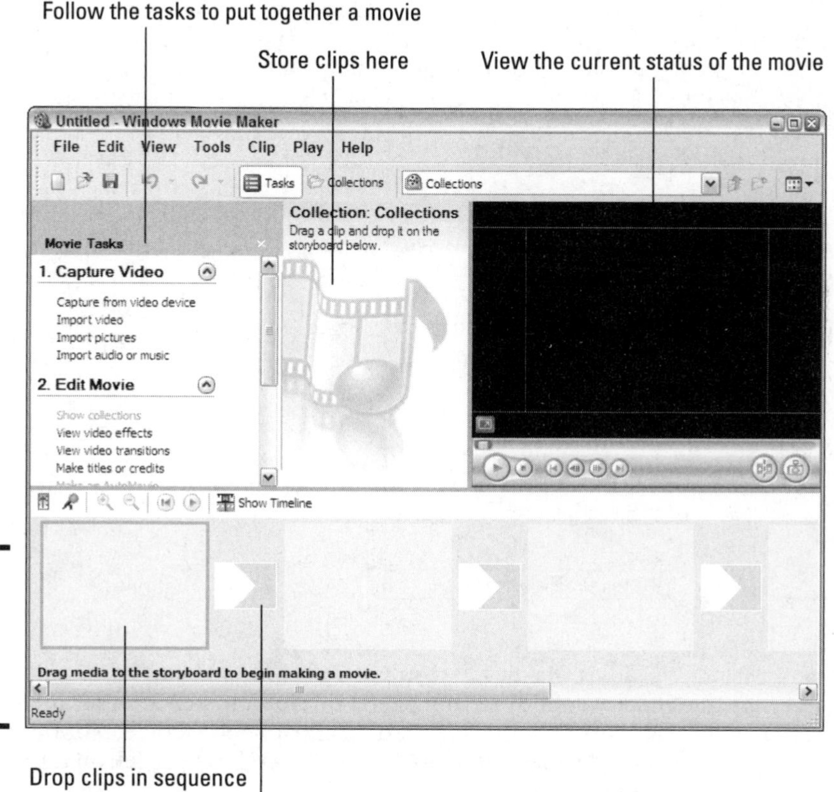

Figure 2-1: Windows Movie Maker as it starts.

Take a moment to become familiar with the parts of the window. Up at the top, you see three panes:

✦ The pane on the left suggests various *tasks* — steps that you can take to bring in clips, tie them together, add effects like titles, and save your movie. You won't go through every task, but this pane will help remind you what needs to be done next.

- The second pane shows *collections* of movie clips. A collection is a group of related movie clips with a name. You can use collections to organize your movie clips, much as you use folders to organize other types of files.
- The third pane shows you a preview of how your movie looks in its current sorry state. The controls at the bottom should look familiar: They're identical to the controls in Windows Media Player.

If you click the icon marked Collections, the left-most pane shows you all the collections of clips that Windows Movie Maker has at its disposal, as shown in Figure 2-2. The collections are arranged just like Windows folders — and that's the easiest way to think of them.

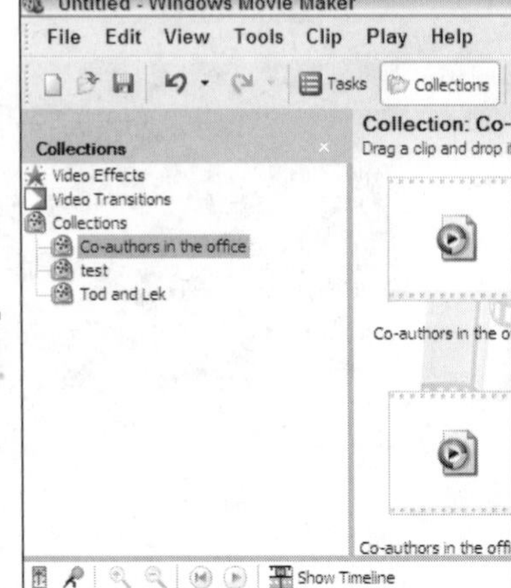

Figure 2-2: Store clips in Windows Movie Maker's collections.

Windows Movie Maker lets you put collections inside other collections, just as the Windows file system lets you put folders inside other folders. To put collection X inside collection Y, drag the icon for X on top of the icon for Y. To create a new collection inside collection Z, right-click on collection Z, and choose New Collection.

Below the three panes is the *workspace.* As you assemble movie clips into a whole movie, this area displays the state of your work and lets you control it. The workspace can appear as a *storyboard,* which shows the first still picture of each clip with room for transitions between the clips, or as a *timeline,* which superimposes a clock over the sequence of clips, with separate tracks for video, audio, and text titles.

Gathering Clips

Before you can edit video, you must get some clips into your computer. D'OH.

In general, you have four choices:

- **Beg, borrow, or steal existing clips.** The Web's full of video clips that you can use. No doubt your friends have marvelous cute clips of Little Dufous spilling ice cream on his blue suede shoes. Any MPG, AVI, WMV, or other video file; any MP3, WMA, WAV, or other audio file; any JPG, GIF, BMP, or other picture file — they're all fair game.
- **Fire up the Webcam.** WMM has all the controls you need to capture video from a cheap (or an expensive!) Webcam. Yes, you can usually connect your multi-zillion pixel digital camera or recorder directly to your PC and use it as a Webcam.
- **Use your digital video recorder.** You can bring in clips from any digital video recorder with a FireWire connection, using the tools supplied with WMM. Anything you can see on that tiny video screen will look great pulled into your PC — and because it's digital, the quality should be outstanding.
- **Go analog.** Whether you're trying to retrieve old predigital camcorder clips, movies from a VCR, or even a direct feed from your television or satellite TV box, WMM can transform anything you see in the analog world into a file that can be edited and saved. But you have two major problems to deal with. First, you have to buy a gizmo that translates TV output into digital signals. (The cables I mention at the beginning of this chapter do the trick, but you can also buy a video card or a translation box.) Second, the quality of digital video generated by analog signals tends to be, uh, less than stellar. If you think you can use WMM as a replacement for a TiVO or Windows Media Player's ability to directly record digital broadcasts, think again.

If the clip you want already sits on your computer (or on another computer on your network), adding it to WMM's collections is easy — just choose File⇨Import into Collections.

You can mix and match clips from all of those sources.

If you don't have all the gadgets you need — or don't know how to operate them — ask your dealer for assistance.

Recording "live" with a Webcam or other camera

What, you don't have an extra six or seven hundred bucks to spend on a digital video recorder? I bet you'll be surprised at the quality of video you can make with a very inexpensive Webcam, or (in some cases, at least) with a plain, still digital camera. Here's how:

1. **Plug in the camera.**

   If the camera's working correctly, Windows responds with a beep-beep sound telling you that a new USB device is up and ready. If the camera isn't working right, you may need to rifle through the documentation to get its drivers set up properly.

2. **In Windows Movie Maker, click the line under Movie Tasks that says Capture from Video Device.**

   Windows Movie Maker opens the Video Capture Wizard shown in Figure 2-3.

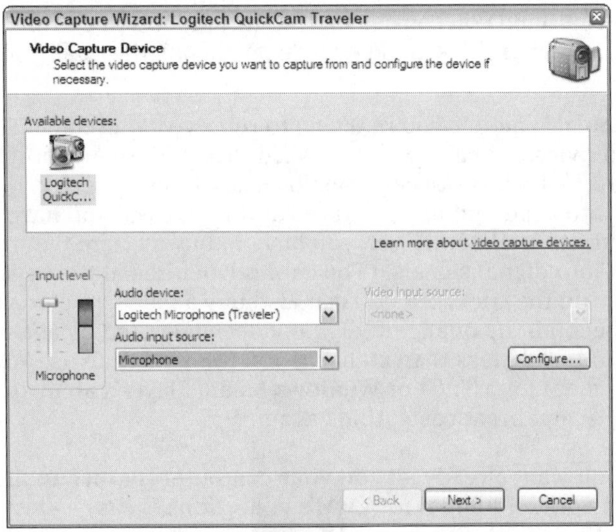

Figure 2-3: The Video Capture Wizard captures clips either from a camera or from recordings stored on digital video recorders.

3. **Choose the camera you want to use for "live" shooting, and click Next.**

4. **The wizard asks you to enter a filename for the captured video and to pick a folder to put it in. Do so, and then click Next.**

   The wizard wants you to choose a file format for the recorded clip (see Figure 2-4). If you're recording "live" with anything but a digital video recorder, your only choices are Microsoft's proprietary WMV format. ("Other settings" allows you to pick what kind of WMV format will be used.)

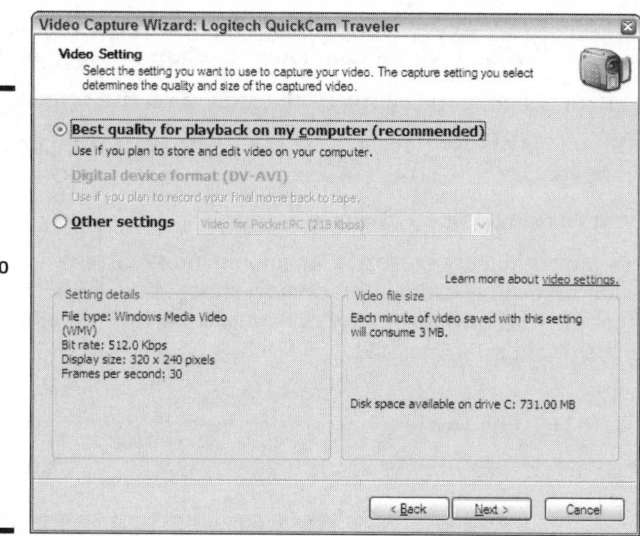

Figure 2-4: Unless you're working with a digital video recorder, you must use WMV format — although you can change quality.

5. **Unless you can live with relatively grainy video clips, select the Best Quality for Playback on My Computer (Recommended) radio button, and then click Next.**

   The wizard presents you with a surprisingly full-featured "live" video-capture program, as shown in Figure 2-5.

Figure 2-5: WMM's "live" video capture program is amazingly easy to use.

6. **When you're ready to start recording, click the Start Capture button. When you've finished with a clip, click the Stop Capture button.**

   The length and size of the captured file appear on the screen.

7. **Repeat Step 6 as many times as you like — or until you run out of hard drive space.**

8. **When you're done, click Finish.**

   Windows Movie Maker returns to its main window, shown in Figure 2-6, divides the recording you just made into short clips, adds the clips to the collection, and clears the way for you to continue making your movie. Er, project.

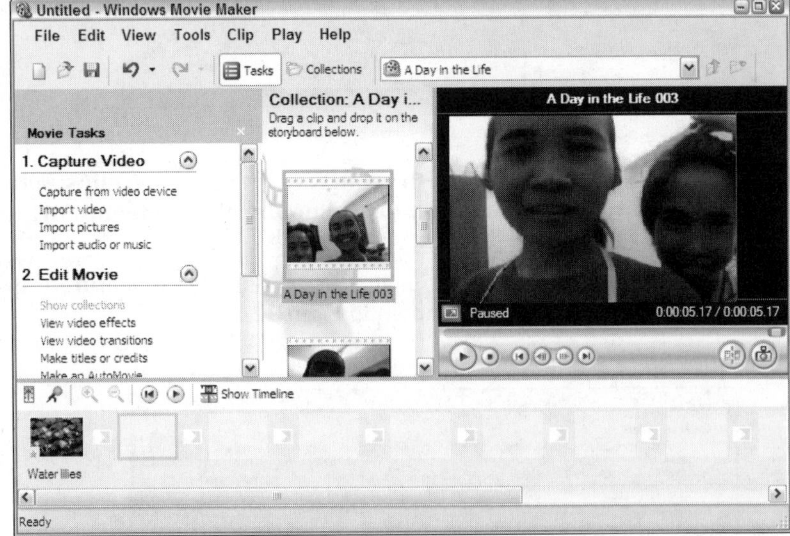

Figure 2-6: The recording gets chopped into clips, with all the pieces assembled in the collection associated with the current project.

How does Windows Movie Maker know where one clip ends and another begins? It looks for a complete change in the image between two consecutive frames of the recording. Whenever it observes that, it closes the video clip that it was recording and starts a new one. This separates your recording into smaller, logically divided segments.

Look back at the Record dialog box shown in Figure 2-5. See the check box labeled Create Clips When Wizard Finishes? That check box controls the behavior you just saw. If you deselect that check box, Windows Movie Maker stores the entire recording in one clip.

Capturing digital video recordings

So you got one of those fancy 10,000 megapixel digital video recorders for your birthday. You have years of continuously recorded videotapes — no detail of your life is too trivial to miss — and you want to transfer all of them onto your PC so that you can use Windows Movie Maker to add titles and transitions, and to cut out the parts where you're snoring.

Good. You've come to the right place.

Transferring recorded movies from your video recorder to the PC is surprisingly easy — in fact, it's only trivially more difficult than making a "live" recording, as detailed in the preceding section.

Here's how to do it:

1. **Plug in your video camera.**

   If you've never plugged your camera into your computer before, you may have to read the manual and run the CD that came with the camera to get the drivers working.

2. **Windows may spontaneously ask if you want to Capture Video/Using Windows Movie Maker 2. If you get that option, click it. If not, start WMM and click the Tasks line that says Capture from Video Device.**

   If you go the second route, you have to select your video recorder from the wizard's offerings (refer to Figure 2-3).

3. **The wizard asks you to enter a filename for the captured video and to pick a folder to put it in. Do so, and then click Next.**

   Then the wizard wants to know what format you want to use (refer to Figure 2-4).

4. **For maximum video quality, choose DV-AVI. That's the "raw" format your video recorder uses. Converting the video into WMV format (which happens if you make any other choice) will result in degradation of the final picture. Click Next.**

   The wizard brings up a capture screen similar to the "live" screen, but one that includes controls for the camera, as shown in Figure 2-7.

5. **Use the controls underneath the picture to play, pause, and move forward or backward on the movie inside the digital recorder. When you're ready to start recording — which is to say, when you're ready to start transferring video from the digital recorder into your computer — click the Start Capture button. When you want to stop transferring from the digital recorder, click the Stop Capture button.**

   WMM keeps track of the length and size of the captured video.

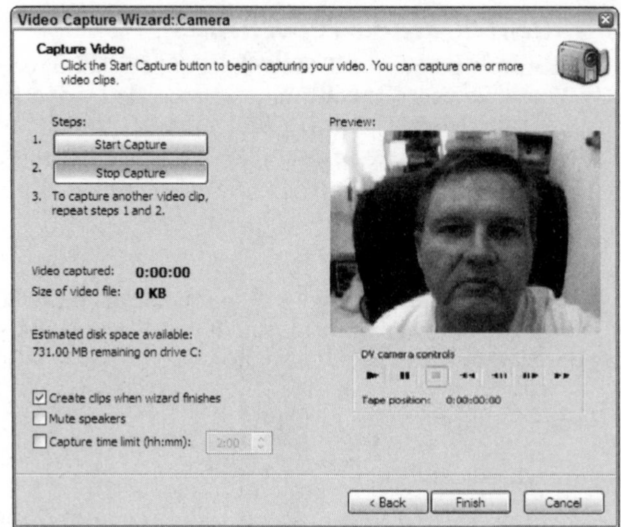

Figure 2-7: The capture screen for retrieving movies from the digital recorder works much like the analogous screen for "live" recordings.

6. **Repeat Step 5 at will. When you're done, click Finish.**

   Windows Movie Maker returns to its main window (refer to Figure 2-6), divides the recording you just made into clips, and adds the clips to the collection.

It's almost as easy as saying, "Lights! Camera! Action!" Except that you don't have to worry about blowing a $100 million budget, over-running a 32-day shooting schedule, and/or keeping your stars out of each others' trailers.

Assembling a Movie

A *project* is a file that contains your work on a movie. In effect, a project *is* a movie, either completed or in development. A *clip* is a piece of a movie (or music or a still picture). In the preceding sections, I show you how to create clips with a camera or Webcam. When the clips are ready, you assemble the clips to create a project.

Creating a project

Here's how to put together a project, er, a movie:

1. **If you've already started working on a movie (say, you've already followed the instructions in the preceding section and recorded a bunch of clips), choose File⇨Save Project, give your project a name, and click Save. If you're starting out fresh, choose File⇨New Project. Then immediately choose File⇨Save and save the project.**

In either case, you have a project ready to go.

2. **Choose a clip from one of your collections and drag it to the storyboard at the bottom of the window.**

To see all the collections available to you, click the Collections icon and WMM shows you a cascading list of collections (see Figure 2-8).

Figure 2-8: Click the Collections icon to see all the collections available.

An image of the clip appears in the first slot of the storyboard.

3. **Drag one or two more clips to the unoccupied part of the storyboard.**

An image of each one appears in the workspace.

You can insert a clip between two existing clips. Just drag it between the two clips.

4. **When a clip is in the workspace, you can move it to a different position. Click the clip, drag it to the place where you want to insert it, and release.**

When you need to move a clip a long way, dragging can be clumsy and error-prone; cutting and pasting is more convenient. To cut and paste, right-click the clip that you want to move and choose Cut. Then right-click the clip *before which* you want to place this clip, and select Paste.

To delete a clip from the workspace, right-click the clip and choose Delete.

5. **To save your project, choose File➪Save Project.**

Congratulations. You're well on your way to becoming a film legend.

Playing a clip or a movie

Have you wondered how you're supposed to tell which clip is which from the tiny images in the Collection pane? It's actually easy because you can see what's in any clip by playing it in the monitor.

To play a clip, select it either in the Collection pane or in the workspace. Then click the Play button under the monitor. When you've seen enough, click the Stop button to stop the playback. (See Figure 2-9.)

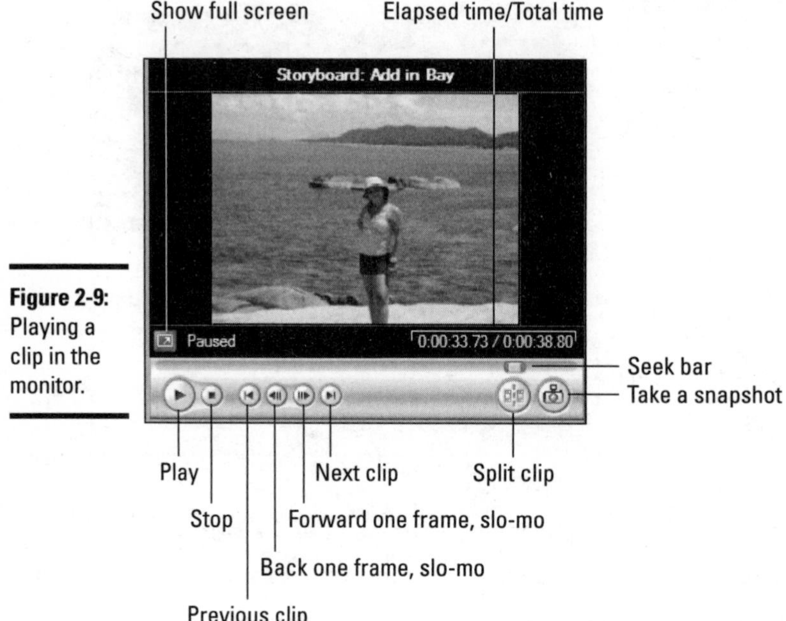

Figure 2-9: Playing a clip in the monitor.

As you play a clip, the pointer on the *seek bar* moves across the bar to show how far the monitor has progressed through the clip. The number near the monitor's lower-right corner shows the elapsed play time for the entire movie, to the nearest hundredth of a second.

The other buttons below the monitor are as follows:

- ✦ **Stop:** Stops playing the clip and deselects the clip.
- ✦ **Back:** Selects the preceding clip.
- ✦ **Previous Frame:** Positions the monitor to the previous frame, moving backward one frame at a time in slow motion.
- ✦ **Next Frame:** Positions the monitor to the next frame.

- **Forward:** Selects the following clip.
- **Full Screen:** Expands the monitor to fill the whole screen. The seek bar and control buttons are not visible. While in full screen, you can control the monitor with these keys (they work in the normal display mode, too):
  - **Play or Pause:** Spacebar
  - **Stop:** Period (.) key
  - **Back:** Ctrl+Alt+Left Arrow
  - **Previous Frame:** Alt+Left Arrow
  - **Next Frame:** Alt+Right Arrow
  - **Forward:** Ctrl+Alt+Right Arrow
  - **Leave Full Screen Mode:** Esc
  - **Split Clip:** Ctrl+Shift+S
- **Split Clip:** Splits a clip in two (see the "Splitting and combining clips" section, later in this chapter).

You can also play your entire movie on the monitor. Choose Play⇨Play Storyboard (or Play Timeline, if the workspace shows a timeline).

Viewing storyboard and timeline

The storyboard and the timeline are two different ways of viewing a movie.

The *storyboard* view represents each clip in the movie with a thumbnail image, as shown in Figure 2-10. Storyboard view is useful for assembling and rearranging clips.

Figure 2-10: Storyboard view of the workspace.

The *timeline* view represents each clip with a thumbnail image set in a space whose width is proportional to the clip's length, as shown in Figure 2-11. A timeline above the thumbnails helps you judge the playing time of each clip. Timeline view is useful for trimming the beginnings and ends of clips. It's also helpful for adding titles and sound.

To switch between the storyboard and timeline view, click Show Timeline or Show Storyboard, up at the top of the workspace.

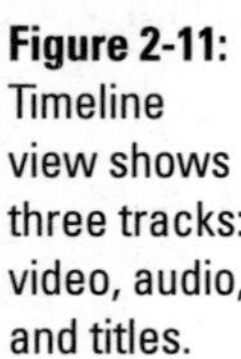

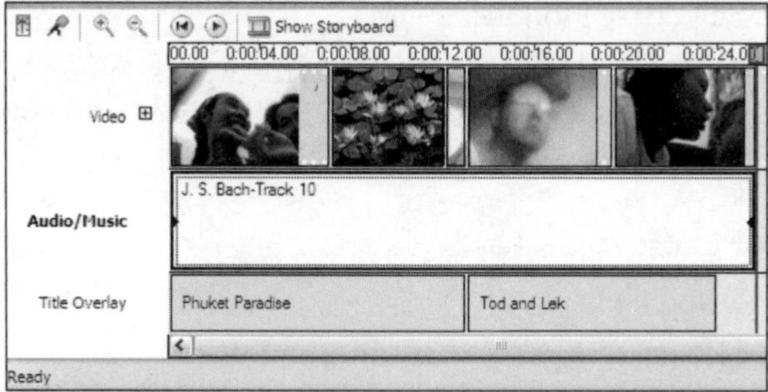

Figure 2-11: Timeline view shows three tracks: video, audio, and titles.

Trimming a clip

Windows Movie Maker lets you *trim* individual clips — remove pieces at the beginning or end of the clip, to make it shorter. You can trim video or sound clips while in timeline view.

The hack-n-slash approach to trimming couldn't be simpler: While in timeline view, click on the clip you want to trim, and then drag either the left or the right edge of the clip inward, toward the center. WMM makes the trim quickly and easily — and it's reversible. If you ever decide to "undo" the trim, repeat the process, but drag the edge back outward, to its original position.

Making a precise trim — where you pick the exact frame that marks the beginning and the ending of the clip — doesn't take much more effort than the hack-n-slash approach. To trim either end of a clip with a bit of finesse, follow these steps:

1. **Make sure Windows Movie Maker shows you the timeline at the bottom of the screen (if necessary, click Show Timeline at the top of the workspace).**
2. **Click on the clip in the timeline that you want to shorten.**

   The first frame of the clip appears in the monitor.
3. **Move the monitor's seek bar to the point where you want to trim the clip. You can choose from several ways to do this:**
   - Click the Play button, and then click the Pause button when the clip reaches the right point.
   - Drag the seek bar's pointer to the right position. The monitor displays the frame at the spot in the clip where you release the pointer.
   - Click the Previous Frame and Next Frame buttons to move the pointer (and the monitor) backward and forward one frame at a time.

4. **When the seek bar's pointer is correctly positioned at the precise frame you want to use as the starting point for this clip, choose Clip➪Set Start Trim Point to trim the start of the clip to that point.**
5. **Move the monitor's seek bar to the point where you want to end the clip.**
6. **Choose Clip➪Set End Trim Point to trim the end of the clip to that point.**

   When you trim a clip, the remaining part expands to fill the entire seek bar. If the workspace is in timeline view, the clip contracts in the timeline so that only the trimmed part is shown.
7. **If you trim too much from a clip, choose Clip➪Clear Trim Points to start over.**

If you drag a clip from the Collection pane to the workspace and trim it, and then you drag the same clip into the workspace again, the second copy is *not* trimmed. You can trim it differently if you want to.

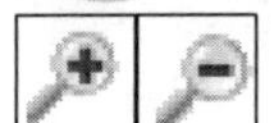

To see more detail in the timeline view, click the *zoom in* icon. To see a larger span of time in less detail, click *zoom out*.

Making transitions and adding effects

Windows Movie Maker gives you dozens of ways to manage the transition from one clip to the next. You can fade out the end of one clip while fading in the beginning of the next clip. You can wipe the screen, or shatter the last frame in a clip before moving on to the next.

Best of all, adding a transition to a movie takes only a few clicks. Here's the easiest way:

1. **Make sure Windows Movie Maker shows you the storyboard at the bottom of the screen (if necessary, click Show Storyboard at the top of the workspace).**
2. **Click View➪Transitions.**

   WMM shows you the Video Transitions pane, in the middle, as shown in Figure 2-12.
3. **Click and drag a transition from the Video Transitions pane to a location between any of the clips.**

   The transition you specify will be used to go from the first clip to the second.
4. **To see the effect of the transition, click Play on the monitor.**

   You can delete a transition by right-clicking it and choosing Delete.

Figure 2-12: You can choose from dozens of transitions between clips.

In addition to the dozens of transitions available in Windows Movie Maker, you can also change the appearance of an individual clip: Make it brighter or darker, rotate or mirror it, turn the color askew (to great effect with "old time" sepia), speed the clip up or slow it down.

To apply an effect to a clip, click Tools➪Video Effects, and then click and drag the effect you want onto an unsuspecting clip. Play it in the monitor, and see what you think!

Splitting and combining clips

You can split or combine clips in two ways: In the workspace (either storyboard or timeline view) and in the Collection pane. When you split or combine clips in the workspace, the effect is similar to trimming a clip: Only that use of the clip is affected. When you split or combine clips in the Collection pane, you actually split or combine the files that store the clips. This affects all projects that use the clips, now or in the future.

Splitting a clip in the workspace is useful if you want to insert a still picture or another clip in the middle of a clip. Combining clips in the workspace is not as common as splitting a clip, but it is possible if you want to do it.

Splitting/combining clips in the workspace

To split a clip in the workspace, follow these steps:

1. **Click the clip that you want to split.**
2. **Set the monitor's seek bar pointer to the position where you want the split to occur.**

3. **Click the monitor's Split button.**

   The storyboard shows two clips: one for the original clip up to the point of the split; the other for the remainder of the clip.

These clips exist only in the workspace; the clip in the collection (and on your hard drive) is not affected.

To combine two or more consecutive clips in the workspace, hold down the Shift key and click the first and last of the clips. Then choose Clip⇨Combine. Again, the clips in the collection, and on your hard drive, aren't harmed.

Splitting/combining clips in the Collection pane

Splitting and combining clips in the Collection pane is useful for organizing your clips. For example, you may need to split a clip because Windows Movie Maker failed to recognize a new clip between shots when recording. You may need to combine clips because Windows Movie Maker started a new clip where a new shot did not begin.

To split a clip in the Collection pane, select the clip in that pane. Move the seek bar's pointer to the split point that you want, and then click the monitor's Split button.

To combine clips in the Collection pane, select the clips in the Collection pane, right-click, and select the Combine command.

You can combine clips only if they were recorded consecutively or were previously split from a single clip.

Typing titles

Superimposing text over your clips — or adding standalone title or credit clips — ranks as the simplest of WMM tricks, and the text formatting options boggle the imagination. Here's how to add titles:

1. **Put your movie together first.**

   It's easiest to add titles when you nail down the location and duration of each clip in advance.

2. **Click Tools➪Titles and Credits.**

   WMM asks where you want to add a title, as shown in Figure 2-13.

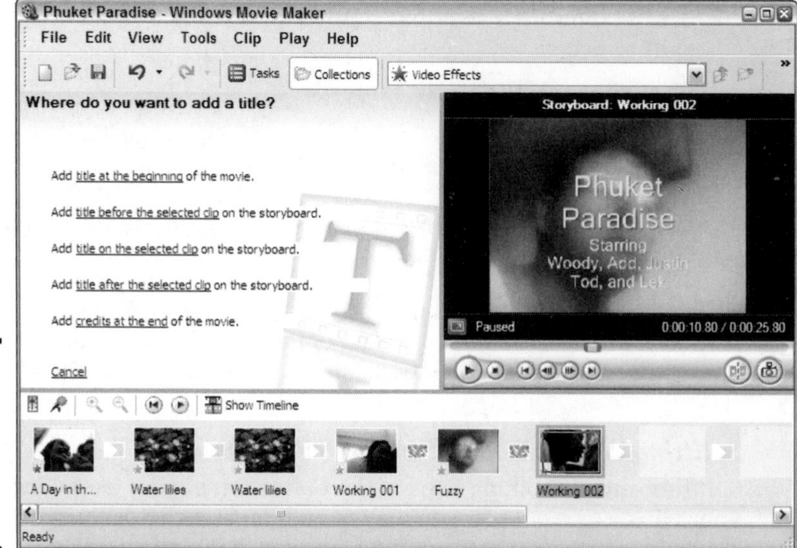

Figure 2-13: Adding text to your movie only takes a few clicks.

3. **Choose the type of text you want to add. If you want a title on a specific clip, make sure you click on the clip down in the workspace before clicking the Add Title on the Selected Clip link.**

   WMM presents you with two boxes (see Figure 2-14).

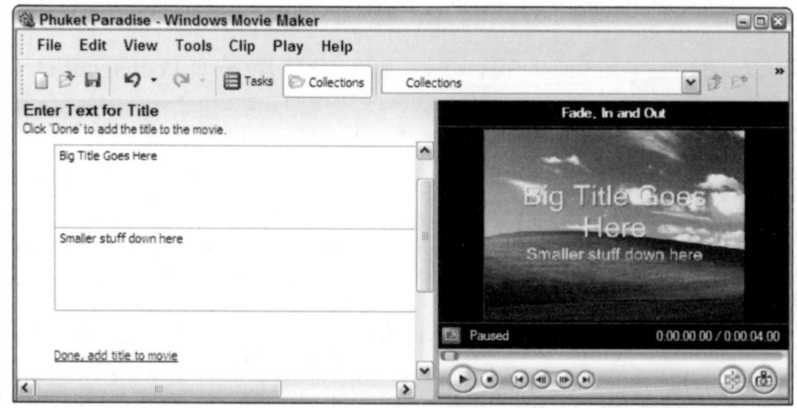

Figure 2-14: WMM automatically puts text you type in the top box in a larger font.

4. **Type the text you want.**

   Text that you type in the top box appears in a larger font, near the top of the screen. Text in the lower box shows in a smaller font, underneath. Look for a preview in the monitor.

   At the bottom of the Enter Text for Title pane, you'll find two options: Change the Title Animation, and Change the Text Font and Color. You may need to scroll down to see them. Try both of them: Titles can fade in and out, fly, flash, or scroll. Text can appear as transparent, in any color, any font. Seriously kewl.

5. **When the text looks good, click Done, Add Title To Movie.**

   WMM places the title where you asked. To see it, use the monitor to play the movie or the clip.

Using sound clips

You can narrate your movie and save the narration so that it plays whenever you view the movie. Windows Movie Maker stores the sound clip on your hard drive as a WMA audio file.

Recording a narration

To record a narration, follow these steps:

1. **Open the project you wish to narrate. Make sure you're in timeline view by choosing View⇨Timeline if necessary.**

   It's easier to see what's happening if you expand the workspace at the bottom of the screen — just click on the bar at the top of the workspace and drag it upward — so that you can see the Audio/Music track. That's where the narration will go.

2. **When you're ready to record, choose Tools⇨Narrate Timeline.**

   Windows Movie Maker opens the Narrate Timeline dialog box, as shown in Figure 2-15.

3. **Make sure your microphone is connected and working.**

   If the mike's live, you see the Input Level indicator bobbing up and down.

   Click the Show More Options link if you want to record from a different microphone, or if you want to mute the speakers so that any sounds you currently have in the movie don't tromp over your narration.

4. **Click the Start Narration button to start recording.**

   Windows Movie Maker plays the movie as you record so that you can synchronize your narration with it.

Figure 2-15: Your narration goes into the Audio/Music track of the timeline.

5. **When you're done, click the Stop Narration button.**

   Windows Movie Maker opens a Save dialog box. Choose a filename and location for the recording and click the Save button. After Windows Movie Maker saves the file, it returns to the main window, and your narration appears in the Audio/Music track.

6. **You can make another recording or click Done to close the dialog box.**

You can't synchronize narration with a single clip selected in the workspace. To get the same effect, create a separate project that contains the clip, and synchronize the narration to it.

Adding a sound clip to a movie

To add a sound clip to a movie, drag the sound clip from the current collection to the appropriate point in the workspace. This is essentially the same operation as adding a video clip, but note the following differences:

- ✦ Sound clips are visible only in timeline view and can be added or managed only in timeline view.
- ✦ Sound clips appear below video clips (refer to Figure 2-15).
- ✦ You can't leave spaces between video clips in the timeline, but you can leave spaces between sound clips. This enables you to set each sound clip's exact position relative to the movie's video clips.

You can play a sound clip by selecting it and clicking the monitor's Play button; the sound plays along with the video. You also can trim a sound clip the same way you would trim a video clip. Click the sound clip, and then use the monitor or the trim handles in the workspace's timeline.

Importing clips from other sources

You can use video clips, sound clips, and still pictures from other sources in your movies. For example, you can use pictures captured with the Scanner and Camera Wizard (see Book VII, Chapter 3) or sound tracks ripped from a CD by Windows Media Player (assuming you don't violate any copyright restrictions; see Book VII, Chapter 1). You also can download all three types of material from sources on the Web.

To import a clip or still into Windows Movie Maker, it must reside on your computer. If the clip is on the Web, you must download it to your computer first.

The usual CYA (Cover Your, ah, Patootie) applies: If you plan to distribute your movie publicly or use it for commercial purposes, you cannot use copyrighted material without the copyright holder's permission. If in doubt, see your attorney for guidance.

When you have the file, here's how to put it in your movie, er, project:

1. **Click the Collections button on the main toolbar so you can see WMM's collections (as in Figure 2-2).**
2. **Click on the collection that you want the clip to go into.**
3. **Choose File⇨Import into Collections.**
4. **Find and select the file that you want to import, and then click the Open button.**

   Windows Movie Maker adds the file to the collection that you selected.
5. **When the clip or still is in the current collection, you can click and drag away.**

The only technical restriction on importing clips is that they must be in one of the recording formats that Windows Movie Maker knows how to handle. Here is a list of the more common formats that work:

- **Video clips:** `.AVI`, `.WMV`, `.MPEG`, `.MPG`, `.MP2`, and `.WMV`
- **Audio clips:** `.WAV`, `.WMA`, and `.MP3`
- **Still pictures:** `.BMP`, `.JPEG`, `.JPG`, and `.GIF`

While writing this book, I had no end of problems importing WMV files that were created by Windows Movie Maker. WMM freezes and you have to use Windows itself to shut it down. (Press Ctrl+Alt+Del, and then on the Applications tab of the Task Manager dialog box, click the line marked Windows Movie Maker, and click the End Task button.) Any unsaved changes to your project disappear. *Caveat emptor.*

Saving the Movie

After you edit a movie to your satisfaction, you probably want to show it to other people. When you choose File⇨Save Project or File⇨Save Project As, Windows Movie Maker stores the movie as a project (a so-called `.MSWMM` file) that can be watched only in Windows Movie Maker. Blech. If you want your friends to be able to view it, either they have to run Windows Movie Maker, or you have to convert the movie into a form that other folks can use.

Microsoft, bless its pointed little head, only allows you to save your movies in two formats: Microsoft's proprietary WMV video format; and the huge (but very high quality) DV-AVI format, which most video recorders use. (WMM also lets you burn a CD in HighMAT format, but HighMAT is just a minor marketing tweak of the WMV format.) If you're trying to save your movie as an MPG file, or an AVI, or burn a DVD directly, you're outta luck. The best you can do is save it as WMV (or DV-AVI), and then scour the Internet and try to find a program that will convert WMV (or DV-AVI) to a format that you can use.

To let others view your movie, follow these steps:

1. **Choose File⇨Save Movie File.**

   Windows Movie Maker opens the Save Movie Wizard, as shown in Figure 2-16.

2. **Unless you want to put the movie back on your digital video recorder, choose My Computer and click Next.**

   You can always burn it on a CD, e-mail it, or copy it to the Web later.

3. **WMM lets you choose a filename and location for the movie. Do so. Click Next.**

   I recommend saving movies to some folder other than My Videos. Otherwise, they are hard to distinguish from your clips, which are stored in the My Videos folder and also use the file extension `.WMV`.

4. **The next screen gives you only one choice for movie quality. (Isn't that ridiculous?) Click the line that says Show More Choices. WMM spills the beans and shows you the full range of options shown in Figure 2-17.**

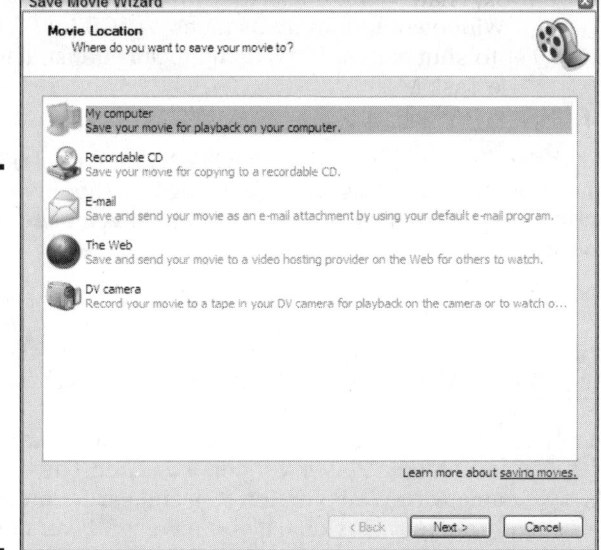

Figure 2-16: For the greatest flexibility, tell WMM that you want to save the movie for playback on your computer.

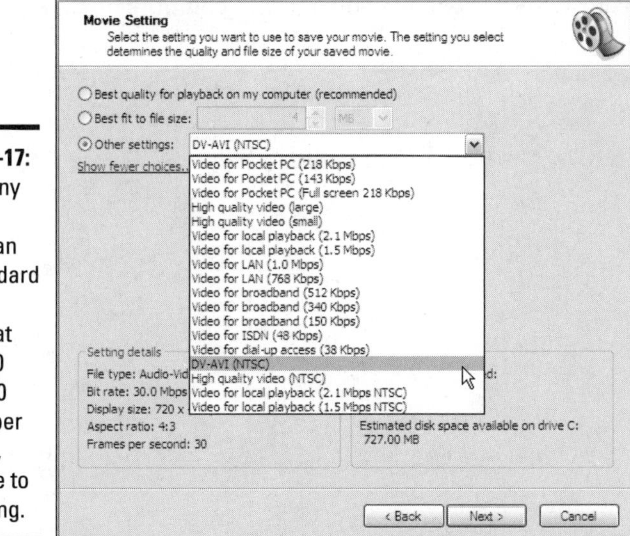

Figure 2-17: To see any options other than the standard WMV format (at 640 x 480 pixels, 30 frames per second), you have to go hunting.

5. **Leaf through the options on offer and choose the quality setting most appropriate for this movie.**

Huge? Yeah. A five-minute video might take up 50MB in the default WMV format. The same video could require as much as 1GB in DV-AVI. The DV-AVI file runs 20 *times* larger that WMV, by no means unusual for DV-AVI.

6. **Click Next.**

   Converting the project to a movie file can take a long, long time. Several Ice Ages may pass. Ultimately, you see a dialog box that invites you to play the movie when you click Finish. (As if you haven't seen it enough times already.)

7. **Click Finish.**

Anyone running Windows can view the movie later by double-clicking on the file. This starts Windows Media Player, which plays the movie.

If you create a movie in WMV format with Windows Movie Maker, you can play it only with Windows Media Player version 9 or later. The original version of Windows XP came with WMP version 8 — and earlier incarnations of Windows ran positively ancient versions. If you have WMP version 8 or 9, you can download version 10 from `www.microsoft.com/windows/windowsmedia/download/default.asp` — but be aware that it will take a long, long time if you have a dial-up connection. So don't wait until Christmas morning to make sure your WMV file will play on another computer, okay?

Chapter 3: Discovering Digital Cameras and Recorders

In This Chapter

- **Choosing a camera**
- **Buying a camera**
- **Printing photographs**
- **Sharing your shots**
- **Troubleshooting**

Windows XP stands light years ahead of Microsoft's earlier operating systems in its ability to handle images. Most of its capabilities aren't really new, but Windows XP makes many things easy that used to require a lot of technical knowledge and a lot of work.

In this chapter, you discover everything you need to know to choose a digital camera, hook it up with your PC, and move pictures from the camera to the PC where you can store, edit, and print them with just a couple of clicks.

Choosing a Camera

Before you can have fun with your images, of course, you need to get them into your computer. You have a lot of options:

- You can use a *conventional (or film) camera* to record images on film and then request the film processor to return the images to you on computer media — typically a CD. Having the photo processor burn a CD while developing the film costs only a couple of bucks — and you may get a small free application thrown in to do some rudimentary editing. Or you can scan prints, if all else fails. When I talk about conventional cameras in this book, I'm talking about the kind that produce images on regular, ol' everyday film. Silver halide.

- You can use a *digital camera* like the one shown in Figure 3-1 to record images in electronic memory and then transfer them into your computer. When I talk about digital cameras in this book, I mean a camera that produces images as files, one image at a time, and stores the files inside the camera.

Figure 3-1: The 5.24 megapixel DSC-F707 Cybershot digital camera from Sony.

Photo courtesy of Sony Electronics, Inc.

- You can use an *Internet camera* (a Webcam) like the one shown in Figure 3-2 to feed live images directly into your computer and capture them as either still frames or movie clips. When I talk about Internet cameras here, I'm talking about the ones that have to be tethered to a computer. They have no capability to store images.
- You can use an analog or digital *video camera* (a camcorder) like the one shown in Figure 3-3 to record movie clips on tape, and then feed them into your computer from the camera or from a playback device. When I talk about video cameras/camcorders in this book, I'm talking about the kind that internally store moving images.

Strictly speaking, Internet cameras are digital cameras. So are many video cameras. Video camcorders can take still shots, just like digital cameras, and many digital cameras can make video clips — although you may be less than impressed with the quality of the results, in both cases. Then again, strictly speaking, Dummies are smart. But I digress.

Figure 3-2: The SiPix iQuest Dual Cam is a full-featured USB video camera, video-conferencing camera, and digital camera all in one.

Understanding digital cameras

You use a digital camera just like a conventional one, but it records images in electronic memory, not on film. Instead of sending a roll of film to be processed and printed, you simply copy the images onto your computer. Then you can erase the camera's memory and use it again.

Digital cameras have sorted themselves roughly into four categories:

- **Point-and-shoot cameras:** The simplest and least expensive type. Most point-and-shoot cameras have inexpensive lenses, often made of plastic, and often with no means of adjusting the focus. They're good for casual photography and for taking pictures to use on your personal Web site.

Figure 3-3: CCD-TRV98 Sony Hi8 Handycam Camcorder.

Photo courtesy of Sony Electronics, Inc.

- **Advanced viewfinder cameras:** More capable than point-and-shoots, and more expensive. Their design is essentially the same, but they have more features and use higher-quality parts. For example, advanced viewfinder cameras have more sophisticated all-glass lenses and generally focus the lens automatically.
- **Zoom-lens reflex (ZLR) cameras:** These cameras have a zoom lens that is permanently attached. The viewfinder's image is formed by the same lens that takes the picture, rather than by a separate optical system. Because these cameras are designed for advanced amateur photographers and professionals, they tend to offer better quality and more features than advanced viewfinder cameras.
- **Single-lens reflex (SLR) cameras:** The most capable kind. And the most expensive. These cameras work like the ZLR cameras, but they feature interchangeable lenses. Many of them are based on conventional SLR cameras, adapted to use digital imaging instead of film.

This brief summary should give you a good idea of which type of camera is most appropriate for you, but it doesn't begin to cover the variety of features that camera manufacturers have developed. Becoming a fully informed buyer in this market takes weeks of research.

Unless you enjoy digging into obscure technical details, seek advice from a well-informed friend or a retailer whom you trust.

Resolution

A digital camera forms its image on a sensor that contains a square grid of tiny, light-sensing areas called *pixels*. *Resolution* refers to the number of pixels the sensor has, measured in millions of dots, or megapixels (abbreviated MP). The more pixels, the more detail the camera can record. The more detail, the larger a print you can make without the individual pixels becoming noticeable (see Table 3-1).

Table 3-1 Resolution and Acceptable Print Size

Camera Resolution	*Produces High Quality Prints up To*
1 megapixel	3 x 5 inches
2 megapixel	4 x 6 inches
3 megapixel	5 x 7 inches
4 megapixel	8 x 10 inches
5 megapixel	11 x 14 inches
8 megapixel	14 x 17 inches
24 megapixel	30 x 36 inches or bigger

Megapixels constitute an important part of the shopping equation, but they aren't the only part. After you get past 2 to 3MP, the quality of the lens becomes every bit as important as the number of pixels.

What about RAW?

Traditionally, most cameras save pictures in JPG format. JPG represents a decent balance between image quality and file size, and just about every kind of software recognizes JPG.

Not so with RAW. The RAW file format (actually, it's a loosely defined bunch of formats) captures information from every single pixel inside the camera. When it comes to quality, what RAW sees is what you got. Full stop.

Unfortunately, every camera manufacturer creates RAW files in different ways, and the files themselves can be big — say, twice the size of a good-quality JPG file. But if you work in the, uh, RAW, you can edit the every detail that the camera can muster directly, without bumping into the pre-editing inherent in JPG.

RAW files are a pain in the neck. Not every camera can generate RAW files, and for daily use, you won't want to hassle with them. They produce tremendous results, however, and they're just one more reason why megapixels don't tell the whole story.

Having more resolution than you need gives you leeway to crop out the unimportant parts of an image and still get a good-quality print. Those extra pixels cost money, of course.

Zoom lens

A *zoom lens* lets you vary the angle of view that your camera takes in by increasing or decreasing the lens's magnification. Most advanced viewfinder cameras have this feature, as do all ZLRs and SLRs. The better ones cover a wider range. Most point-and-shoot cameras do not have a zoom lens.

The zoom lens feature is also known as *optical zoom*. Many cameras offer *digital zoom,* which simply enlarges an image by making each pixel bigger. Digital zoom isn't very useful. You can get the same result by enlarging the final image.

Focusing and stabilizing

Many point-and-shoot cameras have a lens with one or a few fixed focus settings that give reasonably good results over a range of distances. If you're looking at a camera with one setting for close-ups and another for general shots, you are dealing with a fixed-focus camera.

Better cameras adjust the focus automatically — they *auto-focus* — to give the sharpest result at any distance. Auto-focusing cameras generally can be held closer to the subject than fixed-focus ones: sometimes down to a few inches, which can be useful if you want to photograph small objects like flowers or coins.

As an added feature, some advanced cameras let you deal with special photo situations — where the auto-focus just doesn't work very well — by adjusting the focus manually. Typically, auto-focus has problems when the subject of the shot isn't at the middle of the picture; when the subject is very bright, very dark, or low-contrast; when you're taking the picture through glass or water; or when you want to emphasize a small part of a picture by giving it the sharpest focus — a small flower standing quite some distance in front of a face, for example.

Image stabilizers work wonders, even on digital still cameras. By electronically adjusting to compensate for camera shake, a stabilizer can keep you from capturing a blurry mess. You can shoot in low light, shoot from a bus, shoot while jumping with a bungee cord, and your pictures turn out great. Given a choice between a higher-resolution camera — one with more megapixels — and one with image stabilization, go for the stabilizer, every time.

Exposure control and flash

All digital cameras adjust the exposure automatically to suit different light levels. The better ones have more sophisticated circuits that produce good results under a wider range of conditions. Better cameras also give you some control over exposure, either by taking a picture that's lighter or darker than what the camera thinks is ideal, or by allowing you to set the exposure controls (the aperture and shutter speed, for those technically inclined) yourself.

Many cameras have a built-in electronic flash that fires automatically when needed. Better cameras have more powerful and flexible flashes, and offer you various types of control. You may be able to turn off the built-in flash and attach a separate electronic flash of your choice, for example.

Digital cameras are notorious for overly powerful or utterly wimpy flash systems — and far too frequently the same flash is too powerful under one set of lighting conditions and doesn't work worth squat under slightly different conditions. If you're willing to schlep around a standalone flash unit (called an *external flash*), look for a camera that has a *hot shoe* (also called a *synchro-flash terminal*) — a place to plug in and control a standalone flash. Using an external flash with simple techniques like *bouncing* (aiming the flash at a white ceiling or wall) can make a world of difference in the quality of your pictures, and in most cases the camera does all the work.

Image storage and transfer

Really inexpensive cameras store images in built-in memory. When the memory is full, you must transfer the images to your computer to make room for more. If you're at the rim of the Grand Canyon and your computer is at home, this can be, uh, awkward.

Better cameras use removable memory media, often shaped like little cards. When one memory card fills up, you just pull it out and insert a new one. Different cameras use different types of memory cards; all of them work about equally well.

The price of removable memory cards continues to fall precipitously. If you can hold off on buying an SD card, CompactFlash, xD, or Memory Stick, by all means do so. They'll only get cheaper. And bigger.

Most recent cameras have a USB interface for transferring images to your computer. USB is easy and fast, but the whole setup can be clumsy, especially if you want to plug your camera into the wall to avoid draining the batteries during file transfers.

If you buy a camera that uses memory cards, spend an extra $20 or so for a card reader that plugs into your computer's USB port. You can then slide the camera's memory card into the reader and treat it like any other disk drive. Windows XP will identify it immediately. I've used the Kodak 6-in-1 card reader for years, and it works like a champ, but many cheaper generic readers work well, too.

Plugging your camera's memory card into a USB or PCMCIA reader virtually eliminates compatibility problems (see the next section). More than that, you don't have to worry about the dog tripping over the camera's power cord or USB cable, knocking the camera off your desk. I know. My Beagle broke my Nikon Coolpix that way, and it cost hundreds of dollars to get it fixed. Blech!

Compatibility

Windows XP provides direct support for many digital cameras, but not for all of them. If you happen to own a camera that Windows XP doesn't support, it's not a big deal; you may have to use the application provided with the camera to move pictures onto your PC, instead of the Scanner and Camera Wizard built in to Windows XP itself. If you're buying a new camera, though, direct support in Windows XP is a feature you should consider.

Look and feel

Yeah, cameras have look and feel, just like computer applications do. And it's important. The best camera in the world won't do you much good if you can't use it easily. If you're always pushing controls the wrong way, or you can't quite find a comfortable way to hold the camera when you're taking a shot, that camera isn't for you.

It's always wise to try out a camera in a quiet, unpressured environment before you buy it. And in case you miss something important, buy from a dealer who will let you exchange your purchase if you change your mind. For these reasons, buying from a reputable local dealer can be a good move, even if a discounter on the Web offers you a better price.

Using conventional cameras

If you don't want to buy a digital camera, you can take pictures with a conventional film camera and have the photofinisher digitize them. The photofinisher may return the digitized images to you on a CD-ROM or may post them on a secure Web site from which you can download them.

If you're a casual photographer, this approach lets you get your pictures online without buying a new camera. If you're an advanced user, it may be attractive because the best film cameras still produce better results than the best digital cameras. By having the photofinisher do the digitizing, you get the best of both worlds: digital images for their ease-of-use, and negatives/positives for the highest-quality results.

On the other hand, digitizing with a photofinisher is relatively slow, because you have to wait for the film to be processed. It is expensive because you have to pay for film, processing, and digitizing. And you may have to change photofinishers to get the service if the company you currently use doesn't offer digitizing.

Plugging Webcams

A Webcam (also called a *Web camera* or *Internet camera*) is like a little video camera designed to work only while attached to a computer. All Webcams nowadays come with USB interfaces — plug one into a USB port on your PC, and you're off to the movies — or an 802.11 connection that communicates with your wireless network.

Some people use Webcams to publish a continuous, live video feed through a Web site. Popular feeds include pictures of fish in a tank, waves on a shore, burglars breaking into houses, and . . . uh, let's just leave it at that. Other popular uses are video conferencing and recording still pictures or short movie clips to include in e-mail. And MSN Messenger ties into Webcams with a click and a sigh. I know lots of people who comb their hair every morning, for a change, on the off chance that they'll be Messengered with a Webcam.

Webcams are generally less expensive than digital picture-taking cameras, but are also more limited because they work only when plugged into an operating computer. Their resolution is low: typically 320 x 240 to 640 x 480 pixels (with as many as 1 million pixels for snapshots). The lens, image quality, and color accuracy are adequate for the camera's intended purpose, but may be poorer than a point-and-shoot camera.

If you want to get images into your computer quickly and easily, and you don't need high quality, a Webcam may be just the thing for you. They're pretty darn cheap, to boot.

I use my Webcam as a kind of 3D scanner. Instead of trying to get decent scans of small items (such as coins and computer parts), I just set the subjects on a black background, hook up the Webcam, and it's all done in a second.

Panning digital video camcorders

Digital video camcorders have taken over the earth. Where I used to see hordes of bleary-eyed tourists staring into viewfinders, snapping rolls of 35 mm film, I now see hordes of bleary-eyed tourists staring into washed-out LCDs, taking videos of stationary objects. "Wave your hand, Aunt Martha!" That's what passes for motion these days.

The digital camcorder field changes so quickly it's impossible to give general guidelines to manufacturers, styles, or even technologies, which seem to evolve week to week. But a few issues stand out, year after year, camera after camera.

If you go looking for a digital camcorder, get good answers to these questions before you buy:

- **Will the camcorder work in low light?** This seems to be the Achilles heel of most camcorders. Don't rely on the manufacturer's claims or specifications. Look for comments from unbiased reviewers and (better) real people.
- **Can you use the buttons?** Ergonomic problems bedevil still camera designers. Camcorder engineers have all their problems, and many more. Most camcorders have so many complicated controls, placed so close together, with ambiguous or nonexistent labels, that you need to lug along the owner's manual just to shoot a pic.
- **How long will the battery last? Really?** Camcorder batteries are notorious for going dead at the wrong time — and low batteries can lead to all sorts of anomalous behavior. If you think your camcorder needs to be fixed, try it with a new battery. You may be pleasantly surprised.
- **Can you see *anything* in bright light?** Those LCD screens are a lost cause when there's the tiniest bit of glare, but many cameras also use hard-to-see lights to show various settings, or step you through the more complicated procedures.
- **What about color?** Most camcorders have a lot of trouble matching human skin tones, in particular, when moving from shady to bright locations. Shifting from natural to artificial light can turn a person green.

Tips from the Dummies School of Hard Knocks:

- Don't even bother buying a camcorder without a stabilizer.
- The still shots produced by a camcorder will never measure up to (even mediocre) stills from a real digital camera — the technology is completely different.
- If you want decent sound, plan on paying extra for a real microphone.
- And, just like with still cameras, good optical zoom means something; digital zoom doesn't.

Most camcorders use Mini-DV tape, but a few alternatives exist. If you go for one of the other storage media, keep in mind that it may be hard to find a mini-DVD disc or MicroMV tape in Upper Slobovistan.

How to Buy a Camera/Camcorder

Here's my 60-second guide to buying a digital camera or camcorder:

1. **Decide whether you want a still camera or a camcorder.**

   Unless you can afford both a good digital camera and a good digital camcorder, this may be the most difficult decision. Ultimately, you have to decide how you want to use the pictures. Still cameras take lousy videos. Camcorders take lousy stills. If you want a telephone or a PDA, pick the phone or PDA on its own merits; digital photos just come along for the ride.

2. **Narrow your choices down to two or three models.**

   I recommend that you take a look at reviews in the major magazines, and on Web sites such as `www.pcworld.com` and `www.pcmag.com`. Photo magazine pieces are great, too, but unless you look at a side-by-side review that compares many cameras, you may be swayed by a tiny new feature which may or may not be all it's cracked up to be.

3. **Search the Web for comments.**

   A few minutes spent with Google — particularly Google Groups — can save you days of headaches. While you can't believe everything you read online, if you see ten complaints about low-level photos with a camera you've chosen, you should think twice about buying it.

4. **Search the Web for prices and keep a list of the lowest ones.**

   When you have a short list of cameras you're interested in, it's easy to run a quick price comparison. Everybody has their favorite shopping sites, but I always check `www.mysimon.com`, `www.shopping.com`, `www.pricegrabber.com`, `www.nextag.com`, and `www.bizrate.com`. I also drop by `www.amazon.com`, both to see what customers say and to see if Amazon's prices are competitive.

   Don't overlook `www.nextag.com`. They show you historical prices for the camera, so you can see how rapidly the price is decreasing (see Figure 3-4). A recent, fast descent may mean that the camera's ready to be replaced with a newer model.

5. **After you have a good idea of what you want and how much it costs, you can shop anywhere with confidence.**

   Local discount stores may have the camera cheaper (don't forget to factor in shipping costs). Camera shops might charge a few dollars more, but their help — and the knowledge that you're supporting a local business — could well be worth spending a few extra dollars.

Don't forget the batteries

Digital cameras eat batteries for lunch. The Energizer Bunny might last only 20 minutes in a normal camera, particularly one being used at night. You need rechargeable batteries.

If you have a choice in the type of battery you buy, consider:

- **Lithium ion (Li-ion):** These batteries recharge faster and hold their charge longer. But they cost more, and you can't recharge them as many times as with other types of batteries.
- **Nickel Metal Hydride (NiMH):** These batteries are slow on the uptake and discharge quickly, but they aren't as expensive and can be recharged many more times than Li-ion batteries. NiMH batteries are measured in milliamp-hours (mAh) per charge: a 1,800 mAh battery will last 12.5 percent longer than a 1,600 mAh battery on one charge.
- **Nickel Cadmium (NiCad):** These batteries are the dogs — slow to charge, quick to die, they degenerate (each progressive charge gets less effective) and die much sooner than Li-ion or NiMH.

Also, consider spending extra for a fast recharger. If you have to wait eight hours to recharge your batteries, and each set lasts 20 minutes — well, you do the math.

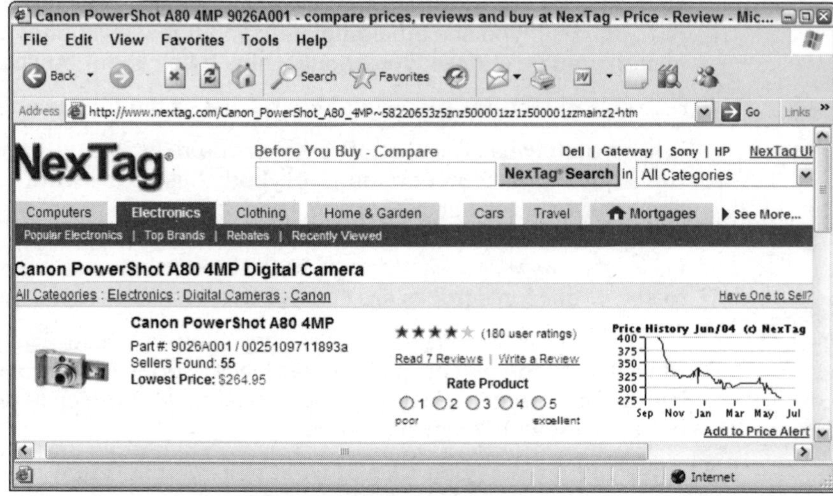

Figure 3-4: NexTag.com includes a historic review of the camera's price.

Moving Images to Your Computer

How you transfer images to your computer depends on the type of camera you're using.

If you're using a conventional camera and your images were scanned by the photofinisher, transferring images is easy: Simply put the CD-ROM in a handy CD drive and copy the files, or go to the photofinisher's Web site and follow its directions. Rocket science.

If you're using a video camera, you should first try the interface in Windows Movie Maker, which I discuss in Book VII, Chapter 2. If you bump into a problem and you're looking for answers, start with the camera manufacturer's Web site. See Table 3-2.

Table 3-2 Major Camera Manufacturers' Web Sites

Manufacturer	*U.S. Web site*
Canon	`www.canon.com`
Intel	`www.intel.com`
Kodak	`www.kodak.com`
Logitech	`www.logitech.com`
Minolta	`www.minolta.com`
Nikon	`www.nikon.com`
Olympus	`www.olympus.com`
Panasonic	`www.panasonic.com`
Philips	`www.philips.com`
Sony	`www.sony.com`

You can use any one of three procedures to bring images from digital cameras and Internet cameras into your PC:

- ✦ With Internet cameras and digital cameras supported by Windows XP, using the Windows XP Scanner and Camera Wizard is the simplest way.
- ✦ With any digital camera, you can use the file-transfer application provided with that camera.
- ✦ With any digital camera that uses memory cards, you can transfer images by putting the card — most likely a SmartMedia or CompactFlash card — in a memory card reader.

Use the Scanner and Camera Wizard to transfer images stored in the memory of a digital camera to your PC or to capture still images from an Internet camera as follows:

1. **Plug the camera into the appropriate port on your computer.**

   If it's a digital camera, turn it on. You may have to move the camera's controls to some particular setting; consult the camera's instructions for transferring images.

2. **The Windows Scanner and Camera Wizard may start automatically at this point. If it doesn't, choose Start➪My Pictures to display the contents of the My Pictures folder in Windows Explorer.**

   When you start Windows Explorer this particular way, it displays some special *task lists* in its left pane, as shown in Figure 3-5.

Figure 3-5: Windows Explorer with the picture task pane.

3. **From the Picture Tasks list, choose Get Pictures from Camera or Scanner.**

   If Windows asks which scanner or camera you want to use, select the icon that represents your camera, and then click OK. The wizard displays a welcome box.

4. **Click Next to display the dialog box shown in Figure 3-6.**

   If you're connected to a Webcam, the Preview panel shows the live image captured by the camera. Each time you click the Take Picture button, the wizard captures a still image. The images appear in the Pictures panel.

   If you're connected to a digital camera, the process is very similar, but the Pictures panel shows the pictures stored in the camera's memory.

   If any of the pictures are not right-side up, you can rotate them. Click a picture to select it, and then click one of the rotate buttons under the Pictures pane to rotate the picture a quarter turn right, a quarter turn left, or a half turn.

   Notice the small check box above each picture. Select the check boxes for the pictures that you want to save and/or clear them for the pictures you don't want to save. You can use the Clear All and Save All buttons for convenience.

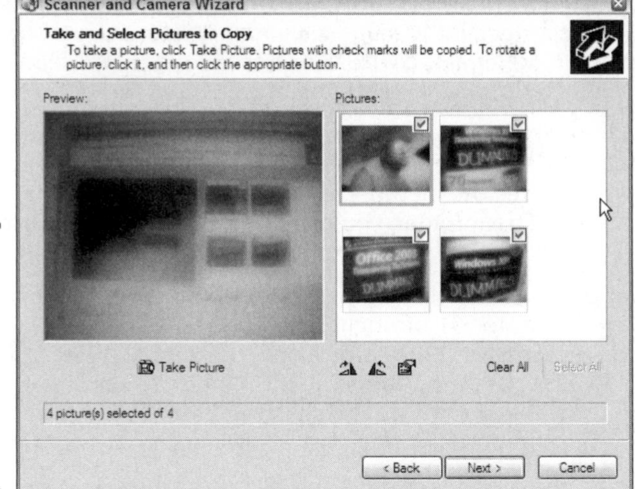

Figure 3-6: Scanner and Camera Wizard, Take and Select Pictures to Copy.

5. **Click Next.**

   The wizard displays the dialog box shown in Figure 3-7.

6. **In the Type a Name text box, enter the name you want to give the first picture you're saving.**

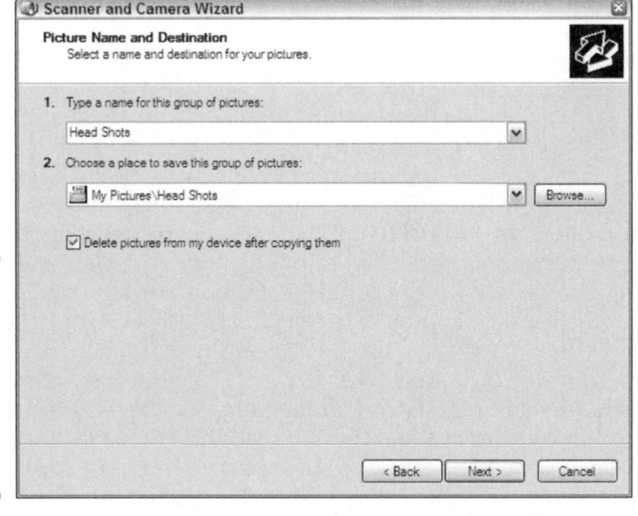

Figure 3-7: Scanner and Camera Wizard, Picture Name and Destination.

If you're saving several pictures, the wizard gives each one a unique name. For example, if the name you enter is "Head Shots" and you're saving three pictures, the wizard names the pictures "Head Shots," "Head Shots 001," and "Head Shots 002."

The wizard automatically stores the pictures in the My Pictures folder, in a subfolder with the name you entered. If you entered "Head Shots," for example, it stores the pictures in the My Pictures\Head Shots folder. If you want a different folder, you can choose one with the Browse button or the Choose a Place drop-down list.

This wizard is remarkably smart. For example, if you store pictures named Head Shots 001 through Head Shots 123, then download another bunch of pictures with the same name, the wizard picks up with Head Shots 124, and goes from there. Also, if you try to copy across the same picture twice, the wizard will catch the gaffe and offer to replace the copy on the computer, or to give it a new name.

Notice the check box labeled Delete Pictures from My Device After Copying Them. If you're using a digital camera, selecting this check box deletes the pictures from the camera's memory. It deletes only the pictures that it transferred — that is, the ones you selected in the wizard's previous screen.

If you're using a Webcam, the camera has no memory, but the wizard gets the same result by keeping copies of the pictures itself. If you don't select the check box, the next time you use the wizard, the pictures you saved will still be in the Pictures pane. If you do select the check box, the next time you use the wizard, the pictures you saved will not be there.

7. **Click Next.**

   The wizard copies the pictures to the folder you chose and displays the dialog box shown in Figure 3-8.

8. **Click Next, and then click Finish.**

   You can follow the wizard to publish pictures on the Web, but if you do (surprise, surprise!), you'll be led by the nose to a Microsoft Web site that will charge you for the privilege. Do yourself a favor. Save yourself some time. See the section, "Sharing Your Pictures with Others," later in this chapter.

If Windows XP doesn't recognize your camera, the least-hassle alternative, by far, is a memory card reader. These cheap little devices plug into your computer's USB port. Simply stick your camera's memory card (probably an SC card, a CompactFlash card, an xD card, or a Memory Stick) into the card reader, and Windows XP thinks you have a new hard drive. Files on the camera's memory card are treated just like any picture files in Windows.

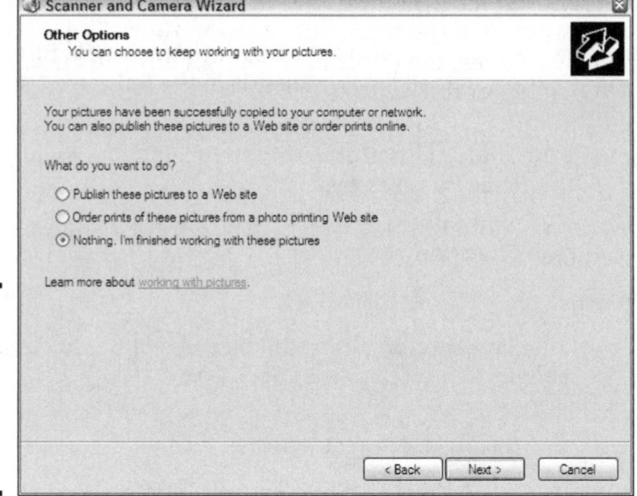

Figure 3-8: Scanner and Camera Wizard, Other Options.

You may also want to try the software that shipped with the camera to transfer images from the camera to your PC. Most digital cameras come with such an application. Install the application and follow its instructions. Good luck.

If Windows XP *does* support your camera directly, you may still want to take a look at the camera's file-transfer application anyway. Many of these applications have additional functions that Windows XP does not provide, such as remotely setting some of the camera's controls.

Printing Pictures

Windows XP provides several ways to print photos and other images. If you have a photo-quality printer, you can use Windows XP's Photo Printing Wizard to print pictures from the My Pictures folder.

In my experience, the Photo Printing Wizard does a good job in producing quality prints, within the imposed size limitations. (You can print only a handful of standard sizes: full page, 4 x 6, and so on.) If you need a very high-quality print, or if you want a size that isn't in the wizard's repertoire, you have to use Photoshop, Windows Paint, or some other image-editing program.

Printing with the wizard

To use the Photo Printing Wizard

1. **Choose Start⇨My Pictures.**

   This opens a copy of Windows Explorer with the My Pictures folder in the right pane and task list commands in the left pane (refer to Figure 3-5).

2. **Navigate to the folder containing the picture(s) you want to print, and then click the Print Pictures task.**

   This starts the Photo Printing Wizard. The wizard displays a "welcome" page. Ho hum.

3. **Click Next.**

   The wizard displays thumbnails of the pictures in the folder, as shown in Figure 3-9. Above each picture is a check box.

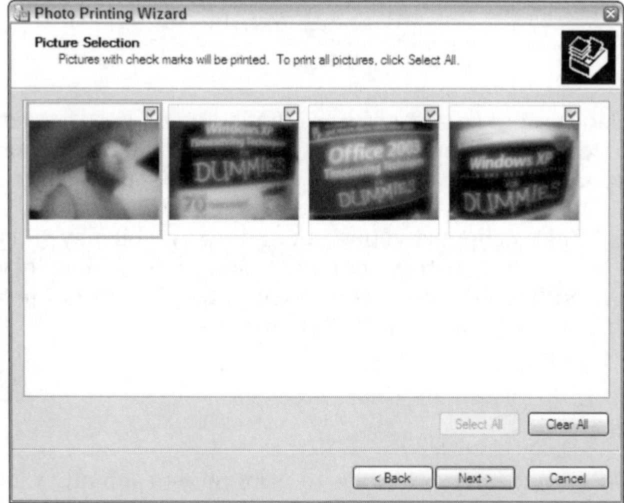

Figure 3-9: Photo Printing Wizard, Picture Selection.

4. **Select the check boxes next to the pictures that you want to print, and deselect the check boxes for any pictures that you do not want to print. Click Next.**

   The wizard displays a panel of printing options. This panel lets you select the printer to use (if you have more than one printer). Clicking the Printing Preferences button opens a dialog box that enables you to set options such as the type of paper you're printing on, the level of print quality you want, and whether to print in black and white or color. The options displayed depend on the type of printer you have.

5. **Choose the printer you want to use, and then click Next.**

   The wizard displays a page that lets you select a layout and set the number of times to print each picture (see Figure 3-10).

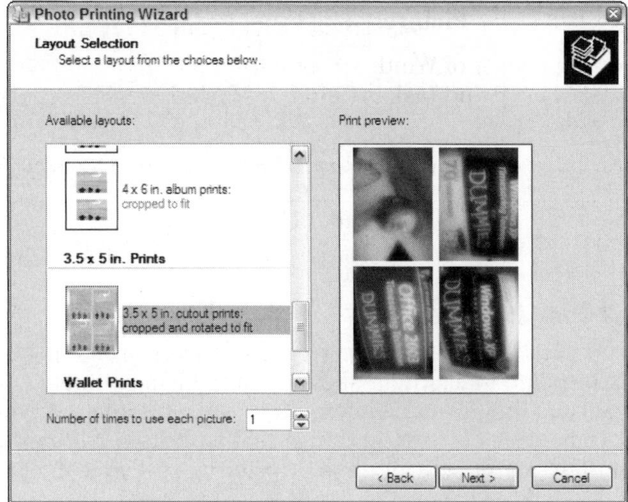

Figure 3-10: Photo Printing Wizard, Layout Selection.

You can choose among a full-page layout (one print per page) and several options that put two or more smaller pictures on a page. The latter options are useful if you selected several images or told the wizard to print a picture more than once.

6. **Choose the picture layout you want, and then click Next.**

   The wizard displays a panel with a progress bar while it prints and then displays a panel that says it is finished.

7. **Click Finish to close the wizard.**

Advanced printing software

The Photo Printing Wizard is okay for making an unmodified print of an entire picture. But suppose you want to print just part of a family portrait to omit the rude gesture one of your kids was making? Or suppose the light in your backyard made Aunt Gertrude's face look a little green, and you want to make the color balance more flattering? Want to chop your ex's head off (in a legally and ethically acceptable manner, of course)? It's easier than you think.

The Photo Printing Wizard can't do those things, but many commercial photo-printing programs can. If you're interested in capabilities like these, look into programs like Adobe Photoshop (the professional's choice), Jasc's Paint Shop Pro, MGI Software's PhotoSuite, and Ulead PhotoImpact. See Table 3-3 for some URL listings.

Table 3-3 Commercial Photo Printing Programs

Program	*URL*
Photoshop	www.adobe.com/products/photoshop/main.html
Paint Shop Pro	www.jasc.com
PhotoSuite	www.photosuite.com
Ulead PhotoImpact	www.ulead.com/pi/runme.htm

Printing via the Web

You can send your pictures to a service that makes prints on standard photographic paper and mails them back to you. The convenience is unbeatable, and the quality of the prints can be better than a photo-quality printer provides. And some services can do things that a photo-quality printer can't — such as printing poster-size pictures or printing on coffee mugs.

Such services predate Windows XP, but Windows XP adds a new level of convenience: You can access a service right from Windows itself.

To see how this works

1. **Choose Start⇨My Pictures.**
2. **Open a subfolder that contains some pictures you want to print.**

   If you don't want to print pictures now, open any subfolder. You can explore the process without committing yourself or spending any cash.
3. **Click the Order Prints Online command in the Picture Tasks list.**

   This starts the Online Print Ordering Wizard. The wizard first displays a Welcome dialog box.
4. **Click Next to display the dialog box shown in Figure 3-11.**

   The dialog box in Figure 3-11 lists the pictures in the folder you chose. A check box next to each picture's name indicates whether you want to order prints of that picture.
5. **Select or deselect the check boxes to choose the pictures that you want to print. Click Next.**

   The wizard displays the dialog box shown in Figure 3-12. This dialog box lists companies whose printing services are currently available through the wizard.
6. **Select the company that you prefer and click Next.**

   At this point, the printing service's Web server takes over, so the details of the process depend on which service you chose. Each of them leads you through a sequence of pages in which you select the services you want, give your address, and arrange to pay.

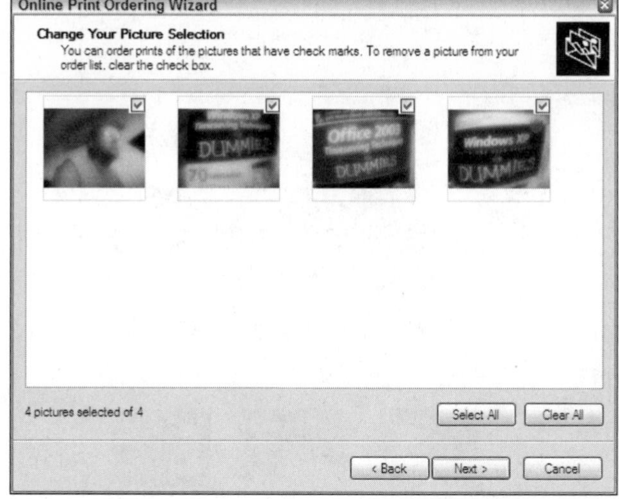

Figure 3-11: Photo Printing Wizard, Change Your Picture Selection.

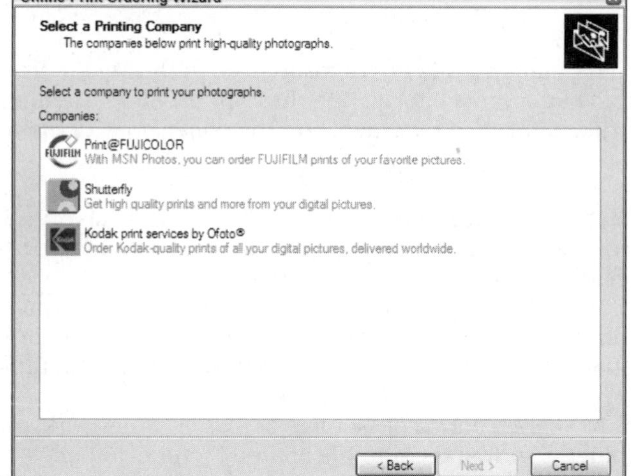

Figure 3-12: Online Print Ordering Wizard, Select a Printing Company.

Storing Pictures in Your Computer

The Windows Explorer View menu lets you select several different views of your pictures. The Thumbnails view (click View➪Thumbnails) and the Filmstrip view (see Figure 3-13) are particularly useful. Try both to see which you prefer.

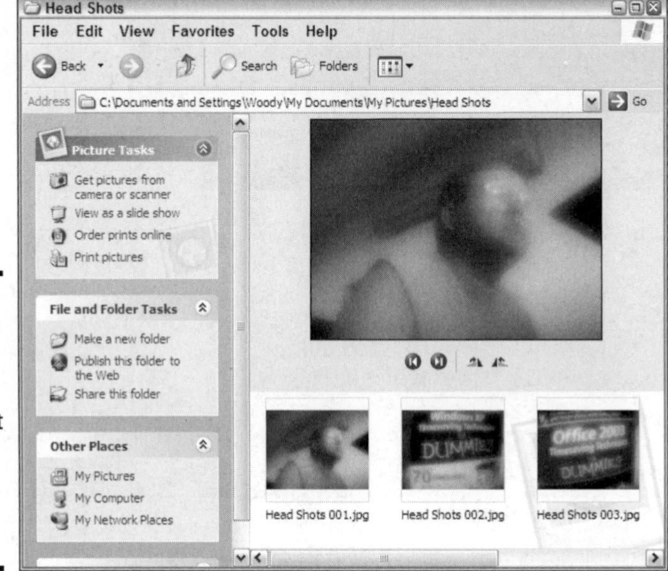

Figure 3-13: Filmstrip view shows you an enlargement of one picture and thumbnails of the rest.

The plain old Details view is not quite so plain in the My Pictures folder. It displays some additional information that you may find useful: The date each picture was taken, if recorded, and the dimensions of the picture in pixels.

When your pictures are in the My Pictures folder, you can organize them any way you want. For example, you can put them in one folder for "Vacations," one for "The Kids," one for "Blackmail" (just kidding), and so forth. You can create two or more levels of folders if you want. As long as you keep your folders inside the My Pictures folder, they inherit the My Pictures folder's task lists, and they show the same additional information in the Details view.

If you want to share a bunch of pictures across your network, put them in a separate folder and drag them to the Shared Pictures folder.

Sharing Your Pictures with Others

When you have some nice pictures on your computer, naturally you want to share them with other interested people. You can share pictures in several ways, the most popular being by e-mail, by burning pictures to CD, or by posting them on a Web site.

E-mail

People frequently send picture files as *attachments* to e-mail. See your mail reader's documentation for instructions on how to do this. If you use a Web-based mail service, check the Web site's help pages.

If you're using Outlook Express, you can find full details in Book III, Chapter 2.

Many Internet Service Providers and Web-based mail services limit the amount of data that you may attach to an e-mail message. The limits vary but are typically in the range of half a megabyte to a few megabytes. Many single picture files are small enough to send — at least, if you aren't using a high megapixel camera — but such a limit may restrict the number of pictures you can attach to one message.

Microsoft has a tremendous tool called the Image Resizer PowerToy, which you can use to quickly reduce the resolution — and the size — of picture files. I have full details in Technique 55 of *Windows XP Timesaving Techniques For Dummies* (Wiley Publishing, Inc.). Look for the program at `http://microsoft.com/windowsxp/pro/downloads/powertoys.asp`.

CD-ROM

If you have a CD writer, you can easily copy pictures to CDs. A CD has enough space to hold several hundred or even thousand pictures.

To burn pictures on your CD-R or CD-RW drive, see Book I, Chapter 5.

HighMAT

Microsoft would have you believe that High MAT (High Performance Media Access Technology) is taking the world by storm. In fact, the world has largely greeted HighMAT with a high-performance yawn, but in some cases it may be worth your consideration.

In theory, you burn a HighMAT CD, give it to a friend, the friend pops it into their HighMAT compatible CD player (of which there are a few), and the pictures on the CD get displayed as a slide show, typically under the command of a remote control. It's kind of like Windows Explorer's View as Slideshow option, except the CD player doesn't need to be running Windows.

To date, HighMAT supports only JPG pictures, WMV videos, and MP3 and WMA audio files. If you have GIFs or MPGs, you're out of luck. Only a few manufacturers (notably Panasonic) make HighMAT-compatible CD players. If you want to play with HighMAT, by all means go ahead. But don't pay extra for it.

In a pinch, you can use compact USB flash drives or even diskettes for lower-quality pictures. Don't expect to get more than a handful of pictures on one diskette, though — fewer if you have high-quality shots. Remember that a floppy can hold only 1.44MB of data — a pittance compared to the lovely 2GB USB flash drive keychain you carry around, eh?

A Web site

Many Internet Service Providers maintain Web servers where their subscribers can post their Web sites with personal material. You can use such a Web site to "publish" your pictures. Anyone who knows where to look can see them, of course, which you may or may not consider a good thing.

Check your service provider's Web site for information about its file-hosting policies and instructions for uploading files.

You can also find independent companies, other than your ISP, that provide Web-hosting services for a very reasonable fee. I've had good luck over the years with `www.dundee.net/isp/hosting.htm` and `www.futurequest.net/Services`. You need to figure out how to set up your own Web page, but both Dundee and Futurequest have full instructions — and live human beings — to help.

Some organizations don't necessarily offer Internet access, but make a business of publishing other people's files for them on the Web. Different organizations offer different types of service.

One of the most interesting services is photo hosting. A photo hosting service typically lets you upload your pictures to a private area on its Web site. You then can choose the people who may have access to your area.

Two inexpensive services you can check out are at

- `www.myfamily.com`
- `www.webshots.com`

Setting a Picture as Desktop Background

The desktop background is the picture that Windows XP displays when no other windows are open. See Book II, Chapter 1, for details.

Setting your own picture as the desktop background is easy: In Windows Explorer, right-click on the picture and choose Set as Desktop Background.

If your picture's dimensions (in pixels) are no more than half those of the screen, Windows XP tries to fill the screen with as many copies of the picture as necessary. This technique is called *tiling*. Otherwise, Windows XP stretches or shrinks the picture to fit the desktop.

A tiled background picture looks best if its dimensions go evenly into the display's dimensions. For example, a tiled background on a 1280 x 1024 display might use a 640 x 480 picture (2 x 2 tiles) or a 320 x 240 picture (4 x 4 tiles). Conversely, if you have a small picture (say, a 320 x 240 image from a Webcam) and you want it to fill the entire desktop, you need to expand the size of the picture so it matches whatever resolution you're running on your monitor.

Most commercial picture editors allow you to change a picture's dimensions. Windows Paint can do this too, although the procedure is awkward:

1. **Start Paint by selecting Start➪All Programs➪Accessories➪Paint.**
2. **Choose File➪Open and open the picture that you want to stretch or shrink to fit on the desktop.**
3. **Choose Image➪Attributes and make a note of the width and height, in pixel, of the image. Click OK to return to Paint.**

   Figure 3-14 shows that my Webcam shot measures 320 x 240 pixels.

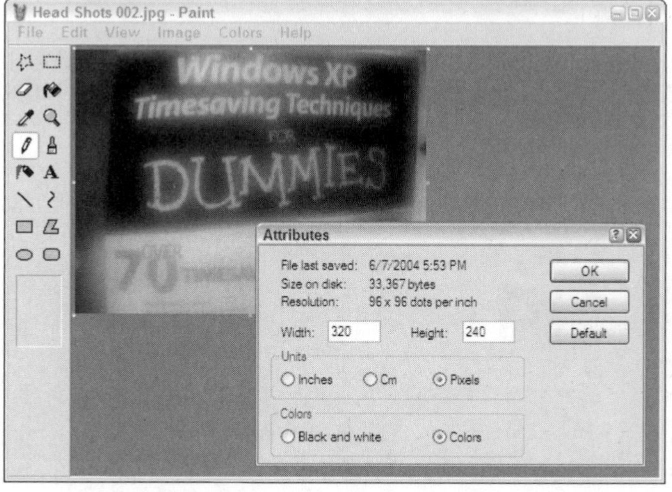

Figure 3-14: Expanding a Webcam shot to fill the entire Windows desktop.

4. **Choose Image➪Stretch Skew to bring up the Stretch and Skew dialog box, as shown in Figure 3-15.**

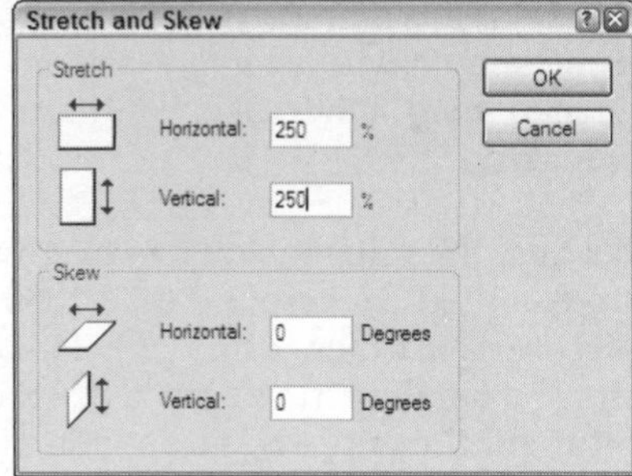

Figure 3-15: Enter the percentage change necessary to make the image fit on the desktop.

Now comes the hard part. You have to figure out what percentage increase (or decrease) of the current image will stretch (or shrink) the image to occupy the entire Windows desktop.

In this particular case, I'm running a laptop at 800 x 600 pixels. So the 320 x 240 pixel Webcam shot has to be stretched/increased by 250 percent (250 = 800 / 320) in the horizontal direction, and also increased by 250 percent (250 = 600 / 240) in the vertical direction.

5. **Type the percentage change in the current image size that will make the image fit on the Windows desktop, in both the horizontal and vertical directions. Leave the Skew boxes at zero. Click OK to return to Paint.**
6. **Click File⇨Save As and save the file as a Bitmap. Click Save to return to Paint.**

   As shown in Figure 3-16, I save the modified picture as `Desktop.bmp`. (Make sure that you select one of the Bitmap formats in the Save As Type drop-down list.)

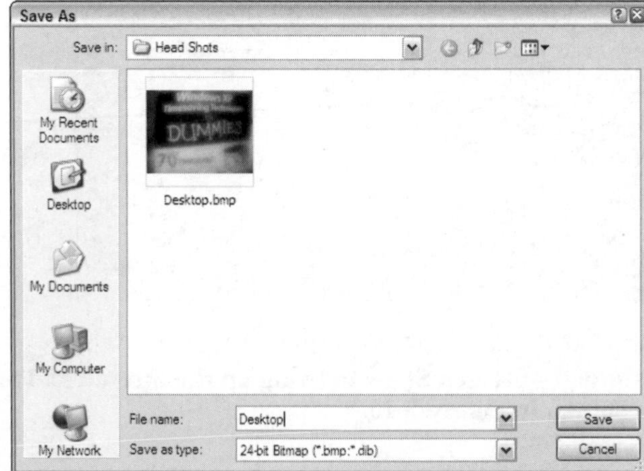

Figure 3-16: Save the stretched (or shrunk) picture as a bitmap.

7. **In Paint, choose File⇨Set As Background. Then choose File⇨Exit to return to Windows.**

   You can choose either (Tiled) or (Centered) — if the picture fits the desktop exactly, both choices do the same thing. Your picture appears as the new Windows desktop.

If you want to go back to your old desktop, right-click any open space on the desktop, choose Properties, and then in the Theme box, choose your old theme.

Troubleshooting

Here are some suggestions to try if you have a problem with one of the procedures described in this chapter:

- ***I plugged my camera into the computer, but the Scanner and Camera Wizard doesn't believe it's there.***

  Be sure the cable is secure at both ends, the camera is turned on, and its batteries are charged.

  If your camera's controls must be set a certain way to permit a transfer, be sure they are set.

  If you haven't used this camera with Windows XP before, read the manual and install the drivers that undoubtedly shipped on a CD with the camera. If all else fails, install and use the file-transfer application provided with the camera.

- ***I displayed the My Pictures folder in Windows Explorer, but the left pane doesn't show the Picture Tasks list — just the usual map of my folders.***

  Exit Windows Explorer and start it again directly from the Start menu. (Choose Start⇨My Pictures.) This is the easiest way to make it display the Picture Tasks list.

- ***My pictures look pretty good on the screen, but when I print them, they look awful.***

  The quality of many color inkjet printers leaves a lot to be desired, but you can do some things to help. To make adjustments to your printer, choose Start⇨Printers and Faxes, right-click on the printer in question, and choose Properties.

  Use the highest-quality settings available: Superior will produce a much better image than Normal.

Use an appropriate paper. Paper formulated for printing photos on inkjet printers is best. Any coated (glossy) paper is likely to work better than ordinary printer paper. Photo quality paper produces the best results of all.

Be sure you have a photo printer. Many older color inkjet printers are designed for printing things like business charts, with large areas of solid color. They can't handle the subtle gradations of a photograph very well.

- ***This is fascinating, and I want more information about one of the topics you discussed.***

  See the answer to the next question.

- ***I'm totally confused!***

  Lots of information about digital photography is available on the Internet.

I cover digital photography extensively (and even answer questions!) on my Web site, www.AskWoody.com. You can also pick up *Digital Photography For Dummies*, 4th edition, by Julie Adair King (published by Wiley Publishing, Inc.).

You can find more sources of information through your favorite Web search engine by searching for keywords like "digital photography tutorial." If you don't have a favorite search engine, try www.google.com.

Book VIII

Windows Media Center

"Wait a minute... This is a movie, not a game?! I thought I was the one making Keanu Reeves jump kick in slow motion."

Contents at a Glance

Chapter 1: Windows Media Center: Should You Buy One?

In This Chapter

- **Finding out what Windows Media Center Edition really is**
- **Discovering how MCE computers are different from those of mere mortals**
- **Knowing what you should look for in an MCE computer**

From the moment you start Windows Media Center Edition, Microsoft wants you to think that you have a special version of Windows. Even the splash screen says "Media Center Edition."

Here's the cold, hard truth: Windows Media Center Edition (which I call *Media Center* or *MCE* in this book) is just a program that runs on Windows. It's a big program. It's a fancy program. But it's just a program — like, oh, Windows Media Player, or Internet Explorer, or Windows Movie Maker.

Microsoft's marketing approaches change from hour to hour, but at this moment, there's one little problem with MCE: You can't go out to your Friendly Local Software Shoppe and buy a copy of Windows Media Center Edition, take it home, and slap it on your PC. Microsoft doesn't sell MCE in a box. Instead, Microsoft teams up with select hardware vendors who sell entire Media Center systems. If you want MCE, you have to buy the whole kit 'n caboodle from an authorized dealer — PC, video, TV tuner, monitor, sound system, wireless remote control, keyboard, and a warm cat to sit on the TV.

Here are two reasons why:

- ✦ Microsoft has high hardware demands for Media Center Edition — fast video cards, lots of memory and hard drive space, and the like — so it doesn't want to take on the headaches of supporting zillions of varieties of less-than-stellar pieces of hardware.
- ✦ Microsoft makes more money that way.

Stop me if this starts to sound like Apple's old approach to limiting the market.

Oh. I lied a little bit. In fact, Microsoft does let software developers install and use MCE on their PCs. The folks who subscribe to MSDN — Microsoft's Developer's Network — get the latest version of MCE on their CDs, along with every other piece of software Microsoft makes. So if you hear about people installing MCE on cobbled-together PCs (I won't mention the folks at, oh, `http://xpmce.com` by name), they're undoubtedly using the MSDN version of Windows MCE.

As this book went to press, Microsoft announced that plain "white box" PC manufacturers will be able to bundle MCE with their systems. There were rumors circulating that Microsoft may also allow video board manufacturers to bundle MCE with their products (presumably with a remote control) too. If that happens, and you're wondering whether it's worth the money to pay more for MCE, read the next section, "Do You Need MCE?" There are no easy answers — but you have plenty of options.

Do You Need MCE?

If you have to ask the question, you don't.

MCE draws people in with its incredible interface; its power; its seductive, immersive multimedia capabilities; its position as the physical and logistical center of all your audio and visual equipment — and the ability to control all of that and more with a remote from across the room.

Windows at ten feet.

MCE sneaks up and grabs you by the throat. If you don't get it, you don't need it. But if you do. . . .

Here's what MCE offers that most people want:

- ✦ The ability to record TV shows with instant action replay (yes, it'll keep recording the halftime show while you watch Justin Timberlake again), easy recording setup via a program guide, and a tiny TV mini-screen that appears just about everywhere you might want it.
- ✦ The full spectrum of Windows Media Player capabilities (they're extensive — see Book VII, Chapter 1), with a gorgeous user interface, all accessible via remote.
- ✦ One central location for all your photo stuff — transferring pics and videos from a camera, playing videos, ripping and burning CDs and DVDs, leafing through photos, running slideshows, making prints.
- ✦ Internet Explorer, sorta, on a big screen, controlled by remote.

- All the bells and whistles you would expect from a souped-up PC that's wired for sound. And video. If you have good audio or video equipment, you'll want to control it through MCE.

That said, MCE isn't for everybody. In particular, it has these drawbacks:

- **Bugs:** Windows Media Center Edition is now up to version 3.0 which, by traditional Microsoft standards, means that most of the bugs have been shaken out — and backward compatibility is already a problem.

  MCE has gone through more than its fair share of bugs. With deep hooks into Windows XP, Windows Media Player, Internet Explorer, and a half-dozen lesser luminaries in the Windows pantheon, MCE falls prey to bugs in many of the major Windows applications. If swatting bugs and rebooting your computer gives you the willies, give MCE a pass.

- **Limitations:** As of this writing, MCE supports only a single tuner, so picture-in-picture or record-one-station-while-you-watch-another features don't work. You can drive a TV screen from your MCE system, but you can't control another PC. An hour of recorded TV takes up more than a DVD's-worth of space, unless you use the "Fair" quality setting.

  Of course, the biggest limitations center around digital rights management, and they aren't all exclusive to MCE. If you record a TV show on your MCE system (in "Fair" quality, of course), can you burn it to DVD and then watch the DVD on a neighbor's DVD player? On another PC? If you rip a CD that you bought on your MCE computer, can you play the tracks on your iPod? Can you play them on the computer in the bedroom? Can your son take them to school on his portable? Sure, you can use MCE to buy music from Napster and other companies that give Microsoft a cut, but if you buy a song from iTunes, can you play it on your Media Center PC? Tough questions. If they concern you, ask people who own and use MCE (at, for example, `http://xpmce.com`) before you buy.

- **Unconvinced Partners:** After all these years, you'd think that media providers would flock to the Microsoft money machine and march to the MCE drums. Embarrassingly, not all of them have. For example, even ESPN — which commands a premium position in MCE's Online Spotlight — doesn't have its act together, at least as of this writing (see Figure 1-1).

- **A Big Price Tag:** MCE isn't the only game in town.

Most TV and FM tuner-card manufacturers these days include recording and playback capabilities: I'm impressed by the latest ASUS TV FM tuner card with its bundled software and remote — a simple, cheap package that provides much of MCE's TV functionality without duplicating Windows Media Player.

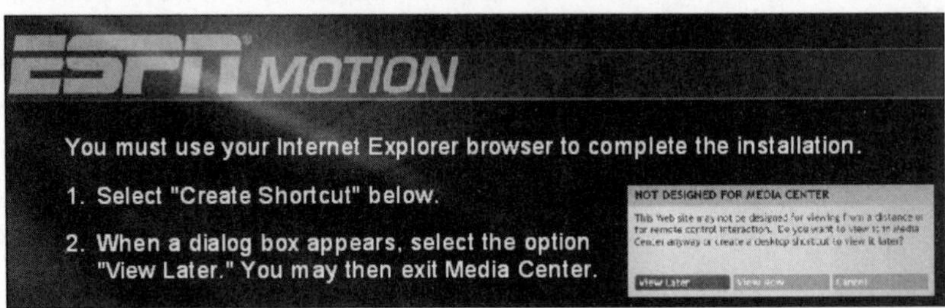

Figure 1-1: ESPN Motion, as highlighted in MCE's Online Spotlight, is "Not Designed For Media Center."

Then there's the crop of USB-based TV tuner/recorders that go in like a snap, take up almost no room, and cost a pittance. AVerMedia led the charge, but others have followed.

That said, Windows Media Center Edition remains the 800-pound gorilla of the genre. When DirecTV decides to do a deal to make its services available on PCs, you can expect that Microsoft will step to the head of the line. Same with NBC and ESPN. Time Warner may be another story, but . . . if you want to stay near the bleeding edge of computerized home entertainment content, MCE's the product of choice.

What's in an MCE PC?

So what do you get when you buy a Windows Media Center PC? Pretty close to the best of everything:

- ✦ A very fast processor with lots of memory, a big hard drive, and lots of USB and FireWire ports. But you expected that.
- ✦ A top-notch TV (and radio) tuner card with built-in MPEG-2 support. (In other words, the tuner card itself has to translate an incoming TV signal into a compressed MPEG-2 video stream, so that the computer doesn't have to worry about it.) Microsoft spends more time and energy nailing down TV/FM tuner cards than any other MCE component, and for good reason: They can make or break a good multimedia system.
- ✦ A fast, reasonably capable graphics card. (Minimum 4X AGP for you techies.) Most MCE computers have graphics cards that can connect to both a computer monitor and a TV, simultaneously. Some have DVI connectors. Most can connect to both the standard "yellow" composite video jack on a TV and an S-VHS jack.
- ✦ A reasonably fast CD/DVD drive. Most have burners.

✦ A high-quality sound card. Most MCE PCs are hooked up to a surround-sound (5.1 or 7.1) speaker system, consisting of five (or seven) speakers with a subwoofer. You almost always get "line out" (plain old stereo) and "digital audio out" (high quality multi-channel sound) connectors, too.

✦ Both a LAN connection and a modem. Microsoft wants you to connect to the Internet — and a fast connection "improves the Media Center experience." It also keeps you from thinking about throwing your remote at the screen.

✦ A remote. To throw at the screen, of course.

All of those jacks and ports (see Figure 1-2) will give you a headache, guaranteed. If you have trouble putting together a cable TV box with a VCR, stereo, and a fancy TV, you ain't seen nuthin' yet.

Figure 1-2: The Niveus AVX, like most Windows MCE PCs, comes packed with connectors of every imaginable description.

How to Buy a Media Center PC

Easy. Take a big wad of cash down to Fast Eddy's PC Emporium, spread it out on a desk, point to a Media Center PC, and say, "I want one of those."

There are lots and lots of manufacturers who would like to take your order. ("Would you like fries with that, sir?") Here's the best way I know to buy a Media Center PC:

✦ Break out Excel and keep track of all the details while you're shopping.

✦ *Don't* start in a discount computer shop. The impulse-buying urge for MCE computers runs way off the scale — if you start in a discount emporium, you may be tempted to buy something you don't want, or pay too much for something you do. Think chocolate cake and red Ferrari, all rolled into one.

✦ Start online with a couple of the big manufacturers. Gateway (www.gateway.com) has a good selection. HP/Compaq (www.hp.com, shown in Figure 1-3), Sony (www.sony.com) and Dell (www.dell.com) offer MCE with many of their desktop computers. Browse around a bit.

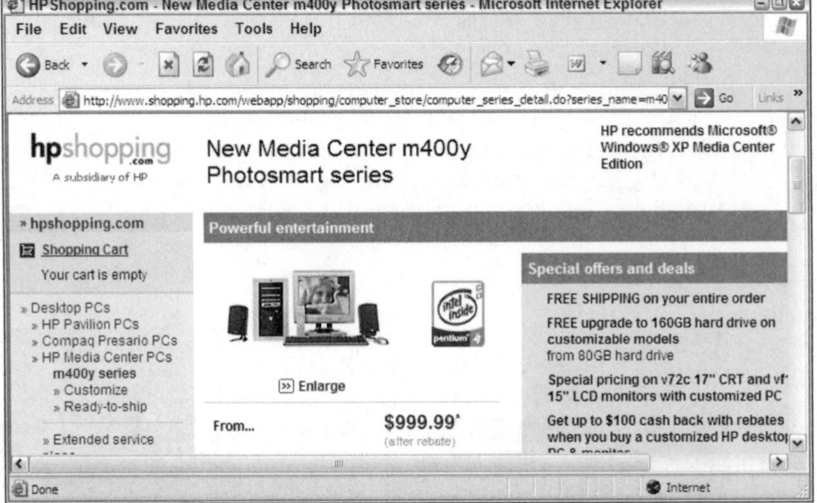

Figure 1-3: Sometimes you have to look pretty hard to find MCE computers on the major manufacturers' sites.

✦ Armed with a good knowledge of what's available and how much it costs, you're ready to take on the most zealous (or ambivalent) sales droids: Go ahead and hit the local stores.

Keep a few things in mind:

✦ Go for quiet. One complaint I hear, over and over again, is that MCE computers are big, ugly, and noisy. Niveus (www.niveusmedia.com) is my favorite for quiet, capable MCE computers.

✦ Don't pay more for the fastest processor. MCE computers depend on all of their components for speed, and the amount of memory — not the speed of the processor — seems to be the chief bottleneck.

✦ If you're intimidated by the thought of putting the machine together, buy from a local supplier who will install it for you.

That one tip alone could save you the price of this book, over and over again.

Chapter 2: Setting Up a Media Center PC

In This Chapter

- **Figuring out where all those %$#@! wires go**
- **Getting Media Center Edition adjusted**
- **Making Windows safe for MCE**

By the time you finish putting together your first Windows Media Center system, you may swear off assembling PCs ever again. In fact, one of the very best reasons for buying an MCE system from a local store is that you can hire the company that sold you the unit to put it together for you.

A friend of mine recently told me that he was getting out of the computer business because it's just gotten too complicated. He made that announcement — you guessed it — immediately after assembling a Windows Media Center PC. 'Course, he built it from scratch. Definitely a fool's task.

Media Center PCs combine all of the frustrations of assembling a complicated PC with the joys of figuring out how to attach your satellite box, where to hook up the speakers, which stack of books to stick under the TV, how to keep all the wires from pulling each other out, and what to do with the subwoofer. The only saving grace? You don't have to worry about a VCR.

Probably.

Organizing the Normandy Invasion

So you have eight big boxes sitting on your living room (or dorm room or office) floor, and the first debilitating pangs of buyer's remorse have set in.

That's normal. Not to worry.

The folks at the computer store sold you everything that you need. But I can *guarantee* they forgot a couple of items that you will surely want. Before you assemble the beast, you need to run out and pick up what they forgot.

In particular, you need

- **A UPS (uninterruptible power supply):** If the sales droid let you walk out of the shop without a UPS, he should be lashed. No, a surge protector isn't good enough. You need a UPS big enough to handle your computer and any other sensitive hardware that's hanging around: TV, network hub, DSL or cable modem, scanner, external drives or USB hubs — the whole nine yards.

No, you don't need to plug your printer into a UPS — and you should *never* plug a laser printer into a UPS. Laser printers draw a tremendous amount of power; a laser printer will probably blow out your UPS when it starts, and even if your UPS doesn't end up a heap of smoldering goo, if the power goes out, the UPS will die in seconds from the laser printer's power drain.

- **Lots of power strips:** The ones that plug into the UPS don't need surge protection, but any that plug straight into the wall should have surge protectors.

Anything with a "brick" that converts AC to DC (which you commonly find with laptop computers, telephones, modems, and the like) doesn't require a surge protector. But each brick will invariably take up two (or even three) slots on a power strip.

- **A roll of masking tape and a fine-point permanent-ink marker:** You should mark the end of every cable as you connect it: Wrap a piece of tape around the wire and write down where it's going. That way, when you look at a power strip with five plugs in it, you can tell which one goes to your PC and which one goes to your TV. You'll also be able to tell your left-front speaker from the right rear without pulling the speaker cable out from under the rug.

If you save a snapshot of the final array of cables — even if you only use your Webcam — you'll have a good record of which cable went where, in case your three-year-old nephew decides to pull a few cables off the back of the TV.

- **Those little plastic gizmos that bundle cables together:** They're cheap, and they'll keep you from going nuts. By the time you're done, the back of your PC is going to look like a wiring bundle down the fuselage of a 747.

- **Video cables that are long enough to go where they need to go:** Before you assemble the beast, block out precisely where the PC will go, where the monitor will go, and where the TV (if you have one) will go. Then figure out how long the video cables must be. Then dig into the box and see if the cables you got are long enough. I bet they aren't, particularly if you're connecting a TV. When you go out shopping, make sure you get the right kind of cables.

You can try to figure out if you need a composite RCA cable, an S-VHS cable, a DVI cable, or a reversible 3-plug mini-DIN with imploded wombat RJ-945, but why sweat the hard stuff? If you have any doubt at all about what kind of cable you need, haul out your digital camera and take close-up shots of the connectors on the back of your computer and on the back of your TV. Then schlep the camera to the shop, and have the salesperson figure it out. Hey, that's what they're paid to do.

- **Speaker cables that are long enough to go . . . well, you get the idea:** I swear, the speaker cables that ship with Media Center PCs are never long enough. Make sure you get the right kind of connectors on the ends. No, I never pay extra for ultra-fancy cables, but you might want to.
- **A nice bottle of wine:** Need I explain what this is for?

Every Media Center PC goes together a bit differently, and the instructions (for most systems, anyway) cover the details pretty well. In my Dummies School of Hard Knocks surveys, several readers have offered a few key assembly tips that overcome several of MCE's shortcomings:

- MCE (as of this writing anyway) won't allow you to watch one TV show while recording another one. If you ever find yourself in a position where it'd be worthwhile to watch one show while recording another, consider using an old trick: Split the input line. Run one set of cables from the cable box to the MCE PC. But run a second set of cables from the cable box straight to the TV and attach the cables to the Video 1 or AUX input. If you want to watch live TV, just switch the TV over to Video 1, ignoring the MCE PC entirely.

- MCE doesn't work with VCRs. You can think of it as benign neglect. I think of it as a failure to accept ubiquitous legacy hardware. Potato/potahtoe, you know. At any rate, you can still hook up your VCR, and MCE can be, uh, coaxed into recording directly from your old videotapes. The process is not for the timid, but it's covered in depth in *Windows XP Media Center Edition 2004 PC For Dummies*, by Danny Briere and Pat Hurley (published by Wiley Publishing, Inc.). Good book, that.
- Don't hesitate to use your current sound system. If you have a better sound system than the one that ships with your MCE PC, and your old sound system accepts either digital optical cable or coax input, and your MCE PC has either a digital optical or coax output on the sound card, go right ahead and hook it up.

Also remember that you're under no obligation to attach everything. If you don't want to run your television through the MCE PC, you don't have to.

Finally, a note on remote hardware: Some MCE PC systems don't have remote keyboards or mice. I think that's a huge mistake. At least until Microsoft brings more functions into the MCE umbrella, occasional trips out to Windows itself are inevitable — and for those, you're going to want a keyboard and mouse. If your MCE PC sits in a cramped dorm room, running for the keyboard is no big deal, but if you have to get up off the couch and find a chair to put in front of the computer, it's a pain in the neck.

One combination I've come to appreciate comes from a company called Gyration (www.gyration.com, shown in Figure 2-1). Gyration combines a decent small remote keyboard with an MCE-compatible remote that doubles as a mouse — move the remote in the air, and the cursor moves with it. Although I wouldn't want to write a book with the two, for quick trips out to Windows land on an MCE computer, it works remarkably well.

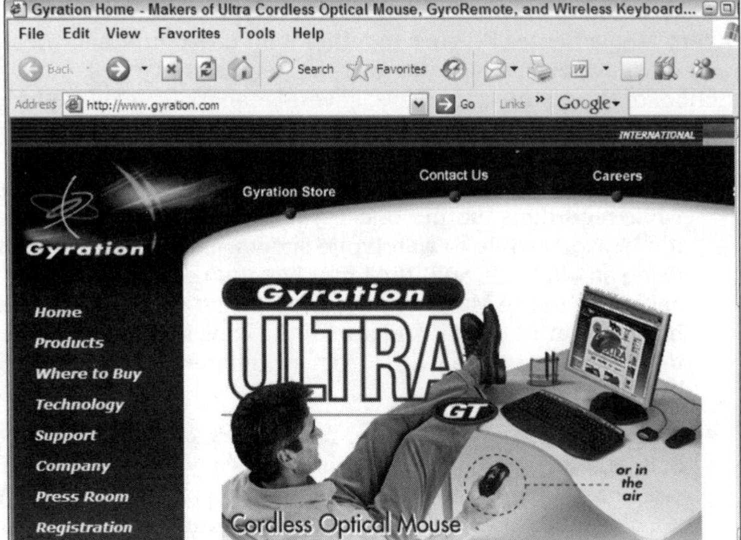

Figure 2-1: The Gyration Media Center Remote and Keyboard let you mouse around without a mouse.

Another product that serves double duty: the Pocket PC Rudeo Control for Windows Media Center Edition (www.rudeo.com, shown in Figure 2-2). The Rudeo converts any Pocket PC PDA into a remote for MCE. That in itself rates about a two on the geek scale where ten equals cool, but in addition to converting a PDA into a remote, the Rudeo also manages playlists, automatically updating your MCE computer as playlists change. That's a Very Big Deal because MCE (at least as of this writing) doesn't have any way to change playlists. If you want to add or change a playlist, do it on your Pocket PC, press a button, and suddenly MCE has a new playlist. Slick. Think 12 on the geek scale.

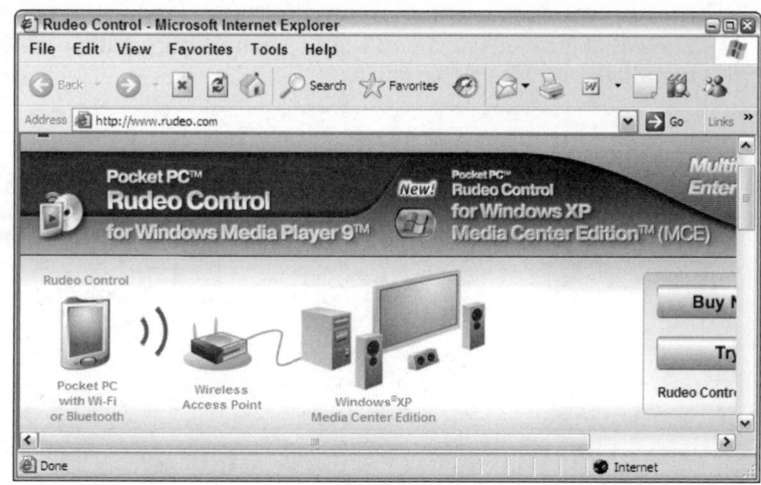

Figure 2-2: The Pocket PC Rudeo Control takes the place of a remote (ho-hum) but it also allows you to change playlists on the fly — a Very Big Deal.

Getting Windows in Gear

The first time you start your new MCE computer, almost anything could happen. Why? Each manufacturer seems to have a different way of introducing you to the experience.

If you have to start out with the MCE Setup routine, skip down to the next section for tips on some of the setup components. But if you have a chance to start with Windows itself, get out a real keyboard and mouse, and spend a few minutes making Windows a much friendlier, more secure place.

Even if you've been using MCE for three years, it would behoove you to run through these steps quickly:

1. **Set up your users.**

   Windows XP lets you set up multiple users, and MCE follows right in step. Each user can choose his or her own playlists, transitions, colors, notification sounds, and the like. The user's name appears in the upper-left corner of the main screen. If you ever wondered how to get rid of the name "Administrator," well, this is the place.

   To set up a new user, follow the instructions (and heed the warnings about Administrator accounts!) in Book I, Chapter 2.

2. **Nail down security.**

   A Media Center PC is a Windows XP Professional PC, and it's subject to all of the security problems that plague "normal" XP users. (In fact, it's subject to more!) You *must* get your new PC locked down by following the Security Center steps (see Figure 2-3) — enable the Windows Firewall, figure out how you want to handle automatic updates, and install an antivirus program.

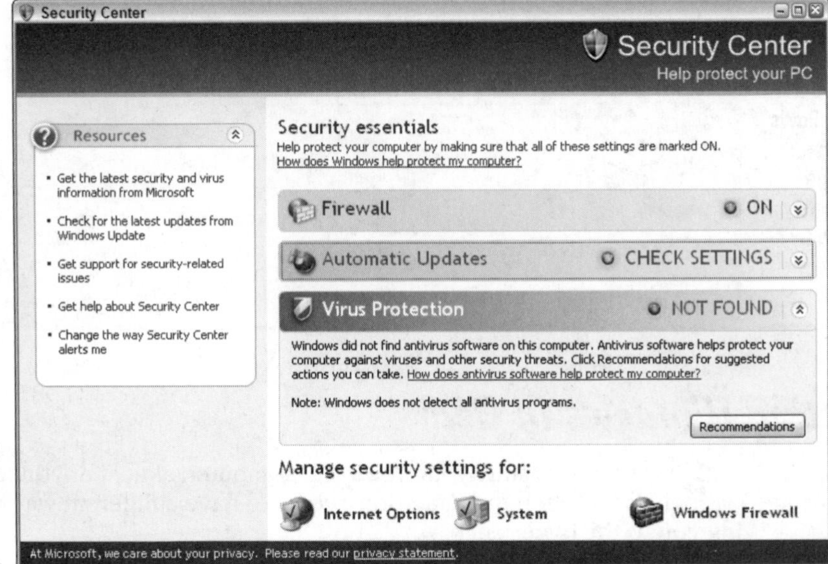

Figure 2-3: Media Center has all the security exposures in Windows XP itself — and then some.

I hate to rain on your parade, but you need to go through the details in Book II, Chapter 3 and onward, to get your system locked down *now*. I don't agree with all of Microsoft's security recommendations — you can see how and why in those chapters — but the minute you're online or connected to a network, you're exposed. There's a very good free antivirus program you can use, if you don't have one already. See Book II, Chapter 6 for more details.

3. **Make Windows show you filename extensions.**

   You'll save yourself all sorts of headaches if you get this one out of the way. See Book I, Chapter 3 for details.

4. **Download, install, and run anti-scumware software and a Registry protection program.**

   Scum is everywhere. At a minimum, you should install Ad-Aware, Spybot S&D, and a simple Registry blocker like Start Monitor. They're all free, and they could all save your patootie. See Book II, Chapter 3.

5. **Run a System Restore point.**

   Right now, when everything is working fine, crank up Windows System Restore and create a restore point. See Book I, Chapter 6 for details on how to do it. Some day you may thank me for that.

That should put Windows in a minimally functional state.

Running Through Setup

When your system starts, you probably see plain, old, boring Windows. If you do, take advantage of the opportunity to get your Windows Media Player set up right.

Unless you've gone through the motions, Windows Media Player has no idea what audio or video tracks are on your computer or on your network — it doesn't know if you *have* songs or videos, or where they might be located. And if Windows Media Player doesn't know about them, Windows Media Center Edition doesn't know about them, either. You can't scan for tracks from inside Media Center, at least as of this writing: You have to be out in Windows proper.

I have full details about scanning for tracks for Windows Media Player in Book 7, Chapter 1 — particularly important details about ripping MP3 tracks from CDs, if you're so inclined — but if you just want to get Windows Media Player to scan for all the audio and video tracks already on your drive and on your network, follow these steps:

1. **Start Windows Media Player.**

   Typically you would choose Start⇨All Programs⇨Windows Media Player, or click on the WMP icon in the Quick Start Toolbar.

2. **Press F3 or choose Tools⇨Search for Media Files.**

   You get the Add to Library by Searching Computer dialog box, as shown in Figure 2-4.

3. **Make sure that the Search On drop-down list shows All Drives, and then click the Search button.**

   Searching for tracks can take an enormously long time. Consider picking up where you left off in *War and Peace*.

4. **When Windows Media Player comes back, consider searching for other track-laden drives on your network by clicking the Browse button. (But only include drives on your network if you expect to have your network up and running 24/7.) Click Search again.**

   When you're done with *War and Peace,* consider cataloging your CD collection.

5. **After Windows Media Player is well and truly done, click Close.**

With Windows finally out of the way, at last you're ready to start Windows Media Center. Press the Start button on your remote, and Media Center Edition (the program) takes over, as shown in Figure 2-5.

Figure 2-4: If you want MCE to know about the audio and video tracks on your computer, or on your network, you have to perform a scan out in Windows itself.

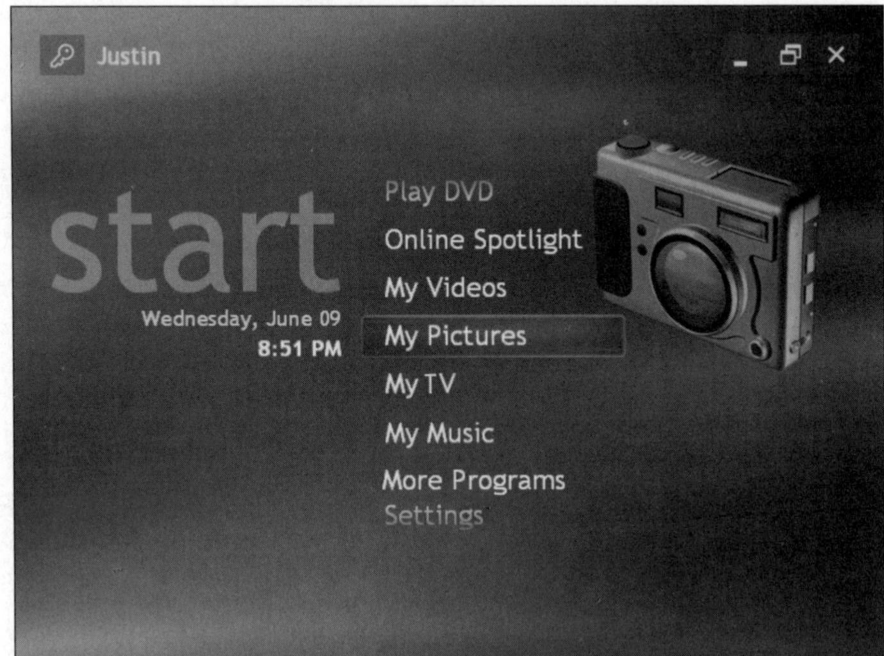

Figure 2-5: Media Center Edition central.

If you've already gone through MCE's setup program (or if your hardware vendor did it for you), you can still get at all of your settings and fix any that you might've messed up (or your vendor might've messed up for you). Here's how to get at the settings:

1. **On the main menu, pick Settings.**

   MCE shows you the gorgeous Settings menu, as shown in Figure 2-6.

2. **From the Settings menu, pick General.**

   The General icon looks amazingly like the original Myst Island cog wheel, doesn't it?

   You get the General settings menu shown in Figure 2-7. Remember where this menu lives. You'll need it someday.

3. **Choose Appearance.**

   MCE shows you the central repository for all of your appearance settings (at least, the appearance settings that aren't controlled directly by Windows). See Figure 2-8.

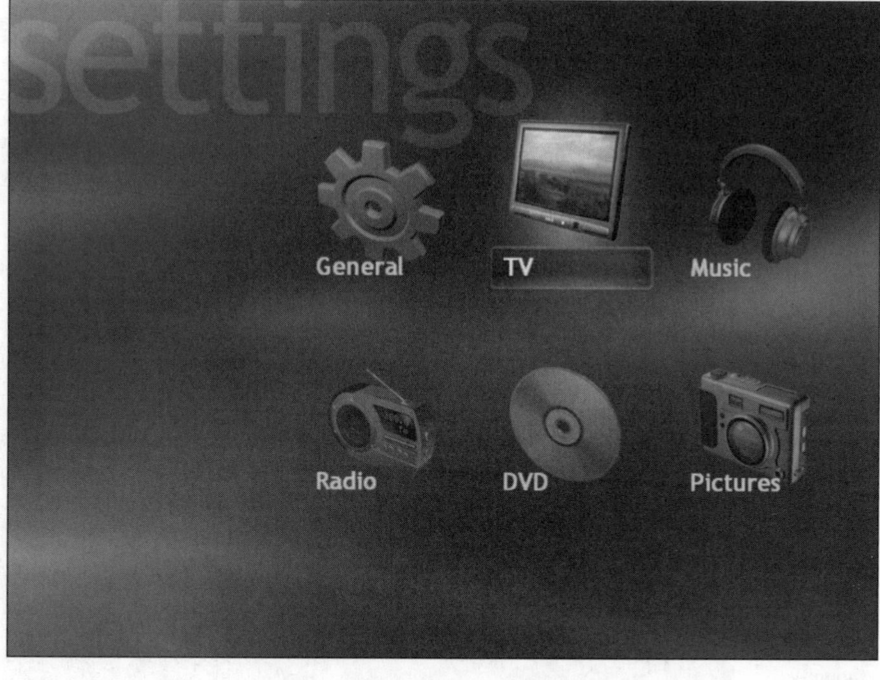

Figure 2-6: All of the settings that you may have chosen during MCE's setup program reside here, so if you made a mistake, you can fix it.

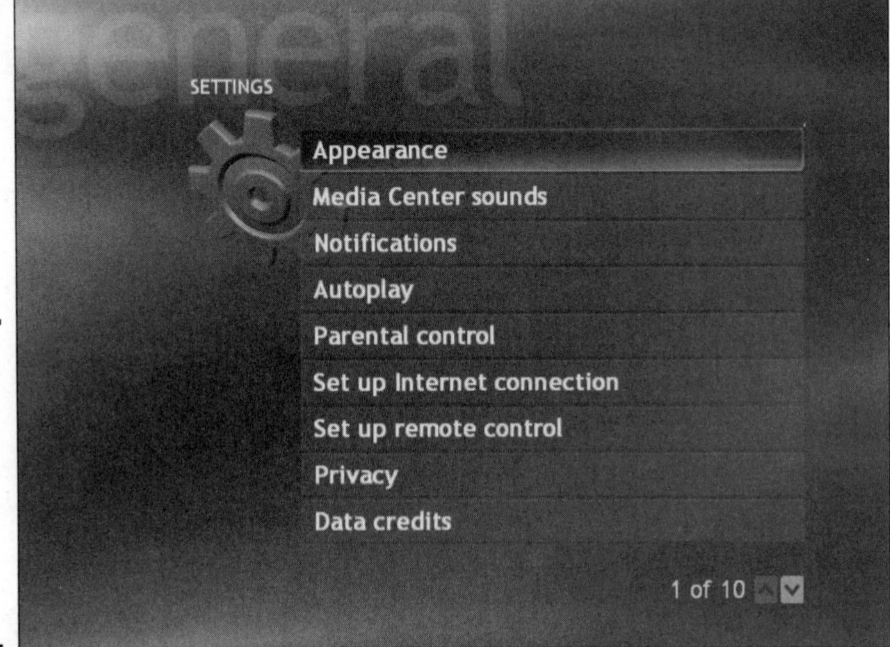

Figure 2-7: When things go bump in the night, this is where you're most likely to change them.

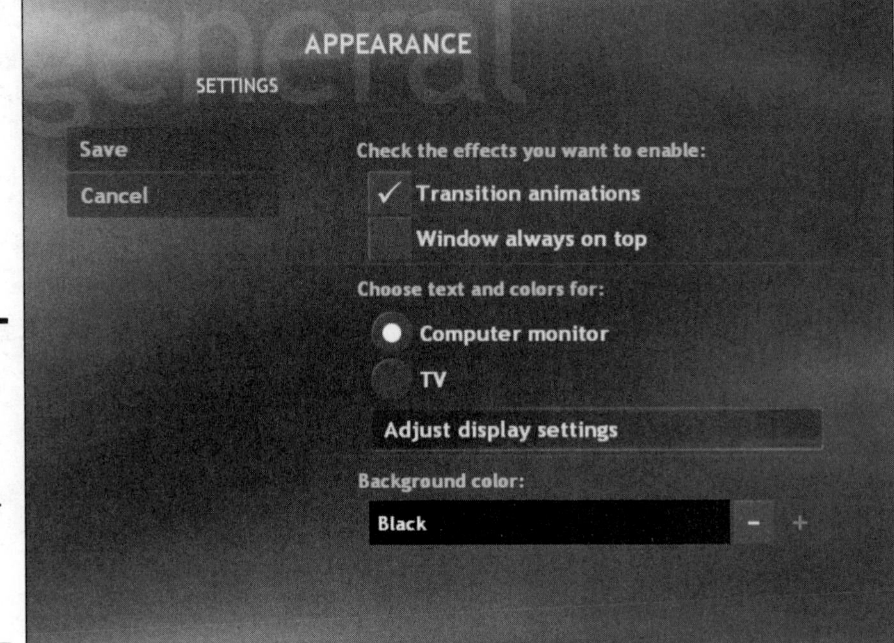

Figure 2-8: The MCE-controlled appearances reside here. Windows, though, still rules the roost.

Don't bother trying to change your monitor settings from here. If you do, MCE warns you, as shown in Figure 2-9, that you're going to visit a Web site that doesn't work very well from inside MCE (Ha! Do you think Microsoft ran out of money when they built the site?), and then unceremoniously dumps you onto a Web site with links to the hardware manufacturers.

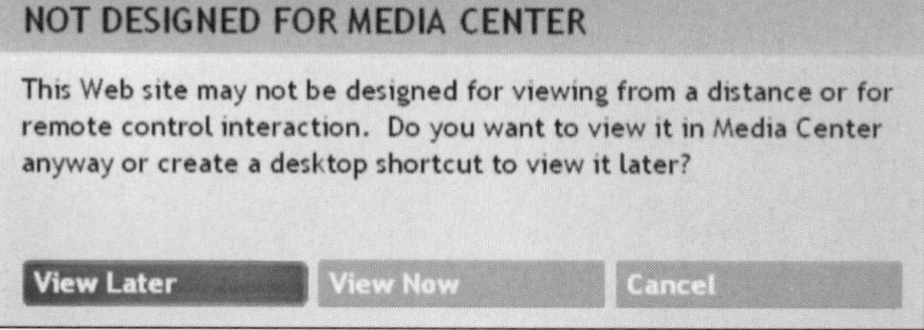

NOT DESIGNED FOR MEDIA CENTER
This Web site may not be designed for viewing from a distance or for remote control interaction. Do you want to view it in Media Center anyway or create a desktop shortcut to view it later?
View Later
View Now
Cancel

Figure 2-9: Microsoft built an MCE support Web site that, uh, doesn't work in MCE.

If you want to adjust your monitor's screen resolution, background, screensaver, and so on, see Book I, Chapter 1.

4. **If you have a TV connected to your MCE system, you should calibrate it. To do so, click the button marked TV, and then click Adjust Display Settings.**

   You will be taken through a thoughtful, accurate series of screens — a wizard, if you will — that does a very good job of adjusting MCE so that it shows good pictures on your TV.

Chapter 3: Running Windows Media Center

In This Chapter

- ✔ **Getting your TV settings right**
- ✔ **Watching recorded TV shows on MCE and plain-vanilla PCs**
- ✔ **Tricking out the other media**

Media Center Edition scores high marks in the usability category: Almost all of MCE sits right at your fingertips, the menus are laid out logically, and the text is pretty easy to read and understand.

Part of the reason why MCE seems so easy to use: Microsoft disabled all the hard parts. If you want to do anything even moderately complex, at least from a technical point of view, you have to pick up a mouse and a keyboard and drop back into Windows itself. Ah well. The price of simplicity.

In this chapter, I step you through a few of the parts of MCE that might prove difficult to follow.

Turning On the Tube

So you bought an MCE PC because you wanted to get something better than a TiVo. Or you wanted to record TV without paying a monthly fee. Am I right or am I right?

Fair enough. When you get right down to it, My TV (see Figure 3-1) and the $20 remote are the two main capabilities that distinguish an MCE computer from just plain ol' Windows XP Home running Windows Media Player. So I take a closer look at My TV in this section.

Getting the Guide

My TV's heart resides in the Guide, as shown in Figure 3-2.

Figure 3-1: My TV, most folks' main reason for buying a Windows Media Center PC.

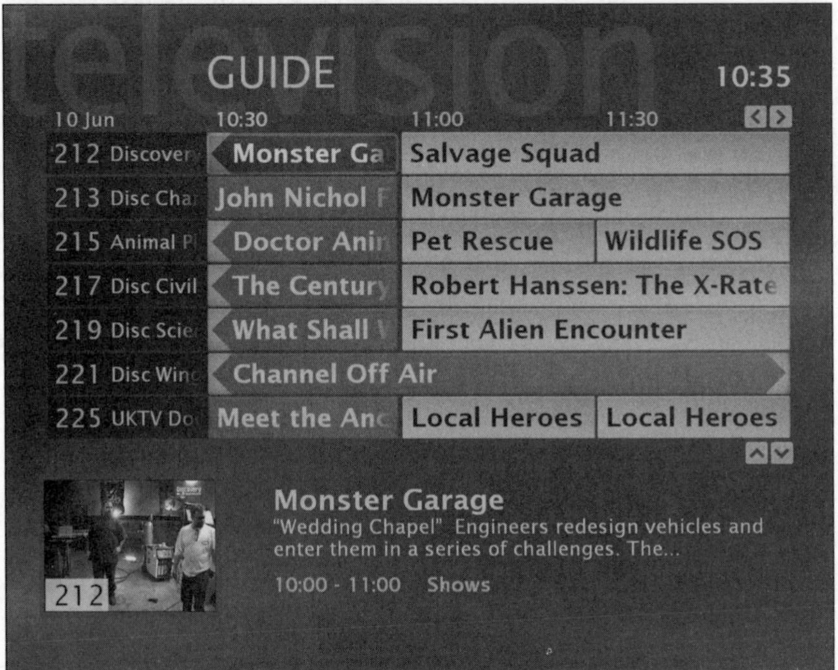

Figure 3-2: The Guide sits at the heart of My TV. Er, Your TV.

To bring up the Guide, press the Guide button on your remote (d'oh!), or from the main screen, choose My TV➪Guide.

The Guide's quite self-explanatory and you will no doubt get the hang of using it in about ten seconds. (Hint: If you have problems, ask your six-year-old). However, a few remote buttons can make your scrolling faster, as Table 3-1 describes.

Table 3-1 Remote Shortcuts in the Guide

Press This Key on the Remote	*And the Guide Does This*
CH + or Channel Up	Move up a page in the Guide (7 channels)
CH – or Channel Down	Move down a page in the Guide
Fast Forward	Advance 3 hours in the Guide
Rewind	Jump back 3 hours in the Guide
Skip	Advance 12 hours in the Guide
Replay	Jump back 12 hours in the Guide

In addition, if you press the remote's Guide button twice, a panel appears at the bottom of the screen, allowing you to limit the Guide — called *filtering* — to certain kinds of programs: News, Sports, Movies, Kids, and Special.

You can add and remove stations from the Guide. When you remove a station, its listing simply doesn't appear when you bring up the Guide (the station's still there, though, and you can watch it). When you add a station, the Guide won't have any information about programming on the station, but you'll be able to use the Guide to record whatever is playing on the station.

Here's how to add and remove stations:

1. **From the main MCE menu, choose Settings➪TV➪Guide.**

   MCE shows you the Guide Settings screen, as shown in Figure 3-3.

2. **If you want to add a channel, click Add Missing Channel, and then Add Channel. Type in a name, and click Next. Then type the channel number and click Add.**

   The process can be rather time-consuming if you have to enter the channel name through the remote, but if you're a victim — er, veteran — of SMS (you know, typing a message on your mobile phone), you should pass through the ordeal unscathed.

   You end up back at the Guide Settings screen (refer to Figure 3-3). If you've added a new channel, the best way to make sure that it "took" is to immediately go into the Edit Guide Listings — in other words, proceed with step coming up next.

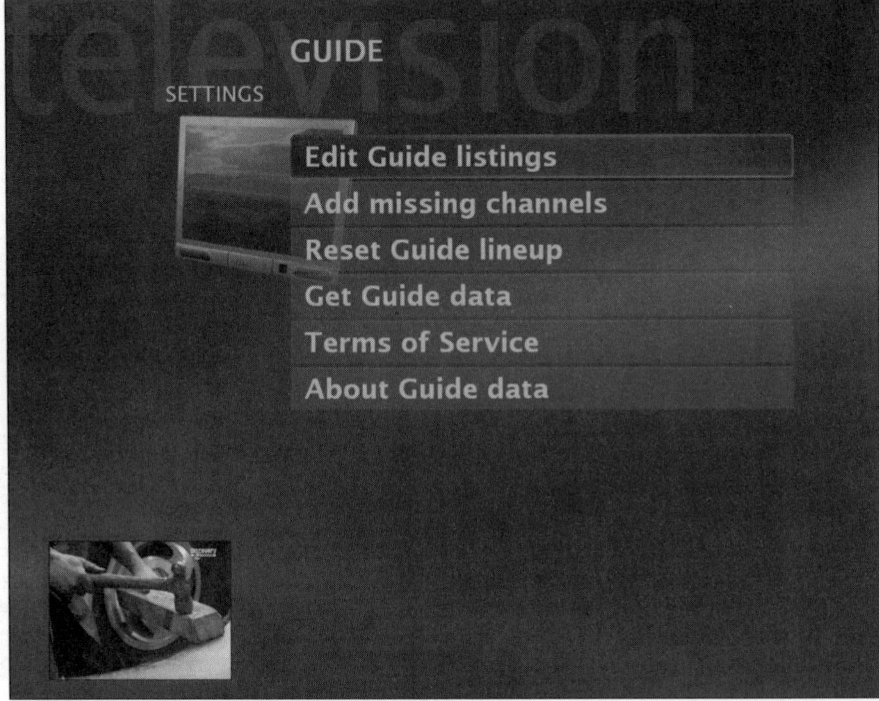

Figure 3-3: To make changes to the Guide, you have to go back through Settings, and then drill down.

3. **Click Edit Guide Listings.**

   MCE shows you a list of all the stations that have either been identified automatically (based on the TV provider that you specified, and/or your zip code), or that you have entered manually (using the preceding step).

4. **Make sure there's a check mark in front of each station that you want to appear in the Guide, and that there's no check mark in front of stations that you want to exclude from the Guide.**

   This setting only affects the station's inclusion in the Guide. You can still watch excluded stations: They just aren't as easy to find.

   If you manually added a station to the Guide list, that means MCE wasn't able to find a schedule for that station. So even if you choose to have the channel listed in the Guide, there won't be any programming information.

5. **When you're done, click Save.**

   You go back to the Guide Settings screen (refer to Figure 3-3).

6. **Now is a good time to update your Guide, so click Get Guide Data.**

   MCE downloads the latest version of the Guide. If you go out to Windows itself, you'll see an icon in the System Tray, down near the clock, that tells you a Guide update is in progress.

7. **Press My TV on your remote.**

   Revert to your reclining position on the couch.

If you ever want to know when your Guide was last updated, go to the main MCE window, and then choose Settings⇨My TV⇨Guide⇨About Guide. The Start Date you see on the screen is the date the Guide was refreshed.

Recording TV

MCE is a great PVR. That's a *Personal Video Recorder* to the unwashed masses — a TiVo-like gizmo, to you and me. Before you start recording TV shows, take a few seconds to make sure your settings reflect the way you want your TV, uh, experience to go. It's seamless.

Man, I hate the word *seamless*. What on earth does it mean? Whenever Microsoft uses the word *seamless,* you know they're trying to sell you something. Hey, you guys in Redmond, listen up! Just give me something that works, okay? I don't care about the seams or lack thereof. Sheesh.

Here's how to get your recording settings straight:

1. **Press My TV on your remote to bring up the My TV screen (refer to Figure 3-1). Then click Settings.**

   MCE displays the TV Settings screen, as shown in Figure 3-4.

2. **Choose Recorder⇨Storage.**

   You see the Storage screen, as shown in Figure 3-5.

3. **Change the settings to allocate as much room as you feel comfortable to your recorded TV shows.**

   If you have a second (or third or fourth) hard drive, use it.

   The Best setting consumes about four times as much hard drive space as the Fair setting. You will see the net effect on recording times as you change the Recording Quality.

4. **Click Save.**

   Your TV recording destiny is sealed. Until you change it, of course. MCE goes back to the Settings screen (refer to Figure 3-4).

5. **Choose Recorder⇨Defaults.**

   MCE's Recording Defaults page appears, as shown in Figure 3-6.

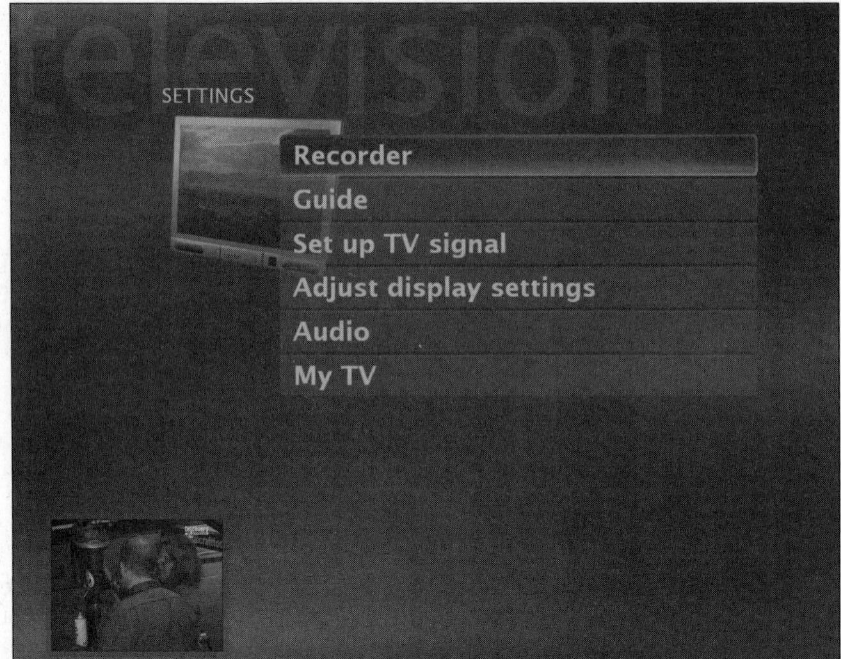

Figure 3-4: TV Settings start here.

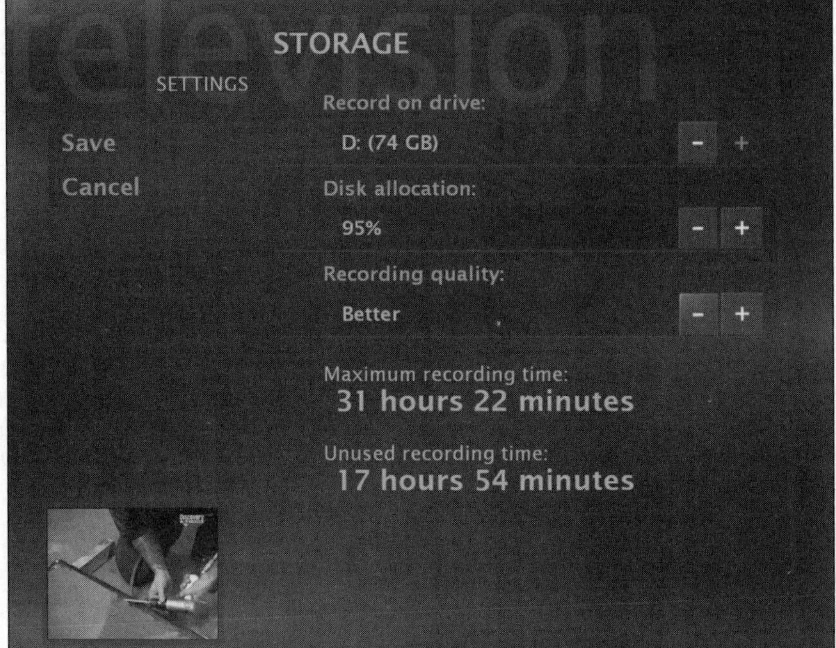

Figure 3-5: Recorded TV takes up gigabytes of space — up to 3GB for a one-hour show — so be careful when you set aside room.

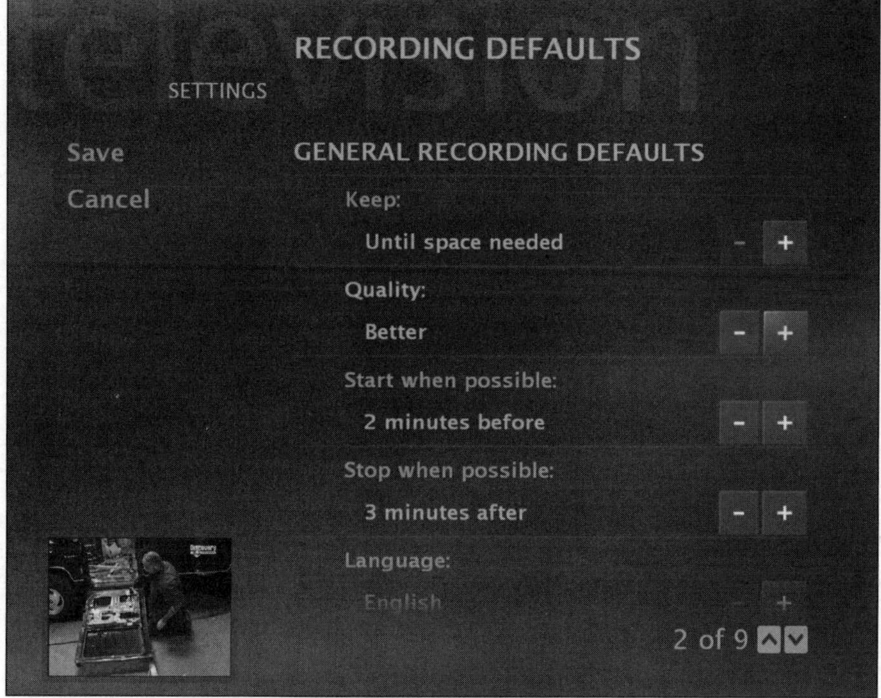

Figure 3-6: Settings for recordings appear here. Don't miss the additional settings — you have to scroll down to see them.

6. **Consider tweaking the start and stop times.**

   Although the big networks almost always start shows precisely on time (except when, say, the news anchor decides to walk off), and your PC's clock should be accurate to the nearest tenth of a second or so, sometimes things go awry and a show starts a shade early or finishes a tad late. Give yourself a tiny bit of breathing room.

   No, there's no way to set the recording default to "Turn off after the last overtime inning" or "Check out when the fat lady sings."

7. **If you do a lot of unattended recording, scroll down with the little up/down arrows and make sure you like the settings for Daily Recording Limit (how many times per day MCE should record a specific show — watch out for *The Prisoner* marathons) If you commonly record multiple shows in the same series, check the Keep Up To setting (how many shows in a given series to keep on the hard drive), the Show Type (don't record reruns), and Record On (which channels to monitor for a specific show).**

8. **When you're done, click Save.**

After your settings look good, recording a show takes less effort than opening a bag of corn chips:

1. **Press My TV on the remote.**
2. **Choose Recorded TV⇨Add Recording.**
3. **Click Guide.**
4. **Click on the show you want to record.**
5. **Press Record on your remote.**

Sometimes, MCE doesn't record a program correctly. ('Fess up. Your trusty VCR didn't always record correctly either, did it?) If you get a message saying the recorder failed, your best bet is to completely restart Windows:

1. **Click the Minimize (-) icon in the upper-right corner.**
2. **Choose Start⇨Shut Down Computer.**
3. **Choose Restart.**

Yes, MCE needs to be restarted from time to time. We're talkin' about Windows here. . . .

Playing recorded TV shows

Playing a TV show on the MCE PC that recorded it couldn't be simpler — the My TV screen (refer to Figure 3-1) walks you through it: Click Recorded TV if you don't immediately see the program you want.

But playing a recorded TV show on a non-MCE computer can be interesting.

One key problem: Digital Rights Management. When MCE records a TV show, it brands the recorded file with whatever restrictions the broadcaster imposes. As of this writing, that may include a restriction that you can play the show back only on the PC on which it was recorded. Heaven only knows what kind of restrictions may come in the future — will it only allow you to play a program on alternate Thursdays, or within a day of when it's recorded? Who knows. We ain't talkin' VHS videotape here.

You can move the recorded TV file (it's a `*.dvr-ms` file, located in `C:\Documents and Settings\All Users\Shared Documents\Recorded TV`) by any convenient method — burn it on a DVD, copy it across a network, send it by e-mail, etch it on papyrus. After you get the file on a new machine, you have two choices for playing it, providing the Digital Rights brand allows you to play it at all:

- Play it directly with Windows Media Player 10.
- Play it sooner or later with Windows Media Player 9. If you have to use WMP 9, check out the Microsoft Knowledge Base article at `http://support.microsoft.com/?kbid=810243` for an explanation and a file that you'll need to get it to run. You'll also need to install Windows XP Service Pack 1 or 2 before WMP 9 can read the files.

Oh. You can't use MCE-recorded TV in Windows Movie Maker. At least as of this writing, Movie Maker doesn't understand `*.dvr-ms` files. Something else the guy at the computer shop didn't tell you, eh?

Getting the Most out of Other Media

Most of the rest of Windows Media Center Edition relies on the good services of Windows Media Player, so if you know the quirks of Windows Media Player, you can usually bypass analogous problems in Windows Media Center.

Take MP3 ripping, for example.

Unless you specifically change things, Windows Media Center allows you to rip CDs — copy music from an audio CD onto your computer — but the songs get ripped into WMA format. Depending on Microsoft's wishes and your PC manufacturer's willingness to kowtow to Redmond, when you rip a CD, the resulting WMA file may be tied up so it will play only on the computer on which it was ripped — or there may be some other restriction, which can vary from song to song and day to day.

The culprit is the Enhanced Playback (gawd, what a euphemism) setting. You can see your Enhanced Playback setting by going to the main MCE window, and then choosing Settings⇨General⇨Privacy⇨Settings (again) to arrive at the Privacy Settings screen shown in Figure 3-7.

Of course, you want to deselect the Enhanced Playback check box in Figure 3-7, but far better (in my opinion) is to have MCE rip CDs into old-fashioned MP3 format. Although MP3 isn't nearly as technically advanced as Microsoft's proprietary WMA — a good-sounding MP3 file is much bigger than the corresponding WMA file — if you stick to MP3, you don't have to worry about licenses, copy restrictions, songs that don't play, and all the headaches inherent in dealing with Microsoft's licensing schemes, now or in the future.

The only way to change MCE so it rips to MP3 format involves running back out to Windows itself, installing a program called an MP3 codec (if you don't have one already), and changing Windows Media Player so it uses MP3. I talk about the process, the pros and the (ahem) cons, in Book VII, Chapter 1, starting in the section, "The MP3 conundrum."

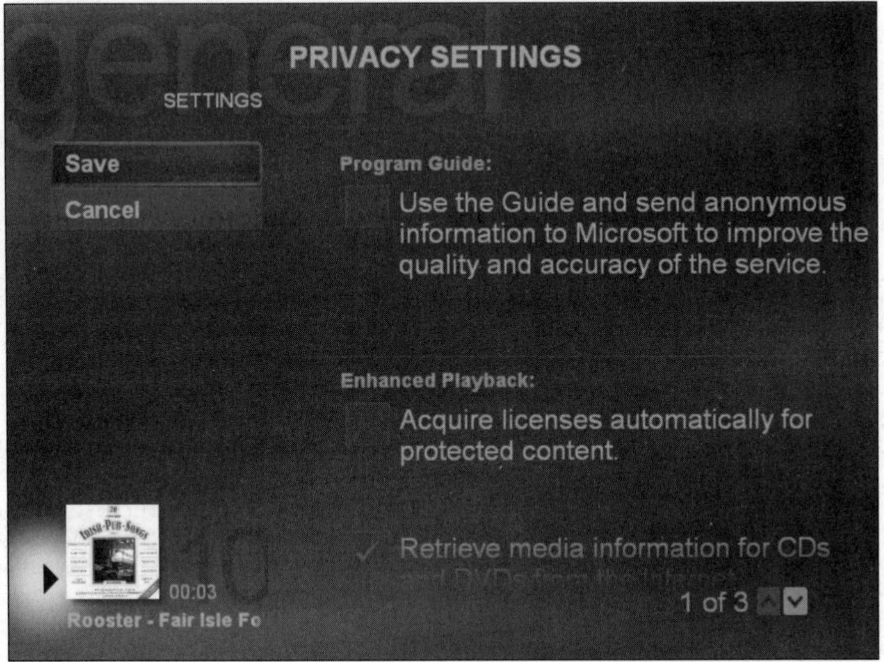

Figure 3-7: The infamous Enhanced Playback setting.

MCE relies on the Scanner and Camera Wizard to get photos into the computer (see Book VII, Chapter 3 for many tricks). And it uses Windows Movie Maker to bring in movies (Book VII, Chapter 2).

The Media Center Edition tiara contains many, many more gems than what I've covered here. If you want to explore MCE's nooks and crannies, I strongly recommend *Windows XP Media Center Edition 2004 PC For Dummies*, by Danny Briere and Pat Hurley (Wiley Publishing, Inc.). It steps you through the key capabilities of MCE, with a special eye toward giving you the greatest amount of flexibility and getting your MCE money's worth.

Book IX

Setting Up a Network with Windows XP

"Frankly, the idea of an entirely wireless future scares me to death."

Contents at a Glance

Chapter 1: Those Pesky Network Things You Have to Know

In This Chapter

- **Finding out why you really *do* want a network, at the office and at home**
- **Comparing client/server (domain) and peer-to-peer (workgroup) networking**
- **Gathering the stuff you need to get started**
- **Networking for Neanderthals**

When business people talk to each other, it's called networking. When computers talk to each other, it's called pandemonium.

This chapter tries to distill 25 years of advances in computer pandemonium, er, networking, into a succinct, digestible, understandable synopsis. I think you'll be pleasantly surprised to discover that even the most obnoxiously inscrutable networking jargon — much of which has made its way into Windows XP — has its roots in simple concepts that everyone can understand.

Understanding Networks

Not long ago, networks were considered esoteric and intimidating, the province of guys in white lab coats, whose sole purpose in life was to allow you to print on the company's fancy laser printer or share that super-fast Internet connection but keep you from seeing your boss's personnel file or the company's budget. Those same guys (and they were always guys, it seems) often took it upon themselves to tell you what you could and couldn't do with your PC — what software you could use, how you could use it, where you could put your data, and so much more. They hid behind a cloak of mumbo-jumbo, initiates in the priesthood of "systems administration."

That's changed a lot. With Windows XP, a network is something that your 13-year-old can throw together in ten minutes. Mine did. (Your results may vary!)

The terminology doesn't help. Ask a network geek — or computer store salesperson — about the difference between a LAN and a WAN, and you'll provoke a tirade of inscrutable acronyms so thick that you need a periscope to see out.

In this chapter, I cut through the bafflegab.

What a network can do for you

Do you need a network?

The short answer: Yes. If you have two or more computers, with one running Windows XP and the other running Windows 98 or later, a network is well worth the hassle. You don't need a fancy one. But you do need one. Consider these facts:

- If you have a network, just about any piece of hardware attached to one computer can be used by the other. That CD-ROM drive on your desktop, for example, can be used by your portable, the same way as if it were connected directly. A printer or (in some cases) a scanner attached to one computer can be shared by all computers.
- All of your computers can use one single Internet connection. With *ICS (Internet Connection Sharing),* you don't need to pay for two Internet accounts or run two connections (over the phone, or via DSL or cable modem) at the same time. If every computer on the network is downloading huge files at the same time, you'll feel the performance hit, of course, but in most normal circumstances, you won't notice at all. And, yes, ICS works well in Windows XP. Very well.
- You can use Windows XP's features on data from other machines, regardless of whether they're running Windows XP. For example, with Windows XP's Explorer, you can view pictures stored on a networked computer as a slide show, even if the pictures are stored on a computer running Windows 98. You can burn a CD with Windows XP's built-in CD burning support, using data from any computer on your network. Even the Windows XP Media Player and Windows Media Center Edition PCs can work with sound and video clips from other machines.
- The easiest, fastest, most reliable way to back up data is to copy it from the hard drive on one machine to the hard drive in another machine on the network.
- You can share documents, pictures, music — just about anything — between the networked computers, with practically no effort. Although very few applications allow you to share individual files simultaneously — Word won't let two people on two different machines edit the same document at the same time, for example — sharing data on networked machines is still much simpler.

How a network networks

All you really need to know about networks you learned in kindergarten:

- Good computers talk to each other over a network. If your computer is on a network, it can play with other computers on the same network. If your computer is not on a network, it can only sit in the corner and play by itself.
- You can see all the computers on your network by looking at Mister Rogers' . . . uh, at Start⇨My Network Places.
- Every computer in a network has its own name — actually, it's a number called an *IP address* — and all the names (er, numbers) are different. That's how computers keep track of each other.
- You can share stuff on your computer. You have two different ways to share. The way you share depends on how the network — uh, kindergarten class — is organized:
    - If you have a really mean teacher (called a *network administrator*), she decides what can be shared. When other kids want to borrow your stuff, they usually have to ask the teacher. I don't talk about this kind of network very much because the teacher makes most of the decisions. Details are in the next section, "Organizing Networks."
    - On the other hand, if the kids are in charge of sharing, each kid can share his stuff in one of two ways. He can put the stuff that he wants to share in a special place that's called *Shared* (such as Shared Documents or Shared Music); or he can tell the computer to just go ahead and share the stuff (using a shared folder, shared drive, or a shared printer).
- Your network can share with other networks, just like kids in your class can share with kids in other classes. The Internet is the biggest class of all. Yippie!
- Unfortunately, some creeps are in other classes, and they may want to take things from you or share something that will hurt you. You have to protect yourself.

When you run into trouble, the advice you hear over and over again (especially in the Windows XP Help and Support Center) is "talk to your teacher," uh, "contact your system administrator." That advice is every bit as useless now as it was when you were five.

When networks work right — which they do about 90 percent of the time in Windows XP — they really are simple.

Organizing Networks

If you want to understand an abstract computer concept, nothing works better than a solid analogy. I use lots of them in this book: A document is like a sheet of paper; a CPU is like a car engine; a modem is like a high-tech hearing aid with a pronounced stutter set to "max" at a Nine Inch Nails concert. You know what I mean.

That's the problem with networks. No really good analogies exist. Yes, you can say that a server is like a gatekeeper, or a hub is like a collection of tap-dancing monkeys at a hyperactive organ-grinder's convention, but all of the analogies fall flat in short order. Why? Because networks are different from what you experience, day to day.

So without benefit of a good analogy, forge ahead anyway.

Understanding servers and serfs

There are two fundamentally different kinds of networks. They both use the same basic kind of hardware — cables, boxes, interface cards, and so on. They both talk the same basic kind of language — Ethernet and something called TCP/IP, usually, but a few renegades speak in tongues. They differ primarily on a single, crucial philosophical point.

In one kind of network, a leader, a top-dog PC, controls things. The leader is called (you guessed it) a server. I still get shivers down my spine at the Orwellian logic of it all. In this kind of network, the lowly serf PCs are called *clients*. Thus, this type of network gets the moniker *client/server*. If you've ever wondered how in the realm of the English language a "client" could be all that much different from a "server," now you know: In the topsy-turvy world of PC networking terminology, a server is really a master.

In the other kind of network, all the pigs, er, PCs are created equal. No single PC dominates — perhaps I should say *serves* — all the others. Rather, the PCs maintain an equal footing. This kind of network is called, rather appropriately, *peer-to-peer,* which sounds veddy British to me. Eh, wot?

Introducing client/server

Client/server networks have one PC, called a server, that's figuratively "on top" of all the others. Figure 1-1 shows a logical diagram of a client/server network. It's important that you not take the diagram too seriously: It only shows the way client PCs are subservient to the server. It doesn't show you how to hook up a network.

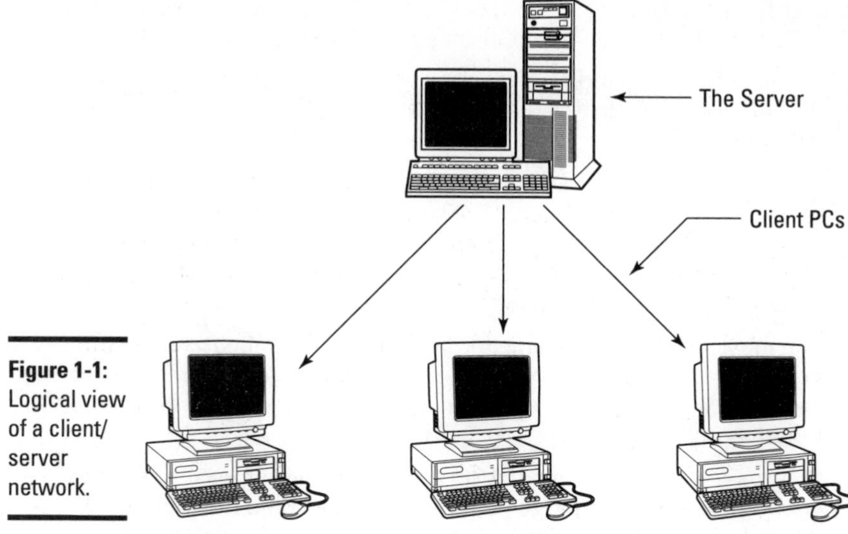

Figure 1-1: Logical view of a client/server network.

Client PCs have some autonomy in a client/server network, but not a whole lot. And a bit of leeway exists in how much security a specific network or server enforces — some less-secure networks may allow Guest accounts, for example, that don't require passwords. But by and large, client/server networks are set up to be secure. They exist to allow computers (and users and peripherals) to talk to each other. But strict limits are rigorously enforced on what individual users can do, where they can go, and what they can see.

Microsoft introduced a new umbrella security system in Windows 2000 Server called Active Directory. It's designed to put control of all client/server security activities in one place. Active Directory is a very complex program — a world unto its own. If you have trouble talking to your network administrator in simple English, you may take some solace in the fact that he has to talk to Active Directory, and the translation can be challenging. The African "click" languages pale in comparison.

In general, you want to use Windows XP/Pro if you're on a client/server network. Yes, you can set up a Windows XP/Home computer to work on a client/server network. No, it isn't worth the effort — or added expense.

In this book, I don't talk about client/server networks (Microsoft calls them *domains*) very much, simply because you don't have much control over them. If you use a client/server network, chances are good that somebody else in your company made the decision to go with client/server. They probably installed your copy of Windows XP — most likely Windows XP/Pro — or bought a new machine rigged to their specifications and configured it to work with your company's network. They also get to fix things when your network connection goes bump in the night. Poetic justice, sez I.

I have to talk about client/server from time to time, though, for three big reasons:

- ✦ You may have an existing client/server network that you want to convert to peer-to-peer. Many Dummies (I'll raise my hand here) installed Windows NT or Windows 2000 client/server networks in their homes or offices, and they're tired of the constant hassles. They need to understand enough about client/server to get rid of it.
- ✦ You may actually need some of the features that client/server offers and not know it. In that case, you are better off to bite the bullet now and get client/server going, instead of struggling with peer-to-peer as an unintentional stopgap.
- ✦ Client/server is the original form of networking (at least in the business environment; you can argue about academia some other time). As such, many networking concepts — and much of the obscure terminology — originated in the client/server cauldron.

Administrator accounts on client computers can make major changes to the client PC in question, but the real action is on the server. If you really want to change things around, you need an Administrator account on the server. That's the seat of power in the client/server milieu.

In a client/server network, the network's Internet connection is (almost) always controlled through the server, using the following:

- ✦ **Windows Proxy Server:** A *proxy server* is a program that allows all the people on a network to share one Internet connection and, at the same time, acts as a *firewall*. A server firewall monitors data as it passes between your network and the Internet, acting as a security barrier.
- ✦ **Microsoft Internet Security and Acceleration Server:** This is a souped-up, extra-charge proxy server.
- ✦ **Other proxy servers:** Many proxy servers are made by companies other than Microsoft. Ositis Software's WinProxy, for example, is used in many companies to protect their client/server networks. (See `www.winproxy.com`. WinProxy works on peer-to-peer networks, too.)

Introducing peer-to-peer

On the other side of the networking fence sits the undisciplined, rag-tag, scruffy lot involved in peer-to-peer computing. In a peer-to-peer environment, all computers are created equal, and security takes a back seat to flexibility.

I like peer-to-peer (see Figure 1-2). Could you tell?

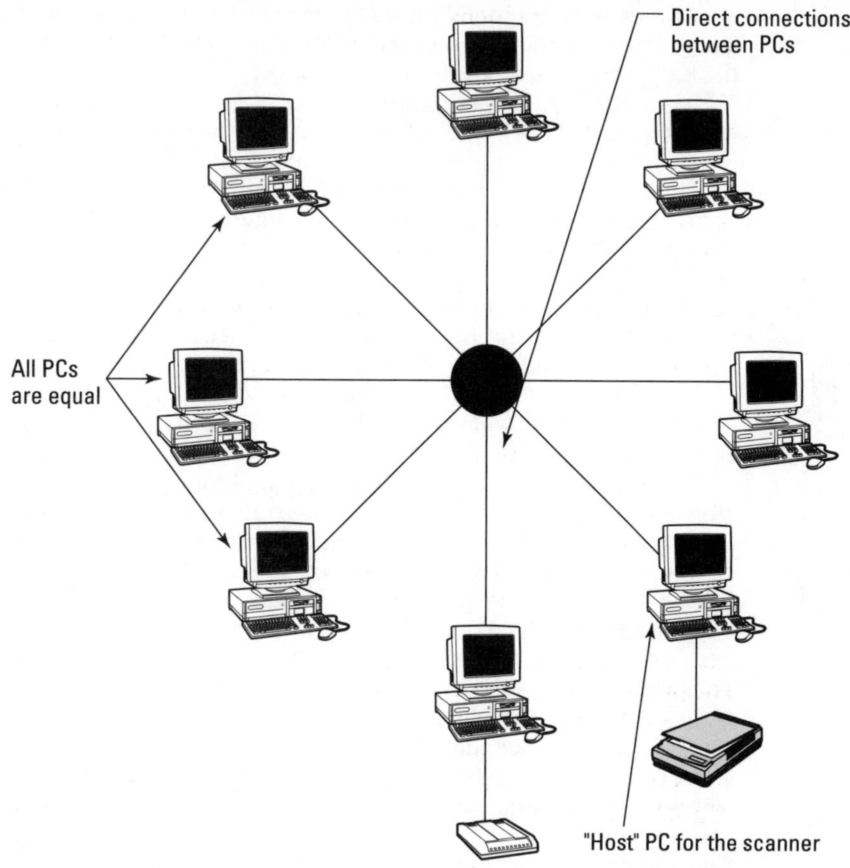

Figure 1-2: Peer-to-peer networks don't rely on a single super PC.

At different times, in different places, Microsoft calls peer-to-peer networks by the following names:

- ✦ Workgroups and/or workgroup networks
- ✦ Small office networks and/or small business networks
- ✦ Home networks

The Windows XP Help and Support Center also, on occasion, refers to peer-to-peer networks as, uh, peer-to-peer networks. They all mean the same thing.

Traditionally, client/server networks (see the preceding section) dangled all of the shared peripherals off the server. Ten years ago, your office's big laser printer was probably connected directly to the server. The massive bank of 2GB hard drives no doubt lived on the server, too. Even today, you hear reference to *print servers* and *file servers* in hushed tones, as if only the server itself were capable of handling such massive processing demands.

Nowadays, you can buy a laser printer out of petty cash — although you better have a line in the budget for toner and paper — and 100GB hard drives fit on the head of a pin. Well, almost.

Peer-to-peer networks dispense with the formality of centralized control. Every authorized Administrator on a particular PC — and most users are Administrators; see Book I, Chapter 2 — can designate any drive, any folder, or any piece of hardware on that PC as shared, and thus make it accessible to anyone else on the network.

In a peer-to-peer network (a *workgroup*), any Administrator on a given PC can share anything on that PC. If you're the least bit concerned about security, that fact should give you pause, high blood pressure, and intense anxiety attacks. Not to mention apoplexy. Say you set up a home office network using the standard Windows XP/Home settings. The network that is installed is a peer-to-peer network with no passwords. That means anyone can walk up to a Welcome sign-on screen, click one of the user names, and immediately designate every drive as shared. The entire process would take less than 30 seconds. From that point on, anybody who can get to any of the computers on the network would have full control over all of the files on the shared drive — anybody can read, change, even delete them permanently, without the benefit of the Recycle Bin.

The primary distinguishing factor among PCs in a peer-to-peer network lies in the shared hardware hanging off an individual PC. Refer to Figure 1-2, for example, and you see that only one PC has a scanner attached to it. Although you may be tempted to call this machine "The PC with the Scanner Hanging off of It," in general parlance, you hear the PC referred to as the scanner's *host*.

Peer-to-peer networks are far more adaptable (computer nerds would say "more robust") than their client/server cousins because they don't rely on any single PC to keep the network running. In a peer-to-peer network, if the laser printer's host PC breaks down, you only need to schlep the printer over to a different PC and install it. You can immediately begin using the printer from any PC in the network. (If auto detect kicks in properly, it's particularly simple: You only need to change the printer in the File➪Print dialog box.) In a client/server network, if the server PC breaks down, you can probably kiss your weekend goodbye.

For many people, *Internet Connection Sharing (ICS)* alone pays for the expense of setting up a network. With ICS, only one PC in the peer-to-peer network connects directly to the Internet, and that one connection is shared, equally and transparently, among all the PCs on the network. The ICS host takes care of all the details.

To the outside world, ICS appears as if you have just one PC connected to the Internet — and it sits behind a big, scary firewall to fend off would-be attackers. To little Johnny, who's using the PC in his bedroom to download massive full-color pictures of anatomically correct Pokemon figures, his Internet connection works just like it always did: slow and cantankerous, with frequent dropped connections and unexplained outages. But at least everybody in the family gets bumped off the Internet at the same time.

At various times in various places, Microsoft calls the PC running Internet Connection Sharing an *ICS host* and/or a *gateway*. Both names mean the same thing. Microsoft also insists on (sporadically) calling certain computers *ICS clients* if they're connected to an ICS host via a peer-to-peer network, even though the term *client* means something quite different in client/server networking. Like I said, networking terminology is all over the map.

Comparing the p-pros and c-cons

If you need to decide between installing a client/server network (Microsoft calls it a *domain*) and a peer-to-peer network (*workgroup* in MS-speak), you should read the two preceding sections for an overview of how each works, and then weigh each of these factors:

- The *C* in client/server stands for complicated, cumbersome, and costly. You, or someone you hire, will spend a lot of time setting up a client/server network. If you have a small network with few employees and one or two applications, you know precisely what machines will be performing which tasks, and you know who needs access to what information and where it's stored, a real pro with extensive Active Directory experience can probably set up your client/server network in half a day. Beyond that, the sky's the limit — and plan on getting your network consultant's home telephone number, because you're going to need it every time you get a new employee, install a new computer, or maybe even begin using a new application.
- Client/server networks can handle enormous volumes of data. High-end servers can juggle hundreds (or even thousands) of client PCs, with data transmission speeds that would bring tears to a lowly peer-to-peer network's eyes. The server can take on additional functions, such as handling e-mail for the entire network (most likely using Exchange Server, another cantankerous Microsoft product that's chock full of features). Data backup and other maintenance tasks that would be a nightmare to coordinate over a peer-to-peer network are all localized. In some client/server networks, applications (such as Microsoft Office) run from the server, so upgrades involve only one copy of the application, not hundreds of copies.

- The *P* in peer-to-peer stands for powerful, painless, and potentially embarrassing. You can have your network up and running in hours — and most of that time will be sweating over cables, interface cards, and other hardware that doesn't work right the first time. When it's up, the network will be reliable and easy to use — and as exposed as a lobster in a glass tank. Unless you go to the trouble of setting up passwords and protecting folders with sensitive data (using the techniques I describe in Book I, Chapter 2), anybody who can sit down at a PC can make all of the PC's contents available to anyone on the network, at any time. Except in extreme situations, not even Windows Firewall will help.

- If you try to install and maintain a client/server network yourself — even with helper tools such as Microsoft's Small Business Server — be aware that it's not nearly as simple as the marketing brochures would have you believe. Many Dummies, this one included, feel that installing and maintaining your own client/server network rates as a low-benefit, high-commitment time sink of the first degree.

Someday, secure networks will be easy to set up and use. That day hasn't arrived yet. Although peer-to-peer networking in Windows XP (specifically Windows XP/Home) has made simple networking a reality, truly secure networks — and really big networks — are still the province of guys in white lab coats.

Making Computers Talk

Getting computers to talk to each other can be as simple as buying a box and some cables and plugging it all together like you do with telephones — or as painful, expensive, and hair-challenging (as in pulling it out by the roots) as any computer pursuit you've ever encountered.

In this section, I step you through the details of setting up a simple, traditional peer-to-peer network with interface cards in each PC, a *hub* (which is an incredibly dumb switch), and a bunch of cable.

After you see the basics, I step you through some of the newer technologies.

For details on actually assembling a network — choosing hardware components, installing and testing them, and then getting Windows XP to recognize the network — see Book IX, Chapter 2.

For the lowdown on wireless networks — surely the simplest kind of network to install — see Book IX, Chapter 3.

Understanding Ethernet

The easiest, fastest, cheapest, most reliable, and most secure way to hook up a peer-to-peer network is also the oldest, least flexible, and most boring. If you want sexy, look somewhere else. If you want an old workhorse, hey, have I got a horse for you: It's called *Ethernet* (see Figure 1-3), and it works like a champ.

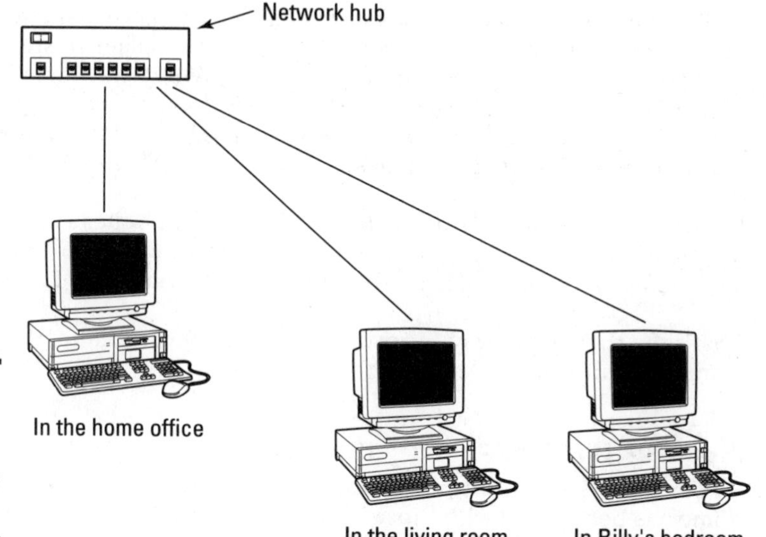

Figure 1-3: A typical Ethernet peer-to-peer network.

Ethernet really isn't that complicated. In the early 1970s, Bob Metcalfe came up with an interesting new way to connect Xerox Alto computers. He called the technique *EtherNet*. The name stuck, give or take a capital N. So did the technology. By modern standards, Ethernet isn't very sophisticated:

- ✦ All the PCs on a network watch messages going over a wire.
- ✦ When PC *A* wants to talk to PC *B*, it shoots a message out on the wire, saying something like, "Hey, B, this is A," followed by the message.
- ✦ PC *B* sees the message on the wire and retrieves it.

Hard to believe, but with a few minor tweaks — like what happens when two PCs try to send messages at the same time, so that they're talking over the top of each other — that's really all there is to Ethernet.

Even harder to believe: PCs using plain, old Ethernet can send and receive messages at the rate of 10 Gbps, or 10,000,000,000 bits per second. Even garden-variety Ethernet systems work at 100 Mbps, or 100,000,000 bits per second. (By comparison, a 56K modem, under the best possible circumstances, receives data at slightly more than 50,000 bits per second.) Things slow down if many PCs are trying to talk to each other at the same time — they start talking over the top of each other — but for a typical peer-to-peer network, 100 Mbps (also called 100Base-T) works great.

Ethernet relies on a *hub* — a box — and cables running from the hub to each PC. The PCs need network cards so that you have a place to stick the cables. The PCs can be using Windows 98 (any flavor), Windows Me, or Windows 2000. Plug it all together, run the Windows XP Home Networking Wizard on your Windows XP machine(s), run a special program that Windows XP sticks on a floppy on the other machines, and your network is ready to use.

It's getting harder and harder to find a plain-Jane hub these days. Most people use a *switch*. The details aren't very important, except that a network switch behaves almost exactly the same way as a hub, only faster.

That's the theory, anyway. Surprisingly, at least 90 percent of the time, it works. I go into all the details in the next chapter.

Adding wireless

What's the biggest problem with Ethernet? The cables. Unless your office or home has been wired with those big eight-wire Ethernet cables, you have to string them across the floor or under the rug, run them up and down staircases, or hang them out the window and pray they don't blow away. Don't laugh. I've done all of that and more.

Wireless networking relies on radio transmitters and receivers in place of Ethernet's cables. You need a wireless base station (which goes by a lot of different names), and wireless network adapters connected to each PC. Sometimes you buy the wireless base station with one or two bundled network adapters.

Wireless networks use the same kind of technology as everyday portable telephones: The part that moves (the telephone handset) communicates with a base that stays put (the phone cradle). Wireless connections suffer all of the problems that you've no doubt encountered with portable telephones: The signal gets weaker as you move farther away from the base station, and at some point it disappears entirely; if the base gets unplugged, everything goes bananas; and other people can eavesdrop on your conversations, unless you're cautious. Ain't no such thing as a free lunch.

I go into detail about wireless networking in Book IX, Chapter 3.

Chapter 2: Building Your Network

In This Chapter

- Getting everything you need to get your network going
- Making a list of what to buy
- Hooking it together
- Convincing Windows XP that your network works
- Using one Internet connection for the whole network

Sharing a printer. Transferring files. Freeing up a phone line. Saving money. Those are great reasons for setting up a network. Snoooooooooore.

I know you really want to get your office or house computers networked so that you can blister your co-workers or friends at Half-Life 2 or Warcraft III. Maybe you want to spend some quality time with your son one Sunday afternoon spraying demons in Doom III. Splat! Don't worry. I won't tell anybody.

So you read Book IX, Chapter 1, and you're convinced that you want to assemble your own network. Good. About 90 percent of the time, in my experience anyway, it's pretty easy to put it all together if you know the tricks. Windows XP really does make networking simple. In this chapter, I show you how.

Planning Your Network

Yeah, you have to plan your network. Sorry.

You have a choice of lots and lots (and lots and lots) of ways to put together networks. The way I show you in this chapter is the way I recommend for first-time networkers who don't want to spend the money to go wireless. It ain't cool. It ain't sexy. It ain't state of the art. But it works.

If you're willing to take the wireless plunge, you should read through this chapter to understand the basic technology, terminology, and how things hang together. Then in the next chapter I show you how to do the wireless thang — whether you tie your wireless network into a wired network or not.

In case you haven't had enough of the arcane terminology yet, this chapter shows you how to put together a *100Base-T Ethernet peer-to-peer network*. There. Now you can impress your friends and neighbors. Harrumph.

Follow the next sections in order, and you'll have your network up and networking in no time.

Blocking out the major parts

To set up a network, you need only a handful of parts:

- ✦ Each PC needs a network adapter.
- ✦ If you're going to have three or more computers in your network, you need a box called a network *hub* or a *switch*. Both hubs and switches are commonly identified by the speed of the connection: a 10/100 Ethernet Switch, for example, handles both 10 Mbps and 100 Mbps network connections. I talk about hubs and switches in Book IX, Chapter 1.

  For a solid, detailed discussion about the differences between hubs and switches, strap on your hip waders and refer to `http://duxcw.com/faq/network/hubsw.htm`.

  If you want to network only two computers, you don't need a hub or a switch. All you need is a special kind of cable called a *crossover cable*. You can buy one — and you only need one — at any store that sells networking cables; just tell them you want an RJ-45 crossover cable to network two PCs. Plug one end of the cable into the network adapter on one PC, and the other end of the cable into the network adapter on the other PC, and you're ready to run the Windows XP Home Networking Wizard. It's that easy.

  Many cable modems and/or DSL modems come with a *broadband router*. If you have a broadband router, you don't need a hub or switch: The router has slots for network cables.

- ✦ You need cables to connect each PC to the hub or switch or router. Take a cable. Plug one end of the cable into the PC's network adapter and the other end into an open slot on the hub. Repeat for each PC. Sounds like the instructions on a shampoo bottle, eh?

A few tricks lurk in the dark corners, as you may imagine, but all in all, if you stick to the simple, old-fashioned (cheap!) equipment, you'll be fine.

Making sure your PCs are good enough

Before you run out and buy networking equipment, double-check and make sure that the PCs you're going to connect are up to the rigors of networking. As a certified (and certifiable) graduate of the Dummies School of Hard Knocks, I have three hard-and-fast rules when choosing PCs to put on a network:

1. Any PC currently running Windows XP will do fine on a network.
2. At least one of the PCs on your network should be running Windows XP. It makes your life much simpler.

3. Any PC currently running Windows 98, Windows Me, or Windows 2000, that works reasonably well — it doesn't crash all the time or run like a slug — is a good candidate for your network, too.

Don't bother trying to connect an older machine — one running Windows 95 or NT 4 or earlier — to your network. With rare exceptions, you spend more time and money getting a new network adapter to work on an old Windows 95 machine than you would pay to throw the slacker PC away (or donate it to a worthwhile charity) and buy a cheap new machine. Why is it so hard to get network adapters to run properly on Windows 95 and NT 4 machines? Millions of analyst hours have been spent pondering that question (both computer analyst and psychiatric analyst, I assure you). It all boils down to a fundamental difficulty in making the network adapter cooperate with the PC. Network adapters make two big demands on PCs: something called an *IRQ* (an internal line for sending information into and out of the PC) and a *base address* (a location inside the PC for the network adapter to stick the information that's coming and going). Both the IRQ and the base address must be unique; the network adapter won't share either with any other part of your computer. If you find yourself in the disastrously unenviable position of trying to get a network adapter card to work in an older PC, do yourself a favor and give up. Life's too short. Have to make it work? Hire an old geezer at a computer shop to wrestle with the problems. I'm an old geezer. I know whereof I speak.

Some folks would have you believe that Macs and Linux PCs will participate in a Windows XP network, with nary a hitch. Sorry, but I don't buy it. Some Macs seem to work well on a Windows XP network, but others can curl your hair. I don't claim to know why. And Linux is . . . well, Linux is Linux, if you know what I mean. If you can get a Linux machine to run on a Windows network, I salute you.

Adding network adapters

Armed with the warnings in the preceding section, you now know which PCs you want to connect to the network.

Each of those PCs has to have a network adapter — basically, a place to plug the network cable. When you shop for network adapters, consider these three points from the Dummies School of Hard Knocks, Graduate Division:

- Your PC may already have a network adapter, and you may not know about it. Believe me, stranger things have happened in the world of network connections. Examine the back of your computer for a receptacle that looks like a place to plug in a telephone, only it's wider. That's an RJ-45 jack. It's the kind you want (see the "Selecting cables" section, later in this chapter, for details).

Unfortunately, some PCs have "dead" RJ-45 jacks. (Don't believe it? I'll introduce you to my IBM Thinkpad someday.) Some manufacturers put jacks in all their machines — presumably that cuts costs — but don't hook up a network adapter unless you pay for one. The only way to tell for sure if a suspect RJ-45 jack is dead or alive is to plug it into a hub and turn on both the hub and the PC. If the light on the hub shows that the PC is online, the RJ-45 jack is alive. No light, no adapter.

✦ If you need to buy a network adapter for your PC, your first choice should be a USB network adapter. They're fast and easy, and they work like champs.

Sometimes USB network adapters interfere with other USB devices. I have a portable, for example, that works fine with a USB network adapter and works fine with a USB mouse, but starts acting like a jilted lover when I put the two together. The only solution I've found is to use the network or use the mouse, but don't even try to use both at the same time.

✦ If USB isn't an option, for whatever reason, you can live with a PCMCIA Ethernet adapter for a laptop, or an old-fashioned Network Interface Card (NIC, pronounced "nick") for a desktop. The PCMCIA card should slide into its slot and just start working. The NIC will require a screw-driver and a bit of patience.

If you don't feel comfortable installing the NIC yourself — and I don't blame you, it's easy to mess up a card if you've never installed one before — have the shop where you bought the card install it. You may have to spend a few extra bucks, but you'll save yourself a lot of grief in the process — and when it's all done, the card should work right, the first time.

It's important that all of the network adapters on your network run Fast Ethernet (or 100 Mbps or 100Base-T). If you have just one adapter card on the entire network that's only capable of the old, slow Ethernet speeds (10 Mbps or 10Base-T), the whole network will run at the lower speed, unless you sink a lot of money into a hub or switch that side-steps the differences. Fast Ethernet adapters are cheap. Use 'em. And if you can afford Gigabit cards and switches (1 Gbps or 1000Base-T), go for it.

Choosing a hub, er, router

A *hub* is nothing more than a box that connects together all the wires in all the cables that are plugged into it. A *router* is a hub with an attitude. A *switch* is a hub that's stuck in its ways.

Before you get bogged down in semantic differences, you need to realize that when most computer geeks talk about hubs and routers and switches, they use the terms interchangeably: Geek A may call a particular box a "hub," whereas Geek B may insist on calling it a "router," and Geek C could call the same box a "switch," and Microsoft might call it a "residential gateway." (A similar box in the wireless world could also be called a "Wireless Access Point," "Wireless hub," "Wireless router," or "Wireless switch," or "Hairless Schnauzer.") In fact, there are differences between hubs, switches, and routers.

Give or take a dotted "i," switches and hubs perform the same job, and you can think of them interchangeably. Routers, on the other hand, have a bit of smarts inside their drab boxes. A *broadband router* is smart enough to handle a fast Internet connection on one end and your network on the other. Plug a cable or DSL modem into a special slot in the router, then plug all your network cables into the other slots, turn on the router, and you're off to the races. The best technical description of broadband routers I've read is at `www.duxcw.com/faq/ics/diffrout.htm`.

Sharing IP addresses

Every computer connected to a network — at least the kind of networks I'm talking about in this book — has to have a number. A lot of mumbo-jumbo is involved, but basically the number is called an IP address, and it uniquely identifies the computer. Every computer on a network has an IP address, and every IP address is different. Easy, right?

Well, not so easy, for a number of reasons, but I'd like to concentrate for the moment on the problem of getting an IP address when you're connected to the Internet. Your Internet Service Provider gives you an IP address. Depending on the kind of Internet connection you have, that IP address may be assigned to you permanently (commonly the case with DSL or cable modems), or you may be assigned a new IP address every time you connect to the Internet.

If you have a permanent Internet connection, you pay for one IP address. In the not-so-good old days, that generally meant you could connect exactly one computer to the Internet: one computer, one IP address, one Internet connection, one bill. If you and your daughter shared a dial-up Internet account, chances are pretty good that both of you couldn't be online at the same time. Your daughter would dial up and get an IP address assigned; but if you dialed up and tried to get a second IP address assigned at the same time, the Internet Service Provider probably prohibited it. (Some ISPs would hand out more than one IP address to a particular account simultaneously, but they were pretty few and far between, and you paid for the privilege!)

Ultimately, the question of billing for Internet access hinges on IP addresses — who gets an address, and when, and how much they have to pay for it.

That's why IP address sharing is so popular. With Windows XP's Internet Connection Sharing, all of the PCs on your network share a single IP address: The PC that's running the Internet Connection Sharing program takes care of all the details. With cable or DSL or satellite modems connected to broadband routers, all of the PCs on your network share a single IP address, and a little computer inside the router takes care of keeping things coordinated. As far as your Internet Service Provider knows, you only have one computer connected to the Internet — after all, the ISP has only doled out one IP address.

When you work with home networks, the crucial decision you have to make is how to hook up the Internet. You can choose between two general approaches:

- ✦ You can connect the Internet to one computer, and then have that computer share its Internet connection with all the other computers on the network (see Figure 2-1).
- ✦ You can connect the Internet to the network box (typically a router) so all the computers on the network go through the network box to get to the Internet (see Figure 2-2). Many DSL and cable modems have built-in broadband routers, so a single box — a *residential gateway* — takes care of all the details.

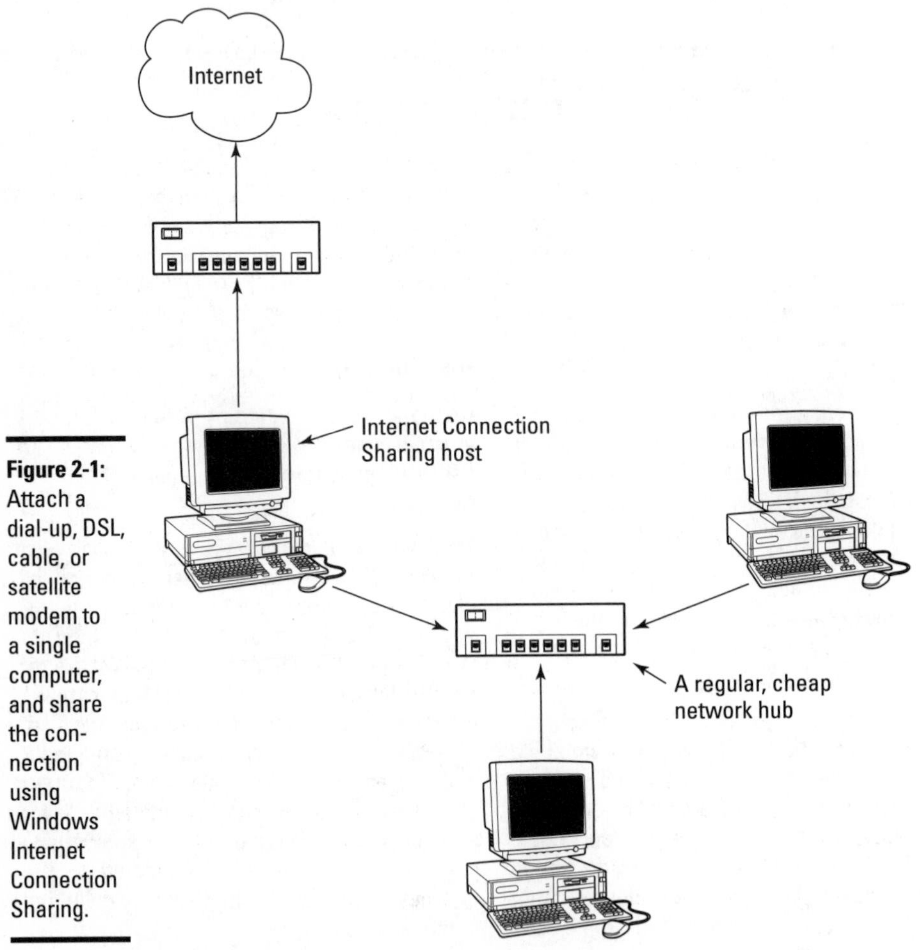

Figure 2-1: Attach a dial-up, DSL, cable, or satellite modem to a single computer, and share the connection using Windows Internet Connection Sharing.

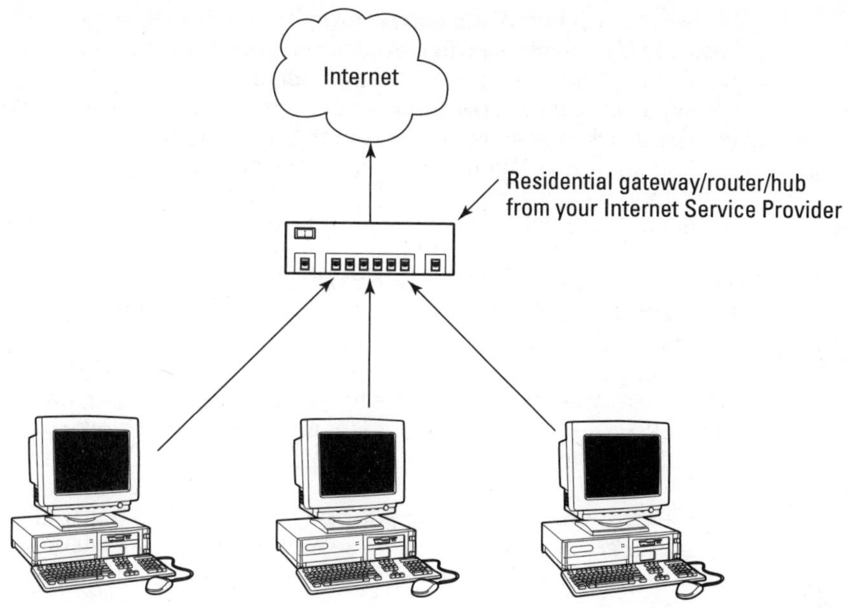

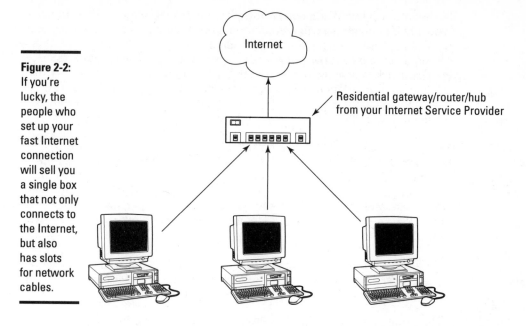

Figure 2-2: If you're lucky, the people who set up your fast Internet connection will sell you a single box that not only connects to the Internet, but also has slots for network cables.

Sometimes you can choose which approach you want to take. But you may be stuck with the first approach if

- ✦ You use a dial-up modem. Almost all dial-up modems connect to a computer, not a network box, and there isn't much you can do about it.
- ✦ You have a DSL or cable modem, you don't want to buy a different one, and it will only connect to a computer (typically through a USB port).
- ✦ The folks who put together your Internet connection supply a DSL or cable modem, you can't change the modem (or don't want to go to the hassle of changing it), and it will only connect to a computer (typically through a USB port).

Windows XP includes a very solid program called *Internet Connection Sharing* that makes it easy to share one computer's Internet connection among all the computers on the network. ICS turns that one PC into an Internet Mother Hen (that's a technical term). The anointed ICS PC interacts with the Internet. All the other PCs on the network interact with the ICS PC. To the outside world, you have only one connected PC. But all of the other PCs in your network think they're on the Internet, too, thanks to the ICS Mother Hen. Clever. And effective.

On the other hand, if you connect the Internet to your network's router — typically by plugging a cable modem or DSL modem into a special slot on the back of the router — the Mother Hen functions may be taken over by the router, or by the cable or DSL modem. The net result: The computers on your network interact with the router, the router interacts with the cable or DSL modem, the modem talks to the Internet, and to the outside world, you have only one connected PC. All of the PCs on your network think they're connected directly to the Internet, thanks to the hardware Mother Hen.

Things get really nasty when a network has two or more Mother Hens, and they both think they're in control: One fights for all the chicks, the other fights for all the chicks, then they both start looking at *each other* as chicks, and . . . all hell breaks loose. You think a catfight looks bad, you should see what these Mother Hens do to each other. At least 90 percent of all the confusion I've seen in setting up a network has to do with two or more Mother Hens fighting for control.

(Okay, okay. Computer geeks don't call them Mother Hens. They're called *DHCP servers.* But they sure act like Mother Hens — mean ones, at that. More about battling Mother Hens later in this chapter.)

If your DSL or cable Internet Service Provider offers a single box that combines the functions of a DSL modem and a router, you're in luck. Just plug the phone line or cable in the back of the box, and then plug in the network cables for all of your PCs, and you're off and running. The main advantage? There's only one Mother Hen.

When you get a cable, DSL, or satellite connection, usually the company that sets up the connection will sell or lease you a modem that works with the line. If the modem seems reasonably priced (check at your Friendly Local Computer Shoppe), and it has a network connection (sometimes called a LAN connection, a network interface, a 100Base-T connection, a CAT-5 connection, and/or an RJ-45 jack) that can plug into a broadband router, go for it. On the other hand, if the modem only has a USB connection — and it will thus only plug into a single computer — consider carefully whether you want to funnel all your network's Internet activity through a single computer.

Personally, I used the first approach (Internet Connection Sharing) for years, with very few problems. When you connect one computer to the Internet, and share that connection among all the other computers on your network, there's one big advantage: It's easy to reconfigure the Internet connection when something goes wrong. If your cable or DSL connection goes down, you can dial out on any handy modem and get the system reconfigured in minutes. I also found that ICS had far fewer problems with battling Mother Hens.

Increasingly, though, I've come to rely on the second approach (connecting the cable/DSL modem directly to a broadband router). With the Internet connection going directly through the router, I don't have to worry about one PC going down and taking all Internet access with it. There are some technical advantages to running off the router and a few security advantages. Mostly, though, putting my cable/DSL modem on the broadband router shares my fast Internet connection with all the PCs in the network, without having them bog down the one dedicated to Internet Connection Sharing. Of course, the price I pay is constantly battling with all of these *prima donna* Mother Hens.

Your DSL or cable Internet Service Provider may get hot under the collar if it discovers that you've hooked up more than one computer to the Internet, to allow more than one person on your network to use the Internet at the same time. Such inappropriate behavior may circumvent their obscene, extortionate billing policies, and the ISP may demand that you ante up. Aside from the sheer audacity of it all — you should tell 'em to take a flying leap, as far as I'm concerned — technically, you only have one computer connected to the Internet. Whether it's a PC running Windows XP Internet Connection Sharing or the little computer inside an IP Address Sharing broadband router, only that one, single computer is talking to your Internet Service Provider's computer. That may provide little solace if the ISP has a monopoly in your area and you have to play by their rules. But it's a fact, nonetheless.

So how do you choose a switch or a router? That depends on how you want to hook up the Internet. Specifically

- ✦ If you're going to connect the Internet to one computer and use Internet Connection Sharing, and you won't ever need wireless access, go for the cheapest, plain 10/100 Ethernet switch you can find. Make sure it has enough slots for all of the network cables that connect to your network's PCs, now and in the future — if in doubt, multiply the current number of cables by two.
- ✦ If the company that provides an Internet line to you — typically a cable TV company or a phone company — has a single box that connects to the cable or phone line, and lets you plug network cables from all your PCs into the back, get it. You'll save so much hassle fighting with Mother Hens that the unit will pay for itself in no time. (Some locations are fortunate enough to have retailers who sell these boxes, too, but be careful to get one that will work with your specific Internet line.)

  If you ever decide in the future to add wireless networking, it's comparatively easy to plug a dumb wireless access point into the hub.

- ✦ In all other cases, I strongly recommend that you get a *wireless broadband router* (also known as a *wireless Internet gateway*). These network boxes have slots to plug in network cables; a unique slot to plug in your cable or DSL modem; and a wireless (radio frequency) base station, similar to the one in your cordless telephone. Even if you don't anticipate ever running wireless, or the prospect of getting broadband lies clouded in the future, the added cost of getting everything in one box is minuscule. You can save a few pennies by cutting back on features, but it just isn't worth the bother. Go for the whole enchilada.

At the time this book went to press, I was using two different Wireless "802.11g" wireless broadband routers, for two different networks, and they work like a-ringin' a bell. They both have four RJ-45 slots for network cables, one slot for a cable or DSL modem, and rabbit ears to handle wireless access. Sweet. Cheap, too. My kind of hardware.

Selecting cables

To get your network running, you have to connect each PC to the hub with cables. (Again, I talk about wireless connections in Book IX, Chapter 3.) Ethernet — the kind of network that you're building — can run over many different kinds of cables. I won't tell you about all of the different options because I want you to get one, specific kind of cable.

There's a problem, though, and it all comes down to networking's lousy terminology. This specific kind of cable goes by five (or six or seven) different names. It looks a bit like a telephone cable. Telephone cable has four wires in it, but this particular kind of Ethernet cable has eight wires inside.

The ends of the cable have little plastic snap-in connectors, much like telephone wire connectors, except they're wider (they have to hold eight wires instead of four, eh?). The connectors on the end are called RJ-45 connectors, and that's the easiest way to reliably talk about the kind of cable you want — tell anyone trying to sell you cable that you want good quality network cable with RJ-45 connectors.

The cable itself is frequently called "RJ-45 cable" (in honor of the connectors at the ends), but you may also find that it's called 10Base-T cable (or 100Base-T or even 10/100Base-T cable), Twisted Pair Ethernet ("twisted pair" being old-fashioned telephone lingo for the innards of a common phone line, although it sounds considerably more interesting), TPE, Unshielded Twisted Pair (UTP) 10Base-T, IEEE 802.3 UTP cable, Category 5 cable, and heaven only knows what else. I tend to call the cable "Cat-5" Or "Cat-5e".

Category 5 refers to the quality of the cable. If you're offered Category 3 cable, don't bother. It costs about as much as Category 5, but may not be able to handle the blazing speeds that you want to install.

You need one piece of Cat-5 cable for each PC in your network. (If you're going to connect your cable/DSL modem to directly to the hub, you need a piece of Cat-5 for the modem, too.) The cable has to be long enough to stretch from the PC to the hub. When in doubt, overshoot: A cable that's too long can be coiled up and stuffed behind a desk; a cable that's too short can be painted black and studded with sharp steel spikes to make a stylish necklace. Or so I'm told.

Scoping out the installation

Measure twice, cut once. That's awfully good advice, even in the electronic era.

If you've been following along so far in this chapter, you should be armed with a concrete idea of what pieces you need to make your network network. Now it's time to figure out exactly where those pieces go. Physically. In meatspace. Keep these tips in mind:

- ✦ If you're going to connect the Internet to a single PC, and share that connection across the network, the PC that's connected to the Internet must be running Windows XP. In meatspace terms, that means you need to have a pretty hefty machine located next to a telephone jack, your DSL, or your cable modem.
- ✦ On the other hand, if you're going to connect your cable, DSL, or satellite modem directly to a broadband router, the router *doesn't* have to be close to the cable/DSL/satellite modem. You just run a regular Cat-5 network cable between the modem and the router.
- ✦ If you're going to burn CDs or DVDs on a CD-R or CD-RW or DVD-RW drive, you'll thank your lucky stars if that machine is running Windows XP. Plan on attaching your CD burner to a Windows XP machine.
- ✦ Other than those two provisions (Internet connection and CD-R/RW placement), I've found no particular reason to stick a specific peripheral on a specific PC. A networked printer, for example, works fine whether it's attached to a Windows XP machine or a Windows 98 machine.
- ✦ The switch or router can go anywhere. Once in a blue moon you may want to watch the lights on the panel dancing, just to make sure that all of your machines are talking to each other, but you really don't need to put the hub on your desk. If you want a light show, get a flashlight. It's cheaper and marginally more interesting.

There's a theoretical limit to the length of the Cat-5 cable connecting the hub, switch or router to a networked PC: 100 meters, or about 330 feet. If you go much farther than that, you may have problems with the whole network crashing. When you figure out where your hub is located, keep that in mind — and the fact that I'm talking about the length of the cable itself, not distances "as the crow flies." If you get stuck, talk to your friendly local hardware purveyor about connecting a switch through an "uplink port." It's an easy, cheap way to set up a second switch that's connected to the main hub/switch/router, and cables can go another 100 meters from the satellite switch.

Installing Your Network

You have your PCs ready to go — network adapters installed and waiting. The hub's sitting in a box on the floor. All of that cable makes quite a mess, and your spouse is starting to wonder, out loud, just what in the Sam Hill you expect to do with all of it. Yep. You're ready.

If you are trying to convert an existing network to a Windows XP-style peer-to-peer network, beware of a few additional wrinkles. Follow the instructions in the "Troubleshooting" section at the end of this chapter.

Here's a simple, 17-step process for getting your new network up and running with a minimum of fuss and hassle:

1. **Set up each of the PCs. Get the network adapters installed, but don't plug in the network cables (the Cat-5 cable) just yet. Connect the peripherals. Test each machine to make sure that it's working.**

   If you're going to be sharing an Internet connection through one PC, get that PC connected to the Internet, and make sure everything is working fine.

2. **Turn off all of the PCs, unplug the modems — both from the power outlet and from the phone line/cable/satellite feed — and let everything sit for at least 30 seconds.**

   Yeah, that sounds weird, but do it.

3. **With all of the power off, put the hub, switch, or router where it's going to go, and connect all the Cat-5 cables, both at the hub and at each individual PC.**

   If you have a cable, DSL, or satellite modem, make sure that it's connected to the phone line or cable TV line, and also make sure that it's plugged into the PC (if the Internet connection is going to be shared from a single PC) or the broadband router (if you're connecting it to a router).

   Broadband routers have only one, specific place where you can plug in a cable/DSL modem. That location frequently sits next to the "normal" slots, so read the documentation (or at least squint at the back of the hub!) to make sure you plug your cable/DSL modem into the right slot.

   If you have a dial-up modem, make sure that the phone line is plugged in.

4. **If you have a cable/DSL/satellite modem, stick the modem's power plug in the wall, turn it on, and wait for the lights to stop flashing.**

   That establishes the DSL/cable/satellite modem as the Mother of all Mother Hens. It also gives the modem a chance to run out to the Internet and gather anything it needs.

5. **Plug in the hub, switch, or router and wait for the lights to stop dancing.**

If your router wants to be a Mother Hen, it should work out its differences with the modem at this point.

6. **Pick a PC and turn it on. If you're going to connect to the Internet through one PC and share the connection with all the others, turn on the PC's modem if need be, and then turn on that PC.**

   Don't turn on the others. Just this one. If the PC's connected to the Internet, and you're going to share the connection, log on to the Internet and leave the connection on. Verify that the light on the hub for that PC comes on — in other words, make sure that the network adapter and cable for that PC are working okay. Now's the time to sort out connection problems: If the light doesn't go on, chances are good that a cable is loose or a NIC isn't installed correctly. Fix the problem now. When the light comes on at the hub, this PC's done — put a fork in it.

7. **One by one, repeat the process in Step 6 for each of the other PCs on the network.**

   Make sure that all the peripherals attached to the PCs are working — print test pages on the printers; slap CDs in CD drives and make sure they're working. Anything that you want to share on the network should be up and running.

8. **If you're going to use Internet Connection Sharing, go over to the PC that will be connected to the Internet. If you aren't going to use ICS, pick a Windows XP machine at random. Choose Start➪All Programs➪Accessories➪Communications➪Network Setup Wizard.**

   You see a Welcome screen. Ho-hum. Click Next. You see a reminder screen. Ho-hum. Click Next.

9. **In the Network Setup Wizard's Select a Connection step (see Figure 2-3), you have three choices:**

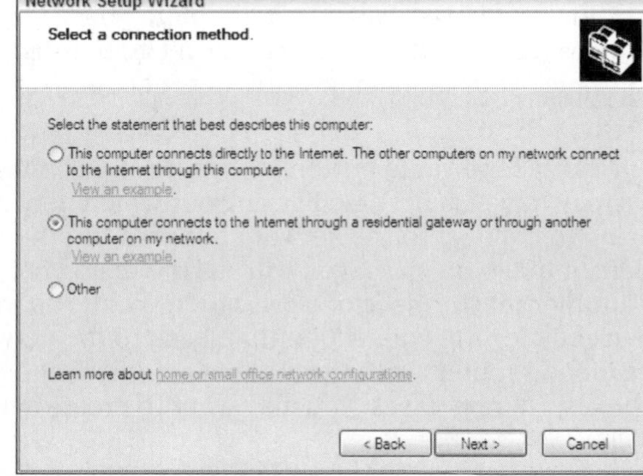

Figure 2-3: Configuring a networked computer to use a cable/DSL/satellite modem.

- If you're going to connect to the Internet through this particular PC, and share that Internet connection among all the PCs on your network, select the first radio button. (I know that isn't exactly what the button says, but that's what Microsoft means.) If you select this radio button, Windows sets up Internet Connection Sharing on this computer.
- Select the second radio button if (a) you already have Internet Connection Sharing set up on one computer on your network, or (b) you have a cable/DSL/satellite modem hooked up to your broadband router.
- You should only select the last radio button if your Internet connection isn't working yet, or if you have a weird setup where every computer on the network has its own, independent Internet connection (for example, if every computer on the network uses its own modem).

This is one of the most obfuscating dialog boxes in Windows-dumb, er, -dom. Microsoft's terminology stinks, and the pictures that you get when you click View an Example don't help at all. The main question is whether your (dial-up/DSL/cable/satellite) modem connects to one computer, and you share that connection among all the computers on the network — or if you stick the modem on the network's router and let the computers on the network share it. If the modem attaches to one computer, select the first radio button. If the modem attaches to the router (or if you just plug your cable wire or DSL phone line into your router), select the second radio button.

10. **Pick one of the radio buttons, and then click Next.**

    If you selected the first radio button in the Select a Connection dialog box, you told Windows XP that you wanted to set up Internet Connection Sharing through this PC. Windows isn't smart enough to pick your Internet connection out of all the connections on your PC, so you see a dialog box like the one shown in Figure 2-4. This dialog box is a little confusing because it lists your network adapter in addition to your potential Internet connection(s). Rest assured that Windows hasn't gone totally bonkers — you just need to pick your modem or other Internet connection out of the proffered list.

    If you selected the second radio button in the Select a Connection dialog box, Windows may have a hard time figuring out which network connection you're using to connect to the network box that has the cable/DSL/satellite modem. If that's the case, you will see the dialog box shown in Figure 2-5 — another masterpiece of obfuscation. Windows wants you to select the check box for the connection that leads to the network box (usually a broadband router) with the modem attached, and deselect the other check boxes. (In rare cases, you may want to create a network bridge to connect two separate networks together. If you think you fall into that category, click Learn More about Network Bridging, and strap on your hip waders — it's rough going.)

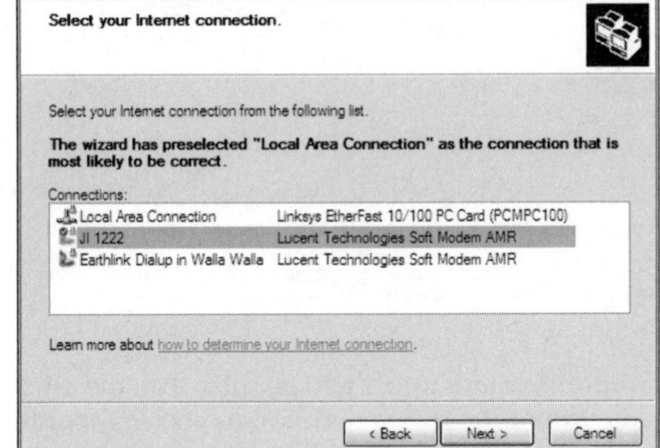

Figure 2-4: Choose the Internet connection, not the network adapter.

Figure 2-5: Select the check box for the connection that leads to the cable/ DSL/satellite modem, and deselect all the others.

11. **Select or deselect the appropriate check boxes, and then click Next.**

    The wizard asks you to fill out a name for the computer and a description (see Figure 2-6). The description doesn't mean much; it shows up in the Start⇨My Network Places dialog boxes, and that's about it. The computer name, on the other hand, is used behind the scenes for a hundred different purposes. That's why it has to be unique on the network — no two computers can have the same name.

Network Setup Wizard

Give this computer a description and name.

Computer description: Sacrificial Lamb

Examples: Family Room Computer or Monica's Computer

Computer name: THINKPAD

Examples: FAMILY or MONICA

The current computer name is THINKPAD.

Learn more about computer names and descriptions.

< Back | Next > | Cancel

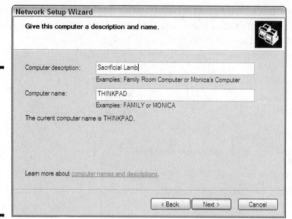

Figure 2-6: Choose a good, short computer name. The description doesn't matter much.

Keep your computer names short and simple. You may find yourself typing the name from time to time. Although you're theoretically allowed to use periods in the name, along with slashes, dollar signs, underscores, and a handful of additional oddball characters — I keep expecting to see amulets and chicken entrails to appease the WinGods — you're best to stick with simple letters and numbers.

12. **Type in a computer name and click Next.**

    The wizard asks for a network name, suggesting MSHOME or possibly HOME (see Figure 2-7). You need to enter the same network name for every computer on the network. Unless you have a very, very good reason for changing the network name, leave it alone.

Network Setup Wizard

Name your network.

Name your network by specifying a workgroup name below. All computers on your network should have the same workgroup name.

Workgroup name: MSHOME

Examples: HOME or OFFICE

< Back | Next > | Cancel

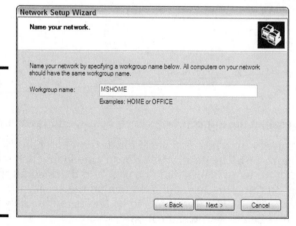

Figure 2-7: Use the name that Windows suggests, unless you absolutely must change it.

13. **Type in a network name (or just leave the one that's there) and click Next.**

    The wizard wants to know if you want to make files and printers (and other peripherals, such as CD/DVD burners) on this computer available to other computers on your network. This sounds scary, but in most cases it isn't: The only files that are automatically shared with other computers are the ones that you intentionally place in the Shared Documents folder. Windows Firewall, which you should run at all times, offers an extra layer of protection.

    ASKWOODY.COM

    If you're ultra-paranoid, or if you're setting up a computer that will be attached to a network that could be accessed by anybody — for example, a computer in an Internet cafe — you might want to turn off file and printer sharing.

14. **Click the Turn on File and Printer Sharing button, and click Next.**

    The wizard tells you what it's going to do (see Figure 2-8).

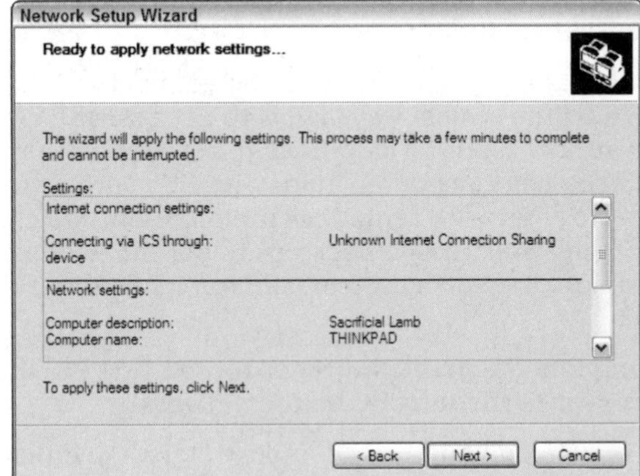

Figure 2-8: Final warning before the network connections are established.

15. **Click Next.**

    It may take forever, but by the time your PC comes back up for air, the network will be ready — on this PC. If you are installing Internet Connection Sharing and this PC will provide the connection, the wizard installs the ICS program, other programs that are necessary for sharing the Internet connection, as well as the firewall that sits between your network and the Internet. The wizard also sets up the Shared Files folders for every user on the PC and shares all of the printers attached to the PC. As the wizard says (see Figure 2-9), you're almost done, but you have one crucial last step.

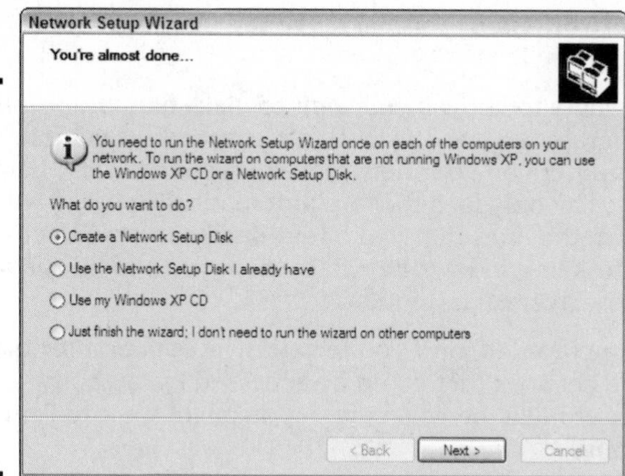

Figure 2-9: If any computer on your network is not running Windows XP, create a Network Setup diskette.

16. **If all of the PCs that you're going to connect to your network are running Windows XP, you're home free — you can select the Just Finish the Wizard; I Don't Need to Run the Wizard on Other Computers radio button, click Next, and you're done.**

    On the other hand, if any one of the PCs on your network is *not* running Windows XP, the easiest way I know to get a non-XP PC hitched up to the network is via the Windows XP-generated Network Setup diskette. So if you have any non-Windows XP PCs on your network, select the Create a Network Setup Disk radio button, and click Next. Windows XP takes you through the steps to put the Windows XP Network Setup program on a diskette and run it on other PCs on your network.

17. **After you complete the preceding steps for the first PC, the others go quickly. Hop over to the next PC on the network:**

    - If the PC is running Windows XP, choose Start➪All Programs➪Accessories➪Communications➪Network Setup Wizard. Run through the Network Setup Wizard again, beginning with Step 8, with two exceptions. In Step 9, do not select the first radio button. And in Step 16, select the Just Finish the Wizard; I Don't Need to Run the Wizard on Other Computers radio button.

    - If the PC is running any other version of Windows, put the Network Setup diskette in the disk drive, choose Start➪Run, type **a:\netsetup.exe**, press Enter, and follow the instructions. If you run Network Setup on Windows Me, for example, you see the dialog box shown in Figure 2-10. Click Yes, and you're home free, give or take a couple of whirring hard drives and a restart or two.

Repeat Step 17 for every computer on your network. When you're done, you're, uh, done. The network should be networking. Try choosing Start➪My Network Places and make yourself at home. Try printing on a networked printer. Betcha bucks to buckaroos that it sets itself up just that easily.

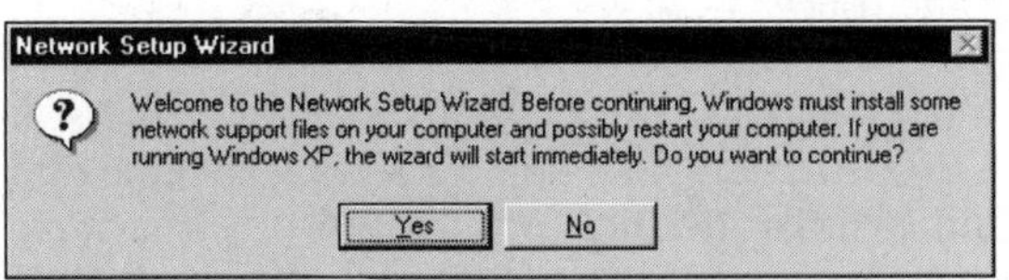

Figure 2-10: Windows XP Network Setup disk, run under Windows Me.

Troubleshooting

I've encountered three general types of problems — or should I say opportunities? — while working with Windows XP peer-to-peer networks.

Two Mother Hens fighting

Man, you ain't seen nuthin' 'till you've seen two fighting Mother Hens.

Many cable/DSL/satellite modems these days get attached directly to broadband routers. In fact, that may be the most common configuration: It's cheap, effective, flexible . . . and sometimes infuriating.

Many cable/DSL/satellite modems are set up as DHCP servers — Mother Hens — that expect to dole out IP addresses to each computer on the network. Many cable/DSL/satellite modems assign themselves an IP address of 192.168.1.1, and then hand out IP addresses starting in that range.

Unfortunately, many broadband routers are also set up as Mother Hens. They, too, expect to hand out IP addresses. Many of them assign themselves an IP address of 192.168.1.1, and expect to hand out IP addresses starting in that range.

What's wrong with this picture?

Well, if you power up your modem, and it assigns itself an address of 192.168.1.1, and then you power up your broadband router, and it assigns *itself* an address of 192.168.1.1, you suddenly have an enormously unstable situation. It's as if two different clones of Paula Zahn were forced to sit down and talk to each other. And when the unsuspecting PCs come up for air, seeking a Mother Hen to assign them an IP address, the feathers start flying.

Here's my favorite solution. Start your router, and then start a PC attached to the router. Follow the manufacturer's instructions to get into the router from the PC (usually you crank up Internet Explorer and type **http://192.168.1.1**). Then change the router's starting IP address to, say, 192.168.2.1. Make sure you update and reboot the router.

While it's possible to go diving into the DHCP server settings on the router or on the modem, there's really no need. By setting the starting IP address on the router to something different from the starting IP address on the modem, you move each of the Mother Hens into their own, separate hen house. End of fighting. All is right in the world.

Installing peer-to-peer over client/server

If you already have a network, and you want to install Windows XP networking, I congratulate you on an excellent choice. Did the same thing myself. I had a Windows 2000 client/server network running on my office machines, and it was such a headache. Oy! I could tell you such stories.

Anyway, I found a sequence of steps that works very well if you're trying to install a Windows XP peer-to-peer network over the top of an existing Windows 2000 (or presumably Windows NT) client-server network. The clients can be running any flavor of Windows, from version 95 on up. Of course, you won't be able to get the Windows 2000 (or NT) server working on the network, but you can get any other networked computers to switch over to peer-to-peer quite easily.

Here's what I did:

1. **Shut down all the machines on the network. Dead cold.**
2. **Start a Windows XP machine.**

   If you're going to use Internet Connection Sharing, start the ICS host. Otherwise, pick a Windows XP machine at random.
3. **Start one — and only one — of the PCs on the existing network.**

   (Note that this cannot be the server. It won't convert to peer-to-peer unless you completely replace the operating system.)
4. **On the Windows XP machine, follow the steps mentioned in the earlier section, "Installing Your Network," to get the new network going. Make sure that you generate a Network Setup diskette.**

5. **Take the Network Setup diskette to the old network machine and run it. Restart the old network machine. It should be connected to the peer-to-peer network.**
6. **Repeat Step 5 on every machine that you want to move from the old to the new peer-to-peer network.**

When you're done, the PCs on the new peer-to-peer network will still be able to access shares (folders, drives, and printers) on the old client/server network, although you have to supply a valid user I.D. and password when you try to access them. To find the old network's resources, follow these steps:

1. **Choose Start⇨My Network Places.**
2. **In the Network Tasks pane, pick View Workgroup Computers.**
3. **In the Other Places pane, pick Microsoft Windows Network.**

Similarly, PCs on the old client/server network can find shares on the new peer-to-peer network. On Windows 98, Me, NT 4, or 2000 computers, double-click the My Network Places icon on the desktop, and then choose Entire Network. Again, you may be required to supply a valid user I.D. and password when you try to access the shares.

You may be able to bypass the user I.D./password requirement for shares on a Windows XP machine if you activate the Guest account on that machine. To do so, see Book I, Chapter 2.

Networking on the road

Most of the time when I travel, I need to hook together two PCs. Guess it's the writer in me, but I've spent hours — days, weeks — trying to get PCs paired up in the field. Direct cable connect. Laplink. USB-to-USB adapters. A dozen other hardware and software kludges. I've resorted to e-mailing files to myself more times than I care to admit.

Suddenly, with Windows XP peer-to-peer networking, it's easy. I mean, really easy.

If you're on the road and you need to plug your PC into a "foreign" network, there's absolutely nothing to it, as long as your portable and the foreign network are running Windows XP peer-to-peer networks. Plug an RJ-45 cable into the portable's network adapter, plug the other end into an available slot on the hub, turn on the portable, and ba-da-boom-ba-da-bing, the whole operation takes maybe 30 seconds.

More than that, though, if I'm carrying two portables that I need to network, all it takes is a crossover cable. (For a discussion of crossover cables — basically, an RJ-45 cable with one pair of wires crossed — see the section, "Blocking out the major parts," earlier in this chapter.)

Whenever I pack two portables, I carry a little one-meter long crossover cable. If I need to network the portables, I plug one end of the cable into the network adapter on one portable, the other end on the other portable, and suddenly my Windows XP peer-to-peer network is right there with me. Everything I can do on the "big" network in my office works precisely the same way on the road.

Absolutely phenomenal.

Chapter 3: Putting the Why in Wi-Fi

In This Chapter

- Finding out why wireless may be right for you
- Setting up a wireless network
- Connecting to a wireless network — anywhere, anytime
- Understanding wireless (in)security

I remember the first time I tried to install a wireless network in my home office.

It was an unmitigated disaster. I live in a three-story concrete townhouse. I put the *wireless access point* (the base station — the thing with rabbit ears on top) on the middle floor. As long as my laptop sat right next to the WAP, everything worked great. The minute I moved it downstairs or upstairs — or even walked into the stairwell — it died. Completely, totally, utterly gone. No amount of futzing with the rabbit ears helped. It's like the bunny turned belly up, and that's all she wrote.

Times change. The minute 802.11g equipment became available in my neck of the woods, I ran out and bought another wireless base station, er, WAP. And therein lies a story. . . .

802.11g

I bought an 802.11g wireless broadband router and a PC plug-in card for the laptop. I paid less than $150 for the whole shooting match. Installation was a breeze. I shut down every PC on my network, unpacked the router, unplugged my (very) old hub, plugged in the new hardware, brought up the PCs — and all of my hard-wired network cable connections worked. Fair enough, but that's not much of a big deal: I expected any replacement for the old hub to work right the first time.

So I plugged the wireless card into the laptop, powered it up. Windows XP Pro recognized it, installed the driver, told me the card was available . . . and it worked. I mean, right then and there, not having done a thing, Internet Explorer picked up the network connection, reached out across my peer-to-peer network, through my DSL modem, and started pulling pages off the Web — much to my amazement.

I took the portable up and down the stairs and ran McAfee's Speedometer (`http://us.mcafee.com/root/speedometer.asp`) to judge how fast my Internet connection was running. Depending on my location, the speed was within 25 percent of the speed of the hard-linked connections. I couldn't believe it.

So what is 802.11g? It's a wireless access method that's been around for a long time, but only recently has it become so ubiquitous that mere mortals could afford it. Other than that, all you really need to know is that it works on the same 2.4 GHz bandwidth as many telephones and other wireless devices; that it blasts through concrete walls considerably better than its predecessor, 802.11b (see Table 3-1); and that it runs about five times as fast as 802.11b — more than fast enough to keep up with a good cable modem or DSL connection. Oh, and it has a horrible name that's just as senseless as 99 percent of the names in the computer business.

Table 3-1 Those 802 Numbers

This Standard	*Rated (Theoretical) Speed*	*Realistic Speed*	*My Recommendation*
802.11b	10 million bits/sec	4 million bits/sec	Don't bother. The signal doesn't reach as far as 802.11g, and it's slower.
802.11g	50 million bits/sec	20 million bits/sec	The sweet spot. Backward compatible with 802.11b, so if you have an old wireless card, it'll work with your 802.11g base station. But it uses the same frequency range as cordless phones.
802.11a	50 million bits/sec	20 million bits/sec	Not as popular as 802.11g (at least this week), thus more expensive. Not compatible with 802.11b or 802.11g, so that notebook adapter that you buy for your 802.11a network at home probably won't work when you go to Starbucks. Uses a much higher frequency than cordless phones.
802.11w	200,000 million bits/sec	400,000 million bit/sec	The "w" stands for "Woody." Hey, these names don't make any sense, so why not create your own?

So, what about Bluetooth?

Bluetooth is a horse of a different color.

The wireless networks I talk about in this chapter are designed to replace wired "local area networks." They need to haul a lot of data over a fairly long distance — say, across a building or even many buildings.

Bluetooth, on the other hand, deals with relatively small amounts of data traveling over a short distance — perhaps ten meters. It's built for connecting headphones to telephones, or speakers to sound systems, or palm computers to notebooks.

To put it another way, if you want to transmit data from a dial-up modem (perhaps a GPRS modem in a mobile phone) to a nearby computer, Bluetooth works great. But if you need to send broadband across the room, you need to haul out the bigger Wi-Fi guns.

Installing a Wireless System

If you've never dealt with a network before, read Book IX, Chapter 2 to make sure you understand the basics. If you think of a wireless network as being very similar to a "regular" wired network, with radio waves in place of network cables, you're pretty close to the mark.

Here we go with the stupid terminology again.

Every computer in a wireless network has to have a *wireless adapter*. A wireless adapter is just a radio receiver/transmitter, similar to the kind in cordless telephones. Most commonly, wireless adapters plug in to USB ports, PCMCIA notebook ports (the flat ones about the size of a pack of playing cards), local area network ports ("RJ-45" slots, the kind you normally plug network cables into), or they go inside the computer as a PCI card.

Many hand-held computers (such as Pocket PCs) also support wireless adapters that plug into the slot used for Compact Flash memory cards.

Most wireless networks also have a *wireless access point* — a WAP — that acts much like a base station for a cordless telephone. (A WAP isn't technically necessary because you can instruct wireless adapters to talk to each other, much as you would use walkie-talkies. But if you plan to run much data over your wireless network, it's far better to run everything through a WAP.)

If you already have a wired network set up, adding a wireless base station, er, WAP is as simple as plugging one in to your existing hub (router, switch, whatever) and adjusting the bunny ears. If you don't have a wired network already, I urge you to follow the advice in Book IX, Chapter 2, and start with a *wireless broadband router* (also known as a *wireless Internet gateway* or just a *wireless router*). The wireless broadband router acts as a wireless base station, but it also has slots for regular wired network cables, and a special slot to connect your cable/DSL/satellite modem.

The location of the wireless access point matters — the stronger the signal, the faster data travels over the waves. My suggestions:

- ✦ If you know which computers will use wireless the most, put the WAP as close as you can to them. If you don't know which computers will drive the largest volume (or you don't know where the high-volume computers will be located), put the WAP as close to the physical center of the coverage area as you can.
- ✦ Do not put the WAP right next to a wall. Move it away from the wall by at least six inches. Don't put one on the floor, or directly attached to the ceiling, either.
- ✦ Remember that metal, water (read: fish tanks), and concrete affect signal strength. Wood and drywall don't matter much. Glass, brick, and stone sit somewhere in between.
- ✦ Try hard to connect your cable/DSL/satellite modem to the WAP by a regular network cable. Although it may be technically possible to go wireless, there's no reason to bog down the wireless system with the highest-volume link in your network.

- ✦ That said, remember that your wireless broadband router (er, wireless Internet gateway, uh, wireless router) doesn't need to be located, physically, right next to the cable/DSL/satellite modem. As long as you can stretch a cable between them (up to 100 meters/300 feet or so), you're fine.
- ✦ WAPs and cordless phones don't mix. I've heard that microwave ovens can cause interference, too, although I've never had the problem. If you have something that operates on the 2.4 GHz frequency — and most cordless phones do — it may give your wireless network heart flutters.

To plug a wireless broadband router into a network, follow the detailed instructions in Book IX, Chapter 2. If you follow those instructions, and the ones in the user's manual, and you can't get anything to work right (particularly, if you reboot a computer or two and it doesn't work right), see my discussion of fighting Mother Hens in the "Troubleshooting" section of that chapter.

Wireless Zero Configuration

Ya gotcher ears on, good buddy? 10-4 that.

Truckers do the wireless thang. You should too.

Microsoft has developed a program and set of de facto standards that fall under the sobriquet *Wireless Zero Configuration*, or WZC. Almost all modern network adapters can use WZC — and many of them, surprisingly, work.

If all goes well, here's how you connect a PC to your new wireless network:

1. **Make sure your WAP is installed and all the lights are blinking.**
2. **If you have a wireless adapter that goes inside your PC, put it in. Start your PC. If you have a wireless adapter that plugs into a USB port, or PCMCIA slot, stick it in.**

   Chances are good that the Found New Hardware Wizard will appear. Follow the instructions, insert the CD that came with the adapter, and get the new hardware installed, as shown in Figure 3-1.

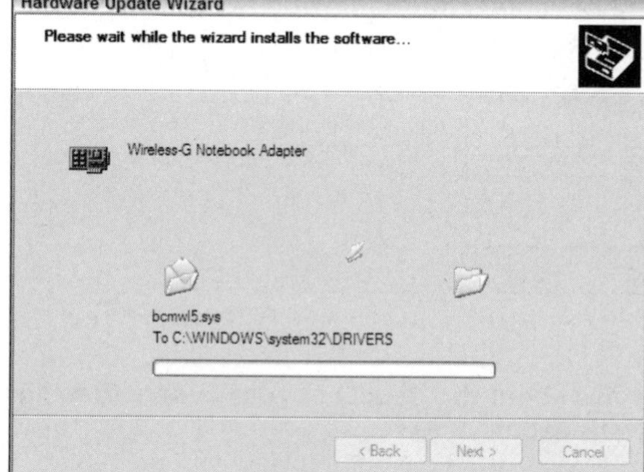

Figure 3-1: Install your wireless adapter.

3. **Windows alerts you that a wireless network is available. Click the icon in the Notification Area (down near the clock) and Windows shows you the Choose a Wireless Network dialog box, as shown in Figure 3-2.**

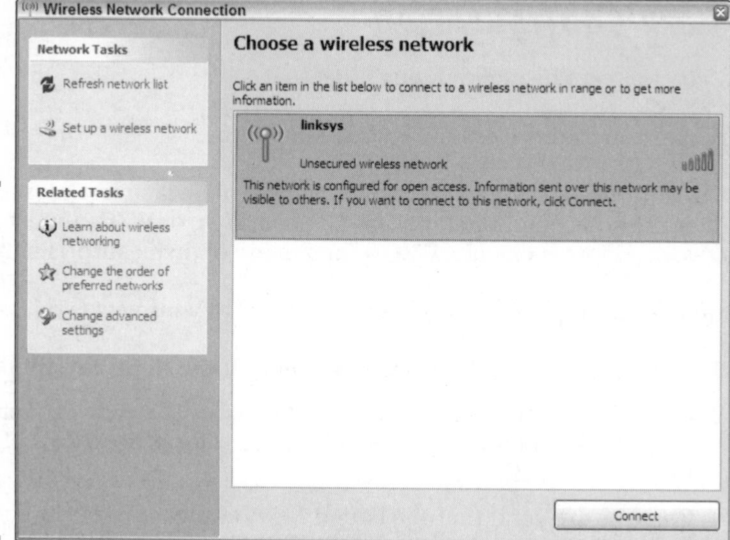

Figure 3-2: All available wireless networks that are "broad-casting" their system I.D. appear in this dialog box.

4. **Click the Connect button.**

   Using Wireless Zero Configuration, Windows hooks you up to the wireless network (see Figure 3-3).

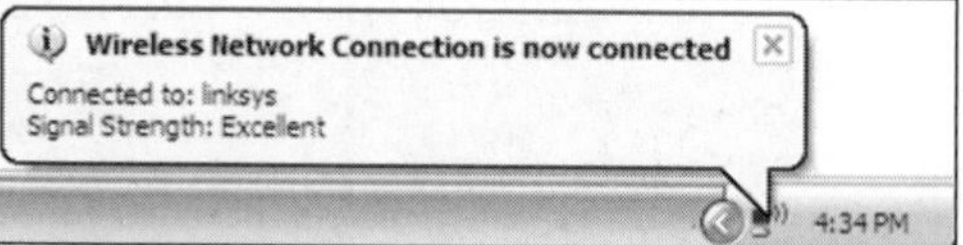

Figure 3-3: You're in. Just like that.

5. **If you're curious about the details of your connection, just click the icon in the Notification Area.**

   Windows shows you a status report like the one shown in Figure 3-4.

Windows keeps constant watch for new networks that broadcast their system I.D.s. If you walk into a Starbucks and you suddenly see a notification that there's another system available, hooking into the system is as simple as clicking the icon in the Notification Area, clicking on the new network, and clicking Connect.

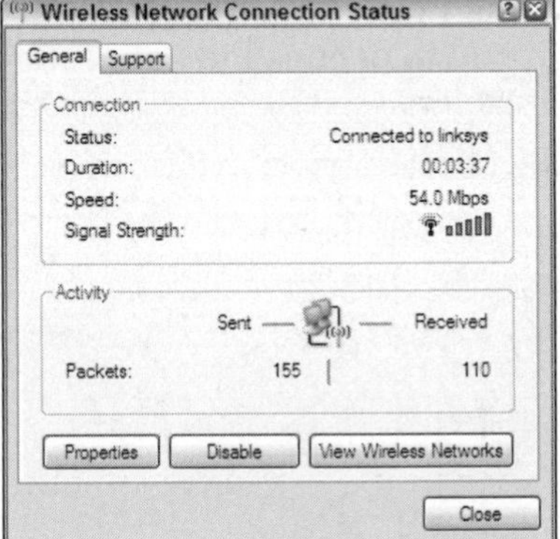

Figure 3-4: Wall to wall an' ten feet tall. Er, the signal strength runs 5 bars — the MAX!

If you're connected to more than one network at a time, Windows automatically routes and reroutes Internet traffic over the fastest connection. That can play havoc when you're near two networks that have nearly-identical Internet response times. To keep Windows from automatically flip-flopping between networks, follow these steps:

1. **Double-click the wireless icon in the Notification Area.**

   You see the Wireless Network Connection Status report in Figure 3-4.

2. **Click the Properties button, and then click the Wireless Networks tab.**

   Windows brings up a list of all the networks that it will connect to automatically (the Preferred Networks list, as shown in Figure 3-5).

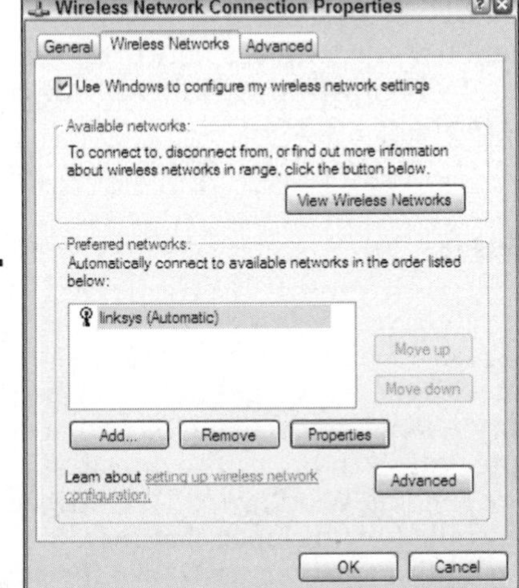

Figure 3-5: A list of the networks that Windows will automatically connect to.

3. **Click the network that you don't want to connect to automatically, click the Properties button, and then click the Connection tab in the Properties dialog box that appears.**

   You see the Properties dialog box, as shown in Figure 3-6.

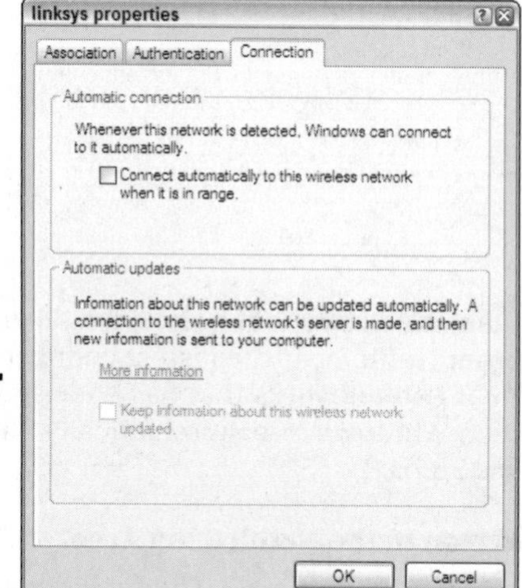

Figure 3-6: Disable automatic connection here.

4. **Deselect the Connect Automatically to This Wireless Network When It Is in Range check box. Click OK twice.**

   Windows will no longer consider this wireless network when it's jockeying for a faster Internet connection.

For much, much more information about wireless networks, see *Wireless Home Networking For Dummies*, by Danny Briere, Walter Bruce, and Pat Hurley (published by Wiley Publishing, Inc.).

Securing a Wireless Network

Lemme tell ya a story.

There's a teensy little problem with the network that I describe in this chapter. It has absolutely no security — anybody walking by with a notebook computer and a wireless adapter card can break into my system in less than three seconds. In fact, if they're running Windows XP, Windows will take it upon itself to not only tell the would-be interloper that there's a "hot" network available for the pillaging, but will also actually take the guy with the notebook through the steps to get hooked up.

When I first set up this precise network, Guy Wells, a friend of mine (who's also a contributor for this book) dropped by the house. As he puts it, "I turned on my laptop to show Woody and Justin a photo of my house. With absolutely no prompting on my part, while we were looking at the photo, Windows XP reached out, identified Woody's nice new 802.11g network, connected to his network, found his fast ADSL connection, signed me on to MSN Messenger, and started pulling down some monster files I had queued for download. We just sat and watched. The ADSL connection was completely red-lined less than a minute after I booted my portable. Absolutely no effort required. It worked as well as if my portable were hard-wired directly into his network. 802.11g has a reputation for working at long distances, so I tried an experiment. I walked down to the main road about 100 meters away from his house. I opened the laptop. Windows XP identified the network, logged me on, and started downloading again."

That's how I first discovered how insecure wireless networks can be.

The first law of wireless networks: Any default installation of a wireless network is absolutely, completely, totally, utterly wide open and vulnerable to the most casual eavesdropping.

If you have a wireless network, you *must* protect it:

- **Change the wireless router's password.** Every manufacturer ships wireless routers with the same password. Unless you change yours, anybody who can log on to the router can break into it.
- **Change the system I.D. and don't broadcast it.** Wireless routers ship with default system I.D.s, like *linksys* or *default*. If the router broadcasts the system I.D., it alerts Windows XP PCs with wireless adapters about its existence — that's where the *linksys* in Figure 3-2 came from: I was using the default system I.D. and my router was broadcasting it.
- **Limit access to specific wireless adapters.** Every wireless adapter has a number called a MAC address. (No, it doesn't have anything to do with Apple computers or McDonalds hamburgers.) If you have a wireless adapter, look at it. You'll see its MAC address printed on the bottom. Wireless routers allow you to specify which MAC addresses can use the router.

  Unfortunately, it's very easy for bad guys to "spoof" MAC addresses — to make it appears as if they have a specific MAC address when they don't.

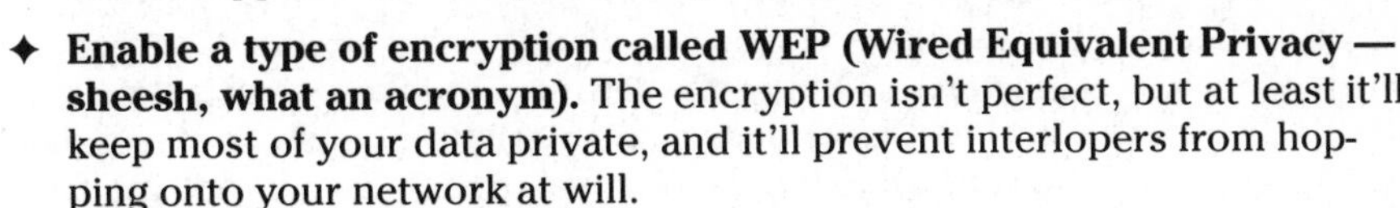

- **Enable a type of encryption called WEP (Wired Equivalent Privacy — sheesh, what an acronym).** The encryption isn't perfect, but at least it'll keep most of your data private, and it'll prevent interlopers from hopping onto your network at will.

WEP slows down your connection, but it ensures that people can't sniff your transmissions and read them as easily as this page. If you're paranoid, consider changing your WEP key every week or so.

Each manufacturer has a different routine, and the specific interface changes all the time. But as of this moment, the Linksys WRT54G router can be changed like this:

1. **Log on to the router by following the instructions in the box.**

   You need to use Internet Explorer to get in. Child's play, once you have the address, default user I.D., and password. The router puts you on the first page, called Setup, as shown in Figure 3-7.

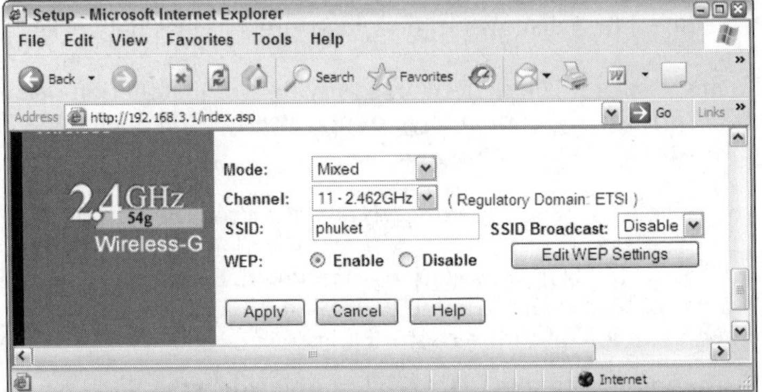

Figure 3-7: The Linksys WRT-54G router setup routine.

2. **Type a new, unique name in the SSID text box. (That's your new system I.D.) In the SSID Broadcast drop-down list, choose Disable, and then select the Enable radio button to enable for WEP encryption.**

   That covers all of the major security bases.

3. **Click the Edit WEP Settings button.**

   The router comes up with a key generator, as shown in Figure 3-8.

4. **In the WEP Encryption drop-down list, choose 128 Bits 26 Hex Digits. Type a password in the Passphrase text box, and click the Generate button.**

   The four keys you see are your WEP keys. Take a screen shot to make sure you remember the setting. (To take a screen shot, press Alt+PrintScr, start Paint by choosing Start➪All Programs➪Accessories➪Paint, and then choose Edit➪Paste to paste the image into Paint. Save and then print the resulting picture.)

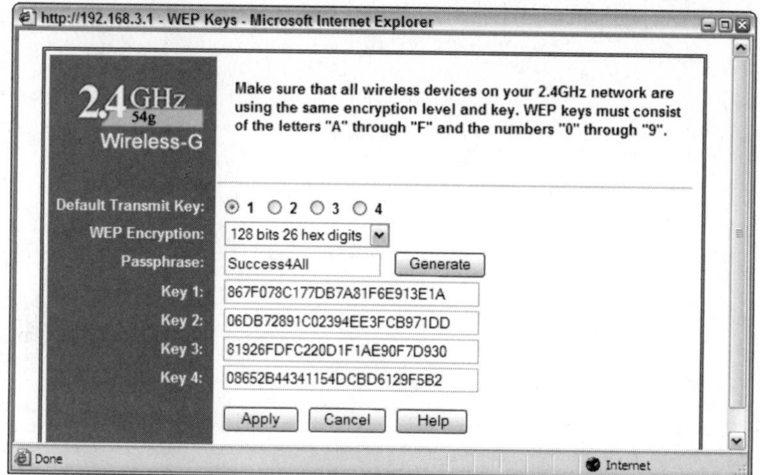

Figure 3-8: Generate a 128-bit encryption key.

5. **Click Apply.**

   The router's settings are changed. Any computers that were attached to your wireless network get bumped off, without warning.

6. **Click the Security tab, and then type a new Router Password.**

   This is the password you need to get into the router.

7. **Click Apply again.**

   The router tells you the changes are successful.

8. **Click the Advanced tab, and then the List tab.**

   Enter the MAC addresses of the network adapters that you want to allow on your wireless network.

9. **Click Apply again.**

   Better remember that password!

Chapter 4: Protecting Your Privacy

In This Chapter

- Protecting against identity theft
- Knowing how much privacy is too much
- Keeping cookies in check

It's a jungle out there. On the one hand, the bad guys (and they're almost always guys) in black hats keep churning out bad programs that crash systems, erase drives, clog the Internet with millions of bogus messages, and bring down major Web sites with amazing ease.

On the other hand, these companies (and they're almost always companies) keep tons of information about you and your online habits, manipulating and collating and slicing and dicing the information to turn yet another cyberbuck.

Add to the stew the enormous upsurge in phishing, where clever spammers convince you, by sheer will and a good story, to divulge private information, and then steal your identity — and your money.

It's fitting that the last chapter in this book tackles the single most important problem facing Windows XP users: privacy. The privacy problem has dogged users since the earliest days of computing, and it's a problem that will not go away.

Identity Theft

The U.S. Department of Justice has an excellent overview of identity theft and how it can affect every computer user at `www.usdoj.gov/criminal/fraud/idtheft.html`.

DOJ starts with a simple statement: "Be stingy about giving out your personal information to others unless you have a reason to trust them, regardless of where you are."

I would add to that: "and regardless of who *they* are."

In these days of ever-more-clever phishing attacks (see Book II, Chapter 3), where thousands of people are tricked every day into handing out private information over the Internet, caution pays.

More than that, supposedly private databases get compromised all the time. I'm not talking about school mailing lists. I'm talking about phone numbers, credit card numbers, medical records, bank accounts, Social Security numbers, and lists of passwords by the hundreds of thousands. Data that should stay private gets out with alarming frequency.

Of course, you're smart enough to recognize a phishing message, even if it looks just like an official e-mail from PayPal. Of course you're smart enough to not type anything into a Web page that springs up when you click on a link in a message, even if it says it's a real Wells Fargo logon site. But are you smart enough to know when you're using a public terminal that's being keylogged? I'm not.

Keylogging programs keep track of everything that you type on a PC. Many keylogging programs successfully hide their activities — unless you know exactly where to look, you'll never know that a keylogger is running. For details, see `http://en.wikipedia.org/wiki/Keylogging`.

Defending Your Privacy

I continue to be amazed at Windows users' odd attitudes toward privacy. People who wouldn't dream of giving a stranger their telephone numbers fill out their mailing addresses for online service profiles. People who are scared to death at the thought of using their credit cards online to place an order with a major retailer (a very safe procedure, by the way) dutifully type in their Social Security numbers on Web-based forms.

Windows XP — particularly through its ancillary services, such as .NET Passport and MSN Explorer — gives you unprecedented convenience.

That convenience comes at a price, though: Everything you do with .NET Passport or MSN — or just about any commercial site on the Web, for that matter — ends up stored away in a database somewhere. And as the technology gets more and more refined, your privacy gets squeezed.

Do you have zero privacy?

"You have zero privacy anyway. Get over it."

That's what Scott McNealy, CEO of Sun Microsystems, said to a group of reporters on January 25, 1999. He was exaggerating — Scott's been known to make provocative statements for dramatic effect — but the exaggeration comes awfully close to reality. (Actually, if Scott told me the sky was blue, I'd run outside and check. But I digress.)

Consider: With Windows XP, you're forced to activate (no personal information collected); persistently urged to register (lots of personal info there); confronted with in-yer-face prompting to sign up for a Passport (hey, you need it for Hotmail and MSN Messenger); and given an, uh, opportunity to purchase fine products from Microsoft "partners" in the Windows Catalog list. When you crank up the Windows Media Player, you're immediately connected to a Microsoft Web site, where you're offered the opportunity to order music from the Mother $hip. When you're in My Pictures, you're offered the opportunity to order prints. Click on MSN Messenger's Chat icon, and you can sign up to get into the Chat rooms for a small monthly fee.

Marketing, marketing, marketing.

Privacy concerns extend beyond the Microsoft Marketing Marvel, of course. A lot of money can be made in collating, filtering, and dishing out personal information, in any usable form. To date, Microsoft isn't the worst offender — not by a long shot.

Understanding Web privacy

Windows XP in general, and Internet Explorer 6 in particular, give you an unprecedented level of control over your privacy on the Web. One key capability: the Platform for Privacy Preferences (P3P) privacy policy.

P3P technology allows Web designers to tell you what they're going to do with the information that they collect from you. That information is stored in a uniform, machine-readable way. P3P Web sites give specific answers to nine questions:

- Who is collecting the data?
- Exactly what information is being collected, and can the information be traced to a specific individual?
- For what purposes is the information collected — why does the site need it?
- Which information is being shared with others?
- Who are these data recipients?
- Can users make changes in how their data is used?
- How are disputes resolved?
- What is the policy for retaining data?
- Where can the detailed policies be found in human-readable form?

Most commercial Web sites have set up formal P3P statements. If you ever want to see a Web site's privacy policy, follow these steps:

1. **Bring up Internet Explorer (choose Start⇨Internet Explorer) and navigate to the site.**
2. **Choose View⇨Privacy Report.**

   You see a list of all the files that go into making up the current Web page (see Figure 4-1).

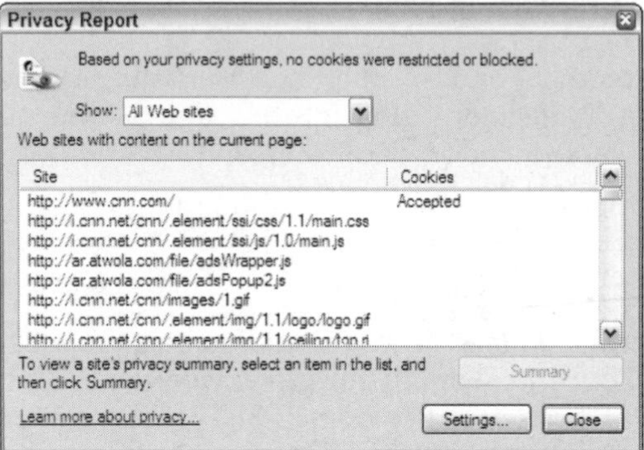

Figure 4-1: The CNN.com main page brings in more than 100 files, including one called www.cnn.com/cookie.crumb.

Note that many Web pages use advertisements that originate on other Web sites. You may be surprised to discover that an ad appearing on `www.abc123.com` came from `www.def456.com`, and `www.def456.com` may not have the same privacy policy as `www.abc123.com`. For example, a recent look at `www.msn.com` — the Microsoft Network main Web page — revealed ads from atdmt.com (see Figure 4-2), an advertising company with a P3P policy that's very different from Microsoft's.

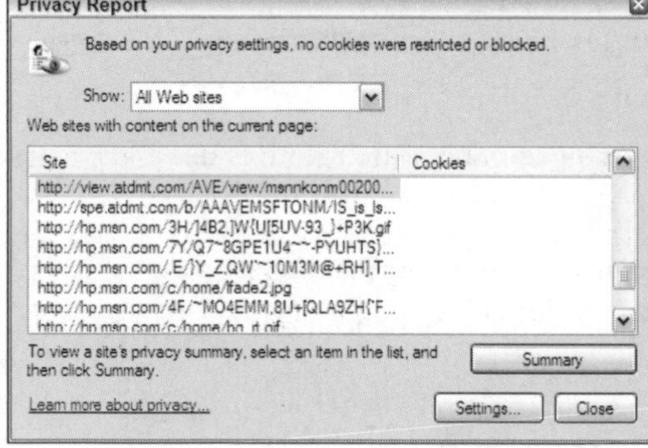

Figure 4-2: The MSN main Web page includes content from atdmt.com.

3. **Select the site that interests you and click the Summary button.**

   The site's P3P statement appears. In Figure 4-3, I bring up Atlas DMT's privacy policy, which includes cookie tracking across multiple sites, and collecting credit card and financial information.

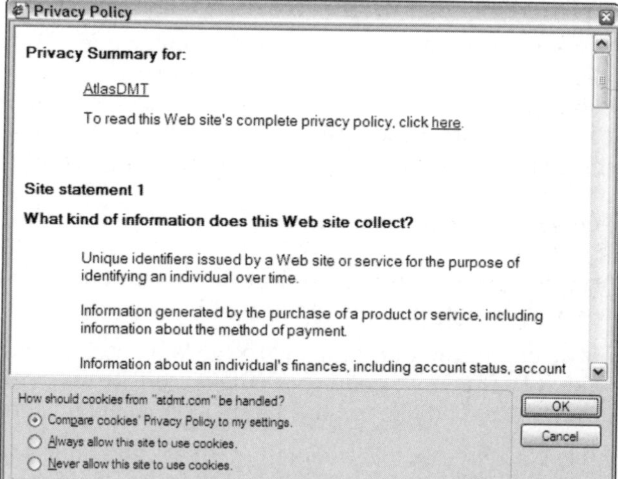

Figure 4-3: Atdmt.com — Atlas DMT — tracks the sites that you have visited over time, a privacy plundering that you wouldn't expect from the main MSN Web site.

4. **Click the underlined text to look at any statements that concern you.**

   Some of the statements are quite innocuous. Others may give you pause. Atlas DMT, for example, makes no bones about the fact that it tracks you, personally, across any sites that you visit, and collects information about what you buy, how you pay for it, and other financial information. I bet you didn't expect that Atlas DMT was watching the last time you visited `www.msn.com`.

Although you have every reason to expect that a Web site will live up to its stated P3P policy, you have no absolute guarantee.

If you find yourself sitting on a Web site that doesn't have a privacy policy, write to `webmaster@` the site (for example, `webmaster@askwoody.com`) and complain. Loudly. Although P3P technology is hardly infallible, it's a good step in the right direction — one that's long overdue, in my opinion — and Webmeisters who balk at implementing it should be convinced of the error of their ways.

Keeping Cookies at Bay

So what's a cookie, anyway? Inquiring Dummies want to know.

A *cookie* is a text file that a Web site stores on your computer. Why would a Web site want to store a file on your computer? To identify you when you come back. It's really that simple.

Consider the case of D. Dummy, D. Dummy's computer, and a Web site that D. Dummy visits — say my hometown newspaper's site, `www.phuketgazette.net`. The *Phuket* (say *poo-KET*) *Gazette* uses cookies to keep track of when readers last visited its Web site, so that readers can click on a button and see what's happened since the last time they looked at the site. Nifty feature.

Here's how cookies come into the picture:

1. D. Dummy decides he wants to look at the *Phuket Gazette*'s site, so he types **www.phuketgazette.net** in Internet Explorer and hits Enter.
2. D. Dummy's computer starts talking to the Web site. "Howdy y'all!" (Did I mention that D. Dummy's computer comes from Texas? Details, details.) "I'm D. Dummy and I'd like to take a look at your main page."
3. The *Phuket Gazette* site, `www.phuketgazette.net`, starts talking back to D. Dummy's computer. "Hey, D. Dummy! Have you been here before?" (Actually, the *Phuket Gazette*'s site is a whole lot more polite than that, but you get the idea.)
4. D. Dummy's computer runs out to its hard drive real fast and looks for a text file called — bear with me here — `DDummy@www.phuketgazette.txt`. It doesn't find a file, so D. Dummy's computer says to the Web site: "Nope. I don't have any cookies here from y'all."
5. The *Phuket Gazette* site pulls off its shoes and socks, starts counting fingers and toes, and then says to D. Dummy's computer, "Fair enough. I figure you're user number 1578462. Store that number away, wouldja, so that I can identify you the next time you come back here? And while you're at it, could you also remember that you were last here at 11:36 AM on December 14?"
6. D. Dummy's computer runs out, creates a new file called `DDummy@www.phuketgazette.txt`, and puts the number 1578462 and 11:36 AM on December 14 in it.

The *Phuket Gazette* site's main page starts to come up on the screen, D. Dummy scans the headlines, and then heads off to do some shopping. Two hours (or days or weeks or months) later, dear old D. Dummy goes back to `www.phuketgazette.net`. Here's what happens:

1. D. Dummy types **www.phuketgazette.net** in Internet Explorer and hits Enter.
2. D. Dummy's computer starts talking to the Web site. "Howdy y'all! I'm D. Dummy and I'd like to take a look at your main page." Texans.
3. The *Phuket Gazette* site, `www.phuketgazette.net`, says to D. Dummy's computer. "Hey, D. Dummy! Have you been here before?"
4. This time, D. Dummy's computer runs out to its hard drive and finds a file called `DDummy@www.phuketgazette.txt`. D. Dummy's computer says to the Web site: "Gee willickers. I have a cookie from you guys. It says that I'm user number 1578462 and I was last here at 11:36 AM on December 14."
5. That's all the *Phuket Gazette* Web site needs to know. It flashes a big banner that says, "Welcome back D. Dummy!" and it puts together a button that says "Click here to see everything that's happened since 11:36 AM on December 14."

Note that the *Phuket Gazette* site could also keep track of user 1578462 — stick an entry in a database somewhere — and accumulate information about that user. (They don't, but they could.)

No doubt you've been told that cookies are horrible, evil programs lurking in the bowels of Windows that will divulge your credit card number to a pimply teenager in Gazukistan and then slice and dice the data on your hard drive, shortly before handing you over, screaming, to the Feds. In fact, your uncle's sister-in-law's roommate's hairdresser's . . . and so on probably told you so himself. Well, guess what? A cookie is just a text file, placed on your hard drive by a Web page. Nothing sinister about it.

A cookie can be retrieved only by the same site that sent it out in the first place. So the *Phuket Gazette* can put cookies on my hard drive, but only the *Phuket Gazette* can read them. There's a trick, though. See the sidebar, "The Doubleclick shtick," for details.

To understand how cookies can pose problems, you have to take a look at the kind of information that can be collected about you, as an individual, and how big a squeeze that puts on your privacy.

When you visit a Web site, the site can automatically collect a small amount of information about you:

- Your computer's address. (Actually, the IP address; see Book IX, Chapter 2 for details.) If you use a dial-up Internet connection, the computer's address changes every time you dial up. But if you have a permanent

Internet connection — with DSL or a cable modem — your address probably doesn't change. That means a sufficiently persistent data-mining program can (at least in theory) track your activities over long periods of time.

- The name of the browser that you're using, its version number, and the name of your operating system — in other words, the Web site will know that you're using Internet Explorer 6 and Windows XP. No biggie.
- The address of the Web page that you just came from.

That isn't a whole lot of information, but it comes along for the ride every time you visit a Web site. You can't do anything about it. When you're on a site, of course, the site can keep track of which pages you look at, how long you stay at each one, what buttons you click, and so on.

In addition, the site you're visiting can ask you for, quite literally, anything: size of your monthly paycheck, mother's maiden name, telephone numbers, credit card numbers, Social Security numbers, driver's license numbers, shoe sizes, and your dowdy Aunt Martha's IQ. If you're game to type in the information, the Web site can collect it and store it.

That's where things start getting dicey. Suppose that you go to one Web site and enter your e-mail I.D. and credit card number and then go to another Web site and enter your e-mail I.D. and telephone number; if those two sites share their information — perhaps through a third party — it's suddenly possible to match up your credit card number and telephone number. See the sidebar, "The Doubleclick shtick," to see where we're all headed.

Microsoft, of course, gathers an enormous amount of information about you in its Windows XP registration database, its Passport database, the MSN user database, and on and on. As of this writing, it doesn't appear as if Microsoft has attempted to correlate the data in those databases. Yet.

Windows XP and Internet Explorer 6 give you the tools to clamp down on unnecessary cookies. They're tied directly to the P3P policy published by conscientious Web sites (see the section, "Understanding Web privacy"). To set higher hurdles for cookies, follow these steps:

1. **Start Internet Explorer by choosing Start⇨Internet Explorer.**
2. **Choose Tools⇨Internet Options, and then click the Privacy tab.**

   You see the Internet Privacy dialog box, as shown in Figure 4-4.
3. **Adjust the slider up or down, to allow more or fewer cookies to be placed on your PC.**

   If a cookie gets blocked, a small icon appears at the bottom of the Internet Explorer screen. Click on it to see which cookie was blocked and why.

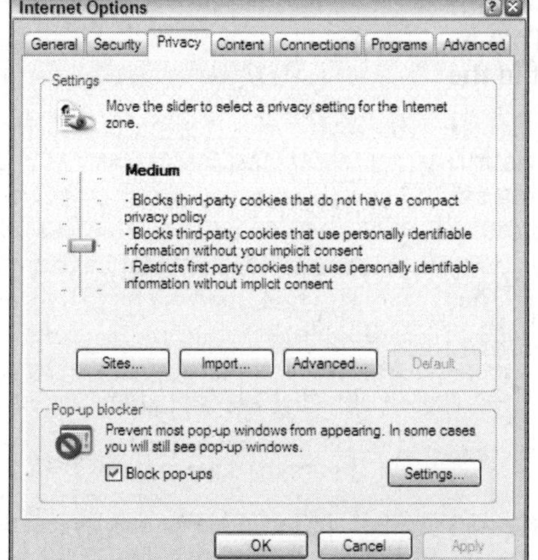

Figure 4-4: Internet Explorer's cookie handling is tied directly to the site's P3P policies.

4. **If you want to block all the cookies on a particular site — or allow all the cookies on a specific site, for that matter — click the Sites button and enter your manual overrides on the Per Site Privacy Actions dialog box, as shown in Figure 4-5.**

Figure 4-5: To accept all cookies from a specific site, type the address of the site and click Allow.

For in-depth, knowledgeable updates on cookie shenanigans, drop by `www.cookiecentral.com`.

The Doubleclick shtick

A Web site plants a cookie on your computer. Only that Web site can retrieve the cookie. The information is shielded from other Web sites. ZDNet.com (the *PC Magazine* Web site) can figure out that I have been reading reviews of digital cameras. Dealtime.com knows that I buy shoes. But a cookie from ZDNet can't be read by Dealtime, and vice versa. So what's the big deal?

Enter Doubleclick.com. As of this writing, both ZDNet.com and Dealtime.com include ads from a company called Doubleclick.com. Don't believe it? Use Internet Explorer 6 to go to each of the sites, and choose View➪Privacy Report. Unless ZDNet or Dealtime has changed advertisers, you see Doubleclick.com featured prominently in each site's Privacy Report.

Here's the trick. You surf to a ZDNet Web page that contains a Doubleclick.com ad. Doubleclick kicks in and plants a cookie on your PC that says you were looking at a specific page on ZDNet. Two hours (or days or weeks) later, you surf to a Dealtime page that also contains a Doubleclick.com ad — a different ad, no doubt — but one distributed by Doubleclick. Doubleclick kicks in again and discovers that you were looking at that specific ZDNet page two hours (or days or weeks) earlier.

Multiply that little example by ten, a hundred, or a hundred thousand, and you begin to see how cookies can be used to collect a whole lot of information about you and your surfing habits. There's nothing illegal or immoral about it. Just realize that Big Brother Doubleclick may be watching, no matter where you go online.

Encrypting E-mail

Bill G. does it. George W. does it. Even Arthur C. Clarke, basking in a shack in Sri Lanka, does it. Maybe you should, too.

Very nearly all the e-mail in the world goes out "in the clear." Just about anybody with a passing interest can look at your messages, reroute them, and snoop to their heart's content. If they're smart, you'll never even know it happened.

The simplest way to protect your mail from prying eyes is by using encryption. And the simplest form of encryption comes in your e-mail program:

✦ If you use Outlook 2003, Outlook 2002 (which comes with Microsoft Office XP), Outlook 2000 (from Office 2000), or Outlook Express (from Windows XP and Internet Explorer 6), choose Tools➪Options, bring up the Security tab, and select the Encrypt Contents and Attachments for All Outgoing Messages check box. Follow the instructions to create a digital certificate and you'll be in business.

✦ If you don't use any flavor of Outlook — or you'd rather not rely on the most commonly used e-mail encryption routines — check out Pretty Good Privacy at `http://web.mit.edu/network/pgp.html`. It's free for personal use and it's, uh, pretty darn good. Unless you believe that some unnamed government agencies have already cracked it. . . .

Protecting Personal Privacy

A few more important privacy points, which all good Dummies should follow:

✦ In the U.S., with very few exceptions, anything you do on a company PC at work can be monitored and examined by your employer. E-mail, Web site history files, even stored documents and settings, are all fair game. At work, you have zero privacy anyway. Get over it.

Why use your company e-mail I.D. for personal messages? C'mon. Drop by `www.yahoo.com` or `www.hotmail.com` or any of dozens of other Web sites for a free e-mail I.D.

Internet Explorer saves copies (in a *cache*) of Web pages that you've accessed, to make things faster if you look at the same page again. IE also maintains 20 days' worth of history, listing the sites you've visited. Clear them both by starting Internet Explorer (Start➪Internet Explorer), choosing Tools➪Options, and choosing the appropriate buttons under the General tab.

✦ You can surf the Web anonymously. It's easy. Check out `www.anonymizer.com` for a free anonymizer toolbar. Be aware of the fact, though, that surfing anonymously still leaves a trail on your PC. To get rid of the trail, follow the instructions in the previous paragraph to clear the history and cache.

✦ You can send e-mail anonymously, too — nobody will be able to trace it back to its source. Look at `www.gilc.org/speech/anonymous/remailer.html`. It's particularly valuable for journalists. Whistle-blowing friends of mine inside a, uh, certain company in Redmond use it all the time.

Keep your head low and your powder dry!

Index

Symbols & Numerics

A

B

C

D

E

F

J

K

L

M

N

O

P

Q

R

S

T

U

V

W

X

Y

Z

Notes

Notes

Notes